DUN & BRADSTREET'S
GUIDE TO
$YOUR INVESTMENTS$™: 1987

NANCY DUNNAN

1817

HARPER & ROW, PUBLISHERS
New York
Cambridge
Philadelphia
San Francisco
Washington
London
Mexico City
São Paulo
Singapore
Sydney

To Miss Fay Swartzendrover, an Iowa teacher

Grateful acknowledgment is made for permission to reprint:

"Fixed Income Securities" table from *The Complete Bond Book* by David M. Darst. Copyright © 1975 by McGraw-Hill, Inc. Reprinted by permission of McGraw-Hill, Inc.

"Calculating Growth Rates" table from *Security Analysis,* Fourth Edition, by Benjamin Graham et al. Copyright © 1962 by McGraw-Hill, Inc. Reprinted by permission of McGraw-Hill, Inc.

"Before You Undertake Arbitration" table from *How to Talk to a Broker* by Jay Pack. Copyright © 1985 by Cloverdale Press, Inc. Reprinted by permission of Harper & Row, Publishers, Inc.

List appearing in Chapter 30, "Betting on a Declining Dollar," from the March 1985 issue of *The Market Letter.* Reprinted by permission of Shearman Ralston, Inc.

"How Bond Interest Compounds" table from *The Complete Book of Bonds* by Robert Holt. Copyright © 1980, 1981 by Robert Lawrence Holt. (1981: Harper & Row, Publishers, Inc.) Reprinted by permission of Waterside Productions, Inc.

"What Are Earnings Worth?" table from *Shaking the Money Tree: How to Find New Growth Opportunities in Common Stocks* by Winthrop Knowlton and John L. Furth. Copyright © 1972 by Winthrop Knowlton and John L. Furth. Reprinted by permission of Harper & Row, Publishers, Inc.

"Comparing Money Market Funds and Treasury Bonds at Different Interest Rates: $100,000 Investment" table and "Comparison of $100,000 Investment in Tax-Free Money Market Fund and Bonds at Different Interest Rates" table. Copyright © and published by Medical Economics Company, Inc., at Oradell, New Jersey 07649. Reprinted by permission.

"Greenmailing: 1984" table in Chapter 34 reprinted from *U.S. News & World Report,* June 25, 1984. Copyright © 1984, *U.S. News & World Report.* Reprinted by permission of *U.S. News & World Report.*

"The Power of Compound Interest" table, "How Compounding Boosts Returns" table, "How to Calculate the Effect of Inflation" table, and "Compounding Factor with Annual Contributions" table. Reprinted with permission from *Encyclopedia of Banking and Financial Tables,* copyright © 1980, 1986, Warren, Gorham & Lamont, Inc., Boston, MA. All rights reserved. Reprinted by permission of Warren, Gorham & Lamont, Inc.

Designer: Gayle Jaeger

ISSN   73-18050
ISBN   0-06-055045-7   87 88 89 90 91 RRD 10 9 8 7 6 5 4 3 2 1
ISBN   0-06-096111-2(pbk.) 87 88 89 90 91 RRD 10 9 8 7 6 5 4 3 2 1

CONTENTS

ACKNOWLEDGMENTS

Standard & Poor's Corp., New York, NY: Carl Ratner, Joseph L.
    Oppenheimer
Dow Theory Letters, San Diego, CA: Richard Russell
Farkouh, Furman & Faccio, New York, NY: Fred C. Farkouh
Seidman & Seidman, New York, NY: Joe Needelman
Silberberg Rosenthal & Co., New York, NY: Jay J. Pack
Shearman Ralston, Inc., New York, NY: Thomas B. Shearman
Noddings, Calamos & Associates, Inc., Oak Brook, IL: Thomas C. Noddings
Oppenheimer Industries, Inc., Kansas City, MO: Joseph F. Intfen
Wright Investors' Service, Bridgeport, CT: Hari Kapadia
Glickenhaus & Co., New York, NY: David Maisel

Special thanks to:
    Helen Moore, Harper & Row, Publishers
    Kathy Hom
    Ellen Flaherty

PART ONE

STARTING OFF

- Advice for 1987
- Building your personal investment pyramid
- Your bank or money market fund
- Using a central asset account
- How safe is your money?
- Directory of major types of investments

1 INTRODUCTION

Following 1985, a year of unprecedented stock and bond market gains, 1986 continued on in the same vein with lower interest rates propelling the prices of stocks and bonds upward, so that as of March 31, 1986, their combined value reached $3.86 trillion, up $928 billion over the previous 12 months.

As we go to press in June 1986, the Dow Jones Industrial Average has hurtled above 1800, and interest rates have crashed to their lowest levels since 1977–78, which in turn has fueled a bull market in bonds, the likes of which has never been seen. The extension of commodity futures, speculation in bond futures, and stock index trading has added volatility factors to both these markets.

Any discussion of the near-term economy in this highly speculative and charged atmosphere must begin with what Felix Rohatyn, senior partner of Lazard Freres, the investment banking company, has called "the most favorable economic event of the last 20 years, the collapse in oil prices." Rohatyn makes the point that "The current collapse . . . is the equivalent of having a multibillion-dollar tax cut without increasing our deficit." Indeed, economists predict that lower oil prices will keep the inflation rate down, thus allowing both interest rates and the U.S. dollar to remain low. Much of America's business in turn is expected to expand and prosper from reduced energy costs. All factors combined are likely to support a favorable atmosphere for continuing rising stock prices, at least during the next 12 months.

Advice for 1987

Although no one can predict with certainty what the economy will do in 1987, these five principles are ones upon which you can base your investments for the year.

- **Accumulate stocks** of leading corporations which are financially strong and can weather economic slowdowns; select those which have demonstrated strength in the past.
- **Note that a low inflation rate** combined with moderate interest rates (below 8%) creates a favorable atmosphere for rising common stock prices.
- **Give careful thought** to those areas of the marketplace that institutional investors may regard as "controversial" but that may nevertheless be moving toward wider investor acceptance. These areas include: hospital management companies, savings and loans and savings banks, semiconductor manufacturers, the smokestack companies, oil and gas and energy companies.
- **Focus on the underlying assets** of the stocks that you buy and hold, not on their prices in the marketplace. Think as a corporate acquirer does, not as a passive investor.

- **Follow the takeover game** and its circular pattern as it moves from industry to industry, from oils to natural gas pipelines to media and publishing. As we go to press, retail stores and advertising companies are moving into the spotlight of takeovers. This is an increasingly important part of the world of Wall Street, and no area seems to be exempt from the excitement of the takeover game.

There was a time when all an investor had to do was to pick attractive stocks or bonds. Now you're faced with a bewildering variety of packages: combinations of shares or units that are almost always better for the salesperson than for the investor. In most cases, they involve hefty commissions, and their profits are the result of guesses or tax benefits more than of competent corporate management. *They are speculations, not investments.* That's why it's so important to accentuate the negative. For successful investing:

DON'T become involved with special "opportunities" until you've developed a balanced portfolio. Stay away from futures, indexes, tax shelters, most new issues, and trick combinations of debt and equity. These are dominated by professionals who have more skill, knowledge, and money than do most individuals.

DON'T go for "super" tax shelters that offer high, fast write-offs involving borrowed funds. Some of these deals take as much as 25% off the top, and the new tax bill puts an end to most.

DON'T follow the crowd. The majority opinion is invariably wrong. Every major market advance has begun when pessimism was loudest and prices lowest. Get the facts, use common sense, and make your own decisions.

DON'T neglect quality. In this type of market, the stocks of major corporations are the ones favored by institutions that account for two-thirds of all transactions on the New York Stock Exchange.

DON'T dash in and out of the market. If you are smart and lucky enough to win 60% of the time, the cost of commissions will cut those profits in half.

DON'T average down: i.e., don't buy more shares when the price of the stock declines. Usually, this will only increase your losses. The best stocks to buy are those hitting new highs.

DON'T be in a hurry to invest your savings. If you miss one opportunity, there will be another—just as good and possibly better—along soon.

DON'T sell America or American corporations short. Despite huge federal deficits and political rhetoric, we are still the most powerful nation on earth and our corporations are the strongest and most profitable for shareholders.

DON'T fall in love with your stocks. There is always a time to be in a stock and a time to be out. With few exceptions, stocks become overpriced, and no tree ever grows to the sky.

DON'T buy exciting concepts which you or your broker do not understand. As adviser John Train counsels, "The small investor is typically moved by ignorance and passion and hypnotized by the movement of a stock without knowing whether his shares are worth $10 or 50¢."

DON'T buy investments that make you nervous. This is doubly important with the special packages that Wall Street concocts for almost every type of security or partnership. Study the package thoroughly and look for hidden costs.

Always remember that even though the bull market may continue there will certainly be severe corrections along the way. Be certain that your portfolio is properly diversified to accommodate these corrections.

WHY INVESTORS SHOULD BE OPTIMISTIC

To get the proper perspective on the stock market, study the figures presented in the tables. The Dow Jones Industrial Average (DJIA) high in 1950 was 235, and since then the indicator has moved up steadily, though erratically. Over the past 35 years, the market value of these stocks has grown by more than a factor of seven. Keep this in mind for the future.

For the past year the trend has been generally upward because of lower interest rates and the improving domestic economy.

Keep in mind that the DJIA records only the data for 30 large companies so it does not provide a comprehensive picture. It is no longer an accurate barometer of the total stock market, which now includes hundreds of new firms, most of which are in faster growing and more profitable industries. Based on past performance, the DJIA will continue to rise: to a possible 2,000 in 1987 and 2,250 by 1990. These are, of course, mechanical projections, but they are based on facts without prejudice or sales-oriented interpretations.

There is one thing every investor must accept: over the short term, the market is usually puzzling and, for most people, frustrating. This is understandable, because the trading action reflects the fears, hopes, biases,

**DOW JONES
INDUSTRIAL AVERAGE
YEAR END CLOSINGS**

1950	235
1955	488
1960	616
1965	969
1970	839
1975	852
1980	964
1985	1546

SOURCE: Richard Russell, *Dow Theory Letters.*

and greed of individuals, primarily a group of professional money managers who thrive on "action" reflecting rumors, headlines, and unsubstantiated projections. This irrationality can drive an intelligent investor bananas, so you must learn to be patient. As Warren Buffett, chairman of Berkshire Hathaway, Inc., advises: "No matter how great the talent or effort, some stocks just take time: you can't produce a baby in one month by getting nine women pregnant."

There are many reasons for optimism:

- Inflation is under control and can be expected to be under 5% for the foreseeable future.
- Congress is taking steps to lower the deficit.
- With greater prosperity, America will export more goods and reduce the trade deficit.
- Most major corporations have streamlined their operations: selling surplus plants, concentrating production facilities, dropping unprofitable and marginal products, and in many cases cutting personnel and compensation. They are now in a position to make more money for stockholders.
- Most important, the majority of companies are financially stronger, with improved cash flow from liberalized depreciation, lean inventories, greater use of computers, stricter policies, and more realistic plans.

Look what has happened to many quality stocks in the past 3 years as shown by these values for their shares:

STOCK PRICES

COMPANY	SPRING 1983	SPRING 1984	SPRING 1985	SPRING 1986
Chubb Corp.	33	46	70	77
Bristol-Myers	36	48	60	76
Clorox	24	26	35	52
Coca-Cola	50	55	68	108
Dun & Bradstreet	60	67	86	106
Exxon Corp.	34	40	51	58
IBM	119	129	134	153
Ralston Purina	23	28	41	63

SOURCE: The Wall Street Journal.

As is stressed throughout this book, there are always profitable investments for those who are willing to do their homework, insist on strict standards, buy when shares are undervalued and sell when they become fully priced, or, when a mistake is made, sell them quickly at a small loss.

Quality, value, and timing will be explained in detail later, but when you invest in shares of *quality* corporations (generally companies that are financially strong, are leaders in their fields, and have fairly consistent records of high, profitable growth), you will *almost always* make money over a period of time.

Here's why:

Quality

If a company earned 15% on stockholders' equity (the money invested by shareholders), it ends the year with 15¢ per dollar more. The dividend payout is generally about 5¢ per share. That leaves 10¢ to be reinvested for future growth. Thus the underlying value of the corporation doubles in about 7.5 years. The same 15¢ rate of return will produce double earnings and often double dividends. Eventually these extra values will be reflected in the price of the common stock. That's why the best investments are shares of companies that keep on making a lot of money.

Value

With *value* (the ratio of tomorrow's price to today's market quotation), the profits will come by buying when the stock is underpriced and selling when it becomes fully valued. Even if you buy too soon, you will profit as long as the company prospers.

Timing

Timing purchases and sales enhances profits and reduces losses. As is explained by many examples, the key points of timing can be determined by technical analysis—primarily by charts, but often by other indices.

Keep in mind that when you buy any stock as an *investor* you are acquiring a share in a business enterprise because you feel that it is worth holding regardless of any short- or intermediate-term action. When you buy a security as a *speculator,* you are assuming that someone else will pay more; the sooner, the better.

Successful investing takes time and patience. Dramatic moves, up or down, are exciting, but they seldom last, and they are usually followed by equally sharp reactions.

THE MAGIC OF COMPOUNDING

The Rule of 72

One thing that's worth repeating has to do with the impact of compounding, or earning income on income by prompt reinvestment of all interest, dividends, and realized capital gains. As shown in the accompanying tables, savings can mount at an astonishing rate over the years. For a quick calculation on how long it takes to double your money, use *the rule of 72:* divide 72 by the yield. Thus, at 9%, it will take 8 years; at 10%, about 7 years; at 12%, 6 years.

Compounding is most rewarding with pension funds, where there are no taxes to pay until withdrawal, but it's always useful with personal savings or with shares of mutual funds. With annual contributions of $2,000 to an Individual Retirement Account, a 30-year-old who invests at a 12% yield can count on a whopping $863,320 at age 65.

SUCCESSFUL INVESTING

Your Investments is written for the concerned investor who now has, or can look forward to, savings of $25,000, is willing to spend time in research and review, and can make logical, fact-based decisions.

THE POWER OF COMPOUND INTEREST

A REGULAR INVESTMENT OF $100 PER YEAR, INVESTED AT:	WILL, COMPOUNDED ANNUALLY AT THE END OF EACH YEAR, GROW TO THIS SUM AFTER THIS NUMBER OF YEARS:							
	5	10	15	20	25	30	35	40
6%	$564	$1,318	$2,328	$3,679	$5,486	$7,906	$11,143	$15,476
8	587	1,449	2,715	4,576	7,311	11,328	17,232	25,906
10	611	1,594	3,177	5,727	9,835	16,449	27,102	44,259
12	635	1,755	3,728	7,205	13,333	24,133	43,166	76,709
14	661	1,934	4,384	9,102	18,187	35,679	69,357	134,202
16	688	2,132	5,166	11,538	24,921	53,031	112,071	236,076

To get the corresponding total for any other annually invested amount (A), multiply the dollar total given above for the yield and the number of years by $\frac{A}{100}$. Example: you plan to invest $75 per month, $900 a year. What capital sum will that provide after 35 years, at 12% compounded annually? Check where the lines cross for 12% and 35 years: $43,166 $\times \frac{900}{100}$ = $388,494. Note: The totals will be greater if: (1) the deposits are made at the beginning of the year; (2) compounding is more frequent.

SOURCE: Reprinted with permission from *Encyclopedia of Banking and Financial Tables,* copyright © 1980, 1986, Warren, Gorham & Lamont, Inc., Boston, MA. All rights reserved.

This approach is quite different from the "sure-fire" formulas "revealed" by some financial wizards and the gloom-and-doom forecasts of self-styled "experts." Most of these people make more money from their books, lectures, reports, and letters than they do from following their own advice.

The record proves them wrong, especially when they downgrade or neglect the strength, growth, and profitability of American corporations. They tell you to buy gold at $800 an ounce, yet its price falls below $300 and fluctuates far more widely and rapidly than the stock market. They tout "stocks of the future" at $2 per share and headline their wisdom when they soar to $20 or higher in a few months. But they seldom mention the majority of the selections that fail to fulfill their promise and end up either bankrupt or merged.

ANOTHER VIEW OF COMPOUNDING

RATE OF RETURN	AVERAGE ANNUAL RETURN ON ORIGINAL INVESTMENT				
	5 YEARS	10 YEARS	15 YEARS	20 YEARS	25 YEARS
6%	6.8%	7.9%	9.3%	11.0%	13.2%
7	8.1	9.7	11.7	14.3	17.7
8	9.4	11.6	14.5	18.3	23.4
9	10.8	13.7	17.6	23.0	30.5
10	12.2	15.9	21.1	28.6	39.3
11	13.7	18.4	25.2	35.3	50.3
12	15.2	21.0	29.8	43.2	64.0

INVESTMENT PERFORMANCE

For the investor, the last year or so has been difficult because of the sharp fluctuations in stock prices. The stock market averages—Dow Jones and Standard & Poor's—bounced up and down and generally trended lower because of the relatively poor performance of a few major corporations. Except for special situations, such as stocks of takeover candidates, the winners were medium-sized corporations and utilities and debt issues with high yields. The most successful investors were those who managed their portfolios: taking modest profits, selling at small losses, and switching, for income, to convertibles, bonds, or other debt issues.

For 1987, the targets are:

■ *For income:* 11% total returns with corporate and government bonds; with utility stocks, 8 to 9% dividends plus 3 to 4% appreciation.

■ *For total returns:* 14% with discount bonds, 11% interest plus 3% rise in value toward maturity or lower interest rates; with quality stocks, 5% dividends and 10% average annual appreciation.

These targets are not headlines written for promotion or publicity. They are based on the results attained by suggested buying and selling as outlined in this guide.

As stressed throughout the pages that follow, for successful investing, the basic concepts are: (1) it is wise to buy quality stocks when they are undervalued and corporate prospects are improving; with this approach, you will *always* make money over the long term of an investment program; (2) the key factor is the corporation, not the stock; as long as the company retains its quality rating, its shares will be worth more . . . in time; the action of the stock, as shown by its market price, is temporary; the value of the "good" corporation will continue to increase because management knows how to make more money; (3) the wise investor switches a portion of savings to debt issues when the market plateaus or begins to decline; the long-term record of the sample portfolios proves the worth of these principles: average annual returns of close to 20%, so your money has doubled in less than 4 years.

By contrast, here's what two creditable experts say about successful investing:

■ Benjamin Graham, whose books have become standard texts: "Investment must be based on thorough analysis and must promise safety of principal and a satisfactory return. Lacking one of these, it is a speculation."

■ T. Rowe Price, who built one of the major money management firms: "I do not have the ability to guess the ups and downs of the stock market averages or the trends in individual stocks. Most fortunes are built on ownership of successful business enterprises over a long period of time."

HOW TO CALCULATE THE EFFECT OF INFLATION

YEARS FROM NOW	4%	5%	6%	7%	8%
5	1.22	1.28	1.34	1.40	1.47
10	1.48	1.63	1.79	1.97	2.16
15	1.80	2.08	2.40	2.76	3.17
20	2.19	2.65	3.21	3.87	4.66
25	2.67	3.39	4.29	5.43	6.85
30	3.24	4.32	5.74	7.61	10.06

SOURCE: Reprinted with permission from *Encyclopedia of Banking and Financial Tables,* copyright © 1980, 1986, Warren, Gorham & Lamont, Inc., Boston, MA. All rights reserved.

According to a recent study, the people who get rich are those who started by absorbing themselves in their business, trade, or profession; when they acquired substantial assets, they became active investors using the same guidelines that helped them to succeed: *knowledge, concentration,* and *stick-to-itiveness.* The people who failed in their quest for wealth were those who scampered after get-rich-quick schemes.

INFLATION IS NO LONGER A THREAT

Successful money managers (and many economists) believe that inflation is not likely to be a destructive force for the next few years. A 5% rate is irksome but not awesome. With a current base of $10,000, you will have to have $12,800 in 5 years and $16,300 in 10 years to buy the same goods and services.

But inflation works both ways because it boosts the yields on investments. At a modest 10% rate of return, that $10,000 will grow to $16,600 in 5 years and to $25,900 in a decade (with compounding). So the smart investor is still ahead of the game.

A final thought from Warren Buffett to keep in mind as you develop and fine-tune your investment portfolio during 1987: "Should you find yourself in a chronically leaking boat, energy devoted to changing vessels is likely to be more productive than energy devoted to patching leaks."

BUILDING YOUR OWN INVESTMENT PHILOSOPHY (OR PYRAMID)

A few years ago, the world of investing was a far simpler one than it is today: investment choices were pleasantly limited and only a few basic concepts governed the ways in which you could make (or lose) money. If you were terribly conservative, you put your hard-won earnings in the local bank where you earned 5.00%; or perhaps your family broker bought some stock in AT&T or a carefully selected public utility company. If you were willing to assume a little more risk, you might have moved out of the **blue chip** arena into more speculative growth stocks. If you wanted a steady stream of income, you merely purchased high-quality corporate or government bonds and waited for the interest to roll in. But the only choices available for the general investor were basically stocks, bonds, and the bank.

But it's 1987 and no longer quite so easy. Several years of deregulation in the financial industry have brought about sweeping changes; the rules that governed this business for at least half a decade have given way to a very competitive atmosphere. In addition, **inflation, disinflation,** and fluctuating interest rates have multiplied investment opportunities as well as risks. Once relegated to the three basic choices, today you face a bewildering array of products and institutions: **certificates of deposit (CDs), money market funds,** interest-bearing bank accounts, **options,** and **index futures** as well as the traditional **stocks, bonds,** and savings account. And the number of people vying to sell you one of these "products" is rapidly growing. Your local bank and stockbroker are no longer the only two games in town. They are, in fact, becoming more and more closely intertwined, especially as the **one-stop financial account** grows in popularity. Banks are steadily moving into the world of stocks, money market accounts, and other "nonbank" services, while brokers are now selling CDs and offering discount brokerage services. **ATMs** are located in supermarkets and gas stations. Shearson and American Express have joined hands, Sears and Dean Witter are coupled, and Prudential Insurance and Bache now work in tandem.

The proliferation of investment choices has made wise decision making far more complicated, and now more than ever before information and knowledge are absolutely essential. In fact, the world of finance is changing so rapidly that unless you are up to date and well informed, you'll be left in the dust. That is why *Dun & Bradstreet's Guide to $Your Investments$* can make the difference between a well-informed decision and pure guess-work. It helps you determine if you're better off buying a bank CD or a Treasury bond; making a play in commodity futures or looking for takeover targets; using your broker's research or following the **charts.**

Whether you're a new investor or a sophisticated money manager who

blue chip: the common stock of a well-known national company with a history of earnings growth and dividend increases, such as IBM or Exxon

inflation: an increase in the average price level of goods and services

disinflation: a reduction in the rate of still ongoing inflation

certificates of deposit: also called CDs or "time certificates of deposit," these are official receipts issued by a bank stating that a given amount of money has been deposited for a certain length of time at a specified rate of interest. CDs are insured by the U.S. government for up to $100,000.

money market fund: a mutual fund that invests only in high-yielding, short-term money market instruments (U.S. Treasury bills, bank certificates of deposit, commercial paper, etc.). Shareholders receive competitively high interest on their shares.

option: the right to buy (call) or sell (put) a certain amount of stock at a given price (strike price) for a specified length of time.

index future: a contract to buy or sell an index (Standard & Poor's, for example) at a future date. An index is a statistical yardstick that measures changes compared to a base period. The New York Stock Exchange (NYSE) Composite Index of all NYSE common stocks is based on a 1965 average of 50. Note: an index is *not* an average.

stock: a security that represents ownership in a corporation.

bond: a security that represents debt of an issuing corporation. The issuer is required to pay the bondholder a specified rate of interest for a specified time and then repay the entire debt (also known as face value) upon maturity.

the one-stop financial account: also known as a central assets or combo account, it combines your brokerage, money market fund, and checking account with a credit card. Offered by both banks and brokerage houses, some central asset accounts include forms of life insurance, mortgages, travelers checks, etc.

ATMs: automated teller machines, located primarily in banks. Upon insertion of a magnetically coded bank

has weathered numerous **bull and bear cycles,** this vital reference brings you more data on the more familiar vehicles, introduces you to new products, and, finally, offers you the best in smart money-making strategies as followed by the professional investment community.

If you are relatively new to the world of investing, or if you're somewhat rusty, we suggest that you read Section One carefully. Those of you who have been buying stocks and bonds for some time and know the basics can proceed directly to Section Two.

BECOMING A SAVVY INVESTOR

Before you plunge into your pocket and buy 100 shares of a reportedly "hot stock" or set up a personally tailored investment program with a **stockbroker** or **money manager,** it's wise to take a few moments to decide your answers to three key questions:

1 What do I want to derive from such a move or investment?
2 How much can I sensibly afford to invest?
3 What are my major financial goals?

Random purchases of stocks, bonds, and tax shelters may initially seem rewarding but are unlikely to fulfill your long-range goals. In order to get the most out of your investment dollar, the answers to these three questions and some background preparation are essential. The four homework assignments below can produce large benefits in the long run, enabling you to make better investment decisions whether you make them on your own or with professional guidance.

KNOW THY WORTH

Before making any type of investment expenditure, whether it's buying a stock, bond, or house, you must know your **net worth.** This is one of the first questions most stockbrokers, money managers, and bank mortgage officers ask. If you're like most people, uncertain of the precise answer, don't panic. Figuring out your net worth is easy. All you need is a free evening, a calculator, your checkbook, bills, and a record of your income. Then, follow these two easy steps:

1 Add up the value of everything you own (your **assets**)
2 Subtract the total of all you owe (your **liabilities**)

The amount left over is your net worth. You can use the worksheets on the following pages as guidelines for arriving at the correct amount. When figuring your assets, list the amount that they will bring in today's market, which could be more or less than you paid for them originally. Assets include cash on hand, your checking and savings account balances, the cash value of any insurance policies, personal property (car, boat, jewelry, real estate, investments), and any **vested** interest in a pension or retirement plan. Your liabilities include money you owe, charge account debts, mortgages, auto payments, education or other loans, and any taxes due.

FINDING YOUR NET WORTH

Date _____
ASSETS

Cash on hand	$_____
Cash in checking accounts	_____
Savings accounts, money market fund	_____
Life insurance, cash value	_____
Annuities	_____
Retirement funds	
IRA or Keogh	_____
401-K Plan	_____
Vested interest in pension or	
profit-sharing plan	_____
U.S. savings bonds, current value	_____
Investments	
Market value of stocks, bonds,	
mutual fund shares, etc.	_____
Real estate, market value of real	
property minus mortgage	_____
Property	
Automobile	_____
Furniture	_____
Jewelry, furs	_____
Sports and hobby equipment	_____
Equity interest in your business	_____
Total assets:	$_____

Date _____
LIABILITIES

Unpaid bills	
Charge accounts	$_____
Taxes, property taxes, and quarterly	
income taxes	_____
Insurance premiums	_____
Rent or monthly mortgage payment	_____
Utilities	_____
Balance due on:	
Mortgage	
Automobile loans	_____
Personal loans	_____
Installment loans	_____
Total liabilities	$_____
Assets	$_____
Minus liabilities	_____
Your net worth:	$_____

identification card, the computer-controlled machine will automatically dispense the amount of cash that you request and indicate the status of your account on a viewing screen. No teller is necessary and the majority of ATMs are open 24 hours.
charts: price and volume trends as well as general movement of the stock and bond markets, of economic cycles, of industries, and of individual companies are recorded continually on charts. A chartist is one who believes that

KNOW WHERE THY WORTH IS GOING: BUDGETING

A budget, like ants at a picnic, is universally unappealing. It's a very rare person who likes either one, yet each has its place. Some form of budgeting should be part of your overall investment plan. It's not only a good way of knowing how much you're spending and on what, but it is also a sensible means of setting aside money for investing, our primary concern in this book. If you need help in establishing a budget for investing, use the worksheet on page 14. In order to budget dollars for investing, try setting aside a certain dollar amount on a regular basis, even if it's not an impressively large number. Mark it immediately for "savings/investing." Ideally you should try to save 5 to 10% of your annual income; if you make more than $60,000 a year, aim for 15%. Don't talk yourself out of budgeting for investing simply because it is a nuisance to keep track of what you spend. You'll be convinced of the wisdom of saving and the advantages of **compound interest** if you take a look at the table on the next page, which shows what happens to $1,000 over 20 years when you put it in an investment yielding 5¼% and the income earned is reinvested or compounded.

past history as expressed on a chart gives a strong clue to the next price movement. A chartist "reads" the lines to tell what a stock has done and may do.

bull and bear cycles: the up-and-down movements of the stock market. A *bull* is one who believes that prices will rise and buys on that assumption. A *bull market* is a period when stock prices are advancing. A *bear* is one who believes that security or commodity prices will decline. A *bear market* is marked by declining prices.

stockbroker: an agent who handles the public's orders to buy and sell securities, commodities, or other properties. A broker may be either a partner of a brokerage firm or a registered representative, in which case the individual is merely an employee. A broker charges a commission for services.

money manager: one who handles all aspects of your finances, including stocks, bonds, insurance, savings, tax shelters, etc.; usually charges a percentage or a flat fee rather than commissions.

net worth: total value (of cash, property, investments) after deducting outstanding expenses or amounts owed.

asset: a possession that has present and future financial value to its owner.

liability: a debt; something owed by one person or business to another.

FREQUENCY OF COMPOUNDING	1 YEAR	5 YEARS	10 YEARS	20 YEARS
Continuous	$1,054.67	$1,304.93	$1,702.83	$2,899.63
Daily	1,054.67	1,304.90	1,702.76	2,899.41
Quarterly	1,053.54	1,297.96	1,684.70	2,838.20
Semiannually	1,053.19	1,295.78	1,679.05	2,819.21
Annually	1,052.50	1,291.55	1,668.10	2,782.54

KNOW THY GOALS AND PRIORITIES

After you've accumulated money to invest, your next homework assignment is to decide what you want to accomplish by investing. If you were to take a trip to Europe or travel by car across the country, you would bring along a good road map. Such should also be the case with investing, only the road map would consist of financial, not geographical, destinations. When you travel through the south of France, you decide what towns, cathedrals, or vineyards you want most to visit, how long it will take you to get there, and approximately what it will cost. The same procedure should be applied to your financial journey through life. Your highlights or destination points may include some of these:

- Establishing an investment portfolio
- Reducing taxes
- Building a nest egg for emergencies
- Preparing for retirement
- Paying for a college education
- Buying a house, car, boat
- Traveling or taking a cruise
- Investing in art or antiques
- Adding on a room or swimming pool
- Setting up your own business

Goal-setting, you will discover, enables you to take firm control of your financial life, especially if you actually write your goals down. The process of listing goals on paper, although perhaps awkward at first, forces you to focus on how you handle money, how you feel about risk versus safety. Divide your goals into two sections: immediate goals (those which can be accomplished in a year or less) and long-range goals.

If you're in your twenties and unmarried, your immediate goals could be:

- Obtain a graduate degree
- Join a health club
- Save for summer vacation
  Longer-term ones:
- Buy a car
- Set up a brokerage account or buy shares in a mutual fund
- Purchase a co-op or condo with a friend

If you're married and raising a family, the goals might shift to include:

vested: the nonforfeitable interest of a participant in a pension plan. You will not lose that portion of your benefit should you leave the job.

compound interest: the amount earned on the original principal plus the accumulated interest. In this way, interest on interest plus interest on principal grows more rapidly.

- Buying a house
- Setting up educational funds for children
- Building a growth portfolio

Individuals closer to retirement tend to seek other goals:

- Shift bulk of portfolio to safe income-producing vehicles
- Increase contribution to retirement plan
- Find appropriate short-term tax shelters
- Set up a consulting business; incorporate

Regardless of your age or income, individual goals make it easier and more meaningful to stick to a budget and to save for investing. Putting aside that 5 to 15% every month for an investment program suddenly has a very tangible purpose—one that you personally decided upon.

YOUR CASH FLOW

WHERE IT COMES FROM		WHERE IT GOES	
INCOME	ANNUAL AMOUNT	EXPENSES	ANNUAL AMOUNT
Take-home pay	$_____	Income taxes	$_____
Bonus and commissions	_____	Mortgage or rent	_____
Interest	_____	Property taxes	_____
Dividends	_____	Utilities	_____
Rent	_____	Automobile maintenance	_____
Pensions	_____	Commutation or other transportation	_____
Social security	_____	Insurance	
Annuities	_____	Homeowners or renters	_____
Tax refunds	_____	Life	_____
Other	_____	Disability	_____
Total	$_____	Child care	_____
		Education	_____
		Food	_____
		Clothing	_____
		Household miscellaneous	_____
		Home improvements	_____
		Entertainment	_____
		Vacations, travel	_____
		Books, magazines, club dues	_____
		Contributions to charities or organizations	
		Total	$_____
		Surplus or deficit	$_____

cash equivalents: the generic term for assorted short-term instruments such as U.S. Treasuries, CDs, and money market fund shares, which can be readily converted into cash.

government or municipal bonds: a contract of indebtedness issued by the U.S. Treasury, federal agencies, or state and local governments which promises to pay back the principal amount plus interest at a specified date.

Treasury securities: bonds issued by the U.S. Treasury, federal agencies, and state and local governments. The term includes: *U.S. Savings Bonds; Treasury bills*, which have a face value of $10,000, are sold at a discount, and mature in 1 year or less; *Treasury notes*, which have a face value of $1,000 or $5,000 and mature in 1 to 10 years; *Treasury bonds*, which mature in 10 to 30 years and have a face value of $1,000; and *municipal bonds* (see above). Interest on Treasuries is exempt from state and local income taxes; interest on municipals is exempt from state, local, *and* federal taxes.

zero coupon bond: a bond which pays no current interest but is sold at a deep discount from face value. At maturity, all compounded interest is paid and the bondholder collects the full face value of the bond (usually $1,000).

BUILDING YOUR INVESTMENT PYRAMID

Once you know why you want to invest, you are ready to think about your investments as part of a pyramid in which each level builds upon the earlier ones. This approach to investing offers a carefully designed, diversified system that provides for financial growth and protection regardless of your age, marital status, income, or level of financial sophistication. As you can see by looking at the illustration, you begin your financial program on the pyramid at *Level One,* the Security Level. It is the lowest in terms of risk and the highest in safety. As your net worth grows, you automatically move up to the next level, increasing both the amount of risk involved and the potential for financial gain.

Level One covers life's basic financial requirements and includes:

- An emergency nest egg consisting of cash or **cash equivalents** such as savings account, CDs, money market funds
- Health, life, and disability insurance
- A solid retirement plan, including an IRA or Keogh

Before leaving this level, you will have saved enough cash or cash equivalents to cover a minimum of 3 to 6 months' worth of living expenses. This minimum is your emergency reserve, and when you've achieved this goal, you're financially solid enough to advance to *Level Two.*

Level Two, also known as the Safety of Principal level, is devoted entirely to safe income-producing investments such as corporate, **government, or municipal bonds; Treasury securities;** longer-term CDs; **zero coupon bonds;** and real estate; all of which are described in this book.

Although safety is key at this step, the **liquidity** factor emphasized in *Level One* is now traded off for a higher return or **yield.** And because some of these items, notably zero coupon bonds and CDs, are timed to **mature** at a definite date, they provide ideal means to meet staggering college tuition bills and retirement costs.

INVESTMENT PYRAMID

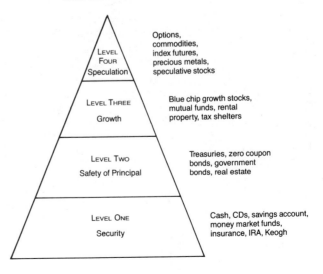

LEVEL FOUR
Speculation
Options, commodities, index futures, precious metals, speculative stocks

LEVEL THREE
Growth
Blue chip growth stocks, mutual funds, rental property, tax shelters

LEVEL TWO
Safety of Principal
Treasuries, zero coupon bonds, government bonds, real estate

LEVEL ONE
Security
Cash, CDs, savings account, money market funds, insurance, IRA, Keogh

liquidity: ability of an asset or security to be quickly converted into cash.

yield: the income paid or earned by a security divided by its current price. For example, a $20 stock with an annual dividend of $1.50 has a 7.5% yield.

mature: when a bond or note comes due and its face value must be paid.

mutual fund: an investment trust in which an investor's dollars are pooled with those of hundreds of others; the combined total is invested by a professional manager in a variety of securities.

tax bracket: the percentage rate at which the top dollar of an income is taxed.

tax shelter: an investment which allows an investor to realize significant tax benefits by reducing or deferring taxable income.

takeover candidate: a company about which there is speculation that it may be acquired by another corporation.

commodities: goods, articles, services, and interests in which contracts for future delivery may be traded. Futures contracts range from precious metals, food, and grain to U.S. Treasuries and the Swiss franc.

Money to buy real estate is also included, not only because it gives you a place to live but also because historically real estate has appreciated significantly in value. At the same time, it offers tax benefits in the form of deductions for mortgage interest payments and real estate taxes.

Level Three involves investing for growth. At this point you can afford to be more adventuresome, more risk-oriented, and less conservative; and this book shows you how to turn away from liquidity and assured income and toward growth and blue chip stocks, conservative **mutual funds,** rentable property, and, depending upon your **tax bracket, tax shelters.** If you find you're interested in the stock market, this is the ideal time to join an investment club and learn by doing so.

Level Four, the pinnacle of the pyramid, is given over to the riskiest of investments that may or may not yield spectacular returns. These include speculative stocks, stocks in new companies, **takeover candidates,** options, **commodities,** index futures, gold and precious metals, and tax shelters designed to provide tax losses—all vehicles discussed in detail in the following chapters.

HINTS FOR THE BEGINNING INVESTOR

- Don't think you're going to get rich immediately. It takes time and wisdom to become a winning investor.
- Start by investing only in stocks of leading companies. They have proven track records, there is a lot of research on them, and there is always a buyer if you should wish to sell.
- Buy a stock *only* if you can state a reason why it will appreciate in price or pay high dividends; merely feeling good about an issue is not a solid enough reason to justify purchase.
- Don't churn your own account so that commissions eat up any profits. Even if the average commission is only 5%, your stock will have to move up at least 10% to be even.
- Spread out your risks. Every company has the potential to be a loser some of the time.
- Decide on the maximum amount that you're willing to lose and stick to it.
- When you lose, if you do, try to determine why your security went down.
- Read about investing and investments as often as possible.

3 PARKING PLACES FOR YOUR MONEY:
Banks and Money Market Funds

Throughout your investment life there will be many times when varying portions of your assets should be kept liquid, that is, readily available. The traditional savings account simply won't do anymore; the interest rate is far too low and is locked in by federal regulations, although ceilings on interest rates are scheduled to end during 1986. Fortunately, you have an abundance of other options.

capital: also called capital assets, it refers to property or money from which a person or business receives some monetary gain.

Interest-bearing accounts are best for the portion of your money that calls for sure income and preservation of **capital** as illustrated on Level One of your investment pyramid. Reserves for unexpected emergencies, parking places while you're looking for more rewarding opportunities, call them what you will—income holding accounts are available at banks, thrift institutions, brokerage firms, mutual funds, and even insurance companies. They consist basically of debt holdings with yields that are about 2 to 3% below those of quality bonds and are often insured by the federal government. Banks may offer toasters, blenders, electric coffee pots, and other free gifts in order to attract your savings dollars.

Regardless of the giveaways, the premise is the same: whether you invest in savings accounts, certificates of deposit, or money market funds, you will always get back the same number of dollars you put in plus interest unless, of course, you make an early withdrawal, in which case you may be penalized. The income earned is taxable at the highest rate, which means that if inflation advances more rapidly than interest rates, the purchasing power of both the principal and the interest will decrease every year. Here are your choices:

AT YOUR BANK

Banks now offer a wide variety of accounts with varying interest rates, so it pays to check several in your area before making a decision. Although it's time-consuming, it can mean as much as 1 to 2% difference in the interest earned on your account.

PASSBOOK SAVINGS

Fewer and fewer banks are offering the old-fashioned passbook savings account to their new customers. Most have replaced it with a *statement account* which provides a monthly or quarterly computerized update of your savings transactions. A statement account typically has a higher minimum deposit requirement than the $0.00 to $25 required to open a passbook account. Most passbook savings accounts still pay 5.25% at commercial banks but often 5½% at a savings and loan. Most statement accounts pay 5.25%. However, the mandated lid has been removed on what rates banks can pay. The total yields will be based on: (1) the starting date set by the bank, sometimes the day of deposit but more often the first of the succeeding month; (2) the method of compounding. As shown by the table, faster reinvestment can be beneficial: at 12%, $1,000 savings earns $175 more when compounded daily than when compounded annually.

But the terms can be tricky when there are withdrawals, as shown by this example, which, for easy figuring, uses a 5% interest rate and a 360-day year.

On April 1, Mr. F deposited $5,000 in a passbook account. On May 1, he withdrew $4,000. On June 1, he added $10,000. On June 30, he took out $1,000, leaving a balance of $10,000. When the interest is based on the lowest balance during the quarter ($1,000), the return will be $50 a year, or $12.50 for the 3 months.

In another savings and loan that used FIFO (first in, first out), Mrs. G made the same deposits and withdrawals on the same dates. Under this format, each withdrawal is deducted from the balance at the start of the quarter and, in sequence, from later deposits. Here the two withdrawals totaled $5,000, so this sum was deducted from the opening $5,000 and there was no earned interest on these savings. But on the $10,000 kept for 1 month, the interest was $41.66.

In a bank that offered daily interest on the exact sum in the account, the total interest was $70.70. This was earned on the balances: in April, $5,000; in May, $1,000; in June, $11,000 for 29 days and $10,000 for one day.

NOW ACCOUNTS

A NOW (Negotiable Order of Withdrawal) account is an interest-bearing checking account wherein the rate of return is the same as with passbook accounts, but it usually requires a minimum $1,000 balance and may involve a monthly service charge and a computerized printout of transactions rather than a return of canceled checks.

HOW COMPOUNDING BOOSTS RETURNS
$1,000 Savings; 360-Day Year

YIELD	DAILY	MONTHLY	QUARTERLY	ANNUALLY
8%	$1,083	$1,083	$1,082	$1,080
9	1,094	1,093	1,093	1,090
10	1,105	1,104	1,104	1,100
11	1,163	1,115	1,115	1,110
12	1,295	1,127	1,126	1,120

SOURCE: Reprinted with permission from *Encyclopedia of Banking and Financial Tables,* copyright © 1980, 1986, Warren, Gorham & Lamont, Inc., Boston, MA. All rights reserved.

In order to earn interest on your NOW account, you are required to maintain the minimum balance set by the bank. If you fall below this amount you will lose interest and in some cases be subject to additional charges. With a NOW account, you can write an unlimited number of checks.

SUPERNOW ACCOUNTS

A variation of the NOW account is the SuperNOW account that pays a higher yield and requires a bigger balance, usually $2,500, with a return to the low passbook rate if this is not maintained. Monthly service fees run from $5 to $20, and there are often extra charges for each check written or deposited and for the use of the automatic teller. Shop around, because there may be bargains for those over 65 or when a new branch is opened. SuperNOWs pay whatever interest rate the bank wishes to offer.

MONEY MARKET DEPOSIT ACCOUNTS

FDIC: Federal Deposit Insurance Corporation, an independent agency of the U.S. government whose basic purpose is to insure bank deposits. Depositors are covered for up to $100,000, regardless of how many accounts they have, at an insured bank.

Offered by most of the nation's banks, money market accounts provide competitive interest rates as well as liquidity, and like all bank accounts, including the NOW and SuperNOW, are insured up to $100,000 by the **FDIC.** Originally you needed a minimum of $2,500 to open a money market deposit account, but that amount is being lowered each year. Starting in 1986, there is no legal minimum deposit requirement. However, banks have the option to set their own minimum deposit requirements.

Yields and penalties for falling below the minimum vary from bank to bank. The interest that you earn is less than that offered by regular money market mutual funds (which we'll discuss next), because banks are required to keep on deposit in the Federal Reserve Bank up to 12% of the balance of these accounts. Bank money market accounts tend to pay competitive rates, slightly below those of Treasury bills (T-bills). The rate changes periodically (often weekly) along with changes in short-term interest rates.

RECENT INTEREST RATES FOR MONEY MARKET INVESTMENTS

INSTRUMENT	YIELD
Money market fund	6.09%
Tax-free money market fund	3.76
90-day Treasury bills	5.95
180-day Treasury bills	6.06
Bank money market accounts	5.94
6-month CDs	6.49
1-year CDs	6.74
30-month CDs	7.08
Passbook savings account—bank	5.25
Savings and loan or thrift accounts	5.50

SOURCE: © Donoghue's *Moneyletter* ($87 per year; P.O. Box 540, Holliston, MA 01746).

In this type of account you are allowed to write only three checks per month to a third party, although you may withdraw cash in person as often as you like. Some banks also allow use of ATMs for transfer of money, but money market deposit accounts are not intended to replace checking accounts.

CERTIFICATES OF DEPOSIT (CDs)

The CD, also called a "time certificate of deposit," is an official receipt issued by a bank stating that a specified sum of money has been deposited for a specified period of time at a specified rate of interest. CDs are widely accepted among investors, companies, and institutions as a highly negotiable short-term investment vehicle and are insured up to $100,000. Although CD rates, terms, and size vary from bank to bank, in general they consist of:

- 7- to 31-day CD with the yield tied to that of a 13-week T-bill
- 91-day CD with interest rate tied to that of a 13-week T-bill
- 6-month CD to yield about ¼% above the average T-bill rate for the most recent 4-week period
- 30-month CD with a fixed rate, typically 1% higher than that of shorter maturity accounts

In most cases, the big type in the ads shows the compounded yield, which will, of course, be paid only when the CD is held to maturity. There are penalties for early withdrawal, but these are waived when:

- The owner dies or is found to be mentally incompetent
- The time deposit is in a Keogh or IRA retirement plan and the depositor is over 59½ years old

Many banks have started to offer adjustable rate CDs, in which case the interest rate fluctuates weekly along with the average T-bill rate. For CDs of 32 days or more, issued after October 1983, there is no federally imposed ceiling on either the interest rate or the minimum size of the deposit. Banks are free to set their own numbers. CD minimums range from $500 up to $5,000 and more. Those that are $100,000 or over are called "jumbo CDs." A number of banks will let you buy a "designer CD," one in which you set your own maturity date, so that you can time it to come due when your child goes off to college or perhaps for when you retire or will need a lump sum.

💲 HINT: Before you buy a long-term CD, check out the Treasury-note interest rate. T-note interest is free from state and local taxes.

When buying any type of CD, take the time to check out how frequently the bank compounds the interest and ask what the effective annual yield is. It can make an important difference, as you can see from the table on the next page.

MONEY MARKET MUTUAL FUNDS

Money market funds are pooled investments offered by mutual funds, insurance companies, brokerage firms, and almost every type of financial

EFFECTIVE ANNUAL YIELD

CD INTEREST RATE	7%	8%	9%	10%	11%	12%
Compounded						
Annually	7.000	8.000	9.000	10.000	11.000	12.000
Quarterly	7.186	8.243	9.308	10.381	11.462	12.551
Monthly	7.229	8.300	9.381	10.471	11.572	12.683
Weekly	7.246	8.322	9.409	10.507	11.615	12.734
Daily	7.250	8.328	9.416	10.516	11.626	12.748

institution. Basically, they invest your money in *liquid assets:* Treasury bills and notes, CDs, commercial paper, repurchase agreements, bankers' acceptances, etc. In an effort to boost yields and to attract new clients, some sponsors have expanded their portfolios to include foreign debt, special packages of long-term bonds, and, in separate units, short-term tax-exempt securities. The goal is always to keep all your money working all the time and earning competitive interest rates.

Money market funds pay daily interest that is compounded by immediate reinvestment, permit sales and purchases at net asset value (without commissions), and charge management fees that appear modest but can add up to hefty profits . . . for the managers.

Back in the early 1980s, their yields were over 15% but they have recently ranged from about 6 to 7%. *Repeat:* all money market funds are best for parking places while deciding on more rewarding holdings:

- *With the broker,* for holding interest/dividends and proceeds of sales of securities while waiting for new opportunities
- *With an investment company,* for deposit of new savings and reinvestment of income
- *With institutions,* to gain income on reserves or to accumulate enough money for other commitments

➤ BENEFITS In addition to high yields and relative safety, money market mutual funds offer:

- *Daily income.* Dividends are credited to your account each day, which means that your money is always working for you.
- *Liquidity.* There is no minimum investment period, and there are no early withdrawal penalties. Money generally can be withdrawn by telephone, mail, or wire, or by writing a check.
- *Stability of principal.* Most money market funds have a constant share price (generally $1.00; occasionally $10.00). This makes it easy to determine the value of your investment at any time.
- *No fees or commissions.* When you open your account, all your money goes to work immediately.
- *Small minimum investment.* Some funds require as little as $500 to open; most minimums are between $1,000 and $2,000. In general,

funds do not require shareholders to maintain the minimum investment as an average balance, but they do impose a limit with respect to how low your balance can go.

- *Safety.* Your money is used to buy prime debt of well-rated corporations or the U.S. government and its agencies. If you choose a fund that invests only in U.S. government securities, your yield will be ½ of 1% or so lower, but you can count on Uncle Sam's guarantee. Money market funds bought through your stockbroker and various central management accounts are protected by **SIPC** (Securities Investor Protection Corporation). This is because shares of money market funds are in fact securities (not cash). They are protected by SIPC against the brokerage firm's failure but *not* against declines in the value of the securities (or shares) themselves.

- *Checkwriting.* Most funds offer this service for free, although some require that checks written be at least $250 or $500.

- *Continual high yields.* If rates drop, you will receive the higher interest rate for about a month afterward until the high yielding securities are redeemed. With a bank, the yield changes more frequently, usually on a weekly basis.

SIPC: Securities Investor Protection Corporation, established by Congress to provide customers of most brokerage firms with protection similar to that provided by FDIC for bank depositors, in the event that a firm fails.

MORE ABOUT YIELDS

The yield of a money market fund changes on a daily basis and is never fixed or guaranteed because it reflects the current money market rates earned by the underlying securities that make up the fund's portfolio. The yield that you receive as an investor in the fund is net of the expenses of the fund; in other words, the costs of running the fund (management fees and administrative expenses) are subtracted from the daily gross.

When the manager anticipates that the cost of money will fall, he believes that he must invest new money for a lower yield, so he tries to extend current maturities . . . occasionally as long as 60 days. When he feels that the cost of money will rise soon, he expects to make new investments at a higher rate, so he shortens maturities. This strategy is effective when interest rates are swinging; but when they are relatively stable, there is only a small difference between the 7-day and 30-day yields.

The spreads are small, roughly about ½ of 1% between the high and low average yield. That's only $50 a *year,* so it seldom pays to make frequent switches. Pick a reputable sponsor and stick with one fund *unless* you want the extra safety of U.S. government debt, which yields less. Almost all funds invest in similar securities, so that temporary advantages reflect timing and over a year or so tend to even out.

When the average maturity moves within a narrow range for several weeks, interest rates are likely to remain stable. When the maturity jumps, say from 37 to 40, the professionals look for a decline in the cost of money. Vice versa when the time frame falls.

Timing tip: buy new shares after 3 P.M. You will pay the closing price and get interest for that day.

net asset value (NAV): used in connection with investment companies or mutual funds which compute their assets daily by adding up the market value of all securities owned by the fund. All liabilities are deducted and the balance divided by the number of shares outstanding. The NAV per share is the figure quoted in the papers for mutual funds. **amortization:** gradual reduction of a debt by a series of periodic payments. Each payment includes interest on the outstanding debt and part of the principal.

All money market funds price their shares at $1.00 each—or $10.00 occasionally. The stated yield, as reported weekly in the financial press, reflects the interest earned on investments. But the methods of calculating the value of the underlying assets and the earned income vary. The base is the **net asset value (NAV)** per share. This is determined by subtracting all liabilities from the market value of the fund's shares and dividing the result by the number of shares outstanding. Here are the most widely used systems of calculation:

➤ AMORTIZED COST   This technique values each security at cost at the time of purchase and assumes a constant rate of **amortization** to maturity of any discount or premium. It does not take into account the impact of fluctuating interest rates on the market value of the holdings. The concept is that since the securities will be held to maturity, price is not important.

Example: DD Fund invests $10 million in 8.75% 6-month commercial paper. It expects to get the money back plus interest. But if the cost of money should rise to 9.75% in the next month, the market value of the $10 million holdings will decline. A new investor might pay $1.00 for a share worth 99¢.

To keep the share value at a constant $1.00, the fund must lower the daily dividend by the amount of the change in the underlying values. With a large fund, the effect is minuscule. A 1-day drop in the NAV might decrease the dividend rate by only $\frac{1}{200}$ of 1%.

But other funds investing at a higher rate will report a better yield, so some DD shareholders will redeem their shares and buy shares of the higher yielding funds with new investors. If this continues, the DD fund will be in trouble.

➤ MARK TO THE MARKET   This is similar to an equity mutual fund. At the end of each day, the managers value the shares. The "pure interest" yield is computed to reflect the interest income earned on the portfolio. Then they (1) **mark** their holdings **to the** day's closing **market** prices; (2) figure the per-share capital appreciation or depreciation; (3) add or subtract the gain or loss from the pure interest yield to arrive at the "actual yield."

mark to the market: the value of any portfolio based on the most recent closing price of the securities held.

A variation of this is to mark to market on a variable NAV basis. This does not factor in capital gains or losses but adjusts the NAV (the price of the fund shares paid by investors).

➤ STRAIGHT-LINE ACCRUAL · This recognizes pure interest income only and does not reflect market value fluctuations, so it provides stability of principal and yield.

➤ INTEREST   Mutual funds lend your money for short periods of time, and the fund collects interest on these loans, paying it out to you, the shareholder. The money you deposit in a bank money market account is not invested in any one area; it becomes part of the bank's general assets. Money market mutual funds are required to pay out all their earnings after expenses to shareholders and tend to pay higher rates than banks. Banks are required to pay only the rate that they decide upon and post. The more competitive the banking atmosphere, the higher the interest rates.

HOW MONEY MARKET FUNDS ARE QUOTED

FUND	AVERAGE MATURITY (DAYS)	AVERAGE YIELD	
		7-DAY	30-DAY
Liberty U.S. Government Money Market Trust	38	5.48%	5.62%
Dean Witter/Sears Liquid Asset Trust	62	6.28	6.34
Dean Witter/Sears U.S. Government M.M.T.	68	5.66	5.84
Dreyfus Liquid Assets	58	6.18	6.21
Fidelity Cash Reserves	64	6.22	6.32
Kemper Money Market Fund	40	6.35	6.42
Merrill Lynch CMA Money Fund	64	5.50	6.46
Merrill Lynch Ready Assets Trust	65	5.25	6.33
Shearson Daily Dividend	39	5.95	6.05
T. Rowe Price Prime Reserve	33	6.03	6.11
T. Rowe Price U.S. Treasury	38	5.39	5.53
Donoghue's Money Fund Average™	48	5.89	6.04

SOURCE: Donoghue's *Money Fund Report®* of Holliston, MA 01746. The data provided is from the July 29, 1986, period. This data was obtained from the money funds on July 30, 1986.

If your account is with a bank that has FDIC or a savings and loan that has FSLIC, it is insured up to $100,000 per account. Money market mutual funds with your stockbroker are insured by SIPC. Money market mutual funds purchased directly from the fund are not insured unless the fund itself indicates that it is insured.

THE MONEY MARKET: WHAT IT IS

Contrary to popular belief, the money market does not exist in the heart of Wall Street, or in London, Brussels, or even Washington D.C. Nor is it housed in an impressive Greek revival building. The money market runs throughout the country and

---

MAJOR USES OF MONEY MARKET FUNDS

- As a place to accumulate cash for a large expenditure, such as a house, car, taxes, vacation
- As a place to deposit large amounts of cash received from the sale of a stock, property, inheritance, a bonus, etc.
- As an investment for your IRA, Keogh plan, or custodian account for dependents

is made up of large corporations, banks, the federal government, and even local governments.

When any of these institutions need cash for a short period of time, they borrow it from this seemingly elusive money market by issuing **money market instruments.** For example, the U.S. government borrows through Treasury bills, large corporations through commercial paper, and banks via jumbo CDs.

These instruments are purchased by other large corporations, banks, and even by extremely wealthy investors. The instruments pay high interest rates because the dollar amounts involved are so large, the maturity lengths are so short (one year or less), and the borrowers are well-known and considered excellent risks. It is these money market instruments, not stocks and bonds, that constitute a money market mutual fund's portfolio.

THE ISSUE OF SAFETY

All investors want to know how safe their money market fund or account is. It's very safe. But every investment has some degree of risk, as we've emphasized elsewhere. Money market funds have an excellent safety record, primarily because they invest in short-term securities of the government and large institutions.

money market instruments: short-term credit instruments such as Treasury bills, commercial paper, bankers' acceptances, CDs, repurchase agreements, etc.

WHAT THE MONEY MARKET MUTUAL FUNDS BUY

Bankers acceptances: drafts issued and sold by banks with a promise to pay upon maturity, generally within 180 days or less

Certificates of deposit: large-denomination CDs sold by banks for money deposited for a minimum time period, i.e., 14 days, 91 days, etc.

Commercial paper: unsecured IOUs issued by large institutions and corporations to the public to finance day-to-day operations, usually in amounts of $100,000 for up to 91 days

Eurodollar CDs: dollar-denominated certificates of deposit sold by foreign branches of U.S. banks or by foreign banks; payable outside the United States, the minimum is generally $1 million, with maturities of 14 days or more

Government-agency obligations: short-term securities issued by U.S. government agencies

Repurchase agreements (also called "repos"): short-term buy/sell deals involving any money market instrument (but usually Treasury bills, notes, and bonds) in which there is an agreement that it will be resold to the seller on an agreed-upon date, often the next day. The money market fund holds the securities as collateral and charges interest for the loan. Repos are usually issued as a means for commercial banks and the U.S. government securities dealers to raise temporary funds. Some degree of risk is involved—the possibility that the issuing party may be unable to make its payment. For example, if a bank sells T-bills to a money market fund and the bank fails, the fund will probably never see the interest on the repos, although it would, of course, receive the principal and interest from the actual T-bill.

The basic principle to keep in mind is: the shorter the maturity of an investment, the lower the risk. Money market mutual funds invest in short-term securities.

Two other factors contribute to their superior safety. *One,* money fund managers continually analyze and compile ratings of the strength of the issuers of money market instruments. Whenever an issuer's credit rating declines, the name is deleted from the acceptable list.

Two, the **SEC** regulates the funds, requiring annual independent audits, detailed data in the fund's **prospectus,** and other disclosure requirements.

SEC: the Securities and Exchange Commission, established by Congress to protect investors in their security transactions. **prospectus:** a summary of data on an issue of securities that will be sold to the public, enabling the public to evaluate the security and decide whether or not to buy it. The SEC requires certain information to be set forth in every prospectus.

SELECTING THE RIGHT MONEY MARKET FUND

Although there are over 100 money market mutual funds, they fall into three basic types. Knowing which one is best for meeting your investment goals will help narrow down the search.

- *General funds.* Available from your stockbroker or directly from the fund itself, general funds invest in nongovernment money market securities.
- *Government only funds.* Also available directly or from a broker, government only funds limit their investments to U.S. government or federal agency securities. Because their portfolios are backed by the "full faith and credit" of the U.S. government, they are regarded as less risky; consequently, they have lower yields than general funds.
- *Tax-free funds.* Available directly or from a broker, tax-free funds restrict their portfolios to short-term tax-exempt municipal bonds. Their income is free from federal tax but not from state and local taxes. These are generally advisable only for investors in the 28% tax

---

CASH MISMANAGEMENT ACCOUNTS

In their efforts to develop new packages more profitable to the sponsor, some fund managers are offering special deals that involve unusual activities: moving part of their portfolio into debt investments by short-term loans to shareholders, based on home equity. These are actually second (or third) mortgages, dangerous to the borrower as well as to other shareholders. The interest charges are high, the paperwork substantial, and the rationale questionable.

Whenever you are offered such special "opportunities," check the costs and terms yourself and do not rely on the salesperson's explanation. In most cases, you will find that the costs are higher than those readily available elsewhere and that the services will be provided by an outside organization that will be difficult to monitor and almost impossible to control.

Money market funds are convenient and can keep your money working, but they are not always the best investments for income.

bracket. Their yields are, of course, much lower, generally about half those of a regular money market fund.

Here there are few changes in the weekly returns because the supply of bonds and trading is limited. If you make a substantial investment in these funds, check the quality and maturity of the underlying bonds. To boost returns, some managers hedge on quality and buy intermediate and long-term issues, which leads to less liquidity and flat yields.

When interest rates rise, the value of debt securities usually falls, but less so with long-term municipals. Their prices react slowly. As a rule, the spread between the returns of long-term municipals and short-term taxable issues should be at least 2 percentage points. *Tax-free money market funds are more appealing now that other ways of sheltering income have been limited by the new tax ruling, although their yields are typically lower.*

BANK ACCOUNTS VS. MONEY MARKET FUNDS

credit card: plastic card issued by a bank or financial institution that gives the holder access to a line of credit to purchase goods or to receive cash. Repayment may be required in full in 30 days or in installments.

debit card: a deposit access card. It debits the holder's bank account or money market account immediately upon use in purchasing. There is no 30-day period in which to pay. It is done immediately and electronically upon purchase.

There's still competition between money market funds and bank accounts, but the choice will increasingly depend on extras: *with banks,* free checking services or gifts; *with institutions,* discounts on brokerage services, no-fee **credit and debit cards,** extended line of credit, direct deposit of pension and dividend checks, and so on.

In many cases, you can arrange to tailor your account to your own and family needs, so once you have determined your resources, ask for advice from the experts. With a mutual fund, you can switch to other funds under the same management and take advantage of other services such as low-cost life insurance, monthly checks at retirement, and computerized accounting. With a bank account, the big benefit is convenience:

- Easy access at a number of local offices
- Instant interest as new deposits are credited immediately. With funds,

---

COMPARING MONEY MARKET FUNDS AND TREASURY BONDS AT DIFFERENT INTEREST RATES: $100,000 INVESTMENT

INVESTMENT	6%	8%	10%	12%	14%	16%
Money market fund	$133,823	$146,933	$161,051	$176,234	$192,541	$210,034
U.S. Treasury 14¾, '89	157,010	160,156	163,562	167,170	171,103	175,310
U.S. Treasury 11⅞, '89	158,606	160,455	162,830	165,400	168,709	172,440
U.S. Treasury 8¼, '90	161,140	161,057	161,899	162,931	165,287	168,264
U.S. Treasury 15¾, '01	176,108	164,141	161,547	156,685	161,319	164,214
U.S. Treasury 7⅝, '07	183,730	164,444	159,318	151,464	156,063	157,108
U.S. Treasury 11¾, '10	183,205	165,488	161,102	155,392	158,936	160,377

SOURCE: © Medical Economics Co., Inc., Oradell, NJ 07649.

it takes a couple of days for the mail to get through and up to 10 days more for the check to clear, so that you can lose as much as a third of your monthly income.

■   Local merchants will accept checks drawn against your account but may balk at cashing one drawn on the fund's bank.

■   In Connecticut and New Hampshire, income from money market funds is taxed as dividends, but there's no tax on bank savings/investment accounts.

BANK CDs/ACCOUNTS VS. T-BILLS

When you can afford to invest $10,000, compare the 6-month money market certificates with Treasury bills. In most cases (especially in states where there are income taxes), the T-bills will be a better deal. Here's the calculation:

1. Since T-bills are sold at a discount, use this formula:

$$D = \frac{L \times SY}{360}$$

D = discount per $100 face value
L = life-span of security
360 = number of days in financial year
SY = stated yield

With a 180-day T-bill and a 9% yield,

$$D = \frac{180}{360} = 5 \qquad 5 \times 9 = 4.50$$

Subtract the 4.50 ($450) from $10,000 to get $9,550 cost.

2. The true yield of the T-bill is more, because T-bill trading uses a 360-day year, but your money works 365 days and the stated yield is based on the cost.

$$TY = \frac{D}{C} \times \frac{365}{L}$$

TY = true yield
D = discount
C = cost
L = life-span of security

With that 180-day T-bill, a yield of 9% and a cost of $9,550, the true yield is 9.56%.

$$TY = \frac{4.50}{9550} = 4.71$$

$$\frac{365}{180} = 2.03 \qquad 4.71 \times 2.03 = 9.56\%$$

3. Interest on T-bills is exempt from state and local income taxes. That on the certificate is fully taxable.

4. If the certificate is cashed in early, there's a penalty. With T-bills, there's an active aftermarket so you will get more than you invested since the sales price includes accumulated interest—unless there's a sharp rise in interest rates.

COMPARISON OF $100,000 INVESTMENT IN TAX-FREE MONEY MARKET FUND AND BONDS
AT DIFFERENT INTEREST RATES

INVESTMENT	3.5%	4.75%	5.7%	7%	8%	9.25%
Tax-free money market fund	$118,769	$126,116	$132,254	$140,255	$146,933	$155,635
Tampa Solid Waste 7¼, '89	139,338	139,690	140,169	141,007	141,760	143,008
W.Va. Bldg. Revenue 3½, '91	139,439	137,165	135,981	135,310	134,994	135,621
San Antonio Water 5¼, '94	147,864	141,293	138,064	137,011	135,644	136,459
NYC PHA 3¾, '96	150,286	140,517	135,666	133,707	129,255	129,011
Wash. Cty. (Okla.) Medical 6¼, '03	172,146	153,714	149,556	146,909	141,612	140,949
Michigan Mtg. 9¼, '09	173,453	151,541	151,072	149,462	145,573	144,614

SOURCE: © Medical Economics Co., Inc., Oradell, NJ 07649.

How is the minimum balance calculated? On any one day? On the average daily balance? The average will usually work out better and avoid extra costs if there's a 1-day drop in your total.

To compare the yield between a 91-day bank CD and a 91-day T-bill, refer to the example and heed this advice from Donoghue's *Moneyletter:*

- If you have $25,000 or more, you will earn more with the T-bill, despite the $35 or so transaction costs.
- If you have less than $25,000, you'll earn more with the bank CD.

FOR FURTHER INFORMATION

For a complete list of money market mutual funds with their toll-free numbers and initial investment requirements:

The Investment Company Institute
1600 M Street N.W.
Washington, D.C. 20036
1-202-293-7700

For information on safety and funds:

"A Beginner's Guide to Mutual Funds:
Money Fund Safety Ratings"
Institute for Econometric Research
3471 North Federal Highway
Fort Lauderdale, FL 33306
1-305-563-9000

For a list of funds that invest only in U.S. guaranteed securities:

Donoghue's Moneyletter
P.O. Box 540
Holliston, MA 01746
1-617-429-5930

Among the better known funds in this category are:

Capital Preservation Fund
1-800-227-8380

Fidelity U.S. Government Reserves
1-800-544-6666

Government Investors Trust
1-800-336-3063

Merrill Lynch Government Fund
1-800-225-1576

Funds without specific dollar minimums:

Cash & Plus Trust
1-800-345-1151

First Trust Money Market Mutual Fund
1-800-621-4770

Funds requiring only $500 initial deposits:

Daily Cash Accumulation
1-800-525-9310

Franklin Group Money Funds
1-800-632-2180 (in California)
1-800-227-6781 (outside California)

Tax-exempt funds:

Dreyfus Tax-Exempt Money Market Fund
1-718-895-1206
1-800-645-6561 (outside NY)

Franklin Tax-Free Income Fund
See Franklin Group above

Lexington Tax-Free Daily Income Fund
1-800-526-4791

Insured money market fund:

Vanguard Insured Money Market Portfolio
1-800-523-7025 (outside Pennsylvania)
1-800-362-0530 (in Pennsylvania)

NEWSLETTERS

Call or write for sample issues if you are interested in receiving continual data on the funds.

Donoghue's Moneyletter
See above
Twice a month; $87 per year includes two semiannual directories

Money Fund Safety Ratings
Institute for Econometric Research
See above
Monthly; $49 per year

4

THE CENTRAL ASSET ACCOUNT:
One-Stop Shopping

If you have a brokerage account, a money market fund, and a major credit card, as well as some type of checking account, you may find it useful and economical to wrap it all together and put it into a combo, or central assets, account. In this way, all your financial transactions will be handled under one roof—at a bank or brokerage firm—which saves you time, red tape, and sometimes money, too.

A typical central assets account consists of one versatile package which can include stocks, bonds, your IRA, money market fund, and credit or debit card transactions. But you must be able to meet the minimum amount set by the brokerage firm or bank, which ranges from $5,000 to $20,000.

For a yearly fee ($25 to $100) the sponsoring bank or brokerage firm will provide unlimited checkwriting privileges on a money market account; an American Express, Visa, or MasterCard account; a line of credit; a securities brokerage account; and an all-inclusive monthly statement. An important additional benefit, known as the "sweep" feature, automatically transfers or sweeps any idle cash (from the sale of a security, from a CD that matured, or from dividends) into a high-paying money market fund. This system not only relieves you from keeping track of the money but more importantly, prevents any loss of interest between transactions.

The combo plans were pioneered by Merrill Lynch in 1977 when it launched its Cash Management Account (CMA). Others soon followed Merrill's lead, and today most large brokerage firms, many of the smaller houses, and even a few discount brokerage firms offer some form of umbrella plan.

Although each firm advertises "unique features," all comprise seven basic ingredients:

- A brokerage account in which securities can be bought and sold at regular commissions
- Automatic investment of idle cash into money market funds
- A checking account, usually with free checks; minimum amounts vary
- A debit or credit card that can be used for purchases, loans, or cash
- A line of credit, i.e., the privilege of borrowing against your credit or debit card
- Quick loans secured by the margin value of the securities held in the account, with interest charged at slightly above the broker call rate
- Composite monthly statements showing all transactions and balances

Here's how a central assets account works. Let's say you have 300 shares of Eastman Kodak that you want to sell. You call your broker and direct him or her to make the transaction. Money from the sale is immediately invested in a money market fund, where it earns around 8%. The transfer of money from your securities account to the money market fund is done automatically by computer.

CENTRAL ASSET ACCOUNT	MINIMUM OPENING INVESTMENT	ANNUAL FEE	SWEEP OF FUNDS	RETURN OF CANCELED CHECKS	CARD	EXTRA FEATURES	TELEPHONE NUMBER
Merrill Lynch Cash Management Account	$20,000	$50	All funds, daily	No	Visa debit	No minimum requirements for checks	1-800-262-4636
Dean Witter Active Assets Account	$20,000	$50	All funds, daily	No	Visa debit	Sears Allstate Insurance	1-800-722-3030
Shearson Financial Management Account	$15,000	$100	$1,000+, daily; Less than $1,000, weekly	No	American Express Gold credit	Envoy Travel Service; Check cashing at American Express offices	1-800-522-5429
Prudential Command Account	$10,000	$50	All funds, daily	No	Visa debit	Discounts on certain items	1-800-222-4321
E. F. Hutton Asset Management	$10,000	$80	$1,000, daily; $100 to $1,000, weekly; $1 to $100, monthly	Yes	American Express Gold credit	No minimum requirements for checks	1-800-334-4636
Paine Webber Resource Management Account	$15,000	$100 (card); $60 (no card)	$500, daily; Less than $500, weekly	Yes	Master Gold credit	Insurance for travel	1-800-762-1000

Account	Minimum	Annual Fee	Sweep	Checks	Card	Features	Telephone
Smith Barney Vantage Account	$20,000	$100 (card) $40 (no card)	$1,000, daily Less than $1,000, weekly	Yes	American Express Gold credit	Check cashing at American Express offices	1-800-522-9300
Kidder Peabody Premium Account	$25,000	$75	$1,000, daily Less than $1,000, weekly	No	Visa debit	Nil	1-800-221-1808
A. G. Edwards Total Asset Account	$20,000	$50	$500 or more, daily Rest, weekly	No	Visa credit	Nil	1-212-952-7200 collect
Advest Cash Reserve Account	$5,000	$25	Daily if over $100	No	Visa debit	Nil	1-212-747-4700 collect
Fidelity Ultra Service Account	$10,000 cash or $20,000 securities	$36	All funds, daily	Yes	Master debit	Nationwide ATM access; discount brokerage service	1-800-343-8721
Citibank Focus Account	$10,000	$60	All funds, daily	Yes	Visa debit	Discount brokerage service; nationwide ATM access	1-800-752-0800
Charles Schwab One Account	$5,000	None	All funds, daily	No	Visa debit	Discount brokerage service	1-800-227-4444

Then a few weeks later you write a check for $800. You do so against your money market fund, leaving a balance of several thousand dollars. You felt this was an adequate balance—and it was, until you had a sudden emergency and needed to use that amount plus $1,500. So your broker arranged for a loan using your remaining securities as collateral. This was done in your margin account. By having an umbrella account, you avoided hours of time and miles of red tape that customarily are involved in obtaining a bank loan.

Many of the larger brokerage firms offer customers one of several funds in which to park their idle cash: a regular money market fund; a U.S. government fund, which is slightly safer but also has lower yields; and a tax-free money fund for those in high-tax brackets.

The traditional monthly statement includes:

- A list of securities held in the account
- Securities bought or sold with an indication of profit or loss
- Amount of commission paid to the broker
- Dividends received
- Interest received from the money market fund
- Number of money market fund shares
- Amount of margin loans, either advanced or paid off
- Credit and debit card transactions
- Data required in preparing your income tax returns

Before you leap into a central assets account, check out the following:

- Minimum required to open the account
- Annual fee
- Commission charged
- Margin loan rate
- Method for handling debit and credit card transactions
- Frequency of sweeps into money market funds
- Number of money market funds to choose from
- Minimum amount for writing checks
- Clarity of monthly statements
- Any extras offered

You should also keep in mind some of the disadvantages of this type of account. First of all, most components of a combo account are available elsewhere. Credit card holders already have credit lines and cash advances. Debit cards can be a disadvantage because they provide a shorter "float period"—that is, less free credit time than that for a standard credit card. With the latter, you can stretch your credit or payment time up to at least 30 days, sometimes 60 or 90.

Interest rates on margin loans are sometimes higher than rates on other types of loans. Margin loan rates are determined by what banks charge the brokers for borrowed money. This is called the "broker loan rate," which is usually the same as the bank's prime rate. (Check to make certain that your margin account rate is not more than 2% higher than the broker loan rate.)

Your stocks in a margin account are held "in street name," which means in the broker's firm. You cannot, therefore, put your stock certificates in your vault. You may also be subject to "margin call" if you use the assets in your account to the point where you have no more credit and/or if the value of your portfolio falls below a minimum amount. Then your broker will ask you to reduce some of the loan. If you cannot come up with the cash or additional securities, your broker may have to sell some of your remaining stock.

Some investors find that such easy access to money and loans makes it possible for them to spend more than they should. If you fall into this category, then steer clear of the central assets account.

FOR FURTHER INFORMATION

The Better Business Bureau in many areas has free material on central asset accounts, banks, and brokerage services. Contact your local office.

If you live in New York, write to:

The Better Business Bureau of New York
257 Park Avenue South
New York, NY 10010

They will send you a free copy of the brochure, "Choosing a Central Assets Account."

5

THE SAFETY FACTOR

Continental Illinois; Washington Public Power Supply (WHOOPS); John Muir; Baldwin United Charter; Penn Square; Home State—all recent nightmares of the financial world because they failed the investing public.

These debacles have caused even the most trusting investors and savers to question how safe their securities and cash are in the nation's banks, savings and loans, and brokerage firms—and rightly so.

BANKS

Over the past 4 years, more banks and savings and loan associations have been liquidated or merged than in any time since the Great Depression. The number of commercial and savings banks on the Federal Deposit Insurance Corporation agency's trouble list is now in excess of 1000—and in 1985 the FDIC closed 120 banks.

THE FACTS

Most of the country's commercial and savings banks are insured by the Federal Deposit Insurance Corporation (FDIC); only 676 are not. FDIC is an independent government agency. To be eligible for membership in FDIC, a bank must meet certain standards and be regularly examined by both federal and state agencies. Member banks pay insurance fees, which in turn are invested in federal government securities. This constitutes the FDIC's insurance fund. In addition, the FDIC may borrow several billion dollars from the U.S. Treasury, even though it has never had to do so in the more than 50 years since it was established.

Of the 3,460 savings and loan associations in operation, 2,900 are insured by Federal Savings & Loan Insurance Corporation (FSLIC); 475 are covered by state insurance, and 25 are privately insured. There are 61 savings and loan associations that have absolutely no insurance at all.

Most credit unions (84%) are insured by the National Credit Union Administration (NCUA); others, by state agencies.

The FDIC, FSLIC, and NCUA are all backed by the federal government, and money insured by them is considered extremely safe. Those which are state or privately insured do not have the backing of the federal government.

So make certain that you bank at a *federally insured institution* and keep in mind that depositors, *not* accounts, are insured up to $100,000, including interest and principal. That means that even if you have four accounts in one institution, you are insured up to a total of only $100,000, not $400,000.

Four types of accounts are insured separately from other accounts that you may have in one institution. Each is insured individually for $100,000. They are: IRAs, Keoghs, testamentary accounts, and irrevocable trusts.

If a federally insured institution fails, regulators will liquidate the assets, and insured depositors will be paid in 7 to 10 business days. If you have money in excess of the $100,000 insured limit, however, you will have a pro rata stake for that portion in excess of $100,000, along with other creditors, and you may or may not get that portion of your money back.

BANK CHECKUP

You can protect your money by taking these steps:

1   Get a copy of your bank's annual report and financial statements

---

GOVERNMENT PROTECTION

FEDERAL DEPOSIT INSURANCE CORPORATION
- Guarantees depositors for up to $100,000: $3 billion credit line with the U.S. Treasury
- Insured deposits: $1.3 trillion
- Fund's assets: $17.0 billion
- Consumer hotline: 1-800-424-4334
- Address for more information on evaluating your bank: 550 17 Street, N.W., Washington, D.C. 20429

FEDERAL SAVINGS AND LOAN INSURANCE CORPORATION
- Guarantees depositors for up to $100,000: U.S. Treasury will provide up to $750 million should FSLIC need more money
- Telephone: 1-202-377-6933
- Address for more information on evaluating your S&L: 1700 G Street, N.W., Washington, D.C. 20429

NATIONAL CREDIT UNION SHARE INSURANCE FUND
- Guarantees depositors for up to $100,000: $100 million credit line with U.S. Treasury
- Insured deposits: $85 billion
- Reserves and equity capital: $1.14 billion
- Telephone 1-202-357-1050
- Address for more information on your credit union: 1776 G Street, N.W., Washington, D.C. 20456

STATE PLANS
- 27 states and Puerto Rico sponsor their own insurance programs to cover 3,903 state-chartered institutions:
  Arizona, California, Colorado, Florida, Georgia, Idaho, Illinois, Indiana, Iowa, Kansas, Maryland, Massachusetts, Minnesota, Missouri, Nevada, New Jersey, North Carolina, Ohio, Pennsylvania, Rhode Island, Tennessee, Texas, Utah, Virginia, Washington, West Virginia, and Wisconsin
- They are *not* covered by federal insurance

2   Request and read the "Report of Condition" on your bank. It will tell
    how much the bank is making, what its loan portfolio is made up of,
    and what percentage of loans are nonperforming. Order from:

    FDIC
    Data Base Room 3070-F
    550 17 Street, N.W.
    Washington, D.C. 20429

3   Request and read "Uniform Bank Performance Reports," which
    compare banks within a certain state or county. They cost $25 each.
    Order from:

    Federal Financial Institutions Examination Council
    U.B.P.R.
    Dept. 4320
    Chicago, IL 60673

4   David C. Cates, president of Cates (Bank) Consulting Analysts, Inc.,
    gives these guidelines for determining a bank's safety:

■   Excessively rapid growth of commercial loans—
    indicates a bank that hasn't enough expert people to check credit
    ratings and make loan assessments
■   Unusually high loan portfolio yields—
    indicates that the bank may be making risky loans
■   Increased reliance on funds outside the bank's natural market—
    suggests lack of client support and a pulling out of outsiders at the
    first sign of trouble
■   How solid is the bank's loan portfolio?
    Determined by comparing nonperforming assets (loans that are 90+
    days overdue or are no longer accruing interest) to total loans, the
    FDIC bank standard being 1%
■   Could the bank handle a run?
    Look for a loan-deposit ratio of no more than 70% and a minimum
    of 5% in cash or short-term investments.

BROKERAGE FIRMS

The 1970 Securities Investor Protection Act covers investors through its
nonprofit Securities Investor Protection Corporation (SIPC). This is not a
government agency, nor is it a regulatory agency. Rather, it is funded
through assessment of dealer members. If a member brokerage firm fails,
then SIPC appoints a trustee to liquidate the firm and perhaps transfer
customer accounts to another broker. (If the firm is a small one, SIPC may
decide to cover losses from its funds immediately.)

    If it has the securities on hand, the liquidating firm will send the
securities registered in customers' names directly to them. If it does not
have enough securities to meet all customer claims, the customers will

receive them on a pro rata basis and any remaining securities will be met in cash.

If the brokerage house in liquidation does not have enough securities or funds to settle all claims, the rest will be met by SIPC—up to $500,000 per customer, including $100,000 in cash.

Not everything is covered by SIPC, only cash and securities, that is, stocks, bonds, CDs, notes, and warrants on securities. Commodities and commodity options are not covered. Shares in money market mutual funds *are* covered by SIPC.

With some brokerage firms it is possible to extend your coverage by opening a second account as a joint account with your spouse, as a trustee for a child, or as a business account, because each account receives full protection—$500,000.

Keep in mind that SIPC covers losses due to the failure of the firm, not losses because investments turned out to be poor quality or because securities fell in price.

THE REPOS ISSUE

The March 1985 failure of an Ohio savings and loan association—Home State Savings of Cincinnati—stemmed directly from the collapse of an obscure Florida bond dealer, E.S.M. Government Securities of Fort Lauderdale. On March 4, the SEC closed down E.S.M., charging that the firm had huge losses and was defrauding customers. As it turned out, the Cincinnati savings and loan association was not the only loser. Beaumont, Texas, had $20 million at stake; Toledo, Ohio, and nine other cities are still trying to collect $76 million.

There have been other similar cases in which the government securities market has crippled savings and loan associations, cities, and even major banks: notably Chase Manhattan Bank, which lost $117 million with Drysdale Government Securities, a Wall Street firm that was forced to close its doors in 1982.

These and other failures, the result of a falling domino effect or daisy-chain reaction, center around the complex U.S. Treasury securities market and, in particular, "repos," or repurchase agreements. Repos allow large investors and dealers to trade cash for packages of Treasury bills and long-term bonds. A repo agreement takes place when one party sells government securities to another, with an agreement to repurchase them later on at a higher price, which includes interest.

A number of city or municipal managers use repos to loan idle cash overnight or for several days, at rates somewhat above T-bill rates. In the past, repos were regarded as almost risk-free, because the dealer backed them with Treasuries as collateral. But some dealers have failed to place the collateral with the designated trustee; in fact, some apparently use the same collateral to back more than one loan.

The number of government security dealers has grown concomitant with the increasing size of the federal debt. In fact, the government securities market is by far the largest U.S. security market: the daily trading volume has reached the $60 billion mark. One reason for spreading concern is that firms trading only in government securities are not required to register with the SEC, although a movement is underway to impose some sort of regulation.

In the meantime, about the only way investors can protect themselves is to take possession of their collateral when turning over the cash.

FOR FURTHER INFORMATION

If you have a complaint or question about your bank, write to the Consumer Services Division of your State Banking Commission or Department.

If you live in New York, write to:

> Consumer Services Division
> New York State Banking Department
> Two World Trade Center
> New York, NY 10047

An overview of the financial condition of many commercial banks, savings and loans, and credit unions is provided for a modest fee by:

> Veribanc, Inc.
> P.O. Box 2963
> Woburn, MA 01888
> 1-617-245-8370

For information about a brokerage firm and its insurance:

> Office of Consumer Affairs
> Securities & Exchange Commission
> Washington, D.C. 20549

For information about SIPC and what it covers:

> SIPC
> 900 17th Street N.W.
> Washington, D.C. 20006
> 1-202-223-8400

6

A BRIEF DIRECTORY OF INVESTMENTS

The following several pages list all the major vehicles available to the average investor. This directory should be your base of operations. Refer back to it as you read further in the book and come across terms you have not encountered before, or if you need more specific information.

The Directory will tell you:

- The name of the investment
- Pages in this book where it is described in full
- Its risk factor and position on the investment pyramid (pages 15–16)
- How much money you will need to buy or invest in it
- Where to purchase it

PAGES IN THIS BOOK	INVESTMENT	DESCRIPTION	WHERE TO BUY	GOAL
314–316	Annuity	Provides regular, guaranteed income payments for life or set time period	Life insurance companies	Retirement income
31	Asset Management Account	One-stop financial plan that includes brokerage account, checking, debit and credit card, money market fund	Brokerage firms, banks, insurance companies, mutual fund companies	Interest income
20	Certificate of deposit (CD)	Receipt for set sum of money left in bank for set period of time at an agreed-upon interest rate; at end of period, bank pays deposit plus interest	Bank, credit union, savings and loan associations, brokerage firms	Interest income
25	Commercial paper	Short-term unsecured notes sold by large corporations	Brokerage firms, bank holding companies, corporations	Interest income
	Commodities (see Futures contracts)			
69–75	Common stock	Security that represents ownership in a company	Brokerage firms, directly from company in a few cases	Income and/or appreciation
76–83	Convertible	Bond, debenture, or preferred share of stock which may be exchanged by owner for common stock, usually of same company	Brokerage firms	Income and/or appreciation
87–92	Corporate bond	Debt obligation of corporation	Brokerage firms	Income

PYRAMID LEVEL	RISK LEVEL	PROS	CONS	MINIMUM OR RECOMMENDED $
2	Low	Safe; minimum guaranteed rate of interest in regular annuity; variable has higher fluctuating rate; can usually borrow cash value at low rates	May pay very low interest rates; high sales commissions reflected in low returns	Varies
1	Low	Reduces record-keeping; offers margin loans; centralized approach to money	Annual fee; high initial investment; may push you to trade or make unnecessary loans	$5,000 to $20,000
1 or 2	Low	Insured up to $100,000 by federal government; competitive interest rates	Penalty for early withdrawal; interest rates may rise while your money is locked in	$500
1 or 2	Low	Competitive yields; backed by credit of the borrowing company	Not collateralized by assets of issuing company; riskier than CD; no secondary market	$25,000
3	Medium	Potential for high rate of return	Market risks; not insured or protected by government; value fluctuates daily	$1,000+
3	Average	Combines safety of bonds and preferred stock with potential of capital appreciation of common stock	Lower yield than similar quality nonconvertibles; sell at premiums to the conversion value of the common stock	$5,000
2	Average	Receive fixed return over long period of time; assured return; high quality available with bond ratings	May be called in prior to maturity	$5,000

PAGES IN THIS BOOK	INVESTMENT	DESCRIPTION	WHERE TO BUY	GOAL
207, 215	Futures contracts	Contracts covering sale of financial instruments or physical commodities for future delivery; includes agricultural products, metals, T-bills, foreign currencies, and stock index futures (i.e., S&P 500)	Commodity futures exchanges; commodities' futures broker	Short-term trading profits
306–310	IRA	Individual Retirement Account that is tax-advantaged	Banks, brokerage firms, credit unions, insurance companies, mutual fund companies	Retirement income
310–311	Keogh plan	Retirement plan for self-employed that is tax-advantaged	Same as IRA	Retirement income
19–20	Money market deposit account	A type of money market fund at a bank or savings and loan association with limited checking privileges	Banks, savings and loan associations	Interest income
20–27	Money market mutual fund	An investment company which buys short-term money market instruments	Mutual fund companies, brokerage firms, insurance companies	Interest income
107–111	Mortgage-backed securities	Securities representing a share ownership in pools of mortgages; backed by federal, state, or local governments; include Ginnie Maes, Fannie Maes, Freddie Macs, etc.	Securities dealers, occasionally issuing institution	Interest income and retirement income

PYRAMID LEVEL	RISK LEVEL	PROS	CONS	MINIMUM OR RECOMMENDED $
4	High	High potential through use of leverage; taxed at favorable rate	Highly speculative; subject to volatile markets; must constantly monitor position	$2,000
1	Varies	Contributions up to $2,000 are deductible each year for those without private pension plans; deduction phased out for others as income rises; totally abolished for joint filers with incomes above $50,000 and for singles above $35,000	Withdrawals before age 59½ generally penalized 10% and are subject to taxes	$250
1	Varies	Contributions up to maximum of 15% of income or $30,000 are tax-deductible each year; account grows tax-free until withdrawn; can also have IRA	Same as above	$250
1	Low	No federal regulation of rates: banks can set their own; insured by federal government up to $100,000; no withdrawal penalties; can withdraw by check, ATM, or in person	Minimum balance required; limited checkwriting; monthly fees	$1,000 to $2,500
1	Low	High short-term interest rates; no withdrawal penalties; handled by professional money managers; checkwriting privileges	Not insured except in rare cases; no growth potential	$1,000
2	Low	Backed by government or government agencies; high yields; liquidity; receive regular prorated monthly income	Subject to interest rate fluctuations; payments dwindle and eventually cease as mortgages are paid off	$1,000 if in a mutual fund; $25,000 otherwise

PAGES IN THIS BOOK	INVESTMENT	DESCRIPTION	WHERE TO BUY	GOAL
112–117	Municipal bond	Debt obligation of state, city, town, or their agencies	Banks, brokerage firms	Tax-free income in most cases
118–127	Mutual fund	Investment trust in which your dollars are pooled with those of hundreds of others and invested by professional managers in stocks or bonds	Mutual fund companies, brokerage firms, insurance companies	Income and/or appreciation
18–19	NOW account	Negotiable order of withdrawal interest-bearing checking account	Banks, savings and loan associations	Interest income
222–231	Options	The right to buy (call) or sell (put) a stock at a given price (strike price) for a given period of time	Brokerage firms	Appreciation
84–86	Preferred stock	Stock sold with a fixed dividend; if company is liquidated, has priority over common stock	Brokerage firms	Income
304	REIT	Real estate investment trusts; corporation or trust that invests in or finances real estate: offices, shopping centers, apartments, hotels, etc.; sold as securities	Brokerage firms	Appreciation
17–18	Savings account	Account in which money deposited earns interest	Banks, savings and loan associations, credit unions	Interest income
19	SuperNOW account	Interest-bearing bank account	Banks, savings and loan associations, credit unions	Interest income
92–93	Treasury bills	Short-term U.S. Treasury securities; maturities: 13, 26, 52 weeks	Federal reserve banks, commercial banks, brokerage firms, U.S. Treasury	Interest income

PYRAMID LEVEL	RISK LEVEL	PROS	CONS	MINIMUM OR RECOMMENDED $
2	Low (on bonds rated A or better)	Interest earned is tax-free at federal level and in state and city where issued	Return is lower than on taxable bonds; subject to price fluctuations	$5,000
2 or 3	Varies	Professional management; diversification reduces risk; can switch from one fund to another within a family of funds; wide selection; low minimums	Not federally insured; subject to fluctuations in the stock market and in interest rates	$1,000
1	Low	Funds in account earn interest; unlimited checking; federally insured up to $100,000	Interest rates are low; must maintain minimum balance	$300 to $3,000
4	High	Large amount of leverage possible; inexpensive way to speculate	Can lose entire investment premium paid if underlying stock becomes worthless in time	$2,000
2	Varies	Fixed rate of return; safer than common stock dividends	Dividend is never increased	$2,000
3	Average	Provides participation in real estate with small amount of money	Subject to fluctuations of real estate and the stock market	$2,000
1	Low	Federally insured up to $100,000; guaranteed yield; can be used as collateral	Low interest rates; minimum balance required in some cases	$5 to $100
1	Low	No federally imposed ceiling on interest rate if minimum maintained; insured by federal government up to $100,000; checkwriting privileges; liquidity	Minimum balance required to earn top interest rates; fees or penalties imposed if balance falls below minimum	$2,500
1 or 2	Low	Backed by U.S. government; interest earned is exempt from state and local taxes	Sold at auction, so you will not know yield at time of purchase	$10,000

PAGES IN THIS BOOK	INVESTMENT	DESCRIPTION	WHERE TO BUY	GOAL
93	Treasury bonds	Long-term U.S. Treasury securities; maturities: 10 years or more	Same as T-bills	Interest income
93	Treasury notes	Medium-term securities of U.S. Treasury; maturities: not less than 1 year and not more than 10 years	Same as T-bills	Interest income
115–116	Unit investment trust	Fixed portfolio of securities deposited with a trustee; offered to public in units; categories include municipal bonds, corporate bonds, public utility common stocks, etc.	Brokerage firms, sponsor	Income and/or appreciation
95–97	U.S. Savings Bonds	Debt obligation of U.S. Treasury designed for small investor	Banks, savings and loan associations, Federal Reserve banks, U.S. Treasury	Interest income
196–199	Warrant	Gives holder right to purchase a given stock at a stipulated price over a fixed number of years	Brokerage firms	Appreciation
103–105	Zero coupon bond	Debt instrument; sold at discount from face value with no (zero) annual interest paid out; capital appreciation realized upon maturity; includes TIGERS, CATS	Brokerage firms, banks	Appreciation

PYRAMID LEVEL	RISK LEVEL	PROS	CONS	MINIMUM OR RECOMMENDED $
2	Low	Backed by U.S. government; interest earned is exempt from state and local taxes	Some interest-rate risk	$1,000
2	Low	Backed by U.S. government; interest earned is exempt from state and local taxes	Some interest-rate risk	$1,000 (4 years+); $5,000 (less than 4 years)
2 or 3	Average	Diversification; professional selection; usually can redeem units; available in small dollar amounts	Portfolio is not managed; most have 25–30 year maturities	$5,000; occasionally $1,000
1	Low	Guaranteed principal and interest; if held 5 years, return is 85% of the average yield on 5-year Treasury security with a 7.5% minimum guaranteed; exempt from state and local income taxes; may defer federal tax; registered, so it can be replaced if lost or stolen	Generally lower rate of interest than available elsewhere	$25
4	High	An inexpensive way to invest; if primary shares go up, so will warrant; can exercise warrant at any time	If warrant expires, lose all your investment; always sells at a premium over common stock	$1,000
3	Average	Low initial expenditure leads to balloon payment upon maturity; know exact amount that you will receive	Yields lower than for regular bonds; must pay taxes annually as though you received interest	$1,000

THE INVESTOR'S ALMANAC

Have you just come into a windfall? Did a relative leave you an unexpected inheritance? Or perhaps you're a bit weary of traditional investments—stocks, bonds, mutual funds, and the like. Maybe you've been thinking about beginning a small collection. The urge to try something a little different lurks in the minds of even the most staid investors and it tends to bubble forth in healthy markets.

There are endless numbers of "offbeat" investment choices if you are willing to be experimental. The Investor's Almanac, which is a new feature this year, highlights three of the most timely offbeat choices. These do not come with a guarantee that you'll make a huge killing, but on the other hand you most certainly will have fun learning about a new field, and, of course, you may see a solid return on your investment over the long term.

Before you invest in any one of the three Investor's Almanac selections, spend some time doing background preparation. A suggested reading list is provided. If you know your own experts or collectors in these areas, consult with them for advice and additional suggestions. In terms of the two collectibles we have selected (and any other antiques or works of art you may be considering):

- **Buy only what you like.** If later on the value should fall or if you decide to sell only part of your collection and keep this particular item, you should be left with something you love.
- **Focus on something.** Random collecting tends to be less valuable over the years. Decide on an art form or category. Then try to specialize in an artist, period, craftsman, or country. Unrelated individual pieces have less marketability than a cohesive collection.

- **Set aside a limited dollar amount.** You can revise this amount annually. Don't take all your money out of your money market fund or sell your IBM stock to move into exotic investments. If you suddenly should need cash when everything you have is tied up in antique silver, platinum, or art pottery, you will be forced to sell, and if at the time prices are low, you will have made a poor investment decision. It's always best to diversify.
- **Buy in your price range.** If your resources are modest to start with, then begin small. As circumstances and finances improve you can always go after more elaborate and expensive items. It is unwise to take a second mortgage to make your first purchase.

ANTIQUE SILVER

In the current environment, very few collectibles offer the investment opportunity afforded by antique silver. There are several reasons for this, the key one being that the price of silver is low. It is selling between $5 and $6 an ounce, well below the $50 price reached in 1979–80. Pieces by little-known yet good silversmiths are still within reach—from $750 to $2,000. A top quality teapot by a well-known artisan is in the $8,000 to $10,000 range. In addition, the dollar is still fairly strong vis-à-vis the British pound, making British antique silver a particularly interesting choice at this time.

You can easily compare antique prices with their modern counterparts. An original pair of Georgian candlesticks, for example, will sell for between $1,000 and $2,500 while a new pair at Tiffany & Co. in New York are likely to be $5,000 to $10,000.

Another reason for considering silver is that most antique pieces are sold to dealers. Where dealers are involved, prices tend to be lower; where individual collectors are heavily involved, they tend to run up prices.

WHERE TO BUY

Stick with reliable dealers and the leading American and British auction houses. The latter have regular auctions. You may contact them directly or look for their announcements in the newspapers and antique magazines (see below).

WHAT TO LOOK FOR

1   Select pieces that are tops in weight and quality. There's not much investment advantage in collecting a number of second rate pieces. Good, legitimate English silver pieces have been hallmarked since about 1300. The hallmark, a stamplike indication, represents the silversmith's mark, the sterling standard (Lion = England, Thistle = Scotland, Crowned harp = Ireland), the assay office (or town), and the year the piece was made. You can identify hallmarks in any one of several books on the topic or in auction house catalogs. Lightweight pieces generally have poorer detail and workmanship.

2   The breath test: Breathe on the cartouche (any decorative bordered area of the piece, not to be confused with the hallmark or maker's stamp) as you would to fog a mirror. If you see lines or seams, then the piece has been repaired and is lower in value.

3   Do not buy pieces that have been heavily repaired or that have cracks or splits. Small dents, however, can be repaired and should not put you off purchase.

4   Focus on a silversmith (see list on page 52) or a type such as spoons, wine labels, snuff boxes, porringers, trays, goblets, bowls, candlesticks, baby utensils, etc. Or, look for regional pieces or pieces from a given period. Art Nouveau silver (from the 1880s and '90s), for instance, is still plentiful.

LEADING AUCTION HOUSES

IN THE UNITED STATES:
Christie's
  502 Park Avenue
  New York, NY 10022
Sotheby's
  1334 York Avenue
  New York, NY 10021
Phillips
  406 East 79th Street
  New York, NY 10021
C.G. Sloan & Co.
  919 E Street, N.W.
  Washington, DC 20004
Richard W. Skinner, Inc.
  585 Boylston Street
  Boston, MA 02116
DuMouchelle's
  409 East Jefferson Avenue
  Detroit, MI 48226
Garth's Auctions
  2690 Stratford Road
  Delaware, OH 43015

IN THE UNITED KINGDOM:
Christie's
  8 King Street
  London SW1, England
Christie's South Kennsington
  85 Old Brompton Road
  London SW4, England
Sotheby's
  34–35 New Bond Street
  London W1, England

IN FRANCE:
Hotel Drouot
  Rue Drouot
  75009 Paris, France

IN SPAIN:
Sotheby's
  Plaza de la Independencia #8
  Madrid 1, Spain
Duran
  Serrano 12
  Madrid 1, Spain

IN ITALY:
Sotheby's
  Via Monte Giordano 36
  00186 Rome, Italy

LEADING SILVERSMITHS (LISTED ALPHABETICALLY)

AMERICAN	John Abbot(t)
	Jeremiah Andrews
	Eleazer Baker
	Jedediah Baldwin
	Roswell Bartholomew
	Joseph Barton
	Clement Beecher
	Ephraim Brasher
	Benjamin Burt
	John T. Curran
	Tunis Dubois
	John Ward Gilman
	William Haverstick
	Samuel Kirk
	Edward C. Moore
	Paul Revere
	Nathan Storrs
	Peter van Dyck
	Samuel Williamson
BRITISH	G. W. Adams
	Joseph Angell
	Edward Barnard
	William Chawner
	Paul de Lamerie
	John Emes
	Rebecca Emes
	William Gibson
	Robert Hennell
	Samuel Hennell
	John Langman
	John Mortimer
	Charles Rawlings
	Charles Reily
	George Storer
	Paul Storr
	William Summers
	Edward Wood

FOR FURTHER INFORMATION

Marvin D. Schwartz. *Collectors Guide to Antique American Silver.* New York: Doubleday & Co, 1975.

SILVER: SHOULD I OR SHOULDN'T I?

PROS
↑ Potential price appreciation
↑ Joy of ownership
↑ Can use certain pieces
CONS
↓ Value can always fall
↓ Silver pieces are not particularly liquid
↓ Insurance for theft is expensive

Dorothy T. Rainwater. *Encyclopedia of Silver Manufacturers.* New York: Crown Publishers, 1980.

Margaret Macdonald-Taylor. *Dictionary of Marks.* New York: Hawthorn/Dutton, 1962, $6.95 paperback.

Katharine Morrison McClinton. *Collecting American 19th Century Silver.* New York: Charles Scribners & Sons, 1968.

C. Louise Avery. *Early American Silver.* New York: Russell & Russell, 1930; reprinted 1968.

Seymour B. Wyler. *The Book of Old Silver: English, American, Foreign.* New York: Crown Publishers, 1937; $14.95.

Ralph & Terry Kovel. *A Directory of American Silver, Pewter and Silver Plate.* New York: Crown Publishers, 1961.

Baile DeLapperiere. *Silver Auction Records.* Norwalk, CT: Hilmarton Manor Press, annual.

AMERICAN ART POTTERY

From Amish quilts to primitive portraits, Shaker benches to Pennsylvania Dutch hex signs, Americans have always been intrigued by the products of their fellow local artists. Although many of these American works today command extraordinarily high prices, there are a few as yet undiscovered pockets left for collectors. One of these is American art pottery, although it is not totally unknown by any means. Savvy investors have already amassed extensive collections of vases, bookends, cache pots, etc. Still, there's much left that's affordable—you can start as low as $250 for a medium-quality piece—and values are on the rise.

Initially stimulated by the famous Arts and Crafts Movement in England, artisans began to react against factory-produced items. Then, in 1876, the Centennial Exhibition introduced Japanese as well as French design to this country. The two events led to a blossoming of art pottery studios throughout the United States during the 1880s and 1890s. The best known among these pioneer studios were Rookwood, Newcomb, Dedham, and Grueby (see box).

Today, the pieces by these early studios and

A SHORT DIRECTORY OF LEADING ART POTTERY FACTORIES AND POTTERS IN THE U. S.

Arequippa A small but important California pottery.

Chelsea Ceramic Art Works Founded 1866 in Massachusetts. Moved to Dedham in 1896 and pottery known as Dedham pottery. Potter: Hugh C. Robertson.

Cincinnati Art Pottery Center of work after the Philadelphia Centennial Exhibition of 1876. Potter: Mary Louise McLaughlin.

Dedham Pottery See Chelsea Ceramic Art Works.

East Liverpool Center of activity in Ohio from about 1840 to 1900. Potters: James Bennett, Benjamin Harker, and Isaac W. Knowles.

Fulper Pottery Factory Established in Flemington, New Jersey, in 1805. Made common housewares until 1910; then introduced art pottery line under the name Vasekraft.

Grueby Faience Co. Established in Boston in 1894 by William H. Grueby. Other potter: George P. Kenrick.

Lonhuda Potter Founded in 1892 by William A. Long in Steubenville, Ohio. Potter: Laura A. Fry.

McCoy Pottery Established in Roseville, Ohio, in 1899. Specialized in cookie jars and birdbaths.

Newcomb Pottery Art pottery was taught to women at Newcomb College, the women's division of Tulane University, starting in 1896. Potters: Ellsworth Woodward and Mary G. Sheerer.

George Ohr Biloxi, Mississippi, ceramicist whose work was not known by the public until 1972 when 6,000 of his pieces were found in a warehouse. Ohr died in 1915.

Rookwood Pottery Established in Cincinnati in 1880. Potters: Mrs. Maria Longworth Nichols (later Mrs. Bellamy Storer), Albert T. Valentien, and Kataro Shirayamadani.

Frederick Rhead Came to the United States from England and worked in many potteries, including Weller, Roseville, Jervis, and even the University of Cincinnati Art School.

Roblin A California pottery active during the 1880s and 1890s.

Roseville Pottery Company Established in Zanesville, Ohio, in 1898. Did imitations of Rookwood, Grueby, Fulper.

Van Briggle Artus Van Briggle (1869–1904) painted porcelain at the Rookwood Pottery in Cincinnati but later moved to Colorado Springs, Colorado, where he established his own pottery.

Vasekraft See Fulper Pottery Factory.

Weller Pottery In Zanesville, Ohio, late 19th century. Potters: Samuel Weller, John Lessell.

their name potters bring the best prices and are the hardest items to find. For example, those by George Ohr are worth between $1,000 and $10,000, while in 1985 at a Christie's auction in New York, a Grueby piece sold for $20,000.

BUILDING A VALUABLE COLLECTION

Experts all agree that the best way to build a worthwhile collection is to focus on an artist, a studio, or a type of design. Look for signed pieces or factory marks, and try to build based upon recognized signatures. You may also specialize according to type of piece, such as bookends, vases, inkwells, bowls, or cookie jars.

Various designs and motifs were popular with certain artists or factories. You may wish to concentrate on those pieces of pottery adorned with lilies, daisies, snakes, or tulips.

The most important factor to keep in mind is quality. If you cannot afford a $2,000 piece, start by buying smaller, less well-known works and then trade up. The true investment quality of an American art pottery collection is found in the better known, more expensive pieces, but you certainly do not need to begin on that level.

- Repaired pieces, of course, are less valuable as an investment. If you place the pottery under an ultraviolet lamp you can detect signs of any patching. That doesn't mean you should not purchase the piece, but it should be less expensive than one that has not been repaired.
- Avoid: pieces with fuzzy lines, chips, hairline cracks, mismatched details.

POTTERY: SHOULD I OR SHOULDN'T I?

PROS
↑ Prices are rising
↑ Some pieces can be used
↑ Joy of ownership
CONS
↓ Prices could decline
↓ Not especially liquid
↓ Insurance is expensive
↓ Pieces could be stolen or damaged

Although fakes are not common in this area of collectibles, if you have any questions about the authenticity of a piece, check with a certified appraiser or museum expert (see For Further Information).

WHERE TO BUY

Local dealers, estate sales, auctions, and other collectors.

FOR FURTHER INFORMATION

Paul Evans. *Art Pottery of the United States.* New York: Charles Scribners & Sons, 1974.

Ralph & Terry Kovel. *Kovel's New Dictionary of Marks: Pottery & Porcelain.* New York: Crown Publishers, 1981.

For museum catalogs, contact:

The American Ceramics Art Society
1775 Broadway
New York, NY 10019

This association has several meetings a year as well as exhibitions.

American Art Pottery Association
P.O. Box 714
Silver Spring, MD 20901

Publishes a newsletter for members: *American Art Pottery*

GENERAL INFORMATION ON ART POTTERY AND ANTIQUE SILVER

In order to find a reliable appraiser, write to the following association for a free directory:

American Society of Appraisers
P.O. Box 17265
Washington, D.C. 20041

General reading material:

Antique Trader
P.O. Box 1050
Dubuque, Iowa 52001

The Art/Antiques Investment Report
120 Wall Street
New York, NY 10005

Art & Antiques Magazine
89 Fifth Avenue
New York, NY 10003

The Connoiseur
224 West 57 Street
New York, NY 10019

The Magazine Antiques
980 Madison Avenue
New York, NY 10021

The Official Sotheby Park Bernet Price Guide to Antiques & Decorative Arts. New York: Simon & Schuster, 1985.

BUYING AT AUCTION

Both antique silver and American art pottery can be found at dealers, shops, galleries, and shows. In each of these situations you will have plenty of time to make up your mind. Yet excellent collectibles can also be found at auctions, where the gavel swings fast. Decisions must be made quickly. There's no time for hesitation. Return visits and sleeping on it overnight are not in the picture. Despite the pressurized atmosphere, serious collectors cannot afford to shy away from auctions. The very piece you've been looking for is apt to appear.

If you follow these guidelines, you'll be able to minimize your mistakes and come away with the right piece at the right price.

BEFORE THE AUCTION

1   Do your homework. Study up on the item for which you'll be bidding. Be able to spot quality. Know what the price range is for the type of piece you're considering.

2   Make a written list of what items you *really* want. Stick to it. Avoid giving in to "auction fever."

3   If there is a catalog for the auction, purchase it in advance. It will give dollar estimates as well as descriptive material on items for sale. During the auction, write down what each item sells for and use the catalog as a guideline in the future.

4   Attend the preview held before the sale. Study the items on display and make notes in your catalog of their size, age, condition, etc.

5   Set a dollar limit for yourself before the auction.

6   If you are unable to attend the auction personally, you may be able to submit a bid, giving the top limit you're willing to pay. Telephone bidding is also possible in some instances. Inquire.

AT THE AUCTION

1   After registering, you'll be given a number and something to bid with, most likely a paddle.

2   Find out what the incremental dollar amounts are; some auctioneers move up by $10; others by $100. You'll need to know.

3   Listen to the bidding carefully. "Silver looking" is not the same as "sterling silver." Don't bid until you are at ease with the auctioneer's voice and patter.

4   Set a dollar limit on what you will bid for each item.

5   Don't be the first to bid on an item you want. Auctioneers often set an arbitrary opening price which may turn out to be artificially high, in which case it will drop if there are no bidders. So, watch who else is bidding. You don't want to be bidding against yourself. Come in as you sense the price rising or that it's near the top.

6   Take cash or your checkbook. Credit cards are generally not an acceptable form of payment.

7   Legally you are obliged to take what you successfully bid on at an auction. If you have second thoughts or change your mind, some auction houses will let you return an item, generally if you shoulder the cost of resale. However, this is the exception rather than the rule. You should plan on putting your money where your bid was. And don't forget some means of transporting your purchase home. Most auction houses don't deliver.

PLATINUM

There's an often overlooked precious item that's silvery-white, metallic, and scarcer than gold or silver. It's called platinum and it's an interesting long-term investment because of its important industrial uses as well as its favorable supply/demand situation.

Used in industry because of its resistance to corrosion, its unusually high melting point (3216°F), and its malleability, platinum's world-wide demand now far outpaces its supply. The annual supply is only 80 tons; 15 times more gold and 125 times more silver are generally produced each year.

In 1985 demand was so great that there was a 100,000-ounce deficit. Demand had increased by about 7% whereas supply grew by less than 1%. South African exports accounted for approximately 85% of supply to the West. Sales by the Soviet Union, the second largest producer, actually fell from the previous year. The two major South African producers, the Rustenburg Mines and the Impala Mines, are working close to capacity.

PLATINUM'S USES

The metal plays a vital role in three major industries: automotive, petrochemical, and power. It is virtually irreplaceable in these areas and the U.S. government has classified platinum as a strategic metal.

➤ AUTOMOTIVE INDUSTRY Platinum's most important application is in the automotive field where it is used in catalytic converters, which reduce the emission of carbon monoxide to meet pollution control standards. In 1974, when these devices were introduced on a nationwide scale in the United States, demand for platinum rose

---

PLATINUM: SHOULD I OR SHOULDN'T I?

PROS
↑ Offers a hedge against inflation
↑ Rarer than both gold and silver
↑ Has excellent industrial applications
↑ Is rising in price

CONS
↓ Wide price fluctuations
↓ Political problems could affect price (turmoil in South Africa could force prices higher as well)
↓ Earns no interest

---

about 50%. Automotive usage today represents 35 to 40% of total demand in the West.

A similar situation to that of 1974 may be in the offing. Starting in 1988, the European Economic Community will phase in auto emission standards comparable to those in the United States and Japan. The plan will run through 1993. This is expected to boost demand for the metal by 15 to 20% and could lead to additional stockpiling, which in turn would help raise the price.

➤ CHEMICALS Platinum is used in the production of nitric acid for synthetic fertilizers and explosives, petrochemicals, fragrances, and drugs. It is also used in converting coal into synthetic fuels.

➤ PETROLEUM REFINING Oil refineries are boosting their use of platinum in order to eliminate lead from gasoline and jet fuel.

➤ FUEL CELLS The fuel cell, an advanced means of generating electricity, could become one of the biggest users of platinum. The device is still under development and will eventually be used to convert chemical energy to electrical energy, with platinum as a catalyst in the process. Fuel cells are currently being used to supply electric power for NASA's space shuttle program.

➤ JEWELRY Platinum jewelry is popular in Japan because platinum is purer and scarcer than gold or silver. Combination jewelry consisting of 18 carat yellow gold and platinum is increasing.

➤ OTHER USES Because of its resistance to heat, platinum is used to melt glass for camera lenses, in medicine, and in electronics.

FACTORS THAT COULD CAUSE A RISE IN PLATINUM PRICES

- Increased inflation
- A declining U.S. dollar
- Sharply mounting U.S. budget deficits
- Rise in bank failures

PLATINUM DEMAND BY APPLICATION

	1980	1981	1982	1983	1984	1985
				(000 oz.)		
Western World Total						
Autocatalyst	680	640	645	615	795	875
Chemical	260	250	260	245	260	225
Electrical	210	185	170	175	190	200
Glass	140	100	85	105	140	140
Hoarding	—	—	45	90	170	260
Jewelry	560	755	765	715	775	810
Petroleum	130	140	65	20	15	15
Other	350	360	285	215	285	285
TOTALS	**2,330**	**2,430**	**2,320**	**2,180**	**2,630**	**2,810**
Japan						
Autocatalyst	210	190	170	170	170	175
Chemical	10	10	10	10	15	15
Electrical	15	15	20	20	30	40
Glass	40	50	45	60	75	60
Hoarding	—	—	—	5	15	35
Jewelry	440	625	620	560	625	675
Petroleum	15	15	15	15	20	15
Other	210	245	170	110	190	215
TOTALS	**940**	**1,150**	**1,050**	**950**	**1,140**	**1,230**
North America						
Autocatalyst	440	430	455	420	590	650
Chemical	115	50	80	100	100	75
Electrical	145	70	70	90	95	80
Glass	50	20	10	15	30	40
Hoarding	—	—	40	40	30	130
Jewelry	15	15	15	15	15	15
Petroleum	140	55	20	15	15	10
Other	75	60	20	25	35	30
TOTALS	**980**	**700**	**710**	**720**	**910**	**1,030**
Rest of Western World Including Europe						
Autocatalyst	30	20	20	25	35	50
Chemical	135	190	170	135	145	135
Electrical	50	100	80	65	65	80
Glass	50	30	30	30	35	40
Hoarding	—	—	5	45	125	95
Jewelry	105	115	130	140	135	120
Petroleum	(25)	70	30	(10)	(20)	(10)
Other	65	55	95	80	60	40
TOTALS	**410**	**580**	**560**	**510**	**580**	**550**

Hoarding is the long-term holding of metal for investment. In this review we define hoarded metal as investment bars and coins weighing 10 oz. or less. The miscellaneous "other applications" sector in the above table includes some larger bars or ingots acquired for investment purposes, especially in Japan.

SOURCE: Platinum Guild International (USA), Inc., 14 East 60th St., New York, NY 10022.

FACTS FOR INVESTORS

- Platinum is the most precious metal in the world.
- It is the only precious metal that has ever traded at over $1,000 per ounce. In 1980 it hit $1,047 per ounce; the peak for gold was $850 per ounce.
- Since World War II, the U.S. government has formally recognized the strategic importance of platinum by stockpiling it for defense purposes.
- Annual supply is 15 times less than gold.
- Only 4% is currently acquired by investors, compared with 54% for gold.

Platinum is sold in 1-, 10-, and 50-ounce bars by the major brokerage firms. Although you can take physical delivery of the metal, it is not required; a "certificate accumulation plan" is more convenient. Here the dealer holds the metal for you while the certificate allows you to buy or sell, generally by telephone. Most dealers charge a modest annual storage fee plus commission.

There is a new platinum coin on the market, called the Noble. It is 1 ounce and is available from coin dealers or directly from: Ayrton Metals, Ltd., 30 Ely Place, London EC1, England.

Platinum is a liquid investment and can readily be sold back to the coin dealer or stockbroker. However, it is subject to wide market fluctuations and requires a willingness to assume risk.

FOR FURTHER INFORMATION

Read the commodity columns in the *New York Times*, *Wall Street Journal*, and *Barron's* on a regular basis.

Platinum Guild International, Inc.
14 East 60 Street
New York, NY 10022

Ask to be placed on the mailing list. You will receive periodic material on activity in the field of platinum as an investment.

For a free copy of *Platinum 1986,* a 52-page pamplet, write to:

Johnson Matthey
c/o Thomas L. Richmond, Inc.
888 Seventh Avenue
New York, NY 10106

PART TWO

TYPES OF SECURITIES

Today, there are so many special packages, combinations, separations, and truncations of securities that it's hard to tell the players without a scorecard. Yet despite their fancy names and enticing promises and projections, there are still only two types of basic investments and speculations: *equity,* where you become part owner of the enterprise and share in its success or failure, and *debt,* where you loan money to the corporation. Commodities and options and futures are sideshows.

Diversification—buying stocks and bonds and holding cash or shares in a money market fund—makes people feel more secure. If you tend toward being a conservative investor, you'll benefit from diversification.

Speculators, on the other hand, grab at any opportunity that appears to offer a high, usually quick, profit on a small outlay. They are concerned with sudden actions that will raise the price or lower the value if they sell short. They like to gamble.

The wise choice is to keep changing your portfolio in tune with the times and future trends: "to every thing, there is a season and a time to every purpose under the heaven."

The following chapters outline the major types of securities that usually stand by themselves but are always the core of those sparkling, glibly promoted "investment opportunities":
- Common stocks
- Convertibles
- Preferred stocks
- Taxable bonds
- Tax-exempt bonds
- Mutual funds

7

GUIDELINES FOR PORTFOLIO-BUILDING

The world of finance is complex, competitive, subject to outside economic and political pressures, and dominated by shrewd, powerful people who control billions of dollars. For most Americans who can save only a few thousand dollars a year, making money in such an arena sounds difficult, if not impossible.

Yet almost everyone can be a successful investor if he or she takes time to set specific objectives, to learn the facts, to adhere to proven profitable rules, to be patient, and, most important, to use common sense. There will be times when success comes quickly, but over the long term, making money requires careful planning and conscientious management.

Unfortunately, some people are unwilling or unable to recognize the importance of these fundamentals. A few may be lucky with speculations, but most of these adventurers lose more often than they win.

As depicted in this guide, a successful investor is one who achieves over a period of time better-than-average returns on investments. In general, you can obtain an average annual yield of 10% using stocks and bonds, and if you manage your money wisely, you can hope for even higher returns in strong markets. Such rewards will not come every year with every investment, but if you build and maintain a plan, let your profits run, take quick, small losses and stay flexible, you can increase your assets with prompt reinvestment of all income and realized appreciation. It's not easy, but it can be done.

How you manage your money depends on the type of individual you are and, in turn, how you choose specific financial goals. In the broad sense, the choices are between sleeping well or eating well; income or growth; managing your money or letting someone else do it. For most people, the first choice is the most important: *if any investment or speculation causes you to worry, do not make it; or if you have already done so, sell it . . . at any price. Money by itself is never as important as peace of mind. You can never be a successful investor when you are fearful!*

The rules that follow apply primarily to securities, but the same principles apply to real estate, producing oil/gas properties, and other enterprises that require capital. When you are in a high tax bracket, it's also wise to consider the tax consequences, but even then, the most successful holdings are sound investments on their own.

For convenience, let's categorize investors in three broad groups: *conservative, aggressive,* and *speculative.* By and large, portfolios should reflect each approach, the emphasis shifting with market conditions and your available resources.

➤ CONSERVATIVE The *conservative* investor seeks safety and income in order to preserve capital and to earn a moderate but sure return. In most cases, he or she looks at the yield and pays little heed to the impact of taxes and inflation.

The *very* conservative investor buys and holds through up and down markets, through shifts in rates of return, and with little regard to the potential growth of the assets. Bonds are purchased at issue and held to maturity; large sums are kept in insured savings accounts with little attention to the rates of return; stocks are retained until forced to sell through outside, nonfinancial pressures such as the need for cash, estate planning, or to supplement retirement income.

The conservative approach provides peace of mind, but it's poor protection against what appears to be inevitable inflation and low interest rates. With the cost of living rising at less than

4% a year, the real purchasing power of every $1,000 is cut to $822 in 5 years and to $703 in 10 years.

The *fairly* conservative investor puts money into: (1) fixed assets, such as certificates of deposit, short-term bills, notes, or bonds; or (2) fixed-income bonds when available at a discount and with maturity in the not-too-distant future; recognizing the importance of flexibility he or she shifts with the trend in interest rates; or (3) steady-income stocks such as quality utilities that keep boosting dividends.

➤ AGGRESSIVE The *aggressive* investor targets total returns: modest income plus appreciation: say, 4% income plus 15% or more average annual price gain. In most cases, the investment is held for 6 months so that the profits will qualify for low capital gains tax, but our investor does not hesitate to sell when he or she feels a fair profit was achieved and future prospects, for the company and the market, are questionable. The enterprising investor looks for quality corporations that have long and fairly consistent records of higher earnings, aiming to double his or her money every 5 years.

➤ SPECULATIVE The *speculator* takes the most risks, buying and selling frequently in an effort to achieve the largest gains in the shortest length of time or buying very low and holding on for a long time to sell very high. Greater reliance is placed on technical analysis, hunches, and rumors. The speculator recognizes the probability of losses on many of his or her holdings and hopes that the profits on the winners will be large enough to keep the bottom line favorable.

The speculator may not always be gambling but is always trying to outwit others. As long as a speculator uses only money he or she can afford to lose, does research, and watches carefully, that speculator may do well but also must be lucky.

In the current market environment, companies which get taken over or buy back their own shares are favorite speculations (see Chapters 19 and 34).

FINANCIAL DOVETAILING: COORDINATE INVESTMENTS WITH FINANCIAL PLAN

All your investments should be considered as part of your total financial and estate planning.

Savings are essential to help you reach your goals of economic security and money-carefree retirement, but it is not enough to set aside money sporadically. You must not only save regularly but must make every one of those dollars work as hard after you earn it as you worked to gain it in the first place. Too many people have too many assets in holdings that fail to meet this basic criterion. And too few people make their first monthly check to themselves: for investment in their personal pension plan or other savings account.

After you have finished this book, review all your investments and rate them according to their actual and potential income and appreciation each year for the next 2 years. Then start developing a step-by-step plan to achieve your personal and family financial goals. Keep your plan flexible so that shifts can be made as resources and goals change. You can set goals in dollars or percentages.

The results are up to you. As you will soon learn by experience, the rules for success in investing are the same as those in any successful enterprise: get the facts, make logical assumptions and projections, act decisively, and stick to your plan until and unless circumstances change or you become convinced that another approach can be more rewarding. *Nothing is more harmful to successful investing than frequent shifts of basic policy. Making money requires persistence and patience.*

Because of the wide scope of investment targets, approaches, techniques, and opportunities covered in *Your Investments,* some of the rules may seem contradictory. In practice they seldom are, because most of them are intended to apply to different types of investors or different investment situations.

There is no mysterious key to unlocking success in the stock market as so many "experts" would have you believe. Whether investment or speculation, it's a business of common sense, courage, knowledge, and patience ... with a reasonable amount of luck.

DEVELOPING YOUR PORTFOLIO

Much of the information you need to analyze stocks and develop your own personal investment strategy is readily available from annual reports, investment services, the *Wall Street Journal, Barron's,* and the financial pages of major newspapers. And that's before you even consult a broker, who may inundate you with research reports, given the chance. Yet you can start on your own *if* you learn the basic methods for judging a security's value and then use the more sophisticated techniques discussed later.

First, for general reference, arm yourself with a copy of *Standard & Poor's Stock Guide* and the *Standard & Poor's Stock Reports,* or with *The Value Line Investment Survey.* Then take time to review the four general types of common stocks, but remember: they are not mutually exclusive.

THE TYPES OF STOCK AVAILABLE

- *Blue chip stocks* represent ownership in a major company that has a history of profitability and continual or increasing dividends with sufficient financial strength to withstand economic or industrial downturns. Examples: IBM, General Electric, Exxon, Du Pont, Sears.
- *Growth stocks* represent ownership in a company that has had relatively rapid growth in the past (when compared with the economy as a whole) and is expected to continue in this vein. These companies tend to reinvest a large part of their earnings in order to finance their expansion and growth. Consequently, dividends are small in comparison with earnings. Examples: Digital Equipment, Advanced Micro Devices, Wendy's.
- *Cyclical stocks* are common stocks of companies whose earnings move with the economy or business cycles. They frequently have lower earnings when the country is in a slump and higher earnings when the economy is in a recovery phase. Examples of cyclical industries: aluminum, automobiles, machinery, housing, airlines.
- *Income stocks* have continually stable earnings and high dividend yields in comparison with other stocks. Income stocks generally retain only a small portion of earnings for expansion and

growth, which they are able to do because there is a relatively stable market for their products. Examples: public utility companies, international oil companies, food processors.

Now you're ready to start selecting stocks for your own personal portfolio, keeping the following key consideration in mind: *every investment involves some degree of risk.* Stocks vary in their degree of risk depending upon the stability of their earnings and/or dividends and the way they are perceived in the marketplace.

The general rule is that your return is correlated to risk: the greater the risk, the greater the expected return.

FACTORS IN STOCK SELECTION AND APPRAISAL

The eight analytic tools briefly described below are used most often in stock selection and appraisal.

➤ EARNINGS PER SHARE For the average investor, this figure distills the company's financial picture into one simple number. Earnings per share is the company's net income (after taxes and preferred stock dividends) divided by the number of common shares outstanding. When a company is described as growing at a certain rate, the growth is then usually stated in terms of earnings per share.

Look for a company whose earnings per share have increased over the past 5 years; 1 down year is acceptable if the other 4 have been up. You will find earnings per share in *Value Line, Standard & Poor's,* or the company's annual report.

➤ PRICE-EARNINGS RATIO (P/E) This is one of the most common analytical tools of the trade and reflects investor enthusiasm about a stock in comparison with the market as a whole. Divide the current price of a stock by its earnings per share for the last 12 months: that's the P/E ratio, also sometimes called the "multiple." You will also find the P/E listed in the daily stock quotations of the newspaper. A P/E of 12, for example, means that the buying public is willing to pay 12 times earnings for the stock, whereas there is much less interest and confidence in a stock with a P/E of 4 or 5. A company's P/E is of course constantly changing and must be compared with its own previous

P/E's and with the P/E's of others in its industry or category.

It is important to realize that the P/E listed in the paper is based on the last 12 months' earnings; however, when you talk to Wall Street professionals, they refer to the earnings of the current year which is unfolding. So when considering a stock to buy or sell, remember to focus on its future, not its past.

Although brokers and analysts in general hold varying views on what constitutes the ideal P/E, a P/E under 10 is regarded as conservative. As the P/E moves above 10, you start to pay a premium. If the P/E moves below 5 or 6, it tends to signal uncertainty about the company's prospects.

Try to buy a strong company with favorable prospects and a conservative P/E before other investors become interested in it and run it up. Sometimes growth industries, for example, semiconductors, fall into economic slumps and may provide this type of investment opportunity.

➤ BOOK VALUE This figure, also known as stockholder's equity, is the difference between a company's assets and its liabilities, in other words, what the stockholders own after all debts are paid. That number is then divided by the number of shares outstanding in order to arrive at book value per share. The book value becomes especially important in takeover situations, which are described in depth in Chapter 34. If book value is understated, i.e., if the assets of the company are worth substantially more than the financial statements say they are, then you may have a real bargain which the marketplace has not yet recognized.

➤ RETURN ON BOOK VALUE This number measures how much the company earns on the stockholders' equity in the company and thus is also called "return on equity" (ROE). A company's total net income, when expressed as a percentage of total book value, is the return on equity, which is especially useful when comparing several companies within one industry.

➤ THE DIVIDEND Check the current and projected dividend of a stock, especially if you are building an income portfolio. Study the payouts over the past 5 years as well as the current dividend. There are times when a corporation plows most of its earnings back into the company to ensure its future growth, in which case the dividend will be small. Typically, the greater the current yield, the less the likelihood of price appreciation. However, it's best if a company earns $5 for every $4 it pays out.

➤ VOLATILITY Some stocks go up and down in price like a yo-yo, while others trade within a relatively narrow range. Those that dance about obviously carry a greater degree of risk than their more pedestrian brothers and sisters. The measurement tool for price volatility is called *beta* and it tells how much a stock tends to move in relation to changes in the Standard & Poor's 500 stock index. The index is at 1.00, so a stock with a beta of 1.5 moves up and down $1\frac{1}{2}$ times as much as the Standard & Poor's index, whereas a beta of 0.5 is less volatile than the index. To put it another way, a stock with a 1.5 beta is expected to rise in price by 15% if the market rises 10%, or fall by 15% if the Standard & Poor's index falls by 10%. You will find the beta for stocks given by the investment services as well as by good stockbrokers.

➤ TOTAL RETURN Most investors tend to think about their gains and losses in terms of price changes, not dividends, whereas those who own bonds pay attention to interest yields and seldom focus on price changes. *Both approaches are mistakes.* Although dividend yields are obviously more important if you are seeking income, and changes in price play a greater role in growth stocks, the total return on a stock makes it possible for you to compare your investment in stocks with a similar investment in corporate bonds, municipals, Treasuries, mutual funds, etc.

To calculate the total return, add (or subtract) the stock's price change and dividends for 12 months and then divide by what the price was at the beginning of the 12-month period. For example:

> An investor bought a stock at $42 a share and received $2.50 in dividends for the next 12-month period. At the end of the period, the stock was sold at $45. The total return was 13%.

Dividend	$2.50
Price appreciation +	3.00
	$5.50
	divided by $42 = 13%

➤ NUMBER OF SHARES OUTSTANDING If you are a beginning investor or working with a small portfolio, look for companies with at least 5 million shares outstanding. You will then be ensured of both marketability and liquidity, because the major mutual funds, institutions, and the public will be trading in these stocks. You are unlikely to have trouble buying or selling when you want to. In a smaller company, your exposure to sharp price fluctuations is greater.

DOS FOR SUCCESSFUL INVESTING

DO investigate BEFORE you invest. Do not buy on impulse, hunch, or rumor. Make all investments according to your specific plan, preferably one that shows buying and selling zones and percentage allocations of funds according to your goals for income and/or growth.

Always write down the information that you have, and if there are gaps, get help from the library or your broker.

A poor selection will not only cost you money but will cause unnecessary mental anguish. Take nothing for granted. Get the facts lest the lack of facts gets you.

DO limit your purchases until your forecast is confirmed. When you feel you have latched onto a winner, buy a half position even if it means buying less than a round lot. You may lose a few points' profit by waiting, but you will minimize your losses. Watch its action in the marketplace and when your judgment appears accurate, buy the other half of your position.

DO focus on the downside risk. If a stock's dividend, asset value, or price history clearly indicates a limited downside risk, then it's probably a good investment. The most important aspect of buying stocks is not how much you can make but how much you could lose.

DO look for rewards double the risks. Buy only stocks that have twice as much potential of rising as probability of falling. Base this decision on past performance and future prospects.

The prices of all investments are affected by psychology and prospects. Neither can be measured precisely, but it is possible to calculate the potential rewards (if all goes well) and the degree of risk (if things turn sour).

This *reward-to-risk ratio* is the basis for all successful speculations. With securities, amateurs can develop their own ratios but will probably do better to rely on professional advisory reports and recommendations. With commodities, currency, etc., expert assistance is imperative until you become knowledgeable and are able to devote time to research and analysis that can project those reward-to-risk ratios.

You should never act until conditions are favorable in the economy, in the trading market, and in your own investment strategy. *Remember: "favorable" may mean BUY in a bull market, SELL or HEDGE in a bear market.*

Here's how to project reward-to-risk ratios. You feel that a stock (or any other type of easily traded property) now at 40 has the potential of moving up to 60. Or there's a risk of a decline to 35. The reward-to-risk ratio is 20 points up vs. 5 points down: a healthy 4:1 ratio.

You buy and the stock goes to 55. The potential gain is now only 5 points, but the risk is still 20 points down. That's a dangerous 1:4 ratio and a signal to sell or, possibly, to enter a stop order.

Be careful not to sell too soon when the ratio shifts from, say, 5:1 to 4:2.5. You will limit your profit potential and end up with relatively small gains.

DO buy only stocks quoted regularly in *The Wall Street Journal, New York Times, or Barron's*. You want a ready market that will attract other investors.

DO investigate AFTER you invest. There is no such thing as a permanent investment. (Even IBM has bounced up and down over the years.) This caveat applies especially to small companies that show great promise at the outset but all too soon fall by the wayside.

In this research, compare the current data with that which you got when you first acquired the holding. If the results have failed to attain the goals you set, consider selling. And if they have exceeded your projections, double-check to decide whether the company's prospects are favorable.

DO watch trends: of the economy, of the stock market, of industry groups, and of the stocks in which you are interested. The stock market leadership changes almost monthly, so what was favorable in January may be sliding in June.

THE IMPORTANCE OF REWARD/RISK RULES

The value of setting parameters when you speculate is shown by the results of a study of 1,100 speculators over 10 years:

- Only 5% scored sizable gains over the entire period.
- The majority stayed optimistic despite losses. As a group, they were 21 times more likely to ride a falling stock all the way down than hang on to a rising stock until it reached a peak price. Worst of all, a substantial percentage poured good money after bad and lost savings earmarked for a new house, car, or other major expenditure.

DO set realistic goals and target prices when you make the original commitment. Roughly, these should be 35 to 50% higher than your cost, and the time frame should be 24 to 36 months. Once in a while, a stock will zoom up fast, but investments usually move up slowly and steadily, with interim dips, to new highs.

DO diversify, but not too much. As a rule of thumb, a $100,000 portfolio, should have no more than 10 securities, with no more than 20% in any one company or industry. However, you can put as little as 5% of your assets in special high-risk situations. Above $100,000, add one new security for each additional $10,000.

When you spread your dollar too thin, you lessen your opportunities for profit. You will always do better with a 20-point gain in one stock than with a one-point rise in 20 holdings, if only because of the commissions.

DO try to stay flexible: to make the most profitable use of your money at any specific period. When debt issues yield over 12%, part of your savings should be in bonds or money market funds. When the yields drop, take your profits and invest the proceeds in quality common stocks where the chances of appreciation are greater.

Keep a list of 10 "future" investments and review them periodically to determine whether any offer greater prospects for faster rewards than the holdings that you now have. This list should include stocks, convertibles, bonds, and, when appropriate, tax shelters. Don't switch as long as the original investment is profitable and appears to have logical prospects of reaching your goals.

DO watch the timing, and never be in a hurry to spend your money. If you miss one opportunity, there will be another soon.

When trading is active, buy at the market price. If you're dealing with a stock that is beginning to attract attention, you may save a point or two by waiting for a temporary dip. But if you are convinced that this is a wise investment, make your move, even if there is a decline later.

When there's little trading, place your order at a set price and be willing to wait a while.

Check technical indicators of the market, the industry, and the stock: charts, ratios, moving averages, areas of support/resistance, breakouts, and so on. These, too, can help you choose between two similar securities.

DO be patient. This is always a basic factor in successful *investing*. Never flit from one stock to another. This will make your broker rich, but it will cut your potential profits and, unless you are very wise and very lucky, will not increase your capital. Four trades a year, at an average cost of 1% of stock value, equals 4% income. (If you deal with a discount broker, you may save a few dollars.)

In normal markets, it takes a quality stock 2 to 3 years to move from undervaluation to overvaluation. Always remember that by definition investments are long-term commitments and rarely create millionaires overnight.

One of the major faults of amateurs is that they try too hard to make too much money too fast. As with most business decisions, take your time. Once in a great while, a stock will take off and rush up, but in most cases appreciation is slow, and often erratic. It is possible to project long-term trends but only rarely short-term action.

DO upgrade your portfolio periodically. Review all holdings quarterly and usually plan to sell at least one security every 6 months. Replace the weakest securities with those having greater potential. Be slow to sell winners, because this will leave you with less profitable holdings. On the average, a successful portfolio will be turned over every 5 years: about 20% annually.

Each time, check target prices: moving them up if corporate progress justifies; down if there have been problems. Always keep in mind that the name of the game is PROFIT, not breaking even.

DO average up when you choose well. Buy more shares as the price of the stock rises. Be sure that there's a solid basis for future optimism and buy judiciously.

DO use leverage when prospects are good and interest rates are not too high in your margin account. In this type of account, you can buy $2 worth of stock for every $1 in cash you have on deposit. Government bonds can be purchased with as little as 10% in cash. The cost of borrowing can often be offset by the interest that you earn from these bonds.

DO set selling prices, preferably stop-loss orders at 15 to 20% below your cost or the recent high. This is discussed in greater detail later, but it is a key factor in successful investing. It is just as important to keep losses low as to keep profits high. At times, this can be a tough decision, so that action should be taken only after you have learned the real reason for the price decline. If the company runs into temporary difficulties, don't panic. But if research (yours or your broker's) concludes that profits will be below projections, it's usually smart to sell now. You can always buy back later.

DO stand by your investment rules. Once in a while, it will pay to make exceptions, but be cautious about such actions. If you feel that you must buy another security, try to use new money. In successful investing, rules should seldom be broken.

DON'TS FOR SUCCESSFUL INVESTING

DON'T invest in a vacuum: without a systematic, sensible, long-range plan for your personal, business, and retirement savings. Wise planning is easy, enjoyable, and rewarding. Lack of planning leads to mistakes which can be more costly than spending the time to understand the fundamentals of investing.

DON'T be overly conservative or overly speculative. This means limiting the portion of your savings allocated to fixed asset/income investments, such as money market accounts,

SELECT LIST OF QUALITY STOCKS THAT HAVE SURVIVED
Standard & Poor's List: 1976 and 1986;
All ranked A or A+

Apparel
Angelica Corp.
Nordstrom, Inc.
U.S. Shoe Corp.
V.F. Corp.

Beverages
Anheuser-Busch Co.
Coca-Cola

Chemicals
Betz Labs
Nalco Chemical

Construction
Masco Corp.

Diversified
Ametek, Inc.
MMM
National Service Industries

Drugs, Cosmetics
Bard (C.R.) Inc.
Becton Dickinson
Bristol-Myers
Gillette Co.
Pfizer, Inc.
SmithKline Beckman
Upjohn Co.

Electrical
Emerson Electric
General Electric

Electronics
IBM

Food
CPC International
Dart & Kraft
General Mills
Pillsbury Co.
Quaker Oats

Machinery & Equipment
Diebold, Inc.
Dover Corp.

Printing, Publishing
Dun & Bradstreet
Dow Jones & Co.
Knight-Ridder
Meredith Corp.

Retailers
Dayton Hudson
Federated Dept. Stores
Maytag Co.
Melville Corp.
Winn Dixie Stores

Tobacco
American Brands
U.S. Tobacco

Utilities
Central & Southwest
Consolidated Edison
Iowa Resources
Panhandle Eastern
Rochester Telephone
Sonat, Inc.
Texas Utilities

Miscellaneous
Josten's, Inc.
Rubbermaid, Inc.

SOURCE: Standard & Poor's.

preferred stocks, and bonds bought at par. These can be safe, but unless they are bought at a discount, they rarely grow in value. Always consider most of these holdings as temporary parking places while you wait for more rewarding opportunities.

Similarly, do not take unnecessary risks with marginal or speculative securities.

DON'T be overly optimistic or pessimistic: about the market and/or the securities that you own. Even the best corporations falter now and then: their growth slows or their markets change. The smart professionals recognize when this occurs and also when the stock price soars to an unrealistic level. When any stock becomes clearly overvalued by your standards, sell or set stop-loss orders. Never be lured by the "greater

---

GOOD ADVICE

For long-term investments in the stock market, keep these "lessons" in mind:
- If the prospects look overly favorable, review your homework.
- Change is inevitable: in the economy of the world, the United States, each industry, and every corporation.
- The more dynamic the market, the greater the percentage of new winners . . . and, often, old losers.
- In any market cycle, leaders seldom repeat their prior success.
- Once any stock has been dropped by the institutions, it will take time for a meaningful recovery, usually at least one year, often longer.
- A stock that has had a sensational rise (or even a modest one) is likely to plateau for many months. It takes at least two consecutive quarters of better earnings to build investor interest.
- High earnings growth is difficult to sustain. A 20% gain with $10 million profits is $2 million; with $100 million, it's a whopping $20 million.
- In today's performance-oriented environment, portfolio managers pay too much heed to short-term results and lose sight of long-term trends and corporate management policies.

SOURCE: Based on *Portfolio Manager's Weekly*, Donaldson, Lufkin & Jenrette.

CONSIDER INCREASING OR DECREASING YOUR POSITION IN AN INDIVIDUAL STOCK WHEN . . .

- The price changes substantially
- New management takes over
- Earnings increases or decreases are announced
- A new product comes on line
- A merger or acquisition takes place
- The company is listed or removed from being listed on one of the exchanges
- Antitrust action is brought against the company
- Dividends are increased, cut, or completely canceled
- The P/E multiple changes
- The stock is purchased or sold by the institutions
- The company spins off unprofitable divisions or subsidiaries

REVIEW YOUR PORTFOLIO WHEN . . .

- There's a significant move up or down in the stock market
- Prime and other bank interest rates change
- There's a new tax law
- The dollar becomes substantially stronger or weaker in the international market
- There's been a major scientific breakthrough
- Regulatory agencies adopt a new policy
- Inflation rate changes
- There's a change in political leadership
- Foreign-trade restrictions are put into effect
- A new international trade agreement is reached
- New rules are passed on margin accounts
- War begins or ends
- The economy changes from boom times to recessionary times, or vice versa
- Bond interest rates change
- Level of government spending changes

fool theory''—that the price will keep rising because someone else will be foolish enough to pay far more than the stock is worth. When you have a pleasant profit, it will usually pay to cash in.

So, too, with pessimism. The stock market will fluctuate and at times dip to unjustified lows. This will unleash the doomsayers, who can always find some reason to predict the doleful consequences of their own ineptitude. *Don't sell America—or American business— short.*

According to one survey, 75% of all investment advisory services are wrong more often than they are right. Once you have done your own research, check the corporate record and make your own projections.

DON'T try to buck the market. There will be exceptions, but in a bull market, almost all stock prices will go up. Vice versa in a bear period. Significant changes take time, and while there are always down periods, the trend of the stock market has been up twice as often as it has been down.

DON'T rush to buy bargains, regardless of the pressure from your adviser or broker. When a stock is at a low price, there is usually a reason. It may not appear to be logical, but major investors are either skeptical or uncomfortable. They will not start buying until their peers do so. Once you spot a bargain, wait until the price and volume start to rise and then proceed cautiously, buying in small lots even if it costs more money.

DON'T average down. A stock that appears to be a good buy at 20 is seldom more attractive at 15. When there's a decline in your current favorite, either your research is inaccurate or your access to the latest information is inadequate. Have your broker check the research department. If you are wrong and keep buying as the price declines, you'll only compound your mistake.

DON'T assume that a quality rating will continue. With cost squeezes, foreign competition, governmental regulations/edicts, and fast-changing financial and market conditions, even stable corporations can become less attractive in a few months. To see how quickly quality stocks can change, check the table from Standard & Poor's on page 66 that shows that only 49 of over 400 stocks retained their prime rating from 1976 to 1986.

DON'T heed rumors. Wall Street is a center of gossip, hopes, and fears, but a rumor is *never* a sound reason for investment decisions. By the time you hear or read it, the professionals have made their move. If it's a quality stock, don't worry.

DON'T forget that a stock does not care who owns it. The price per volume of the trading of its shares is the result of forces far stronger and wealthier than you are or probably ever will be.

DON'T look back. There's no way that you can reverse your decision. If your judgment was wrong, there's nothing that you can do about it except to learn from it.

8 | COMMON STOCKS

Over the long term, the best total returns—income plus appreciation—come from ownership of common stocks of high-quality, growing, profitable corporations. You gain by: (1) constantly higher underlying values; (2) ever-increasing dividends; and (3) rising prices reflecting greater popularity.

In periods of high interest, greater profits can temporarily be attained with fixed income securities: CDs and money market accounts, high coupon bonds bought for income and low coupon bonds bought at discounts. But the core of every investment portfolio should be shares of financially strong companies whose managements know how to achieve profitable growth. Here's why:

If a corporation earns 15% on stockholders' equity (the money invested by shareholders), it ends the year with 15¢ per dollar more. After payment of a 5¢-per-share dividend, 10¢ is reinvested for future growth: research and development, new plants and equipment, new products and markets, etc. Thus, the underlying value of the corporation doubles in about 7.5 years. Eventually, these gains will be reflected in the price of the common stock. That's why the best investments are shares in companies that continue to make the most money!

ADVANTAGES OF COMMON STOCKS

➤ GROWING VALUES Stocks are *live* investments. The good ones *grow*. Bonds and savings are *dead* investments. Their basic values remain static. (*Note:* This doesn't mean that you should

Common stock: A security that represents ownership in a corporation.

always be fully invested in common stocks, no matter how rewarding. For maximum investment returns, it's important to be flexible.)

The market value of a common stock grows as the corporation prospers. This growth keeps pace and, it is hoped, exceeds the erosion of inflation. The face value of bonds remains the same, so that over the years, their real value, in terms of purchasing power, decreases.

By contrast, the prices of bonds are almost completely controlled by interest rates and take effect immediately. When the cost of money rises, bond values drop to maintain competitive returns. Vice versa when interest rates decline. Bonds are traded by yields; stocks by what investors believe to be future corporate prospects.

Certainly, the stock market fluctuates, but the long-term trend has *always* been up, and there has been a better than 3:1 edge for the years of gain versus those of decline. Right now, most analysts look for the greatest gains in history, because by traditional standards, most common stocks are undervalued.

➤ MAXIMUM SAFETY Quality stocks are as safe as bonds are. As long as the corporation meets quality standards—financial strength, growth, and profitability—your money is safe. The company will continue to pay dividends, usually with periodic increases; and with higher earnings, the value of its shares will increase. If a well-known corporation pays dividends for more than 40 years, its stock is certainly as durable as its bonds.

➤ EFFECTIVE TAX SHELTER The earnings that are *not* paid out to shareholders in dividends represent tax-deferred income. These profits are reinvested to make the company grow and prosper. As long as you own stock in a profitable company, your money is growing. You will pay no taxes on these "gains" until you sell.

COMPARATIVE INVESTMENT RETURNS
Total Investment Return—Price Appreciation Plus Income

	CUM. LAST 5 YEARS ANNUAL RATES	1985	1984	1983	1982	1981
Stock Market Averages						
S&P 500	14.6%	31.6%	6.2%	22.5%	21.5%	−4.9%
Dow Jones industrials	15.9	33.5	1.3	26.0	27.1	−3.6
Dow Jones utilities	20.3	27.6	25.5	21.8	22.2	5.7
Bond Market Averages						
Dow Jones corporate bonds	17.5	27.1	15.7	8.7	38.5	1.1
U.S. government bonds	18.7	29.1	16.7	2.2	41.0	8.7
Municipal bonds	13.0	20.0	10.6	12.9	48.0	−17.0
Reserve Funds						
U.S. T-bills (90 days)	10.2	7.6	9.8	8.8	10.8	14.1
CD's (90 days)	11.1	8.0	10.4	9.1	12.3	15.9
Money market funds	11.0	7.7	10.0	8.6	12.1	16.8

SOURCE: Data compiled by Wright Investors' Service, 1985.

> ➤ LIQUIDITY Common stocks traded on major stock exchanges can be quickly bought or sold at clearly stated prices, the ranges of which are quoted in the financial press. You can instruct your broker to buy or sell at a specific price or at "market," which will be the best price at-

HOW QUALITY STOCKS CAN GROW

COMPANY	SHARES	1982 PRICE	VALUE	1985 PRICE	VALUE	TOTAL DIVIDEND	TOTAL RETURNS
Dillard Dept. Stores	100	$6.57	$657	$37½	$3,750	$24	$3,774
Dreyfus Corp.	100	18.87	1,887	86½	8,650	297	8,947
Strawbridge/Clothier	100	9.11	911	41⅜	4,137	161	4,298
Ames Dept. Stores	100	5.58	558	25⅜	2,537	26	2,563
Harcourt Brace Jov.	100	18.25	1,825	74½	7,450	300	7,750
Wilmington Trust	100	10.25	1,025	38	3,800	275	4,075
Ennis Business Forms	100	6.59	659	23	2,300	78	2,378
Midlantic Banks	100	14.12	1,412	43¾	4,375	313	4,688
Giant Food	100	8.43	843	26½	2,650	117	2,767

(Includes stock splits)

SOURCE: Standard & Poor's.

tainable at that time. The complete transaction will take five working days, but immediately after the transaction, you can get exact data from your broker.

➤ GROWING DIVIDENDS This is important for investors who want ever-higher income. Almost all quality companies keep boosting their payouts because of higher earnings.

DISADVANTAGES OF COMMON STOCKS

There are, of course, risks with ownership of common stocks. The risks are far less with quality corporations and, to a large degree, can be controlled by setting strict rules for selling and by using common sense. As long as the company continues to make more money, its stock price is likely to rise, but this may take time, often longer than you are prepared, financially or mentally, to accept.

➤ THE RISK OF PERMANENT LOSS OF CAPITAL You may lose all your profits and some of your capital if you speculate in "poor" stocks (and, occasionally, if you do so with quality stocks). The problem is *you*. When you speculate in high-flying stocks which are temporarily popular, the odds are against success. Only a few strong-minded people have the courage to sell such stocks when they become overpriced. When such equities start down, many people hang on in hopes of a comeback. This seldom happens.

Speculations in stocks should be limited to half of the money you can afford to lose.

FINDING WINNERS

➤ CONTINUITY For investors who place safety first, the best common stocks are those of companies that have paid dividends for 40 years or more. There are many familiar names: Anheuser-Busch, Bristol-Myers, Chesebrough-Pond's, Heinz (H. J.), Johnson & Johnson, Melville Corp., Philip Morris, and Woolworth.

But continuity is not necessarily a mark of quality. Some of the real old-timers, such as utilities, are monopolies. Their continuing profits may be the result of their market position rather than managerial ability. And despite their famous names, neither Philip Morris nor Woolworth are quality corporations.

Always check a company's records to see if: (1) the dividends have increased fairly consistently as the result of higher earnings; (2) the company has been able to move ahead in recent years and appears likely to do even better in the near future. It's great to do business with an old store, but only if the merchandise is up to date and fairly priced.

➤ INSTITUTIONAL OWNERSHIP These are stocks chosen by the "experts"—managers of mutual funds, pension plans, insurance portfolios, endowments, etc. With few exceptions, these are shares of major corporations listed on the New York Stock Exchange.

Institutional ownership is no guarantee of quality, but it does indicate that some professionals have reviewed the financial prospects and for some reason (not always clear) have recommended purchase or retention. Without such interest, no stock can move up.

In most cases, the companies must meet strict standards of financial strength, investment acceptance, profitability, growth, and, to some extent, income. But institutions still buy name and fame and either move in after the rush has started or hold on after the selling has started. Use the list on page 74 as a checkpoint for companies that appear attractive. If the stock is owned by more than 50 institutions, you'll be in good (but not always the most profitable) company. Information is available in Standard & Poor's *Stock Guide*, Moody's *Handbook of Common Stocks, The Value Line*, and analyses available from brokerage firms and some investment advisory services.

Institutions are not always smart money managers, but since they account for 70% of all NYSE transactions (and a high percentage of those on the AMEX and OTC), it's wise to check their portfolios when you consider a new commitment. Every investment portfolio should contain at least three stocks whose shares are owned by 250 institutions.

If you want to track portfolio changes, watch for reports on actions of investment companies in *Barron's Monthly Stock Digest* and the quarterly summaries published by *Lipper Analytical Services* and *Wiesenberger Services.*

But be cautious. The public information comes months after decisions have been made.

By the time you get the word, prices may have risen so much that your benefits will be comparatively small. Or you may be buying right before the portfolio managers on Wall Street, realizing their mistake, start selling.

➤ MOST PROFITABLE COMPANIES An important standard of safety is high and consistent profitability. It can be determined by calculating the rate of return on shareholders' equity, a minimum annual average of 11%. By sticking to these real winners, you will always make a lot of money . . . in time.

The table to the right shows how one investment advisory firm projects winners in the next couple of years, listing companies that are expected to achieve high total returns because of higher profits and, currently, undervaluation.

COMMON STOCKS FOR INCOME

If you are looking for income only, common stocks may not always be the best investment. In periods of high interest rates, bonds and CDs will provide higher returns. But unless those fixed-income securities are bought at a discount, they will seldom appreciate in value, so that your total returns will be limited.

The right kinds of common stocks can provide income plus appreciation and with lower taxes can net more money. Under present laws, all income is taxed at the same rate, since the favorable short-term capital gains rate was eliminated in the 1986 tax bill. This means investors can concentrate on sound fundamentals when selecting stocks, rather than on tax consequences. In addition, income stocks have greater appeal than in the past since the lower tax rates enable investors to keep a greater percentage of this income.

CALCULATING RATES OF RETURN

To reach your target goals, you should monitor your rate of return on each investment, which will, it is hoped, be a profit, but will occasionally be a loss. To make this calculation, divide the

WHERE BIG EARNINGS GAINS ARE PROJECTED FOR 1987

COMPANY	EST. 1987 E.P.S. GAIN	1985–86 PRICE RANGE	CURRENT PRICE
Abbott Laboratories	19%	$55-19^{15}/_{16}$	$53
American Int'l Group	48	141–65	139
Becton, Dickinson	21	$59^{1}/_{2}-19^{3}/_{4}$	59
Boeing	16	$64^{7}/_{8}-36^{1}/_{8}$	61
Church's Fried Chicken	25	$20^{1}/_{4}-11^{1}/_{4}$	12
Corning Glass Works	31	$81^{1}/_{2}-34^{1}/_{8}$	62
Dayton-Hudson	16	$58^{1}/_{2}-29^{3}/_{8}$	48
Digital Equipment	19	$98-42^{5}/_{8}$	98
Dow Chemical	18	$60^{7}/_{8}-27$	54
Eastman Kodak	95	$64^{3}/_{8}-40^{15}/_{16}$	57
Gulf + Western	43	$71^{7}/_{8}-27^{3}/_{4}$	66
Household Int'l	15	$47-32^{1}/_{4}$	43
Johnson & Johnson	17	$73^{3}/_{4}-35^{1}/_{8}$	70
K-Mart	15	$57^{3}/_{8}-30^{5}/_{8}$	54
Limited Inc.	42	$34^{1}/_{4}-8^{5}/_{8}$	31
Marion Laboratories	31	$49-10^{1}/_{4}$	48
Merck & Co.	19	$113^{1}/_{2}-45^{1}/_{8}$	113
Philip Morris	17	$76^{7}/_{8}-36$	73
RJR Nabisco	21	$55^{1}/_{8}-24^{3}/_{4}$	53
Squibb Corp.	15	$123^{3}/_{4}-49^{3}/_{4}$	123
Syntex Corp.	15	$72^{3}/_{4}-23^{3}/_{4}$	72
Texas Instruments	57	$148^{1}/_{4}-86^{1}/_{4}$	116
Thomas & Betts	17	$48^{1}/_{8}-33^{1}/_{2}$	44
Tonka Corp.	15	$32-6^{3}/_{8}$	31
Tracor Inc.	29	$28^{1}/_{3}-16$	21
Upjohn	18	$103^{3}/_{4}-33^{3}/_{8}$	90
Walgreen Co.	17	$39^{1}/_{2}-21^{1}/_{2}$	37
Wal-Mart	23	$53^{7}/_{8}-18^{15}/_{16}$	46
Woolworth (F.W.)	17	$49-18^{1}/_{3}$	43

SOURCE: Standard & Poor's *The Outlook,* August 20, 1986.

INCOME STOCKS WITH GROWTH POTENTIAL

| COMPANY | CURRENT YIELD (%) | 3- to 5-YEAR DIVIDEND ÷ | | | DIVIDEND GROWTH RATES | | 3- TO 5-YEAR TOTAL RETURN | | 3- TO 5-YEAR APPRECIATION POTENTIAL | | FINANCIAL STRENGTH RATING |
		CURRENT PRICE ($)	TIMELINESS	SAFETY	LAST 5 YEARS	NEXT 5 YEARS	LOW	HIGH	LOW	HIGH	
Alex & Baldwin	3.4%	$40	3	3	11%	15%	13%	23%	45%	65%	B+
Amer. Home Products	3.7	83	2	1	12	11	9	14	20	15	A++
Big Three Ind.	3.6	25	3	3	15	10	15	27	60	140	A
H&R Block	3.5	40	2	3	9	14	7	18	15	75	B++
Citizens & South. Corp.	3.6	26	2	2	32	15	11	20	35	90	B++
Colt Industries	3.7	68	3	3	13	10	11	20	30	90	A
Commerce Clrg Hse.	3.9	54	2	2	18	10	7	15	20	65	A+
Cross A.T.	3.8	38	3	2	15	12	8	18	20	70	A+
Dibrell Bros.	4.6	26	3	3	17	13	10	23	35	110	B++
Emerson Electric	3.3	84	3	1	11	10	11	16	35	65	A++
Harsco	3.4	27	3	1	10	16	17	23	65	105	A+
Hartmarx	3.5	26	3	3	14	14	10	20	35	90	B++
Ipco Corp.	3.3	12	3	3	20	12	10	22	35	110	B
Marine Midland	4.1	50	1	3	14	13	7	16	10	60	B
Philip Morris	3.6	64	1	1	22	16	12	17	40	70	A+
RJR Nabisco	3.5	43	3	1	11	10	14	19	50	85	A++
Service Master	3.3	27	3	2	25	19	13	22	50	105	A+
Transtechnology	3.5	19	3	3	21	11	15	23	60	110	B
U.S. Tobacco	6.1	32	3	2	19	16	17	25	55	120	A+

SOURCE: Value Line, May 30, 1986 (© 1986 Value Line, Inc.).

INSTITUTIONAL FAVORITES

Owned by More than 500 Institutions
American Express
American Home Products
Bristol-Myers
Coca-Cola
Du Pont (EI)
Exxon Corp.
General Electric
IBM
MMM
Philip Morris
Sears, Roebuck

Westinghouse Electric
Xerox Corp.
Owned by 400 to 500 Institutions
Anheuser-Busch
Dun & Bradstreet
ITT Corp.
Lilly (Eli)
Royal Dutch Petroleum
Santa Fe Southern Pacific
Travelers Corp.
Owned by 250 to 400 Institutions
Chase Manhattan

Corning Glass
Federal Express
General Mills
Heinz (H.J.)
Marsh & McLennan
Schering-Plough
Time, Inc.
Toys R Us
Wal-Mart Stores
Walt Disney Co.
Waste Management

SOURCE: Standard & Poor's.

---

total end value by the starting value, subtract 1, and multiply by 100:

R = Rate of return
EV = Value at end of period
BV = Value at beginning of period

$$R = \frac{EV}{BV} - 1 \times 100$$

In early January, Sol Smith bought 100 shares of OPH stock at a cost of $3,315 (price plus commissions and fees). During the year, OPH pays dividends of $3 per share. In December, the stock is at 45. For that year, the rate of return is 44%.

$$R = \frac{4500 + 300}{3315} = \frac{4800}{3315}$$

$$= 1.44 - 1 \times 100 = 44\%$$

If Sol had held the stock for 2 years and the dividends rose in the second year to $3.50 per share but the stock price stayed at 45, the rate of return would be 32%.

$$\frac{4500 + 300 + 350}{3315} = 1.64 - 1 \times 100 = 64\%$$

But since this was over 2 years, the annual rate would be half 64%, or 32%.

To make similar calculations with a time-weighted rate of return (where the rates of return vary and there are additional investments over a period of time), use the same general formula but calculate each time frame separately.

Sam Smith started the year with a portfolio worth $10,000. He reinvested all income. At the end of March, it was worth $10,900; on June 30, it was up a bit to $11,100. On July 1, Sam added $1,000. At the end of the third quarter, the value was $13,500 and savings totaled $15,000 at year-end. Here's how he determined the return.

$$\text{March 30:} \quad \frac{\$10,900}{10,000} = 1.09, \text{ or } 9\%$$

$$\text{June 30:} \quad \frac{11,100}{10,900} = 1.01, \text{ or } 1\%$$

$$\text{September 30:} \quad \frac{13,500}{12,100} = 1.12, \text{ or } 12\%$$

$$\text{December 31:} \quad \frac{15,000}{13,500} = 1.11, \text{ or } 11\%$$

Now use the quarterly figures according to the formula:

$$1.09 \times 1.01 \times 1.12 \times 1.11 = 1.37 - 1 = 37\%$$

Thus, 37% is the time-weighted rate of return, but the average rate of return is much lower.

A SAMPLING OF COMPANIES RATED A+ THAT HAVE INCREASED DIVIDENDS FOR TEN CONSECUTIVE YEARS

Abbott Laboratories*
Albertson's, Inc.
American Home Products*
American Water Works
Anheuser-Busch*
Arkla, Inc.

Bairnco Corp.
Bard (C.R.)
Bell Canada*
Brooklyn Union Gas

Centel Corp.
Cincinnati Financial
Citizens Fidelity*
Clorox Co.
Coca-Cola*
Consolidated Natural Gas*

Dow Jones & Co.*
Dun & Bradstreet*

Emerson Electric

Federated Dept. Stores*
First Alabama Bancshares
First Kentucky National*

Flowers Industries
Fourth Financial

Gannett Co.*
General Electric*
General Mills*

Heileman (G.) Brewing*
Hillenbrand Industries
Hubbell, (Harvey) "B"*

Johnson & Johnson*

Kellogg Co.*
Knight-Ridder Inc.

Lilly (Eli)*

McDonald's Corp.
Melville Corp.*

National Service Industries
Noxell Corp. "B"*

Philip Morris*
Pillsbury Co.*

PNC Financial*
Procter & Gamble*

Quaker Oats*

Ralston Purina*
Rubbermaid, Inc.

Schlumberger, Ltd.
Service Master Industries
Sonat, Inc.
Strawbridge/Clothier
Sunwest Financial Services*

Texas Commerce Bankshares*
Texas Utilities*
Transalta Util. "A"
TRW, Inc.
Tucson Electric Power*

Universal Leaf Tobacco*
U.S. Tobacco*

V.F. Corp.

Winn-Dixie Stores*

Zions Utah Bancorp

* Has paid dividends for 50 consecutive years.

SOURCE: Standard & Poor's.

9

CONVERTIBLES:
Income Plus Appreciation

With convertible securities (CVs), investors can have their cake and eat it too. These hybrids combine the security of principal and fixed income of debt issues with the growth potential of common stocks. It's a tough combination to beat.

As the name implies, CVs can be swapped for shares of common stock, usually of the same company, at specific ratios and until a specified date. There are two types of CVs:

Debentures, which are secured by the overall assets of the corporation and generally sold at $1,000 each and redeemable at par.

Preferred stocks, which are not quite as safe as debentures because, in the case of corporate liquidation, they will be secondary to bonds although ahead of common stock. They may not have a set maturity date or price but are sold at lower prices, typically $25 to $100 each.

In most cases, CVs are callable prior to maturity, often after the first 2 years.

Note: When the term "convertible" (CV) is used, it refers to both debentures and preferred stocks, but always check the provisions of call and conversion, because there can be exceptions.

Broadly speaking, CVs are a conservative way to play the equity market and an aggressive approach to the fixed income field. The yields are fair to good; welcome gains are possible from a rise in the price of the related common stock; and in down markets, the declines are likely to be less than those of market averages. Most CVs are more attuned to equity (common stock) than to debt (bonds), because the ultimate worth is tied to the ability of corporate management to make more money.

With CVs, there are two value determinants: investment value and conversion value.

Convertibles: Bonds, debentures, or preferred stock that may be exchanged or converted into common stock.

➤ INVESTMENT VALUE This is the estimated price, usually set by an investment service company, at which the CV would be selling if it had no conversion feature. This is supposed to be a floor price under which the CV will not fall regardless of the action of the related stock. This value moves with the prevailing rate of interest: *down* when interest rates rise, and *up* when they fall. Thus, when the stock is selling below its conversion rate, an 8% CV issued at par ($1,000) will trade at about 70 ($700) to give a 12% yield to maturity when the return on straight bonds is 12%. Similarly, a CV with a high 11% coupon might sell at 110 ($1,100) when bond yields are 10%. *But in sharp bear markets, that floor can be breached.*

➤ CONVERSION VALUE This is the amount the CV is worth if exchanged for shares of the common stock. A debenture that is convertible into 25 shares of common stock has a conversion value of $1,000 when the stock is $40 per share. If the price of the stock is $32 at the time of issuance, the conversion value is $800 (25 shares × 32) and the conversion premium is 25%. ($1,000 ÷ $800 = 1.25).

If the price of the stock goes up 25%, from 32 to 40, the CV's market price will rise at a slower rate, say 20%, to $1,200.

If the price of the stock falls to 24, the price of the CV will decline less because its value will be cushioned by its investment value. Typically, the decline would be about 20%, to $800. This is well above the conversion value of $600 (25 shares × 24); the conversion premium would move up to 33% ($800 ÷ $600 = 1.33).

CVs are issued primarily in buoyant markets. To established firms, they can be money-savers because their interest or dividend rates are lower than those of straight debt issues. To small new firms seeking additional capital for expansion, they provide investors with

THE NODDINGS-CALAMOS LOW-RISK CONVERTIBLE BOND INDEX, POSITIONS HELD ON JUNE 30, 1984

COMPANY NAME	BOND DESCRIPTION	BOND PRICE	CURRENT YIELD	STOCK BETA	S&P STOCK RANK
Allied Corp.[1]	7.75–05	92.00	8.4%	1.15	A–
Allied Stores	9.50–07	112.50	8.4	.80	A+
American General	11.00–07	123.50	8.9	.85	A
American Medical Int'l.	13.00–01	147.00	8.8	1.35	A
Barnett Banks of Florida	12.25–06	124.00	9.9	1.00	A
Burlington Industries	5.00–91	79.12	6.3	.95	B+
Celanese Corp.	9.75–06	104.00	9.4	.90	B+
Chase Manhattan	6.50–96	70.50	9.2	.95	A–
GTE Corp.	10.50–07	100.00	10.0	.85	A+
Inexco Oil		74.75	11.4	1.45	B+
Kaneb Services[2]	8.75–08	89.00	9.8	1.25	A–
Leggett & Platt	8.125–01	94.00	8.6	.90	A–
McKesson Corp.	9.75–06	95.75	10.2	.80	A
Merrill Lynch	8.875–07	102.00	8.7	1.75	B+
Nat'l. Convenience Stores	9.00–08	88.00	10.2	1.05	A–
Nat'l. Medical Enterprises	12.625–01	103.50	12.2	1.40	A
Newell Cos.	8.75–03	85.50	10.2	.85	A–
Paine Webber[3]	8.00–05	90.50	8.8	2.00	B+
Pogo Producing	8.00–05	72.50	11.0	1.15	B+
Quaker State Oil	8.875–08	96.00	9.2	1.25	B+
Reynolds Industries[4]	10.00–08	107.50	9.3	.95	A+
SCOA Industries	10.00–07	118.50	8.4	.90	A+
Seagram Co. Ltd.	8.25–08	101.75	8.1	1.05	A
Southwest Airlines	10.00–07	121.00	8.3	1.10	B+
United Telecommun.[5]	5.00–93	69.00	7.2	.90	A+
Viacom International	9.25–07	105.00	8.8	1.30	B+
Walter, Jim Corp.	5.75–91	82.50	7.0	1.10	B+
Averages (27 positions)			9.1%	1.11	

[1] Bond trades as Textron.
[2] Bond trades as Moran Energy.
[3] Bond trades as CIGNA Corp.
[4] Bond trades as General Cinema.
[5] Bond trades as United Utilities.

SOURCE: Thomas C. Noddings, *Low Risk Strategies for the High Performance Investor.* Chicago: Probus Publishing Co., 1985.

extra security and still retain the potential for appreciation.

All CVs are a form of debt, so they require regular payments of interest or dividends—not easy when the company is struggling to show a profit. And when they are converted, they will dilute shareholders' equity. *As with all types of securities, the key factor is quality.*

To repeat, the conversion value of a CV is the price at which the CV must sell to equal the

TYPICAL NEW CONVERTIBLE BOND ISSUES, 1983

	LOW-RISK	AGGRESSIVE
Price	100	100
Interest rate	6¼%	8¼%
Years-to-maturity	20	20
Issue size, $ million	100	20
Yield advantage	4%	10%
Conversion premium	15%	25%
S&P investment grade	A	B
Straight bond equivalent yield	8½%	12%
Investment value	70	65
Investment value premium	43%	54%

SOURCE: Thomas C. Noddings, *Low Risk Strategies for the High Performance Investor.* Chicago: Probus Publishing Co., 1985.

price of the stock, i.e., the number of shares received on conversion times the price of stock. You pay a premium to make the conversion. To calculate, use this formula:

CV = conversion value of the convertible

PC = price of the common stock

SC = number of shares by conversion

PV = current price of the convertible

$P = dollar premium you pay

P = percentage of premium

$$CV = PC \times SC$$

$$PV - CV = \$P$$

$$\frac{\$P}{CV} = P$$

Example: Nifty, Inc., convertible debenture 8% due in 2006, rated A, is selling at 100 ($1,000). Each bond is convertible into 32 shares of common stock, which is trading at 30. To find the percentage of premium:

$$CV = 30 \times 32 = 960$$

$$1000 - 960 = 40$$

$$\frac{40}{960} = 4.16\%$$

This is a low premium for a CV of such a well-rated corporation. If future prospects are good and the stock is attracting investor interest, such a CV could be a worthwhile investment.

Note: In boom times, new issues of CVs often carry high premiums because of the hope that the company will do well and the value of its common stock will rise sharply. But remember that CVs are issued when the underwriter feels that they can command the maximum price.

CALCULATING CONVERSION PREMIUM

1. Market price of debenture		$1,000
2. Yield @ 8%		$ 80
3. Conversion ratio		25
4. Conversion price: $\dfrac{\#1}{\#3} = \dfrac{1,000}{25}$		40
5. Market price of stock		32
6. Conversion value: #3 × #5 = 25 × 32		$ 800
7. Conversion premium: $\dfrac{\#1-\#6}{\#6} = \dfrac{1,000-800}{800}$		25%

SOURCE: New York Stock Exchange.

BENEFITS TO THE ISSUER

In judging the merits of any new investment, consider the benefits to the corporation. With common stock, shareholders are partners; with bonds, they are creditors. With CVs, they are in between: potential shareholders with hopes sustained by a promise of steady income. CVs are a call on the stock, so no gains can be achieved unless the corporation grows profitably.

Generally, CVs enable the corporation to:

➤ SELL STOCK AT A HIGHER PRICE THAN COULD BE OBTAINED WITH A STRAIGHT ISSUE To raise $10 million through an equity offering, a company would have to sell 100,000 shares of common at $100 (disregarding financing costs). Since CVs usually command a premium of about 15%, the $10 million could be raised by selling CVs at 115. When converted, they would require only 85,000 shares of common. In effect, the corporation is selling common stock at higher than current prices, and without presently diluting equity.

➤ OBTAIN BETTER FINANCIAL TERMS That is: (1) interest rates as much as 4% below those of straight bonds; on a $10 million issue, this means annual savings of $400,000; (2) bond interest (payable on debentures) is tax-deductible as a cost of doing business; dividends (on preferred or common stock) are paid with after-tax dollars; (3) more gradual dilution of the common stock: the company hopes that the funds obtained from the CVs will enable greater and more profitable growth; when the price of the common stock rises above the conversion price, CV holders will start to convert and the dilution will be largely offset by higher earnings. Eventually, through call, conversion, or redemption, the debt will be wiped out.

Note: Some corporations have used CVs to borrow millions of dollars with no, or little, interest. In May 1980, when yields of new corporate bonds were 14%, Wang Laboratories floated $50 million of 8% debentures with a conversion price of 38% when the common stock was at 33. For such a fast-expanding computer company, this 17% premium was in line, so that the issue sold out quickly. Investors were happy with the modest yield and prospects of long-term appreciation.

But in October, before the first interest date, Wang called the entire offer. Since the stock was selling between 51 and 64, investors averaged gains of 47%. But this was far below the 72% profit that they would have made if they had bought the stock directly. The big winner was Wang, because the company had the use of the $50 million for 6 months without paying a cent of interest. This saved the company about $2.6 million.

Similar "opportunities" have not been so rewarding. When Digital Equipment tried to force an exchange a few months after the new issue of 8⅞% CVs, investors balked. They pointed out that this would dilute the number of shares of common stock by 12% and dumped their shares. When the stock price fell 10 points, the swap was canceled.

Now that Wall Street is wary of trick deals, they are not likely to be repeated with listed corporations, but they may be used by small companies, especially when underwritten by swinging brokers and/or syndicates. After all, they are legal—and can be very profitable!

CHECKPOINTS FOR CVs

With all CVs, the primary consideration should be the quality of the issuing corporation, which means that management should be able to achieve profitable growth by earning at least 12% on stockholders' equity (your money) and the company should be financially strong and the securities widely traded, preferably on the NYSE or AMEX.

Concentrate on companies rated B or higher by Moody's or Standard & Poor's. Any corporation with a lower rating is speculative, may not be able to pay the interest or dividends, and probably has dim prospects for profitable growth.

If the stock is speculative, the CV will be risky too. If it's the stock of a stodgy company, the conversion privilege won't be worth much. Buy CVs only from companies whose common stocks you want to own on the basis of quality and value.

➤ BREAKEVEN POINT This is the time needed to make up the difference between the income of the CV and the dividend of the related common stock. Let's say that the 8% debenture is trading at 70 ($700). That's a current yield of 11.4%. Each CV can be converted into 25 shares of common; so when the stock is trading at 32, the conversion value is $600. The difference is $100.

Since the interest is $80 and the dividends total $50 (at $2 per share), there's a spread of $30. Divide 100 by 30 to get 3.3. This is the number of years it will take for the extra income from the interest to make up the conversion premium. Professionals look for CVs in which the spread can be offset in 3 to 4 years.

➤ DURATION OF THE CONVERSION PRIVILEGE Sometimes the conversion period may be too short to permit the common stock to appreciate enough for swapping to be worthwhile. Unless the premium is small, be wary of CVs that will be redeemed in less than 5 years. You may still be able to count on substantial price appreciation if the current price is well below par.

In some cases, the best returns will come from discount CVs. It's true that new CVs are offered at par without commission, so you save a few dollars. But the premium will be fairly high and it will take time—2 or 3 years at a minimum—for the spread to be narrowed. When you buy discount CVs of a quality company, you'll be getting a bargain in bear markets, and the relatively high yields will ease the temporary paper losses.

➤ CALL PROVISIONS Traditionally, most CVs cannot be redeemed for several years—usually

2 years—after issue. That provides protection for a while but can cut profits if the price should soar.

Example: Back in 1978 when airlines were making money and their stocks were popular, Pan American 9⅞, '96, convertible into 166.67 shares of stock, were trading at $1,791.70 when the stock was at 10¾. The bond redemption price was $1,086.20. This was the time to take a profit. A few months later, when Pan Am stock fell to 6, the CVs were down to $1,000, so some people missed out . . . and so did holders of the common stock.

When CVs have provisions for a sinking fund, it is a guarantee that the company will retire a portion of the issue annually by buying at par or when the price is below par. Either way, this ensures market support and usually a higher price. Once in a while, a cash-shy company may swap a sinking fund issue for one that won't be redeemed for some years. In such a switch, there can be a welcome premium: with Lockheed 4¼, '92, the exchange called for a new issue, at 75, for the old debt trading at 56.

➤ TIMING OF CONVERSION The investor should make the swap when the income from the dividends on the common stock is greater than the interest of the debentures or the dividends of the preferred, if the quality of the earnings is high.

Example: PDQ $4.00 preferred is convertible to 1.05 shares of common stock. Owners of 100 shares of preferred are sure of $400 annual income. By converting, they can own 105 shares of common stock that, with a $5.00 per share dividend, brings in $525. But they must be sure that the common dividend is secure and, preferably, likely to increase.

➤ MARKETABILITY All types of CVs have limited investor acceptance. As a result, their trading volume is modest and prices can swing several points between transactions. This is an important consideration if you have to sell in a hurry. Take a look at the daily quotations for a week or so. If the prices move widely, be doubly cautious unless you can tie up your money for a long time.

➤ TAXES When the conversion is made, the holding period for federal income taxes is the time that you held *both* securities. If you bought the CV 2 months before converting, there are no tax consequences. If you sell at this point, the profit will be short-term. But if you wait until 6 months after the original purchase, the gains become long-term.

➤ LOWER COMMISSIONS As bonds, CVs are traded for commissions that are below those for an equal dollar amount used to buy stock (unless you use a discount broker). To purchase five CVs at 80 might cost $25. The same $4,000, used to acquire 200 shares of stock at 20, would cost more than twice as much.

On the other hand, the $25 will be a minimum charge for two CVs, and when the purchase involves more than five bonds, the per-unit cost may be only slightly more.

INVESTMENT COMPANIES

If you have limited capital or prefer to let someone else make the selections, there are investment companies that use a substantial portion of their assets to buy CVs and, in some cases, to write options. Three of these are funds with fixed capitalization (closed-ends), and their shares are traded on exchanges just like stocks. These shares typically sell at a discount from net asset value (the worth of the portfolio holdings). Investors are skittish because they believe that the fund would have to sell current holdings to take advantage of new opportunities.

The discounts can be profitable. When they narrow, the values of the shares will increase and, since the income is based on a discounted price, the yields can be relatively high: that is,

---

BABY BONDS

The latest Wall Street promotion for debt issues is "baby bonds," priced at $25 each to attract small investors. Most of these are convertible debentures, e.g., a 12%, '08 issued by DiGiorgio Corporation, a food distribution and processing firm.

These can be worthwhile *long-term* holdings, but because their markets are limited, their interim prices can fluctuate widely, forcing a loss if you have to sell before maturity.

RISK–REWARD ANALYSIS WITH CONVERTIBLES
Common Stock: 20; Debenture: 90, 10% Yield, Convertible to 40 Shares Common

	PROJECTIONS OF STOCK PRICE IN 6 MONTHS					
	10	15	20	25	30	40
Hedging With Common Stock						
Estimated bond price	72	80	90	104	122	160
Profit (loss): CV	(1,800)	(1,000)	0	1,400	3,200	7,000
Stock	1,500	750	0	(750)	(1,500)	(3,000)
Interest: CV	500	500	500	500	500	500
Profit (loss)	200	250	500	1,150	2,200	4,500
Annualized rate return	+4%	+6%	+11%	+26%	+49%	+100%
Hedging With Call Options						
Estimated bond price	72	80	90	104	122	160
Estimated call price	0	0	0	5	10	20
Profit (loss): CV	(1,800)	(1,000)	0	1,400	3,200	7,000
Calls	600	600	600	(900)	(2,400)	(5,400)
Interest: CV	500	500	500	500	500	500
Profit (loss)	(700)	100	1,100	1,000	1,300	2,100
Annualized rate return	−17%	+2%	+26%	+24%	+31%	+50%

SOURCE: Noddings, Calamos & Associates, 2001 Spring Road, Oak Brook, IL 60521.

TIPS ON CVs

- Usual minimum investment is $1,000.
- Shares can be purchased directly from the fund or from a stockbroker.
- Read the fund's prospectus before investing.
- Check the quality of the fund's underlying stocks.
- Convertibles offer a hedge against volatile changes in the stock market.
- Automatic reinvestment of distribution into additional fund shares is available.
- If you invest in a family of funds and your yield declines, you can switch to higher-yielding funds within the family.

LEADING CONVERTIBLE BOND MUTUAL FUNDS

	% APPRECIATION 12/31/85 TO 5/31/86
Dreyfus Convertible Securities (800-645-6561)	20.9%
American Capital Harbor Fund (800-421-5666)	18.07
Dean Witter Convertible Bond (800-221-2685)	17.31
Value Line Convertible Fund (800-223-0818)	16.46
Putnam Convertible Income Growth (800-354-5487)	15.38
Noddings, Calamos Income Fund (800-251-2411)	14.75
Convertible Yield Securities (800-231-0803)	14.21
Phoenix Convertible Fund Series (800-243-1574)	14.04

an 8% yield on shares selling at a 20% discount equals a 10% rate of return.

HEDGING WITH CVs

For professional traders, CVs offer excellent vehicles for hedging—buying one security and simultaneously selling short its related security. The hedge is set up so that if the market goes up, one can make more money on the purchase than one can lose on the sale, or vice versa if the market goes down. Such trading is best in volatile markets (of which there have been plenty in recent years).

Here's an example cited by expert Thomas C. Noddings: The CV debenture carries a 10% coupon and is convertible into 40 shares of common stock. The CV trades at 90; the common at 20. *Buy* 10 CVs at 90 at a cost of $9,000; sell short 150 common at 20—$3,000. Since the short sale requires no investment, the cost is $9,000 (not counting commissions). Refer to the risk-reward analysis on page 81 to see what can happen in 6 months.

- *If the price of the stock falls to 10,* the CV's estimated price will be 72, so there will be a loss of $1,800 ($9,000 − $7,200). But 150 shares of stock can be acquired for $1,500, for a profit of $1,500. Add $500 interest (10% for 6 months) and the net profit is $200.
- *If the price of the stock dips to 15,* the CV will sell at 80 for a $1,000 loss, but this will be offset by the $750 profit on the stock plus $500 interest for a return of $250.
- *If the price of the stock holds at 20,* the CV will stay at 90. There will be no profit on either, but the $500 interest will represent an annualized rate of return of 11%.
- *If the stock rises to 25,* the CV will be worth 104 for a $1,400 profit, but there will be a $750 loss on the shorted stock. With the $500 interest, there'll still be a $1,150 profit.
- *And if the stock soars to 40,* the CV will trade at 160 for a whopping $7,000 gain, which will be offset by a $3,000 loss on the stock but enhanced by the $500 income for a total of $4,500 on that $9,000 investment—all in 6 months!

SELECTED CV DEBENTURES WITH LISTED OPTIONS

COMPANY OR ISSUE	NUMBER OF SHARES PER $1,000 BOND	MAY 1986 PRICE OF CV
Burroughs Corp. 7¼%; 2010	12.88 shares	$105
Caesars World 6⅞%; 2006	43.54	94
ENSERCH Corp. 10%; 2001	35.01	101
Federal Nat'l Mtg. 4⅜%; 1996	50.94	155
Grace (W.R.) 6½%; 1996	33.76	187
Heinz (H.J.) 7¼%; 2015	28.42	116
Humana Inc. 8½%; 2009	26.46	110
IBM 7⅞%; 2004	6.51	127
Limited Inc. 7½; 2010	31.87	138
Morgan (J.P.) 4¾%; 1998	25.00	208
PepsiCo 4¾%; 1996	47.24	416
Prime Motor Inns 6⅝%; 2011	22.41	111
Rockwell Int'l 4¼%; 1991	86.96	384
Union Carbide 10%; 2006	45.54	115
Wendy's Int'l 7¼%; 2010	45.87	116
Xerox Corp. 6%; 1995	10.87	97

SOURCE: Standard & Poor's.

Says Noddings: "Selling short stock against undervalued CVs can eliminate risk while offering unlimited gains if the stock advances."

Best bet with hedges of CVs: Try out the "if projections" on paper until you are sure that you understand what can happen. By and large, the actual transactions will follow these patterns. At worst, the losses will be small; at best, the profits will be welcome.

WRITING CALLS WITH CVs

Noddings also shows how to write calls with CVs. This is a conservative way to boost income and, when properly executed, involves minimal risks and fair-to-good gains. Since the CVs represent a call on the stock, they provide a viable base. Let's say that a $1,000 par value CV debenture can be swapped for 40 shares of common; the CV is at 90; the stock at 20; the calls, exercisable at 20, are due in 6 months and carry a premium of 2 ($200) each.

Buy 10 CVs for $9,000 and sell three calls. (Since the CVs represent 400 shares of stock, this is no problem.) The $600 premium will reduce the net investment to $8,400.

- *If the stock jumps to 40,* the CV will sell at 160 for a $7,000 gain. Add $500 interest to get $7,500 income. But there will be a $5,400 loss because the calls will have to be repurchased with a deficit (tax advantageous) of $1,800 each. The net profit will thus be $2,100.

Warning: Writing calls on CVs is *not* for amateurs. To be worthwhile, this technique should: (1) involve a substantial number of shares (at least 300); (2) be done with the aid of a knowledgeable broker who watches for sudden aberrations in price spreads; (3) be initiated with adequate cash or margin reserves that may be needed to buy back calls early; (4) be handled only by individuals in a high enough tax bracket to benefit from the short-term losses.

FOR FURTHER INFORMATION

"Understanding Convertibles" (28 p.)
New York Stock Exchange
11 Wall Street
New York, NY 10005

Thomas C. Noddings. *Low Risk Strategies for the High Performance Investor.* Chicago: Probus Publishing Co., 1985.

Thomas C. Noddings. *Superhedging.* Chicago: Probus Publishing Co., 1986.

10

PREFERRED STOCKS:
Corporate America's Choice

Preferred stocks are middle securities that carry preference on all income available *after* the payment of bond interest and amortization and *before* dividend payments on the common stock. The dividend is usually secure for the life of the issue, and if a payment is skipped because of corporate losses, it will be paid later when profits become available.

Unless they are convertible to common stock, preferreds cannot provide the ever-higher income of equity investments in growing profitable companies. With straight issues, the market prices are keyed to the yield and move opposite to the cost of money: UP when interest rates drop; DOWN when they rise. Unlike bonds, where the accumulated interest is added to the sales price, preferred stocks are traded at the quoted price and the dividends are paid only to those who own the shares on the record date as set by the terms of the original issue, usually quarterly.

For individuals, all income is taxable, but the attraction is the low price for fixed income holdings, typically, $25 to $100 per share.

In selecting preferred stocks, use the same basic criteria used for all debt investments: *quality* of the issuing corporation as shown by financial strength and profitability; *value* as indicated by the yield; *timing* that takes into account the probable trend of interest rates and the possibility of an early call. Then:

- **Deal with a brokerage firm that has a research department that follows this group of securities.** Many registered representatives are not familiar with preferreds, will not be able to provide pertinent information, and may charge higher commissions than for transactions involving common stocks or bonds.

- **Recognize the inherent volatility because of limited marketability.** Preferreds listed on a major stock exchange may drop (when you want to sell) or rise (when you plan to buy) 2 or 3 points the day after the last quoted sale. If you have to sell in a hurry, this can be expensive. Preferreds sold over the counter (OTC) may fluctuate even more because of their thin markets. As a rule, place your orders at a set price or within narrow limits.

CALCULATING BENEFITS OF PREFERRED STOCK INVESTMENTS

Assumptions: 12% preferred stock dividend rate; 85% corporate tax exclusion on dividends; 46% corporate tax rate.

1 What is the effective after-tax rate of the dividend?
   12% dividend − 12% (1 − .85 [.46]) = 11.31% after-tax return

2 Should you borrow to invest?
   Borrowing cost: 16% (1 − 46) = 8.6%
   Effective yield − borrowing cost = 11.31% − 8.60% = 2.71%

3 How much after-tax yield improvement can I expect?
   Money market investment after-tax rates:
   12% (1 − 46) = 6.48%
   11.31/7.56 − 1 = 74.5% after-tax yield improvement

SOURCE: © Donoghue's *Moneyletter* ($87 per year, P.O. Box 540, Holliston, MA 01746).

Preferred stock: A company's senior stock, which has first claim on profits for the payment of a dividend. The dividend does not rise or fall with profits.

CHECKPOINTS FOR PREFERRED STOCKS

In selecting preferred stocks, look at these factors:
➤ QUALITY Choose those rated BBB or higher by Standard & Poor's. The difference in yield between a high- and not-so-high-rated issue can be small when you shop around.

But if you are willing to take greater risks, you can boost your income by buying BB-rated Philadelphia Electric $4.40 at 30 for a 14.7% yield.

Usually, but not always, the higher rating will be given to companies with modest debt. Since bond interest must be paid first, the lower the debt ratio, the safer the preferred stock. If you like to dig into annual reports, look for utilities with balanced debt and then check the preferred stocks, typically several issues with varying dividends so that you can fit the purchase to your savings.
➤ CALL PROVISION This provision allows the company to redeem the shares, usually at a few points above par and typically after 5 years. When the original issue carries a high yield, say over 12%, the company may find it worthwhile to retire some shares when: (1) it can float new debt/preferred at a lower rate, say 9%; (2) corporate surplus becomes substantial. In both cases, such a prospect may boost the price of the preferred by a point or two.

With large established companies, there's little need to worry about shenanigans, but watch out with: (1) preferreds of small struggling corporations where there may be special call or conversion provisions in small type; (2) utilities that take advantage of obscure provisions in their charters to save interest costs. What they do is use other assets to call in the preferred prior to that 5-year date. You may still end up with a modest profit, but chances are that the redemption price will be less than that at which it was selling earlier, so the investor loses.
➤ SINKING FUND This permits the corporation to buy up a portion of the outstanding preferred shares each year so that the entire issue is retired before the stated maturity date. That is, starting 5 years after the original sale, the company buys back 5% of the stock annually for 20 years. The yields of such preferreds will usually be slightly less than those for which there is no such provision.

If you decide to speculate with preferred stocks of marginal or small companies, especially those in "hot" new industries, spend a few extra minutes checking the small print to be sure that your rights are protected by:
➤ FULL VOTING RIGHTS Preferred shareholders should not be shut out from having a say in the

---

SELECTED STRAIGHT PREFERRED STOCKS

COMPANY	DIVIDEND	STANDARD & POOR'S RATING	RECENT PRICE	RECENT YIELD
Alabama Power	$ 9.00	A−	$100	9.0%
Chase Manhattan	7.60	A+	93	8.1
Du Pont (E.I.)	3.50	AA	48	7.2
Macy (R.H.)	4.25	AA−	101	4.2
NY State E&G	8.48	BBB	24	8.8
Pacific Gas & Electric	1.20	A−	14	8.4
San Diego Gas & Electric	4.65	A−	36	13.0
Transcontinental Gas	6.65	BBB−	88	7.5
U.S.G. Corp.	1.80	AA−	120	1.5
Wal-Mart	2.00	AA	179	1.1

SOURCE: Standard & Poor's.

management of the company. The NYSE lists only preferreds with the right to vote if the company gets into trouble.

There is no payment of dividends on the common stock until there is adequate working capital and a surplus sufficient to pay preferred dividends when corporate earnings lag.

➤ RESTRICTIONS ON NEW PREFERREDS OR BONDS Regulations that prohibit management from issuing new securities until they are approved by two-thirds of preferred shareholders.

NEW TYPES OF PREFERREDS

With their ever-sharper marketing skills, financial officers, with a nudge from Wall Street, have developed special types of preferred stocks to attract new capital:

- **Convertible, redeemable preferreds.** These were introduced by Wells, Fargo & Co., a bank holding company, to raise additional capital. The shares, offered at $50 each, pay a regular dividend for the first 5 years. Then the investor can swap for common stock at a price 5% below the market value. And to sweeten the deal, the bank will redeem 4% of the 700,000 preferred shares annually. This has helped to hold the market price above that of comparable issues; and if the common shares continue to appreciate, there will be an extra bonus from capital gains.

- **Adjustable preferreds**—where the quarterly dividends fluctuate with interest rates under a formula that resets the payments at either a premium or discount from one or more measurements of Treasury securities.

HOW TO MAKE 24 TO 36% A YEAR

Sharp traders may get as many as 12 dividends a year by rolling over preferred stocks. By buying shares just before the dividend date, they get the full payout. They sell the next day

---

PREFERRED STOCK
PROS
↑ Generally pays higher dividends than common; quoted as percentage of original investment
↑ Receive your dividend before common stockholders
↑ Dividends generally cumulative; if dividend skipped, made up in future
↑ Know what your dividend income is
↑ Possibility of capital gain in price of stock
CONS
↓ If company's earnings increase, you don't share in increases; dividend fixed, with few exceptions
↓ Call provisions allow company to redeem your stock at stated price

---

and buy another preferred with an upcoming dividend payment date. Because of the commission costs and need for constant checking, this technique is difficult for amateurs but can work well when deals involve 500 shares or more with hefty discounts on all transactions.

With 12 annual dividends, the theoretical yield could be 36%. Practically, however, most people are willing to settle for eight checks annually. If we assume a 12% yield (not always readily available), we find that the return—at 3% per quarter—can be 24%.

Timing is the key. After the payout date, the price of the preferred will drop almost as much as the value of the dividend. A 12% preferred might thus trade at 100 before the dividend date and drop back to just over 97 the next day. If you sell, you take a small loss (tax deductible), so your total income will be less. If you wait a week or so and are lucky in a strong market, you may be able to sell at 100. If you have the time and money, you should still be able to make 18% or more a year with sharp trading.

11 TAXABLE BONDS

If you want to protect your principal and set up a steady stream of income, then bonds, rather than stocks, are the answer. Income is in fact traditionally the most important reason people own bonds, which generate greater returns than CDs, money market funds, and stocks. They also offer greater security than most common stocks since an issuer of a bond will do everything possible to meet its bond obligation. Interest on a corporate bond must be paid before dividends on common or preferred stocks of the same corporation, and it's payable before federal, state, and city taxes. This senior position helps make your investment safer. A corporation, on the other hand, can and often does decide to cut back or eliminate its dividend.

Bonds, unlike stock, are debt. They can best be described as a contract to pay money. When you buy a bond, you loan money to the issuer and in return receive a certificate stating that the issuer will pay a stated interest rate on your money until the bond matures. The date of maturity is predetermined and ranges from 1 to 40 years. The interest rate received is called the coupon rate and is usually paid twice a year. At the date of maturity you get back the full purchase price, or face value, which is also called "par" and is usually $1,000.

Many investors think of bonds as being stable in price, almost stodgy. Not true. When they are first issued they are sold at face value, but afterwards they move up and down in price, trading either above or below par, at a premium or at a discount, in response to changes in interest rate markets.

Taxable bond: A security that represents debt of an issuing corporation. Issuer is required to pay bondholder a specified rate of interest for a specified time and then repay the entire debt.

Note: Although bonds are issued at par ($1,000), in the financial pages of newspapers they're quoted on the basis of $100, so always add a zero to the price; for example, a bond quoted at $108 is really selling at $1,080.

Bonds are issued by corporations, the U.S. government and its agencies, and by states and municipalities. The latter, also called "munis," are discussed in Chapter 13 on tax-exempt bonds.

In the last few years, the proliferation of new bond products has turned the bond markets into a three-ring circus. New products such as zero coupon bonds, zero convertibles, delayed payment bonds (which pay no interest for the first 5 or 6 years), and others have all been used to raise capital in extraordinarily innovative ways.

In addition, the introduction of bond futures and options on these futures has turned the traditionally conservative bond markets into areas of intense speculation. For the average investor, this host of new and fascinating products provides new opportunities, and as long as he or she exercises caution and investigates carefully, there's money to be made. The increased action in bonds also opens the door to trading them for appreciation as well as investing for income.

Every portfolio should contain some corporate or government debt holdings, and when the investor is in a high tax bracket, personal savings should include tax-exempts (more on this later). With *new issues,* you can count on high income for many years; with *outstanding securities,* you can be sure of excellent total returns; with *mortgage-backed debt,* you can count on monthly checks or sure appreciation through prompt reinvestment of income; and with *special types of bonds,* you can receive extra benefits from variable yields, indexing of the interest rate, and certain appreciation from a very low cost.

CORPORATE BONDS

For the issuing corporations, bonds are a relatively inexpensive way to obtain funds for capital improvements and expansion. The interest paid to bond holders is a tax-deductible business expense, so the cost of a 12% bond for a firm in the 34% tax bracket is only 7.92% (12 × 66%).

BOND YIELDS

Like stocks, bonds fluctuate in price, with their market value changing any number of times a day in reaction to interest rate movements. This is because the only way the bond market can accommodate the changes in interest rates is by changing the price of bonds. If you buy a bond at par ($1,000) and its coupon rate is 10%, you will receive $100 each year in interest payments. If rates move up, then the same corporation will issue new bonds yielding a higher rate, say 10½%. The older bonds then fall in price, perhaps to $960, in order to keep the yield competitive. (The yield is the equivalent of 10½% on the new bond because of the $40 saved when buying it at $960.) On the other hand, if new bonds pay less interest, then older bonds rise in price, because they immediately become more desirable due to their higher coupon rates.

ATTRACTIVE FEATURES OF BONDS

➤ CURRENT RETURN The issuer cannot reduce the interest rate unless it files under the bankruptcy code, so you'll receive your payments in good times and bad.

➤ SENIORITY Interest on a corporate bond must be paid before dividends on common and preferred stocks.

➤ CAPITAL GAINS If you buy a bond at discount (below $1,000 face value) and you either sell or redeem it at a profit, this gain is taxed at the ordinary income rate.

➤ SAFETY Ratings are available on corporate

bonds that help determine how safe they are as an investment.

SIZING UP THE MARKET

As with all securities, there are some disadvantages to bonds, especially when purchased at par (usually when issued).

➤ LIMITED APPRECIATION Bond values move in the opposite direction to interest rates: UP when interest rates fall and DOWN when rates rise. The recent rises and falls in interest rates have sent bond prices moving like yo-yos, so the bond market is no longer the safe harbor it once was. If you buy a bond today and interest rates fall, you'll make a profit if you sell. On the other hand, if rates climb back up, you'll lose if you have to sell your bond before maturity.

➤ EROSION BY INFLATION Since bonds have set interest rates and pay back the principal at a future date, they do not offer a hedge against inflation.

➤ CORPORATE REVERSES Corporate financial woes can hurt bonds. Two prime examples: Chrysler and Navistar. Stick with high-rated companies, A or above (see table of quality ratings).

➤ FIXED RATE OF RETURN Stockholders have an opportunity to enjoy increased dividends, whereas bondholders do not receive interest rate increases with the exception of those holding floating-interest bonds.

➤ CALLS Most corporate bonds are sold with a "call" feature that allows the issuer to redeem the bond before maturity. The conditions of a call are given to the SEC when the bonds are first issued to the public. Bonds are not usually called in if the current rate of interest is the same or higher than the bond's coupon rate.

However, if interest rates fall below the bond's coupon rate, it is likely to be called in, because the issuer can now borrow the money elsewhere at a lower rate. When this happens you lose your steady stream of income. You can protect yourself from calls by purchasing bonds with "call protection," which guarantees that the issue will not be called in for a specific number of years, say 10.

➤ DIFFICULTY OF COMPOUNDING Unless you buy shares in a bond fund or zero coupon bonds, there can seldom be automatic reinvestment of interest as with stock dividend reinvestment plans. *One partial solution:* instead of depositing interest checks in a low-yielding savings or NOW account, add to your shares of your money market fund. As long as the return stays close to that of the bonds, you'll be OK. But when the fund pays 8% vs. 12% for the bonds, try to add to the interest check and make new commitments.

➤ LIMITED MARKETABILITY With taxable bonds, there are two major markets: (1) the New York Stock Exchange, where a relatively small number of debt issues of major corporations are traded with daily quotations; (2) the over-the-counter market, dominated by bond dealers who handle U.S. government bills, notes, and bonds; debt of smaller companies, and special offerings and packages via bid and asked prices.

With small lots (under 25 bonds), the prices can fluctuate widely from day to day or even within a given trading day. The spreads between the offers by the buyer and seller normally run from ⅜ to ½% in strong markets, up to 3% in weak markets, and even more with little-known issues. *Unless you have special knowledge, buy only bonds or debt issues whose trading is reported in the daily financial press.*

WHAT TO LOOK FOR IN SELECTING BONDS

Value depends on two factors: the quality of the issuer and the rate of interest. Bonds of a solid, successful corporation are certainly a better investment than bonds of a weaker firm. The interest rate factor must also be considered: if you buy a bond with a fixed rate of interest, say 8%, and rates rise to 10 or 11%, the bond will decline in value. The three areas to consider when selecting bonds are:

➤ QUALITY RATINGS This is essential in choosing bonds for investments. In most cases, investments should be made only in A or better rated debt. You can get extra interest each year with lower quality bonds, but your risks are greater.

The ratings are made by statistical services that analyze the financial strength of the corporation, project future obligations, and determine the degree of protection of payments for both interest and principal. By and large, the

HOW BONDS ARE RATED

GENERAL DESCRIPTION	MOODY'S	STANDARD & POOR'S
Best quality	Aaa	AAA
High quality	Aa	AA
Upper medium	A	A
Medium	Baa	BBB
Speculative	Ba	BB
Low grade	B	B
Poor to default	Caa	CCC
Highly speculative default	Ca	CC
Lowest grade	C	C

Ratings may also have + or − sign to show relative standings in class.

two top services, Moody's Investors Service and Standard & Poor's, reach the same conclusions about each bond.

Prices for high-grade bonds reflect money market conditions and interest rates. Farther down the quality scale, however, bond prices are more closely attuned to business conditions and the financial prospects of the corporation. Medium-grade Baa and BBB bonds are the lowest category that qualifies for commercial bank investments.

Watch for changes in ratings of all types of bonds. Upgrading is beneficial, so the market price will probably rise (and the yield dip) a bit; downgrading signals possible trouble, so the value will decline. Shifts are not too important so long as the rating is A; but with any B category, be wary.

➤ TERMS Most debt issues of both the federal government and corporations carry a fixed coupon with a fixed date of maturity. But there will occasionally be serial bonds wherein a portion of the issue will be paid off periodically. Usually, the earlier the redemption date, the lower the interest rate—¼ to ½%, or so. These can be useful when you have a target date for need of money. Serial bonds are widely used with tax-exempt issues.

➤ CORPORATE COLLATERAL This is the property behind each bond. There are two basic types: "senior" or "secured" bonds and "junior" bonds.

INTEREST RATES

YEAR	TREASURY BILLS*	PRIME RATE†	CORPORATE BONDS‡	MUNICIPAL BONDS§
1940	0.04	1.25	3.07	2.50
1950	1.22	2.50	2.71	1.98
1960	2.95	4.50	4.54	3.73
1970	6.46	6.75	8.21	6.51
1980	11.51	21.50	12.02	8.51
1985	7.49	9.50	11.41	9.18

* Annual average on 3-month bills.
† End of the year.
‡ AA rated annual average.
§ Annual average.

SOURCE: Standard & Poor's.

Senior bonds are backed either by the company's real estate—these are mortgage bonds—or by equipment—called equipment certificates. Junior bonds are backed only by the promise of the issuer to pay interest and principal. The seniority ranking becomes most important when default or insolvency occur. Senior-obligation-backed bonds receive preferential treatment.

Unsecured bonds or debentures are backed only by the general credit standing of the issuing company. The investor should translate this credit into the company's ability to pay annual interest and amortization plus the principal sum when due. The projection should consider recent historical ratios and trends and should apply to the *total* debt.

In practice, with respect to most bonds, the ability of the corporation to pay is much more important than theoretical security, because legal obstacles to investors collecting a bond's security in the event of insolvency are often formidable and time-consuming and can quite possibly require litigation.

▶ HOW TO MEASURE BOND QUALITY *A handy formula for determining investment-grade bonds* is the number of times total annual interest charges are covered by pretax earnings for a period of 5 years.

	BEFORE FEDERAL INCOME TAXES	AFTER FEDERAL INCOME TAXES
Industrial bonds	5×	3×
Public utility	3×	2×

CHANGES IN BOND RATINGS

Up:	Heller (Walter) International	from BBB to A+
	Wang Laboratories	from BBB to A−
Down:	Chase Manhattan	from AAA to AA
	Commercial Credit	from A to BBB

SOURCE: Standard & Poor's *Bond Guide.*

HOW TO READ THE QUOTES

Unlike most stocks, many bonds have thin markets, trading only now and then. That means when you look for quotes in the newspaper, they may not be listed. The trading transactions of bonds that you should consider owning are listed in financial publications: daily in major newspapers; weekly in *Barron's* and other specialized publications.

Corporate bonds: The accompanying table shows a listing for AAA-rated A.T.&T. with a coupon of 3⅞% and a 1990 maturity date. The last quotation was 89½ ($895.00) and, during

HOW CORPORATE BONDS ARE QUOTED

STANDARD & POOR'S RATING*	ISSUE	CURRENT YIELD	SALES 1000s	HIGH	LOW	CLOSE	CHANGE
AAA	A.T.&T. 3⅞, '90	4.3%	167	89⅞	89⅜	89½	—

* The rating is not shown in the press.

SOURCE: Barron's June 23, 1986.

the day, the high price was 89⅞ and the low 89⅜, with the last sale 89½ unchanged from the price of the last sale on the previous day. Overall, 167 one thousand dollar bonds changed hands.

Each bond paid $37.85 annual interest, so the current yield was 4.3%. Investors were willing to accept this modest return because they knew that in about 3 years, each bond would be redeemed at 100 ($1,000) for a capital gain of 10½ ($105.00). The yield to maturity was competitive with that of new issues.

Government bonds: Traded OTC these are quoted in thirty-seconds (3.125), with bid and asked prices daily. (*Barron's* lists the high, low, and last price; volume; and yield.) The quotations are per $1,000 face value. The first line in the table shows notes due in 1989 with a coupon of 8%, a bid price of 101.22 ($1016.88), and an asked price of 101.26 ($1018.13) with a yield of 7.24%. The investor who holds them to maturity will get about $18 per bond because they will be redeemed at par.

HOW GOVERNMENT DEBT IS QUOTED

ISSUE	BID	ASKED	CHANGE	YIELD
8 1989 Feb.	101.22	101.26	−.4	7.24
9 1994 Feb.	106.15	106.23	−.24	7.82
12 2008–13 Aug.	136.5	136.13	−1.7	8.36
7¼ 2016 May	96.26	96.30	−.28	7.51

SOURCE: The New York Times.

The 12% bond, due to mature between 2008 and 2013, provides a 8.36% yield and is trading far above par because the coupon (12%) is much higher than new Treasury issues of similar maturities.

With all government debt, there is no early call, as there may be with corporate issues. You can always be sure that you can keep the bond to maturity.

BOND YIELDS

Yield is a matter of definition and objective.

➤ NOMINAL, OR COUPON, YIELD This is the interest rate stated on the bond: 10%, 11.25%, etc. It depends on the quality of the issuing corporation and the prevailing cost of money at the time the bond is issued.

➤ CURRENT YIELD ON THE PURCHASE PRICE This is the rate of return per year that the coupon interest rate provides on the *net* price (without accumulated interest) at which the bond is purchased. It is *higher* than the coupon yield if you buy the bond below par and *lower* if you buy the bond above par.

➤ YIELD TO MATURITY Since maturities vary and the current yield only measures today's return, the bond market relies on the yield to maturity (YTM). It is the total return and includes both interest and gain in price. Put another way, it is the rate of return on a bond when held to maturity. It includes the appreciation to par from the current market price when bought at a discount or depreciation when bought at a premium. To approximate the YTM for a discount bond:

1　Subtract the current bond price from its face value.

2 Divide the resulting figure by the number of years to maturity.

3 Add the total annual interest payments.

4 Add the current price to the face amount and divide by 2.

5 Divide #3 by #4.

Example: A $1,000 9% coupon bond due in 10 years is selling at 72 ($720). The current yield is 12.5% ($90 ÷ $720); the YTM is about 13.7%.

$$\$1,000 - 720 = 280$$

$$280 \div 10 = 28$$

$$28 + 90 = 118$$

$$720 + 1,000 \ (1,720) \div 2 = 860$$

$$118 \div 860 = 13.7\%$$

The YTM is the yardstick used by professionals, because it sets the market value of the debt security. But to amateurs, the spread—between current and redemption prices—is what counts, because this appreciation will be taxed at the low capital gains rate. You get a competitive return while you wait . . . usually over 8 years because with shorter lives, the current yield is modest: e.g., A.T.&T. 3⅞, '90 at 70. That's a current yield of 5.5%, but in 6 years, there will be a $300 per bond capital gain.

➤ DISCOUNT YIELD This is the percentage from par or face value, adjusted to an annual basis, at which a discount bond sells. It is used for short-term obligations maturing in less than 1 year, primarily Treasury bills.

It is roughly the opposite of YTM. If a 1-year T-bill sells at a 12% yield, its cost is 88 ($8,800). The discount yield is 12 divided by 88, or 13.64%.

PROTECTION AGAINST PRICE DECLINES

The point to keep in mind about price advances and declines of bonds is: do not buy long-term bonds and think you can get your money back without a loss. If you cannot invest for an extended period of time, switch instead to short-term obligations. In general, the shorter the term of a bond, the lower the yield but the smaller the price swings.

You can protect yourself against price declines to some extent by purchasing high-grade bonds at discount, i.e., below face value. This is especially true if maturity is not far away.

$ IF YOU DARE: To get the highest yields, invest for the shortest time possible while rates are rising. When rates have peaked, sell and buy longer term bonds to lock in those higher yields.

$ HINT: Rather than having all bonds come due at the same time, own a spread of bonds to come due every year or so. That way you'll periodically receive cash which you can reinvest to keep the cycle going. Spreading out maturities also tends to average out the effects of price changes.

➤ TO REDUCE RISK There's really only one reliable way to reduce loss of principal due to rising interest rates, and that's not to buy bonds. Secondly, do not buy long-term bonds. Diversification through a bond mutual fund or unit investment trust will also help reduce risk (see Chapter 13) or maintain a broad-based bond portfolio.

Deeply discounted corporate bonds are useful when trying to get your money back on a certain date—say to meet college tuition bills. By buying a bond selling for 80¢ on the dollar, you'll get back $100 when it matures. In the meantime, you've had the benefits of annual interest income.

U.S. GOVERNMENT BONDS

These are the principal types of U.S. Treasury securities bought by individual investors. In order of maturity, they are:

➤ U.S. TREASURY BILLS These mature in 91 days, 6 months, 9 months, and 1 year. They come in bearer form with a minimum face value of $10,000 but are sold at a discount. Smaller units can be traded in the after market.

T-bills are at a price that reflects the yield as set by bids from major institutions. Thus, a 1-year 9% bill will be bought for $9,100 and redeemed for $10,000 12 months later. This gain is interest and is thus taxable at the full federal income tax rate, but it is not subject to state and local income levies.

Individuals can buy T-bills via a form available from the nearest Federal Reserve bank. This is done by making a noncompetitive bid (to arrive by mail on Friday or, by appearing in person, before 1:30 P.M. on the day of the auction).

The price that you pay will be the average of all competitive offers from large institutions that buy millions of dollars' worth each week. With the form, enclose a personal certified check or an official bank check drawn on a bank in the Federal Reserve district. The check should be made payable to the "Federal Reserve Bank of (District)." A third-party check endorsed by you to the Fed will not be accepted.

A few days after the auction, the Fed bank will mail you a "discount" check representing the difference between the purchase price and the face value of the bills. With this will be a receipt as proof of your purchase.

If you bought the bills directly from a Federal Reserve bank, notify your local commercial bank when you want to transfer ownership. Then, fill out Treasury Form PD 4633 and send it to the address on the form. The T-bills will be sent to your bank, which will complete the transfer. If you buy the bills through a bank or broker, let them handle the details.

➤ U.S. TREASURY NOTES These mature in from 1 to 5 years, are issued in bearer form, and pay interest semiannually.

➤ U.S. TREASURY BONDS These come in medium term (5 to 10 years) and long term (10 to 40 years). Interest is paid semiannually.

➤ U.S. TREASURY TAX ANTICIPATION BILLS AND CERTIFICATES These are issued to mature a few days after federal income tax payment dates (April 15, June 15, etc.). They can be used to pay income taxes at par (or with full interest to maturity), thereby giving the taxpayer a bonus of several day's interest. They are designed for large corporations with large tax bills.

FEDERAL AGENCIES' DEBT

There are well over 100 series of notes, certificates, and bonds issued by federal agencies as instrumentalities of the U.S. government: Federal Intermediate Credit Banks, Federal Land Banks, Banks for Cooperatives, Federal Home Loan Banks, etc.

They are backed by the full faith and credit of Uncle Sam and carry maturities from a few months to many years. They are among the highest quality securities available. Their yields are as high as, and often higher than, those of most Aaa- or Aa-rated industrial bonds.

Problems: In odd lots, government agency bonds may be less liquid than corporates, so you could take a small loss if you have to sell quickly. The point spread between bid and asked prices has been as high as ½ of 1% versus a normal spread of ¼ of 1%. *But most people buy bonds for long-term holdings.*

MAKING PROFITS WITH BONDS

Broadly speaking, the mechanics of buying and selling listed bonds (those traded on the NYSE and AMEX) are similar to those of stocks. You enter an order with your broker, who arranges for it to be executed at the best price. With small lots (less than 10 for active issues, 25 for others), it's best to set a price that you are willing to pay or accept. As the table on the next page shows, bond prices can shift sharply, so if you give a market order, you may lose money.

Unless you are determined to own a specific issue, buy from your broker's inventory. Tell your broker the quality rating, the approximate maturity, and the amount of money that you have to invest, and let your broker give you suggestions. This can save you as much as $20

TO DEFER INCOME WITH T-BILLS

Since Treasury bills are sold at a discount price, i.e., less than face value, and redeemed at maturity or full face value, they do not pay an annual interest. The return equals the difference between the purchase price and the face value. In the example below, Mrs. Y will not have to pay taxes until her T-bill matures in 1987, which is to her advantage since she expects her income will be lower in 1987.

Example: Mrs. Y buys a $10,000 1-year bill in February 1986. The interest rate is 6.2%, so she pays $9,380 and will receive $10,000 at maturity. Because of the prepayment of interest via the discount, her real yield is 6.6%. When Mrs. Y cashes in, February 1987, she will receive $620 on a cash investment of only $9,380.

PRICE SHIFTS

The exact moves depend on the quality and maturity of the bond and the tenor of the market, but here are some general figures that can be used in projections.

For bonds priced to yield 11.5% with these maturities, the percentage price gains will be:

MATURITIES	INTEREST RATE DECLINE	
	−1%	−3%
2½ years	+0.21	+0.65
7 years	+0.50	+1.16
20 years	+0.83	+2.86

a bond in buying and, if you are a good customer, nearly as much in selling.

➤ ACCRUED INTEREST With both government and corporate bonds, the accrued interest must be taken into account. The holder of the bond on the stated interest payment date is entitled to collect the entire amount of the interest since the previous coupon date. Thus, the buyer will have to pay the seller extra. *Example:* 10 corporate bonds are sold at 79¾. The seller receives $8,046.67: the $7,975 price plus $71.67 interest (not counting commissions).

Since most investors buy bonds for income, the compounding of interest, over a period of time, will provide more than half the total return. It's easy for professionals to reinvest the interest but difficult for amateurs to do so because of the small sums involved. With 10 bonds at a 10% yield, the semiannual interest is $500—only enough to buy one deep discount bond.

Alternatives:
1 Schedule your savings so that you will have extra money to add to the interest.
2 Buy shares of bond funds that provide automatic reinvestment.

As shown by the table to the right, compounding with a pension or trust fund can still be a powerful force over the years.

YIELD CURVE

A yield curve is a diagram that illustrates the relation between rates of return and maturities

of similar fixed-income securities. Analysts use different patterns to decide which type of bond to buy at certain periods.

To draw a yield curve, professionals set out the maturities on graph paper on a horizontal line, from left to right, starting with the shortest maturities (30 days) and continuing over days or years to the most distant (30 years). Then they plot the yields on the vertical axis and connect the dots with a line that becomes the yield curve.

The shape of that curve is affected by how investors *expect* interest rates to change. If they think interest rates are going to climb, they put their money in short-term securities while they wait. At the same time, borrowers get their dollars before the cost of money rises. Both responses tend to push short-term interest rates down and long-term rates up—not always im-

HOW BOND INTEREST COMPOUNDS AT 12% ANNUALLY FOR $10,000 INVESTMENT

TIME	SEMIANNUAL INTEREST	CUMULATIVE GROWTH
6 mos.	$ 600	$10,600
1 year	636	11,236
1½ years	674	11,910
2 years	715	12,625
2½ years	758	13,383
3 years	803	14,186
3½ years	851	15,037
4 years	902	15,939
4½ years	956	16,895
5 years	1,014	17,909
5½ years	1,075	18,984
6 years	1,139	20,123
6½ years	1,207	21,330
7 years	1,280	22,610
7½ years	1,357	23,967
8 years	1,438	25,405
8½ years	1,534	26,929
9 years	1,616	28,545
9½ years	1,713	30,528

SOURCE: Robert Lawrence Holt, *The Complete Book of Bonds.* New York: Barnes & Noble Books, 1985.

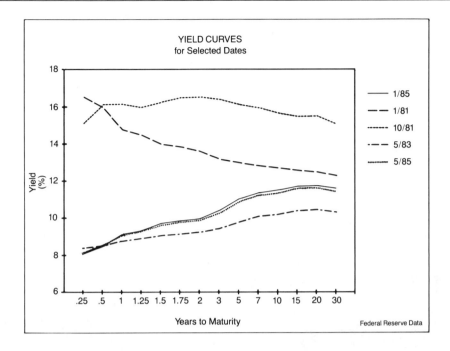

YIELD CURVES
for Selected Dates

Yield (%)

Years to Maturity

Federal Reserve Data

1/85
1/81
10/81
5/83
5/85

YIELD CURVES

This illustration shows the yield curve for a number
of selected dates, starting in January 1981 when
short-term Treasury yields were close to 17% and
just above 12% for those with 30-year maturities.
By October 1981, the highest yields were available
for Treasuries in the maturity range of 2 to 3
years, as illustrated by the 10/81
line.

The last three lines (5/83, 1/85, and 5/85) all
follow the more typical yield curve of lower short-
term rates and higher long-term rates for debt
issues.

SOURCE: Standard & Poor's.

mediately, but always over a reasonable time
span.

Let's suppose you want to invest $10,000
in debt issues for 10 years. You have these
choices:

- A 6-month T-bill that will be rolled over
  at each maturity
- A 2-to-3-year Treasury note which, at
  maturity, will be turned into a 7-to-8-year

note, at a somewhat more rewarding yield
IF the projection proves out

- A 10-year bond to be held to redemption.
  This would be best if you expect interest
  rates to decline or stay about the same.
- A 15-to-20-year bond to be sold at the end
  of 10 years, best if you project lower costs
  of money. But the longer out the maturity,
  the greater the risk.

The yield curves are most useful when they
are kept up to date and checked to find the
trends. If you are chart minded, ask your broker
for copies from the research department, or
purchase them from the sources listed at the
end of this chapter.

U.S. SAVINGS BONDS

Savings Bonds are a safe and extremely easy
way to save and, thanks to a recent upgrading
of interest rate formulas, they are a better
investment than they were a few years ago.
They are backed by the full faith and credit of
the U.S. government, and, like zero coupon
bonds, are inexpensive, entail no commissions,
and permit postponement of taxes. Their yields,
compounded semiannually, are flexible.

Series EE savings bonds sell for one-half
their face value: from $25 for a $50 bond to

$5,000 for a $10,000 bond. Maximum investment: $30,000 face value per calendar year.

The interest on EE bonds is 5.5% the first year and then moves up ¼% every 6 months until the fifth year. After the fifth year, the interest rate is equal to 85% of the average yield paid on 5-year Treasury notes. In addition, the government guarantees a minimum of 6% on bonds held 5 years or longer, which protects you against sharp drops in interest rates. You receive the accrued interest as the difference between the purchase price and the face value when you hold the bond to maturity. Interest is exempt from state and local taxes and deferred from federal tax until cashed in. Even then you can further delay paying federal taxes by swapping series EE bonds for series HH bonds.

$ HINT: Because their interest is credited only twice a year, redeem EE bonds right after their 6-month anniversary; if you redeem prior to that date, you will lose several month's interest.

If you still hold Series E and H savings bonds, cash them in or roll them over into EEs or HHs. On the old issues, no interest will be paid 40 years after the original date: before April 1952 for Es; before May 1959 for Hs.

Series HH bonds, issued in denominations

EE SAVINGS BONDS

PROS
↑ Safe; principal and interest guaranteed
↑ No fees or commissions
↑ If lost, replaced free of charge
↑ If held 5 years or more, get floating rate of interest with minimum of 6% guaranteed
↑ Federal taxes deferred
↑ No state or local taxes
↑ Market value does not drop when interest rates rise as with other bonds

CONS
↓ Floating rate minimum available only if bond held 5 years
↓ Cannot be used as collateral
↓ Limited purchase: $30,000 face value in one year per person
↓ Other vehicles may pay higher rates

DEADLINES FOR INTEREST ON E BONDS

DATE OF ISSUE	DATE OF MATURITY
May 1941–April 1952	May 1981–April 1992
May 1952–January 1957	January 1992–September 1996
February 1957–May 1959	January 1996–April 1998
June 1959–November 1965	March 1997–August 2003
December 1965–May 1969	December 1992–May 1996
June 1969–November 1973	April 1995–September 1999
December 1973–June 1980	December 1998–June 2005

No interest will be paid after maturity. The bonds may be exchanged for Series HH bonds within one year after maturity.

---

from $500 to $10,000, pay 6% over a 10-year period to maturity. You get the interest twice a year by a Treasury check and, at redemption, receive only your original purchase price. There's a penalty for early redemption when bought for cash but not when exchanged for E or H bonds. Maximum investment: $20,000.

When you swap for EEs or HHs, the interest on the old E or H bonds—unlike that from savings accounts, money market funds, and similar investments—does not have to be reported to the IRS annually until you cash them in. By swapping, you can postpone the tax on the accumulated interest for as long as 10 years. At that time, the amount of the accrued income is stamped on the face of the HH bonds and, from then on, you must pay taxes on the semiannual payments. Fill out PD Form 3523 to make the transfer.

$ HINT: Buy bonds at the end of the month so that you can start out with income, because the interest is credited from the first day.

LOCATING LOST SAVINGS BONDS

If you've lost your savings bonds, get form PD 1048, an Application for Relief, from the U.S.

Treasury. Write down as much information as you have: serial number, issuance date; name, address, and Social Security number of the original owner. Mail the form to Bureau of Public Debt, 200 Third Street, Parkersburg, WV 26106. Even with the partial data, they may be able to locate or replace the bonds.

GOVERNMENT RETIREMENT BONDS

These are issued in denominations of $50, $100, and $500 through Federal Reserve Banks and the U.S. Treasury. They are designed for investment of funds in Individual Retirement Accounts. They pay 9% interest, compounded semi-annually.

CORPORATE NOTES

Investors who want competitive yields and flexibility should find out about corporate notes. These are debt issues by major corporations that, in many cases, tailor the maturities to meet your time schedule: 133 days, 2 years and 3 months, etc.

General Motors Acceptance Corporation (GMAC) offers both short- and medium-term notes. The short-term debt is bought at a discount (interest is deducted on issue, and the investor receives face value at redemption). Longer-term debt is on an interest-bearing basis.

SPECIAL DEBT ISSUES

The old days when a bond was a bond are gone, replaced with an amazing variety of special issues involving extra inducements, flexible rates, indexing, and no interest. At the outset many of these were offered by secondary corporations (with the aid and advice of friendly underwriters) but these "opportunities" are increasingly being offered by well-known, well-rated companies. In most cases, they are best suited to wealthy investors, but on occasion, they can be rewarding for those with modest savings. Always check all details in the prospectus.

➤ EQUIPMENT CERTIFICATES These are floated by airlines and railroads to finance the purchase of new planes or rolling stock. Their yields are excellent and there's little chance of a default, because the company would then be out of business. Certificates are issued in serial form, so they mature at different dates. As the units are in large denominations, these are only for the wealthy or large fiduciary holdings.

➤ OPTIONAL MATURITY These are bonds that can be redeemed anytime after the first 5 years or so. This provision protects the investor against unfavorable shifts in the cost of money by setting a floor on the value of the debt.

➤ FHA-BACKED BONDS These are private debt issues 90% guaranteed by the Farmers Home Administration. The proceeds are used to finance business acquisition, plant expansion, or equipment purchases when the project is in a rural area and shows promise of providing permanent jobs.

For investors, these bonds provide longer maturities and the assurance that Uncle Sam will make good on any loan in default. To the borrower, they offer a lower interest rate than could be obtained on the borrower's own credit.

➤ EUROBONDS These are issued by foreign subsidiaries of U.S. companies. They pay 50 to 100 basis points (0.5 to 1%) more than similarly rated domestic bonds.

Since these have heavier sinking funds than do most U.S. issues, there's less risk of loss of capital when interest rates rise. Buy only in units of 10 or more, because these bonds are sold in a dealer's market oriented to major investors.

➤ YANKEE BONDS These are foreign issues floated in dollars. They include debt of governments, governmental agencies, and publicly owned corporations. Their yields are good, and there are possibilities of extra profits due to shifts in exchange rates, but their marketability is limited. You had better know something about the issuer or have a money-savvy adviser.

➤ FOREIGN BONDS These are issued in native currencies and so are subject to the fluctuations in their value against the dollar. The stronger the dollar, the lower the real value of the bonds and the interest paid. The yields are a bit higher than those of American debt, but so are the risks.

Remember, too, that with most foreign firms, accounting practices are different and are usually more liberal than those permitted by American agencies and CPAs.

➤ FLOATING-RATE DEBT These are adjustable rate notes where the interest rate changes every

2 years to a level at a preset percentage of the prevailing yield of 2-year Treasury notes. With BankAmerica notes, due in 1989, the yield is 105% of the base. Great when interest rates are rising, but not so attractive when they are likely to decline.

A variation is the *extendable note* where the maturities can be stretched out at the option of the issuer. IBM notes permit three extensions in 12 years. At the normal maturity, the investor can cash in at par or can keep the notes with interest to be paid at the then current rate.

➤ USABLE BONDS These are special types of debentures that are sold with a detachable warrant to buy the common stock by using the bond, instead of cash. The maturities for the bonds run from 10 to 20 years; those of the warrant, 5 years. With higher interest rates, most bonds sell at a discount, so the warrant can be exercised at savings of 15 to 25%. As the warrants expire, the demand for the debentures forces up their prices. To speculate, buy the warrants; to invest, buy the usable bonds.

FLOWER BONDS FOR RETIREES

One of the best investments for affluent senior citizens is a package of "flower" bonds. These are U.S. government obligations that carry low coupons (because they were issued years ago) and so are selling at discounts.

Their benefits: they will be accepted at face value in paying estate taxes when they are owned by a person at death. If you are in your seventies, or are responsible for some older

---

FLOWER BONDS TO REDUCE ESTATE TAXES

ISSUE	RECENT PRICE	RECENT YIELD
4¼s, Aug. 1987–92	90.31	5.62%
4s, Feb. 1988–93	91.9	5.24
4⅛s, May 1989–94	91.10	5.28
3½s, Feb. 1990	91.4	5.27
3s, Feb. 1995	91.12	3.99
3½s, Nov. 1998	91.5	4.33

SOURCE: Barron's.

---

person, check this opportunity. The savings are not great, but they can be welcome. These are no longer being issued but are available in the secondary market.

Example: February 4% bonds, due from 1988–93, are trading at 91.9 ($912.81). Aunt Hettie, age 83, buys 10 bonds for $9,128 plus commission. If she dies the next year, her estate will be credited with $10,000 against federal taxes.

CALL PROTECTION

To attract major investors for long-term commitments, corporations (but not the U.S. government) usually include call protection with new bond issues. This provides that the debt cannot be redeemed for the first 5 or 10 years, and then only at an above-par price: e.g., Pacific T&T 15s, 2020 at 112.17. In effect, the call price guarantees a profit to the original purchaser.

But that call price may also mean a loss to the investor who buys in the after market when the bond price is high as the result of lower interest rates. If the Pacific T&T bonds should rise to 119, management might consider exercising that call when new bonds could be floated with a 12% coupon. Corporate treasurers begin to think about refunding when the current interest rate is 2% below that of the old coupon, especially when there are many years to maturity.

When the price of bonds moves above the call price, the professionals sharpen their pencils and calculate the yield to call rather than the yield to maturity. This will often show a favorable spread of 50 basis points. Even with a redemption below the market price, a high yield will more than compensate for the capital loss. Du Pont 14s, 1991 at 111⅜ and callable at par, had a yield to call of 11.24%, better than the yield to maturity of comparable issues.

SINKING FUND PROVISIONS

Often millions of dollars are borrowed in any one bond issue, so quite obviously that amount of money must be available when the bond matures. In order to retire some of that enormous debt, some issuers buy back part of the debt, leaving less to be paid off at one time. In the process they shrink the debt. The money used to do this repurchasing is called a sinking fund. When a bond issue sets up a sinking fund, it means that the corporation must make periodic predetermined cash payments to the trustee of the debt.

With a sinking fund, the corporation pays less total interest. With a 25-year issue set up to buy back 3.75% of the debt annually, 75% of the bonds will be retired before maturity. This means that the average life of the bonds will be about 17 years, not the 25 years anticipated by the investor. And, again, the proceeds may have to be reinvested at a lower yield.

A similar situation to the early-call provision is the use of the "funnel." This allows the company to satisfy sinking-fund requirements for its entire mortgage debt by zeroing in on and retiring bonds of a single issue. Obviously, the called bonds will be those with the highest coupons. The same threat of early retirement applies to some preferred stocks.

Another special situation with sinking funds is "doubling the option." This allows the corporation, at the time interest payments are due, to call up twice the normal number of shares at a special call price. Thus, with a 6% sinking fund started in the fifth year, this will amount to an annual call of 12% of the entire issue. To the investor, this would be worthwhile only if the call price were well above par.

A sinking fund adds a margin of safety in that the purchases provide price support and enhance the probability of repayment. But it narrows the time span of the loan so that there will be less total income for the long-term investor. Sinking funds benefit the corporation more than the bondholder.

Watch out for:

- Call provisions for high-coupon utility bonds. With Niagara Power 10⅝s, '85, the *big type* in the prospectus set the call price at 103.54 after 1981, but the *small type* referred to a replacement fund, a reserve for the repair and maintenance of mortgaged property, to be used to redeem the bonds at any time. So, 4 years *before* the anticipated protection date, investors had to turn in their bonds.
- Bonds selling close to their call price when the call date is near or past. Such debt issues tend to move like short-term

---

> ## THE SINKING FUND
>
> This specifies how certain bonds will be paid off over time. If a bond has a sinking fund, then the company must redeem a certain number of bonds annually before maturity to reduce its debt.
> - *Advantage:* bondholders get their principal back earlier than the maturity date
> - *Disadvantage:* if coupon rate is high, bondholders will not want to retire bond early
>
>   If your bond is called in, you will be notified by mail and in the newspaper. You *must* take your money, because interest will cease at the specified time.

---

holdings when the market is moving up; like long-term ones when the trend is down.

LEVERAGE WITH BONDS

With taxable bonds, it's possible to borrow as much as 95% of the purchase price. This is wise only with large investments where the interest is deductible. But leverage can work both ways: it's great when the value of the bonds remains stable or rises but can be costly when interest rates rise and the loan costs more and the bond is worth less. *Do your homework first!*

Example: In June 1984, Investor X bought $400,000 in U.S. Treasury notes at 13⅞% due August 1989 at par. She borrowed 95% of the money from her margin account at her broker's. The interest rates at which she borrowed varied between 9 and 12%, changing weekly in relation to the broker loan rate. (Brokers are obliged to charge customers at least ½% more than the rate at which they borrow from their banks. The rate at which brokers borrow is known as the broker loan rate. See Chapter 20 on leverage).

In March 1986, after an extraordinary and historic change in interest rates, Investor X sold her $400,000 in T-notes at $118 for a long-term gain of $72,000. Her original cash investment was only $20,000. During the period that the investor held the notes, she never paid her

FIXED-INCOME SECURITIES

	MINIMUM PURCHASE	MATURITY RANGE	LIQUIDITY	INTEREST	WHERE AVAILABLE
Short Term					
U.S. Treasury Bills	$ 10,000	3–12 months	Best	Discount*	Brokers, banks, Federal Reserve Banks
Local authorities	1,000	3–12 months	Average	Straight	Banks, brokers
FNMA notes†	10,000	30–360 days	Good	Discount	Major dealers
Federal intermediate credit	5,000	270 days	Good	Straight	Banks, brokers
State and local government notes	5,000	1–12 months	Average	Straight	Banks, brokers
Bankers' acceptances	5,000	1–270 days	Average	Discount	Banks, brokers
Negotiable CDs	100,000	1–12 months	Average	Straight	Banks, brokers
CDs	10,000	1 year	Penalty for early withdrawal	Straight Compounded	Banks, savings and loan associations, Credit Unions
	1,000	30 months	See above	See above	Banks, savings and loan associations, Credit Unions
Commercial Paper	100,000	1–270 days	Average	Straight	Dealers
Medium Term					
U.S. EE bonds	25	10 years	Poor	Discount	Banks, U.S. Treasury
U.S. HH bonds	500	10 years	Penalty for early withdrawal	Straight	Federal Reserve
U.S. Treasury notes or bonds	1,000	1–30 years	Good	Straight	Banks, brokers
Federal financing bank notes or bonds	1,000	1–20 years	Good	Straight	Banks, brokers
Farmers Home Administration notes or certificates	25,000	1–25 years	Average	Straight	Banks, brokers
GNMA securities or certificates‡	5,000	1–25 years	Average	Straight	Banks, brokers
GNMA pass-throughs‡	25,000	14–17 years	Good	Straight	Banks, brokers
Federal land bank bonds	1,000	1–10 years	Good	Straight	Banks, brokers
Corporate notes or bonds	1,000	1–30 years	Good	Straight	Brokers
Eurobond bonds or notes	1,000	3–25 years	Average	Straight	Foreign banks
Long Term					
Housing Authority bonds	5,000	1–40 years	Good	Straight	Banks, brokers
Federal Home Loan Mortgage certificates	100,000	15–30 years	Average	Straight	Banks, brokers
FNMA bonds†	$ 25,000	2–25 years	Average	Straight	Banks, brokers

	MINIMUM PURCHASE	MATURITY RANGE	LIQUIDITY	INTEREST	WHERE AVAILABLE
State or local government notes or bonds	5,000	1–30 years	Average	Straight	Brokers
International Bank: Reconstruction or Development; Asian; Inter-American notes or bonds	1,000	3–25 years	Average	Straight	Banks, brokers
Foreign notes or bonds denominated in dollars, issued by U.S. and foreign corporations	1,000	1–20 years	Average	Straight	Brokers, overseas banks
Corporate preferred stock	25	No maturity	Average	Quarterly dividends	Brokers

* On discount basis: with 1 year, $10,000 bill @ 10% = $9,000.
† Federal National Mortgage Association.
‡ Government National Mortgage Association

SOURCE: Based on David M. Darst, *The Complete Bond Book.* New York: McGraw-Hill, 1982.

broker more than the 13⅞% she was receiving as interest on the Treasury notes. As a matter of fact, during most of the time, there was always close to a 2% profit, known as a positive carry.

SWAPPING BONDS

To the serious (and affluent) investor, swapping bonds can be profitable: a capital loss can reduce taxes; a higher yield can boost income; a wise switch can raise quality and extend the maturity of the debt.

Example: Dapper Dan owns 25 Telex Bonds, 9%, due in 1996—at par ($25,000). Their current price is 85: (25M × $850 = $21,250). He gets an annual income of $2,250 with a 10.6% annual yield.

Seeking a tax loss, Dan sells them for a $3,750 loss ($25,000 − $21,250 = $3,750). This loss can be used against any capital gains he may have, or half of it ($1,875) may be used as a deduction against ordinary income (see Chapter 35 on taxes).

Dan buys 25 Sears 10¾s, due 2013 at 82.

He thus has replaced his bonds with a better quality investment and established a tax loss.

If you have a sizable loss in bonds, consider swapping if the results are beneficial and help you to meet your investment objectives.

BOND FUNDS

Many of the negatives of bonds can be eased, if not eliminated, by buying shares of bond funds. They come in all types, packages, and styles and are available as load or no-loads, open- or closed-end, conservative or speculative, straight or mixed, and so forth.

Shares can be purchased for as little as $1,000, with smaller increments later. Most funds encourage automatic reinvestment of interest for compounding—something that individuals rarely do on their own.

The yields may be a bit less than those available from direct investments, and the professional management may leave something to be desired; but you get diversification, convenience, detailed reports, and the opportunity to switch to other funds (bond or stock) under the same sponsor. These are explained further in Chapter 14 on mutual funds, but to help you make the best choice, here are some checkpoints:

➤ GET THE PEDIGREE OF THE SPONSOR Dealing in bonds is a special art that requires different types of analyses from those used with stocks. The future projections always factor in the anticipated cost of money, and in normal markets this is difficult to forecast, almost impossible in erratic periods. Look for a backup team of analysts and traders experienced on debt issues, who have lived long enough to understand the vagaries of the bond market.

➤ EVALUATE THE PORTFOLIO For safety, choose funds with the most A or better-rated holdings. For good income, look for those with lower-quality (but not too low) issues. For high returns, use "junk" bond funds (as explained in the next chapter). A couple of big winners will offset the inevitable losers.

➤ CHECK THE PERFORMANCE OVER AT LEAST 10 YEARS Long enough to include both bad and good years for debt securities. Choose the fund that scored highest according to your specific objectives.

➤ DETERMINE THE AVERAGE PRICE OF BOND HOLD-INGS Or have the fund do it for you. If this is low, it means that when interest rates decline, the bounce-up will be greater than if the average price was higher.

➤ LOOK FOR FREQUENT DISTRIBUTIONS A fund that pays monthly ensures a steady cash flow. If this is reinvested, compounding will be at a more rewarding rate. Buy right before the distribution-declaration date.

➤ CHECK THE REPURCHASE PRICE If the fund buys only at the lower side of the price spread, you will lose a few dollars when you cash in. At redemption, Nuveen pays a bid side price; Merrill Lynch pays the offering price as long as

the fund is one in which the firm makes a market.

FOR FURTHER INFORMATION

"Basic Information on Treasury Bills" is available from your nearest Federal Reserve Bank or from:

> Federal Reserve Bank of New York
> 33 Liberty Street
> New York, NY 10045

Purchase yield curves from:

> United Business Service
> 208 Newbury Street
> Boston, MA 02116
> 1-617-267-8855

> William O'Neil & Co.
> P.O. Box 24933
> Los Angeles, CA 90024
> 1-213-820-2583

For more information on bonds:

> "How the Bond Market Works" (28 p.)
> Standard & Poor's Corporation
> 25 Broadway
> New York, NY 10005

> "Facts About Zero-Coupon U.S. Treasury Physical Strips"
> Government Bond Trading Dept.
> L.F. Rothschild, Unterberg, Towbin
> 55 Water Street
> New York, NY 10041

> "U.S. Savings Bonds—Fifty Questions & Answers"
> U.S. Savings Bond Division
> Washington, D.C. 20226

> David M. Darst. *The Complete Bond Book.* New York: McGraw-Hill, 1982

THE BOND BONANZA:
Zeros, Junk, and the Mae Family

During the last several years there's been an amazing proliferation of out-of-the-ordinary bonds and bond packages. Some are excellent, others highly speculative; yet, all are interesting and at some point you may find one of them entirely suitable for your investment goals. Zeros, for instance, are an excellent choice if you know you will be needing a lump sum of money at a certain date in the future. Junk, or lower quality bonds, offer top interest rates but in turn you give up a large degree of safety. Securities backed either fully or partially by the various members of the Mae family, Ginnie, Freddy, Fanny, etc., are appropriate when you are looking for favorable yields with reduced risk. The pros and cons of each are described below.

ZERO COUPON BONDS

These bonds, offered by both corporations and the U.S. government, are sold at a deep discount from face value and pay no interest. Worthwhile? Yes, as long as you understand the facts. These bonds are "stripped" of their interest coupons, but when they mature you get this interest back in a balloon payment; in this respect they are much like EE savings bonds. In other words, they are fully redeemed at par

> **Zero coupon bonds:** Instead of paying annual interest, they are sold at a large discount from face value and at maturity you receive a significant capital appreciation—a 30-year zero issued at 4 ($40) will return 100 ($1,000) upon maturity.
> **Junk bonds:** Lower quality bonds that pay high interest rates.
> **Mae family:** Various mortgage-backed securities either sponsored or partially guaranteed by a handful of government agencies or private corporations, such as the Government National Mortgage Association (GNMA) and the Federal Home Loan Mortgage Corporation (Freddie Mac).

or face value. For example, a zero coupon Treasury recently selling for $121 will be worth $1,000 upon maturity in 2004. That is a yield to maturity of 11.25%. The annual appreciation (or undistributed interest) is subject to tax. *You must pay taxes* all along the way, just as though you had actually received the interest payments. Zeros tend to be volatile in price because of this compounding effect; in fact, since there are no interest payments to cushion market swings, zeros can fall dramatically when interest rates rise. Therefore, if you buy zeros, plan to hold them to maturity.

Zeros make most sense in tax-advantaged accounts such as IRAs and Keoghs so you can avoid paying taxes every year on interest that you don't actually receive. Recently, for example, a 30-year STRIP (explained later on) was available for $1,970.76, yielding 10.65%. In an IRA this would be worth $44,000 in 30 years.

Use zeros also when saving for a specific goal, such as college tuition payments, retirement, a vacation home, etc. If you use zeros to finance a child's college education, have your broker select those that come due the same year your child turns 18.

TYPES OF ZEROS

➤ CORPORATE ZEROS These are riskier than federal government zeros, but they also offer higher returns. They are backed only by the credit of the issuing corporation, so stick to those with A ratings in order to protect your investment.
➤ GOVERNMENT ZEROS TIGERS (Treasury Investment Growth Receipts) are packaged by Merrill Lynch. Salomon Bros. has CATS (Certificates of Accrual on Treasury Securities). LIONS (Lehman's Investment Opportunity Notes) are

THE POWER OF COMPOUNDING: HOW MUCH $1,000 IN ZEROS WILL GROW, BEFORE TAXES, AT VARIOUS COMPOUNDING RATES

	SEMIANNUAL COMPOUNDING RATE					
MATURITY	**8%**	**9%**	**10%**	**11%**	**12%**	**13%**
5 years	$1,480	$1,552	$1,629	$1,708	$ 1,791	$ 1,877
10 years	2,191	2,411	2,653	2,918	3,207	3,523
15 years	3,243	3,745	4,322	4,984	5,744	6,614
20 years	4,801	5,816	7,040	8,513	10,286	12,416

SOURCE: Merrill Lynch, 1986.

the latest addition to the feline family. All are actually certificates issued by custodian banks, which hold in an irrevocable trust the federal government bonds that have been stripped of their coupons and then sold by brokers.

STRIPS (Separate Trading of Registered Interest and Principal Securities) are issued directly by the Treasury, and therefore are safer than other zeros. Yields are slightly less than those of TIGERS, LIONS, and CATS because of their greater degree of safety. STRIPS do not involve a commission or fee.

➤ MORTGAGE-BACKED ZEROS These are backed by securities issued by Ginnie Mae, Fannie Mae, and Freddie Mac (see page 108). The securities are secured by mortgages which are AAA rated. You'll see some of them referred to as ABCs, which stands for agency-backed compounders. *Caution:* you may not get to hold your mortgage-

backed zero until maturity if mortgages are paid off early.

➤ MUNICIPAL ZEROS These are discussed in Chapter 13.

➤ ZERO COUPON CONVERTIBLE BONDS A hybrid vehicle in which you can convert the bond into shares of stock of the issuing company. In most cases, bonds can be called in after just 2 years.

➤ ZERO COUPON CERTIFICATES OF DEPOSIT These are really CDs, but sell at discount and do not pay current interest.

HINT: Buy zeros that are the last callable issues in a particular series to partially protect yourself against call provisions.

A Word of Caution: In 1985, a group of Michigan investors filed a class action suit against Merrill Lynch, claiming that the brokerage firm "fraudently omitted to disclose" important facts about TIGERS. The group said Merrill Lynch

THE POWER OF COMPOUNDING: HOW MUCH $1,000 IN TIGERS WILL GROW AT VARIOUS COMPOUNDING RATES

	SEMIANNUAL COMPOUNDING RATE				
MATURITY	**10%**	**11%**	**12%**	**13%**	**14%**
5 years	$1,629	$1,708	$ 1,791	$ 1,877	$ 1,967
10 years	2,653	2,918	3,207	3,524	3,870
15 years	4,322	4,984	5,744	6,614	7,612
20 years	7,040	8,513	10,286	12,416	14,975

SOURCE: Merrill Lynch, 1986.

ZERO COUPON TREASURY BONDS

PROS

↑ Lock in stated yield
↑ Maturity dates can be tailored to meet future needs
↑ Call protection available
↑ Predictable cash payment
↑ U.S. government guaranteed
↑ Tax-deferred in retirement accounts
↑ No reinvestment decisions
↑ Less expensive than most bonds

CONS

↓ If interest rates rise, you're locked into a lower yield
↓ Inflation erodes purchasing power of the bond's face value
↓ Commissions and/or sales markups not always made clear
↓ Many zeros have call provisions permitting issuer to redeem them prior to maturity

gations (bond interest payments). It also comprises established blue chip companies that have been forced into heavy debt in order to fend off a takeover or to finance their own leveraged buyout. Default is not out of the question, which is why you should invest in junk bonds only through a mutual fund, where the element of risk is diversified, unless you have sufficient money with which to speculate.

JUNK BOND MUTUAL FUNDS

The sponsors of junk bond funds are quite apt to play up the diversification point and de-emphasize the risks involved. They make much of the fact that their portfolios are diversified and continually monitored so that issues in trouble can be jettisoned. This is, of course, absolutely true *if* the portfolio manager is astute. But there's another risk involved—the risk of changing interest rates. Like any fixed income security, junk bond funds are vulnerable to broad changes in interest rates, and as those rates rise, the value of the fund falls. (Renewed inflation would boost interest rates.)

The high-yield funds tracked by Schabacker

sold the zeros with "undisclosed excessive markups" and did not reveal that the TIGERS could be retired by the U.S. Treasury in 2006 rather than 2011. In addition, they claimed the firm did not provide a prospectus.

Since then, the SEC has ordered that the net yield *after* commissions be disclosed on confirmation slips for all zeros.

HIGH-YIELD OR JUNK BONDS

With Treasury bond yields at their lowest point in years, and rates on other fixed income vehicles such as CDs declining well into single-digit territory, it's not surprising that large numbers of investors are overlooking previous standards of quality in their quest for higher yields. A solution for many is the so-called high-yield or junk bond which yields substantially more than higher quality bonds. These extra 1 or 2 points, however, march in tandem with extra risk.

Junk bonds are those rated BB or lower by Standard & Poor's and Baa or lower by Moody's. Some have no ratings at all. The world of junk bonds comprises new or old companies with uncertain earnings coverage of their fixed obli-

HOW JUNK BONDS FARED IN 1986

COMPANY	STANDARD & POOR'S RATING	PRICE (LOW OF 1984)	PRICE SPRING 1986
Caesars World: 12.5%; 1990	B	$83	$107
Chrysler: 8.875%; 1995	BBB	68	96
Cleveland Electric: 9.85%; 2010	BBB+	62	98
McLean Industries: 12%; 2003	B−	73	84
Philadelphia Electric: 15.375%; 2010	BBB−	92	118
United Merchants and Manufacturers: 9.5%; 1995	CCC	65	79

SOURCE: Standard & Poor's.

Investment Management had an average yield of 12% during the first quarter of 1986 versus 10% for corporate bonds. The top five "junk" funds for January through April 1986 were:

FUND NAME	YIELD
Putnam High Yield Trust I	12.9%
Oppenheimer High Yield Fund	12.8
YES Fund	12.7
Bullock High Income Shares	12.7
Bull & Bear High Yield Fund	12.7

But what about default? It's always a possibility, but not an overwhelming one. According to Salomon Bros., between 1977 and 1985 only 1.3% of all bonds with BB or lower ratings went bankrupt. If one bond in a fund defaults, it means a decrease in the overall fund yield, certainly less of an impact than if you owned the bond directly. However, the fund share price will also reflect the decline in the value of the defaulted bond.

MUNICIPAL JUNK BONDS

The high-yield municipal bond funds are another matter altogether, since tax revisions have made some municipals taxable. Check each fund's prospectus for its policy on taxable munis. The best performers among the high-yield municipal funds for the first quarter of 1986 were:

FUND NAME	YIELD
Vanguard Muni High Yield	8.00%
Fidelity High Yield Municipals	8.25%
Prudential-Bache High Yield Municipals	8.20%

Junk bond munis are regarded as riskier than corporates. Corporates are frequently issued by new companies without a past history of earnings. Theoretically, these companies are on their way up. Munis that are low rated are more often than not the result of a fundamentally risky situation.

Fund managers try to cut risks primarily by diversifying their portfolios according to both bond type and bond rating. A number of them limit their holdings of any one issue to 5% of the fund's total assets. Others offset risk by adding a mixture of investment-grade bonds. More frequent review of the portfolio—monthly or quarterly—is another risk-cutting technique. In selecting a junk bond fund, if you're concerned with risk, determine the portfolio mix and

management's position. Don't shy away solely because there are nonrated issues: some smaller municipalities have local appeal and/or do not request a rating from S&P or Moody's.

UNIT INVESTMENT TRUSTS

Unit investment trusts are closed-end investment companies. Because they have fixed portfolios, their yields are more predictable than those of a mutual fund. However, they have far less flexibility in terms of adjusting the portfolio and getting rid of poor bonds. Since they are not actively managed, *investors are at risk* should there be a default. "The unit investment

---

DEBT FOR EQUITY

There are two types of this new development:

1 Defeasance: used by corporations to discharge debts without actually paying them off prior to maturity. The company arranges for a broker to buy a portion of the outstanding bond issues for a fee. The broker then: (1) exchanges the bonds for a new issue of corporate stock with a market value equal to that of the bonds; (2) sells the shares at a profit. The corporate balance sheet is improved without harming operations or prospects.

2 Debt for equity: Manufacturers Hanover, in need of additional capital, issued 10-year 15⅛% notes with attached equity contracts mandating conversion into common stock at the lower of $55.55 per share or the 30-day average closing price prior to conversion—with a floor of $40 per share.

For the investors, this worked out well. When interest rates dropped, they could sell each $1,000 note for $1,200 for a $200 profit. They could then reinvest the $1,000 in other securities which they could turn over to the bank as collateral to replace the now detached equity contracts. They could look for profits on the new investments and eventually on the common stock.

trust is fine for quality bonds, but should be avoided for junk issues," warns Peter Hegel, bond expert at Van Kampen Merritt.

MORTGAGE DEBT: THE MAE FAMILY

High yields, safety, and convenience, that's what the various mortgage-backed securities in the Mae family offer. These securities, which are shares in pools of mortgages, are often called *pass-throughs* because the sponsor who packages the loans passes through the income (minus a modest fee) directly to investors. Payments are monthly and yields tend to be 1.5+ points higher than those on comparable Treasury bonds, largely because the monthly payments include principal as well as interest. In this respect the Mae family does not behave like regular bonds, where you receive a return of principal upon maturity. Instead you receive monthly checks that reflect both interest *and* principal.

Ginnie Maes, other than U.S. Treasury issues, are the only securities that carry the direct full faith and credit guarantee of the U.S. government. Others in the Mae group carry an indirect guarantee.

GINNIE MAEs

"Ginnie Mae" stands for Government National Mortgage Association, a wholly owned corporation of the U.S. government, which functions as part of the Department of Housing and Urban Development. The objective of Ginnie Mae is to stimulate housing by attracting capital and guaranteeing mortgages. A GNMA certificate represents a portion of a pool of 30-year FHA- or VA-insured mortgages. The GNMA provides payment of interest and principal on a monthly basis.

When a homebuyer takes out a mortgage, the house is pledged as collateral. The bank or savings and loan pools this loan with others of similar terms and rates, thus creating a package of mortgages worth $1 million or more. Ginnie Mae reviews the mortgages to make certain they pass certain standards and then assigns a pool number. Stockbrokers and others sell participations or certificates to the public.

Homebuyers make their payments (interest and principal) to the bank, which deducts a handling fee as well as a Ginnie Mae insurance fee. The rest of the money is "passed on" to the investors from the mortgage bankers.

Because GNMA certificates carry the guarantee of the U.S. government, they have made mortgage investments especially safe. And, since certificates can be traded in the dealer market, they also offer liquidity.

The minimum investment for a GNMA is $25,000, with $5,000 increments thereafter. Monthly interest is considered ordinary income and is taxed, whereas monthly principal payments are considered a return of capital and are exempt from taxes. Monthly payments are not uniform—they are based on the remaining principal in the pool. As the mortgage pool gets paid down, you receive the stated coupon interest on a declining amount of debt. In other words, each month the proportion of interest received is slightly less and principal slightly more. Over the long term, GNMAs are therefore self-liquidating.

You can purchase Ginnie Maes for less than $25,000 through mutual funds (discussed later in the chapter) or you can buy older Ginnie Maes in the secondary market. Older Ginnie Maes have lower coupon rates and have been partially paid down.

$ WARNING: Ads for Ginnie Maes and their mutual funds often claim they are totally safe and 100% government guaranteed. This is not true. Ginnie Maes are *not* completely risk-free.

■ The government does *not* guarantee the yield.

QUOTATIONS FOR GINNIE MAEs

INTEREST RATE	BID	ASKED	YIELD
8%	73–02	73–10	12.43%
9	77–22	77–30	12.66
10	83–06	83–14	12.73
11	88–28	89–04	12.74
12	94–08	94–16	12.84
13	99–15	99–23	12.96
14	104–24	105–08	13.02

This is digested. Quotes are in 32nds: 88–28 equals $888.75.

SOURCE: Barron's.

MORTGAGE-RELATED SECURITIES

SECURITY	MINIMUM ORIGINAL DENOMINATION	PAYMENTS	GUARANTEE	GUARANTOR	UNDERLYING ASSETS
Government National Mortgage Association (Ginnie Maes)	$25,000 $1,000 in mutual funds	Monthly	Interest and principal	Full credit USA	Pools of FHA and VA loans
Federal Home Loan Mortgage Corp. (Freddie Macs)	$25,000 $1,000 in mutual funds	Monthly	Interest and ultimate payment of principal	Federal Home Mortgage Loan Corp.	Conventional and seasoned FHA and VA loans
Mortgage-backed securities of Federal National Mortgage Association (Fannie Maes)	$25,000 $1,000 in mutual funds	Monthly	Interest and principal	Federal National Mortgage Assn.	Conventional and seasoned FHA and VA loans
Collateralized mortgage obligations (CMOs) of Freddie Macs and private issuers	$1,000 to $25,000	Monthly or semiannual	Specified minimum obligations	Issuer	Mortgages or mortgage
Private issues by banks, thrifts, homebuilders	$1,000 to $25,000	Monthly	Interest and ultimate payment of principal	Private mortgage insurers	Conventional home loans

SOURCE: Federal National Mortgage Association.

- The government does *not* protect investors against declines in either the value of the fund's shares or the yield.
- The government, however, *does* indeed protect investors against late mortgage payments as well as foreclosures. If homeowners default, you will still receive payments.

If you're considering Ginnie Maes, don't expect to get the 12 to 14% you saw advertised last year. Assuming inflation remains low and interest rates don't shoot back up, yields will be much lower as homeowners eagerly pay back their mortgages and refinance at lower rates.

This reduces the Ginnie Mae's life span and investors actually receive less than they anticipated. Bear in mind that the average 30-year Ginnie Mae is repaid in about 12 years.

For investors who don't want to invest $25,000, Ginnie Maes are available through unit investment trusts and mutual funds for as little as $1,000. Although minimum investment in a unit trust is generally only $1,000, once the trust's portfolio is assembled, it's set. The portfolio manager cannot make adjustments, so if interest rates drop you face exactly the same dilemma as you do in owning a GNMA certificate.

**HIDDEN RISKS IN GINNIE MAEs
FOR RETIREES**

- If you spend each monthly check you are using up both interest and principal.
- You may want to reinvest. Finding a better rate with equal safety is often difficult.
- Monthly checks are not all the same, which is worrisome if you're expecting a set dollar amount to live on.

GINNIE MAE MUTUAL FUNDS

The advantage of a fund over a unit trust is that portfolio managers can shift the maturities of the certificates in the fund to reflect changing economic conditions. For example, if it appears inflation is returning, they will move to shorter maturities to protect the return. And, in certain types of funds, part of the portfolio can be shifted into other types of investments. The Kemper U.S. Government Securities Fund, for instance, also invests in intermediate Treasury bonds.

Funds are best for those who want high current income rather than capital appreciation. But plan on a long-term play, since these funds are volatile and subject to market risks.

In seeking high yields, many GNMA funds use almost speculative strategies, investing in put and call options, interest rate futures contracts, etc. Others invest in mortgage-related securities that do not carry the full government guarantee. Check the prospectus, and remember that a fund's shares may go down in value as well as its yield.

Ginnie Mae funds are offered by many of the large family funds, including Vanguard, Lexington, Franklin, Kemper, Fidelity, and Shearson-American Express.

➤ IN AN IRA Denis Jamison, vice president of Lexington Management Corp., points out that for every 1% change in interest rates, the value of the average Ginnie Mae fund will move in the opposite direction almost 6%. Therefore, advises Jamison, Ginnie Maes are well suited to tax-deferred portfolios, where regular contributions over a period of time cushion the negative effect of price swings.

FREDDIE MACs

Freddie Mac (Federal Home Loan Mortgage Corp.) issues its own mortgage-backed securities, which are called PCs or participation certificates. Freddie deals primarily in conventional mortgages, which may have private insurance but, unlike Ginnie Maes, are not guaranteed by the government. If homeowners do not make their mortgage payments on time, you will receive your monthly payment on time, but you may have to wait several months to a year to receive your share of the principal. Even though they're not quite as secure as GNMAs, they are considered very safe. Because of the discrepancy in safety, Freddie comes cheaper than Ginnie.

Freddie Mac PCs are sold for $25,000. Since the market is dominated by institutional investors, there are fewer mutual funds: Vanguard (Valley Forge, PA) and Federated Investors (Pittsburgh) are two. The US AA Income Fund (San Antonio) divides its assets between Ginnie and Freddie.

FANNIE MAEs

The Federal National Mortgage Association is a shareholder-owned corporation that buys conventional mortgages, pools them in $1-million lots, and sells them in $25,000 units. You are guaranteed your interest and principal payment each month, even if homeowners do not meet their obligations. Although not backed by the full faith and credit of the U.S. government, Fannies are triple-A rated by both S & P and Moody's.

Both Freddie Mac and Fannie Mae are corporations chartered by Congress and are *not* officially part of the federal government. Therefore they do not carry the unconditional guarantee of Ginnie Mae. One advantage this discrepancy in safety brings is a slightly higher yield. Another is that the mortgage pools are larger than the Ginnie Mae pools. The more mortgages, the more accurately you can predict how fast the principal will be returned.

CMOs

CMOs (Collateralized Mortgage Obligations) were introduced in 1983 by the Federal Home Loan Mortgage Corp. Their advantage is a more predictable payout of interest and principal. Instead of buying mortgage

---

ESTIMATING A FANNIE MAE'S YIELD TO MATURITY

A Fannie Mae with: 10% coupon
price of 85 (85% of par)
11.76% current yield
25 years to maturity

1 Divide the amount of the discount by the number of years to maturity.

$$\frac{100 \text{ minus } 85 = 15}{25} = .60$$

2 Divide the result by 2 to factor in discounting.

$$.60 \div 2 = .30$$

3 Add this number to the current yield.

$$.30 + 11.76 = 12.06$$

4 This is your approximate current yield: 12.06%.

SOURCE: Fact Magazine 2/85.

---

securities directly, you buy a GNMA or Freddie Mac bond. Each bond is divided into four classes, having different dates of maturity ranging from 3 to 20 years. Investors receive semiannual interest payments, *but,* and here's the difference, principal payments are initially passed through only to those investors in the shortest maturity class. Once that group has been paid in full, principal payments go to the next class. In the fourth and final class, investors get all interest and all principal in one lump sum.

These certificates generally have slightly lower yields than the regular pass-throughs, because the size and length of payments can be more accurately determined and you have some protection against prepayments. CMOs are $25,000 for all but the longest maturing class, which can be purchased for $1,000.

SONNY MAEs

These bonds are backed by fixed-rate single-family home mortgages. Proceeds are used to subsidize below-market-rate mortgages for those buying a house for the first time. These are regular bonds, not pass-throughs, and therefore pay interest only until they mature. They are all rated AA by Moody's and are exempt from federal taxes for everyone and from state and local taxes for those living in New York State.

SALLIE MAEs

Created in Congress in 1972 to provide a nationwide secondary market for government guaranteed student loans, Sallie (the Student Loan Marketing Association) is to students what Ginnie is to homeowners. It issues bonds, rather than certificates, based on a pool of loans. Each bond is backed by Sallie Mae, and since its assets are made up of loans that have a government guarantee, these bonds are regarded as almost as safe as Treasuries. However, and this is key, this federal backing is only implied, not explicit. They yield about ¼ of 1% more than equivalent Treasury bonds.

Sallie Mae is a publicly owned company although it is chartered by the government. Its stock trades on the New York Stock Exchange. Originally issued at $20 per share, it recently was trading at $48½. The need for student loans is expected to continue through the 1980s.

NELLIE MAEs

The New England Education Loan Marketing Corp. is a nonprofit corporation created by the Commonwealth of Massachusetts to provide a secondary market for loans in Massachusetts and New Hampshire. The loans are federally guaranteed.

Nellie Mae's AAA-rated bonds, which mature in 3 years, are sold in $5,000 denominations. They are exempt from federal taxes and, for those who live in Massachusetts and New Hampshire, from state and local taxes. Depending upon the type of bond you buy, the interest rate is either fixed or variable. The variable rate is tied to rates on 3-month Treasury bills.

A Word of Caution: Although these bonds are highly rated, the secondary market is extremely small. If you need to sell prior to maturity, you may have difficulty.

GRANNIE MAEs

Under this plan, homeowners who are 55 or older can sell their property and continue to live in it with a lifetime lease. This allows them to benefit from the equity in their house. Most homeowners sell to their children, but it is possible to sell to other investors. The money from the sale is then used to buy an annuity in order to supplement the sellers' income. Monthly rent is paid from the annuity. Grannie Mae (the Family Backed Mortgage Association) is a private company that works with local lenders. (See Chapter 38 on retirement for more about annuities.)

Another plan is offered by the American Homestead Mortgage Corp. Its Individual Retirement Mortgage Account sets up lifetime monthly payments for older people. In this system, the owners keep the title to their house and receive as much as $700 per month.

$ HINT: General rule of thumb: the higher the rate on the mortgages in a pool, the faster the pool will liquidate.

FOR FURTHER
INFORMATION

For a report on government zeros, send $1.00 to:

> The Donoghue Organization, Inc.
> P.O. Box 540
> Holliston, MA 01746

"An Introduction to Zero Coupon Bonds" (8 p.) is available free of charge from:

> Thomson McKinnon Securities, Inc.
> One State Street Plaza
> New York, NY 10004
> Attn: Don D. Nardone, V.P.
> 1-212-482-7090

To determine the yield on your GNMA investment at any time, consult *Financial Pass-Through Yield and Value Tables for GNMA Mortgage Backed Securities*, available for $38.00 plus shipping and handling from:

> Financial Publishing Co.
> 82 Brookline Avenue
> Boston, MA 02115
> 1-617-262-4040

Similar tables available for Freddie Mac pools ($35.00 plus shipping and handling) and Fannie Maes ($26.50 plus shipping and handling).

For more on Grannie Maes, write:

> Family Backed Mortgage Association
> 2585 Ordway Building
> One Kaiser Plaza
> Oakland, CA 94612

13 TAX-EXEMPT BONDS

Tax-exempt bonds (also called municipals) are debt issues of states, local governments, and certain public authorities. Their interest is free of federal income taxes; and when the bonds are issued in the investor's state of residence, they are also exempt from local and state income levies. Debt issues of Puerto Rico, Guam, and the Virgin Islands are tax-exempt in all 50 states.

REDUCED SUPPLY/VOLUME

For a number of years the federal government has sought to reduce the number of local government bonds issued, maintaining that because the interest on these bonds was exempt from federal income tax, the government lost billions in revenues. In 1980, $47 billion of municipals were issued, but by 1983 the dollar amount had soared to $83 billion, and by 1985 it topped $161 billion. The Fed viewed the mushrooming of munis as providing unfair tax loopholes for the wealthy investor as well as preventing Washington from collecting its fair share of taxes. Consequently, the restrictions written into the Tax Reform Bill of 1986 are expected to sharply reduce the number of municipals issued each year.

Tax reform has made the municipal bond market one of the few legitimate shelters left in town. But it has also dramatically reduced the volume as well as the types of bonds that state and local governments can issue. So, unless you do your homework, you could be in for some surprises.

CATEGORIES OF MUNICIPAL BONDS

In broad terms, the bill divides municipals into four categories.

➤ GENERAL OBLIGATION BONDS (GOs) Also known as public purpose bonds, these have not been touched much by reform. The bill maintains the historic tax-exempt status for these bonds, which are sold to finance roads, schools, and government buildings. However, these issues, which are the most conservative of the municipals, are now tax-exempt only when no more than 10% of their proceeds is used by a private entity. Under the old rules, GOs were tax-exempt unless more than 25% of the proceeds benefited a private entity.

General obligation bonds are the most common and generally the safest municipals. They are backed by the full taxing power of the issuer. The payment of their interest and redemption is a primary obligation, so they usually have the highest safety ratings but often the lowest yields.

➤ INDUSTRIAL DEVELOPMENT BONDS (IDBs) As soon as more than 10% of the dollars raised by the sale of a muni is used by a private entity, the bond is classified as an industrial development bond. Under the old law, IDBs (or nongovernmental-purpose bonds) were subject to a state-by-state cap of $150 per person or $200 million, whichever was greater. In 1987, under the revision, most IDBs are subject to a $75 per person cap or $250 million.

IDBs are issued by states or authorities to finance construction of plants, buildings, and facilities that are then leased to private firms such as Exxon, K-Mart, McDonalds, etc. Because of the backing by major firms, many of these issues carry top ratings.

To permit small investors to participate, brokerage firms offer packaged industrial development bonds in limited partnerships at $5,000 per unit. The income increases with the gross revenues from the tenant. The after market is limited; there's little diversification, and costs and fees tend to be high. Investigate carefully before purchasing.

$WARNING: If you buy an IDB issued after August 7, 1986, beware: the interest earned is treated as a "preference" item and must be added to your taxable income *if* you are required to calculate the alternative minimum tax (AMT). This new ruling means that IDBs are suitable for those not likely to be subject to the AMT. The one exception: bonds issued by private, nonprofit hospitals and universities; these so-called 501(c) bonds are not taxable.

$HINT: As compensation for the fact that the interest income, by its nature as a "tax preference," may be subject to the 21% alternative minimum tax, industrial development bonds pay a slightly higher yield than general obligation or public purpose bonds.

➤ TAXABLE MUNICIPALS The new law eliminates issuance of tax-exempt bonds for what Congress deemed nonessential purposes, such as pollution control facilities, sports stadiums, convention and trade shows, industrial parks, and parking facilities. For the most part, these bonds will be exempt from state and local taxes where issued, even though they're subject to federal taxes.

In order to win over investors who traditionally purchased Treasury and corporate bonds, these taxable municipals are being conservatively

---

PRE-AUGUST 7 BONDS

PROS
↑ Virtually the only tax shelter available
↑ Higher yields than Treasury bonds in many cases
↑ Excellent ratings
↑ Especially valuable in states with high local taxes

CONS
↓ Market too new to evaluate
↓ Dominated by institutional investors
↓ Limited market if selling bonds before maturity
↓ Lower tax rates reduce attractiveness

---

designed to assure top rankings from Moody's and Standard & Poor's. And yields so far are 1 to 2 percentage points higher than those on Treasury bonds with similar maturities.

➤ PRE-AUGUST 7 BONDS You can avoid the problems that accompany newly issued municipals by purchasing bonds issued prior to August 7, 1986. These are generally not taxable. A number of firms are packaging pre-August 7 bonds, especially during the transitional years while the new law is being phased in. In the meantime, the supply of older bonds is dwindling because of aggressive purchases by both bond mutual funds and trusts. As is always the case, the demand is boosting prices and lowering yields.

TAXES AND THE INVESTOR

There's no question but that the overall reduction in income tax rates makes tax-exempt income less important to greater numbers of people. But the most negative aspect for both the average investor and the market in general stems from the provisions covering the alternative minimum tax (AMT). According to the terms of the new bill, interest earned on all newly issued IDBs, with the sole exception of those issued by private, nonprofit hospitals and universities (called 501(c) bonds), is subject to a 21% AMT for individuals and a 20% corporate AMT. (This is, of course, dependent on whether the taxpayer is subject to the AMT.)

The new provisions impact most heavily on banks, which in the past were major purchasers of munis, having the ability to take an 80% deduction from the interest costs entailed in buying and carrying municipals.

$TAX HINT: Municipal bond income is taxable under certain circumstances for some retirees. Up to half of a retiree's benefits can be taxed if municipal bond interest income plus adjusted gross income plus half of Social Security payments is more than $32,000 for couples or $25,000 for singles.

BUYING MUNICIPAL BONDS

■ If, after calculating your tax rate, you find that municipals turn out to be advantageous, then start with general obligation bonds. These bonds typically yield less than riskier municipals because they are the most conservative.

- All municipals are sold with legal opinions attached to their offering circulars. These will tell you if the issue is tax-free or not.
- As with all investments, the number one checkpoint is *quality,* best indicated by the ratings set by Moody's and Standard & Poor's.

    For investments, buy only bonds whose ratings start with an A. They are safe, and in most cases, their yields will be only slightly lower than those of poor-quality bonds.

    For speculations, a Baa rating involves as much risk as anyone seeking income should take. If you want to gamble, do not buy tax-exempt bonds unless you are very experienced and very rich. (For lower rated bonds, see Chapter 12 on junk bonds.)

    Once in a while, you may be asked to buy unrated issues: those from municipalities that are so small or have such modest debt that they have never had to bother with the paperwork of statistical services. If you personally know the community and its officials, these can be OK, but keep the maturities short, because you will have difficulty selling in a hurry and may incur local criticism.

- In a state that has local or state income taxes, the interest on municipal bonds issued in that state is exempt from these levies as well as the federal income tax. Thus, if you live in New Jersey, try to buy bonds issued there.

CHECKPOINTS FOR TAX-EXEMPTS

➤ MATURITY DATE   For bonds with the same rating, the shorter the maturity, the lower the yield and the greater the price stability. Unless you plan to buy municipals regularly, it is usually prudent to stick to those with maturities of less than 10 years. In many cases, these will be older bonds selling at a discount (more on that later). Select maturities according to your financial needs and time schedule. If you plan

to retire 8 years from now, pick a discount bond that will mature at that time.

➤ MARKETABILITY   The most readily salable municipals are general obligation bonds of state governments and revenue bonds of large, well-known authorities. Smaller issues have few price quotations, and the cost of selling, especially in odd lots, can be more than half the annual interest income.

➤ CALL PROVISION   Larger issues usually permit the bonds to be redeemed, at a price above par, after the first few years. With older low-coupon issues, there's no problem, because they will be selling below par. But with high-coupon issues, when interest rates decline, watch out. The bond that is trading at 115 might be callable at 105, so it could pay the issuer to refinance at a lower rate.

➤ YIELD DISPARITIES   If you buy more than 10 bonds, shop around. It's best to buy from your broker's inventory; but even if you do, you will find wide differences with debt of comparable ratings.

➤ TYPES OF BONDS   Prior to 1983, there were two types of tax-free bonds; *bearer,* where the investor detached coupons and sent them in or through a bank to receive the interest; and *registered,* with the name and owner identified on the face of the certificate or, more likely, in a central filing system. Today, all bonds are issued in registered form and thereby cost less to handle, usually eliminate printed certificates, and require lower transfer and custody fees.

BONDS SUBJECT TO PERSONAL ALTERNATIVE MINIMUM TAX

- General obligation issues in which more than 10% of the proceeds is used by a private entity
- Single- and multi-family housing bonds
- Student loan bonds
- Bonds financing small industrial development projects
- Bonds for airports and other ports not owned by local governments

> DEAL ONLY WITH A REPUTABLE BROKERAGE FIRM If you get a hard sell on tax-exempts, especially by phone, be *very* cautious. You will always be safer with your regular broker.

> TAKE ADVANTAGE OF SERIAL MATURITIES Unlike most corporate bonds, which usually have the same redemption date, municipals mature serially: a portion of the debt comes due each year until the final redemption. You can buy maturities to fit future needs: for college tuition, retirement, etc.

$HINT: If you're in the 28% top tax bracket, then an 8% tax-free municipal is equal to an 11% federally taxed bond.

MUNICIPAL BOND MUTUAL FUNDS

For small investors, one of the best ways to buy municipals is through a mutual fund. Mutual funds provide diversification (by type, grade, coupon, and maturity), continuous professional management, the opportunity to add with relatively small dollar amounts, the ability to switch to other funds under the same sponsorship, and, most importantly, prompt reinvestment of interest to buy new shares and benefit from compounding.

Unless you have over $10,000 and are willing to watch the market, a fund is the best way to invest in munis. The yields may be lower than you could obtain yourself, but then again you won't be tempted to spend the income if you reinvest. Minimum investments are generally $1,000. (See Chapter 14 for details on selecting mutual funds.)

In a fund, which is open-ended, the portfolio contains bonds with varying maturities. The manager then buys and sells bonds in order to improve returns, switching from short- to long-term maturities when yields are high and doing the opposite when yields decline. When interest rates shift quickly, some funds do extremely well; some do not. Keep in mind that your income from the fund will fluctuate, unlike a unit trust (explained below) where the yield is locked in.

MUNICIPAL BOND UNIT TRUSTS

These are closed-end funds with a fixed portfolio of municipal bonds that usually remain in the trust until maturity, unless they are called. The trust aims to lock in the highest yield possible on good-quality issues at the time of the initial offering. The units are registered in the name of the holder; and monthly, quarterly, or semi-annual checks are mailed out to the holder. A few have reinvestment privileges.

TAX-EXEMPT BOND FUNDS AND UNIT TRUSTS

FUND	YIELD	BOND QUALITY	MINIMUM INVESTMENT	MANAGEMENT FEE
Dreyfus Tax Exempt	9.06%	A	$2,500	0.60%
Fidelity Municipal	9.08	BBB	2,500	0.40
T. Rowe Price Tax-free	7.98	BBB	1,000	0.50
Scudder Managed Municipal	9.08	A	1,000	0.50
TRUST				
Glickenhaus Empire Fund Insured #194	7.78%	AAA	$1,000	4.90%
Merrill Lynch #371	9.16	A	1,000	4.00
John Nuveen National Trust #340	9.04	A	5,000	4.90
Paine Webber Long-Term #188	9.15	A	1,225	4.50
Smith Barney #116	9.50	A	1,463	4.25

SOURCE: Standard & Poor's *The Outlook*

TEN TAX-EXEMPT BOND FUNDS

Calvert Tax-Free Reserves	800-368-2748
Dreyfus Tax-Exempt Fund	800-645-6561
Fidelity Municipal Funds	800-544-6666
Financial Tax-Free Income	800-525-8085
New York Muni Fund	212-747-9210
T. Rowe Price Tax-Free	800-638-5660
Scudder Municipal Funds	800-225-2470
Stein Roe Municipal Funds	800-621-0320
Value Line Tax-Exempt Fund	800-223-0818
Vanguard Municipal Funds	800-662-SHIP

MUTUAL FUND VS. UNIT TRUST

- A managed mutual fund is generally a better investment for those who expect to sell in less than 10 years. The shares react quickly to fluctuating interest rates. Check the 1-, 5-, and 10-year performance records of several before investing.
- Unit trusts are best for long-term holdings, especially when the initial yield is high.

When the bonds mature, are sold (rarely), or are called, the principal is returned to the unit holders as a return of capital. If the sponsor feels a bond is endangering the trust's interest, it can be sold and proceeds paid out. Unit trusts, of course, are vulnerable to market risks: rising interest and early call on bonds in the portfolio.

Units can be sold in the secondary market, but doing so entails a commission and the bid-asked spread. If interest rates have fallen, you could make a profit, but if they've gone up, you may not get back your original investment. Unit trust prices are based on the price of the securities in the portfolio and are determined either by the sponsor or by an independent evaluator. Nuveen, for instance, which has a number of trusts, sets the price on a daily basis. Although unit prices are not quoted in the newspaper, you can call the sponsor for this figure.

There are two kinds of trusts: general and state. General trusts include bonds from various states and territories, while state trusts have bonds only from a single state, hence the name "single state unit trusts." Income generally is free from state and local taxes in the issuing state as well as from federal taxes.

Unit trusts have a one time sales charge that typically ranges from 2 to 5% plus annual fees in the neighborhood of 0.15%. Both these costs are factored into the yield. Mutual funds, on the other hand, may be load or no load. Most have larger annual fees, averaging about 0.8%.

$HINT: If you pay high state and/or local income taxes, look into single state bond funds that invest only in that state. Whether you select a bond mutual fund or a unit trust, read the portfolio first and determine the minimum rating set by management. Beware of any fund with a large portion of its holdings in issues with a B rating. (See Chapter 12 on junk bonds.)

MUNICIPAL BOND UNIT TRUSTS

Glickenhaus & Co. (Empire Fund) (New York City)	212-953-7800
Merrill Lynch (New York City)	call any local office
John Nuveen & Co. (Chicago)	800-221-4272
	312-621-3188
Van Kampen Merritt (Philadelphia)	800-523-4556
	215-523-4556

MUNICIPAL BOND INSURANCE

Years ago, investors never doubted that a municipal bond issuer would make the returns on principal and interest. Then, along came the default of Washington Public Power System, or "Whoops." Now, an increasing number of tax-free issues, as well as mutual funds and trusts, offer insurance for additional peace of mind. According to the Chicago-based bond counsel firm of Chapman & Cutler, less than 1% of the municipals issued since the Depression have defaulted. Of those defaults, approximately 77% occurred with bonds issued to finance revenue-producing facilities such as utilities, bridges, and nuclear power plants.

To insure its bonds, the issuer pays an insurance premium ranging between 0.1 and 2% of total principal and interest. In return, the insurance company will pay the principal and interest to the bondholders should the issuer default. Policies for new issues cannot be cancelled, and the insurance remains active over the lifetime of the bond. With a bond fund or unit trust, the insurance is generally purchased for the entire portfolio. The oldest insurers are American Municipal Bond Assurance Corp. (AMBAC) and Municipal Bond Insurance Association (MBIA). Both are AAA rated by Standard & Poor's.

Once a bond is insured, it is given an AAA rating by S&P *even if the bond has a BBB rating.* So remember that if you are purchasing an AAA insured bond, it may really be a BBB bond with insurance.

Insured municipal bonds pay lower yields, usually .1 to .5 percentage points less than comparable uninsured bonds. If the insurer's rating drops, then so do the ratings of all the

---

INTEREST RATE RISK

Interest rate risk is a greater problem for municipal bonds than defaults. According to Value Line Investment Service, a 20-year bond with an interest coupon of 9% that is trading at par declines in value by 8.6% when interest rates rise 1 percentage point; it rises in value by 9.9% when rates decline 1 percentage point. This volatility increases as the bond's maturity lengthens and its coupon rate declines.

---

issues that the company has insured. This happened to the $6 million of tax-exempts insured by Industrial Indemnity Co. after S&P dropped its rating of the parent company, Crum & Forster (a division of Xerox Corp.) from AAA to AA.

▶ MONOLINE VS. MULTILINE Before you invest in an insured bond, you would do well to understand how the insurers work. Monoline companies, such as Financial Guaranty Insurance Co. (FGIC), AMBAC, and Bond Investors Guaranty (BIG), are the result of one-time capital infusions from their parent companies. From then on, they use revenues stemming from a single line of insurance and other contracts. Multiline companies, on the other hand, such as MBIA, are formed from the association of member insurance companies. Their cash reserves stem from other lines of insurance, such as life, property, casualty, etc., underwritten by the various members. Most experts feel the multiline approach is safer because of the distribution of risk.

14 MUTUAL FUNDS

The world of mutual funds grows larger every year, with money mangement firms becoming as aggressive as food and drug companies, offering broader services and special packaging for every purpose and purse. In addition to the traditional pooled investments in stocks and bonds, there are now mutual funds for mortgage pass-throughs, short-term debt, options, precious metals, foreign securities, new issues—you name your goal or area and if there isn't a fund already available, just wait a few months.

The tremendous growth and popularity of funds is due in part to the expansion of personal pension plans that require fiduciary involvement, but it's also due to frustration with the erratic fluctuations of stocks and stock groups. More people are buying more shares in mutual funds than ever before, taking advantage of diversification, compounding of income, professional management, and liquidity. Unless you have full-time to devote to managing your investments, it's quite likely that at one time or another you'll buy shares in a fund. Since there are hundreds to select from, read the following before making your final decision.

All mutual funds operate fairly much the same way. They sell shares to the public at net asset value (NAV) price. The money received is then pooled and used to buy various types of securities. So when you buy into a fund you are really buying shares in an investment company, but the assets of this company consist not of plants or equipment but of stocks, bonds, and cash instruments.

As the owner of mutual fund shares you will receive periodic payments provided your fund does well. Of course, if the fund has a poor year, you stand to lose money.

Funds are either open- or closed-end. In an *open-end fund,* shares are continually available to the public at a price that represents the underlying asset value of the shares. The price is referred to as NAV. (NAV per share equals the total net assets of the fund divided by the outstanding shares.) The fund's shares are continually increasing or decreasing in number depending upon sales to the public.

A *closed-end fund* is like a corporation. It has fixed capitalization and makes one initial issue of stock. After that it trades in the open market on the major exchanges. Prices are determined by supply and demand: when buyers are plentiful, the price rises, and vice versa.

Mutual funds can also be categorized as load or no load. *Load* funds are *sold,* primarily by registered representatives of brokerage firms but also by qualified-by-law individuals who work full- or part-time.

A sales charge, typically 8.5%, is deducted from the amount of your investment. Thus, with a $10,000 purchase, the dollars that go to work for you are reduced to $9,150. The real cost is therefore 9.3%. The broker handles all details.

On large purchases, made immediately or under an installment plan, the commissions are lower, usually on a sliding scale down to about 4% on a single $100,000 purchase or commitment.

$HINT: For estate and gift-tax purposes, shares of load mutual funds are valued at the *bid* price (without commissions), not the *asked* price (which includes the sales cost).

No-load funds are *bought,* directly from the sponsoring company with no sales charge. You handle everything.

Mutual fund: An investment company that raises money by selling its own stock to individual investors and investing proceeds in a variety of securities.

HOW MUTUAL FUND SHARES ARE QUOTED

FUND FOUNDERS GROUP	52 WEEKS		CLOSE	WEEK'S CHANGE	INCOME*	CAPITAL GAINS
	HIGH	LOW				
Growth *n*	8.77	6.28	6.37	−0.08	0.157	2.505
Income *n*	15.18	13.72	13.87	+0.01	1.273	0.232
Mutual	11.56	9.74	9.98	−0.07	0.426	0.706
Spec. *n*	37.11	22.88	23.54	−0.13	1.90	1.395

*Last 12 months. *n* = no load.

SOURCE: Barron's.

There is usually no redemption charge, but some no-loads have recently set a 4% fee for early sales, and, with SEC approval, the costs of distribution of promotional material such as prospectuses have recently been levied against the shareholders instead of being absorbed by management.

With both types of funds, there are administration fees that run from 1 to 2% of the value of the fund assets. This seems small, but it can eat up a good chunk of your investment income. With $100,000 invested, an $8,000 annual return could be reduced by $750 every year.

There are seldom significant differences in the performance of funds with similar objectives, but the no-loads are better buys. With $10,000, and fund shares quoted at $10 each, you can buy 1,000 shares of a no-load but only 920 shares of a load fund with an 8% sales commission. At the end of 20 years, the load fund must earn an average of ¾ of 1% more than the no-load to provide the same return.

DISTRIBUTION OF INCOME

Mutual funds distribute money to investors in two ways: income dividends and capital gains distributions. *Income dividends* represent the interest and/or dividends earned by the fund's portfolio, minus the fund's expenses. *Capital gains distributions* represent a fund's net realized capital gains—when there are profits in excess of losses on the sale of the portfolio securities. Both income dividends and capital gains distri-butions can be automatically reinvested in the fund, usually at no cost.

To qualify for an exemption from corporate income taxes, a fund must meet these tests:

- At least 90% of its gross income in any taxable year must consist of dividends, interest, and capital gains from securities.
- Not more than 30% of gross income in any taxable year may be from sales of securities held under 3 months.
- The fund must distribute to its shareholders as taxable dividends at least 90% of its *net* income for any taxable year, excluding long-term capital gains (which may be distributed or retained, in whole or in part). When distributed, they are taxable to the shareholder.

VARIETY OF FUND OBJECTIVES

Mutual funds come in all sizes, shapes, and combinations. It is extremely important that you match your personal investment objectives with those of the fund. The following list summarizes the broad objectives and should be read carefully in order to familiarize yourself with the various terms or bits of jargons the funds use to describe what they do with your money.

➤ MAXIMUM CAPITAL GAINS OR AGGRESSIVE GROWTH, CAPITAL APPRECIATION, OR PERFORMANCE FUNDS These funds are highly risky and volatile and often have dramatic price swings. They seek maximum capital apprecia-

TOP RETURNS

Best-performing mutual funds through March 31, 1986. Increases include reinvestment of all capital gains, distributions, and dividend income.

OVER 1 YEAR

Fidelity Overseas	123.2%
Zenith Capital Growth*	92.7%
GAM International*	90.9%
Alliance International	88.0%
FT International*	81.9%
Putnam International Equities	81.3%
Transatlantic*	80.5%
PaineWebber Atlas	80.2%
Kemper International	78.1%

OVER 5 YEARS

Fidelity Magellan	284.2%
Vanguard Qualified Dividend 1*†	264.4%
Oppenheimer Target	250.5%
Quest for Value*	236.0%
Loomis-Sayles Capital*†	220.3%
Lindner Dividend*†	218.8%
Phoenix Growth	211.2%
Sequoia*†	199.4%
Franklin Utilities	198.4%

OVER 10 YEARS

Fidelity Magellan	1,762.8%
Quasar Associates*†	966.9%
Twentieth Century Select*	964.3%
Lindner*†	945.8%
Twentieth Century Growth*	930.1%
American Capital Pace	898.4%
Evergreen*	873.5%
Over-the-Counter Securities	798.4%
Loomis-Sayles Capital*†	772.3%

* No sales charge.
† Closed to new investors.

SOURCE: Lipper Analytical Services, Inc.

tion through the use of investment techniques involving greater than ordinary risk, such as borrowing money in order to provide leverage, short selling, hedging, options, and warrants.

➤ GROWTH FUNDS These invest for long-term capital appreciation and future income, principally in common stocks.

➤ GROWTH AND INCOME FUNDS These aim to provide long-term capital growth and to generate current income. They invest primarily in large, stable companies with good performance records.

➤ BALANCED FUNDS These funds have a stated policy determining the balance in the portfolio between bonds, preferred stocks, and common stocks. The objective is current income and preservation of capital.

➤ OPTION/INCOME FUNDS These seek high current return by investing primarily in dividend-paying common stocks on which call options are traded on national securities exchanges. Current return generally consists of dividends, premiums from expired call options, net short-term gains from sales of portfolio securities on exercises of options, and profits from closing purchase transactions.

➤ INCOME FUNDS These concentrate on preferred and common stocks that pay high dividends, plus bonds with high yields. These funds are not averse to capital gains, but it's a secondary consideration.

➤ CORPORATE BOND FUNDS Emphasis is normally on income rather than growth. It's important to check the bond ratings before investing. There are two main types of bond funds: (1) *unit trusts*, which buy a package of bonds and make no changes in the portfolio so the fund or trust is self-liquidating; the advantage: you are certain of the same yield, but if interest rates rise, the values of the bonds decline; (2) *managed trusts*, where the managers try to gain extra profits by shifting holdings in anticipation of changes in interest rates. (See chapters on bonds.)

➤ MUNICIPAL BOND FUNDS These invest in tax-exempt bonds issued by states, cities, and other local governments. Interest obtained from these bonds is passed through to shareholders free of federal tax. The types of municipal bond funds are the same as for corporate bond funds.

➤ MONEY MARKET MUTUAL FUNDS Also called liquid asset or cash funds, their primary objective is to make higher interest securities available to investors who want immediate income and high safety. (See Chapter 3.)

There are also a number of special funds that have grown in size and popularity during the past several years. They include:

➤ GINNIE MAE MUTUAL FUNDS These sell mortgage-backed securities. Their primary objective is income. Some funds use somewhat risky techniques to boost yields. (See Chapter 12.)

➤ FOREIGN OR GLOBAL FUNDS These invest in overseas companies and/or American companies that do a substantial portion of their business abroad. (See Chapters 29 and 30.)

➤ HIGH-YIELDING FUNDS These buy "junk" bonds of troubled corporations. The interest rates are high—over 15%—and the hope is that the company will get squared away so that the prices of the bonds will rise for substantial capital gains. (See Chapter 12.)

➤ INDEX FUNDS These are composed of securities that make up a stock market average such as Standard & Poor's Composite 500 Stock Index and are selected on a proportional basis. The idea is that by owning the average, you will do as well as the overall market. Some funds try to beat the market by indexing only 200 of the most profitable Standard & Poor's corporations.

There's no research, commissions are few because of the small turnover, and the management fee is a low $^2/_{10}$ of 1% of share value. Usually, however, there's a sales load of 8.5% and a quarterly maintenance fee of $6, no matter how many shares you own. These were popular in 1981–82 before the market rise but faded fast when greater gains could be scored with individual stocks. Recently, they have been used primarily by managers of major pension funds who could afford to accept mediocre results.

➤ SECTOR FUNDS These are the latest opportunities. They are designed to "concentrate capital where maximum growth is anticipated: to offer exceptional investment opportunities for the 80s and beyond." They include separate funds for gold and precious metals, service economy, technology, health care, and energy. To a degree, they are initiated to keep major funds from growing too unwieldy.

➤ SOCIALLY CONSCIOUS FUNDS With these, investments are not made in stocks of industries involved in areas that some people consider immoral, unethical, or questionable. Provident Fund for Income won't buy shares of companies in liquor or tobacco. Dreyfus Third Century buys only shares of corporations producing products for safety, purity, health, education, housing, environment, minority hiring, civil rights, or consumer protection. With such investments, you have to sacrifice performance

for ideals. That's not exactly a profitable financial criterion.

➤ FUND FUNDS These are mutual funds that invest in other mutual funds. The idea is to keep moving out of poorly performing funds into those with the best current record. As usual, this is a better sales concept than investment vehicle. And you have to pay two management fees and hope that the "professional" managers are shrewd enough to time their investments profitably.

➤ COMMODITIES FUNDS These offer shares in professionally managed portfolios of commodities futures contracts. The commissions or charges are high, but similarly managed private portfolios, with broad diversification and computerized controls for signaling buy and sell points, have produced good results. (See Chapter 23.)

➤ ROYALTY TRUST FUNDS With this fund, the trustee deposits a defined package of income-generating assets of oil and gas wells. The royalties are paid on the output. They are recognized by tax authorities as real assets and thus are not the same as royalties that are paid on land ownership.

The royalties come off the top from gross income and are subject to operating expenses or a fraction of the net profit of the wells. They

---

NEWSLETTERS

One of the latest gimmicks involving mutual funds is advisory reports that provide information and recommendations for buying and switching fund investments. They concentrate on aggressive growth funds that can rack up 50 to 75% gains in a good year. These are high-risk, high-volatility funds, so timing can be important.

Most letters are issued monthly and some offer telephone service (for an extra fee). They are not cheap, typically about $125 a year.

If you like to trade in an effort to profit from short-term swings, these could be worth the money. But they are for speculators, not investors. (See Newsletters, page 127.)

are not subject to corporate income tax so that they typically provide a steady 12% return as long as the wells produce.

Caution: Many funds offer shares at $2,000 each for pension funds. But the IRS could call the payments unrelated business income, which is by law taxable. It's difficult to determine which portion of a return is capital and which is tax-sheltered.

➤ INCOME PARTNERSHIP FUNDS The income derives from producing oil and gas properties that have been in production for 5 to 15 years with reserves of 10 years or more. The partnership does no drilling. If the general partner is honest and capable and does not take too much off the top, these can work out well. See the chapter that discusses tax shelters for checkpoints, and buy shares only with money that you will not need until the wells run dry.

Keep in mind that there are scores of other types of mutual funds. Some are described in other chapters relating to specific types of securities. Before you commit any savings, do your homework and make sure that you understand what you are getting into.

CLOSED-END FUNDS

Closed-end funds are investment opportunities with all the benefits of standard mutual funds plus chances for extra profits and tax savings.

Here's why:

➤ CONCENTRATION These limited capital funds generally concentrate their holdings in securities in special areas: American General and Bancroft on CVs; ASA on gold, etc. When these groups are popular, you get gains plus diversification.

➤ DISCOUNT PRICES Shares are often traded below net asset value (NAV), apparently because investors feel that the fixed capitalization limits management's ability to take advantage of profitable opportunities. It would have to sell current holdings, possibly at a loss. Straight mutual funds do not have this problem, because they have a constant inflow of new savings.

Such spreads can provide extra profits because: (1) you are buying at a bargain price. When shares of New American Bond Fund are trading at a discount of 19.3%, you are paying $32 for $39.65 worth of assets. If that spread narrows to 10%, you score well even though the worth of the underlying assets remain the same.

CLOSED-END FUNDS

FUND	NET ASSET VALUE	PRICE	PERCENT DIFFERENCE
Stock Funds			
Adams Express	16.92	15⅞	−6.2
Gen. American	16.27	16⅝	+2.2
Source	31.20	29⅝	−5.0
Tri-Continental	23.46	22½	−4.1
Convertible Funds			
Amer. Capital	30.57	31¼	+2.2
Bancroft CV	24.17	22½	−6.9
Castle CV	29.57	29⅜	−0.7
Special Equity Funds			
ASA	62.68	59⅜	−5.3
Japan Fund	13.68	12½	−8.6
New American	39.65	32	−19.3
Bond Funds			
Amer. Capital	18.38	17⅞	−2.7
Drexel Bond	15.65	16¼	+3.8
Lincoln Natl.	22.13	19¼	−13.0

SOURCE: Barron's.

(2) With income-oriented funds, the yield is based on the lower market value of the portfolio: e.g., with dividends averaging 10% and shares with a $10 NAV selling at $9, that $1 income becomes 11.1%.

➤ RETIREMENT PLANNING Closed-end funds, when bought at a discount, can be useful after quitting work when income becomes more important.

ADVANTAGES OF MUTUAL FUNDS

➤ DIVERSIFICATION Unless you have $40,000, it is almost impossible to have a properly diversified portfolio. It's costly to buy in odd lots and if you buy round-lot shares of quality corporations, your average per share cost will be about $40, so you can own only about 10 stocks—the minimum for a cross section of securities.

➤ SYSTEMATIC SUPERVISION Mutual funds have the personnel, research, facilities, and experience to handle efficiently all details of stock transactions, dividends, rights, proxy statements, and other details of ownership of securities. Well-run funds mail dividend checks promptly, provide accurate year-end summaries for income tax purposes, and are always ready to answer questions . . . on the 800 toll-free phone line.

➤ PROFESSIONAL MANAGEMENT The records of some fund managers leave much to be desired, but their performances overall have been superior to those of stock market averages. They have time and experience and access to information that is needed for profitable investments and, at times, for rewarding speculations.

➤ SWITCHING PRIVILEGES When a management company sponsors more than one type of fund (and most do), all shareholders have the privilege of swapping on a dollar-for-dollar basis as the market outlook and personal needs change. This usually involves a fee of $5 per transaction.

JUDGING MUTUAL FUNDS

As with all types of investments, the number one factor is the competency of management as measured by the ability to meet or surpass stated goals fairly consistently over a fairly long period of time: at least 5 and preferably 10 years with mutual funds.

Be wary of highly publicized, aggressively promoted funds, especially those with a "gimmick."

The risks do not vanish simply because there's self-styled professional management. They are gambling and may be lucky—for a while. But super performances are seldom repeated. The high-flying Oppenheimer Fund scored a whopping +58.1% total return in 1983, but in the first quarter of 1984, it was down 17%. If you go for such swingers, get out when performance lags. Just as with "hot" stocks, the

HOW TO ANALYZE A MUTUAL FUND

	MARCH 31	JUNE 30	SEPTEMBER 30	DECEMBER 31
Investment Position				
Cash				
Common stocks				
Bonds and preferreds				
Income				
High dividends				
Modest dividends				
Growth or low dividends				
Quality				
NYSE blue chips				
NYSE average				
AMEX				
OTC established				
OTC new issues or hi-tech				
Vulnerability				
Percent of total in largest holding				
Percent of total for 5 largest holdings				
Percent of total for 10 largest holdings				

first loss (when the downtrend is confirmed) is the cheapest. You can judge the future by checking the stocks shown in the last quarterly report and watching how they are falling.

Study the performance in both up and down markets. Several major funds have never been first in any one year, but they do better than the market in good periods and lose less in bear markets. One of the best guides is the annual *Forbes* magazine report in the late August issue. This rates funds on the basis of performance in both rising and falling markets. To get a high score, the fund must perform consistently, in relation to other funds, in all three up and down periods. Adjustments are made to prevent exceptional performance (good or bad) in any one period from having undue influence on the fund's average performance—calculated separately for both up and down markets. Data include reinvestment of realized capital gains but not of income. Other financial publications provide similar comparisons, but because they are keyed to relatively unsophisticated readers they tend to highlight short-term results. Popular periodicals such as *Money* and *Sylvia Porter's Personal Finance Magazine* also track fund performance on a monthly basis.

➤ INVESTMENT PORTFOLIO In their annual and quarterly reports, the management companies provide information on the securities bought and sold, the percentage of assets in cash or equivalents, in bonds, in preferred stocks, etc., and a list of the 10 best and worst performers during the reporting period. Only rarely do they show when the securities were acquired—so the popular holdings may have been bought right before the end of the quarter, not in the first month when their prices were lower.

With all types of funds, check points such as these:

- **Amount of cash.** Any fund that holds large sums in liquid assets after the start of a confirmed bull market is not making the best use of its assets.
- **Big name stocks** (Exxon, GM, IBM, Merck) in large blocks for long periods. There are times when these favorites are severely undervalued, but they generally represent security and reputation, not profitable growth.
- **Unfamiliar companies** whose shares are traded on the AMEX and OTC. These are almost always speculations. Their stocks

are volatile so that you cannot look—or even hope—for consistently superior performance.

- **Big winners and big losers.** These are usually listed in annual reports and sometimes in quarterly statements. What you want to watch for is when these stocks were bought and sold. Were the big gainers bought years or months before upswings? Were losers sold quickly after definite downturns or held tenaciously for years?
- **Where assets are concentrated.** Most funds make their significant gains with a few stocks but keep a high total with modest returns (and small losses) from the rest of the portfolio. Check the emphasis over a couple of years. Over the long term, proper selection can pay off, but for the short run, too great concentration can be devastating if a couple of major holdings bomb.
- **The relation of the results to the stated goals.** A fund that opts for income may have most of its money in high-dividend-paying utilities or bonds. In periods of rising interest rates, changes are hard to make and will reduce real returns.

➤ SIZE The larger the assets of a mutual fund, the smaller the amount each investor pays for administration. If you choose funds with assets over $50 million, this should not be important. The management fee of $250,000 to $275,000 for operational charges should be adequate to pay for able management and staff.

Stay away from funds whose assets have been under $50 million for over 10 years. If the fund hasn't grown, its performance must have been so poor that new shares could not be widely sold. If it's a new fund, there's no track record.

Conversely, when a fund becomes huge (over $500 million), there's a tendency for the managers to confine their investments to a relatively few major corporations that have millions of shares outstanding. In order not to upset the market, large commitments must be purchased or sold over a period of time and so may not always be traded at the most advantageous prices.

This lack of agility makes it difficult for major funds to beat the averages. In a sense, they are the market. By contrast, smaller funds

CONTRARY STRATEGY

In timing their purchases of shares of mutual funds, most investors look for the funds with the best records over the long term and then check recent performances and make their choices.

Says *Indicator Digest:* "This is wrong. The opposite strategy is more rewarding. Buy the funds that have performed worse, particularly after a substantial market move in either direction."

Their proof: in the market correction from early fall 1983 through spring 1984, the most depressed funds were those that performed best in the prior bull market and over some time previously. Their reasoning:

- The top performing funds grow too big to be efficient. They can no longer make meaningful investments in small companies.
- Their managers move to better jobs or are too busy being interviewed by the media.
- Success may be owing to emphasis on fads and fashions. Favorites tend to fade when long-neglected securities start to become popular.

can score welcome gains if they pick three or four winners. But large funds are likely to be more consistent in their returns.

➤ TURNOVER This shows the dollar amount of stocks sold in relation to total assets. Thus, if a fund had assets of $100 million and sold $75 million in stocks in one year, the turnover would be 75%. This is high and may indicate that the fund managers either are speculating for short-term profits or are being anxious about the possibility of generating big commissions to reward a related brokerage firm or registered representative who pushes the sale of fund shares.

$HINT: A rapid turnover may mean that a substantial portion of the realized gains will be short term and thus taxable, on your return, at the highest rate. A fund with a turnover of over 100% will almost always have more short-term than long-term capital gains.

FUND SERVICES

Not all funds offer all services, but here are some of the most frequently available extras:

➤ AUTOMATIC REINVESTMENT This means that all dividend and capital gains disbursements will be automatically and systematically reinvested to compound your earnings. This can be beneficial, because there's magic in compound interest. With a total average annual return of 12%, your money will double every 6 years.

$HINT: This automatic reinvestment is a form of dollar cost averaging, but it may not always be in your best interests. Mutual funds pay their largest dividends in capital gains when the stock market is relatively

THE PROSPECTUS

You must read the prospectus before investing in a fund. Although it may appear formidable upon first glance, a half-hour with this step by step guide will crystalize the entire process and enlighten you about the fund. Here's what to look for:

- What the fund's investment objectives are. These will be spelled out at the beginning.
- A risk factor statement.
- What strategies will be used to meet the fund's stated goals.
- The degree of diversification. How many issues does it hold?
- What is the portfolio turnover? A low rate, below 60 or 70%, reflects a long-term holding philosophy, whereas a high rate indicates an aggressive strategy. The average is around 80%.
- Fees and expenses. Check in particular the cost of redeeming shares and management's fees. The latter should not exceed 0.75% per year.
- Rules for switching within a family of funds and fees, if any.
- Restrictions. Will the fund sell securities short, act as an underwriter, engage in selling commodities or real estate? What percentage of total assets is invested in any one security? Be wary of a fund that is not adequately diversified.

high. Instead of reinvesting at the high level, you may do better to take the cash and wait for the market to decline. Your cash will buy more shares.

➤ BENEFICIARY DESIGNATION With both single-payment and contractual plans, you can name your beneficiary by means of a trust agreement. This will ensure that the investment goes directly to your designated heir when you die, with none of the delays and expenses of probate. Consult your lawyer, because some states prohibit this transfer.

➤ LIFE INSURANCE Available, as term life, with long-term contractual plans. The insurance guarantees that your survivors will receive the full amount of your investment commitment. Or, for convenience, you can buy the coverage with your savings via regular deductions. There is usually no medical exam; the age limit to start is 55 and the total investment required is $18,000.

➤ OPEN ACCOUNT This enables you to invest whenever you have extra funds or receive regular payments (social security or pension). The money buys shares immediately in fractional units. This arrangement is excellent for IRAs and Keoghs.

It's also possible to set up withdrawals, directly or indirectly through special checks. The minimum payout is usually $500.

Note: Most no-load funds require that your signature be guaranteed by a commercial bank or brokerage firm. They want to be sure that the person redeeming shares is the lawful owner.

➤ REGULAR INCOME CHECKS These are available (by the month, quarter, or other specified period) in several ways: (1) by buying shares in several funds, each with different dividend months; (2) by arranging for regular quarterly dividends to be paid in monthly installments; (3) by opting for a fixed income each month by permitting the sale of some shares to supplement the dividends. In addition, most funds will ease your tax reporting—and taxes—by providing print-outs to show that the redeemed shares were those with a loss or with the least capital gains.

➤ LOAN PROGRAM Some funds permit share-holders to use their investments as collateral for loans at interest rates tied to the broker's call money rate. The minimum loan is $5,000 on a 50% margin. There are no set repayment terms, and you can arrange for the interest to be paid from income or capital of your holdings.

➤ INFORMATION AND SERVICE Almost all investment companies provide 800 numbers, so you can make toll-free calls to learn about prices, minimum investments, charges, and types of other funds available for switching. And you can also get forms for setting up pension programs, etc.

KEEPING TRACK OF YOUR MUTUAL FUND FOR TAX PURPOSES

		INVESTMENTS			REDEMPTION				
	DATE	NO. SHARES	COST	TOTAL	DATE	NO. SHARES	PRICE	PROCEEDS	SHARES LEFT
Purchase	1/82	200	$12	$2,400	12/83	100	$8	$800	100
	12/82	50	7	350					
	2/83	200	5	1,000	12/83	100	8	800	100
Reinvest.	12/83	50	9	450					

	REDEMPTION TAX RECORD				
NO. SHARES	DATE PURCHASED	DATE REDEEMED	COST	SALES PRICE	GAIN OR (LOSS)
100	1/82	2/83	$1,200	$800	($400)
100	2/83	2/84	500	800	300

FOR FURTHER INFORMATION

GENERAL DIRECTORIES

Individual Investor's Guide to No-Load Mutual Funds
American Association of Individual Investors
612 North Michigan Avenue
Chicago, IL 60611
1-312-280-0170

An annual guide with evaluative data on 300 funds, $19.95.

The Mutual Fund Almanac
The Donoghue Organization
P.O. Box 540
Holliston, MA 01746
1-617-429-5930

Annual with data on 850+ funds, $23.

The Dow Jones-Irwin Mutual Fund Yearbook
Dow Jones-Irwin
1818 Ridge Road
Homewood, IL 60430
1-312-798-6000

Wiesenberger's Investment Companies
The Wiesenberger Investment Companies Service
1633 Broadway
New York, NY 10019
1-212-977-7453

Mutual Fund Fact Book
The Investment Company Institute
1775 K Street N.W.
Washington, D.C. 20006
1-202-293-7700

NEWSLETTERS

The Peter Dag Investment Letter
Peter Dag & Associates, Inc.

65 Lake Front Drive
Akron, OH 44319
1-216-644-2782

Published every three weeks. Gives fund timing and switching advice.

NoLoad Fund X
235 Montgomery Street
San Francisco, CA 94104
1-415-986-7979

Lists top performers by investment goals.

Mutual Fund Forecaster
3471 North Federal Highway
Fort Lauderdale, FL 33306
1-305-563-9000

Ranks funds by risk and profit potential.

Telephone Switch Newsletter
P.O. Box 2538
Huntington Beach, CA 92647
1-714-898-2588

Monthly. Gives timing and switching advice.

United Mutual Fund Selector
United Business Service Co.
210 Newbury Street
Boston, MA 02116
1-617-267-8855

Monthly. Tracks major funds.

For sampling of newsletters:

Select Information Exchange
2095 Broadway
New York, NY 10023
1-212-874-6408

A financial publications subscription agency providing a group of trial subscriptions to various investment newsletters. One trial group comprises 12 different mutual fund services for $12. SIE also monitors performance of advisory publications.

PART THREE

INVESTMENT ANALYSIS

Now that you are well acquainted with the various types of securities available, the next step of course is deciding which ones to select for your personal portfolio. Do you want common stocks? If so, which ones? Perhaps you would benefit from bonds or convertibles. Yet selecting the best and avoiding the worst requires skill and knowledge. That's where investment analysis enters the picture.

In this section you will learn the various techniques used by the experts in selecting all types of securities. You will come to know how to recognize the potential profit in stocks, bonds, and mutual funds, and how to spot the winners and avoid the losers. Among the topics covered are:

- Finding quality
- Reading a company's balance sheet
- Getting the most out of statistics
- Following technical analysis
- Studying the charts
- Finding top takeover targets

RANKINGS

The number one criterion for successful investing is *always quality.* In the stock market, quality is determined by the corporation's investment acceptance, financial strength, profitability, and record of growth. Refer to *Standard & Poor's Stock Guide* or *Value Line Investment Survey* to find the ratings assigned to companies on the basis of past performance in earnings and dividends, corporate creditworthiness, and the growth and stability of the company.

The Standard & Poor's categories range from A+ (highest) to A (high), A— (above average), B+ (average), B (below average), B— (lower), to C (lowest). With the exception of banks and financial institutions, which are rated NR (no ranking), most publicly owned corporations are listed. *Never invest in any company rated below B+,* and always check recent earnings to make certain that the quality rating is still deserved.

The Value Line Investment Survey is a weekly service that reports on 1,700 stocks classified into 92 industry groups. A report on each industry precedes the individual stock reports. Each stock is given two rankings: one for "timeliness," i.e., the probable relative price performance of the stock within the next 12 months; and one for "safety," i.e., the stock's future price stability and its company's current financial strength. Within these two categories each stock is assigned a rank from 1 (the highest) to 5 (the lowest). Here's what the rankings mean:

➤ VALUE LINE TIMELINESS

RANK 1 (highest) Expect the stock to be one of the best price performers relative to the 1,700 other stocks during the next 12 months.

RANK 2 (above average) Expect better than average price performance.

RANK 3 (average) Expect price performance in line with the market.

RANK 4 (below average) Expect less than average price performance.

RANK 5 (lowest) Expect the poorest price performance relative to other stocks.

➤ VALUE LINE SAFETY

RANK 1 (highest) This stock is probably one of the safest, most stable, and least risky relative to the 1,700 other stocks.

RANK 2 (above average) This stock is probably safer and less risky than most.

RANK 3 (average) This stock is probably of average safety and risk.

RANK 4 (below average) This stock is probably riskier and less safe than most.

RANK 5 (lowest) This stock is probably one of the riskiest and least safe.

It sounds as though it is easy to pick growth stocks, but true growth equities are relatively rare, because their companies must combine growth with profitability.

Example: In base year 1, on a per-share basis, the stock's book value is $10.00; earnings $1.50; dividends 50¢; leaving $1.00 for reinvestment. This boosts the book value, in year 2, to $11.50 per share. At the same 15% return on equity, the per-share earnings will be $1.75 and dividends will be 60¢, leaving $1.15 for reinvestment. And so on.

At the end of only 4 years, on a per-share basis, the book value will be $15.25; earnings, $2.30; dividends, 90¢; with $1.40 put back into the business. Thus, the underlying worth of this quality company is up 52.5% and, in normal markets, such profitable growth will bring a much higher valuation for the stock.

HOW A QUALITY INVESTMENT GROWS

	PER SHARE			
YEAR	BOOK VALUE	EARNINGS	DIVIDENDS	REINVESTED
1	$10.00	$1.50	$.50	$1.00
2	11.50	1.75	.60	1.15
3	13.25	2.00	.76	1.25
4	15.25	2.30	.90	1.40

Compare these projections with the past records of several of your most successful holdings and you'll see why quality stocks are always worth more . . . eventually. The truest, most valuable growth companies are those that continue to report ever-higher revenues and earnings and, as a result, greater book values.

In choosing growth stocks, weigh carefully the record, over at least 5 and, preferably, 10 years, and then project a realistic future—as was done in the table. *The best choice is a company that combines a strong past with prospects for an equally strong—or stronger—future. Add a little luck and you'll be smiling in 24 to 30 months, or less in a strong market.*

DON'T CONFUSE GROWTH WITH PRICE

Investing for growth is wise so long as the price that you pay does not get out of line. The problems come from Wall Street, not the corporation whose shares you own. In their infinite "wisdom," the analysts swing from unsupported optimism to equally false pessimism.

When growth stocks become popular, as they did in the early 1970s, institutions kept buying with little or no regard to value. Everything was keyed to the "future," which, as you've probably learned by personal experience, is usually more hyperbolic than rational. This is mass mania, not investing. The higher the price of the stock, the greater the buying . . . for a while. Sure, corporate profits keep rising, but the price-earnings ratios soar faster, to absurd multiples of 40 or 50.

The problem is *hope* based on what some analysts predict. Too often, their predictions

bear little relation to facts. Over the short term, there will always be periods when the value of a stock is overinflated (time to sell) or overdepressed (time to consider buying). But in the long run, corporate growth and profitability will be the determinants for investors.

GUIDELINES FOR SMALL GROWTH FIRMS

Throughout *Your Investments,* you'll find checkpoints that can be valuable in making money with your investments. With small, unseasoned companies, you are always taking extra risks, but the reward can often be worthwhile. To keep the odds in your favor, use these guidelines:

- **Read the annual report backward.** Look at the footnotes to discover whether there are significant problems, unfavorable long-term commitments, etc.
- **Analyze the management's record** in terms of growth of revenue and earnings and, especially, return on stockholders' equity.

CALCULATING GROWTH RATES

ANNUAL RATE OF EARNINGS INCREASE PER SHARE	JUSTIFIED P/E RATIOS			
	5 YEARS	7 YEARS	10 YEARS	15 YEARS
2%	15	15	13	12
4	17	17	16	16
5	18	18	18	18
6	19	19	20	21
8	21	22	24	28
10	23	25	28	35
12	25	28	33	48

Note that there should be only a small premium when a low growth rate remains static over the years. A 5% annual gain in EPS justifies the same P/E no matter how many years it has been attained. But when a company can maintain a high rate of earnings growth, 10% or more, the value of the stock is enhanced substantially.

SOURCE: Graham and Dodd, *Security Analysis.* New York: McGraw-Hill, 4th ed., 1962.

- **Find a current ratio** of assets to liabilities of 2:1 or higher. This indicates that the company can withstand difficulties and will probably be able to obtain money to expand.
- **Look for a low debt ratio** with long-term debt no more than 35% of total capital. This means that the company has staying power and the ability to resist cyclical downturns.
- **Compare the price of the stock** and its price-earnings ratio to those of other, larger companies in the same industry. If they're lower, this may be a sleeper. If the multiple is above 20, be wary. Such stocks tend to be volatile.
- **Look for stocks with strong management,** little debt, and a return on investment high enough to generate internal growth.
- **Concentrate on companies whose earnings growth rate has been at least 20%** annually for the past 5 years and can be projected to be not much less for the next 2 years.

Keep in mind that: (1) you are buying the future of the company; (2) increasing revenues are not enough (the real test is increasing profits); (3) the stock market is built on hype, and that's easy with new companies that do not have a long, successful record.

DON'T OVERLOOK ESTABLISHED COMPANIES

The corporation does not have to be young to have growth potential. There are opportunities with old companies where there's new management, a turnaround situation, or R&D-based developments. Analyst James Wolpert lists these ever-important developments:

- **Strong position in an evolutionary market.** Find an industry or market that is bound to move ahead and check the top half dozen corporations. The leaders are probably the best bets, but do not overlook the secondary companies. They may provide a greater percentage gain on your investment.
- **Ability to set prices at profitable levels.** This is important in service industries where greater volume can bring

proportionately higher profits as overhead remains relatively stable. The same approach applies to companies making or distributing branded merchandise.

- **Adequate funds for R&D.** With few exceptions, future growth of any corporation is dependent on finding new and better products, more efficient methods of doing business, etc. Look for a company which is building for that sort of future.
- **Control of a market.** IBM is in a dominant position, not because of price, but because of its ability to engineer new computers and office equipment and to provide good, continuing service at reasonable cost to the customer.
- **Strong technology base.** This is a valuable, but not essential, asset. Growth companies usually start with expertise in specific areas and then move out into other products and markets.
- **Growing customer demand.** This means a total market that is growing faster than the GNP. In the early years of new items, almost any company can prosper, because the demand is greater than the supply. Later, when production has caught up, the strong, better managed firms will survive and expand their positions.
- **Safety is always important,** but with common stocks, the foremost consideration should be profitable growth: in assets, revenues, and earnings.

RISING EARNINGS AND DIVIDENDS

Despite some temporary setbacks, American business has continued to make more money and to pay out higher dividends. To a degree, these gains have reflected the impact of inflation, but over the years, the progress has been strong and relatively steady.

In selecting stocks, check the corporate record of earnings and dividends. The best buys will be companies that have outperformed and appear likely to continue to outperform the averages, not for just a year or two but fairly consistently over a 5-year period. The greatest profits are made with shares of corporations that make the most money.

■ **Look for a high compound growth rate:** at least 15 to 20% annually. Compounding means that every year earnings are 20% higher than in the prior year. The table shows a theoretical example of earnings growth of 20% compounded annually.

Example: To find earnings growth for any one year, subtract the earnings per share of the prior year from the earnings per share of the year in question. Then divide the difference by the base year (i.e., the prior year) earnings.

In 1986, Eckveldt Technology earned $1.20 per share. In the prior year, it earned $1.00 per share.

$$\begin{array}{r} \$1.20 \\ -\ 1.00 \\ \hline 0.20 \end{array} \div \$1.00 = 20\% \text{ growth rate}$$

In the next year, in order to maintain a 20% growth rate, Eckveldt would have to report an increase of 20% of $1.20, or $1.20 × 0.20% = 0.24¢. Therefore, earnings expectations are $1.44 per share in the third year ($1.20 + 24¢ = $1.44). Tables for compound growth rates are available from your stockbroker.

EARNINGS GROWTH RATE
■■■■■■■■■■

Year 1	$1.00 × 20% = 0.20 = $1.20
Year 2	$1.20 × 20% = 0.24 = $1.44
Year 3	$1.44 × 20% = 0.29 = $1.73
Year 4	$1.73 × 20% = 0.35 = $2.08

Look for the trend of earnings as reported for two consecutive quarters. If profits fall, find out why. The decline may be temporary and reflect heavy investments in new products or markets. But if the drop indicates real trouble, consider selling if you have not already done so. *Never fall in love with any stock.* If the corporate prospects are dim, why hang on? If you are convinced that it is still a quality company, you can buy back at a lower price.

Similarly, if profits rise, be just as curious. If they are the result of higher sales and lower costs, this could be the start of something big.

But if the improvements come from accounting changes, it's less impressive.

HOW TO DETERMINE REAL GROWTH AND PROFITABILITY

In selecting stocks for managed accounts, Wright Investors' Service relies heavily on two fundamental measurements of corporate growth and profitability: *earned growth rate* (EGR) and *profit rate* (PR). These reveal the ability of management to make the money entrusted to them by stockholders grow over the years.

➤ EARNED GROWTH RATE   The EGR is the annual rate at which the company's equity capital per common share is increased by net earnings after payment of the dividend—if any. *It is a reliable measure of investment growth because it shows the growth of the capital invested in the business.*

$$E = \text{earnings}$$

$$D = \text{dividend}$$

WHAT ARE EARNINGS WORTH?
■■■■■■■■■■

ANNUAL GROWTH RATE	WHAT $1.00 EARNINGS WILL BECOME IN 3 YEARS AT GIVEN GROWTH RATE	THE P/E RATIO YOU CAN PAY TODAY TO MAKE 10% ANNUAL CAPITAL GAIN AND EXPECT P/E RATIO IN 3 YEARS TO BE	
		15×	30×
4%	$1.12	12.6	25.3
5	1.16	13.1	26.2
6	1.19	13.4	26.8
7	1.23	13.9	27.7
8	1.26	14.2	28.4
9	1.30	14.7	29.3
10	1.33	15.0	30.0
12	1.40	15.8	31.6
15	1.52	17.1	34.3
20	1.73	19.5	39.0
25	1.95	22.0	44.0

SOURCE: Knowlton and Furth, *Shaking the Money Tree.* New York: Harper & Row, 1979.

BV = book value

$$EGR = \frac{E - D}{BV}$$

The book value is the net value of total corporate assets, i.e., what is left over when all liabilities, including bonds and preferred stock, are subtracted from the total assets (plant, equipment, cash, inventories, accounts receivable, etc.). It is sometimes called stockholders' equity and can be found in every annual report. Many corporations show the book value, over a period of years, in their summary tables. A good growth company will increase its equity capital at a rate of at least 6% per year. The accompanying table shows why American Home Products (AHP) qualifies as a top growth company.

To determine the EGR for AHP in 1983, take the per-share earnings of $3.99 and subtract the $2.40 dividend to get $1.59. Then divide this by the book value at the *beginning of the year:* $11.78. Thus, the EGR for that year was 13.5%:

$$EGR = \frac{3.99 - 2.40}{11.78} = \frac{1.59}{11.78} = 13.5\%$$

➤ PROFIT RATE The PR is equally important in assessing real growth, because it measures the ability of the corporate management to make money with your money; it shows the rate of return produced on shareholders' equity at corporate book value. It is calculated by dividing the earnings per common share by the per share book value of the common stock, again at the *beginning of the year.*

PROFITABILITY OF AMERICAN HOME PRODUCTS

YEAR	BOOK VALUE	PER SHARE EARNINGS	PER SHARE DIVIDENDS	EGR
1978	$6.57	$2.21	$1.33	13.4%
1979	7.37	2.51	1.50	13.7
1980	8.39	2.84	1.70	13.6
1981	9.62	3.18	1.90	13.3
1982	10.61	3.59	2.15	13.6
1983	11.78	3.99	2.40	13.5
1984	13.70	4.39	2.64	13.4
1985	15.14	4.70	2.90	11.8

SOURCE: Wright Investors' Service.

PROFITS: PHANTOM AND EXTRA

It's nice to be able to report debt reduction, but the wise investor should check how this is accomplished. One of the newest methods is to swap bonds for stock. This is like buying back the mortgage on your home. You can save current dollars, but you will lose the benefit of the old low interest rate.

Example: A wily investment banker accumulates large amounts of old low-coupon bonds that have been selling at deep discounts, say 70¢ on the dollar. The banker then swaps this debt for shares of common stock, which are then sold to the public . . . at a modest profit. On its books, the corporation shows a "profit" because the price of the bond was far below the face value that would have to be paid at the future redemption date.

Similarly, watch out when a company keeps reducing its debt by new stock offerings. Since the interest is a business expense, the net cost is about half that of the same dollars paid out in dividends. When debt is repaid from the proceeds of new common stock, the same dividend rate requires greater after-tax profits.

Using AHP as an example:

$$PR = \frac{3.99}{11.78} = 33.9\%$$

AHP's EGR and PR were above the averages for the DJIA stocks for 1983: PR of 9.8%; EGR of 3.5%. The consistently strong record of AHP was a major reason for the rise in the stock price, from 28 in mid-1981 to 54 in early 1984.

CHECKPOINTS FOR FINDING GROWTH AND PROFITABILITY

- **Improving profit margins.** This is an excellent supplementary test because wider PMs almost always indicate larger earnings per share *soon.*

STANDARD & POOR'S A−, A, or A+ RATED STOCKS LISTED ON THE NEW YORK STOCK EXCHANGE WITH DIVIDEND AND EARNINGS PER SHARE INCREASES FOR 1981–1985

Aerospace Industry
McDonnell Douglas
Rockwell International

Apparel
Hartmarx

Automotive
Genuine Parts

Beverages and Bottlers
Anheuser-Busch
Coca-Cola
MEI Corp.

Business
Pitney Bowes

Chemicals
Clorox Co.
Morton Thiokol

Construction
Avery International
Sherwin-Williams

Drugs, Cosmetics
Abbott Laboratories
American Home Products
Gillette Co.
Johnson & Johnson
Lilly (Eli)
Pfizer, Inc.
SmithKline Beckman
Squibb Corp.
Tambrands, Inc.

Electrical
Emerson Electric
General Electric
E.G.&G., Inc.
Tracor, Inc.
United Industrial

Financial and Bank Industry
BancOne Corp.
Bank of Boston
Bank of New York
Bank of Virginia
Bankers Trust NY

Dreyfus Corp.
Morgan (J.P.)
NBD Bancorp
Republic NY

Foods
Borden, Inc.
Campbell Soup
Con Agra
Dart & Kraft
Dean Foods
Flowers Industries
Heinz (H.J.)
Hershey Foods
Kellogg Co.
Pillsbury Co.
Quaker Oats
Ralston Purina
Sara Lee
Smucker

Health Care
Beverly Enterprises
Community Psych Centers
Humana, Inc.
Manor Care
National Medical Enterprises

Paper, Printing, Publishing
De Luxe Check Printers, Inc.
Donnelley (R.R.) & Sons
Dow Jones
Dun & Bradstreet
Fort Howard Paper
Gannett Company
Harland (John)
Knight-Ridder
Lee Enterprises
Meredith Corp.

Restaurants
Luby's Cafeterias
McDonald's Corp.
Wendy's

Retailers
Albertson's, Inc.
Allied Stores
Ames Department Stores

American Stores
Associated Dry Goods
Dayton Hudson
Family Dollar Stores
Long's Drug Stores
May Department Stores
Mercantile Stores
Payless Cashways
Supermarkets General
Walgreen Co.
Wal-Mart Stores
Weiss Markets
Zayre Corp.

Transportation
Carolina Freight Corp.
Consolidated Freightways
Overnite Transportation

Utilities
ALLTEL Corp.
Baltimore Gas & Electric
Brooklyn Union Gas
Central Hudson
Cincinnati Bell
Delmarva Power & Light
Hawaiian Elec. Indus.
Niagara Mohawk Power
Potomac Electric
Savannah Electric & Power
Southern Co.
Wisconsin Electric Power
Wisconsin Public Service

Miscellaneous
Bandag, Inc.
Collins & Aikman
Josten's, Inc.
Leggett & Platt
Marriott Corp.
Masco Corp.
Maytag Co.
New York Ball Corp.
N.Y. Sealed Air
Philip Morris
Rubbermaid
U.S. Tobacco

SOURCE: Standard & Poor's.

The profit margin shows a company's operating income, before taxes, as a percentage of revenues. It is listed in many annual reports and most statistical analyses. It can be calculated by dividing the net operating income (total revenues less operating expenses) by the net sales. Generally, a PM of 6% indicates a company that deserves further study. Anything below that, especially when it is lower than the previous year, is a danger signal.

The PM has drawbacks. Internal corporate changes can result in a higher figure that is not due to true growth. This could be the result of accounting changes or a shift in distributing, say, from direct sales to wholesalers.

- **Plowed-back earnings.** The fastest-growing companies will almost always be the stingiest dividend payers. By reinvesting a substantial portion of its profits, preferably 70% or more, a company can speed expansion and improve productive efficiency. Any corporation that plows back 12% of its invested capital each year will double its real worth in 6 years.

- **Strong research and development.** The aim of research is knowledge; the aim of development is new or improved products and processes. A company that uses reinvested earnings largely for new plants and equipment will improve its efficiency and the quality of its products, but it will not grow as fast, in the long run, as a company that spends wisely to develop new and better products.

A prime test for aggressive growth management is whether the company is spending a higher than average percentage of its revenues for research, new product development, and new process development. *With good management (and a little luck), dollars spent for R&D constitute the most creative, dynamic force for growth available for any corporation.* It is not unusual for the thousands of dollars used for research to make possible millions of dollars in additional sales and profits.

See the table of selected growth companies for a list of recommended common stocks which can be used as a basis for building a growth portfolio.

WHAT TO WATCH FOR

To spot the nonachievers among companies in a growth industry, look for these danger points:

- **Substantial stock dilution.** When a company repeatedly and exclusively raises funds through the sale of additional common stock, either directly or through convertibles.

    There's no harm in small dilution, especially when there are prospects that the growth of earnings will continue. But beware of any company where there are heavy future obligations that can mean reductions in profits of 30% or more.

- **Vast overvaluation as shown by price-earnings ratios of 30 or higher.** This is a steep price to pay for potential growth. Take your profits or, at least, set stop-loss prices. When any stock sells at a multiple that is double that of the overall market (usually around 12), be cautious unless it's a roaring-up market. Huge price rises are almost always followed by equally huge declines.

RELATING CURRENT PRICES TO FUTURE PROFITS

In making projections of future prices of stocks, although the most important consideration is anticipated corporate earnings, most analysts also check past performance and mix in hope.

One way to make projections is to assume that earnings will continue to grow at pretty much the same rate as during the past decade. This may be true of a few large established corporations with long histories of steady growth, but it is a rash assumption for most smaller companies. The bigger you get, the tougher it is to maintain the same rate of growth. It is a lot easier to add 10% annually to $1 million in profits than to add $10 million to $100 million in earnings!

A reasonable frame of projection reference is 5 years. Many firms now prepare 5-year

A SAMPLING OF GROWTH COMPANIES

| EARNINGS PER SHARE ($) | | | INDI-CATED DIV. $ | 1984-1986 PRICE RANGE | RECENT PRICE | P/E RATIO | YIELD % | | LATEST 5-YEAR GROWTH RATES | | NO. OF EARN. GAINS '80-'85 | INTERIM ■EARN. TREND | ▼PRICE ACTION VS MKT. 11-28-80 TO 8-12-82 | SINCE AUG. 12, '82 | LISTED OPTIONS TRADED |
1984	1985	E1986							SALES	EARN.					
1.67	1.94	2.20	0.84	45¹⁵/₁₆-18³/₈	45w.i.	20.5	1.9	Abbott Laboratories	10%	18%	5	+16%	1.51	1.30	Ph
¹3.45	¹3.65	↑4.25	2.20	81⁷/₈-41	78	18.4	2.8	Bristol-Myers	7	14	5	+11	1.70	1.23	C
2.65	3.05	3.50	1.00	55¹/₂-19³/₄	53	15.1	1.9	ConAgra (May*)	42	18	5	+12	3.02	1.73	···
5.10	5.43	5.85	2.76	92-58¹/₈	84	14.4	3.3	Emerson El. (Sept.)	8	7	5	+3	1.96	0.72	A
2.36	2.36	2.45	0.40	42¹/₈-25¹/₄	29	11.8	1.4	Northern Telecom	17	‡	4	+8	1.62	1.11	T
2.04	2.32	3.20	1.20	61⁵/₈-18⁷/₈	60	18.8	2.0	Syntex (July)	10	16	5	+44	1.62	1.31	C
¹2.51	2.15	2.65	1.36	47-28¹/₄	47	17.7	2.9	Thomas & Betts	5	2	4	-11	1.03	0.99	···

↑ Upward change in earnings estimate or dividend rate since last publication of the Master List; ↓ downward change. *Of following year.

Listed options traded: C-Chicago Board Options Exchange; A-American Stock Exchange; Pac-Pacific Stock Exchange; Ph-Philadelphia Stock Exchange; T-Toronto Stock Exchange.

Price/Earnings Ratios are based on latest shown estimated or actual earnings.

▼ A figure above 1.0 indicates that the stock outperformed the S&P industrial stock price index in this period. It is computed by taking the ratio of the stock's price at the end of the period vs. the beginning of the period and dividing it by the corresponding ratio of the index. The time periods covered are updated periodically to conform to the latest major market cycle.

■ This column compares share earnings of latest six months with those of the corresponding year-earlier period.

‡Not calculable because of a deficit. ¹Restated for the acquisition of Genetic Systems.

SOURCE: Standard & Poor's *The Outlook.*

CHECKPOINTS FOR BARGAINS

Norman Weinger of Oppenheimer & Co., ever on the lookout for bargains, developed special checkpoints for finding undervalued situations. His criteria:

- Current yield 33.3% above Standard & Poor's 400 yield of 4.2%
- Current P/E is 33.3% below Standard & Poor's 400 P/E ratio of 13.1
- Current price to book value is 33.3% below Standard & Poor's 400s of 139%

Benjamin Graham, in his book *Security Analysis*, looks for bargains in stocks, which he defines as the time when they trade at:

- A multiple of no more than twice that of the prevailing interest rate: i.e., a P/E ratio of 16 vs. an interest rate of 8%.
- A discount of 20% or more from book value.

The Growth Stock Price Evaluator on page 139 can be used to make your own projections. It is most useful when studying fast-growing companies with above-average growth rates and cash flow, because it shows that if your growth assumptions are correct, the P/E ratio based on your cost today will be more modest.

Example: The stock of a small high-technology corporation is selling at 30 times current earnings. You estimate that over the next 5 years, earnings will grow at an average annual compound rate of 20%. The table shows that if this projection is correct, the stock will be selling at 12.1 times its anticipated 5-years-hence profits.

This evaluation technique can be reversed. Today the stock is selling at a multiple of 30, but you are not so sure about its future profits. From experience, you are willing to pay no more than 12 times future 5-year earnings for any growth stock. Checking the table, you find that the average annual growth rate must be 20% compounded annually to meet your investment standards. This stock just meets your criteria.

The Growth Stock Price Evaluator does *not* show the *future* price-to-earnings multiple or cash flow. They might be lower than, the same as, or greater than they are today.

There is a built-in offset: when the earnings (or cash flow) growth of a company is uninter-

advance budgets, and with a true growth company, this is a period long enough to balance out temporary dips and yet short enough to be reasonably accurate. If you read such a long-range forecast in an annual report, clip the notes for your research file.

HOW QUALITY PAYS OFF

COMPANY	STOCK PRICE CLOSE OF 1981	STOCK PRICE CLOSE OF 1985	DIVIDEND 1981	DIVIDEND 1985
Health Care Industry				
Hospital Corp. of America	$25.75	$35³/₄	$00.24	$00.57
Humana, Inc.	14.61	31¹/₄	.25	.68
Restaurants and Food				
McDonald's Corp.	29	80⁷/₈	.42	.88
Shoney's, Inc.	8	29¹/₂	.08	.15
Electronics and Electrical				
Emerson Electric	45³/₈	81¹/₂	1.82	2.64
Loral Corp.	16³/₄	36¹/₂	.36	.50
Retail Stores				
American Stores	9	64³/₄	.26	.64
Dayton-Hudson	15	45⁷/₈	.51	.76

SOURCE: Standard & Poor's.

HIGHLY PROFITABLE COMPANIES

| COMPANY | 10 YEAR AVERAGE | | RETURN ON EQUITY |
	EARNINGS/ GROWTH	DIVIDEND/ GROWTH	
Abbott Laboratories	+20%	+35%	25.6
Albertson's, Inc.	+16	+27	22.0
Ames Dept. Stores	+23	+11	23.1
Barry Wright Corp.	+15	+30	18.2
Bob Evans Farms	+22	+26	23.1
Church's Fr. Chicken	+9	+29	22
Community Psychia.	+33	+21	26.5
E.G. & G., Inc.	+22	+22	28.4
E-Systems, Inc.	+15	+29	21.6
Flightsafety Inter.	+28	+11	26.7
Fort Howard Paper	+14	+31	22.1
Harland (John H.)	+21	+30	26.0
Hewlett-Packard	+18	+10	18.7
Loral Corporation	+18	+27	21.2
Medtronic, Inc.	+16	+18	20.4
Miller (Herman)	+25	+18	24.5
Payless Cashways	+18	+12	19.0
Salomon Inc.	+17	+18	25.0
Revco, D.S.	+5	+32	18.7
Schlumberger, Ltd.	+4	+25	24.2
Servicemaster, Inc.	+24	+70	42.9
Shared Medical	+27	+28	33.6
Shoney's, Inc.	+23	+14	23.9
SmithKline Beckman	+20	+41	29.9
Super Valu Stores	+20	+29	25.1
Tandy Corp.	+29	—	29.6
Tracor, Inc.	+15	+16	18.9
United Industrial	+17	+27	23.3
U.S. Shoe	+16	+28	18.3
VF Corp.	+21	+29	27.9
Wal-Mart Stores	+37	+12	35.2
Waste Management	+28	+23	21.1

SOURCE: Wright Investors' Service.

rupted, the price of its stock tends to rise faster than earnings. This is almost always the case when the stock's P/E ratio is still below the stratosphere.

The greatest risk in buying and holding growth stocks lies in overestimating their probable future rate of growth in earnings. Too many investors project recent earnings growth automatically. That's OK if you have access to complete data and can make frequent revisions, but when such forecasts go awry, the price of such glamor issues can collapse. That's why it can be so costly to hold an overpriced equity.

THE GROWTH STOCK PRICE EVALUATOR
How to Weigh Prices of Growth Stocks in Terms of Their Future Gains in Earnings or Cash Flow

| IF— A STOCK NOW SELLS AT THIS MANY TIMES ITS CURRENT EARNINGS OR CASH FLOW: | —AND YOU BELIEVE ITS AVERAGE ANNUAL GROWTH IN EARNINGS OR CASH FLOW PER SHARE (COMPOUNDED) WILL BE: THEN—HERE IS HOW MANY TIMES ITS PROJECTED EARNINGS OR CASH FLOW PER SHARE FIVE YEARS HENCE THE STOCK IS CURRENTLY SELLING AT: | | | | | | |
	10%	15%	20%	25%	30%	40%	50%
12	7.5	6.0	4.8	3.9	3.2	2.2	1.6
14	8.7	7.0	5.6	4.6	3.8	2.6	1.8
16	9.9	8.0	6.5	5.2	4.3	3.0	2.1
18	11.2	9.0	7.3	5.9	4.9	3.3	2.4
20	12.4	10.0	8.1	6.6	5.4	3.7	2.6
22	13.7	10.9	8.9	7.2	5.9	4.1	2.9
24	14.9	11.9	9.7	7.9	6.5	4.5	3.2
26	16.1	12.9	10.5	8.5	7.0	4.8	3.4
28	17.4	13.9	11.3	9.2	7.5	5.2	3.7
30	18.6	14.9	12.1	9.8	8.1	5.6	3.9
32	19.9	15.9	12.9	10.5	8.6	5.9	4.2
34	21.1	16.9	13.7	11.1	9.2	6.3	4.5
36	22.4	17.9	14.5	11.8	9.7	6.7	4.7
38	23.6	18.9	15.3	12.5	10.2	7.1	5.0
40	24.8	19.9	16.1	13.1	10.8	7.4	5.3
42	26.1	20.9	16.9	13.8	11.3	7.8	5.5
44	27.3	21.9	17.7	14.4	11.9	8.2	5.8
46	28.6	22.9	18.5	15.1	12.4	8.6	6.1
48	29.8	23.9	19.4	15.7	12.9	8.9	6.3
50	31.1	24.9	20.2	16.4	13.5	9.3	6.6

WHAT THE NUMBERS TELL YOU:
Balance Sheets Made Simple

The idea is to buy low and sell high. This sounds easy, but it isn't. You must determine what is *low* and, to a lesser degree, what is *high.* That's where value comes in. The surest way to make money in the stock market is to buy securities when they are undervalued and have prospects of appreciation and to sell them when they become fully priced. *Value shows the range in which a stock should be bought or sold and thus provides the base for investment profits.* Value also indicates whether or not, and to what extent, a stock is likely to advance or decline from its present price.

Value is not always what it should be or appears to be. A stock selling at 100 drops to 50 because some institutions lose confidence in the future. The different market values reflect investor optimism or pessimism. If investors look for higher earnings, chances are that the price of the stock will rise. Vice versa with lower profits.

But those earnings are subject to interpretation and, in some cases, to manipulation. With established well-managed firms, earnings usually reflect how many real dollars the company made in a reporting period. With speculative, promotion-minded management, those earnings can be inflated with special adjustments: shifts in depreciation policy, inclusion of one-time gains, and so forth.

Value itself is based on financial "facts," as stated in the corporate reports; the projections rely on analyses of past performance, present strength, and future progress. When you select quality stocks on the basis of value (or undervaluation), you will almost always make money, often quickly with speculative situations; usually slowly with major corporations. To find value,

you must understand the basics of financial analysis, our next step.

HOW TO ANALYZE FINANCIAL REPORTS

Financial analysis is not easy for the uninitiated, but once you get the swing of things, you can pick the few quality stocks from the thousands of publicly owned securities; and if you are speculation-minded, you can find bargains with securities of mediocre or even poor corporations.

Basic figures and ratios show the company's current and prospective financial condition, past and prospective earning power and growth, and, thus, investment desirability.

Publicly owned corporations issue their financial reports on an annual, semiannual, or quarterly basis. Most of the information important to the investor can be found in: (1) the balance sheet; (2) the profit and loss, or income, statement; (3) the change in financial position or the "flow of funds" data. In each of these you should look for:

- *The key quantities:* net tangible assets, changes in working capital, sales costs, profits, taxes, dividends, etc.
- *The significant rates and ratios:* price-earnings multiples, profit rates, growth in net worth, earnings, dividends, etc.
- *The comparison of a corporation with a standard:* that of its industry, the stock market, the economy, or some other broader base.

Here's how to find value (and other important information) for a company. The data and explanations are digested from *Understanding Financial Statements,* prepared by the New

York Stock Exchange. Ask your broker to get you a copy, or write to the address given at the end of the chapter.

INCOME AND RETAINED EARNINGS

Here's where you find out *how the corporation fared for the past year* in comparison with the two previous annual reporting periods: how much money the company took in, how much was spent for expenses and taxes, and the size of the resulting profits (if any) that were available for distribution to shareholders or for reinvestment in the business. Income and retained earnings are the basis for comparison within this company and with firms in the same or similar business.

SALES

How much business does the company do in a year? With public utilities, insurance firms, and service organizations, the term "revenues" is often used instead of sales. In the past year, corporate sales in the sample corporation shown were up $5.8 million, a gain of 5.3%, not quite as good as the 5.5% rise the year before. Net income per share (middle) was also just slightly better: $.4 million (to $9.9 from $9.5), +4.2%. Check these figures against those of the industry and major competitors. They may be better than they appear.

COSTS AND EXPENSES

➤ COST OF GOODS SOLD The dollars spent to keep the business operating. The $3.2 million

STATEMENT OF INCOME AND RETAINED EARNINGS
"Your Company"

MILLIONS	CURRENT YEAR	PREVIOUS YEAR	2 YEARS AGO
	DECEMBER 31 YEAR-END		
Sales	$115.8	$110.0	$104.5
Less:			
Costs and Expenses:			
Cost of goods sold	$ 76.4	$ 73.2	$ 70.2
Selling, general, and administrative expenses	14.2	13.0	12.1
Depreciation	2.6	3.5	2.3
	$ 93.2	$ 89.7	$ 84.6
Operating Profit	$ 22.6	$ 20.3	$ 19.9
Interest charges	1.3	1.0	1.3
Earnings before income taxes	$ 21.3	$ 19.3	$ 18.6
Provision for taxes on income	11.4	9.8	9.5
Net income (per common share for year: current-$5.24; last-$5.03; 2 years ago-$4.97)*	$ 9.9	$ 9.5	$ 9.1
Retained Earnings, Beginning of Year	42.2	37.6	33.1
Less dividends paid on:	$ 52.1	$ 47.1	$ 42.2
Preferred stock ($5 per share)	(.3)	(.3)	–
Common stock (per share: this year-$3.00; last year-$2.50; 2 years ago-$2.50)	(5.4)	(4.6)	(4.6)
Retained Earnings, End of Year	$ 46.4	$ 42.2	37.6

* After preferred share dividend requirements.

more was less than the $5.8 million increase in sales.

➤ SELLING, GENERAL, AND ADMINISTRATIVE EXPENSES The costs of getting products or services to customers and getting paid. These will vary with the kind of business: high for consumer goods manufacturers and distributors because of advertising; lower for companies selling primarily to industry or government.

➤ DEPRECIATION A bookkeeping item to provide for wear, tear, and obsolescence of machinery and equipment, presumably to set aside reserves for replacement. The maximum calculations are set by tax laws. Typically, a straight-line method might charge the same amount each year for a specified number of years. Or, with accelerated methods, the deductions would be higher in the early years.

With companies in the natural resource business, the reduction in value is depletion, again calculated over a period of years.

By changing the type of depreciation, a company can increase or decrease earnings, so always be wary when this happens.

OPERATING PROFIT

The dollars generated from the company's usual operations without regard to income from other sources or financing. As a percentage of sales, it tells the profit margin: a rising 19.5% in the last year compared with 18.5% the year before.

➤ INTEREST CHARGES The interest paid to bondholders. It is deductible before taxes. The available earnings should be many times the mandated interest charges: in this case, a welcome 17 times before provision for income taxes (i.e., $22.6 \div $1.3 = 17).

➤ EARNINGS BEFORE INCOME TAXES The operating profit minus interest charges. When companies have complicated reports, this can be a confusing area.

➤ PROVISION FOR TAXES ON INCOME The allocation of money for Uncle Sam—a widely variable figure because of exemptions, special credits, etc., from about 5% for some companies to 34% for industrial corporations.

➤ NET INCOME FOR THE YEAR: *the bottom line.* This was 4.2% better than the year before— about the same as recorded in the previous period. This was no record breaker and works out better on a per share basis: $5.24 vs. $5.03.

One year's change is interesting, but the true test of management's ability comes over 5 to 10 years.

Use this figure to make other comparisons (against sales: 8.5% vs. 8.6% the year before) and then relate this to returns of other companies in the same industry. The average manufacturing corporation earns about 5¢ per dollar of sales, but supermarkets are lucky to end up with 1¢ against shareowners' equity: the profit rate (PR) explained in the previous chapter. Here, the PR was a modest 13%.

To find the earnings per share, divide the net income (less preferred dividend requirements) by the average number of shares outstanding during the year. This is the key figure for most analysts. It is also used to determine the price-earnings (P/E) ratio: divide the market price of the stock by the per share profits. If the stock was selling at 30, the P/E would be 10—slightly above the average of most publicly owned shares.

➤ RETAINED EARNINGS The dollars reinvested for future growth, always an important indication of future prospects. If the company continues to boost this figure, its basic value will increase. At the same PR, earnings will increase and, eventually, so will the value of the common stock.

Here the company keeps plowing back more: $4.6 million last year vs. $4.5 million the year before. (Subtract the retained earnings at the beginning of year from retained earnings of the previous year; i.e., $37.6 minus $33.1 = $4.5.)

➤ DIVIDENDS The amount paid out to shareholders for the use of their money. The $5 per share paid on the preferred stock is fixed. The payments for the common move with profits: last year up 50¢ per share to $3.00 from the flat $2.50 of the last two prior years.

Note that this statement shows earnings retained as of the beginning and end of each year. Thus, the company reinvested $46.4 million for the future.

BALANCE SHEET ITEMS

Now that you know what happened in the last year, it's time to take a look at the financial strength (or weakness) of the corporation. On page 143 is a typical balance sheet. Use it as the basis for reviewing annual reports of the companies in which you own, or plan to own, securities. The headings may vary according to the type of industry, but the basic data will be similar—and just as important.

CURRENT ASSETS

Items that can be converted into cash within 1 year. The total is $48.4 million this year, $4.2 million more than last year.

➤ CASH Mostly bank deposits, including compensating balances held under terms of a loan—like keeping a savings account to get free checking.

➤ MARKETABLE SECURITIES Corporate and government securities that can be sold quickly. In the current year, these were eliminated.

➤ RECEIVABLES Amounts due from customers for goods and services. This is a net amount after a set-aside for items that may not be collected.

➤ INVENTORIES Cost of raw materials, work in process, and finished goods. Statements and footnotes describe the basis, generally cost or current

BALANCE SHEET
"Your Company"

MILLIONS	DEC. 31 CURRENT YEAR	DEC. 31 PRIOR YEAR	MILLIONS	DEC. 31 CURRENT YEAR	DEC. 31 PRIOR YEAR
Assets			**Liabilities and Stockholders' Equity**		
Current Assets			**Current Liabilities**		
Cash	$ 9.0	$ 6.2	Accounts payable	$ 6.1	$ 5.0
Marketable securities	–	2.0	Accrued liabilities	3.6	3.3
Accounts and notes receivable	12.4	11.4	Current maturity of long-term debt	1.0	.8
Inventories	27.0	24.6	Federal income and other		
Total current assets	$ 48.4	$ 44.2	taxes	9.6	8.4
			Dividends payable	1.3	1.1
			Total Current Liabilities	$ 21.6	$ 18.6
Property, Plant, and Equipment					
Buildings, machinery, and			**Other Liabilities**	3.6	2.5
equipment, at cost	104.3	92.7	Long-term debt		
Less accumulated depreciation	27.6	25.0	5% sinking-fund debentures,		
	$ 76.7	$ 67.7	due July 31, 1987	26.0	20.0
Land, at cost	.9	.7	**Stockholders' Equity**		
Total property, plant, and			5% cumulative preferred		
equipment	$ 77.6	$ 68.4	stock ($100 par: authorized		
			and outstanding-60,000)	6.0	6.0
			Common stock ($10 par:		
Other Assets			authorized-2,000,000;		
Receivables due after 1			outstanding-1,830,000)	18.3	18.3
year	4.7	3.9	Additional paid-in capital	9.6	9.6
Surrender value of insurance	.2	.2	Retained earnings	46.4	42.2
Other	.6	.5	Total stockholders' equity	$ 80.3	$ 76.1
Total other assets	$ 5.5	$ 4.6			
			Total Liabilities, and		
Total Assets	$131.5	$117.2	**Stockholders' Equity**	$131.5	$117.2

market price, whichever is lower. To handle the additional business, these were up over those of the previous year.

PROPERTY, PLANT, AND EQUIPMENT

The land, structures, machinery and equipment, tools, motor vehicles, etc. Except for land, these assets have a limited useful life, and a deduction is taken from cost as depreciation. With a new plant, the total outlays were $11.6 million more, with depreciation up $2.6 million.

➤ OTHER ASSETS Identifiable property is valued at cost. Intangibles such as patents, copyrights, franchises, trademarks, or goodwill cannot be assessed accurately, so they are omitted from the computation of tangible net worth or book value.

If an increase in sales does not follow an increased investment, management may have misjudged the ability to produce and/or sell more goods, or the industry may have reached overcapacity. If a company's plant and equipment show little change for several years during a period of expanding business, the shareholder should be cautious about the company's progressiveness. In this example, both fixed and total assets grew steadily.

LIABILITIES AND STOCKHOLDERS' EQUITY

Divided into two classes: current or payable within a year and long-term debt or other obligations that come due after 1 year from the balance sheet date.

➤ ACCOUNTS PAYABLE Money owed for raw materials, other supplies, and services.

➤ ACCRUED LIABILITIES Unpaid wages, salaries and commissions, interest, etc.

➤ CURRENT LONG-TERM DEBT Amount due in next year. This usually requires annual repayments over a period of years.

➤ INCOME TAXES Accrued federal, state, and local taxes.

➤ DIVIDENDS PAYABLE Preferred or common dividends (or both) declared but not yet paid. Once declared, dividends become a corporate obligation.

➤ TOTAL CURRENT LIABILITIES An increase of $3 million needed to finance expansion of business.

➤ LONG-TERM DEBT What's due for payment in the future less the amount due in the next

year. Although the total was reduced to $20 million, an additional $6 million of debentures were issued.

STOCKHOLDERS' EQUITY (or CAPITAL)

All funds invested in the business by stockholders as well as reinvested earnings.

➤ PREFERRED STOCK Holders are usually entitled to dividends before common stockholders and to priority in the event of dissolution or liquidation. Dividends are fixed. If cumulative, no dividends can be paid on common stock until the preferred dividends are up to date.

Here each share of preferred was issued at $100, but its market value will move with the cost of money: UP when interest rates decline; DOWN when they rise.

➤ COMMON STOCK Shown on the books at par value, an arbitrary amount having no relation to the market value or to what would be received in liquidation.

➤ ADDITIONAL PAID-IN CAPITAL The amount of money received from the sale of stock in excess of the par value.

➤ RETAINED EARNINGS Money reinvested in the business.

➤ TOTAL STOCKHOLDERS' EQUITY The sum of the common par value, additional paid-in capital, and retained earnings less any premium attributable to the preferred stock: what the stockholders own. The increase of $4.2 million is a rise of about 5%—not bad, but not as much as should be the mark of a true growth company.

CHANGES IN FINANCIAL POSITION

This presents a different view of the financing and investing activities of the company and clarifies the disposition of the funds produced by operations. It includes both cash and other elements of working capital—the excess of current assets over current liabilities.

The balance sheet shows that the working capital has increased by $1.2 million (current assets of $48.4 million exceeded current liabilities of $21.6 million by $26.8 million at the end of the year vs. $25.6 million the year before).

Sales and net income were up; the contribution to working capital from operations decreased to $13.6 million vs. $15 million the year before. This was narrowed to $.4 million by the proceeds of the $7 million in long-term debt, $1 million more than the proceeds from the sale of preferred stock the year before.

The difference between the funds used last year and the year before was $1.1 million, reflecting a heavier investment in productive capacity against a larger repayment of long-term debt the year before.

STATEMENT OF CHANGES IN FINANCIAL POSITION
"Your Company"

MILLIONS	DEC. 31 CURRENT YEAR	DEC. 31 LAST YEAR	DEC. 31 2 YEARS AGO
Funds Provided			
Net income	$ 9.9	$ 9.5	$ 9.1
Changes not requiring working capital:			
Depreciation	2.6	3.5	2.3
Increase in other liabilities	1.1	2.0	1.4
Funds provided by operations	$13.6	$15.0	$12.8
Proceeds from long-term debt	7.0	–	–
Proceeds from sale of 5% cumulative preferred stock	–	6.0	–
Total funds provided	$20.6	$21.0	$12.8
Funds Used			
Additions to fixed assets	$11.8	$ .5	$ 6.2
Dividends paid on preferred stock	.3	.3	–
Dividends paid on common stock	5.4	4.6	4.6
Payments on long-term debt	1.0	15.0	–
Increase in noncurrent receivables	.8	.1	.3
Increase in other assets	.1	–	.2
Total funds used	$19.4	$20.5	$11.3
Increase in working capital	$ 1.2	$ .5	$ 1.5
Changes in Components of Working Capital			
Increase (decrease) in current assets:			
Cash	$ 2.8	$ 1.0	$ 1.1
Marketable securities	(2.0)	.5	.4
Accounts receivable	1.0	.5	.8
Inventories	2.4	1.0	1.3
Increase in current assets	$ 4.2	$ 3.0	$ 3.6
Increase in current liabilities:			
Accounts payable	$ 1.1	$ .9	$ .6
Accrued liabilities	.3	.5	.2
Current maturity of long-term debt	.2	.1	.5
Federal income and other taxes	1.2	1.0	.8
Dividends payable	.2	–	–
Increase in current liabilities	$ 3.0	$ 2.5	$ 2.1
Increase in working capital	$ 1.2	$ .5	$ 1.5

With increased capacity, the company should be able to handle higher sales. The additional cash may be a good sign, but when too much cash accumulates, it may indicate that management is not making the best use of its assets. In financially tense times, cash is still always welcome.

SEVEN KEYS TO VALUE

1 **Operating profit margin (PM).** The ratio of profit (before interest and taxes) to sales. The operating profit ($22.6) divided by sales ($115.8) equals 19.5%. This compares with 18.5% for the previous year. (Some analysts prefer to compute this margin without including depreciation and depletion as part of the cost, because these have nothing to do with the efficiency of the operation.)

When a company increases sales substantially, the PM should widen, because certain costs (rent, interest, property taxes, etc.) are pretty much fixed and do not rise in proportion to volume.

2 **Current ratio.** The ratio of current assets to current liabilities: $48.4 divided by $21.6 equals 2.24. For most industrial corporations, this ratio should be about 2:1. It varies with the type of business. Utilities and retail stores have rapid cash inflows and high turnovers of dollars, so they can operate effectively with low ratios.

When the ratio is high, say, 5:1, it may mean that the company has too much cash and is not making the best use of these funds. They should be used to expand the business. Such corporations are often targets for takeovers.

3 **Liquidity ratio.** The ratio of cash and equivalents to total current liabilities ($9 divided by $21.6 = 41.7%). It should be used to supplement the current ratio, because the immediate ability of a company to meet current obligations or pay larger dividends may be impaired despite a high current ratio. This 41.7% liquidity ratio (down from 44.1% the year before) probably indicates a period of expansion, rising prices, heavier capital expenditures, and larger accounts payable.

If the decline persists, the company might have to raise additional capital.

4 **Capitalization ratios.** The percentage of each type of investment as part of the total investment in the corporation. Though often used to describe only the outstanding securities, capitalization is the sum of the face value of bonds and other debts *plus* the par value of all preferred and common stock issues *plus* the balance sheet totals for capital surplus and retained earnings.

Bond, preferred stock, and common stock ratios are useful indicators of the relative risk and leverage involved for the owners of the three types of securities. For most industrial corporations, the debt ratio should be no more than 66⅔% of equity, or 40% of total capital.

In this instance, the long-term debt plus preferred stock is 43.1% of the equity represented by the common stock and surplus, and 30.1% of total capital.

Higher ratios are appropriate for utilities and transportation corporations.

5 **Sales-to-fixed-assets ratio.** Computed by dividing the annual sales ($115.8) by the year-end value of plant, equipment, and land before depreciation and amortization ($104.3 plus $.9 equals $105.2). The ratio is therefore 1.1:1. This is down from 1.2:1 the year before.

KEYS TO VALUE

	CURRENT YEAR	PRIOR YEAR
1. Operating profit margin	19.5%	18.5%
2. Current ratio	2.24	2.38
3. Liquidity ratio	41.7%	44.1%
4. Capitalization ratios:		
Long-term debt	24.4%	20.8%
Preferred stock	5.7	6.3
Common stock and surplus	69.9	72.9
5. Sales to fixed assets	1.1	1.2
6. Sales to inventories	4.3	4.5
7. Net income to net worth	12.3%	12.5%

This ratio helps to show whether funds used to enlarge productive facilities are being wisely spent. A sizable expansion in facilities should lead to larger sales volume. If it does not, there's something wrong. In this case, there were delays in getting production on stream at the new plant.

6 **Sales-to-inventories ratio.** Computed by dividing the annual sales by year-end inventories: $115.8 divided by $27 equals a 4.3:1 ratio. The year before, the ratio was 4.5:1.

This shows inventory turnover: the number of times the equivalent of the year-end inventory has been bought and sold during the year.

It is more important in analyzing retail corporations than in analyzing manufacturers. A high ratio denotes a good quality of merchandise and correct pricing policies. A declining ratio may be a warning signal.

7 **Net-income-to-net-worth (return on equity) ratio.** One of the most significant of all financial ratios. Derived by dividing the net income ($9.9) by the total of the preferred stock, common stock, and surplus accounts ($80.3). The result is 12.3%: the percentage of return that corporate management earned on the dollars entrusted by shareholders at the beginning of each year. Basically, it's that all-important PR (profit rate).

This 12.3% is a slight decrease from the 12.5% of the prior year. It's a fair return: not as good as that achieved by a top-quality corporation but better than that of the average publicly held company. *The higher the ratio, the more profitable the operation.* Any company which can consistently improve such a ratio is a true growth company. *But be sure that this gain is due to operating skill, not to accounting legerdemain or extraordinary items.*

RATIOS AND TRENDS

Detailed financial analysis involves careful evaluation of income, costs, and earnings. But it is also important to study various ratios and trends, both those within the specific corporation and those of other companies in the same industry. Analysts usually prefer to use 5- or 10-year averages. These can reveal significant changes and, on occasion, point out special values in either concealed or inconspicuous assets.

➤ OPERATING RATIO The ratio of operating costs to sales. It is the complement of *profit margin* (100% minus the PM percentage). Thus, if a company's PM is 10%, its operating ratio is 90%. It's handy for comparing similar companies, but not significant otherwise.

PMs vary with the type of business. They are low for companies with heavy plant investments (Ingersoll-Rand) and for retailers with fast turnovers (Eckerd, Jack) and high for marketing firms such as Gillette.

➤ INTEREST COVERAGE The number of times interest charges or requirements have been earned. Divide the operating profit (or balance available for such payments before income taxes and interest charges) by the annual interest charges.

Here the interest (fixed charges) was covered 17.4 times in the past year and 20.3 times in the previous year. This is a high, safe coverage. If earnings declined to only 6% of the past year's results, interest would still be covered. As a rule, a manufacturing company should cover interest five times; utilities, three times.

Keep in mind that when a company (except utilities or transportation firms) has a high debt, it means that investors shy away from buying its common stock. To provide the plants, equipment, etc., which the company needs, management must issue bonds or preferred shares (straight or convertible to attract investors). There are some tax advantages in following such a course, but when the debt becomes too high, there can be trouble during times of recession. All, or almost all, the gross profits will have to be used to pay interest and there will be nothing, or little, left over for the common stockholders.

On the other hand, speculators like high-debt situations when business is good. With hefty profits, interest can be paid easily and the balance comes down to the common stock. Typically, airlines with heavy debt obligations for new planes do well in boom times. An extra 10% gain in traffic can boost profits by as much as 30%.

➤ PAYOUT RATIO The ratio of the cash dividends to per share profits after taxes. Fast-growing corporations pay no or small dividends because they need money for expansion. Profitable companies pay out from about 25 to 50% of their profits. Utilities, which have almost assured earnings, pay out more. But be wary when those dividends represent much more than 70% of income.

It's pleasant to receive an ample dividend check, but for growth, look for companies that pay small dividends. The retained earnings will be used to improve financial strength and the operating future of the company. *And they are tax-free.*

➤ PRICE-TO-BOOK-VALUE RATIO The market price of the stock divided by its book value per share. Since book value trends are usually more stable than earnings trends, conservative analysts use this ratio as a price comparison. They check the historical over- or undervaluation of the stock, which in turn depends primarily on the company's profitable growth (or lack of it).

Because of inflation, understatement of assets on balance sheets—and, in boom times, the enthusiasm of investors—often pushes this ratio rather high. On the average, only stocks of the most profitable companies sell at much more than twice book value. Investors believe that these corporations will continue to achieve ever-higher earnings. But if the stock prices rise too high, their decline, in a bear market, can be fast and far.

➤ PRICE-EARNINGS (P/E) RATIO Calculated by dividing the price of the stock by the reported earnings per share for the past 12 months. Such projections can be made ONLY with stocks of quality corporations with long, fairly consistent records of profitable growth. They will not work with shares of companies that are cyclical, erratic, or untested. There can be no guarantee that these goals will be attained as soon as anticipated. Wall Street is often slow to recognize value and always takes time to come to intelligent decisions.

➤ CASH FLOW A yardstick that is increasingly popular in investment analysis. Reported net earnings after taxes do not reflect the actual cash income available to the company. Cash flow shows the earnings after taxes *plus* charges against income that do not directly involve cash outlays (sums allocated to depreciation, depletion, amortization, and other special items).

A company might show a net profit of $250,000 plus depreciation of $1 million, so cash flow is $1,250,000. Deduct provisions for preferred dividends (if any), and then divide the balance by the number of shares of common stock to get the cash flow per share.

Two types of cash flow are:

Distributable cash flow: the amount of money that the company has on hand to pay dividends and/or invest in real growth. If this is negative, there are problems. If it's positive, fine, *unless* the company pays out more than this figure in dividends and is thus liquidating the firm.

Discretionary cash flow: distributable cash flow minus dividends, i.e., how much money is left to grow with, after allocations for maintenance and dividends. Companies do not actually set aside such funds, but, they must ultimately have the money in some form—cash savings or borrowing.

HOW TO DETERMINE A PRUDENT P/E RATIO

Analysts usually justify their recommendations by adjusting the multiple of the price of the

---

DIVIDENDS AS PERCENTAGE OF EARNINGS: 1986

COMPANY	PERCENTAGE PAYOUT
Allegheny Power	75%
American Can	57
Baltimore Gas & Electric	58
Bank of New York	32
Chesebrough-Pond's	85
Circle K	30
Coca-Cola	53
Dun & Bradstreet	54
Exxon Corp.	53
Paine Webber	35
Ralston Purina	31
Syntex Corp.	43
Tribune Co.	27
U.S. Steel	64

SOURCE: Standard & Poor's *The Outlook,* May 1986.

stock by estimated rate of future growth or by cash flow per share rather than by reported earnings. In both cases, these are attempts to justify a predetermined decision to buy. The projections appear plausible, especially when accompanied by tables and charts and computer printouts. But in most cases, they are useful only as background and not for the purpose of making decisions on the proper level to buy or later to sell. The calculations depend a good deal on market conditions and your own style, but here's one approach for those "supergrowth" stocks that will be suggested by your friends or broker.

Example: According to your financial adviser, the stock of a "future" company now selling at 40 times its recent earnings will be trading at "only 16 times its projected earnings 5 years hence IF the company's average earnings growth is 20% a year." (See Price Evaluator page 139.)

If you are speculating with this type of "hot" stock, you should compare it with other opportunities and on some basis decide how reasonable this projection really is.

A handy formula is:

PRU PER = G R Q M T

PRU PER = Prudent P/E ratio

➤ G = GROWTH The company's projected growth in earnings per share over the next 5 years. The basic compound interest formula is $(1 + G)^5$, where G is the projected growth rate, as shown in the Price Evaluator and prudent P/E multiples table. This omits dividend yields because they are usually small in relation to the potential capital appreciation.

➤ R = RELIABILITY AND RISK Not all projected growth rates are equally reliable or probable. A lower projected growth rate is likely to be more reliable than a very high projected one (30 to 50% a year).

Logically, you can assign a higher reliability rating to a noncyclical company (utility, food processor, retailer) than to a corporation in a cyclical industry (aluminum, machinery, tools).

➤ T = TIME Another factor is the assumed length of the projected growth period. If you can realistically anticipate that the company will continue its rate of growth for the next 10 years, a 10% rate for its stock is more reliable than a 15% rate for a company whose growth visibility is only 3 to 5 years.

If you are uncertain about the corporation's consistency, you should assign it the greater risk.

➤ Q = QUALITY As you know, this is the single most important investment consideration.

➤ M = MULTIPLE OF PRICE TO EARNINGS This is a comparative measurement. The first step is to determine the P/E for an average quality nongrowth stock. This is done by relating the current yield on guaranteed, fixed income investments (savings accounts, corporate bonds) to the P/E multiple that will produce the same yield on the nongrowth stock.

P/E = Price/earnings ratio
D = Dividend as percentage payout of earnings
IR = Interest rate

$$P/E = \frac{D}{IR}$$

PRUDENT PRICE-EARNINGS MULTIPLES FOR GROWTH STOCKS

IF YOU PROJECT EARNINGS PER SHARE (AFTER TAXES) TO GROW IN NEXT 5 YEARS AT AVERAGE COMPOUNDED RATE OF:	WITH THESE QUALITY RATINGS* THESE ARE APPROXIMATE PRUDENT MULTIPLES WHICH REPRESENT THE MAXIMUM CURRENT PRICE TO PAY:				
	B	B+	A−	A	A+
5%	12.0	12.9	13.7	15.0	16.7
6%	12.5	13.4	14.3	15.8	17.4
7%	13.0	14.0	14.9	16.5	18.2
8%	13.6	14.5	15.6	17.1	18.9
9%	14.1	15.1	16.2	17.8	19.7
10%	14.6	15.7	16.8	18.5	20.4
15%	17.4	18.7	20.1	22.0	24.5
20%	20.2	21.8	23.4	25.7	28.6
25%	23.0	24.7	26.6	29.3	32.7
30%	25.2	27.3	29.4	32.5	36.2
35%	28.5	31.0	33.5	37.1	41.5
40%	31.9	34.8	37.7	41.7	46.7

*Standard & Poor's designations. If not rated, use B; if new, untested firm, use a conservative rating based on comparison with similar companies, preferably in the same industry.

SOURCE: Standard & Poor's.

Thus, a stock yielding 8% on a 70% payout of profits must, over a 5-year period, be bought and sold at 7 times earnings to break even on capital and to make as much income as could be obtained, over the same period via the ownership of a fixed-income investment continually yielding 10%:

$$P/E = \frac{7}{10} = 7$$

Note: This is NOT a valid comparison in terms of investment alone. Since the nongrowth stock carries a certain amount of risk in comparison to the certainty of a bond or money market fund, the stock should sell at a lower multiple, probably 5 to 6 times earnings.

Other key items used in analysis are:

➤ EARNINGS GROWTH RATE A formula that gives the rate at which a company's profits have increased over the past several years. You can find the earnings growth rate in annual reports or from your broker. Then divide it by the P/E and compare this number with the Standard & Poor's 500 in order to decide whether to buy or sell. Keep in mind that in good years the average growth rate for the Standard & Poor's 500 stock index has been 16% and the average P/E 8, so that the index for the purposes of this formula should be divided by 2.

For example, let us assume that Company XYZ has an earnings growth rate of 40% per year. Its P/E is 20; its index is therefore 2, only equal to the Standard & Poor's average—nothing to get excited about.

Another company, the LMN Corporation, has an earnings growth rate of 40% also; however, its P/E is 15, so that its index comes out to be 2.6. Because this ratio is above the Standard & Poor's index of 2, it is an apparent bargain.

➤ PERCENTAGE BUYING VALUE This is a variation of the formula developed by John B. Neff of the Windsor Fund. It uses the current yield plus the rate of earnings growth divided by the current P/E ratio. If the result is 2 or more, the stock is worth buying:

CY = Current yield
EG = Earnings growth
P/E = Price/earnings ratio
PBV = Percentage buying value

$$\frac{CY + EG}{P/E} = PBV$$

$$\frac{1.4 + 20}{22} = 9.7\% = BUY$$

$$\frac{8.6 + 2}{7.7} = 1.32\% = SELL \text{ or DO NOT BUY}$$

➤ RETURN ON EQUITY AND P/E: TOTAL RETURN Most investors tend to think about their gains and losses in terms of price changes and not dividends, whereas those who own bonds pay attention to interest yields and seldom focus on price changes. Both approaches are mistaken. Although dividend yields are obviously more important if you are seeking income, and changes in price play a greater role in growth stocks, knowing the *total return* on a stock makes it possible for you to compare your investment in a stock with a similar investment in a corporate bond, municipal, Treasury, mutual fund, etc.

To calculate the total return, add (or subtract) the stock's price change and the dividends received for 12 months and then divide that number by what the price was at the beginning of the 12-month period. For example: an investor bought a stock at $42 per share and received dividends for the 12-month period of $2.50. At the end of 12 months, the stock was sold at $45. The total return was 13%.

Dividend	$2.50
Stock price change	$3.00
	$5.50 ÷ $42 = 13%

➤ CORPORATE CASH POSITION Developed by Benjamin Graham, granddaddy of fundamentalists.

■ Subtract current liabilities, long-term debt, and preferred stock (at market value) from current assets of the corporation.

■ Divide the result by the number of shares of common stock outstanding to get the current asset value per share.

If it is higher than the price per share, Graham would place the stock on his review list.

CHECKPOINTS FOR FINDING UNDERVALUED STOCKS

■ A price that is well below book value, asset value, and working capital per share.

- Ample cash or liquid assets for both normal business and expansion.
- A current dividend of 4.5% or more.
- Cash dividends paid for at least 5, and preferably 10, years without decrease in dollar payout.
- Total debt less than 35% of total capitalization.
- Current dividend protection ratio of at least 1:4 and $1.40 earnings for each $1.00 in dividends.
- A P/E ratio lower than that of prior years and, preferably, below 10 times projected 12-month earnings.
- Earnings now depressed but a strong probability of higher profits in the near future, based on the historical record.
- Assets with heavy depreciation and thus large cash flow. A company that earns $1 per share and that can write off $3 per share actually generates $4 in cash that can be used for future growth.
- Realistically valued inventories. This is difficult to ascertain but can be checked by reviewing annual reports for the past several years.
- Gain-to-loss or risk-reward ratio a minimum of 2:1, i.e., based on past market action and future prospects, the probable price gain should be twice as great as the possible loss: a potential gain of 10 points vs. a possible 5-point decline.

LOW P/Es PAY OFF

Investors often get excited about stocks with high P/Es. They figure the stocks are so popular that their prices will keep on rising. But the facts prove otherwise: stocks with low P/Es (seemingly those with the worst prospects) outperform those with high multiples.

According to a 21-year study by analyst David Dreman, 80% of low P/E stocks scored better than average gains. He concludes that when investors become disappointed with high-multiple stocks, they tend to overreact and dump their shares, so their prices plummet. With low P/E groups, he found that the action is reversed. At the first sure sign of better earnings, their prices move up sharply.

PRICE/SALES RATIOS

There are successful investors who scoff at P/E ratios and prefer a PSR (price-sales ratio). To calculate this, divide the stock price by the per share revenues. Says Kenneth Fisher, a San Francisco money manager, "Stocks can be good buys when the PSR is between 0.75 and 1 and *may* be worthwhile investments when ratios move up to 3—if the corporate prospects are favorable."

Fisher argues that corporate sales tend to fluctuate less than earnings and points out that the P/E ratio is relative in that it can be the same even though the price of the stock has shifted sharply.

HINT: Do not buy any stock with a high PSR. In most cases, this presages a lower price soon. Do consider buying when the PSR is low if the company is financially strong and has prospects of improved earnings.

STOCKS WITH LOW INSTITUTIONAL OWNERSHIP

Most stocks listed on the New York Stock Exchange are more than 15% owned by institutions (such as insurance companies, pension funds, mutual funds, banks), but in the list on page 154, institutions own less than 15% of the outstanding shares of each company. The list can be viewed as one of overlooked values, especially if institutions decide to increase their ownership, thus pushing the prices up. (Institutions tend to follow one another both in and out of a company.) The fact that institutional ownership is low however may be for very valid reasons; therefore, this should not be regarded as a buy list, but merely as one way of finding potentially undervalued stocks.

COMPANIES REPURCHASING THEIR STOCK

When corporations set up a program to buy back their shares, it's a bullish sign. Over a 12-month period, one survey showed, 64% of such stock outpaced the market.

LOW P/E STOCKS

	P/E RATIO ON S&P 1986 EARNINGS ESTIMATE	4/18/86 STOCK PRICE	1986 S&P E.P.S. ESTIMATE	CURRENT YIELD ON INDICATED DIVD. RATE
Coleco Indus.	5.1	17	$3.45	. . .
Chrysler Corp.	5.2	41⅜	8.00	2.4%
Tonka Corp.	6.3	25⅜	4.00	0.3
Manufacturers Hanover	6.3	56	8.85	5.8
Gen'l Pub. Utilities	6.8	19¼	2.85	. . .
Unocal Corp.	7.0	22¾	3.25	5.3
Chase Manhattan	7.1	48	6.75	4.3
Golden West Fin'l	7.1	39½	5.50	0.4
Chemical New York	7.2	54	7.50	4.8
Ford Motor	7.2	83⅜	11.50	4.0
Ahmanson (H.F.)	7.2	65½	9.00	2.1
Houston Indus.	7.4	32	4.40	8.5
Commonwealth Edison	7.5	33⅞	4.50	8.9
Southern Co.	7.5	24⅝	3.25	8.3
First Chicago	7.5	32⅝	4.30	4.0
Philadelphia Elec.	7.6	19½	2.55	11.3
Citicorp	7.6	61½	8.00	4.0
Irving Bank	7.7	52½	6.75	4.0
Texas Utilities	7.7	34	4.50	7.7
Great West'n Fin'l	7.7	46⅝	6.00	2.1
Illinois Power	7.8	28	3.55	9.4
Marine Midland Bks.	8.0	55¼	6.90	3.3
Pacific Gas & Elec.	8.0	22⅝	2.80	8.1
Northeast Utilities	8.0	22¼	2.75	7.6
AZP Group	8.1	31	3.90	8.6
General Motors	8.2	81½	10.00	6.1
Lockheed Corp.	8.2	57½	7.00	1.4
New England El. Sys.	8.2	27¼	3.30	7.0
General Dynamics	8.2	87⅛	10.50	1.1
Bankers Trust N.Y.	8.3	49¼	5.90	3.0
Security Pacific	8.3	39	4.75	3.7
Ohio Edison	8.4	20⅝	2.45	9.3
Bank of Boston	8.5	38	4.45	3.5
National Fuel Gas	8.5	35⅝	4.15	5.8
Texas Commerce Bkshr.	8.6	23¼	2.70	6.7
Niagara Mohawk Pwr.	8.6	25⅛	2.90	8.3
Central & So. West	8.6	32⅛	3.70	6.7
Southwestern Bell Corp.	8.7	91¼	10.40	7.0

SOURCE: Standard & Poor's *The Outlook.*

	P/E RATIO ON S&P 1986 EARNINGS ESTIMATE	4/18/86 STOCK PRICE	1986 S&P E.P.S. ESTIMATE	CURRENT YIELD ON INDICATED DIVD. RATE
First Bank System	8.7	58	$6.70	3.0%
Dayco Corp.	8.8	22	2.50	1.1
RepublicBank Corp.	8.8	29⅛	3.30	5.6
Burlington Northern	8.8	70½	7.95	2.3
Transcon Inc.	8.8	9	1.10	. . .
First Interstate Bancorp.	8.9	66	7.40	3.8
US West Inc.	8.9	94	10.60	6.4
Kansas City Pwr. & Lt.	9.0	28⅝	3.15	8.2
PacifiCorp	9.0	35⅝	3.70	7.1
Equitable Resources	9.0	40	4.40	4.3
NBD Bancorp.	9.0	49¼	5.45	3.2
Consol. Natural Gas	9.1	47	5.20	5.5
Mellon Bank Corp.	9.2	70	7.60	3.9
Armco Inc.	9.2	9¼	1.00	. . .
Diversified Energies	9.2	25	2.70	5.6
Southern Cal. Edison	9.2	31	3.35	7.0
GTE Corp.	9.3	53½	5.75	5.9
Kansas Pwr. & Light	9.3	48⅞	5.25	6.5
Bank of New York	9.4	68⅞	7.35	3.3
Detroit Edison	9.4	18⅞	2.00	8.9
Public Sv. El. & Gas	9.4	37	4.00	7.5
MAPCO, Inc.	9.4	41⅛	4.35	2.4
Puget Sound P&L	9.4	21	2.30	8.1
Household Int'l	9.4	44½	4.70	4.1
Russ Togs	9.5	27⅛	2.85	2.8
Cont'l Telecom	9.5	30½	3.20	5.9
Sperry Corp.	9.5	53⅝	5.60	3.6
ALLTEL Corp.	9.6	34⅝	3.60	5.7
Cyclops Corp.	9.6	60⅛	6.25	1.8
Royal Dutch Petrol	9.6	77	8.00	4.3
First Fidelity Bancorp.	9.6	36⅝	3.80	4.3
NICOR Inc.	9.6	25⅝	2.65	7.0
Primark Corp.	9.7	27	2.85	4.0
Morgan (J.P.)	9.7	86	8.80	2.8
San Diego Gas & El.	9.7	33¾	3.45	6.6
CIGNA Corp.	9.8	69⅞	7.10	3.7
Phillips Petroleum	9.8	10⅞	1.10	9.2
Boston Edison	9.9	52¼	5.25	6.6
American Can	9.9	74⅜	7.45	3.9

STOCKS WITH LOW INSTITUTIONAL OWNERSHIP

	NO. OF INSTITUTIONS HOLDING SHARES	TOTAL SHARES HELD BY INSTITUTIONS (000)	STOCK PRICE	INSTI. HOLDINGS AS A % OF TOTAL SHARES
Advest Group	20	1,350	$19	16%
Amer. Heritage Life	19	300	42	9
Connecticut Energy	15	314	24	9
Green Mountain Power	16	500	24	15
Interstate Power	44	658	25	7
Iowa Elec. Lt. & Power	44	870	24	6
Katy Industries	26	1,532	19	24
Legg Mason, Inc.	23	1,140	29	22
Park Electrochemical	18	1,002	17	19
Rothschild, Unterberg	24	1,263	25	7
Showboat, Inc.	25	1,765	21	35
Tootsie Roll Industries	23	443	59	12
Williams Electronics	12	661	8	8

SOURCE: Standard & Poor's.

Repurchase of a substantial number of shares automatically benefits all shareholders: profits are spread over a smaller total; there's more money for dividends and reinvestments; and there's temporary market support.

During periods of recession, many corporations feel that their stocks are at bargain levels and represent a wise and fruitful use of corporate funds. With shares at 50% of book value, the purchase acquires $2 in assets for every $1 spent. The savings on dividends could be applied against the interest on loans made for the stock purchase.

FOR FURTHER INFORMATION

The Meaningful Interpretation of Financial Statements (by Donald E. Miller)
American Management Association, Inc.

135 West 50th Street
New York, NY 10020

"Understanding Financial Statements"
New York Stock Exchange
11 Wall Street
New York, NY 10005

Louis Engel & Brendon Boyd. *How to Buy Stocks.* Boston: Little, Brown & Co., 1953; Bantam paperback.

Benjamin Graham & David L. Dodd. *Security Analysis.* New York: McGraw-Hill, 4th ed., 1962.

Charles J. Rolo. *Gaining on the Market.* Boston: Little, Brown & Co., 1982.

Andrew Tobias. *The Only Investment Guide You'll Ever Need.* New York: Harcourt Brace Jovanovich Inc., 1978; Bantam paperback.

17   TECHNICAL ANALYSIS

Everyone who wants to be successful in the stock market should understand technical analysis (TA). Although it is more useful for trading than for investing, even die-hard fundamentalists heed charts and other indicators to improve the timing of their purchases and sales. With speculations, TA is essential; with investments, it can enhance profits and reduce losses.

TA is neither as complex nor as esoteric as many people think. It's a tell-it-as-it-is interpretation of stock-market activity. The technician glances at the fundamental values of securities but concentrates on the behavior of the market, industry groups, and stocks themselves—their price movements, volume, trends, patterns; in sum, their supply and demand.

Basically, TA is concerned with what *is* and not with what *should be.* Dyed-in-the-wool technicians pay minimal attention to what the *company* does and concentrate on what its *stock* does. They recognize that over the short term,

the values of stock reflect what people *think* they are worth, not what they are really worth.

Technical analysts operate on the assumption that (1) the past action of the stock market is the best indicator of its future course; (2) 80% of a stock's price movement is due to factors outside the company's control and 20% to factors unique to that stock; (3) the stock market over a few weeks or months is rooted 85% in psychology and only 15% in economics.

THE DOW THEORY

There are a number of technical theories, but the granddaddy is the Dow theory. It is the oldest and most widely used. As with all technical approaches, it is based on the belief that stock prices cannot be accurately forecast by fundamental analysis, at least not for the short term, but that there are trends, indicated by price movements and volume, that can be used successfully. And that these can be recorded, tracked, and interpreted because the market itself prolongs movements: investors buy more when the market is rising and sell more when it's dropping.

This follow-the-crowd approach is essential for traders. It enables them to buy when the market is going up and to sell or sell short when the market turns down. For amateurs, such quick trading can be costly because of the commissions and the need for accurate information. But when properly used, TA can be valuable in timing.

The Dow theory is named after Charles H. Dow, one of the founders of Dow Jones & Company, Inc., the financial reporting-publishing organization. The original hypotheses have been changed somewhat by followers, but broadly interpreted, the Dow theory signals both the beginning and end of bull and bear markets.

TECHNICAL vs. FUNDAMENTAL ANALYSIS

Technical analysis focuses on the changes of a company's stock as illustrated on daily, weekly, or periodic charts. Volume of number of trades is included, and from this "technical" information future price movements are forecast.

Fundamental analysis of industries and companies, on the other hand, centers upon the outlook for earnings and growth. Analysts study such factors as sales, assets, earnings, products, services, potential markets, and management.

Dow believed that the stock market is a barometer of business. The purpose of this theory is not to predict movements of security prices but rather to call the turns of the market and to forecast the business cycle or longer movements of depression or prosperity. It is not concerned with ripples or day-to-day fluctuations.

The Dow theory basically states that once a trend of the Dow Jones industrial average has been established, it tends to follow the same direction until definitely canceled by *both* the industrial and railroad (now transportation) averages. The market cannot be expected to produce new indications of the trend every day; and unless there is positive evidence to the contrary, the existing trend will continue.

Dow and his disciples saw the stock market as made up of two types of "waves": the *primary wave,* which is a bull or bear market cycle of several years' duration, and the *secondary* (or *intermediary*) *wave,* which lasts from a few weeks to a few months. Any single primary wave may contain within it a score or more of secondary waves, both up and down.

The theory relies on similar action by the two averages (industry and transportation), which may vary in strength but not in direction. Robert Rhea, who expanded the original concept, explained it this way: "Successive rallies, penetrating preceding high points with ensuing declines terminating above preceding low points, offer a bullish indication , . . (and vice versa for bearish indication). . . . A rally or decline is defined as one or more daily movements resulting in a net reversal of direction exceeding 3% of either average. Such movements have little authority unless confirmed by both Industrial and Transportation Averages . . . but confirmation need not occur in the same day."

Dow did not consider that his theory applied to individual stock selections or analysis. He expected that specific issues would rise or fall with the averages most of the time, but he also recognized that any particular security would be affected by special conditions or situations.

Dow made the point that "the business community has a tendency to go from one extreme to the other. It is either contracting business under a belief that prices will be lower or expanding under a belief that prices will be higher. It appears to take 5 or 6 years for public confidence to go from the point of too little hope

to the point of too much confidence and then 5 or 6 years to get back to the conditions of hopelessness."

The key indicators of the Dow theory are:

- **A bull market is signaled as a possibility** when an intermediate decline in the DJIA stops above the bottom of the previous intermediate decline. This action MUST BE CONFIRMED by the action of the DJTA. A bull market is confirmed after this has happened and when on the next intermediate rise BOTH averages rise above the peaks of the last previous intermediate rise.

- **A bull market is in progress** as long as each new intermediate rise goes *higher* than the peak of the previous intermediate advance and each new intermediate decline stops *above* the bottom of the previous one.

- **A bear market is signaled as a possibility** when an intermediate rally in the DJIA fails to break through the top of the previous intermediate rise. A bear market is *confirmed* (1) after this has happened, (2) when the next intermediate decline breaks through the low of the previous one, and (3) when it is confirmed by the DJTA.

- **A bear market is in progress** as long as each new intermediate decline goes *lower* than the bottom of the previous decline and each new intermediate rally fails to rise as high as the previous rally.

A pure Dow theorist considers the averages to be quite sufficient to use in forecasting. He sees no need to supplement them with statistics of commodity prices, volume of production, carloadings, bank debts, exports, imports, etc. The course of the stock market is clear when both averages shift from a bear market pattern— or vice versa—IF this is confirmed by another average: DJIA plus DJTA, for example.

INTERPRETING THE DOW THEORY

The Dow theory leaves no room for sentiment. A primary bear market does not terminate until stock prices have thoroughly discounted the worst that is apt to occur. This decline requires three steps: (1) "the abandonment of hopes upon which stocks were purchased at inflated prices"; (2) selling due to decreases in business and earnings; (3) distress selling of sound securities despite value.

Primary bull markets follow the opposite pattern: (1) a broad movement, interrupted by secondary reactions averaging longer than 2 years, where successive rallies penetrate high points with ensuing declines terminating above preceding low points; (2) stock prices advance because of demand created by both investors and speculators who start buying when business conditions improve; (3) rampant speculation as stocks advance on hopes, expectations, and dreams.

These broad swings may take years (1970–74) or happen quickly (1977–78). Markets do not normally go straight up or straight down but, according to Dow, "are subject to periodic interruptions by countermoves that are likely to retrace one third to two thirds of the original move before starting again in the primary direction. Thus, a bull market that rises 30 points will probably lose 10 to 20 points of its gain before resuming its ascent."

There are analysts who scoff at the Dow theory. They point out that the stock market today is vastly different from that in the early years of the century when Dow formulated his theory. The number and value of shares of publicly owned corporations have increased enormously: in 1900, the average number of shares traded *annually* on the NYSE was 59.5 million. Now that's a slow *day's* volume.

The sharpest criticism is leveled against the breadth, scope, and significance of the averages. The original industrial index had only 12 stocks, and today's 30 large companies (despite recent substitutions of IBM, Merck, and American Express) do not provide a true picture of the broad technologically oriented economy. Critics point out that the transportation average is also unrepresentative, because some of the railroads derive a major share of their revenues from natural resources, and the airlines and trucking companies are limited in their impact. Add the geographic disbursement of industry, and transportation is no longer a reliable guide to the economy.

Finally, the "purists" argue that government regulations and institutional dominance of trading have so altered the original concept of

individual investors that the Dow theory can no longer be considered all-powerful and always correct.

To most investors, the value of the Dow theory is that it represents a sort of think-for-yourself method which will pay worthwhile dividends for those who devote time and effort to gaining a sound understanding of the principles involved.

➤ WHAT'S AHEAD In July 1986, Richard Russell, whose *Dow Theory Letters* newsletter is the leading authority on the theory, stated, "This is a market that has had a huge upside run in both stocks and bonds—and it's a market that's still 'out of breath.' When a world-class runner has set a world's record and is exhausted, he parks himself on the grass and cools off. Wall Street does the same thing and is doing it now." (*Dow Theory Letters*, P.O. Box 1759, La Jolla, CA 92038; $225/year)

Yet Russell also pointed out, "It is impossible to predict ahead when writing a book. Events change too rapidly, and by the time the book is published, you could be in a different world."

BROAD-BASED INDICATORS

The major stock market indices—the Dow Jones industrial average, Standard & Poor's 400 and 500, and the New York Stock Exchange composite index—are either limited or weighted so they do not fully reflect what's happening with all stocks. They are useful for continuing comparisons, but more accurate data, especially for timing, are illustrated by broader based indicators, such as those of *Value Line* and *Indicator Digest*. They both report the price movements of *all* stocks traded on the big board.

To see why, study the *Indicator Digest* composite index (see the chart on the next page). Each stock in this has the same weight, so that the percentage changes are equal, without distortions due to the number of outstanding shares and their market prices.

As shown on the chart, over many years the IDA moves more or less with the DJIA but reflects smaller and fewer wide swings. *Remember:* the Dow records the actions of only 30 stocks, all of giant corporations with millions of shares. Thus, if only one or two major stocks, such as GM or IBM, swing 2 or 3 points, the

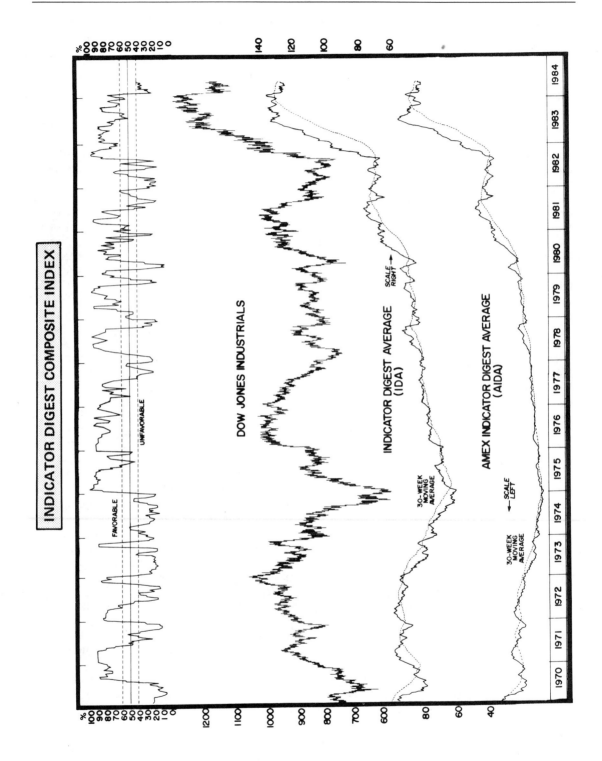

INDICATOR DIGEST COMPOSITE INDEX

FAVORABLE

UNFAVORABLE

DOW JONES INDUSTRIALS

INDICATOR DIGEST AVERAGE
(IDA)

SCALE
RIGHT

30-WEEK
MOVING
AVERAGE

AMEX INDICATOR DIGEST AVERAGE
(AIDA)

SCALE
LEFT

30-WEEK
MOVING
AVERAGE

DJIA will move sharply even though almost all the other 28 stocks stay flat.

For timing, IDA provides clear guidelines (top of chart). When the line moves above 60, the outlook is favorable; when the line moves below 40, the outlook is unfavorable. Note how in 1982 and 1983 the IDA signaled caution but the DJIA kept moving up. But when a downside break came, both indicators fell. Traders rely on such signals to buy and sell quickly; investors use them to delay purchases or to shift from stocks to debt issues. Or vice versa.

For traders, the IDA short-term trading guide (SGA) shows similar checkpoints. This compares the overall market action with a 5-week moving average (MA, top) and with the straight IDA (bottom). For convenience, there are arrows to show when to buy and when to sell.

In this chart, the SGA is at a favorable plus 16 compared with a plus 2 on the MA. This shows the market in mid-May 1984 when there was considerable pessimism about rising interest rates. But, says *Indicator Digest*, the SGA "is one of the prime reasons for our basically bullish stance . . . a 50% long, 50% cash position seems sensible . . . but temper with caution."

➤ NEW HIGHS OR LOWS Over a period of time, at least a week and preferably two weeks, these indicate hope or despair. When there's an ever-increasing number of new highs, the market is moving up; when there continue to be more lows than highs, pessimism is in the saddle. But don't take these numbers as a guarantee of the future, because for a while, they will record many of the same stocks day after day: "A trend in motion. . . ."

Again, these figures are most effective when converted to a chart and compared with a standard average. As long as the high-low indicators stay more or less in step with the DJIA or Standard & Poor's 500, they are simply a handy confirmation. But when the high-low line starts to dip while the averages move up, WATCH OUT: internal market conditions are deteriorating.

Conversely, an upturn in the high-low line while the DJIA is still declining probably indicates impending market strength.

This index of highs and lows exposes the underlying strength or weakness of the stock market, which is too often masked by the action of the DJIA. In an aging bull market, the DJIA may continue to rise, deceptively showing strength by the upmoves of a handful of major stocks; but closer examination will usually reveal

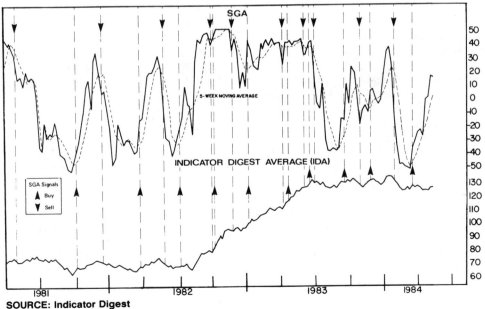

SHORT-TERM TRADING GUIDE (SGA)

SOURCE: Indicator Digest

that most stocks are too far below their yearly highs to make new peaks. At such periods, the small number of new highs is one of the most significant manifestations of internal market deterioration. The reverse is the telltale manner in which the total number of new lows appears in bear markets.

PSYCHO-LOGICAL ATTITUDES

Keeping in mind that "the stock market is rooted 15% in economics and 85% in psychology" (over the short term), it's important to check how investors view the future by such indicators as these:

➤ BARRON'S CONFIDENCE INDEX (BCI) This is published weekly in the financial news magazine. It shows the ratio of the yield on 10 highest-grade bonds to the yield on the broad Dow Jones 40-bond average. The ratio varies from the middle 80s (bearish) to the middle 90s (bullish).

The theory is that the trend of "smart money" is usually revealed in the bond market before it shows up in the stock market. Thus, *Barron's* confidence index will be *high* when shrewd investors are confident and buy more lower grade bonds, thus reducing low-grade bond yields; *low* when they are worried and stick to high-grade bonds, thus cutting high-grade yields.

Many market technicians use the BCI as a *primary* indicator. If you see that it simply keeps going back and forth aimlessly for many weeks, you can probably expect the same type of action from the overall stock market.

➤ OVERBOUGHT-OVERSOLD INDEX (OOI) This is a handy measure of the short-term trend's anticipated duration. Minor upswings or downturns have limited lives. As they peter out, experienced traders say that the market is "overbought" or "oversold" and is presumably ready for a near-term reversal. But remember, the definitions are set by the technician and are not always uniform.

Indicator Digest constructs its OOI with a 10-day accumulation of net advances and/or net declines. On the average, a 10-day total of 1,500 signals overbought conditions when on the "plus" side and an oversold condition when on the "minus" side. But there can be adjustments to the activity of the overall market.

➤ GLAMOR AVERAGE Another *Indicator Digest* special, this shows what is happening with the institutional favorites, usually trading at high multiples because of their presumed growth potential and current popularity (in a bull market). By and large, this is a better indicator for speculators than investors.

➤ SPECULATION INDEX This is the ratio of the AMEX-to-NYSE volume. When trading in AMEX stocks (generally more speculative) moves up faster than that in NYSE (quality) issues, speculation is growing. It's time for traders to move in and for investors to be cautious.

➤ 233 KEY STOCKS This indicator is one of the more useful tools because it measures the market movers from the solid old-time blue chips to the proven growth favorites. Since these generate a large proportion of the market's capitalization and volume, no major market move would be worth its salt without their support. The batting average of this index has been high.

When the 5-week moving average of this stock group rises to over 60%, the outlook is promising; over 70%, look for a durable advance.

➤ ODD-LOT INDEX This shows how small investors view the market, because it concentrates on trades of less than 100 shares. The small investor is presumably "uninformed" (a somewhat debatable assumption) and so tends to follow established patterns: selling as the market rises; jumping in to pick up bargains when it declines. The signal comes when the odd lotter deviates from this "normal" behavior.

When the small investor distrusts a rally after a long bear market, that investor gives a bullish signal: initial selling is normal, but when this continues, it's abnormal and a signal to the pros to start buying.

➤ RELATIVE STRENGTH This is a negative kind of indicator in that it relies on a comparison of the Dow Jones transportation average (DJTA) or the Dow Jones utilities average (DJUA) with the Dow Jones industrial average (DJIA). When these special averages fail to confirm the action of the industrials, watch out.

Examples: Early in 1974, the DJIA advanced sharply, reacted in February, and then rose to a new high in March. But the DJTA topped out at this time and started down below its 13-week MA. This signaled a future decline of the DJIA.

Similarly, the DJUA almost always leads the DJIA. If the DJUA moves opposite to the DJIA, it's a sign of future change: that is, when the utilities rise, the industrials will come along soon. Vice versa: when the DJUA falls, even when the DJIA is still moving up, there'll be a reversal soon.

➤ MOVING AVERAGE LINES A moving average (MA) is exactly what the name suggests—an average that moves with the unit of time covered. A 30-week MA, such as that shown with the IDA composite chart, records the average closing prices of all stocks for the 30 most recent Fridays. Each week, the total changes because of the addition of the latest week's closing figures and the subtraction of those of 30 weeks ago. The new total is then divided by 30 to get the MA.

Technicians use different time frames: 10 days, 200 days, 30 weeks, etc. In most cases, they compare that MA with a regular market average: the DJIA or here the IDA. The MA can serve as a trend indicator:

- As long as the IDA is *above* the MA, the outlook is bullish.
- As long as the IDA is *below* the MA, the outlook is bearish.
- A confirmed downward penetration of the MA by the base index is a *sell* signal: see early 1984.
- A confirmed penetration of the MA is a *buy* signal: see late 1982.

Beware of false penetrations, and delay action until there is a substantial penetration (2 to 3%), upward or downward, within a few weeks. In other words, don't be in a hurry to interpret the chart action: for example, in early 1980, the down penetration did not last long and was followed by a sharp upswing.

Professional money managers more concerned with long-term performance often use a second MA line, plotted for a 10-week span, and also maintain a 3-year MA. The latter is long enough to compensate for stock-market fluctuations and to enable clients to judge the true capability of the investment money manager.

MAs are vulnerable to swift market declines, especially from market tops. By the time you get the signal, you may have lost a bundle, because prices tend to fall twice as fast as they rise.

If you enjoy charting, develop a ratio of the stocks selling above their 30-week MA. When the ratio is over 50% and trending upward, the outlook is bullish. When it drops below 50% and/or is trending down, there's trouble ahead. Like many technical indicators, this is a hybrid: part price index and part breadth indicator.

Two additional comments from experience:

- Think of the MA in terms of juncture points where violation warns of change— coming or sometimes already taken place.
- The longer the time-span of the MA, the greater the significance of a crossover signal. An 18-month chart is more reliable than a 30-day one.

OTHER WIDELY USED TECHNICAL INDICATORS

➤ BUYING POWER TA is designed principally to measure the flow of *market strength*, which is shown by:

- Rising volume in rallies. Investors are eager to buy, so the demand is greater than the supply, and prices go up.
- Shrinking volume on market declines. Investors are reluctant to sell.
  Market weakness is indicated by:
- Rising volume on a market decline. Investors are getting nervous and fear still lower prices.
- Declining volume on market rallies. Investors have little faith in the higher prices.

With this technical approach, volume is the key indicator: it rises on rallies when the trend is up and rises on reactions when the trend is down.

Note: Volume trends are apt to reverse before price trends. Shrinking volume almost always shows up before the top of a bull market and before the bottom of a bear market.

➤ VOLUME AND VELOCITY This is a concept developed by Joseph E. Granville. He combines these in what he calls balance-on-volume.

When a stock closes at a higher price, he adds the daily trading volume to the cumulative net total he maintains. When the stock closes lower, he subtracts. When there's no price change, no volume is recorded.

Granville points out that when volume rises

with price, smart money is buying. When others follow, there will be a strong upmove.

He also relies on velocity: the cumulative volume as a percentage of corporate capitalization. This measures the turnover and thus demand. If a stock has 10 million shares and records cumulative volume of 10 million shares, the velocity is 100%.

➤ MOST ACTIVE STOCKS This list is published at the top of daily or weekly reports of the NYSE, AMEX, and NASDAQ, and it gives the high, low, and last prices and change of 10 to 15 volume leaders. Here's where alert traders spot popular and unpopular industry groups and occasionally stocks.

Forget about the big-name companies such as Exxon, GE, and IBM. They have so many shares outstanding that trading is always heavy. Watch for repetition: of one industry or of one company. When the same names appear several times in a week or two, something is happening. Major investors are involved: buying if the price continues to rise; selling if it falls.

With most actives, watch for:

Newcomers, especially small- or medium-sized corporations. When the same name pops up, major shareholders are worried (price drop) or optimistic (price rise). Since volume requires substantial resources, the buyers must be big-money organizations that have set a course. Once they have provided the blocking, take the ball and move up the field to quick gains.

MOST ACTIVE STOCKS ON NYSE: WEEK JUNE 23, 1986

STOCK	HIGH	LOW	LAST	CHANGE
AT&T	25⅝	24⅝	25⅜	+⅝
CmwE	32⅝	31	32⅝	+1⅝
DartKr	64⅜	55¾	64⅜	+6½
IBM	149⅞	144⅛	147½	−2⅛
CdPac	12½	12	12¼	−⅛
Navistr	9⅛	8	8⅜	−⅞
Safewy	51½	47	48⅜	+½
AMI	18¼	15⅞	17¾	+¾
PhilMr	70	66⅞	69⅞	+1
Motorla	42⅛	37¼	40½	−2

SOURCE: Barron's.

LONDON *FINANCIAL TIMES* INDEX

This is sort of a British Dow Jones industrial average. It records data on the London Stock Exchange: prices, volume, etc. Because it reflects worldwide business attitudes, it's a fairly reliable indicator of what's ahead, in 2 weeks to 2 months, for the NYSE.

There are, of course, temporary aberrations due to local situations, but over many years it has been a valuable technical tool. Since London is 5 hours ahead of New York, early risers benefit the most. One of my old New Jersey neighbors used to leave home at 5 A.M. to get to his Wall Street office to review the British market . . . but not on Monday, because the reports are published only Tuesday through Saturday. Maybe that's why he was able to take early retirement.

Companies in the same industry. Stocks tend to move as a group. Activity in retailers such as Sears and K-Mart *could* signal interest in this field. But wait for confirmation.

Technical services provide quick summaries of the most active stocks. The one prepared every other week by *Indicator Digest* shows the trend in terms of *up* stocks and *down* stocks. It can be easily plotted: on a daily basis, set down the net difference between the number of stocks *up* and the number *down*. If 9 are up, 5 down, and 1 is unchanged, the net is +4. Total the results for the last 30 market days, then divide by 30. On the thirty-first day, remove the oldest data and add the newest. Record the results on your chart. According to *ID,* the time to *buy* is when the indicator is +3 or higher; the time to *sell* is when the indicator falls below −3. Readings in between are neutral.

➤ PERCENTAGE LEADERS This list is published weekly in several financial journals. It's primarily for speculators seeking to catch a few points on a continuing trend.

Its value has recently diminished because of the high gains scored by takeover or buyout candidates. It is still a way to spot some potential

NYSE PERCENT LEADERS

NAME	UPS HIGH	LOW	LAST	CHANGE	PERCENT
Anacomp	4⅝	2¾	4¼	+1½	+54.5%
UNC Res.	5	3¼	4¾	+1½	+46.2
Teledyne	193½	153⅛	193⅜	+40⅛	+26.2
City Inv.	44½	32⅝	41⅝	+8⅝	+26.1
	DOWNS				
SwstForest	22⅛	16⅞	17½	−4½	−20.5
Enterra	20⅝	17	17⅜	−3⅞	−18.2
World Air	4⅝	4	4	−⅞	−17.9
Int. Har wt.	4⅝	3⅞	3⅞	−¾	−16.2

SOURCE: Barron's.

winners and to avoid losers. If you're thinking about making a move, check this list first. You may find that you've made a bundle . . . or have at least found a topic for locker-room comments.

➤ ADVANCES VERSUS DECLINES (A/D) These can be excellent guides to the trend of the overall market and, occasionally, of specific industry or stock groups. The best way to utilize A/D data is with a chart where the lines are plotted to show the cumulative difference between the advances and the declines on the NYSE or, for speculative holdings, on the AMEX. The total can cover 1 week, 21 days, or whatever period you choose, but because you're looking for developing trends it should not be for too long.

The table shows a week where the volume was stable but the trend was down: almost neutral on Monday, a pleasant rise on Tuesday, and then downhill for the rest of the week. A chart will show previous periods and make possible projections.

Many analysts prefer a moving average (MA) based on the net change for the week: 3,844 advances and 4,403 declines for a net down difference of 919. To make plotting easier, you can start with an arbitrary base, say 10,000, so that the week's figure would be 9,081 (10,000 minus 919).

The following week there's a net advance of 1,003, so that the new total would be 10,084, etc. When you chart a 20-week MA, divide the cumulative figure by 20. When you add week 21, drop week 1. *Result:* a quick view of market optimism or pessimism.

To spot trouble ahead, compare the A/D chart with that of the DJIA. If the Dow is moving up for a month or so but the A/D line is flat or dropping, that's a negative signal. Watch out for new highs and lows on the A/D chart. Near market peaks, the A/D line will almost invariably top out and start declining before the overall market. At market lows, the A/D line seldom gives a far-in-advance warning.

Be cautious about using the A/D line alone. Make sure that it is confirmed by other indicators or, better yet, confirms other signals.

RELY ON A CONSENSUS

Until you are very experienced, never rely on one technical indicator. Only rarely can a single chart, ratio, average, MA, or index be 100%

NYSE: ADVANCES AND DECLINES: HIGHS AND LOWS

	MONDAY	TUESDAY	WEDNESDAY	THURSDAY	FRIDAY
Total Issues	2,020	2,021	2,031	1,891	1,997
Advances	758	936	658	739	393
Declines	812	645	960	790	1,196
Unchanged	450	440	413	462	408
New Highs	23	20	20	23	10
New Lows	47	44	65	61	64
Sales (000) shares	86,972	97,798	118,932	125,384	98,351

SOURCE: Barron's.

accurate. There can be false signals or no signals at all (that you can discern). When an indicator breaks its pattern, look for confirmation from at least two other guidelines, preferably those involving other types of information. Then wait a bit: at least 2 days in an ebullient market, a week or more in a normal one. This won't be easy, but what you are seeking is confirmation. These days a false move can be costly.

This emphasis on consensus applies also to advisory service comments and recommendations. If you select only one, look for a publication that uses—and explains—several indicators. Pay attention to the statistics and trends, not the opinions. *The majority of commentaries, by almost all stock market analysts or letters, are wrong more often than they are right—temporarily.*

CHARTS: A VALUABLE TOOL FOR EVERYONE

Charts are a graphic ticker tape. They measure the flow of money into and out of the stock market, industry, or specific stock. They spotlight the highs and lows, how volume rises and falls on an advance or decline, and, in summary form, show the long-term patterns of the market and individual stocks.

Charting is simple; interpretation can be complex. Even the strongest advocates of TA disagree about the meaning of various formations, but they all start with three premises: (1) what happened before will be repeated again; (2) a trend should be assumed to continue in effect until such time as the reversal has been definitely signaled; (3) a chart pattern that varies from a norm (be it a past configuration or an average) indicates that something unusual is happening. More than almost any other area of TA, chart reading is an art and a skill rather than a solid body of objective scientific information. It is an aid to stock analysis, not an end.

Charts are not surefire systems for beating the market but they are one of the quickest and clearest ways to determine and follow trends. But all charts are after the fact. They may not work at precisely the times they are needed most—when the market is putting the finishing touches to a major top or bottom. At most

depths, the chart pattern will be bearish and point to a much lower level of prices. At market tops, it's the reverse.

The best combination for maximum profits and minimum losses is fundamental analysis supplemented by graphic technical analysis. Charts report what volume and price changes occur. Proper interpretation can predict the direction and intensity for change, because every purchase of every listed stock shows up on the chart.

Watch the bottom of the chart as well as the progress lines. This shows volume, and *volume precedes price.* A strong inflow of capital eventually pushes up the price of the stock; an outflow of dollars must result in a decline. To the charted results, it makes no difference who is doing the buying or selling.

Broadly speaking, charts are most valuable to provide corroboration. Once you have more

---

ADDITIONAL ADVICE

From Martin J. Pring, whose book is one of the best on technical analysis:

- *Breadth:* the fewer the issues moving with the market trend, the greater the probability of imminent reversal of that trend.
- *Industry breadth:* using the Barron's reports on 35 industry groups, set up an A/D line by cumulating the difference between the groups that advanced that week and those that declined. Ignore unchanged industries and gold (which moves from other pressures).
- *Tenacity:* if the technical position remains the same for the market or stock, hold to your original opinion but recheck the basic data.
- *Keep it simple:* most things done well are also done simply. If you must resort to complex computer programming and model building, chances are that you have not mastered the basics. The long-term action of the stock market operates on common sense, so the best approaches are always simple.

or less made up your mind to buy, sell, or hold a stock, check the charts. But be careful. Charts are like fire or electricity. They are brilliant tools if intelligently controlled or handled. But they can also be dangerous.

Keeping in mind that charts are not infallible, use them to:

- **Help determine when to buy and when to sell** by indicating probable levels of support and supply, and by signaling trend reversals
- **Call attention, by unusual volume or price behavior,** to something happening in an individual company that can be profitable to investors
- **Help determine the current trend:** up, down, or sideways, and whether the trend is accelerating or slowing
- **Provide a quick history of a stock** and show whether buying should be considered on a rally or a decline
- **Offer a sound means for confirming or rejecting** a buy or sell decision that is based on other information

Remember: charts are history. By studying past action, it is often possible to make a reasonably valid prediction of the immediate future.

WIDELY USED TYPES OF CHARTS

The most commonly used types of charts are point and figure (P&F) and bar charts. For best results, they should be constructed on a daily or weekly basis, but with experience, you may want to supplement these with charts covering months or even years. Printed charts are available for almost every purpose.

If you have time, charting can be fun and highly educational. All you need is a pad of graph paper: plain squares for P&F charts; logarithmic or standard paper for bar charts.

P&F charts are one-dimensional graphics. They show only price changes in relation to previous price changes. There are no indications of time or volume. The key factor is the change in price direction.

Some professionals think that P&F charts are oversimplified and consider them useful only as short-term guides and as a quick way to choose between two or three selections.

In making a P&F chart, the stock price is posted in a square: one above or below another, depending on the upward or downward movement of the price. As long as the price continues in the same direction, the same column is used. When the price shifts direction, the chartist moves to the next column.

In the chart shown here, the stock first fell in a downward sequence from 68 to 67 to 66. Then it rose to 67, so the chartist moved to column 2. The next moves were down to 62, up to 63 (new column), and so on. Most chartists start the new column only when there is a distinct change, typically 1 point, but for longer projections, 2 or 3 points.

Note how a pattern is formed with various resistance levels where the price of the stock stayed within a narrow range (57–56 and later 48–47). The chart signals each shift from such a base: down from 56 to 51; up from 47 to 52.

The best way for an amateur to learn about P&F charts is to copy them. Take a stock which has been plotted for many years and slowly recopy its action on a piece of graph paper. Then draw in the trendlines: the uptrend line on the high points, the downtrend line along the low points. Then draw your channels, which are broad paths created by the highs and lows of a definite trend. (Without a trend your channel will be horizontal.)

POINT AND FIGURE CHART

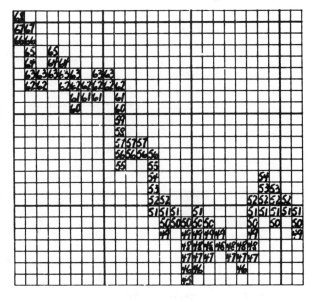

P&F charts have disadvantages: they do not portray intraday action or consider volume. The financial pages report only the high (62), low (59¼), and close (61½). This does not show that the stock might have moved up and down from 60 to 62 several times during the day.

Despite the omission of volume on P&F charts, many technical analysts feel that volume should always be checked once there is a confirmed trend on the chart. Rising volume on upside movements and dwindling sales on the downside usually indicate that the stock has ample investor support. It's always wise to be on the same side as volume.

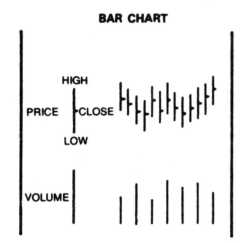

BAR CHART

Bar charts are described in greater detail later. The example here is simplified to show how these graphics record changes in relation to time. The horizontal axis represents time—in a day, week, or month; the vertical coordinates refer to price. To follow volume on the same chart, add a series of vertical lines along the bottom. The higher the line, the greater the volume. On printed charts, adjustments are made so that everything fits into a convenient space.

In plotting a bar chart, enter a dot to mark the highest price at which the stock was traded that day; then another dot to record the low. Draw the vertical line between the dots to depict the price range and add a short horizontal nub to mark the closing price. After a few entries, a pattern will begin to emerge.

UNUSUAL CHARTS

Almost every chartist has favorite configurations. They include such descriptive titles as: the rounding bottom, the flag, the pennant, the tombstone top, the Prussian helmet formation, the megaphone top, the lattice formation, etc. One of the most popular formations is *head and shoulders* (H&S).

Oversimplified, the head and shoulders chart portrays three successive rallies and reactions, with the second reaching a higher point than either of the others. The failure of the third rally to equal the second peak is a warning that a major uptrend may have come to an end. Conversely, a bottom H&S, formed upside down after a declining trend, suggests that an upturn lies ahead.

➤ LEFT SHOULDER This forms when an upturn of some duration, after hitting a climax, starts to fall. The volume of trading should increase with the rally and contract with the reaction. *Reason:* people who bought the stock on the uptrend start to take profits. When the technical reaction takes place, people who were slow to buy on the first rally start buying on the technical reaction.

➤ HEAD This is a second rally which carries the stock to new highs and is followed by a reaction that erases just about all the gain. Volume is high on the rally, yet lower than when forming the left shoulder. *Reason:* inves-

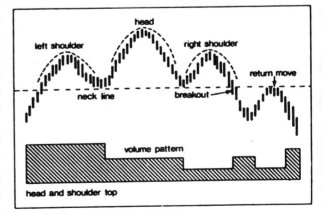

HEAD AND SHOULDERS CHART

tors who missed both the earlier actions start buying and force new highs.

This is followed by another drop as those who hesitated earlier see the second reaction and start acquiring the stock as it is sold by early buyers.

➤ RIGHT SHOULDER The third rally fails to reach the height of the head before the reaction. This is a sign of weakness. Watch the volume. If it contracts on a rally, it's likely that the price structure has weakened. If it increases, beware of a false signal.

➤ BREAKOUT This occurs when the stock price falls below the previous lows. At this point, most of the recent buyers have sold out—many of them at a loss.

No H&S should be regarded as complete until the price breaks out below a line drawn tangent with the lows on the left and right shoulders. This is called the neckline.

INTERPRETING CHARTS

The charts from Securities Research Company (SRC) shown here are typical of those available from technical services. They can be valuable tools to improve the selection of securities and especially the timing of purchases and sales. Similar graphics are available for industry groups and stock market averages.

Do NOT buy any stock when the chart shows a confirmed downtrend. As Blackman says, "Buy UP stocks in UP groups in an UP market." And, unless you are holding for the long term, consider selling when there's a downtrend in the stock, the industry, and the market.

SRC offers two chart books: blue for long-term of 12 years; red for short-term of 21 months. By using both, you get a better idea of the character, history, and probable performance of the stock.

LEGEND CHART: LONG-TERM

➤ CAPITALIZATION (*CENTER*) Information on the corporation: dollars of bonds and preferred stocks (in millions); number of common shares outstanding (in thousands); and book value per common share.

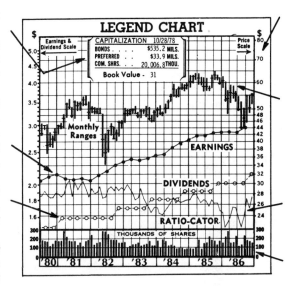

SOURCE: Securities Research Company, A Division of United Business Service Company, 208 Newbury St., Boston MA 02116.

➤ EARNINGS AND DIVIDENDS (*LEFT SIDE*) Per share data scaled from 0 to $5.50.

➤ DIVIDENDS (*NEXT TO BOTTOM*) The annual rate of interim dividend payments. The circles mark the month in which the payments were made. Extra or irregular payouts (not shown) are typed in.

➤ EARNINGS On a per share 12-month-ended basis as shown by the solid black line. Dots indicate whether the company issues quarterly, semiannual, or annual earnings reports.

➤ MONTHLY RANGES (*SOLID VERTICAL BARS*) Shows the highest and lowest prices for the stock each month. Crossbars indicate the closing price.

➤ PRICE SCALE (*RIGHT SIDE*) This is equal to 15 times the earnings and dividend scale, so when the price range bar and the earnings line coincide (mid-1981), the price-earnings ratio is 15. When the price is above the earnings line, the P/E ratio is greater; when below, lower.

➤ RATIO-CATOR A guideline used by SRC. The plottings are obtained by dividing the closing price of the stock by the closing price of DJIA on the same day. The resulting percentage is multiplied by a factor of 4.5 to bring the line close to the price bars and is read from the right-hand scale. The plotting indicates whether the stock has kept pace, outperformed, or lagged behind the general market.

➤ VOLUME (*BOTTOM*) The number of shares traded, in thousands, each month on an arithmetic scale. Watch when there are extremes: high volume with rising prices (mid-1977); low volume with falling values (mid-1981). Volume comes before price.

LEGEND CHART: SHORT-TERM

Here the data are similar to those of the longer term charts but cover the action for only 21 months.

➤ EARNINGS For the last 12 months. Read from the left border to find the changes in dollar-per-share profits.

➤ DIVIDENDS On an annual basis. The "X" indicates the ex-dividend date; the "O," the dividend payment date.

➤ MOVING AVERAGE FOR 39 WEEKS Each dot represents the average of the closing prices of the 39 most recent weeks. When used with the price bars, you can determine trends as well as buying and selling points.

➤ RATIO-CATOR LINE Shows the relative perfor-

mance of the stock. It is calculated by dividing the closing price of the stock by the closing price of the DJIA on the same day and then multiplying by 7.0.

Note: In plotting the short-term chart, the price range, earnings, and dividends are shown on a uniform ratio scale: that is, the vertical linear distance for a 100% move is the same any place on the chart regardless of whether the rise was from $5 to $10 or from $20 to $40. Thus, all charts of all stocks are comparable.

USING CHARTS

Once you have your eye on a stock which from research meets quality standards and appears to have excellent prospects, take a look at its long-term chart. This will give you an idea of how the stock performs through both bull and bear markets.

TRENDLINES

The key to the successful use of charts, and most technical analysis, is the premise that *a trend in force will persist until a significant change in investor expectations causes it to reverse itself.* Or, as Martin Pring puts it, "on the assumption that people will continue to make the same mistakes they have made in the past." To discern that trend, the chartist draws lines connecting the lowest points of an upmoving stock; the highest points of a downmoving stock. This trendline is a reliable indicator about 80% of the time because it predicts the immediate action of the stock or market.

The shrewd trader or investor rises with the trend: buying when there's a confirmed upmove; considering selling when there's a definite downswing. Generally, the stock will move along that line—regardless of the direction. There will be interim bounces or dips, but most stocks hold to that pattern until there is a clear change.

By spotting the trend, you can get an edge in determining your tactics. By keeping your charts up to date, you can project where and, to a degree, how soon or late the market, industry, group, or stock will go.

Trendlines establish bases. The uptrend line

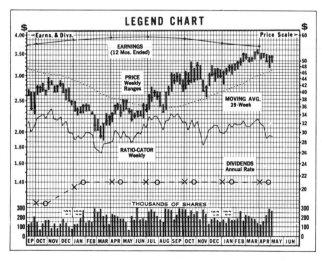

SOURCE: Securities Research Company, A Division of United Business Service Company, 208 Newbury St., Boston, MA 02116

LONG-TERM PROFITABLE GROWTH:

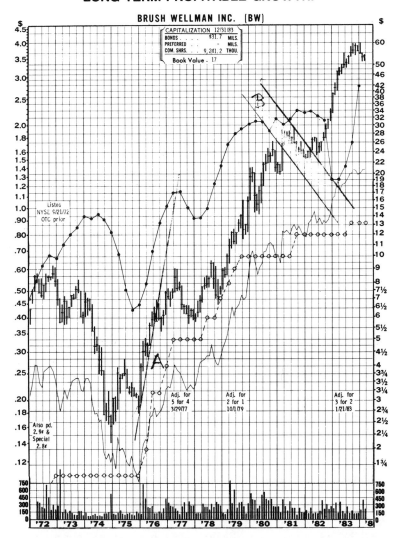

BRUSH WELLMAN INC. (BW)

CAPITALIZATION 12/31/83		
BONDS	$31.7	MILS.
PREFERRED . .	—	MILS.
COM. SHRS. . .	9,241.2	THOU.

Book Value - 17

Listed
NYSE 9/21/72
OTC prior

Adj. for
5 for 4
3/29/77

Adj. for
2 for 1
10/1/79

Adj. for
3 for 2
1/21/83

Also pd.
2.9¢ &
Special
2.8¢

SOURCE: Securities Research Company, A Division of United Business Service Company, 208 Newbury St., Boston, MA 02116

becomes a support level below which an upmoving stock is not likely to fall. The downtrend line marks a resistance level above which the stock is not likely to rise.

Before you invest—or speculate—in any stocks, check the chart and draw trendlines. Buy when the trend is up; hold or do not buy when it is moving down. The best profits always come when you buy an UP stock in an UP industry in an UP market—clearly evident with

trendlines on charts. And, of course, when you sell short, it's the opposite.

➤ LONG-TERM CHART The company is Brush Wellman, a producer of beryllium products. It is rated A— by Standard & Poor's and BAA16 by Wright Investors' Service. These mean that its quality is good but not the best. The long-term debt-to-equity ratio is a safe 31%; there's no preferred, the common stock is listed on the NYSE with 9.2 million shares, and there are

103 institutional investors. For the past decade, the profit rate has averaged a satisfactory 14.8% and projections indicate a higher return on equity in the next 3 years.

Start with the long-term chart to see that this is a *good* investment. After a sharp profit decline in 1974 and 1975, the company started a comeback, and with almost steadily rising earnings (top line), the value of the stock moved almost steadily up, from an adjusted-for-splits 3 to 9, bounced back to 6, onward and upward to 28, a drop back, with the declining market, to 24 in 1981, and since then, an almost uninterrupted rise to a peak of 60 in late 1983.

Clearly, BW proved to be a rewarding investment: since 1976, as the result of three splits, each 100 shares grew to 375; earnings (per adjusted share) rose from $1.02 to $2.77.

The chart shows that the time to buy was in 1976–77 when the trendline (A) rose almost straight up, from around 4 to a projected 22 (shown by the extension of line A), a price reached in 1980.

Periodically, after each sharp rise, the stock fell back. This decline reflected the 50% rule—which is that when a stock moves up significantly, there is likely to be a technical reaction that will lose about half its recent gain. Such setbacks came in 1977 and, after a rise, in 1978 and again in 1980. There is nothing sacred about that percentage; with a quality stock, the drop will usually be less than 50%.

Note, too, that these dips usually followed a stock split. In anticipation of this possibility, traders pushed up the price of the stock and sold out after the announcement.

Long-term investors, gladdened by the extra shares, might hold but at some point should consider selling. Lines B show why. When trendlines are drawn in 1981, they signal a downturn. The stock price fell from around 28 to 22. The trader would use this channel (B) to sell when the price hit the upper line, about 29; to buy when it reached the bottom line, about 23.

Another pattern to watch is the accumulation period: in 1980, when volume stayed high for many months. Usually, the longer the stock holds within a narrow range, the greater the ultimate price rise. It's called "building a base." But with BW, its long history of profitable growth shortened that base period.

It's also interesting that in 1982–83, when BW stock was roaring up, the volume was modest, apparently because this upswing was counter to that of the overall market and, during that period, many institutions were speculating in hi-tech and takeover issues.

Based on the long-term chart, BW was an excellent long-term investment at almost any time after 1975.

➤ SHORT-TERM CHART Now let's assume that it's the fall of 1982. You know that BW is an excellent investment but are not sure about timing your purchase.

The stock is at 24 (before the 3-for-2 split), and its price is rising with somewhat higher volume. Drawing trendlines (C), you project that the stock price could reach 60 (again before the split). To be doubly sure, you review the earnings forecast and find that 1982 profits are expected to be down because of a change in accounting and foreign currency adjustments.

But research shows that in 1983 earnings should improve and could reach a record high in 1984. With the chart signaling optimism, you make your investment in November at 40, receive 50% more shares in January, and then watch the stock soar from 30 (adjusted) to 48 in early summer.

For a trader, this would be a welcome gain, but the high tax bracket investor would prefer to hold for 12 months to take advantage of the lower tax rate. Based on the historic pattern of the stock, the risks are modest. In December, after a short dip, BW shares rose to 56 and in January 1984 hit 60.

Note: It didn't quite happen with BW, but the stock will often stall and fall when it reaches its previous peak price—28 as shown on the long-term chart. At this point, some investors who bought at that then-high price will bail out to break even. This is more likely to occur when there are a large number of shares outstanding and thus big ownership by institutions. Their selling will force down the price of the stock.

When you opt for income, some of the best stocks to buy are those of quality utilities. Charts are not as useful here because the values of these stocks move within a narrow range. They are less vulnerable to cyclical changes than other groups but do respond to shifts in the cost of money: *down* when interest rates rise; *up* when they fall.

BRUSH WELLMAN CORP. (BW)

A leading producer of beryllium containing products and a manufacturer of friction materials used in heavy-duty vehicles.

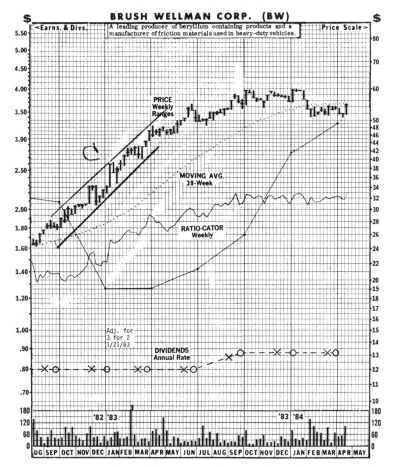

CENTRAL & SOUTH WEST CORP. (CSR)

CAPITALIZATION 12/31/82		
BONDS	$1,710.1	MILS.
PREFERRED	$315.3	MILS.
COM. SHRS.	87,272.8	THOU.

Book Value - 19

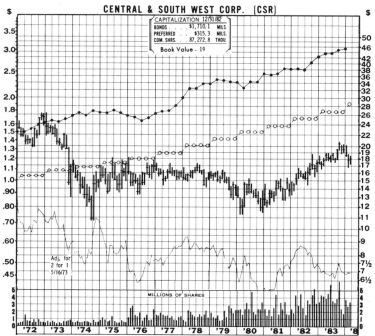

SOURCE: Securities Research Company, A Division of United Business Service Company, 208 Newbury St., Boston, MA 02116

This chart of a quality utility, Central & South West (CSR), shows that after 1974, when earnings flattened, the stock moved with the overall market, but because of ever-higher per share profits—from $1.72 in 1975 to an estimated $3.15 in 1984—the values rose from 15 to 20. There was a sharp drop in 1980 as the result of the superhigh interest rates, but the stock prices generally fluctuated only 2 to 4 points a year.

Next time you plan to buy a utility stock, review the long-term chart to find companies, such as CSR, whose stock prices stay relatively stable over the years. You want income first, then capital gains, therefore stay away from low-rated swinging-in-price utilities. These can be OK for trading but not for investing.

Technical analysis, especially charts, can be a valuable aid to timing. Unless you are extremely optimistic and can afford to tie up your money for a while, *never* buy any stock until its chart is pointing up. And *always* check the chart action before you sell. You may think that the high has been reached, but the chart may disagree and make possible greater gains.

On the other hand, if the chart shows a downtrend, consider selling. If it's a good investment, you can buy the stock back later at a lower price. If it's not, you'll save a lot of money.

Properly utilized, technical analysis can be an important adjunct to fundamental investing and, more often than not, it will keep you humble!

FOR FURTHER INFORMATION

Robert D. Edwards and John Magee. *Technical Analysis of Stock Trends.* Boston: John Magee, Inc., 1966.

Martin Pring. *Technical Analysis Explained.* New York: McGraw-Hill, 4th ed., 1985.

Jeffrey Weiss. *Beat the Market.* New York: Viking Penguin, 1985.

18   TIMING STRATEGIES TO BEAT THE MARKET

Timing the purchase or sale of securities is always tough. It is not overly important to investors seeking long-term gains with quality stocks, but it is imperative with speculations that depend on fast action for quick profits and low losses.

There are two types of timing: *market timing* and *corporate timing*.

MARKET TIMING

Related to the overall stock market, this approach determines whether or not it is a good time to invest in common stocks. Action is taken against the broad background of economic, monetary, and political factors with decisions about specific securities based on earnings, yields, interest rates, and future prospects for the economy.

Market timing is subject to varying interpretations that are usually more emotional than realistic. But since they influence the decisions of major investors, they are important and must be considered even though you may disagree with the conclusions. If the trend of the market is down, be slow to buy and then only for the long term (unless you are bold enough to sell short to take advantage of the confused pessimism). If the trend is up, it's usually time to start buying.

The fundamental investor acts with confidence that the stock market, over a period of time, will adjust to price levels reflecting rational factors: decisions made on the basis of continuing business and economic forecasts. The investor pays little heed to the many psychological and short-run market forces that affect week-to-week and month-to-month fluctuations in stock market prices. With market timing, the fundamental investor works in general areas: low or *buy* ranges and high or *sell* areas.

Market timing is based on the assumption that the prices of common stocks move together and that there are three broad kinds of movements:

➤ MAJOR BULL AND BEAR MARKETS These seldom last less than 2 years. They include many short reversing fluctuations. It's not too difficult to spot long-term trends, but it is difficult to catch interim movements.

The stock market almost always moves to extremes, up to overoptimistic highs and down to overpessimistic lows. Overall, the trend has been UP, but the interim swings are seldom predictable. Some professionals may be right for a year or two (as they will trumpet loudly), but few are smart (or lucky) enough to time their recommendations within 3 or 4 months of the highs or lows. The best that the best analysts can do is to point out the major bull or bear markets.

➤ INTERMEDIATE MARKET MOVEMENTS WITHIN A MAJOR BULL OR BEAR MARKET These usually run several months and are ever-present and ever-changing.

➤ IMMEDIATE SHORT-TERM FLUCTUATIONS OF WEEKS OR DAYS These are of importance only to traders although upsetting to investors on occasion.

There are hundreds of investment timing techniques which attempt to spot and pinpoint all three of these market movements. The conservative investor wants to catch the turn of major bull or bear markets; the less conservative investor watches for intermediate movements; the speculator, along with the professional, plays for the short day-to-day fluctuations. *All serious investors should understand the broad trends and movements of the stock market in order to sharpen their own timing.*

CORPORATE TIMING

This approach zeros in on industries and specific stocks and takes into account earnings, yields, ratios, financial strength, and future prospects. These factors are most important in buying but are also valuable in deciding whether to hold or sell.

Using corporate timing wisely requires self-discipline and adherence to logically determined conclusions, not hunches or rumors or tips. It is as important to avoid losers as it is to pick winners. In a strong market, almost all stocks will move up, but the worthwhile gains will come with the best stocks (except for temporarily popular speculative issues).

Because most stocks move along with their industries, it is important to check group action. Over the years, some industries—especially growth ones—will move ahead at a relatively steady pace, but the year-to-year shifts can be very dramatic.

CYCLICAL-SPECULATIVE STOCKS

This list of stocks (see table) includes those likely to benefit from cyclical upswings and turnaround situations. The risk factor in some of these issues may be relatively high.

Before you make any major commitment, always check the long-term performance and concentrate on industry groups that have bettered the averages. Chances are that they will continue to be winners.

TIMING TECHNIQUES

There are two major techniques involved in timing: *the fundamentalist approach* and *the technical approach.* The latter, which relies on charts and technical indicators, has been discussed in Chapter 17. Both techniques recognize, however, that certain common patterns for successful timing exist.

PRICE SWINGS
On the average, the price of a stock will fluctuate about 25% a year, with utilities moving within a narrower range. Watch that average over a 5-year period, because the changes may be small for a while; but when

CYCLICAL STOCKS

Bankers Trust	Favorable earnings trend; stock remains undervalued
Boeing Co.	Pickup in commercial aircraft orders expected
Borg-Warner	Cyclical businesses to join prospering service lines
Browning-Ferris	Growth in waste disposal activity aids prospects
Burlington Northern	Superior rail, with expanding natural resources base
Circus Circus	Rebound in Nevada gaming benefiting profits
Engelhard Corp.	Favorable prospects for most catalytic products
Interlake	Strong earnings momentum; P/E may expand
Ogden Corp.	Focus on resource recovery should aid earnings
Parker-Hannifin	Strong capital spending helping profits
Raytheon	Strong growth likely in defense electronics
Reynolds Metals	Lower aluminum inventories, firmer prices to aid net
Signal Cos.	Diversified company has sizable earning power
Sonat Inc.	Positioning itself for future oil services upturn
Zurn Industries	Increasing resource recovery business to boost profits

SOURCE: Standard & Poor's *The Outlook.*

the breakout comes, it can be substantial—up or down. For example, *Dow Jones & Co., Inc.* (adjusted for splits): 1979: 8 to 10; 1980: 8.7 to 16; 1981: 15 to 28; 1982: 18 to 35; 1983: 32 to 57.

VOLATILITY

To classify such price movements, analysts have developed volatility ratios. These measure the rate of change in the price of the stock (or group of stocks) against a stock market index and thus indicate volatility.

The best known measure of volatility is "beta," based on the Standard & Poor's 500 stock index. A stock with a beta of 1.25 has 25% more volatility (and thus, to a degree, risk) than does the overall market. This means that the stock is likely to rise or fall 25% more than the general level of the stock market.

Investors should choose low-beta stocks, those rated 1.00 or less. In a down market, their decline will probably be smaller than the average; but in an up market, their gain may be slower and lower. The more aggressive or speculative you are, the higher the beta you should look for.

Such criteria are best for professionals because of the complex calculations, but wise amateurs should check betas with a broker to be sure the stocks fit their plans and risk level.

THE SPREAD BETWEEN YIELDS OF STOCKS AND BONDS

This technique is useful in timing moves from debt to equity, or vice versa. It recognizes that competition between stocks and bonds always exists. It compares the difference between bond interest and stock dividends. It does not take into account any change in prices. This can be important, because stocks can provide total returns—dividends plus appreciation—while bonds, unless bought at a discount, remain at about the same price level. But, of course, the market value of stocks is more likely to decline in bear markets.

SIGNIFICANT CHANGES IN VOLUME

When the number of shares of a company traded for a week or more rises sharply, something may be happening, such as merger

HOW SECURITIES MARKETS CHANGE

INVESTMENT GROUP BOND MARKET	1985	1984	1983	1982	1981
Corporate	+16%	+4%	−2%	+24%	−10%
Municipals	+18	−2	+5	+36	−26
U.S. Long-Term	+16	+2	−9	+26	−5
Stock Market					
Dow Jones Industrials	+28	−4	+20	+20	−9
NYSE Composite	+26	+1	+17	+14	−9
S&P 500 Stock Index	+26	+1	+17	+15	−10
Value Line	+21	−8	+22	+15	−4
Special Stock Groups					
Low-priced stocks	+18	−24	+54	+10	0
Institutional favors	+24	+1	+13	+20	−13
Major Stock Groups					
Financial	+26	+1	+24	+30	−1
Utilities	+24	+10	+13	+6	+10
Transportation	+22	−9	+39	+24	+3

SOURCE: Wright Investors' Service.

YIELDS: STOCKS VS BONDS

YEAR	S&P 500	STOCK YIELDS	BOND YIELDS	DIFFERENCE VS. STOCKS
1970	83.2	3.83	8.21	4.38
1971	98.3	3.14	7.65	4.51
1972	109.2	2.84	7.51	4.67
1973	107.4	3.06	7.71	4.65
1974	82.9	4.47	8.43	3.96
1975	86.2	4.31	8.89	4.58
1976	102.0	3.77	8.57	4.80
1977	98.2	4.62	8.33	3.71
1978	96.0	5.28	8.93	3.65
1979	103.0	5.47	9.80	4.33
1980	118.8	5.26	12.02	6.76
1981	128.1	5.20	14.32	9.12
1982	119.7	5.81	13.73	7.92
1983	160.4	4.40	11.86	7.46
1984	160.5	4.64	12.94	8.30
1985	186.8	4.25	11.41	7.16

SOURCE: Standard & Poor's.

discussions, accumulation of stock by a possible acquirer, a favorable turn in the company's fortunes. If indeed a major development is occurring, some people (corporate lawyers, company executives, accountants, security analysts, etc.) may think they have advance information and rush to buy the stock. They may or may not be correct.

Understanding volume can add to gains and reduce losses: a sharp increase in volume of shares traded may signal a forthcoming rise in price. The effects are usually long-lived in that even after the original enthusiasm plateaus, the price of the popular stock will usually keep going up, at least for a while.

PRICE-EARNINGS RATIOS

As discussed in Chapter 16, on balance sheets, timing can be enhanced by comparisons of price-earnings ratios of the market, of the industry, and of the stock. Professionals *buy* when the multiple, or P/E ratio, is well below the long-term average and *sell* when it rises far above the historic range. This is better in theory than in practice but can be a useful confirmation check.

The problem is that although value timing does tell you when a stock may be over- or undervalued, it cannot indicate when a favorable price movement will occur. Wall Street is slow to change its prejudices. The price changes that

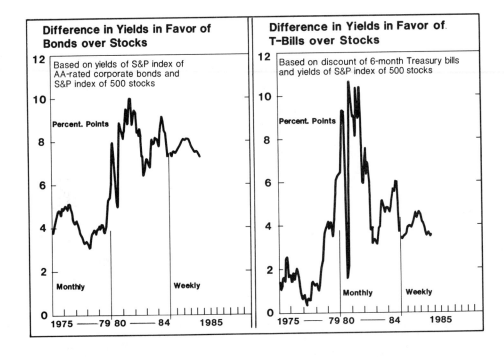

Difference in Yields in Favor of Bonds over Stocks — Based on yields of S&P index of AA-rated corporate bonds and S&P index of 500 stocks. Percent. Points. Monthly / Weekly. 1975 — 79 80 — 84 1985

Difference in Yields in Favor of T-Bills over Stocks — Based on discount of 6-month Treasury bills and yields of S&P index of 500 stocks. Percent. Points. Monthly / Weekly. 1975 — 79 80 — 84 1985

should take place are often slow to come about because they reflect the psychology of the situation rather than the logic of the decisions.

Thus, if you buy a stock with a low P/E that you are convinced is undervalued, you may have to wait: hopefully, only a few months, but possibly as long as one year. Your analysis may be right, but if the timing is too early, you will tie up your money and miss potential profits that could be made elsewhere.

INTEREST RATES

Declining interest rates can often be beneficial for the stock market, since stocks are in competition with bonds and other fixed income instruments. Stocks do not *always* rise when rates fall, but such is the general trend.

Among the major interest-sensitive industries are: banks, savings and loan associations, life insurance, utilities, telephone, and tobacco.

➤ BANKS, SAVINGS AND LOAN ASSOCIATIONS As interest rates come down, the cost of this group's short-term funds likewise decreases, and lower rates tend to boost consumer demand for mortgages and loans.

➤ LIFE INSURANCE Interest rate fluctuations affect the value of these companies' large bond portfolios, which are carried on the books at the original purchase prices; but, of course, the

WELL-REGARDED INTEREST-SENSITIVE STOCKS

	EARNINGS DOLLARS PER SHARE		INDICATED DIVIDEND	YIELD %	CURRENT PRICE	†P/E RATIO
	E1984	E1985				
Electric Utilities						
IPALCO Enterprises	A4.22	4.40	$2.92	8.8	33	7.5
TECO Energy	3.60	3.70	2.20	7.3	30	8.1
Wisconsin Electric Power	A4.35	4.50	2.28	7.1	32	7.1
Life Insurance Companies						
Capital Holdings	4.60	5.15	1.54	3.3	47	9.1
Jefferson-Pilot	3.75	4.05	1.32	3.3	40	9.9
Lincoln National	4.05	4.60	1.84	4.6	40	8.7
Savings and Loan Associations						
Ahmanson (H.F.)	1.75	3.25	1.20	3.8	32	9.8
Golden West Financial	3.75	4.00	0.20	0.8	26	6.5
Great Western Financial	A2.60	3.25	0.88	3.3	27	8.3
Telephone Companies						
Ameritech	A10.17	11.00	6.00	7.8	77	7.0
Cincinnati Bell	A5.74	6.45	3.12	6.8	46	7.1
Pacific Telesis	A8.46	9.25	5.40	7.8	69	7.5
Rochester Telephone	3.75	4.30	2.44	7.2	34	7.9
Southwestern Bell	A9.04	9.65	5.60	7.9	71	7.4
Tobacco Companies						
American Brands	A7.20	8.05	3.75	5.9	64	17.1
Philip Morris	[1]A7.24	9.90	3.40	4.1	82	24.1
Reynolds (R.J.)	6.95	8.50	3.40	4.6	74	21.8

A-Actual. E-Estimated. †Based on estimated 1985 earnings. [1]Incl. $1.19 write-down.

SOURCE: Standard & Poor's The Outlook.

actual value of the bonds declines when interest rates rise, and vice versa.

➤ UTILITIES AND TELEPHONE These stocks are purchased primarily for their yields; however, when interest rates decline, their borrowing costs are greatly reduced.

TARGET PRICES

An essential element of timing is that of setting the target prices for each stock that you buy. Try to set a target price of 25 to 50% above your cost if you are seeking capital appreciation. Allow at least 18 to 24 months for your target price to be reached. If your stock reaches the target price, you must then make one of three decisions:

- Sell and take the profit
- Review the investment and set new, higher target prices, if the outlook for the company is still favorable
- Protect it by setting a stop-loss order 15% below the recent high if your profit is substantial; this avoids the trauma of a wrong decision and loss of gains due to indecision

The time to *buy* is when the projections indicate that, in a fair to good market, the stock will become popular. The time to consider *selling* is when the stock moves into the target range.

Technical indicators can be valuable tools for timing, but they are never substitutes for common sense. If it's a bear market, don't argue. Switch some of your holdings into fixed income holdings. If it's a bull market, move back into quality growth stocks.

$ HINT: When using timing techniques such as those just described, it is a good idea also to check the individual stock's chart, as well as the composite chart for the industry.

GUIDELINES FOR TIMING SELLING

➤ TAKE YOUR PROFITS WHEN YOU HAVE A WORTHWHILE GAIN It is always better to sell too soon than too late. Once any stock has appreciated substantially, the risk is that there will be a quick, sharp decline because it has become overvalued. The only excuse for hanging on in such a situation is the "greater fool theory"—that regardless of how high the price,

a greater fool will come along and buy it from you. But what happens if the bubble bursts and the institutions start to unload? The amateur can lose a lot of money fast. There is nothing wrong with an adequate profit!

➤ SELL WHEN THE ORIGINAL REASONS FOR PURCHASE NO LONGER HOLD There are three basic reasons to buy any stock:

- Your study shows that this is a sound company with good prospects for profitable growth.
- You believe that something good is going to happen: the stock may be split, the company is getting a big new contract, a new, profitable product, acquisition, etc.
- Reports and/or charts show that smart money is moving into the stock.

The last two are usually reasons for a quick rise in the price of the equity. There should be quick action. If there is not, *sell.* You were wrong.

➤ SELL WHEN THE INDUSTRY BECOMES UNPOPULAR In 1981, Wall Street turned sour on aerospace stocks. The industry index started to fall from 200 and by year-end was down to 140. The values of individual stocks kept pace: Boeing, from 42 to 15; General Dynamics, from 43 to below 20; United Technologies, from 65 to 32.

Never argue with Wall Street. The professionals have far more money and clout than any individual. Sell when there is a confirmed downtrend unless you are willing and able to hang on—in this case, about 18 months; then the group average moved ahead as defense securities became popular again. By mid-1983, the index was up to 258; Boeing to 48; GD to 60; and UTX to the mid-70s.

➤ ACT WHEN THE STOCK'S VOLUME REACHES A 6-MONTH HIGH With major corporations, this will show up first on the Most Active List in the newspaper. With smaller firms, check their charts, especially the vertical lines at the bottom. When they grow taller, with higher prices, gains are probable. When they shrink, with lower prices, watch out. The institutions are unloading.

Keep in mind that a rising market needs greater volume to sustain the upmove. Low volume on a decline in the early stages of a bull market is OK because it indicates little selling. But once the market has dropped, low volume means that most investors are holding with hope.

Carefully note the Most Active List in the paper every day and the volume for each stock on the list. (1) Check the quality of the volume leaders. If they are big blue chips, the future is promising. If they are secondary stocks, be cautious. (2) Watch the price changes on the list. The bigger the upmoves, the stronger the market. This also applies to specific stocks. If the gains are fractional, wait for confirmation of the uptrend . . . if any.

And now let's add some advice from Richard Blackman, a New Jersey discount broker and author of *Follow the Leaders*. He's a tough-minded professional who sticks to rules like these. His motto: *A stock does not care who owns it.* Never let emotion override facts.

- **After a big hit.** If you have sold at a hefty profit, take your time before reinvesting, except in a strong market. Do not let your broker talk you into buying another stock until you have reassessed the situation. Stop. Let the market go for a week. Then make sure that the next stock you buy has the potential to gain at least 25% fairly soon. Otherwise, put your dollars in a money market fund and wait until you find another potential winner.

- **After three straight losses.** Says Blackman, "When you strike out three times in a row, get out of the market. If you have been playing by the rules and still lose, it's a poor time to be in the market. Stop kidding yourself and wait for new opportunities that fit your guidelines."

- **After 12 months of a rising market.** At this point, the market and upward moving stocks are likely to pause under the pressure of sales by profit-taking investors. They take control and for a while virtually stop the market from going up.

  "When you judge this time span, do so from the week the uptrend started, not the date you bought the stock," says Blackman. "Check the chart and make believe you bought at the bottom. Then mark your investment calendar one year ahead. . . . This is a tough rule for most investors to accept. It should be used flexibly, but it's backed by common sense and proven-profitable results."

- **When stocks break out of a consolidation pattern.** (See Chapter 17, on technical analysis.) Stocks seldom rise to a peak and then fall off. They usually form a consolidation area wherein the price moves up and down within a relatively narrow range. Charts show this quickly. That's where they are useful. As long as the stock moves within that pattern, *hold*. But the minute there's a confirmed breakthrough on the downside, get ready. If this is validated in the next few days by a further decline, then *sell*.

SIX SELLING SITUATIONS

Sell when the dividend income falls short of your goal. People who need maximum yield on their savings should not hesitate to sell when the return is considerably lower than could be obtained elsewhere. *Always calculate the income on the basis of present value, not on the basis of your initial cost.*

Think about selling when the company announces plans to issue convertible debentures or preferred stock. Eventually, these will dilute the value of the common stock unless the corporation is able to use the money to boost profits. This warning is most significant when the market is booming, because the CVs will command a high price based on investor optimism. (A CV is a bond or a preferred stock which is exchangeable [i.e., convertible] into common stock at a fixed price, usually a price higher than that of the common stock.) (See Chapter 9.)

Unless the company is doing well and is ably managed, CVs will benefit the issuer more than the investor. According to one study of 141 NYSE firms that floated CVs, the common stock of 70% of these firms fell 25% or more within the next 9 months. Later, only about half of these issues moved above their original price.

Sell promptly when your stock runs up on news that it may be taken over because there's no guarantee that the merger will be successful and it's difficult to accurately project future profits. If you have reason to believe that the takeover will be completed and then result in a much stronger organization through a merger for stock in another company, you will make your judgment on a different, sounder basis. *But get all the facts first. That's more* *than most of the people who boosted the price of your stock will have done.*

Get ready to sell when the stock moves up fast. If you're lucky enough to pick a stock that jumps up 50% or so in a couple of months, sell or set up a stop-loss order.

$HINT: *Always sell too soon.* When a stock becomes overpriced, the risks of a severe decline are far greater than the rewards of further gains. Take your profits and run to another stock that will provide similar profits in the future.

In timing the selling of stocks you own, ask yourself, "If I were making a new investment, would I make this investment at this price at this time?" If the answer is an unqualified YES, hold. If you're undecided, check the target price and, if close, consider selling. If the answer is NO, sell at once. Don't set up a situation that will cause you to worry.

Stick with up-moving groups. For the best and usually quickest profits, purchase stocks of popular industries. Once an uptrend begins, it is likely to continue, so that an undervalued industry can get double support when the rise begins. But this momentum can also be doubly detrimental on the downside.

$HINT: If you subscribe to a service that lists opinions of market advisers, divide the

---

WATCH INSIDER TRANSACTIONS

When there are twice as many sellers as buyers in a month or so, something unfavorable must be coming up—at least, the profits will not grow as rapidly as in the past. These data may be published a little late, but they are still strong signals for selling.

Conversely, when the number of purchases by officers or directors is significantly greater than the number of sales, this could be bullish.

In bear markets, these signals are not as accurate, because some insiders may sell for tax or personal reasons. Some executives may unload to get cash to exercise stock options. As a rule: when the ratio of sellers to buyers is under 2:1 for 2 months, it's bullish; when over 3:1, it's bearish.

---

percentage of bulls by the percentage of bears. When the quotient is 75% or higher, watch out. When it's under 40%, consider buying.

Fundamentals of common stock selection do not change much, as you can see from the basic criteria set forth in the opening chapters of this book. Price-earnings ratio, price-to-book value, return on equity, cash flow, and all other ways of calculating value remain useful in different cycles of the stock market. What does change, however, are the external or macroeconomic conditions, such as a strengthening or weakening dollar, inflation or disinflation, high-growth economy or recession. These more global shifts call for a different emphasis in stock selection—specifically a new way of looking at the importance of cash flow per share and book value per share.

The real book value per share, which is also referred to as the net asset value (NAV), reflects the true value of a company's assets if they were sold, also called private marketization or breakup value. A supermarket chain, for example, may own real estate carried on the books at only nominal value instead of its "going market" price. Similarly, mineral or oil and gas reserves, radio and TV stations, and forest reserves are more often than not carried at "stated" book value, which is typically far lower than are the values which could be realized in a breakup sale.

These two key factors—cash flow per share and real net asset value per share—are the main focus of interest in the current game of takeover mania.

TAKEOVER MANIA

American public corporations are owned by their stockholders, yet for decades a large percentage of corporate managements have been more interested in keeping their jobs and perks than in rewarding their stockholders. Dividend increases have been deemed less important than executive salaries, and many managements have ignored the prices at which their stocks were trading. Wall Street analysts have described these managements "as not very stock-minded."

During the past few years, this neglect of stockholder interests has come to a screeching halt. The catalyst for this great change has been takeover mania. One after another, complacent and neglectful managements have found themselves under attack from corporate raiders, leveraged buyout (LBO) specialists, and aroused stockholder groups.

Before we present specific examples of two takeovers, let us review what we mean by cash flow per share and net asset value per share, since these two factors are instrumental in understanding the takeover phenomena.

CASH FLOW PER SHARE

Every corporation needs income from operations to pay for:

- Dividends
- Expansion
- Working capital
- Interest on and repayment of debt

These financial needs are met by both income and depreciation. Depreciation is a noncash charge made against earnings to replace assets as they wear out. Income after taxes and interest charges (but before dividends) is then added to depreciation and is called "cash flow."

Cash flow per share is calculated by dividing the cash flow by the number of common shares outstanding. For example, Phillips Petroleum, which we will discuss in greater depth later on, reported net income of $721 million for the year 1983. Depreciation and depletion for that same year was $985 million. Thus, cash flow was:

$$\begin{array}{r} \$ \ 721 \text{ million} \\ + \ \ 985 \text{ million} \\ \hline \$1,706 \text{ million} \end{array}$$

To determine the cash flow per share, you then divide $1,706 million by the number of shares, i.e., 154,627,000. The cash flow per share was $11.03 (see Standard & Poor's report below).

NET ASSET VALUE PER SHARE

NAV per share, or book value per share, is derived by subtracting all liabilities from total assets (after depreciation) and dividing by the number of shares outstanding. For example, Phillips had total assets as of December 31, 1983, of $13,094 million and total liabilities of $6,945 million.

$$\begin{array}{r} \$13,094 \text{ million} \\ - \ \ 6,945 \text{ million} \\ \hline \$ \ 6,149 \text{ million} \end{array}$$

divided by 154.6 million shares = $39.77 or approximately $40 per share.

However, the real net asset value of a company can be determined only by learning what the assets would sell for in today's market. Here we depart from stated book value and look for:

- Real estate—land and buildings with a substantial current market value
- Lumber and forest reserves
- Oil and gas reserves that are proven and commercial
- Radio and TV stations
- Mineral resources
- Trucks, trailers, railway cars, with substantial resale value
- Retail chains, fast food facilities, textile, metal, and manufacturing facilities; i.e., anything with a profitable "going-concern" value

When we have corrected our assets and arrived at a true picture of net asset value, we can then divide the number of shares in order to find the real net asset, or breakup, value per share:

$$\frac{\text{Total assets adjusted} - \text{All liabilities}}{\text{Number of common shares}}$$

For example, American Broadcasting had net assets of $1,214 million as of December 31, 1983, as stated in its financial reports. This was approximately $42 per share. (See the following Standard & Poor's report.) ABC, however, has since been acquired by Capital Cities Broadcasting, at $118 per share. Apparently the real values of ABC's TV and radio stations as well as its other operations were substantially in excess of either its stated book value or the prices at which its common stock was trading. (See ABC— A Study in Assets, page 187.)

FINDING A TAKEOVER TARGET

Companies with substantial cash flow per share and/or real net asset value per share have been takeover targets in the past and they continue to attract attention from a wide range of potential acquirers. The accompanying Standard & Poor's stock reports illustrate what skillful readers of this guide might look for to discover a takeover target. Indeed professional money managers and security analysts do this sort of cash flow and asset study all the time.

PHILLIPS PETROLEUM—A STUDY IN CASH FLOW

As we see, Phillips had a combined net income and depreciation in 1983 of $11.03 per share. During 1983, the stock sold in the range of $29 to $39 and as of October 1984 sold below $40 per share. In other words, as late as October 1984, less than 6 weeks before the announcement from Mesa, Phillips was still selling at less than four times its cash flow.

On December 4, 1984, T. Boone Pickens, chairman of Mesa Petroleum, and his partners announced they had acquired 5.8% of Phillips common stock and intended to make a tender offer to buy 23 million shares at $60 per share. This would have given the Mesa partners 20% of the common shares and effective control.

After this event, the fat was in the fire. A settlement was reached between Mesa Petroleum and Phillips in which Phillips

Phillips Petroleum

NYSE Symbol P   Options on ASE (Feb–May–Aug–Nov)

Price	Range 1984-5	P-E Ratio	Dividend	Yield	S&P Ranking
Jan. 14'85 44	56¼–33⅜	8	2.40	5.5%	A

Summary

On December 23, 1984 Phillips and Mesa Partners announced a settlement agreement under which Phillips would propose a recapitalization plan to its stockholders and Mesa Partners would terminate its efforts to acquire control of Phillips. The recapitalization plan resembles something of a partial leveraged buyout, with Phillips offering debt securities for a big chunk of its shares outstanding and then selling Phillips employees a big ownership interest in the company. Mesa Partners is to receive at least $53 each for the 8.9 million (6%) Phillips shares it owns.

Current Outlook

Earnings for 1985 (assuming the recapitalization program is implemented) are projected at $4.20 a share, down from 1984's estimated $5.20.

Dividends are expected to continue at a minimum of $0.60 quarterly.

Revenues for 1985 could be down on the sale of assets. Profits also are targeted lower, penalized by the proposed recapitalization and oversupplied markets in just about every part of the petroleum business.

Total Revenues (Billion $)

Quarter:	1984	1983	1982	1981
Mar.	3.96	3.64	3.81	4.23
Jun.	4.05	3.79	4.03	4.07
Sep.	3.74	3.89	4.00	3.90
Dec.	---	4.15	4.06	4.09
	---	15.47	15.89	16.29

Revenues for the first nine months of 1984 rose 3.8%, year to year. Net income gained 35%, to $4.16 a share from $3.10.

Common Share Earnings ($)

Quarter:	1984	1983	1982	1981
Mar.	1.26	0.84	1.26	1.78
Jun.	1.50	1.10	0.96	1.51
Sep.	1.40	1.15	1.00	1.26
Dec.	E1.04	1.61	1.01	1.23
	E5.20	4.71	4.23	5.78

Important Developments

Dec. 23'84—Under Phillips' (P) restructuring plan (to be voted on by shareholders in February or

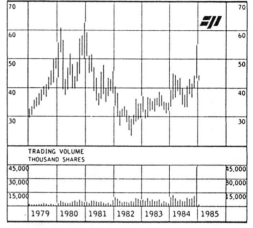

TRADING VOLUME THOUSAND SHARES

March), P would offer to exchange a package of debt securities designed to have an aggregate principal value of $60 a share for about 58.8 million (38%) of its shares outstanding. P would then sell not more than 32 million of its shares to a newly-formed Employee Stock Ownership Plan, and it would spend not less than $1 billion within the year following recapitalization to purchase its common in open market transactions at prices not to exceed $50 per share. Following recapitalization, P would sell about $2 billion of assets and make significant revisions in its capital expenditure programs and its annual operating expenses. P believes that its debt securities and shares outstanding after the recapitalization should be worth about $53 per presently outstanding share.

Next earnings reports due in Jan. & Apr.

Per Share Data ($)

Yr. End Dec. 31	1984	1983	1982	1981	1980	1979	1978	1977	1976	1975
Book Value	NA	40.13	37.70	36.02	32.44	27.57	23.54	20.08	17.77	15.90
Earnings	NA	4.71	4.23	5.78	7.01	5.77	4.61	3.37	2.69	2.25
Dividends	2.35	2.20	2.20	2.20	1.80	1.35	1.20	0.97½	0.87½	0.80
Payout Ratio	NA	47%	52%	38%	26%	23%	26%	29%	33%	36%
Prices—High	56¼	38⅞	40¾	59½	62⅞	50⅝	36⅜	33⅝	33⅛	30⅛
Low	33⅜	29⅜	23½	34	37⅝	29½	26¾	25¾	24¾	18½
P/E Ratio—	NA	8-6	10-6	10-6	9-5	9-5	8-6	10-8	12-9	13-8

Data as orig. reptd. Adj. for stk. div(s). of 100% Jun. 1977. NA-Not Available. E-Estimated.

January 21, 1985
Copyright © 1985 Standard & Poor's Corp. All Rights Reserved
Standard & Poor's Corp.
25 Broadway, NY, NY 10004

Income Data (Million $)

Year Ended Dec. 31	Revs.	Oper. Inc.	% Oper. Inc. of Revs.	Cap. Exp.	Depr.	Int. Exp.	Net Bef. Taxes	Eff. Tax Rate	[2]Net Inc.	% Net Inc. of Revs.
1983	15,249	3,347	21.9%	1,141	985	311	[1]2,277	68.3%	721	4.7%
1982	15,698	3,218	20.5%	2,132	1,086	336	[1]2,100	69.2%	[3] 646	4.1%
1981	15,966	3,409	21.4%	2,664	858	262	[1]2,671	67.1%	879	5.5%
1980	13,377	3,847	28.8%	1,666	838	106	[1]3,240	67.0%	1,070	8.0%
1979	9,503	2,638	27.8%	1,454	647	97	[1]2,136	58.3%	[3] 891	9.4%
1978	6,998	1,827	26.1%	956	460	79	[1]1,713	58.5%	710	10.2%
1977	6,284	1,484	23.6%	1,091	337	82	[1]1,187	56.4%	517	8.2%
1976	5,698	1,264	22.2%	728	304	68	[1]1,031	60.1%	412	7.2%
1975	5,134	1,048	20.4%	694	326	50	[1] 752	54.4%	343	6.7%
1974	4,981	1,001	20.1%	618	274	53	[1] 786	45.3%	430	8.6%

Balance Sheet Data (Million $)

Dec. 31	Cash	Current Assets	Current Liab.	Ratio	Total Assets	Ret. on Assets	Long Term Debt	Common Equity	Total Cap.	% LT Debt of Cap.	Ret. on Equity
1983	906	2,903	2,881	1.0	13,094	5.7%	2,242	6,149	9,636	23.3%	12.1%
1982	793	2,909	2,712	1.1	12,097	5.5%	1,955	5,773	8,603	22.7%	11.4%
1981	895	3,048	3,237	0.9	11,264	8.3%	1,100	5,481	7,318	15.0%	16.9%
1980	1,471	3,694	3,105	1.2	9,844	11.7%	773	4,937	6,214	12.4%	23.4%
1979	1,300	3,386	2,678	1.3	8,519	11.5%	745	4,257	5,477	13.6%	22.6%
1978	1,136	2,492	1,748	1.4	6,935	11.1%	796	3,636	4,893	16.3%	21.1%
1977	327	1,615	1,222	1.3	5,837	9.5%	923	3,087	4,394	21.0%	17.8%
1976	702	1,859	1,082	1.7	5,068	8.5%	839	2,720	3,863	21.7%	16.0%
1975	523	1,621	884	1.8	4,545	8.0%	893	2,424	3,531	25.3%	14.6%
1974	393	1,466	889	1.6	4,028	11.2%	658	2,274	3,013	21.8%	20.2%

Data as orig. reptd. 1. Incl. equity in earns. of nonconsol. subs. 2. Bef. spec. item(s). 3. Reflects accounting change.

Business Summary

Phillips is engaged in petroleum exploration and production on a worldwide basis, and petroleum marketing and refining in the U.S. It also is a major chemical producer, and is developing businesses in other energy fields, including coal, uranium, oil shale, and geothermal power.

Profits	1983	1982
U.S. expl. & prod.	40%	51%
U.S. gas & gas liquids	37%	42%
U.S. ref., mkt. & trans.	10%	9%
Foreign expl. & prod.	17%	13%
Foreign gas & gas liquids	Nil	1%
Foreign ref., mkt., & trans.	2%	2%
Worldwide chemicals	6%	2%
Minerals	−6%	−9%
Other	−6%	−11%

In 1983 net production of crude oil averaged 247,000 barrels a day, net natural gas liquids production 175,000 b/d, net natural gas production 1.3 billion cubic feet a day, crude oil refined 260,000 b/d, and petroleum products sold 505,000 b/d.

Net proved reserves at the 1983 year-end were 1,048 million barrels of crude oil and natural gas liquids and 6,859 billion cubic feet of natural gas.

In October, 1984 Phillips completed the purchase of the energy operations of R.J. Reynolds for $1.7 billion cash. Reynold's energy operations consist mainly of Aminoil Inc. and nonoil operations include Geysers Geothermal Co. Phillips estimated Aminoil's proved reserves of oil and natural gas at about 245,000,000 barrels of oil equivalent, virtually all domestic.

Dividend Data

Dividends have been paid since 1934. A dividend reinvestment plan is available.

Amt. of Divd. $	Date Decl.	Ex-divd. Date	Stock of Record	Payment Date
0.60	Mar. 12	Apr. 30	May 4	Jun. 1'84
0.60	Jul. 9	Jul. 30	Aug. 3	Sep. 1'84
0.60	Oct. 8	Oct. 29	Nov. 2	Dec. 1'84
0.60	Jan. 14	Jan. 28	Feb. 1	Mar. 1'85

Next dividend meeting: mid-Mar. '85.

Capitalization

Long Term Debt: $1,969,000,000.

Minority Interest: $37,000,000.

Common Stock: 154,626,706 shs. ($1.25 par). Institutions hold about 49%. Shareholders of record: 119,800.

Office—Phillips Bldg., Bartlesville, Okla. 74004. Tel—(918) 661-6600. Chrmn & CEO—W. C. Douce. Pres—C. J. Silas. Secy—G. C. Meese. VP-Treas—R. E. Bonnell. Investor Contact—R. L. Howard. (212) 397-9760. Dirs—G. B. Beitzel, M. N. Chetkovich, G. A. Cox, W. C. Douce, J. B. Edwards, R. F. Froehlke, E. D. Kenna, C. M. Kittrell, M. R. Laird, C. C. Laise, D. B. Meeker, C. J. Silas, R. G. Wallace, W. C. Wescoe, D. D. Wharton, F. M. Wheat. Transfer Agent & Registrar—Manufacturers Hanover Trust Co., NYC. Incorporated in Delaware in 1917.

Earl L. Lester, CFA

American Broadcasting

NYSE Symbol ABC   Options on Pac (Feb-May-Aug-Nov)

Price	Range	P-E Ratio	Dividend	Yield	S&P Ranking
Nov. 5'84	1984				
64⅝	77¼–50¼	10	1.60	2.5%	A

Summary

This company operates one of the three national television networks, operates seven radio networks, and owns five TV and 12 radio stations in major cities. It also is engaged in publishing, motion picture production and cable TV programming services. In June, 1984 ABC purchased the remaining 85% interest in Entertainment and Sports Programming Network (ESPN) and other assets for $202 million, then sold a 20% interest in the service to Nabisco Brands for $60 million in October, 1984. Near-term earnings prospects remain favorable.

Current Outlook

Earnings for 1985 are tentatively projected to rise to $7.50 a share from the $6.70 estimated for 1984.

The $0.40 quarterly dividend is likely to be raised in the near term.

Revenues and earnings in 1985 will benefit from stronger broadcast advertising revenues and favorable margins. Publishing gains are expected to continue. Losses from video enterprises are likely to be larger, which should be partially offset by an expected recovery in motion picture results.

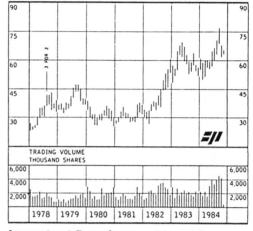

TRADING VOLUME
THOUSAND SHARES

Total Revenues (Million $)

Quarter:	1984	1983	1982	1981
Mar.	837	663	613	541
Jun.	854	755	685	612
Sep.	1,084	660	607	554
Dec.	---	871	760	737
	---	2,949	2,665	2,444

Total revenues for the nine months ended September 30, 1984 advanced 34%, year to year. Largely aided by improved operating profits from broadcasting and publishing, net income gained 30%, to $4.91 a share from $3.76.

Common Share Earnings ($)

Quarter:	1984	1983	1982	1981
Mar.	0.81	0.48	0.84	0.45
Jun.	2.49	2.20	2.06	1.96
Sep.	1.61	1.08	1.22	1.19
Dec.	E1.79	1.69	1.42	1.53
	E6.70	5.45	5.54	5.13

Important Developments

Oct. '84—ABC sold a 20% interest in the Entertainment and Sports Programming Network (ESPN) to Nabisco Brands for $60 million. In June, ABC purchased the 85% of ESPN that it did not already own, plus other assets, for $202 million; it had earlier purchased 15% for $25 million. ESPN is an ad-supported cable TV network available to some 32.7 million subscribers.

Jun. '84—ABC agreed to sell radio station WXYZ-AM Detroit. The company also ended its experimental home video service TeleFirst, which resulted in a second-quarter pretax charge of $15 million.

May '84—ABC sold its leisure attractions division at a pretax gain of $6.6 million.

Next earnings report due in mid-January.

Per Share Data ($)

Yr. End Dec. 31	1983	1982	1981	1980	1979	1978	1977	1976	1975	1974
Book Value²	39.13	35.46	31.45	28.09	24.41	20.78	16.71	13.89	11.56	11.52
Earnings¹	5.45	5.54	5.13	5.18	5.67	4.60	4.03	2.70	0.66	1.95
Dividends	1.60	1.60	1.60	1.60	1.30	1.00	0.73⅜	0.56¾	0.53⅜	0.53⅜
Payout Ratio	29%	29%	31%	31%	23%	22%	18%	21%	81%	27%
Prices—High	69¾	61¼	38¼	39	47⅝	43¼	31½	26⅞	18¼	18⅞
Low	48⅜	26¾	26¾	25⅝	32⅜	23⅛	24	13¼	8¾	7⅝
P/E Ratio—	13–9	11–5	7–5	8–5	8–6	9–5	8–6	10–5	28–13	10–4

Data as orig. reptd. Adj. for stk. div(s). of 50% Oct. 1978. 1. Bef. results of disc. opers. of ⊦0.29 in 1978. 2. Excl. intangibles. E-Estimated.

Standard NYSE Stock Reports
Vol. 51/No. 219/Sec. 3

November 12, 1984
Copyright © 1984 Standard & Poor's Corp. All Rights Reserved

Standard & Poor's Corp.
25 Broadway, NY, NY 10004

American Broadcasting Companies, Inc.

Income Data (Million $)

Year Ended Dec. 31	Revs.	Oper. Inc.	% Oper. Inc. of Revs.	Cap. Exp.	Depr.	Int. Exp.	Net Bef. Taxes	Eff. Tax Rate	[3]Net Inc.	% Net Inc. of Revs.
1983	2,940	361	12.3%	127	56.9	15.5	[2]312	48.8%	160	5.4%
1982	2,641	319	12.1%	116	49.2	16.9	[2]293	45.4%	160	6.1%
1981	2,421	326	13.5%	54	43.8	18.3	[2]297	50.8%	146	6.0%
1980	2,256	319	14.1%	111	35.0	[4]18.3	[2]295	50.3%	146	6.5%
1979	2,029	337	16.6%	128	28.7	17.8	[2]319	50.1%	159	7.8%
[1]1978	1,767	311	17.6%	68	23.1	16.9	[2]271	53.0%	128	7.2%
1977	1,617	260	16.2%	46	21.1	16.1	[2]232	52.6%	110	6.8%
1976	1,342	177	13.3%	29	18.1	15.8	[2]149	51.8%	72	5.4%
1975	1,065	76	7.1%	31	17.4	12.1	[2] 36	52.1%	17	1.6%
1974	986	123	12.5%	52	13.0	7.3	[2]103	51.4%	50	5.1%

Balance Sheet Data (Million $)

Dec. 31	Cash	Current Assets	Current Liab.	Ratio	Total Assets	Ret. on Assets	Long Term Debt	Common Equity	Total Cap.	% LT Debt of Cap.	Ret. on Equity
1983	52	1,109	477	2.3	2,091	7.9%	171	1,214	1,409	12.1%	13.8%
1982	66	945	439	2.2	1,922	9.1%	176	1,098	1,288	13.6%	15.4%
1981	194	963	367	2.6	1,588	9.7%	212	975	1,195	17.8%	15.7%
1980	147	807	291	2.8	1,411	10.8%	220	870	1,092	20.2%	17.8%
1979	213	777	277	2.8	1,274	13.3%	226	760	986	22.9%	22.8%
1978	251	761	258	3.0	1,101	12.2%	192	628	821	23.4%	22.3%
1977	181	650	235	2.8	963	12.0%	199	504	703	28.3%	24.0%
1976	166	609	230	2.6	844	9.3%	188	403	591	31.9%	19.2%
1975	81	468	146	3.2	698	2.6%	194	339	533	36.5%	5.1%
1974	39	398	162	2.5	621	8.3%	106	333	441	24.0%	15.8%

Data as orig. reptd. 1. Excludes discontinued operations. 2. Incl. equity in earns. of nonconsol. subs. 3. Bef. results of disc. opers. and spec. item(s). 4. Reflects accounting change.

Business Summary

American Broadcasting Companies operates the nationwide ABC television and radio networks and owns TV and radio stations in major cities. ABC is also engaged in publishing, motion picture production and video enterprises. The leisure attractions division was sold in May 1984. Contributions by business segment in 1983:

	Revs.	Profits
Broadcasting	89%	$365.3
Publishing	10%	29.2
Video enterprises / scenic attractions and other	1%	−48.7

Five television stations and 12 radio stations are owned and operated in New York City (WABC-TV & AM, WPLJ-FM), Los Angeles (KABC-TV & AM, KLOS-FM), San Francisco (KGO-TV & AM), Detroit (WXYZ-TV & AM, WRIF-FM), Chicago (WLS-TV, AM & FM), Houston (KSRR-FM), and Washington, D.C. (WRQX-FM). At the beginning of 1984, ABC's television network had 210 primary affiliated stations and its radio network served 1,740 affiliated stations.

Farm, business, database, high tech leisure and specialty magazines and books are published by several subsidiaries. Word, Inc. publishes reli-

gious books and materials, and produces and distributes records, tapes, sheet music and instructional materials.

Video enterprises produce programming for video-cassettes, video discs, and cable and subscription TV. Cable program networks include ESPN, Lifetime, ARTS & Entertainment Network, and Satellite News Channel. Theatrical feature-length films are also produced.

Dividend Data

Dividends have been paid since 1950.

Amt. of Divd. $	Date Decl.	Ex-divd. Date	Stock of Record	Payment Date
0.40	Nov. 14	Nov. 18	Nov. 25	Dec. 16'83
0.40	Feb. 13	Feb. 21	Feb. 27	Mar. 15'84
0.40	Apr. 2	May 14	May 18	Jun. 15'84
0.40	Jul. 30	Aug. 20	Aug. 24	Sep. 15'84

Next dividend meetings: Nov. 12 & Feb. '85.

Capitalization

Long Term Debt: $157,359,000, incl. $22,995,000 capital lease obligations.

Common Stock: 28,913,526 shs. ($1 par). Institutions hold about 75%. Shareholders of record: 11,870.

Office — 1330 Ave. of the Americas, NYC 10019. Tel—(212) 887-7777. Chrmn & CEO—L. H. Goldenson. Pres—F. S. Pierce. VP-Secy—J. B. Golden. Treas—D. J. Vondrak. Investor Contact—J. L. Abernathy. Dirs—R. C. Adam, F. T. Cary, J. T. Connor, E. H. Erlick, L. H. Goldenson, A. Greenspan, J. Hausman, L. Hess, G. P. Jenkins, F. S. Jones, T. M. Macioce, M. P. Mallardi, N. T. Pace, F. S. Pierce, E. H. Rule, M. J. Schwab. Transfer Agent—Morgan Guaranty Trust Co., NYC. Registrar—Bank of New York, NYC. Incorporated in New York in 1949.

William H. Donald

agreed to a recapitalization plan providing that (1) Phillips would not spend less than $1 billion to purchase its shares in the open market at prices not higher than $50 per share; and (2) Mesa was to have an option to sell its already acquired shares (5.8%) at $53 per share.

Many Wall Street arbitrageurs and especially Carl Icahn were dissatisfied with this settlement, feeling that only Mesa's shares would be sold for $53 per share and the values in Phillips deserved a higher price. During February, Icahn made proposals to acquire Phillips shares for $55 per share and later for $57 per share. Finally, on February 14, Icahn commenced an offer for 70 million shares at $60 in cash per share.

Then, on March 3, 1985, Phillips capitulated in what is known as the "Icahn Settlement." Under the terms of the settlement, Phillips agreed to issue bonds and notes worth $70 per share in exchange for 72,580,000 of its shares. The company also agreed to raise the dividend on the remaining shares from $2.40 to $3.00. This transaction, in which Phillips created new debt to use in exchange for its common stock, came about because Phillips had substantial cash flow and assets.

We can see from this example how Phillips's cash flow, when directed from other corporate purposes, was used (1) to pay interest on the debt used to buy back its shares at a substantially higher price; and (2) increase dividends on the remaining shares.

AMERICAN BROADCASTING COMPANIES—A STUDY IN ASSETS

In March 1985, Capital Cities Broadcasting made an offer to acquire all the outstanding stock of ABC at $118 per share. Yet in the early days of March, ABC was selling in the marketplace at $69 per share.

Note that the stated book value on December 31, 1983, was $39.13. Cash flow for 1983, which consisted of net income ($160 million) plus depreciation ($56.9 million), was $216.9 million. If we divide this figure by ABC's 28.9 million

shares, we arrive at a figure for cash flow per share of $7.50 in 1983.

How might either of these figures, book value per share of $39.13 or cash flow per share of $7.50, have given any forewarning of the spectacular takeover?

The answer lies *first* in the fact that the Federal Communications Commission's restrictions on the ownership of TV and radio stations had recently been liberalized to a maximum of 12 TV, 12 AM, and 12 FM radio stations. In the past, each broadcaster was limited to 7 TV, 7 AM, and 7 FM radio stations. This was known as the 7-7-7 rule. In effect, the new ownership rule became 12-12-12.

The *second* and far more important fact was that ABC's book value was substantially understated, as noted early on by the astute security analyst John Kornreich of Neuberger and Berman. Writing about ABC in early March 1985, Kornreich stated: "Breakup value is probably in the area of $130 to $140 per share. In fact, the television and radio stations alone would find ready buyers for something in the area of $2 billion or $69 per share."

Weeks before the news of the ABC takeover by Capital Cities hit the public like a bombshell, smart investors and analysts were already focusing on the breakup value as a key consideration.

STOCK BUY-BACKS

A corporate action that has become more prevalent than in the past is a stock buy-back. It, too, bears study because it reflects the shifting action on the part of companies to protect themselves. Many companies, in an effort to raise their earnings per share and the price of their stocks, have been buying back their common shares, either by making public tender offers or by simply going into the open market.

The motives are often clear. Managements, fearing a hostile takeover, try to give their stockholders nearly the same benefits as a takeover by raising their own stock's price.

Here again, as in the case of takeovers, cash

SELECTED COMPANIES WITH STOCK-REPURCHASE PROGRAMS

| | EARNINGS, DOLLARS PER SHARE | | INDICATED DIVIDEND | YIELD % | CURRENT PRICE | REPURCHASE PROGRAMS | | |
	1985	E1986				NUMBER OF SHARES (THOUSANDS)	APPROXIMATE % OF SHARES OUTSTANDING	LATEST PROGRAM ANNOUNCED
★Abbott Laboratories	1.94	2.20	$0.84	2.0	43w.i.	6,000	5	12-85
American Express	3.55	4.90	1.36	2.4	57	10,000	4	4-86
American Standard	0.56	3.20	1.60	4.0	40	3,000	8	2-86
Avon Products	d0.76	2.25	2.00	6.3	32	10,000	14	10-85
Celanese	13.70	15.00	4.80	2.3	208	600	5	1-86
Coleco	3.87	3.45	None	. . .	19	2,000	12	1-86
Ford Motor	9.09	9.75	3.30	4.3	76	1	11	11-85
General Motors Cl. E.	1.57	N.E.	0.40	0.9	46	8,500	13	3-86
Grace (W.R.)	2.82	3.00	2.80	4.9	57	13,600	33	1-86
Holiday Corp.	5.06	5.75	1.16	1.9	61	2,500	10	11-85
Honeywell	6.02	5.65	2.00	2.6	76	5,000	11	2-86
Louisiana Pacific	0.70	1.40	0.80	3.2	25	3,000	8	11-85
§Lotus Development	2.31	2.70	None	. . .	35	1,650	10	2-86
Macmillan	2.04	2.45	0.60	1.3	47	1,500	67	10-85
Martin Marietta	4.36	3.50	1.00	2.3	44	3,000	6	3-86
Questar	3.20	N.E.	1.72	5.7	30	1,000	6	10-85
TransWorld Corp.	2.84	3.00	None	. . .	14	4,000	15	4-86
USLIFE	3.70	4.30	1.12	2.8	40	1,000	5	10-85
United Technologies	2.12	4.80	1.40	3.0	47	10,000	8	2-86
Warner-Lambert	d4.05	3.40	1.56	2.8	55	8	10	11-86

★Master List issue.   §Over the counter.   d-Deficit.   N.E.-No estimate.   E-Estimated.   1Plans to repurchase up to $1 billion of stock.   w.i.-When issued.

SOURCE: Standard & Poor's *The Outlook*, May 28, 1986.

flow and high asset values provide the money for corporate buy-backs of stock. When cash flow per share is high, then cash is obviously available for common stock buybacks.

Large understated assets may enable a corporation to raise cash from sales of those same assets and use the cash to buy back its own stock, thus closing some of the gap between market price and breakup value. (See the table for a list of companies with repurchase programs.)

As we go to press, the U.S. stock market is hurling through the strongest bull market in history. The Dow Jones industrial average is above 1800, a level that would have been unthinkable in the early months of 1985. Disinflation and a historic and precipitous drop in interest rates as well as a collapse in oil prices have combined to create an environment in which common stocks have been revalued in terms of their private market values. Takeovers, leveraged buyouts, and stock buy-backs have fueled these extraordinary changes in stock valuations. It is far from over. Astute investors should be working round the clock in their quest for the many still undiscovered values in the market.

Companies with high NAV and strong cash flows also benefit stockholders because they have the capability to buy back their own shares. The three main reasons behind a stock buy-back are: (1) to fend off hostile takeovers; (2) to boost shareholder values; (3) to increase earnings per share. Therefore, investors are well advised to search for companies already embarked on buy-back programs.

PART FOUR

SPECULATIONS: RISKS AND REWARDS

There are times, and occasions, when a portion of your savings can be used for speculations. When it is, recognize the hazards and limit your commitments to 20% of your capital. If you are smart—and lucky—enough to score, put back half your winnings into a money market fund to build assets for future risks.

Speculations are not investments. This statement sounds simple-minded, but most people fail to make, or understand, the distinction. Investments are designed to preserve capital and to provide income. The decisions are made on the basis of fundamentals: the quality of the corporation and the value of the security. If you set strict standards, do your homework, and buy at a fair price, you will *always* attain your goal.

Speculations involve risks and are profitable primarily because of market fluctuations. *They should be entered into only when you understand what you are doing (or trying to do) and with money that you can afford to lose.* The profits will usually come quickly as the result of shrewd timing, but there are speculations where success depends on an understanding of special securities and situations and patience. Speculative securities should *never* be included in fiduciary portfolios, but they can be valuable with personal holdings to build capital and, perhaps most important, to add excitement to making your money make more money.

Before getting into details about speculations:

- Recognize that there is usually a sound reason why a security is selling at a low price or a high yield. Investors are not interested, so you should be certain that there are facts to justify higher future values.
- Be realistic with new issues, because their market values depend largely on unsubstantiated optimism and hard selling by the sponsoring brokers.
- In making projections, cut in half the anticipated upmove and double the potential downswing. These "values" are seldom based on facts and usually reflect conditions over which you have no control. Once any industry or company becomes unpopular, the prices of its shares can fall rapidly. Conversely, the price rises are likely to be slower than projected by research—your own and that of your broker.

- Speculate only in a rising market unless you are selling short. Worthwhile gains will come when more people buy more shares . . . not likely in a down market.
- Be willing to take quick, small losses and never hold on with hope for a recovery unless there are little-known or -understood reasons for optimism.
- When you pick a winner, sell half your shares (or set a protective stop-loss order) when you have doubled your money.
- Speculate only when you have time to continue research and watch developments, preferably daily and certainly weekly.
- *And, most important, buy a rabbit's foot.*

There are scores of types of speculations. Some of the most popular involving securities are summarized here. By and large, they are related to investments. The *real* speculations, closely allied to gambling, are explained later under futures, commodities, and tax shelters.

There's nothing wrong with modest speculations as long as you understand the risks, have the temperament to accept losses, and use only money you can afford to lose.

On the next few pages you will read about:
- Warrants
- Margin accounts and leverage
- Venture capital and new issues
- Commodities
- Financial futures
- Options
- Stock rights

20 MARGIN ACCOUNTS: Using Leverage

With almost all types of speculations, a key factor in their success is leverage: using borrowed funds to supplement your own commitments. With *real estate,* it's making a small down payment and having a large mortgage; with *securities,* it's buying on margin: using cash, stocks, convertibles, bonds, etc., as collateral for a loan from your broker or banker. When the borrowing is kept at a reasonable level and the interest costs are modest, buying on margin can enhance profits because your money is working twice as hard since you put up only part of the cost. Margin, then, is trading on credit and a way of using borrowing power to take a larger position in the stock market.

Leverage in the stock market is not as simple as it sounds. Successful use of margin calls for sophistication, sufficient resources to absorb substantial losses when the prices of the securities decline, and the temperament to handle debt. Many people must meet these criteria, because in 1984 the margin debt of the NYSE was over $22 billion.

Under the rules set forth by the Federal Reserve Board, the initial requirement for margin on stocks is 50%. Greater leverage is allowed on government bonds, where you can borrow up to 95%. The New York Stock Exchange, however, has stricter requirements. It asks members to demand that investors deposit a minimum of $2,000 in cash or its equivalent in securities in order to open a margin account. That means if you want to buy $3,000 in stock, your initial margin requirement is actually 66⅔%, or $2,000 rather than the $1,500 the Federal Reserve Board requires. Some brokers set even higher standards, especially on low-priced stocks. The New York Stock Exchange also requires that the equity in the account be maintained at 25% at all times, and many brokerage firms require more than 25%. This is called a "minimum maintenance margin."

Example: With $10,000 you buy 200 shares of a stock at $50 each. By using margin, you will have $15,000, so you can acquire 300 shares.

As with most stock market ploys, leverage works best when stock prices rise. If the stock moves up to 55, you will have a $1,000 (10%) profit in your cash account or a $1,500 (15%) gain if you use a margin account. At this point, your cash account assets will be $11,000, so the margin account will be worth $16,500. The equity will be $11,500 ($16,500 minus $5,000). This will be above the maintenance minimum of $3,750, so you can increase your loan.

But leverage works both ways. If your stock starts to slide, you will lose money that much faster. With a 5-point drop in the value of the stock, the cash account loss will be $1,000; that of the margin account, $1,500. If the decline continues so that your equity falls below 25%, your broker will issue a margin call and you will have to come up with more cash or collateral or be sold out.

When the value of the portfolio drops too far, more collateral will be required. And there can be problems with low-priced stocks. In margin evaluation, when the price of a stock falls below a full dollar figure, the next lower round-dollar value is used: that is, when a stock drops from 100 to 99½, its new margin value is 99, a loss of less than 1% of its worth. But a stock trading at 10 that falls to 9⅞ is valued at 9, a 10% loss. Use a margin account cautiously and always keep ample reserves.

Mounting interest charges can take a big hunk out of profits, especially if you hold your stocks a long time. You are charged interest

Margin account: Use of borrowed money to increase your position.

Assuming you put up cash in the amount of $10,000 in each case, you could buy on margin:

- $20,000 worth of *marginable stocks*
- $20,000 worth of *listed corporate convertible bonds*
- $40,000 worth of *listed corporate* and certain *OTC nonconvertible bonds*
- $66,000 face value of *municipal bonds*
- $200,000 face value of *U.S. government bonds*

You can invest on margin in nearly every issue on the New York and American Stock Exchanges and in nearly 2,000 over-the-counter securities. To open an account, you must sign a margin agreement which includes a consent to loan securities. The margin account agreement states that all securities will be held "in street name," i.e., by the broker. The consent to loan means that the broker can lend your securities to others who may want them for the purpose of selling short.

daily based on the *broker call rate,* the rate the banks charge brokers for money. The interest the broker then charges you may run from ½% to 2½% above the broker loan rate, which currently is about *8%.* The more active and the larger your account, the lower the rate is likely to be. Dividends, of course, can help offset some of the interest. A greater offset comes about when you deduct the interest charges from your taxes.

UNDERMARGINED ACCOUNTS

If the value of your margin account falls below minimum maintenance requirements, it becomes undermargined, and even if the deficit is only $4, there will be a margin call. To check when you're approaching this 25% level, divide the amount of your debit balance by 3 and add the result to your net loan. Thus, one-third of

$5,000, $1,666, plus $5,000 equals $6,666. If the portfolio value is less, your account becomes restricted.

If the value of your securities falls below the minimum level and you get a margin call, you must deposit additional cash or securities. If you are unable to do either, the broker will sell enough securities from your account to bring it up to the required level. A margin call does not imply any lack of faith in your ability to pay; nor is it a reflection on your credit.

When your account is at a 25% maintenance level, your withdrawals of cash or securities are limited. If your account has anything above the 25% level, this amount is designated as SMA (special miscellaneous account). It represents the

CALCULATING YOUR YIELD WHEN BUYING ON MARGIN

To determine exactly what yield you get by buying on margin, you must ascertain the return on your actual investment: the *margin equivalent yield.* You can calculate this from the accompanying formula.

The *cash yield* percent (CY%) is the return on securities bought outright. The same formulas can be used for both pretax and after-tax yields.

$$MEY = \left(\frac{100}{\%M} \times CY\%\right) - \left(\frac{100}{\%M} - 1\right) \times DI\%$$

where MEY = margin equivalent yield
  %M = % margin
  CY% = cash yield %
  DI% = debit interest %

Example: You are on a 50% margin base, receive 12% cash yield from dividends, and pay 20% in your debit balance.

$$MEY = \frac{100}{50} \times 12 - \frac{100}{50} - 1 \times 20$$

$$MEY = 2 \times 12 = 24\% - 2 - 1 \times 20 = 20\%$$

$$MEY = 24\% - 20\% = 4\%$$

Thus, the 12% return, with margin, dwindles to 4%.

equity in excess of margin requirements which come from price appreciation, dividends, proceeds of sales, and cash deposits made to meet a margin call. When you have equity in your SMA, and you wish to sell some of your stock and withdraw cash from the sale, there are special rules involved. At this point you can withdraw funds above the maintenance minimum, but you must deposit assets equal to the lesser of (1) 70% of the market value of the securities taken out, or (2) the amount needed to bring the remaining equity back to 50%.

There is one way to get around these rules: *buy and sell on the same day stocks of equal value.* But the 70% retention rule applies if the transactions are made on different days.

The Fed's rules are specific. On same-day deals, if the cost of the stock you buy is greater than the value of the one sold, you deposit 50% of the difference between the two prices. If the new stock is worth less than the old, only 30% of the difference is credited to the SMA.

If the equity drops below 30%, your account becomes *super-restricted.* All purchase and sales, even on the same day, are treated separately, with each purchase requiring 50% margin and each sale releasing only 30% of the proceeds.

§HINT: If you use margin, don't let your equity fall below 50%. In a volatile market, you can get in trouble mighty fast.

Margin rules have been extended to stock indexes and options on CDs and, in some cases, to mutual funds. Individuals are allowed to have more than one margin account at the same brokerage house as long as all but the first are discretionary accounts controlled by the broker

---

> ### DO NOT HAVE A MARGIN ACCOUNT IF:
>
> - You lack the temperament
> - You are dealing in small amounts of money
> - You cannot absorb a loss
> - Your portfolio is primarily income equities
> - You tend to buy and hold stocks
>
> TO MINIMIZE RISKS:
> - Set stop orders above the 30% loss point
> - Borrow less than the maximum
> - Buy on margin only in a bull market

---

or an independent investment adviser; and the introducing broker can maintain margin accounts for the same person if those accounts are cleared by different firms.

The NYSE sets special loan limits for individual issues that show unusual volume, price fluctuations or rapid turnover, to discourage undue speculation.

And again for protection, customers whose accounts show a pattern of "day-trading" (purchasing and selling the same marginable issues on the same day) are required to maintain appropriate margin before the transactions are made.

§HINT: You may use your margin account to borrow from your broker for purposes other than to buy stocks and bonds. The rates are almost always lower than a consumer bank loan. The interest you pay the broker is tax-deductible and there are no monthly payments.

21

WARRANTS

Warrants are pure speculations. Their prices are usually low, so there can be high leverage if the value of the related stock rises. In recent years, with the expansion of the options market, warrants have not been overly popular, but with sharp selection and a strong market, they can be profitable.

A warrant is an option to buy a stated number of shares of a related security (usually common stock) at a stipulated price during a specified period (5, 10, 20 years or, occasionally, perpetually). The price at which the warrant can be exercised is fixed above the current market price of the stock at the time the warrant is issued. Thus, when the common stock is at 10, the warrant might entitle the holder to buy one share at 15.

Since the two securities tend to move somewhat parallel to each other, an advance in the price creates a higher percentage gain for the warrant than for the stock.

Example: Let's say that the warrant to buy one share at 15 sells at 1 when the stock is at 10. If the stock soars to 20 (100% gain), the price of the warrant will go up to at least 5 (400% gain).

But the downside risk of the warrant can be greater than that of the stock. If the stock drops to 5, that's a 50% loss. The warrant, depending on its life span, might fall to ⅛: an 88% decline.

A warrant is basically a call on a stock. It has no voting rights, pays no dividends, and has no claim on the assets of the corporation. It is not registered with the company and is issued in bearer form. If the certificate is lost or stolen,

Warrant: A certificate giving the owner the privilege of buying a specified number of shares of corporate stock at a fixed price, with or without a time limit.

there's almost no way for the broker or exchange to find it.

The "value" of a warrant reflects *hope:* that the price of the stock will rise above the exercise figure. When the stock trades *below* that call price, the warrant has only speculative value: with the stock at 19 and the exercise price at 20, the warrant is, theoretically, worthless. But it will actually trade at a price that reflects the prospects of the company, the life of the warrant, stock market conditions, etc. At one time, when AT&T stock was selling at 44, the warrants to buy shares at 52 sold at 7.

When the price of the stock rises above the specified exercise price, the warrants acquire a tangible value that is usually inflated by speculation. Thus, when that utility stock rose to 52, the price of the warrant soared to 11½.

The closer a warrant gets to its expiration date, the smaller the premium it commands. After expiration, the warrant is worthless. Conversely, the longer the life of the warrant, the higher the premium if there is real hope that the price of the stock will rise.

A variation of this package involves *usable bonds:* debentures with a detachable warrant to purchase stock. The debentures can be used at face value in lieu of cash to pay for the stock at the specified warrant exercise price.

CALCULATING THE VALUE OF A WARRANT

The speculative value of a warrant is greatest when the warrant price is below the exercise price. If the stock moves up, the price of the warrant can jump fast. The table shows guidelines set by warrant expert S. L. Pendergast for the maximum premium to pay. For example, when the stock price is at the exercise price

DUAL-PURPOSE WARRANT

The combination of the flexibility of warrants and the packaging ability of Wall Street has led to a new hybrid: the dual option warrant (Du-Op). They were first issued by Trans World Corp. in mid-1982 and were a sellout despite a quarterly loss of $103 million.

For $22.50, the "investor" received one share of common stock plus one warrant to buy that stock at $25.50 through 1987 plus the provision that, between May 1983 and June 1984, each unit could be swapped for one share of TWC preferred paying 14%. This was an expensive way to raise money but made everybody happy: the investor could count on a floor for the stock because of the conversion to the high-yielding preferred; the speculator could hope for an ample profit. But there were still risks: that the price of the stock would fail to move over 25½ and that interest rates would rise, thus forcing a decline in the value of the preferred.

(100%), pay at most 41% of the exercise price. Thus, with a stock at the exercise price of 30, the maximum price to pay for a warrant (on a one-for-one basis) would be about 12. In most cases, better profits will come when the warrant is bought at a lower price.

Keeping in mind that the market value of any warrant is hard to predict, there's a formula to determine the EV (exercise value):

$$EV = N(P - S)$$

where N = number of shares of stock that one warrant entitles you to buy

P = current price of stock

S = per share price of stock at which warrant can be exercised

Example: ABC Corporation common stock is at 12; the warrant exercise price, on a one-for-one basis, is $3.75. The EV for the warrant is $8.25:

$$1(\$12 - 3.75) = \$8.25.$$

MAXIMUM PREMIUM TO PAY

STOCK PRICE AS PERCENT OF EXERCISE PRICE	WARRANT PRICE AS PERCENT OF EXERCISE PRICE
80%	28%
90	34
100	41
110	46

WARRANTS FOR CAPITAL GAINS

Warrants are generally best in bull markets, especially during periods of great enthusiasm. Their low prices attract speculators who trade for quick gains. At all times, however, use these checkpoints:

➤ BUY ONLY WARRANTS OF A COMMON STOCK THAT YOU WOULD BUY ANYWAY If the common stock does not go up, there's little chance that the warrant's price will advance.

The best profits come from warrants associated with companies that have potential for strong upward swings due to sharp earnings improvement, a prospective takeover, newsmaking products or services, etc. It also helps if they are temporarily popular.

SOME POPULAR WARRANTS

COMPANY	EXERCISE PRICE TERMS	RECENT PRICE OF COMMON	RECENT PRICE OF WARRANT
Atlas Corp.	$31.25	$13	$3½
Golden Nugget	18.00	11	2
Horn & Hardart	18.75	13	4
Lilly (Eli)	75.98	80	26
Lomas Nett Mtge. Inv.	27.00	32	5
Navistar Int'l	5.00	7½	4
Occidental Petroleum	25.00	28	10
U.S.X.	42.00	19	75¢
Webb (Del) Inv. Properties	9.50	8	75¢

SOURCE: Standard & Poor's.

In most cases, the warrants for fast-riding stocks, even at a high premium, will outperform seemingly cheap warrants for issues that are falling.

At the outset, stick with warrants of fair-to-good corporations whose stocks are listed on major exchanges. They have broad markets.

When you feel more confident, seek out special situations, especially warrants of small, growing firms. Many of these "new" companies rely on warrants in their financing. Their actual or anticipated growth can boost the price of their warrants rapidly.

But be wary of warrants where the related stock is limited or closely controlled. If someone decides to dump a block of stock, the values can fall fast.

➤ BUY WARRANTS WHEN THEY ARE SELLING AT LOW PRICES The percentages are with you when there's an upmove, and with minimal costs the downside risks are small. But watch out for "superbargains," because commissions will eat up most of the gains.

Also watch their values and be cautious when their prices move to more than 20% of their exercise figure.

➤ WATCH THE EXPIRATION OR CHANGE DATE After expiration, the warrant has no value. Generally stay away from warrants with a life span of less than 4 years. When you know what you are doing, short-life warrants can bring quick profits if you are smart and lucky. But be careful. You could end up with worthless paper.

➤ AVOID DILUTION If there's a stock split or stock dividend, the market price of the stock will drop but the conversion price of the warrant may not change. The same caveat goes for warrants subject to call. Warrants of listed companies will generally be protected against such changes, but take nothing for granted.

Once in a while, warrants will be reorganized out of their option value. This occurs with troubled corporations taken over by tough-minded operators who are unwilling to pay for past excesses or to provide profits for speculators.

➤ SPREAD YOUR RISKS If you have sufficient capital, buy warrants in five different companies. The odds are that you may hit big on one, break even on two, and lose on the others. Your total gains may be less than if you had gambled on one warrant that proved a winner, but your losses will probably be less if you're wrong.

➤ LOOK FOR SPECIAL OPPORTUNITIES SUCH AS "USABLE" BONDS WITH WARRANTS ATTACHED With such a package, the speculator can acquire the stock either: (1) with the warrants at an exercise price of, say 20; or (2) with the bond on a face value basis (at $1,000, 50 shares at 20). Three years after such an offering, the stock might sell down to 15 with the bond at 60 ($600). The warrants then would be nearly worthless, but the bonds could be turned into a nifty profit because each could be swapped for 50 shares worth $750.

Except in unusual situations, all warrants should be bought to trade or sell and not to exercise. With no income, usually a long wait for appreciation, and rapid price changes, warrants almost always yield quick gains to speculators who have adequate capital and time to watch the market.

SELLING WARRANTS SHORT

In bear markets, the leverage of warrants can be profitable with short sales. Basically, it's the opposite of buying long. You assume that the same relation between the stock and warrants continues when their prices fall.

But short selling is always tricky, and with warrants there can be other problems: (1) limited markets because of lack of speculator interest; (2) exchange regulations—e.g., the American Stock Exchange prohibits short selling of its listed warrants several months before expiration date; (3) the possibility of a "short squeeze": the inability to buy warrants to cover your short sales as the expiration date approaches; (4) the life of the warrants may be extended beyond the stated expiration date, advancing the date when the warrants become worthless, so a short seller may not be able to cover a position at as low a price as was anticipated.

WARRANTS WITH OPTIONS

Swingers use warrants to speculate in options. The costs are low, the risks modest, and the profit potential is high, especially in erratic but uptrending markets.

Example: In October, TP Industries stock was at $14.50, and the warrants, exercisable until August the next year, were at $4.50. Trader

Tom bought 1,000 warrants for $4,500 and sold 10 January options with a striking price of 15 for 1⅜, to net about $1,250 after commissions. If TPI stock stayed the same or went down by January, Tom would let the options expire and sell another 10 calls with an April expiration. If these also expired, he would sell 10 more options with an August closeout date.

If the stock went up, he would buy back the January options and sell 10 April calls at a higher premium, etc. He hoped to sell three sets of options, at an average return of $1,250 each, to net $3,750.

In August, if the stock was at $16.50, the warrants would be worth $2.75. He would sell them for $2,750 and deduct the $1,750 loss from the $3,750 profit on the options for a pleasant $2,000 profit on a net investment of $3,250.

If the warrants expired worthless, he would still be ahead of the game. That's what hedging is all about.

22

MAKING MONEY WITH VENTURE CAPITAL AND NEW ISSUES

NEW ISSUES

The market in new issues—those companies making their first public offering of stock—is one of the most speculative and exciting areas of investing. Taking their cue from the general stock market, new issues roar ahead when the market does, decline when the climate turns cautious, and absolutely die when the market becomes bearish. Right now there's plenty of action in new issues, or initial public offerings (IPOs) as they are called by Wall Street professionals. The prevailing economic policies of President Reagan's administration very much favor entrepreneurship, new ventures, and business in general. Low interest rates in tandem with an expanding economy lure investors and companies alike into the new issues arena. The advance of technology also fosters a continual flow of new inventions in electronics, high tech, medicine, and other areas.

Now and then a large, successful, well-known company will go public—as was the case with Ford Motor Company back in the mid-fifties—but more often than not IPOs consist of small, growing firms whose attraction is their future potential. Few have been in business long enough to establish any real record of competent management, financial strength, or investment acceptance. Some have never seen a profit. The sales pitch is always the same: "This company is a sure winner. Get in on the ground floor." Sometimes it works.

If you'd bought the first public offering of Entertainment Marketing in July 1985 at $2 per share, you would have doubled your money in this Houston-based company within just a month. By mid-1986, when the stock was selling at $6.50, some of the early birds had reaped a 222% profit! An initial investment of $100 in 1981 in Liz Claiborne, the fashion company, is now worth an impressive $1,000. On the other hand, Pizza Transit Authority came out at $2.75 per share and 9 months later was down to a mere dollar.

According to IDD Information Services, the New York firm that studies the field, during the period between 1980 and 1985, just over half the new issues launched were worth more than their initial offering prices by December 31, 1985. Despite the facts, investors continue to be drawn to the new issues market by the dream of huge profits. In 1985, there were over 350 IPOs totaling $8.6 billion; that was second only to 1983's all-time record of $12.5 billion. More companies are expected to go public during 1987 in order to take advantage of soaring stock prices. If you're tempted, if you think you can double your money, know the facts and follow the guidelines below for selecting fledgling companies to back. It is possible to make money in IPOs, but it requires far more research than most investments as well as an understanding of the market. Norman G. Fosback, editor of *New Issues*, favors companies that have reported profits for at least 5 years and whose earnings are trending up.

GETTING IN ON THE GROUND FLOOR

When investors hear about a "hot" new issue, more often than not demand for shares is greater than the supply and it's hard to find shares. Even the largest financial institutions are often limited as to the number of shares they can get. If you are a regular customer, your stockbroker may be able to snare some for you, especially if his or her firm works with the syndicator or is a member of the selling group.

PENNY STOCKS

Most penny stocks have been and still are offered in Denver. They are totally speculations. If you are lucky or related to one of the promoters, you may make a lot of money. But most of these "opportunities" are better for their sponsors than they are for outside speculators. The markets for these shares are more or less controlled; their initial price is "negotiated" by the company, the selling shareholders, and the underwriter and rarely have much relation to value. Most importantly, once the shares have been distributed, there's seldom any sustained interest.

Most penny stocks are brought out by underwriters on a "best-efforts" basis, which puts such issues on shaky ground from the beginning. The promoters seldom pledge a nickel of their own funds to guarantee the selling out of the offering.

There is, however, one saving grace: full disclosure as required by the SEC. Few people bother to read the prospectus to discover that "The offering price . . . bears no relationship to assets, earnings, book value, or other criteria of value. . . . There is no trading market for the securities . . . no assurance that such a market will develop."

The lure is the low price and huge number of shares. For $1,000, speculators can own thousands of shares and profit from a slight price rise (usually initiated by the promoters). But over a period of time (as little as 3 months), the losses can be as sensational, because very few of the companies ever report significant earnings, and once the initial enthusiasm is withdrawn, no one is interested. With all penny stocks, you are shooting dice and the house sets the odds . . . against you.

If you don't get in on the ground floor, you can buy shares in the after market when they are trading over the counter. If it's a weak market, chances are you won't pay much more, if anything; but in a hot market, expect a 20 to 25% increase in the after market. If you are enamored of the issue but cannot buy at a reasonable price, follow the stock's progress carefully. Wait for the first blush to fade and move in when it takes a tumble. Often a new company will lose its initial luster or report lower earnings, thus pushing the price down temporarily.

Remember too that it's always the hard-to-buy issues that receive all the press. There are plenty of less glamorous offerings to pick from. IF the fundamentals are right, these can be equally rewarding.

GUIDELINES FOR SELECTION

Learning about new issues is less difficult than you might think. A number of the larger brokerage firms publish a list of them on a regular basis, but unless you're a major client, you won't hear about them. Your broker or library may subscribe to the bible in the field, *Investment Dealer's Digest,* which lists all IPOs as they are registered with the SEC.

THE UNDERWRITER

Your chances for success will be increased if you select IPOs from reputable investment bankers. First-class underwriters will not allow themselves to manage new issues that are of poor quality or highly speculative. Moreover, if a fledgling company runs into a need for additional financing, a first-rate banker will be ready to raise more capital. Thus, the prime consideration is the reputation of the underwriters. However, this is not written in stone.

The IPO Reporter's top ten performers in 1985 were: Rooney, Pace, Inc.; Whale Securities Corp.; L. F. Rothschild, Unterberg, Towbin; Ladenburg Thalmann Co.; Alex. Brown & Sons; Oppenheimer & Co.; Mosley Hallgarten Estabrook & Weeden, Inc.; Rauscher Pierce Refnes Inc.; Morgan Stanley & Co.; and Giford Securities. Smaller and regional underwriters often do well in their own backyards. Among the best are: Blunt Ellis & Loewi, Advest, William Blair, Piper Jaffray & Hopwood, and Robinson-Humphrey.

THE PROSPECTUS

Once you learn about a new issue, your first investigative step is to read a copy of the prospectus, generally available when an offering is registered with the SEC. (It's also called a ''red herring'' because of the red-inked warning that the contents of the report are not final.) Despite its many caveats, the prospectus will help you form a rough opinion about the company and what it may be worth. Look for:

➤ DETAILS ABOUT MANAGEMENT The success of a company is often determined by the quality of the management team. The officers and directors should have successful experience in the company and/or similar organizations; they should be fully involved in the firm, and not treat it as a part-time activity.

➤ TYPE OF BUSINESS New ventures have the best chance of success in growth areas, such as electronics, retailing, and special services. Manufacturing, specialty retail chains, and savings and loan associations are expected to do well in 1987–88. The risks are greatest with companies in exciting but partially proven fields such as biotechnology, genetic engineering, computer software, etc. These companies are tempting but pay off only after heavy capital investments and successful R&D. Try to invest in an area you know something about or a business located near you. A good prospectus will also list some of the company's customers.

➤ FINANCIAL STRENGTH AND PROFITABILITY Use the following criteria based on the current balance sheet. Glance at the previous year's report to catch any major changes:

■ Modest short-term debt and long-term obligations of less than 40% of total capital: with $40 million in assets, the debt should not be more than $16 million.

■ Current ratio (of assets to liabilities): a minimum of 2:1 except under unusual, temporary conditions.

■ Sales of at least $30 million to be sure that there's a market for products or services. Make a double-check when revenues exceed $50 million. That's the threshold for the big leagues where competition is sure to heighten.

■ High profitability: a return on equity of 20% annually for the past 3 years—with modest modifications if recent gains have been strong. This will assure similar progress in the future.

➤ EARNINGS The company should be able to service its debt. Look for the most recent P/E and compare it with P/Es of competitors, listed in the newspaper. If a P/E is significantly higher than the industry average of a similar sized company, then shares are overpriced. Robert S. Natale, editor of Standard & Poor's *Emerging & Special Situations* newsletter, states that a young company often hasn't had time to produce much in the way of earnings, so instead look for a ratio of total offering price to annual sales. On the whole, this market-capitalization-to-sales ratio should not be greater than 2:7.

➤ USE OF PROCEEDS Check out what the company plans to do with the newly raised capital. It should not be devoted to repaying the debt or bailing out the founders, management, or promoters. Most of it should be used to expand the business. If 25% or more is going toward nonproductive purposes, move on. Avoid firms where management or a founding shareholder is selling a large percentage of the shares: 30% or more. For example, in 1985, the underwriters of Vestron, Inc., a videocassette publisher, had to restructure the deal because the institutional investors were unenthusiastic about the fact that 50% of the IPO was for shares held by Vestron's founder and his family. The Vestrons would have received $100 million in cash. Their shares were withdrawn and the price cut from the $17–$19 range to $13.

$ HINT: Whenever the public is chasing after new issues and creating a shortage, unscrupulous operators and bucket shops tend to fill the void. Beware of telephone solicitations from brokerage firms with names that sound legitimate. These people will offer shares at $1 or $2 and guarantee that they'll be trading at double those prices when they go public. Careful: you're skating on thin ice.

SUCCESSFUL SPECULATING: NEW ISSUES

With both new issues and high-tech stocks, success requires more care and review than with shares of established companies. Typically, there will be spurts of expansion in revenues and profits; then periods of struggle to continue growth and profitability. That means that the prospects and performance must be viewed in a broad context with greater flexibility than would apply to regular investments. Very few of these types of organizations reach a quality rating in less than 10 years.

To be successful with these types of speculations, it's essential to have a clearly defined game plan and to set targets:

- *For investing:* to hold the shares for at least 3 years but to be ready to sell if the price: (1) rises sharply as the result of market popularity of a takeover offer, (2) falls because of declining profits, greater competition, or managerial changes. If you're conservative, sell half your shares when the price doubles; if you're aggressive and confident and can afford to be patient, hold as long as you are

---

WHERE NEW ISSUES COME FROM

- Entrepreneurs who want to make money on modest investments in start-up companies
- Cash-poor but promising firms that do not want to borrow to raise capital
- Cash-poor firms that do not want to sell out to a big company
- Larger or established companies that want to spin off subsidiaries

---

convinced that the company will be a winner.

- *For speculating:* to sell by formula of time or profit: (1) before the fourth Friday after the issue (when most underwriters withdraw their support so that the stock will trade on its own merits); (2) when you have that 50% gain. This is a high return anytime, but if you are still enthusiastic, sell half the stock and get back your capital for another new venture.

Set a stop-loss order about 15% below cost or 10% below its high price. If the stock continues to move up, raise that figure proportionately. But do not lower your protection price. The first loss is almost always the smallest. If you hang on in hope, you will be bucking the odds and end up with a pile of losers in your portfolio. *Two of every three new issues sell below their offering price within the next 12 months!*

$HINT: It's a good sign if the managing underwriter takes warrants in order to purchase shares at a higher price than the initial offering price.

VENTURE CAPITAL

Venture capital, which is often the source of new issues (see page 200), was once the province of the very rich; today the glamor of helping finance a new company is open to nearly every investor. You can purchase a share in a public company that provides venture capital for as little as $5 per share; buy a mutual fund that specializes in start-up companies for $1,000; or go all the way and take a $25,000+ stake in a private placement. Regardless of how much you

---

TAX SAVER

To help small corporations attract investment capital, Congress OK'd a special tax arrangement that allows "investors" to claim an ordinary loss deduction when the shares of a new or small company are sold at a loss or the business fails. The deal must involve a Small Business Investment Corporation with these limitations:

- The shares must be common stock of a U.S. corporation (no convertibles or bonds) issued for money or property, not for other securities.
- The total money or assets received by the corporation, for the stock, must be less than $1 million and used in the business, not for investments.
- The shares must be issued to you or a partnership in which you are a member.

The deduction must reflect a business loss and cannot be used to recover taxes already paid. The limit to the annual loss: $50,000 for a single taxpayer; $100,000 for a joint filer. Above these figures, there are no special tax benefits.

spend, investing in untested companies is guaranteed to make you richer or poorer. There's no middle ground.

Before you get started on your expedition to become a venture capitalist, a few words of caution:

- About 30% of all venture capital deals are winners; that means 70% are not, according to Stanley Pratt, editor of *Venture Capital Journal.*

- Most deals take 5 to 7 years to reach maturity; not a way to make a quick killing. If you don't want to lock up funds over the long term, look elsewhere.

- The majority turn a profit when they either go public or are sold to another company.

- Never place more than 10% of your investment money in venture capital.

SMALL BUSINESS INVESTMENT COMPANIES (SBICs)

These companies, which are federally licensed and regulated by the Small Business Administration, pool the money they raise by selling shares to the public. This money is then used to back small businesses—those with a net worth under $6 million and after-tax earnings of less than $2 million for the preceding 2 years. These fledgling firms can borrow money from an SBIC at relatively low rates. The standard rule of thumb is that they can borrow $4 for every $1 they raise.

There are approximately 500 SBICs. Most are owned by either banks or private groups; a handful, however, are public and their shares trade over the counter or on the American Stock Exchange (see list). On the whole, their results have not been spectacular, although there are always exceptions and continual surprises. In 1980, for instance, Greater Washington Investors sold for 52½¢. Recently it traded between $7 and $9.

SBIC portfolios are frequently well diversified, investing in brand new companies, in second or third round financing, or in companies moving into a new phase. As with a mutual fund, an SBIC tends to be as good as its portfolio manager. Read its annual and quarterly reports and check out its track record. The price of an SBIC's stock reflects the value of its portfolio. Dividends or interest earned from loans can be added to its earnings, used to invest in new businesses, or paid out to shareholders.

VENTURE CAPITAL COMPANIES

A similar route to go is via publicly traded venture capital companies, which are similar to SBICs but, since they are not controlled by the Small Business Administration, have fewer restrictions on the types of investments they can make. Venture capital companies are generally more speculative and carry greater risk than their companion SBICs. Like mutual funds, they raise money by selling shares to the public and then use this capital to invest in new businesses. They trade OTC or on the AMEX and, like regular stocks, are subject to price volatility.

PRIVATE PLACEMENTS

If you're willing to spend $25,000 or more you can participate in a private placement deal and reap either great benefits or great losses. Bankers, CPAs, and stockbrokers often serve as matchmakers or have leads in this area since they know who is trying to raise capital. In a number of cities, venture capital clubs also unite investors

SBICs

Capital Investments, Inc.
744 North 4th Street, Suite 400
Milwaukee, WI 53203
1-414-273-6560
(No NASDAQ symbol)

Clarion Capital Corp.
1801 East 12th Street, Suite 201
Cleveland, OH 44114
1-216-687-1096
OTC: CLRN

First Connecticut SBIC
177 State Street
Bridgeport, CT 06604
1-203-366-4726
AMEX: FCO

The Franklin Corp.
1185 Avenue of Americas
New York, NY 10036
1-212-719-4844
OTC: FKLN

Greater Washington Investors
5454 Wisconsin Avenue
Chevy Chase, MD 20815
1-301-656-0626
OTC: GWII

Vega Capital Corp.
720 White Plains Road, #360
Scarsdale, NY 10583
1-914-472-8550
(No NASDAQ symbol)

PUBLICLY TRADED VENTURE CAPITAL COMPANIES

Allied Capital Corp.*
1625 I Street N.W.
Washington, DC 20006
1-202-331-1112
OTC: ALLC

Blotech Capital Corp.*
600 Madison Avenue,
  21st Floor
New York, NY 10022
1-212-758-7722
OTC: BITC

Capital Southwest Corp.*
12900 Preston Road,
  Suite 700
Dallas, TX 75230
1-214-233-8242
OTC: CSWC

Colorado Venture Capital
885 Arapahoe Avenue
Boulder, CO 80302
1-303-449-9018
OTC: COVC

Corporate Capital
  Resources
32123 Lindero Canyon
  Road
Westlake Village, CA
  91361
1-818-991-3111
OTC: CCRS

First Midwest Capital
  Corp.
1010 Plymouth Building
12 South 6th Street
Minneapolis, MN 55402
1-612-339-9391
OTC: FMWC

T. H. Lehman & Co.
355 South End Avenue
New York, NY 10280
1-212-912-0770
OTC: THLM

Narragansett Capital
  Corp.*
40 Westminster Street
Providence, RI 02903
1-401-751-1000
OTC: NARR

Rand Capital Corp.*
1300 Rand Building
Buffalo, NY 14203
1-716-853-0802
OTC: RAND

The Rockies Fund
8400 East Prentice,
  #560
Englewood, CO 80111
1-303-793-3060
OTC: ROCF

* Has a wholly owned SBIC subsidiary.

with start-up operations. Since private placements are not allowed to solicit the general public, you'll have to find out about them through these and other contacts.

Note: Venture capital partnerships are structured very much like limited partnerships, raising money from institutions and wealthy individuals. Public venture deals (SBICs, mutual funds, and publicly traded venture capital companies) are all regulated by the SEC Act of 1933 in order to protect the small, less wealthy, or less sophisticated investor. Private placements,

on the other hand, are limited to a smaller number of investors (often 35) who meet specified net worth and income standards.

Getting in on a sound private placement before it is closed is almost as difficult as finding it in the first place. After you find a private placement, evaluate it carefully. Study the business plan, consider the potential market. Ask a financial expert to help. A word of caution: you may be asked to put in additional money if the company grows or falters.

MUTUAL FUNDS

There are a few mutual funds that invest part of their portfolios in start-up ventures and provide

MUTUAL FUNDS THAT INVEST IN SMALL, EMERGING COMPANIES

Alliance Technology
  Fund
P.O. Box 997
New York, NY 10268
1-800-522-2323 in NY
  state
1-800-221-5672 out of
  state

American Capital OTC
  Securities Fund
P.O. Box 379
Kansas City, MO 64141
1-800-231-3638

Fairfield Fund
605 Third Avenue
New York, NY 10158
1-800-522-4022 in NY
  state
1-800-323-3032 outside
  state

Fidelity Mercury Fund
82 Devonshire Street
Boston, MA 02109
1-800-225-6190

Keystone S-4 Fund
99 High Street
Boston, MA 02110
1-800-225-2618

The Nautilus Fund
24 Federal Street
Boston, MA 02110
1-800-225-6265

New Horizon Fund
T. Rowe Price Associates
100 East Pratt Street
Baltimore, MD 21202
1-800-638-5660
1-301-638-5660

The Nova Fund
470 Atlantic Avenue
Boston, MA 02210
1-800-572-0006

Putnam Health Sciences
  Fund
P.O. Box 2701
Boston, MA 02208
1-800-225-2465

20th Century Ultra
  Investors
P.O. Box 200
Kansas City, MO 64141
1-816-531-5575

Vanguard Explorer Fund
P.O. Box 2600
Valley Forge, PA 19482
1-800-523-7025

yet another avenue for getting in on the ground floor. The best known is the Nautilus Fund, which helped launch Apple Computer in 1979. Inclusion in the list here does not constitute a recommendation or endorsement. Check past performance records and read the prospectus prior to purchasing shares.

FOR FURTHER INFORMATION

To help you spot the winners and avoid the losers when firms go public, you may want to read one of the following advisory newsletters for background data:

> *Value Line New Issues Service*
> 711 Third Avenue
> New York, NY 10017
> 1-212-687-3217

> *Emerging and Special Situations*
> Standard & Poor's Corp.
> 25 Broadway
> New York, NY 10004
> 1-212-208-8000

> *New Issues*
> Institute for Econometric Research
> 3471 North Federal Highway
> Ft. Lauderdale, FL 33306
> 1-305-563-9000

> *Ground Floor*
> 6 Deer Trail

Old Tappan, NJ 07675
1-201-664-3400

> *Investment Dealers Digest*
> 150 Broadway
> New York, NY 10038-4476
> 1-212-619-5454

For more information on venture capital:

> *Investing in Venture Capital and Buyouts*
> (Sumner Levine, ed.)
> N.Y. Society of Security Analysts
> 71 Broadway
> New York, NY 10006
> 1-212-344-9450

> *National Venture Capital Association: Membership Directory*
> 1655 North Fort Myer Drive
> Arlington, VA 22209
> 1-703-528-4370

> *Venture Capital Journal* (Stanley Pratt, ed.)
> P.O. Box 348
> Wellesley Hills, MA 02181

Contains list of companies that were venture capital sponsored and have gone public.

> *Venture Capital Network, Inc.*
> P.O. Box 882
> Durham, NH 03824
> 1-603-862-3556

A not-for-profit organization, connected with the University of New Hampshire, that introduces entrepreneurs to venture capitalist investors. Specializes in the $10,000 to $500,000 range.

23

COMMODITIES, GOLD, AND CURRENCIES

Commodities are one of the quickest ways to get rich, but they can also be a fast way to lose money. These futures contracts are almost always 100% speculation because with them you must try to guess what will happen in the months ahead with the prices of food products, natural resources, metals, and foreign currencies. The financial futures markets operate much the same way, but since they involve securities, they are discussed in a separate chapter.

Trading in commodities involves active, volatile markets, high leverage, hedging, and short selling. It's a game that requires ample capital, emotional stability, frequent attention to trends, and experience. Everyone should understand trading in commodities markets, but few amateurs should become involved.

In addition to the normal hazards of speculations, there are special risks that are often beyond the ken or control of most participants. With skill and luck, an individual can score high on occasion, but the odds are always against the amateur: *85% of all commodities speculators lose money.* And their aggregate losses are six times as great as their gains. You win only with a few supersuccessful deals.

The techniques can be grasped and utilized if you take time to study the pertinent factors and forces and continue to do your homework. You must be able to accept quick, small losses and let your profits run . . . not easy in these swinging markets.

With commodities, the cash requirements are low: 5 to 10% per contract, depending on the commodity and the broker's standards. Unlike margin for securities which is an interest-bearing cost, margin for commodities is a secu-

Commodities: Transportable articles of commerce, traded on a commodity exchange.

rity deposit. There are no interest payments on the balance, but when the price dips, more money or collateral must be deposited or the position will be closed out.

The lures of fast action, minimal capital, and high potential profits are enticing—but before you start trading contracts for corn, wheat, soybeans, silver, or any other commodity, heed these warnings from professionals:

- **Be emotionally stable.** You must be able to control your sense of fear and greed and train yourself to accept losses without too great a strain.
- **Be ready to risk at least $10,000:** $5,000 at once; the rest to back up margin calls.
- **Deal only with a knowledgeable commodities broker** who keeps you informed of new and potential developments.
- **Recognize that you are always bucking such professionals as General Mills.** These big operators are hedging; you're speculating.

HOW THE MARKET OPERATES

Commodity trading is different from investing (or speculating) in stocks. When you buy a common stock, you own a part of the corporation and share in its profits, if any. If you pick a profitable company, the price of your stock will eventually rise.

With commodities, there is no equity. You buy only hope. Once the futures contract has expired, there's no tomorrow. If your trade turned out badly, you must take the full loss. And it's a zero sum game: for every $1 won, $1 is lost by someone else.

The economic reason for a futures market is hedging (that is, reducing the risk of a commitment by taking an offsetting one). A farmer who borrows money to plant a 5,000-bushel soybean crop in the spring may be asked by his banker to sell a futures contract (5,000 bushels for November delivery). The contract calls for a fixed price, say $6.90 per bushel (quoted in the financial press at 690 cents per bushel). If the price in November is down to $6.50, the farmer loses 40¢ per bushel on the sale but makes up this loss by buying back his contract for less than he received. He comes out even and earns his normal profit on the crop.

On the other hand, a food processor who sells her products throughout the year wants a predetermined cost price for her soybean purchase, let's say, $6.90 per bushel. She buys that November futures contract at $6.90 to lock in her cost. If the price, in November, is $6.50 per bushel, she sells the futures contract at a 40¢ per bushel loss but can acquire the soybeans at below her projected cost to complete a protective hedge.

In most cases, it's not that simple. The opposite side of each transaction is picked up by speculators who believe they can make money by a favorable price change in the months before delivery.

Note: To give you an idea of how professionals cut their risks, many rely on "scalping." With this, the trader buys a position and then immediately tries to sell it for one tick or better. A tick is the least amount of money that a contract can change in price. With gold futures, a tick is $10 for a 100-ounce contract that may be worth $40,000.

STEPS TO TAKE

➤ READ A GOOD BOOK ABOUT COMMODITY TRADING Your broker can provide you with a folder from his firm or the commodity exchanges. Study the books listed in their bibliographies. Then decide if you have the stomach and the funds to start speculating.

➤ GET CURRENT INFORMATION There is no inside information about commodities. All statistics are available in government reports, business and agricultural publications, newsletters, and special service. Always check two or three for confir-mation and then review your conclusions with your broker. It will help to become something of an expert in both the fundamental and technical aspects of a few major commodities. When you become experienced, you can move into other areas where information is not so widely available.

➤ CHOOSE AN EXPERIENCED BROKER Deal only with a reputable firm that (1) has extensive commodities trading services and (2) includes a broker who knows speculations and can guide you. Never buy or sell as the result of a phone recommendation until it has been confirmed in written or printed form.

➤ ZERO IN ON A FEW COMMODITIES Preferably those in the news. Staples such as corn, wheat, and hogs always have strong markets, but the best speculative profits can be made in the active groups, recently natural resources such as metals and petroleum.

➤ AVOID THIN MARKETS You can score when such a commodity takes off, but the swings can be too fast and may send prices soaring, or plummeting, so that the amateur can get caught with no chance of closing a position.

➤ LOOK FOR A RATIO OF NET PROFIT TO NET LOSS OF 2:1 Since the percentage of losses will always be greater than that of profits, choose commodities where the potential gains (based on confirmed trends) can be more than double the possible losses. This is on a net-after-commissions basis, so use a 3:1 reward-to-risk ratio. With small units and small price shifts, the costs can be significant.

➤ PREPARE AN OPERATIONAL PLAN Before you risk any money, test your hypothesis on paper until you feel confident that you understand what can happen. Do this for several weeks so you get the feel of different types of contracts in different types of markets.

With an active commodity, "buy" contracts at several delivery dates and calculate the potential profits if the price rises moderately, say +3%: for an agricultural contract, 21¢ per bushel, from $6.90 to $7.11. This would mean a gain of $3,555, minus $50 commissions, for a net profit of $3,505 on a $1,500 margin (that 2:1 profit ratio).

Next assume that the price drops 3% to $6.69 per bushel. With every 5¢ decline, you must increase your margin by $150, so your invested capital (if you hang on) would be $2,100. The loss would be $1,150 plus commission.

➤ NEVER MEET A MARGIN CALL When your original margin is impaired by 25%, your broker will call for more money. Except in most unusual circumstances, do not put in more money. Liquidate your position and accept your loss. This is a form of stop-loss safeguard. When a declining trend has been established, further losses can be expected.

➤ BE ALERT TO SPECIAL SITUATIONS Information is the key to profitable speculation. As you become more knowledgeable, you will pick up many points, such as:

- If there's heavy spring-summer rain in Maine, buy long on potatoes. They need ideal weather.
- If there's a bad tornado over large portions of the Great Plains, buy wheat contracts. Chances are the wheat crop will be damaged, thus changing the supply and demand.

There are, of course, many other factors to analyze before reaching any final decision. As with everything involving the profit potential of money, knowledge plus luck is important.

➤ TRADE WITH THE MAJOR TREND, AGAINST THE MINOR TREND With copper, for example, if you project a worldwide shortage of the metal and the market is in an uptrend, buy futures when the market suffers temporary weak spells. As long as prices keep moving up, you want to accumulate a meaningful position.

Corollary to this, never average down. Adding to your loss position increases the number of contracts that are returning a loss. By buying more, you put yourself in a stance where you can lose on more contracts if the price continues to drop.

Generally, if the trend is down, either sell short or stay out of the market. And never (well, hardly ever) buy a commodity after it has passed its seasonal high or sell a commodity after it has passed its seasonal low.

➤ WATCH THE SPREADS BETWEEN DIFFERENT DELIVERY DATES In the strong summer market, the premium for January soybeans is 8¢ per bushel above the November contract. Buy November and sell January.

If the bull market persists, the premium

should disappear and you will have a pleasant limited profit. Carrying charges on soybeans run about 6½¢ per month, so it is not likely that the spread will widen to more than 13¢ per bushel. Thus, with that 8¢ spread, the real risk is not more than 5¢ per bushel.

➤ NEVER SPREAD A LOSS Turning a long or short position into a spread by buying or selling another contract month will seldom help you and, in most cases, will guarantee a locked-in loss. When you make a mistake, get out.

➤ DO NOT TAKE A POSITION UNTIL THE PROFIT POTENTIAL IS 8 TO 10 TIMES THE COMMISSION Newcomers are intrigued with the idea that they can make a profit each day that can be partly removed immediately. Just to cover the loss trades and commissions, they have to be right nearly half the time. Such day-trading can be exciting, but it's too fast and volatile for the amateur. Look for trends, not interim movements.

Keep in mind that because of limited capital, most amateurs can hold positions in only 2 contracts. This compares with 18 by the professional.

LOW-RISK TRADING

The MidAmerica Commodity Exchange (MCE) now offers smaller contracts that are one-fifth to one-half the size of full contracts.

This is the result of a survey that showed that 45% of all commodities traders held only $5,000 to $10,000 in equity in their futures trading accounts. With such limited funds, they were able to deal with only 1 or 2 standard contracts if they maintained sufficient equity to allow for adverse price moves. With the new MCE offerings, the amateur can handle up to 10 contracts.

To protect the small speculators, the floor traders try to ensure that only a normal price difference exists between the MCE and the standard contract price. But there are times where there can be significant spreads.

➤ WATCH THE PRICE PEAKS AND LOWS Never sell at a price that is near the natural or government-imposed floor, and never buy at a price that is near its high.

Similarly, do not buy after the price of any commodity has passed its seasonal high or sell after it has dropped under its seasonal low.

➤ RISK NO MORE THAN 10% OF YOUR TRADING CAPITAL IN ANY ONE POSITION And no more than 30% of all capital in all positions at any one time . . . except when you have caught a strong upswing and can move with the trend. These limits will ease the effect of a bad decision. Few professionals count on being right more than half the time.

➤ BE SLOW TO LISTEN TO YOUR BROKER Unless the recommendations are backed by clear-to-you analyses. In most cases, when you get the word, smart traders have made their moves. To be successful, you must anticipate, not follow.

The same caveat applies to professional newsletters. If speculators had followed the 7,500 recommendations made by 16 services, they would have ended −1.43% below the market.

➤ USE TECHNICAL ANALYSIS Especially charts, because timing is the key to speculative success, and, with commodities, what has happened before is likely to be repeated.

SPECULATING IN FOREIGN CURRENCIES

Trading in foreign currencies can be exciting and profitable.

Futures contracts of foreign currency are traded on the International Monetary Market Division (IMM) of the Chicago Mercantile Exchange. Basically, positions are taken by importers and exporters who want to protect their profits from sudden swings in the relation between the dollar and a specific foreign currency. A profit on the futures contract will be offset by a loss in the cash market. Or vice versa. Either way, the businessperson or banker guarantees a set cost.

The speculation performs an essential function by taking opposite sides of contracts, but unlike other types of commodities trading, currency futures reflect reactions to what has already happened more than anticipation of what's ahead.

For small margins of 1.5 to 4.2%, roughly $1,500 to $2,500, you can control large sums of money: 100,000 Canadian dollars, 125,000 Deutsche marks, 12.5 million Japanese yen, etc.

The attraction is leverage. You can speculate that at a fixed date in the future, the value of

SMALL CONTRACTS FOR COMMODITIES/CURRENCY TRADING
MidAmerica Commodity Exchange

COMMODITY	CONTRACT TERMS	VALUE OF MINIMUM TICK	MARGIN	COMMISSION
Soybeans	1M bu/5M bu	$ 1.25	$600/$3,500	$40/$70
Live cattle	20M lb/40M lb	5.00	450/900	50/70
Gold	33.2 oz/100 oz	3.32	400/1,200	50/100
NY Silver	1,000 oz/5,000 oz	1.00	600/3,000	50/125
T-bills	$.5 mil/$1 mil	12.50	750/1,500	50/80
T-bonds	$50M/$100M	15.12	750/1,500	50/80
Swiss francs	62.5M/125M	6.25	800/2,000	50/80
Japanese yen	6.25 mil/12.5 mil	6.25	600/1,500	50/80

For each quantity, the numbers on the left are for the MCE contracts; those on the right are for standard-size contracts.

Margins are exchange minimums; commissions are typical of major brokers.

SOURCE: Forbes, January 30, 1984.

your contract will be greater (if you buy long) or less (if you sell short).

The daily fluctuations of each currency futures contract are limited by IMM rules. A rise of $750 per day provides a 37.5% profit on a $2,000 investment. That's a net gain of $705 ($750 less $45 in commissions). If the value declines, you are faced with a wipe-out or, if you set a stop order, the loss of part of your security deposit. Vice versa when you sell short.

One of the favorite deals is playing crosses, taking advantage of the spread between different currencies: buying francs and selling liras short, etc. For example, when the West German mark was falling faster than the Swiss franc relative to the U.S. dollar, Speculator Stan set up this spread:

April 15: Buys a June contract for 125,000 francs and sells short a June contract for 125,000 marks. The franc is valued at 50.64¢, the mark at 46.03¢. Cost, not including commissions, is the margin: $2,000.

May 27: The franc has fallen to 48.58¢, while the mark has dropped to 43.22. Stan reverses his trades, selling the June contract for francs and buying the mark contract to cover his short position.

Result: The speculator loses 2.06¢ per franc, or $2,575, but he makes 2.81¢ per mark, or $3,512.50. The overall gain, before commissions, is $937.50, a return of 46.9% on the $2,000 investment—in about 6 weeks.

Nowadays, commissions are negotiable and vary from $25 to $75 per contract. At worst, the speculator pays about $150, leaving $787.50 net profit. Now his return is 39.4%.

Warning: IMM is a thin market. Small speculators may not be able to get out when they want at the price they expect. On a one-day trade, the value of a currency can swing sharply, so that the pressure can be intense.

➤ CURRENCY OPTIONS According to some traders, currency options can be the fastest game in town (or perhaps they should say "in the Free World"). The premiums are small, so the leverage is high.

The options, traded on the Philadelphia Exchange, are for five currencies: Deutsche mark (DM), British pound, Canadian dollar, Japanese yen, and Swiss franc. The premiums run from $25 for a short-life out-of-the-money option to $2,000 for a long-term deep-in-the-money call or put.

The option represents the currency value against the dollar, so traders buy calls when they expect the foreign money to gain ground against the dollar and puts when they anticipate the reverse. The options expire at 3-month intervals.

The quotations are in U.S. cents per unit of the underlying currency (with the exception of the yen, where it's $1/100$¢): i.e., the quote for 1.00 DM means 1¢ per mark, and since the contract covers 62,500 DMs, the total premium would be $625.

➤ OPTIONS ON FUTURES These are now available on the Chicago Mercantile Exchange, where the currency futures are already traded. They are similar to regular options except that they give the holder the right to buy or sell the currencies themselves, *not the futures.*

The CME rules permit the speculator to:

- Generate extra income by writing calls or selling puts (but this can be very expensive if you guess wrong and the option is exercised).
- Exercise the option at any time. But once you do so, you may not liquidate your option position with an offsetting option as you can do in futures trading. So you would have to sell to, or buy from, the other party the required number of currency units at the option exercise price.

These options on futures sound risky—but only for the speculator. Business firms use them to hedge the prices of foreign goods at a future delivery date.

➤ FOREIGN CURRENCY CERTIFICATES OF DEPOSIT (CDs) These are offered by currency trading firms in three currencies—yen, Swiss francs, and Deutsche marks—in units of $5,000 with maturities of 3 and 6 months. Those sold by Deak-Perera are insured because the American purchaser converts dollars into the foreign currency and then buys the CDs through the Deak National Bank, headquartered in New York.

These CDs pay interest at a low annual rate: 1½% for the franc-based units; 3½% for those of DMs; and 4⅛% for those denominated in yens. But there can be handsome profits when the exchange rates decline. If the dollar dips

5%, the 6-month Swiss CD will grow by an annualized rate of 12%.

GOLD: THE "MAGIC" METAL—FOR SPECULATORS

To millions of people (very few of whom are investors), gold is the finest form of tangible wealth; the symbol of security against inflation, war, and revolution; and the best investment for ultimate wealth. You may have to do a little trading now and then, but the value of the precious metal is sure to rise.

The validity of this faith was "proven" after January 1975 when gold could first be bought by Americans. The price did rise from $197.50 to close to $900 an ounce but then fast and erratically fell below $300. Since then, it's been bouncing up and down a bit. There are always a few optimists who project another searing, soaring rise, but future profits, if any, will be hard to come by.

There are two kinds of goldbug: (1) the true believers, who insist that the value of this most precious metal will go up because inflation is sure to get worse; in recent years, these zealots have paid dearly for their "faith"; (2) the systems players, who speculate with gold, in some form, by buying low, selling or selling short at an interim high, rebuying to catch a rise, reselling on the way down, and so on . . . until their interest or capital runs out.

Right now, with inflation apparently under control and business profits improving, gold is no longer in the spotlight. Even James Dines, the original goldbug, glooms that "Gold will have to make a helluva run upward to beat the high yields of government bonds."

But, says a precious metals newsletter, "Gold experts were pessimistic about 2 years ago, not long before gold stocks became some of the best market performers." But gold is always a speculation.

If you do succumb to gold fever, here are some choices:

➤ PUBLICLY OWNED AMERICAN AND CANADIAN MINING COMPANIES There are few with holdings elsewhere. The most stable are large and diversified: Homestake Mining (HM), Campbell Redlake, etc. Their shares are traded on major exchanges, so there's always an active market.

But their prices can fluctuate: for HM, in 1981, from an adjusted 32 to 8½ and, in 1982, back up to 32.

The most speculative are "penny" stocks sold on Canadian exchanges. These are shares of small companies that own, or have rights to, mines that can be worked profitably when the price of gold is high or that have been "certified" as having ore reserves. With these, the only sure winners are the promoters.

➤ SOUTH AFRICAN GOLD MINING COMPANIES Their shares are available as American Depositary Receipts (ADRs). They pay a fair dividend, but their prices are volatile because they reflect the estimates of remaining reserves and, of course, the price of gold. In one *month*, the stock of President Steyn shuttle-cocked between 58½ and 45½.

BUT gold mining shares usually lead gold bullion prices, so you might get ahead of the market.

➤ HOLDING COMPANIES *A.S.A. Limited,* a closed-end investment company with some 70% of its assets in South African gold mining shares; *Anglo-American Corporation,* the largest mining finance firm and the number one producer of both gold and diamonds; *Anglo-American Investment Company,* with holdings in a number of gold mines. With all of these, you are buying the equivalent of shares in a mutual fund.

For the years when the price of gold was soaring, these were very worthwhile. Recently, however, the movements have been low, slow, and generally down.

➤ GOLD CERTIFICATES These are papers that spell out ownership of a portion of bulk gold stored in a bank vault: in Switzerland, where there's no U.S. account, no sales tax, and no report to the IRS; in America, usually in Delaware, where there's no sales tax.

Certificates are sold for $1,000 each plus commissions of 2 to 5% plus storage charges—for cash or via an installment agreement. They are not negotiable nor assignable, so they must be sold back to the dealer; but that's better than storing the metal yourself, because there must be an assay before it can be sold.

Beware of bargains: Bullion Reserves sold $60 million in certificates for gold and silver "stored" in Utah. The "investors" lost most of their money, and the promoters were indicted.

➤ GOLD FUTURES CONTRACTS These give the speculator the biggest bang for the buck. They are similar to commodities futures, can be handled by most brokers, and are actively traded on the Comex and IMM.

You can buy and sell 100-ounce contracts with different future delivery dates on a margin of 5 to 15%, usually after a minimum balance. Thus, with gold at $313, for about a $1,600 margin you can control 100 ounces worth $31,300. If there's a 10% price rise to $344 or so, you can double your money, after costs. But if the price falls, you must come up with more cash or collateral.

➤ GOLD COINS These are not to be confused with collectors' items that are judged on rarity and condition. They are primarily South African Krugerrands, Canadian Maple Leafs, Austrian Coronas, and Mexican pesos. They are best for display and pride of ownership because they are hard to sell at a profit.

These glittering coins contain slightly less gold than stated; come in several sizes and, thus, prices; sell at 5 to 8% premium over the quoted value of gold; and are usually subject to a local sales tax. *Exception:* U.S. medallions that are sold tax-free in ½- and 1-oz units, at about 2% above the New York "spot" price. They have no major market for resale.

Note: Deal only with a reputable firm, preferably located in the United States. European coins are easy to fake.

➤ GOLD OPTIONS These are rights to buy or sell futures contracts at a set price before a set date. For a premium, you can buy below or sell above the current market quotation. The leverage is high and the commissions low ($25 round trip) and if gold prices are swinging—and you're lucky—you can make money fast. Or you can lose it even faster.

You can use spreads, which can be profitable if the price stays within preset limits but can be money-losers if there's too wide a move the wrong way.

A variation of these options is the leverage contract, bought with a down payment of 20 to 50% of the total value with the balance covered by an interest-bearing loan. These are private deals with traders who make their own markets. The merchant stands ready to make delivery or reverse the deal if the customer closes out the

position and will liquidate if a margin call is not met promptly.

➤ INSTALLMENT BUYING These are billed as "sure-fire" systems. They require consistent investing with the goal of building substantial holdings. You buy bullion on the installment plan. It is stored abroad or in a state where there are no taxes.

New York's Citibank sets an initial minimum of $1,000 with additions in units of $100. There's a 3% load and a 1% fee on the sale.

Merrill Lynch's Sharebuilder Gold Plan requires a basic $100 with additions in units of $50. The gold is purchased at $1 an ounce above the London price.

There are usually two types of contracts:

- *Unit price averaging,* where the investor agrees to buy a fixed amount of gold regularly, paying less when the price is low, more when high.

- *Cost averaging,* or investing a fixed sum at periodic intervals, buying more when the price is low and less when high. Attractive packaging doesn't change the risks.

GOLD AND PRECIOUS METALS MUTUAL FUNDS

Bull and Bear Golconda
  Investors
11 Hanover Square
New York, NY 10005
1-800-523-9250
1-212-785-0900

Fidelity Select—Precious
  Metals
82 Devonshire Street
Boston, MA 02109
1-800-544-6666
1-617-523-1919

Franklin Gold
155 Bovet Road
San Mateo, CA 94402
1-415-570-3000
1-800-632-2350

International Investors
122 East 42nd Street
New York, NY 10168
1-800-221-2220
1-212-687-5200

Strategic Investments
2030 Royale Lane
Dallas, TX 75229
1-800-527-5027
1-214-484-1326

United Services Gold
  Shares
(also United Services
  Prospector)
P.O. Box 29467
San Antonio, TX 78229
1-800-527-5027
1-512-629-1234

CHECKPOINTS FOR TRADING GOLD OR SILVER

If you are willing to spend time watching trends, dealing in precious metals can often be profitable and will always be exciting. First:

- *Check the broker or dealer* via bank references and written recommendations by customers you know or recognize

- *Contact the Better Business Bureau* and, if you're planning to commit large sums, the attorney general

- *Avoid firms that "guarantee" profits,* or discounts from spot prices or suggest delayed deliveries

- *Get a written explanation of all costs:* for storage, insurance, delivery, etc.

Then, follow these guidelines and heed these warnings:

- *Paper trade for at least one month.* Make decisions, calculate margins, set stop-loss prices, etc.

- *Never commit more than half of your risk capital.* Keep the balance in a money market account for the inevitable margin calls.

- *Limit the possible loss,* on any situation, to 25% of your total account.

- *Check the bulletins and reports of at least three reliable dealers.*

- *Use charts to check price movements and spot trends.*

- *Never give discretionary powers to anyone in the business.*

And if you prefer to let someone else do it for you, there are gold funds (see table on page 213).

24

FINANCIAL FUTURES AND INDEXES

For amateurs, financial futures and stock indexes are becoming one of the riskiest areas in Wall Street. For professionals, all these can be investment tools to hedge positions. Just as agribusinesses rely on commodities futures, so money-oriented firms use financial futures to buy in the current market and sell in the future (or the other way around) to protect their costs or profits.

The speculator takes the opposite side of the contract. It is usually a professional who understands the risks and rewards, but it will increasingly be an individual shooting for a quick gain with minimal capital. *Only 20% of these deals are profitable.*

With all of these special speculations, you have to *guess* right: to correctly predict the short or intermediate movements of the entity. Financial futures involve debt issues whose values move with the cost of money, while the new indexes are tied to stock market averages or small groups of stocks. With tiny margins, as small as $800 to control $1 million, a shift of ½% in the interest rate can double your money, or lose most of your capital.

The margins with the indexes are slightly higher, but the swings can be faster and wider. These packaged pools can give you a startling ride: on one Friday afternoon, the Standard & Poor's index futures dropped $325 per contract on news of an unexpected decline in the money supply. Two minutes later, when the Federal

Reserve Board cut the discount rate, their price roared up $675 per contract.

The swings of financial futures are not quite so dramatic, but the forecast of higher interest rates by only one financial guru can send these contracts down as fast as a punctured balloon. And unlike the stock market, optimistic forecasts are accepted slowly and reluctantly.

If you are a modest investor, skip this chapter. If you have over $100,000 in a portfolio, read it rapidly. If you are a speculator who can afford to lose half of your stake, study the explanations and get more information from a specialist.

FINANCIAL FUTURES

Basically, these are contracts that involve money. They are used by major investors, such as banks, insurance companies, and pension fund managers, to protect positions by hedging: what they gain (lose) in the cash market will be offset by the loss (profit) in the futures market.

The terms and rules of trading are set by the exchanges:

➤ PRICE MOVEMENTS So that we'll all be on the same wavelength, here are some basic data on quotations and price movements of financial futures:

- Prices for contracts for T-bills and CDs are quoted in basis points: increments of $\frac{1}{100}$ of 1%. Thus, a rise or fall of one basis point is $100. Since these contracts are quoted on a 90-day basis, divide by 4 to get $25. Normal daily price limits: $\frac{25}{100}$ of 1% (25 basis points) or $625 per contract above or below the previous day's settlement price. Price limits do not apply to trading in contracts for delivery during a specific month or after the first notice day for deliveries during that month.

Financial Futures: Contracts to deliver a specified number of financial instruments at a given price by a certain date, such as U.S. Treasury bonds and bills, GNMA certificates, CDs, and foreign currency.

Index: A statistical yardstick that measures a whole market by using a representative selection of stocks or bonds. Changes are compared to a base year. Futures are now sold on stock indexes such as the S&P 500.

- Prices of Treasury bond and Ginnie Mae futures are quoted in $^1/_{32}$ point per 100 points: $31.25 per contract. Normal daily limits on price movement: $^{24}/_{32}$ of a point ($750 per contract) above or below the previous day's settlement price.

➤ HEDGING   Mr. Pension Manager holds a large portion of the fund's assets in 10-year Treasury notes. At this time, long-term interest rates are richer than those of short-term obligations, so P.M. will get the best yield by holding to maturity. But he looks for a relative rise in short-term rates and knows that the yields on T-bills will usually rise faster than those of the 10-year notes. And he is mindful that he could be wrong and that the prices of both types of debt could decline.

He has two choices: (1) to shift to shorter maturities as soon as rates begin to rise and thus minimize losses in the T-note portfolio. But he will probably have to accept somewhat lower yields, because his research shows that the yield curve is positive; (2) to wait until yields on both bills and notes rise farther as anticipated, at some future point when the yield curve becomes negative. This would mean a loss on the sale of the 10-year notes.

Here's the strategy as explained by the Chicago Board of Trade: to protect the principal and to hold the return on the long-terms while waiting for the short-term rates to rise, he sells 10-year Treasury futures. As interest rates rise, the loss on the cash Treasury note portfolio is offset by the profit in the futures position. The hedge enables P.M. to sell the notes later at a higher effective price (see table).

This hedge used 71 contracts based on a conversion factor of 1.4269 for a 14.50% coupon due in 9.5 years. If the hedge had been maintained for an extended period, it would have been necessary to reduce the number of contracts as the time to maturity for the T-notes decreased.

In this example, the entire loss was not offset, due to a weakening basis, or negative move, in the spread between the cash and futures prices: here, the basis moved from 31–19 ($31^{19}/_{32}$) to 29–02 ($29^2/_{32}$).

➤ SPREADS   Speculators usually trade financial futures by going long on one position and short on another with both contracts due in the same month. But you can also use spreads: buying one contract month and selling another. This technique is used when there's an abnormal relation between the yields and thus the prices of two contracts with different maturities. These situations don't come often, but when they do, they can be mighty rewarding, because the gains will come from a restoration of the normal spread.

Example: Eagle-Eye notes that June T-bonds are selling at 80–11 (each $^1/_{32}$ of 1% equals $3.125 of a standard $100,000 contract) and that September's are at 81–05. The basis for quotations is an 8% coupon and 15-year maturity.

Having a keen memory, E.E. decides that this $^{26}/_{32}$ difference is out of line with normal pricing. He *sells* the September contract and

---

HEDGING STRATEGY

CASH	FUTURES
Jan. 15	
Owns $5 million 14.5% T-notes due 5/5/89	SELL 71 June 10-year Treasury futures @ 75–21
Current Price: 107–08 (yield 13.13%)	
90-day T-bills (10.85%)	
April 15	
Sell $5 million T-notes @ 99–24 (yield 14.54%)	BUY 71 June 10-year Treasury futures @ 70–22
90-day T-bills (14.80%)	

Results

Holding T-notes for this 3-month period cost the portfolio $375,000 (107–08 minus 99–24).	A gain in the futures position of $352,781 (75–21 minus 60–22 × 31.25) reduces the opportunity loss to $22,218.
The portfolio manager was able to pick up 395 basis points in the purchase of T-bills, for a gain, in interest income, of $49,375.	

buys the June one. In a couple of weeks, prices begin to normalize: the September contract edges up to 81–08 and the June one surges to 80–24. Now he starts to cash in: he loses $^{3}/_{32}$ ($93.75) on the September contract but gains $^{13}/_{32}$ ($406.25) on the June one: $312.50 profit minus commission. With his 10 contracts, E.E. pays for a Florida holiday.

FOLLOW STRICT RULES

If you have money you can afford to lose, time enough to keep abreast of developments in the financial world, strong nerves, and a trustworthy, knowledgeable broker, trading in financial futures may be rewarding and will surely be exciting. Of course, if you're involved with substantial holdings, you probably are already familiar with hedging, so you can stick to protective contracts. Otherwise, follow these rules:

- *Make dry runs on paper for several months.* Interest rates change slowly. Pick different types of financial futures each week and keep practicing until you get a feel for the market and risks and, over at least one week, chalk up more winners than losers.
- *Buy long when you look for a drop in interest rates.* With lower yields, the prices of all contracts will rise.
- *Sell short when you expect a higher cost of money.* This will force down the value of the contracts, and you can cover your position at a profit.

- *Set a strategy and stick to it.* Don't try to mix contracts until you are comfortable and making money.
- *Set stop and limit orders, not market orders.* A market order is executed immediately at the best possible price. A stop order, to buy or to sell at a given price, becomes a market order when that price is touched. A limit order is the maximum price at which to buy and the minimum at which to sell.

OPTIONS ON FUTURES

➤ OPTIONS ON FUTURES These involve far less money than contracts do: roughly, $100 for an option compared to $1,800 for a futures contract. There are no margin calls and the risk is limited to the premium. But these are for professionals and real swingers. If you ride a strong market trend, you can make a lot of money with a small outlay and rapid fluctuations or you can make a modest profit by successful hedging. *Be cautious and limit your commitment.* It's easy to con yourself into thinking you're a genius when you hit a couple of big winners fast, but unless you bank half of those profits, you will lose money over a period of time if only because of the commissions.

➤ OPTIONS ON DEBT ISSUES As with all types of securities or contracts, a *call* is the right to buy at a preset price, usually before a preset date; a *put* is the mandate to sell the same item, again at a preset price at a preset date. The cost of the option is the premium and varies with

CONTRACT SPECIFICATIONS OF FUTURES

	U.S. TREASURY BONDS	10-YEAR U.S. TREASURY NOTES	GNMA-CDR	GNMA II
Basic trading unit	$100,000 face value	$100,000 face value	$100,000 principal balance	$100,000 principal balance
Price quotation	Full points (one point equals $1,000) and 32nds of a full point			
Minimum price fluctuation	1/32nd of a full point ($31.25 per contract)			
Daily price limit	64/32nds (2 points or $2,000) above or below the previous day's settlement price			
Date introduced	Aug. 22, 1977	May 3, 1982	Oct. 20, 1975	1984
Ticker symbol	US	TY	M	GT

SOURCE: Chicago Board of Trade.

the time frame and situation of that exercise price, whether it is *at the money, in the money,* or *out of the money.*

Since the values of debt issues move opposite to interest rates, think backward with these options. Here's how they are quoted and traded:

- Options on T-bills reflect the discount yield. With a 9% yield, the T-bill price basis would be 91 ($9,100). The option might trade at 93, 100 basis points away from the strike price.

- The premiums for bonds are quoted at intervals of $5 each. In trade lingo "6 to 10, 25 up, last 7" for calls offered at 10 basis points of $50 each means that someone is bidding 6 ($30); there are 25 calls available on either side; and the last trade was 7 basis points ($35) an option. If interest rates fall, the price of the call will rise. If they remain stable, the price of the call will dwindle to zero because all options, with set expiration dates, are wasting assets.

SETTING UP HEDGES

Options provide excellent opportunities to set up hedges if you plan your strategy and understand the risks and rewards. Here's an example cited by Stanley Angrist in *Forbes.*

In March, the June T-bond contract is selling at 52–05 (72⅝). Calls, at 72, 74, and 76 are quoted at premiums of 2–06, 1–20, and 0–46, respectively; puts, at 68, 70, and 72 are available at 0–30, 0–61, and 1–54. Wally thinks that the market will remain stable so he makes these paper projections of hedges with a margin of $3,000:

Sell June 72 call	$2,093.75
Sell June 72 put	1,843.75
Total income	$3,937.50

If the T-bond is still worth 72 at June strike date, both options will expire worthless, so Wally has an extra $3,937.50 minus commissions.

Sell June 74 call	$1,312.50
Sell June 70 put	953.13
Total income	$2,265.63

This is less risky, and less profitable, because both options will expire worthless if the last-day price is between 70 and 74.

Sell June 76 call	$ 718.75
Sell June 68 call	468.75
Total income	$1,187.50

If final price is between 68 and 76, Wally

TYPICAL FUTURES, OPTIONS, AND CONTRACTS

CONTRACT	EXCHANGE	ENTRY FEE*	CONTRACT VALUE†
Equity Futures			
Standard & Poor's 500	CMI	$6,000	$81,500
NYSE composite	NYF	3,500	47,700
Financial futures			
Treasury bonds	CBT	1,500	69,688
Japanese yen	CMI	1,500	52,975
Equity options			
Standard & Poor's 100	CBOE	275	16,595
Major market	AMEX	—	12,114
Financial options			
Treasury bonds	CBT	1,500	1 T-bond future

    * Futures: initial minimum margin; Options: average premium for at-the-money option.
    † Recent changes daily.

SOURCE: Exchanges.

Here's how futures and options compare as described by *Commodities* magazine when December T-bond futures were quoted at $72^2/_{32}$ and the options were at a strike price of 72.

October 1: Projection: lower interest rates so higher bond futures prices. Choices: (1) buy T-bond futures at $72^2/_{32}$; margin: $3,000; (2) buy call option at 2–03; $2,000 plus $^3/_{64}$ of $1,000: $2,046.88.

October 4: Futures down to $70^{16}/_{32}$ so need more margin. Call down to $1^{20}/_{64}$ ($1,312.50); no margin call.

October 13: Futures up to $78^3/_{32}$: +$6,000 profit. Call to $6^{15}/_{64}$ ($6,234.38): +$4,187.50 Less than futures, but no margin call.

October 1: Projection: higher interest rates add lower futures prices. Choices: (1) sell futures at $7^2/_{32}$; (2) buy put option at $1^{59}/_{64}$ ($1,921.88).

Futures: after early gain, loss of over $6,000 by October 13. Put: value up to $2^{46}/_{64}$ ($2,718.75) at outset but calls to $^{10}/_{64}$ ($156.25) by 13th. Decline less than $6,000 for futures but need more margin and still in market.

will do OK. He swaps a lower income for a broader price range.

STOCK INDEXES

These are the fastest growing area of speculations and make it possible to play the stock market without owning a single share of stock. They combine the growth potential of equities with the speculative hopes of commodities.

With a stock index, you are betting on the future price of the composite of a group of stocks: *buying* if you anticipate a rise soon; *selling* if you look for a decline. You put up cash or collateral equal to about 7% of the contract value vs. 50% for stocks. All you need is a little capital and a lot of nerve. A minor jiggle can produce sizable losses, or gains. And there are also options that require even less money.

To emphasize the speculative nature of indexes, some brokerage firms advise their registered representatives to limit trading to individuals with net worths of $100,000 (exclusive of home and life insurance).

These are the stock index contracts currently available:

- **Standard & Poor's 500:** stocks of 400 industrials, 40 financial companies, 40 utilities, and 20 transportations issues, all listed on the NYSE. They are weighted by market value. Contracts are valued at 500 times the index: at 160, $80,000. They are traded on the Chicago Mercantile Exchange. Generally, this is the index favored by big hitters, as contracts are extremely liquid and it's widely used to measure institutional performance.

- **Standard & Poor's 100:** a condensed version of the 500 Index (known as OEX). It is weighted by capitalization of the component corporations, all of which have options traded on the CBOE (Chicago Board Options Exchange). The value is 100 times the worth of the stocks.

- **Value Line Futures:** an equally weighted geometric index of about 1,700 stocks actively traded on the NYSE, AMEX, and OTC. Contracts are quoted at 500 times the index. This tends to be difficult to trade because of a thin market on the small Kansas City Board of Trade.

- **AMEX Market Value Index (XAM):** measures the changes in the aggregate market of over 800 AMEX issues. The weighting is by industry groups: 32% natural resources, 19% high technology; 13% service; 11% consumer goods. No one company accounts for more than 7% of the total.

- **AMEX Major Market Index (XMI):** based on 20 blue chip NYSE stocks and price-weighted so that higher-priced shares have a greater effect on the average than lower priced ones.

- **AMEX Oil & Gas Index (XOI):** made up of the stocks of 30 oil and gas companies with Exxon representing about 17%.

- **AMEX Computer Technology Index (XCI):** stocks of 30 major computer companies, with IBM accounting for about half and Hewlett-Packard, Digital Equipment, and Motorola another 16%.
- **NYSE Composite Index (MYA):** a capitalization-weighted average of about 1,500 Big Board stocks.
- **Standard & Poor's Computer & Business Equipment Index (OBR):** capitalization-weighted average of a dozen major office and business equipment companies, with IBM about 75%; Digital Equipment, Wang, Xerox, and NCR about 18%.
- **Pacific Technology Index (PTI):** a price-weighted index of 100 stocks of which 45 are traded OTC. *Very volatile.*

According to Wall Street these indexes, especially the Standard & Poor's ones, enable you to hedge your portfolio.

Example: Jill has a well-diversified portfolio worth $48,000. It's April and she anticipates a market decline but does not want to sell because some of the gains will be short term. The AMEX Major Market Index is at 120, so Jill buys four July 120 puts (4 × $120 × 100) at a premium of 2% ($1,500). By expiration date, if the market falls 10%, the portfolio loses $4,800 in value. But the puts are worth the strike price minus the index value (120 minus 108): $1,200 each or $4,800 total. The net loss is $1,150 vs. a possible $4,800 decline in portfolio worth.

If the index rises 10%, the portfolio will be worth $4,800 more. Subtract the $1,150 cost for the puts and Jill is ahead by $3,650. The $1,150 was insurance.

That's what the brokers tell you, but it's not realistic because: (1) very few investors have a portfolio whose composition is close to that of an index; (2) the changes in the stock values are not uniform. *Repeat: stock indexes are for speculation, not protection.*

Guidelines for dealing in stock indexes:

- *Follow the trend.* If the price of the index was higher than the day before which, in turn, was higher than the previous day, go long. If reverse, sell short.
- *Set stop-loss prices at 3 points below cost.* If they are too close, one erratic move can stop you out at a loss even though the market may resume its uptrend soon.

- *Recognize the role of the professionals.* To date, most contracts have been traded by brokerage houses active in arbitrage and spreads and in hedging large block positions. Only a handful of institutional managers have done more than experiment. So the amateur is competing with top professionals who have plenty of capital and no commissions to pay, and who are in positions to get the latest information and make quick decisions.
- *Study the price spreads.* Contracts for distant months are more volatile. In a strong market, buy far-out contracts and short nearby months; in a weak market, buy the closer months and short the distant ones.

SPECIAL TERMS

- **Arbitrage.** Simultaneous purchase and sale of the same or equivalent security in order to make a profit from the price discrepancy.
- **Contract month.** Month in which a futures contract may be fulfilled by making or taking delivery.
- **Cross hedge.** Hedging a cash market risk in one financial instrument by taking a position in a futures contract for a different but similar instrument.
- **Forward contract.** An agreement to buy or sell goods at a set price and date. Those involved plan to take delivery of the instrument.
- **Mark to the market.** Debits and credits in each account at close of trading day.
- **Open interest.** Contracts that have not been offset by opposite transactions or by delivery.
- **Physical.** The underlying physical commodity.
- **Spread.** Holding opposite positions in two futures contracts with the intent of profit through changes in prices.

- *Be mindful that dividends can distort prices.* In heavy payout months, these discrepancies can be significant.
- *Use a hedge only when your portfolio approximates that of the index:* roughly a minimum of $250,000 (very rarely does a major investor buy only 100 shares of a stock). In most cases, any single portfolio has little resemblance to that of the index.

OPTIONS ON STOCK INDEXES

These are the ultimate in speculations. For a few hundred dollars, you can control a cross section of stocks worth $75,000 or so. The action is fast and exciting. The options, both calls and puts, have expiration dates every 3 months, are quoted at intervals of 5 points, and their premiums reflect hopes and fears, the time premiums declining with the approach of the strike date. There are no margin calls, and the risks are limited.

Example: In May, when the Standard & Poor's 100 index was at 166.97, the June 160 call traded at 9⅜ ($937.50); the September 160 call at 13⅜ ($1,337.50). To break even with the June call, the index would have to rise to 170. Above that, it's all profit. With the September option, the target price would be 174 (to pay for the commissions).

USING HEDGES

Ruth has $60,000 worth of quality stocks and anticipates a drop in the overall stock market. The Standard & Poor's 500 index is at 151.50. She sells short one September contract. By mid-September, the index is up to 153, so she didn't need the protection. She paid $150 for insurance, but the value of her holdings was up about $600.

With volatile stocks, options on the special indexes can be useful. You're bullish (but hesitant) on high-tech stocks. Here's what to do, according to *Indicator Digest:*

- In January, the XCO options index is at 100.79. You buy a March 100 call at 4⅜ and sell a March 105 call at $1^{13}/_{16}$: a net cost of $2^9/_{16}$ points or $256.25 (not counting commissions).

If the XCO trades at 105 or above at expiration (about +4%), you make 2¼ points ($225)—more than an 80% gain. The maximum loss will be the cost of the spread if the index trades at 100 or less at expiration.

With all options on indexes, settlements are made in cash. When the option is exercised, the holder receives the difference between the exercise price and the closing index price on the date the option is exercised. *Watch out:* This can be far from the price the day the assignment notice is received. A hedge can lose on both the long and short side!

25 OPTIONS: All or Nothing

Everyone who owns securities should understand and, at times, utilize options. For *investors,* they can provide extra income and set up tax losses; for *speculators,* they can produce quick profits with small capital, make possible protective hedges, and usually limit losses. But to make money with options, you must work hard, research thoroughly, review often, and adhere to strict rules. To be really successful, you should have ample capital and recognize that, compared with stocks and bonds, the commissions as a percentage of the option prices are high.

Before you allocate savings to any type of options, discuss your plans with your broker, and test out your ideas on paper. If you are not willing to follow your hypothetical choices for several months, get quotations for the previous 13 weeks from files at your library.

Options on major stocks were first listed on options exchanges in 1974. When volume soared, the professionals added financial futures, and when these proved exciting, they combined the two concepts with options on futures contracts. Each new "opportunity" has been more speculative.

The options market is dominated by professionals. In the early years, the prices of most options moved with those of their related securities or commodities, but nowadays with the erratic, fluctuating market, many options trade on their own—or, in some cases, on the dictates of the market makers, whose success depends on their ability to guess option prices.

There are still opportunities for individuals to use options as part of their overall strategy. With careful selections and constant monitoring,

Option: A contract to sell or buy 100 shares of stock at a specified price within a certain time span. If the option is not exercised within that time, the money paid for the option is lost.

selling options can boost annual income by 15% or more; *buying* options can bring quick gains; and both techniques can be used for tax benefits. With options, you have the power of leverage (a small sum can control a large investment); low costs; and a variety of choice (in types of underlying assets, strike prices, and time frames).

Now, let's take a look at the most widely used options—those on stocks of over 300 corporations as traded on four options exchanges: Chicago Board of Options Exchange (CBOE); AMEX Options Exchange; Philadelphia Stock Exchange; and Pacific Stock Exchange. Later, we'll discuss more exotic variations that have been added recently.

Options are a cross between trading in stocks and trading in commodities. They permit holders to control for a specified period of time a relatively large amount of stock with a relatively small amount of capital. They are rights to buy or sell a specified number of shares (usually 100) of a specified stock at a specified price (the striking price) before a specified date (the expiration date).

In effect, options are limited-life warrants. They pay no dividends and, by definition, are diminishing assets. The closer the expiration date, the less time there is for the value of the option to rise or fall as the buyer anticipates.

Buying options is speculation. Selling options can be investing.

The most popular and widely used option is a *call*—the right to buy the underlying stock. A *put* is the opposite—the right to sell the stock. For sophisticated traders, there are complex combinations: spreads, strips, straps, and straddles.

The cost of the option is called the premium. It varies with the duration of the contract, the type of stock, corporate prospects, and the general activity of the stock market. Premiums run as high as 15% of the value of the underlying stock; that is, for a volatile stock selling at 50 ($5,000 for 100 shares), the premium for a call to be exercised 9 months from now might be 7½ ($750) when the exercise price is also 50. Shorter term options on more stable stocks carry smaller premiums: from 2% for those expiring in a month or so to 5% for those with longer maturities. Commissions will cut those returns.

Added caveats: (1) all profits with all options are short-term, so they are taxed at the highest rate; (2) the options market today is quite different from a few years ago: normally, the value of calls dropped ½ point for each point decline in the price of the stock, but in 1984 the average option fell ¾ point for every $1 per share dip in the stock. Since the cost of the option is a fraction that of the stock, the percentage shifts are greater.

DEFINITIONS USED IN OPTION TRADING

➤ STRIKING PRICE The price per 100 shares at which the holder of the option may buy (with a call) or sell (with a put) the related stock.

For stocks selling under $100 per share, the quotations are at intervals of 5 points: 45, 50, 55, etc.

For stocks trading at over $100 per share, the quotations are every 10 points: 110, 120, etc.

New listings are added when the stock reaches the high or low strike price, i.e., at 40, when the stock hits 35 and 25 when the stock falls to 30. When you see a long list of strike prices, the stock has moved over a wide range.

➤ EXPIRATION DATE The Saturday following the third Friday of the month in which the option can be exercised.

➤ PREMIUM The cost of the option, quoted in multiples of $\frac{1}{16}$ for options priced below $3, $\frac{1}{8}$ for those priced higher. To determine the percentage of premium, divide the current value of the stock into the quoted price of the option. When there's a difference between the exercise price of the option and the quoted price of the stock, add or subtract the spread.

Here's how options were quoted in the financial pages when Tandy Corp. (TAN) stock was at 32⅜ (see the table on page 224):

The April 30 call prices ranged from a high of 4¾ ($475) to a low of 2¾ ($275) and a closing price of 3⅛ ($312.50) for a net change from the previous week of −⅛ ($12.50). There were 1,317 sales of contracts for 100 shares each.

The second line lists the action with April 30 puts: a high of $\frac{9}{16}$ ($56.25), a low of ¼ ($25), and a closing price of ⅜ ($37.50). For the week, the net change was $\frac{1}{16}$ ($6.25). There were 996 contracts traded.

Traders looking for quick profits were pessimistic, as shown by the heavy volume in puts: 1,422 contracts for the April 35s and 2,219 for the April 40s. But there were fairly sharp differences of opinion as the April 35 puts were up $\frac{5}{16}$ and the April 40s up ⅜.

Investors were more optimistic and appeared to believe that TAN stock was ready for an upswing: April 40 calls, due in a few weeks, were quoted at ⅛, whereas the farther out October 40s were quoted at 1⅝. Much of the spread, of course, was due to the time factor.

The prices of the options, of course, reflect temporary hopes and fears, but over a month or two, they will tend to move with the underlying stock. But do not rely on this type of projection. The professionals create their own markets and, especially near the expiration date, will move the prices of options sharply in hopes of profiting from their personal positions.

RELATIVE PREMIUMS
As Percent of Price of Underlying Common Stock When Common at Exercise Price

MONTHS TO EXPIRATION	LOW	AVERAGE	HIGH
1	1.8–2.6	3.5–4.4	5.2–6.1
2	2.6–3.9	5.2–6.6	7.8–9.2
3	3.3–5.0	6.7–8.3	10.0–11.7
4	3.9–5.9	7.9–9.8	11.8–13.8
5	4.5–6.8	9.0–11.2	13.5–15.8
6	5.0–7.5	10.0–12.5	15.0–17.5
7	5.5–8.2	10.9–13.7	16.4–19.2
8	5.9–8.9	11.8–14.8	17.7–20.6
9	6.4–9.5	12.7–15.9	19.0–22.2
10	6.8–10.1	13.5–16.9	20.2–23.6
11	7.2–10.7	14.3–17.9	21.4–25.0
12	7.5–11.2	15.0–18.8	22.5–26.2

HOW OPTIONS ARE QUOTED

NAME, EXPIRATION DATE, AND PRICE	SALES	HIGH	WEEK'S LOW	LAST	NET CHG.
Tandy Apr30	1317	$4^3/_4$	$2^3/_4$	$3^1/_8$	$-^1/_8$
Tandy Apr30 p	996	$^9/_{16}$	$^1/_4$	$^3/_8$	$-^1/_{16}$
Tandy Apr35	3872	$1^1/_4$	$^3/_8$	$^1/_2$	$-^3/_{16}$
Tandy Apr35 p	1422	$3^1/_8$	$1^5/_8$	$2^{15}/_{16}$	$+^5/_{16}$
Tandy Apr40	1526	$^3/_{16}$	$^1/_{16}$	$^1/_8$	$-^1/_{16}$
Tandy Apr40 p	2219	$7^7/_8$	$5^7/_8$	$7^7/_8$	$+^3/_8$
Tandy Jul30	426	6	$4^1/_2$	$4^1/_2$	$-^1/_2$
Tandy Jul30 p	805	$1^3/_8$	$^7/_8$	$1^3/_8$	$+^1/_8$
Tandy Jul35	1084	3	2	$2^1/_{16}$	$-^3/_{16}$
Tandy Jul35 p	870	$3^7/_8$	$2^3/_4$	$3^7/_8$	$+^1/_4$
Tandy Jul40	1145	$1^1/_8$	$^3/_4$	$^3/_4$	$-^1/_8$
Tandy Jul40 p	523	$7^3/_4$	$6^1/_8$	$7^3/_4$	$+^3/_8$
Tandy Oct35	346	$4^3/_8$	$3^1/_8$	$3^1/_4$	$-^1/_4$
Tandy Oct35 p	261	$4^3/_8$	$3^1/_2$	$4^3/_8$	$+^3/_8$
Tandy Oct40	137	$2^1/_4$	$1^5/_8$	$1^5/_8$	$-^1/_4$
Tandy Oct40 p	326	$7^7/_8$	$6^1/_2$	$7^3/_4$	$+^1/_4$

Stock price: 32⅜. Table does not show open interest because of space limitations.

SOURCE: Barron's.

One key factor to keep in mind is that the premium at the outset reflects the time factor. This will fall rapidly as the expiration date nears. In the last 3 months of a call, the premium can be cut in half because of the dwindling time.

➤ DIVIDENDS AND RIGHTS As long as you own the stock, you continue to receive the dividends. That's why calls for stocks with high yields sell at lower premiums than do those of companies with small payouts.

A stock dividend or stock split automatically increases the number of shares covered by the option in an exact proportion. If a right is involved, its value will be set by the first sale of rights on the day the stock sells ex-rights.

➤ COMMISSIONS These vary with the number of contracts traded: for a single call, a maximum of $25; for 10 calls, about $4 each. As a guideline, make your calculations, in multiple units, at $14 per contract, less if you use a discount broker.

When you are writing options and income is paramount, it's a good idea to try to work with a base unit of 300 shares of owned stock.

For each side of the transaction the commission per call is about half that of a single option (about $14 versus $25).

You can save commissions when you write calls for a premium of less than 1 ($100). A call traded at $^{15}/_{16}$ ($93.75) will cost $8.39 compared with $25 for one priced at 1 or higher.

➤ RESTRICTED OPTION This occurs when the previous day's price closed at less than 50¢ per share and the underlying stock price closed at more than 5 points *below* its strike price for calls, or more than 5 points *above* its strike price for puts. Opening transactions (buying or writing) calls are prohibited unless they are covered. Closing transactions (liquidations) are permitted. There are exceptions, so check with your broker.

WRITING CALLS

When you write (sell) calls, you start off with an immediate, sure, limited profit rather than an uncertain, potentially greater gain. The *most* you can make is the premium you receive even if the price of the stock soars. If you write calls on stock you own, any loss of the value of the stock will be reduced by the amount of the premium. Writing covered calls (on stock you own) is a conservative use of options. You have these choices.

➤ ON-THE-MONEY CALLS These are written at an exercise price that is at or close to the current price of the stock.

Example: In December, Investor One buys 100 shares of Company A at 40 and sells a July call, at the striking price of 40, for 3 ($300). He realizes that A's stock may move above 43 in the next 7 months but is willing to accept the $3 per share income.

Investor Two is the purchaser of the call. He acquires the right to buy the stock at 40 at any time before the expiration date at the end of July. He anticipates that A's stock will move up well above 43.

Investor One will not sustain a dollar loss until the price of A goes below 37. He will probably keep the stock until its price goes above 43. At this price, the profit meter starts ticking for Investor Two, so let's see what happens if A stock jumps to 50. At any time before late July, Investor Two can exercise his option and pay $4,000 for stock now worth $5,000. After deducting about $400 (the $300 premium plus commissions), he will have a net profit of about $600, thus doubling his risk capital.

But if the price of A stock moves up to only 42, Investor Two will let the call expire and take the loss. Investor One will end up with about $375: the $300 premium plus two dividends of $50 each minus $25 commission for the sale of the call.

If the price of the stock soars, Investor One can still come out ahead if he is willing to come up with cash to keep the stock by buying back the call.

When A stock hits 50 in June, the July call might be quoted at 11⅝. New corporate developments make Investor One enthusiastic about further gains, so he buys back the call for $1,162.50 (plus commission). He takes a cash loss of $862.50 (the $1,162.50 purchase price minus $300 premium) for an after-cost net of about $900. But he has a paper profit on A stock of $1,000 and hopes for a further rise soon.

Investor One can now write a new call at 50, with an October expiration date, for 3 ($300) because of the market optimism. This will reduce his out-of-pocket loss. If the stock is called in October, he is still ahead of the game and he has set up a welcome short-term capital loss.

➤ IN-THE-MONEY CALLS This is a more aggressive technique that requires close attention but can result in excellent profits and tax benefits, especially for those in high tax brackets.

Example: In January, Karen buys 300 shares of Glamor Electronics Co. (GEC) at 105 ($31,500) and sells three June 100 calls at 8 each ($2,400). If GEC stock stays below 108, she keeps the premiums and the stock. If it goes to 110, she can buy back the calls at, say, 11, $1,100 ($3,300 total), to set up a short-term tax loss of $900. Karen then sells the shares (for $33,000) for a $1,500 gain plus dividends. In her 50% tax bracket, that trading adds only $750 to her taxable income—more than offset by the tax loss.

If GEC stock drops below 100, Karen keeps the premiums and starts writing new calls. She won't suffer a loss, because her "real" cost is 97 (105 purchase price minus 8 premium).

➤ DEEP-IN-THE-MONEY CALLS These are calls that are sold at striking prices *below* the current quotation of the stock. Writing them is best when the investor is dealing in large blocks of stock, because of the almost certain commissions which have to be paid when the underlying stock is called. With this approach, the best selection is a stable, high-dividend stock. Your returns may be limited, but they are likely to be sure. Here are techniques used by professionals:

■ *Using leverage:* when the exercise price of the call is below that of the current value of the stock, both securities tend to move in unison. Since the options involve a smaller investment, there's a higher percentage of return and, in a down market, more protection against loss.

Example: Pistol Whip, Inc. (PWI) is selling at 97⅝. The call price at 70 2 months hence is 28, so the equivalent price is 98. If PWI goes to 105, the call should keep pace and be worth 35.

If you bought 100 shares of the stock, the total cost would be about $9,800. Your ultimate profit would be about $550, close to a 5.5% return. If you bought 10 options, the dollar profit would be a 22.4% return on the smaller $2,900 investment. If the stock does not move, you can let it go or buy back the calls at a small loss. If PWI declines, your maximum loss is $2,900, probably much less than that of the stock.

Note: All too often, this is more theory than practice. When an option is popular, it may trade on its own and not move up or down with the price of the stock. This separate value will shift only when the expiration date is near.

When one volatile stock was at 41 in March, the November 45 call was trading at $2\frac{1}{16}$. Three weeks later, when the stock fell to $35\frac{1}{2}$ (-16%), the call edged down to 2: a 3% decline. The professionals had moved in and set their own terms.

But remember that, at times, the price of the call may drop farther in percentage than that of the stock.

A variation of this use of deep-in-the-money calls is to create cost by basing the return on the total income received from premiums plus dividends.

Example: In January, one professional money manager seeking extra income for his fund bought 1,000 shares of Wellknown Chemical at $39\frac{1}{2}$. He then sold April 35 options for $6\frac{7}{8}$ each, thereby reducing the price per share to $32\frac{5}{8}$. He could count on a 45¢ per share dividend before the exercise date.

If the call is exercised, the total per share return will be $7.21 on a 32.62 investment: a 22% gross profit in 4 months. Even after commission, the annual rate of return will be excellent. The stock will have to drop below 33 before there's any loss.

WRITING NAKED CALLS

If you maintain a substantial margin account, have considerable experience, and feel confident that the price of a stock will stay flat or decline, you can write (sell) "naked" calls ... without owning the stock. This is risky, because if the stock hits the strike price before or at the exercise date, you are obligated to deliver the shares which you do not own.

You can, of course, cover your position by buying calls, but if the stock price soars, the loss can be substantial. At best, your premium income will be reduced.

One technique that works well is to write 2 out-of-the-money calls for every 100 shares you own. This gives you double premiums. Do

not go too far out, because a lot can happen in a few months.

Example: You own 300 shares of Pumpernickel at 32. The 35 call, due in 4 months, is 3, but you are not persuaded that the market, or the stock, will rise soon. You sell six calls, pocket $1,800 (less commissions), and hope the stock stays under 35. If it moves to 36, you can buy back three calls for, say, $1\frac{1}{2}$ ($450) and let the stock go. But if the stock jumps to 40, you're in trouble.

RULES FOR WRITING OPTIONS

Here's a digest of rules for successful option-writing.

- DEFINE YOUR GOAL
- WORK ON A PROGRAMMED BASIS
- CONCENTRATE ON STOCKS THAT YOU WOULD LIKE TO OWN
- SET A TARGET RATE OF RETURN
- BUY THE STOCK FIRST
- WRITE LONG-TERM CALLS
- CALCULATE YOUR NET RETURN
- KEEP YOUR CAPITAL FULLY EMPLOYED
- BE PERSISTENT
- WATCH THE TIMING
- PROTECT YOUR CAPITAL
- USE MARGIN TO BOOST PROFITS
- WATCH THE RECORD DATE OF HIGH-DIVIDEND STOCKS
- KEEP A SEPARATE BOOKKEEPING SYSTEM

BUYING CALLS

This is speculating, but with the right selections and timing, it can be a rewarding technique: *good* in an up market and *very profitable* if you are smart and lucky. But you can lose plenty if you're wrong.

The basic problem with buying options is that calls, and occasionally puts, are wasting assets. At expiration date, their values can decline to zero if the stock price moves opposite to your expectations or stays fairly stable.

Example: In May, Fred believes that oil stocks are due to move up. His capital is limited, so he decides to speculate by buying options: 10 December 20 calls of SuperZip Oil at $2\frac{1}{2}$. At the time, SZO stock was at $19\frac{5}{8}$ so, to make money, the December price must be over 23: $2\frac{1}{2}$ plus commissions.

By July, SZO is up to 21 and, in September, roars up to 25 with the December calls at an optimistic 7½. Fred sells his calls and pockets about $4,700.

But if the stock price fell or even stayed about the same, Fred would lose all or most of his money.

Buying options can create false optimism and make you believe that you're smart. Take the case of Ned, who started buying a few single options in early 1982. With the up market, he soon doubled his money. Entranced with the profit prospects, he subscribed to options advisory services and set up charts. By fall, he had nearly $20,000 in positions: three to ten long-term calls on a dozen good-to-quality stocks. When the market kept soaring, he moved into strips and straddles, and, while he had a few losses, most of his gambles were profitable. But, as usually happens, he began to believe his own publicity and took greater risks: bigger commitments with more volatile stocks. In April 1983 when the market dropped, he had a whopping paper loss, and because most of his calls were due to expire that month, there was little time for a comeback. By 1984, Ned was out of the options market "for keeps."

In an up market, buy calls on up stocks on either of these terms:

- Long-term, out-of-the-money options at a low premium, typically 1 or less. By diversifying with four or five promising situations, you may be lucky enough to hit it big with one and make enough to offset the small losses on the others.

- Short or intermediate term in-the-money or close-to-the-money options of volatile stocks: 2 months to expiration date, a stock within 5% of the strike price, and a low time premium. If the price of the premium doubles, sell half your holdings. Advice from one expert: "Never pay a premium of more than 3 for a call on a stock selling under 50 nor more than 5 for one trading over 60. Both prices should include commissions."

Rule of thumb: The striking price of the option and the market price of the stock should change by about one-half as many points as the change in the stock price: for example, if a 30 option is worth 5 when the stock is at 30, it should be worth 2½ when the stock falls to 25, and worth 8 when the stock moves up to 36.

TRADING OPTIONS

The new options market has opened new vistas for speculators. Trading is for cash, so there are no margin calls. The investments are relatively small and the potentials large, and there are always opportunities to hedge. Instead of risking their money in junky low-priced stocks, speculators can get action with the same outlay for options on top-quality equities.

There are scores of speculative situations, so the examples must be limited. Once you get the swing of trading options, find a skillful broker, do your homework, and play the odds. Success in options is a matter of percentages. Because calls are traded daily, there's instant information, and gains or losses can be taken any time during the life of the contract.

You can dabble with one or two calls, but to actually play the options market, you should work with $8,000 a month, spend time enough to make frequent checks, and have a fast, reliable source of information: daily from your broker or weekly from specialists in options.

If you have time to watch developments closely, you can let your profits run, but for most amateurs, the best rule is to set target prices for gains of 15 to 25%—after deducting commissions and depending on the size of your investment, the prospects of the stock market, and the volatility of the stock.

The sale of multiple options against a single stock position can ensure extra protection in a decline, added income if the stock stands still, and bigger returns when there's a modest advance. This works best following a strong market advance, when there's likely to be a temporary lull or fallback.

Example: You own 300 shares of So Long, Inc. (SLI), trading at 25. You believe that the market is topping out, so you sell six calls at premiums of 2½ each: $1,500. Here's what could happen:

PRICE SLI	GAIN OR LOSS	PRICE CALL	GAIN OR LOSS	NET
20	−1,500	0	+1,500	0
25	0	0	+1,500	+1,500
30	+1,500	5	−1,500	0
35	+3,000	10	−4,500	−1,500

PUTS FOR PROFIT AND PROTECTION

In a broad sense, a put is the opposite of a call. It involves the right to *sell* a specified number of shares (usually 100) of a specified stock at a specified price before a specified date. Puts have the same expiration months and price intervals as listed calls. They are most widely used in declining markets to provide extra income, to protect positions, and to speculate on lower stock prices.

The value of a put moves counter to that of the related stock: *up* when the price of the stock falls; *down* when it rises. You buy a put when you are bearish and anticipate that the market or stock will decline. Vice versa with selling puts. As with all options, the value of a put is a wasting asset and will diminish with the approach of the expiration date.

Here again, the attraction of puts is *leverage.* A few hundred dollars can acquire temporary control of thousands of dollars worth of stock. The premiums are generally smaller than those of calls on the same stock because of the lesser demand, reflecting the small number of people who are pessimistic. Sharp traders take advantage of this situation, because they realize that most people tend to be optimistic about the stock market.

➤ SELLING (WRITING) PUTS This provides instant income but involves your responsibility to buy the stock if it sells, before the expiration date, at or below the exercise price.

Example: Ed owns Xanadu stock now selling at 53, well above the purchase price. He's hopeful that the market will keep rising but decides to write a put at 50 for 2 ($200).

As long as the stock stays above 50, the put will not be exercised and Ed keeps the $200 per contract. But once the stock falls below 50, Ed must buy the shares or buy back the put, thus cutting or eliminating the opening profit.

➤ BUYING PUTS These can be used to protect positions and, of course, to score a quick gain. The profits come when the price of the stock falls.

Example: In March, Delphinium becomes skittish about the stock now trading at 47. She buys a July put at the strike price of 50 for 4 ($400). This put has an intrinsic cash value of 3, because the stock is selling 3 points below the exercise price. In effect, she is paying 1 ($100) to protect her position against a sharp market or stock decline.

If Del's prediction is right and the price of the stock drops, the value of the put will rise: to over 7 when the stock falls to 43.

In late July, the stock price is 45, so Del sells the put for 5 for a $100 gross profit. If the price of the stock goes below 43, her profit will be greater.

BUT if Del is wrong and the market soars, with the stock price jumping to 52, she must either sell the put at a loss or, more likely, deliver the stock to the seller of the put at that 50 price. She has a before-cost loss of $100 and no chance to take advantage of the $2 price gain: from the strike price of 50 to the market price of 52.

Buying puts is risky except in a confirmed down market. Do your homework, diversify, take your profits when you double your money, and be ready to accept losses. But shrewd traders can do well in down periods and fairly well in flat markets.

As with calls, the important factor in profitable puts is the related stock. The best candidates for both writing and buying puts are stocks that:

- *Pay small or no dividends.* You are hoping that the value of the stock will decline. Dividends tend to set a floor because of their yields.
- *Sell at high price-earnings ratios.* These are more susceptible to sharp downswings than are stocks with lower multiples. A stock with a P/E of 25 has a better chance for a quick decline than one with a P/E of 10.
- *Are historically volatile*—with patterns of sharp wide swings in their price. Stable stocks move slowly even in active market.
- *Are unpopular with institutions.* At the outset, when selling starts, the price drops can be welcome. Later, however, when panic selling is over, there's likely to be minimal action, because there will be so few buyers.

SPREADS FOR THE SERIOUS

Hedges with options can be a profitable way to pick up a few dollars and/or lessen risks. This involves buying one option and selling another short, both on the same stock. *Your goal:* to capture at least the difference in premiums—at least ½ point between the cost of options exercisable at different dates and/or at different prices. Your cash outlay can be small, because under current margin rules, the long option is adequate to cover the short option: for a ½-point spread, only $50 for both positions. *Make your calculations on paper first,* and make no commitments until you are sure you understand the possibilities or probabilities.

Here's an example involving POP stock priced at 50 in April. The premiums for 50 calls are: for July, 3½; for October, 4.

If POP is below 50 in July, you keep $350 and still own an option worth $250 to $300.

If POP goes up by October, the option will be worth $500 or more, so you have a profit of $850.

If POP is at 60 at the end of July, that month's option will be worth 10, so you have to buy it back at a loss of about $650 plus in-and-out costs. But the October call might be at 14, so you could sell that for a gross profit of $1,000 to offset the July loss.

If the stock falls below 46½, you will lose money unless there's a recovery by October. But with such a stable stock in a rising market, this is not likely. The key factor is the small spread, which keeps the maximum loss low.

Sell July 50 for 3½	+$350
Buy October 50 for 4	− 400
Cash outlay	− 50
Commission	− 25
Total cost	− 75

➤ PERPENDICULAR SPREAD This is based on buying and selling options with the same exercise date but different striking prices.

Example: Easy Rider (ER) is at 101¾. The market is moving up and you are bullish. Sell 10 ER October 100s at 12¼ and buy October 90s at 16⅞. This requires an outlay of $4,625. Your maximum loss will occur if ER plunges below 90.

If it goes to 95, you will still make $375.

MAKING YOUR OWN PUT

Options are flexible and can be combined so that the stock purchases, sales, or short sales protect positions and make profits. Here's an example, by Max Ansbacher, of how to create your own put.

Assume that in late summer, your stock is at 69⅞ and the January 65 call is 9¼. You sell short 100 shares of the stock and buy the call. Here are the possibilities:

- If the stock falls to 55 by the end of January, the call will be worthless, so you lose $925. But your profit from the short sale is $1,487.50 ($6,987.50 sale; $5,500 buy-back cost) = net profit $562.50 (not counting commissions and fees).
- The option limits your risk of loss on the short sale even if the stock price should rise. Thus, if the stock jumps to 100, an unprotected short sale would mean a loss of $3,012.50 ($10,000 purchase price minus $6,987.50 received from the short sale).
- But with a short sale of the stock and a purchase of a call, the loss will be only $437: the purchase price of 9¼ ($925) minus $488 (the spread between the stock price of 69⅞ and the exercise price of 65)—again not counting costs.

At 100 or higher, your profit will be a welcome $5,375, a 120% return on your investment.

If the market is declining, set up a bearish spread. Psychologically, the risk is greater, so it is best to deal with lower priced stocks, selling at, say, 24⅝.

Buy 10 October 25s at 2⅛ and sell 10 October 20s at 5⅜. This brings in $3,250 cash. Since the October 20 calls are naked, you'll need $5,000 margin (but the premiums cut this to $1,750) to control nearly $50,000 worth of stock.

If the stock goes to 22, you will make $1,250. At 20 or below, your profit is $3,250 for a 180% return. With perpendicular spreads, you know results at any one time. With horizontal spreads, there's the added risk of time.

➤ BUTTERFLY, OR SANDWICH, SPREAD In this case you are multihedging. Here's what to do:

in the spring, when your stock, hypothetical Busty Bertha, is at 96¼, with July 80 calls at 17⅛, July 90s at 12⅛, and July 100s at 7⅛, *buy* one July 100 and one July 80 and *sell* two July 90s. This provides $2,425 in cash, but it requires at least $1,000 margin.

If you can set up such a combination, *you cannot lose money.* If the stock ends July at 80 or below, or at 100 or above, the buy and sell sides offset each other.

You make money if BB stock is between 81 and 99 (that profit zone again). At 94, you will lose $800 on the sell side but make $1,400 on the buy side for a $600 gross profit.

At 90, you get the best profit. The July 80 call is worth 10 (a loss of $712.50), and the July 100 expires worthless for a loss of another $712.50. But the two July 90s also expire at zero, so the investor pockets $2,245 on the sell side for a net gain of $1,000, or 100% on the money he put up.

There are dangers in such complex combinations:

- With one call each, the commissions will eat you up.
- Such spreads are difficult to execute at the same time.
- Early exercise by the buyer can destroy the hedge and create a new ball game.
- Lifting a leg of the spread can: (1) increase the risk from temporary market fluctuations, (2) create an unprofitable tax situation. The potential profit on the short side could be larger than the loss on the long side. If both are closed out or expire, the taxes could take all the gains.

Advice: Set up butterfly spreads *only* if you have a shrewd, knowledgeable broker, time enough to watch changes, and money enough to make such speculations worthwhile. Otherwise, your broker will be the winner.

HYBRID OPTIONS/ COMBINATIONS

Hybrid options can be rewarding. But they are dangerous for amateurs and, unless substantial sums are involved, expensive. Here are some examples of the flexibility of combinations of teaming calls and puts.

➤ STRADDLE A double option, combining a call and a put on the same stock, both at the same price, and for the same length of time. Either or both sides of a straddle may be exercised at any time during the life of the option—for a high premium. These are profitable when you are convinced that a stock will make a dramatic move but are uncertain whether the trend will be up or down.

Traditionally, most speculators use straddles in a bull market against a long position. If the stock moves up, the call side will be exercised and the put will expire unexercised. This is more profitable than writing calls, because the straddle premiums are substantially higher than those of straight calls.

But this can be costly in a down market. If the underlying stock goes down, there's a double loss: in the call and in the put. Therefore, when a straddle is sold against a long position, the straddle premium received must, in effect, protect 200 shares.

In a bear market, it is often wise to sell straddles against a short position. The odds are better.

Here's how one self-styled trader did it:

"In January, QRS stock was at 100. This was close to the last year's high and, since the stock had bounced as low as 65, I felt the best straddle was short term so I picked a February expiration date. Simultaneously, I bought a call and a put, both at 100: 5 ($500) for the call and 4 ($400) for the put. With commissions (for buying and selling) of about $100, my exposure was $1,000.

"To make money, QRS had to rise above 110 or fall below 90. I guessed right. The stocks' uptrend continued to 112. I sold the call for $1,300 and was lucky to get rid of the put at $50: profit—$350 in one month!

"I would do OK if the stock fell to 88. Then, the call would be worth ½ but the put would bring at least $1,200, so I end up with about $250.

"The risk was that the stock's price would hold around 100. This would mean an almost total loss. But, from experience, I know that I'll lose on about 25% of my straddles so I have to shoot for a high return on the other deals."

➤ SPREAD A variation of a straddle in which the call will be at a price above the current market and the put at a price below the current market. Essentially, this is a cheaper form of straddle, carrying a lower premium because of the lower risk to the seller.

➤ STRIP A triple option: two puts and one call on the same stock with a single option period and striking price. A strip writer expects the stock to fall in the short term and rise over the long term. He offers to sell 100 shares that he owns above the market price or take 200 shares below the market. The premium is higher than that for a straddle.

➤ STRAP Also a triple option: two calls and one put on the same stock. The writer gets top premium—bullish over the long term, but more negative than the strip seller on short-term prospects.

➤ INSURANCE To protect a profit, buy a put on stock you own. *Example:* your stock has soared from 30 to 60, so you expect a setback. You buy a short-term put, at 60, for $400. If the stock dips to 50, the put will be worth 10 ($1,000), so you sell for a profit of $600 and still own the stock. If the stock keeps moving up to 70, the put expires worthless. You lose $400 but you have a paper profit of $1,000 on the stock, so you are $600 ahead.

➤ LOCK IN CAPITAL GAINS The same technique can be used to lock in a capital gain. By buying the put at 60 for $400, you reduce the stock value to 56. If it falls to 50, you sell the stock at the exercise price of 60 for $6,000. Deduct the $400 premium from the $3,000 profit (from cost of 30) and you still have $2,600. That's $600 more than if you had held the stock until its price fell to 50.

Stock rights are options that permit current shareholders to buy more corporate securities, usually common stock, ahead of the public, without commissions or fees, and typically at a discount of 5 to 10%.

Rights are a convenient way for corporations to raise additional capital at a modest cost. In a sense, they are a reward to shareholders. They are often used by utilities anxious to issue more common stock to balance their heavy debt obligations. The discount makes it possible for investors (who obviously have confidence in the company) to acquire additional shares at a bargain price or to pick up a few extra dollars by selling the rights in the open market. But rights are worthwhile only when the additional money can be expected to generate extra profits to permit the same, or higher, dividends for the additional shares.

To be eligible for rights, you must own the common stock on a stated date. Most offerings must be exercised within a short time, usually less than 30 days, so watch your mail and, if the shares are held by your broker, be doubly alert. Failure to take advantage of this opportunity is foolish and can be costly—causing loss of the actual value of the rights and, if there is a loss in the future, the tax benefit.

Rights have an intrinsic value, but they are also speculative because of the high leverage: a 10% rise in the price of the stock can mean as much as a 30% jump in the value of the right. Or vice versa on the loss side.

Let's assume that the stock is trading at $28 per share; that shareholders get 1 right for

Stock right: A short term privilege issued by a corporation to its existing stockholders granting them the right to buy new stock at a discount from market price

every 5 shares; and that each right entitles the holder to buy 1 new share at $25 each.

$$VR = \frac{MP - EP}{NR + 1}$$

where VR = Value of right
MP = Stock's market price
EP = Exercise price
NR = Number of rights needed to buy one share

To calculate the value of 1 right *before* the ex-date, add 1 to the number of rights:

$$VR = \frac{28 - 25}{5 + 1} = \frac{3}{6} = 0.50$$

Thus, each right is worth 50¢, and the stock at this time is worth that much more to investors who exercise their rights.

After the stock has gone ex-right, there'll be no built-in bonus for the stock; and the right will sell at its own value, or possibly higher, if the price of the stock advances; lower if it declines.

BENEFITS TO SHAREHOLDERS

- **Maintenance of ownership position.** If you like a company well enough to continue as a shareholder, pick up the rights. Historically, 80% of stocks bought with rights outperformed the market in the year following the issue. That's logical; management was optimistic.
- **Bargain price.** When Southwestern Public Service issued 29.2 million rights, the offer permitted shareholders to buy one additional common share at $10.95 for each 10 shares already held. At the time,

the stock was trading at $11.50, so the new shares were available at a 4.8% discount. If you owned 1,000 shares, you could save about $55 on the deal, because there were no transaction costs.

■ **Profits from rights themselves.** If you do not want to acquire more stock, you can sell the rights in the open market: through your broker or through a bank designated by the company. With Southwestern, each right was worth 4⅝¢ ($4.69 for each 100 rights).

Or you can buy rights, either to exercise or to speculate. Trading in rights starts as soon as the offer is announced. For a while, the prices of both the basic stock and the rights are quoted—the latter on a "when issued" (wi) basis, as shown with Hefalump in the table.

As a rule, it's best to buy rights soon after they are listed in the financial press; it's best to sell a day or two before the lapse date. Always look at the total costs: commissions and taxes on the rights and the future sale of the stock. You are dealing in odd lots, so the costs can be significant.

Note: Foreign rights (including those of Canadian corporations) may not be exercised by U.S. residents except in the rare cases in which the issuer has registered the related securities with the SEC. Best bet: sell and avoid possible problems.

SPECIAL BENEFITS

There are two other investment advantages with rights. These give you the opportunity to purchase.

1   The stock with a very low margin in a special subscription account (SSA).

This is a margin account set up to use the rights to buy extra stock within 90 days after the rights issue. To open an SSA, deposit rights—your own or purchased—with your broker.

In addition to no commissions for purchase, the *advantages* are: (1) a 25% margin compared with 50% for stocks; (2) no interest charges, so you can use the full credit balance; and (3) a year to pay if you come up with 25% of the balance each quarter.

Example: You have rights to buy Kwick Kick common, selling at 63, for 56 on the basis of 1 new share for 10 old shares. You acquire 100 rights, so you need $5,600 to complete the purchase. You can borrow up to 75% ($4,200), so you can make the deal with only $1,400 in cash or collateral. Every 3 months you must reduce the outstanding balance by 25%. Once 80% of the purchase price has been paid, you can sell or transfer the stock to your regular margin account.

The *disadvantages* of SSA are: (1) the price of the stock may decline, so you will have to come up with more margin; (2) you cannot draw cash dividends or use the securities for collateral as long as they are in this special account.

Neither the receipt nor the exercise of the right results in taxable income to the stockholder. But you will have to pay taxes on ultimate profits when the stock is sold.

2   Extra rights through additional subscription privileges.

Some shareholders will not exercise their rights, so, after the expiration date, you can buy these rights, usually on the basis of your original allotment. You must

HOW RIGHTS ARE QUOTED

| 52 WEEKS | | | | | WEEK'S | |
HIGH	LOW	STOCK	SALES 100s	YIELD	HIGH	LOW
59	19⅜	Hefalump	132	2.3	57⅜	56¾
20¼	6⅜	Hefalump wi	19		19½	19

indicate your wish to participate in the oversubscription early, preferably when you send in your check for the new shares. Do this yourself, because small orders handled through a major brokerage firm can be lost in the back office.

There is a slight tax break. If the value of the rights received is *less* than 15% of the cost of the stock at the time of the offer, the rights are assumed to be without cost for determining the taxable gain on the sale of the rights and for setting the cost of the new stock.

If the value of the rights is *more* than 15% of the cost of the stock, you must allocate the cost of the rights proportionately: reducing the cost basis of the old stock and raising that of the new securities. *Most investors will do better to sell their rights.*

When stock rights are allowed to lapse, you can take a capital loss if their fair market value, at the date of issue, is 15% or *more* of the market value of the old stock. The loss is proportional to the allocation of rights. If the value of the rights is *less* than 15%, you can take a tax loss only by notifying the IRS in writing, usually more bother than it's worth. Profits or losses on the sale of rights are subject to regular tax rules.

FOR FURTHER INFORMATION

Richard J. Teweles and Edward S. Bradley. *The Stock Market.* New York: John Wiley & Sons, 1982.

Lawrence J. Gitman and Michael D. Joehnk. *Fundamentals of Investing.* New York: Harper & Row, 1984.

PART FIVE

OPPORTUNITIES AT HOME AND ABROAD

These chapters cover several types of investments that require somewhat different analysis or involve out-of-the-ordinary securities. Basically, the criteria are the same: quality and value for selection and timing for purchase or sale.

Historically, most bank stocks have been traded OTC, although today an increasing number are listed on the major exchanges. Nevertheless, along with stocks of public utilities and foreign companies, bank issues march to the tune of a different drummer. Utilities and bank stocks are interest-sensitive, while foreign stocks, of course, are dollar-sensitive.

In this section you will learn about:

■ Banking institutions
■ Public utilities
■ Investing abroad
■ How to take advantage of the declining dollar

27 BANKING INSTITUTIONS

Financial institutions are in the midst of the greatest upheaval in their long history. The traditional image of conservatism, safety, high dividends, slow growth, and stodgy management is changing rapidly.

Banks are: (1) expanding into allied fields, such as consumer finance, trust services, special mortgages, brokerage, and special accounts to compete with mutual funds; (2) taking advantage of loopholes in the law and regulations to buy banks or savings and loan associations, and to set up "branches" far from headquarters.

Nonbanks are building financial supermarkets: Sears not only sells appliances and childrens' clothing, but it now handles stocks and bonds as well as insurance. The Merrill Lynch bull has wandered into greener pastures, where it has found new investment opportunities in everything from securities to mortgages, loans against your home, insurance, mutual funds, and limited partnerships; and the king of credit, American Express, has broadened its credit card and insurance operations to include an investment management firm and a major financial underwriter.

Such diversification makes it difficult to properly analyze the companies whose securities you may want to acquire. One part or division may prosper while another produces substantial losses. For example, after U.S. Steel acquired Marathon Oil, earnings improved based largely on Marathon's contribution while steel operations continued to falter.

These sweeping changes will accelerate in the years ahead: more financial supermarkets, more takeovers, greater branch and interstate banking, expansion of auxiliary services, etc. These can be exciting but may not prove profitable for some time.

The major financial institutions whose stocks are listed on the NYSE—and thus possible investments—still derive the majority of their income and earnings from traditional sources and traditional customers. Comments an officer of a local savings and loan association that was taken over by an out-of-state giant, "We would not have sold out if we felt we could look forward to profitable years. My guess is that, if the new people are smart, and lucky, they will need three years to start becoming profitable."

Furthermore, most of the big banks are still burdened with foreign loans, where payments of interest have been delayed and the repayment of principal has been stretched out. Instead of the superhigh yields that were anticipated when the loans were made, banks must write off a portion of these debts. As indicated by the recent maneuvers with loans to Brazil, Mexico, and

RETURN ON EQUITY OF SELECTED BANK HOLDING COMPANIES

COMPANY	RETURN ON EQUITY	EARNINGS PER SHARE GROWTH
Barnett Banks of Florida	23.56%	16%
Citizens 1st Bancorp	19.58	40
Morgan (JP)	17.97	15
First Wachovia	17.44	17
Bank of Boston	16.60	7
First Atlanta	16.46	7
Bank of New York	15.71	9
Wells Fargo	13.90	10
Citicorp	13.76	9
NBD Bancorp	13.20	13
Mellon Bank Corp.	12.91	3
First Chicago	9.44	−3

SOURCE: Standard & Poor's.

Argentina, it's unlikely that there will be outright defaults, but profits, if any, will be small and delayed.

Basically, all financial institutions try to borrow cheap—through deposits—and lend dear. In the past few years, with superhigh interest rates, this process was reversed: institutions were locked in with low-interest mortgages and forced to pay high yields on CDs. But with help from federal agencies and special accounting, most institutions survived and, generally speaking, are back to their old methods of operation with tighter controls, better credit checks, and, in many cases, more competent management.

Investments in stocks of banks and thrift institutions can be rewarding, but more than ever before, it is important to check the quality of the corporation and the ability of management to make money from operations.

The outlook for banks is currently positive; in fact, the stocks have been outperforming the overall market for some time—ever since interest rates started trending downward. Lower rates, of course, always benefit banks. In addition, loan demand is up, loan losses are less severe, and noninterest income is rising. The informed investor might do well to consider the issues listed in the table on page 236.

28 UTILITIES RISE AGAIN

AN ELECTRIC SHOCK

The utility industry (electric power, gas distribution, and telephone companies) has historically appealed to the conservative investor because of the ever-higher dividends and slow yet steady growth in the value of the stocks. In the past, in fact, investors tended to think of utilities as being in the same safe category as bonds, and together they were the cornerstone of many conservative portfolios. But investing in utilities isn't what it used to be, as countless shareholders have found out by watching their stocks drop through the floor. Financial pressures relating primarily to costly nuclear plant construction have caused investor concern, initially resulting in major price drops for a relatively small number of utilities. Once the selling began, however, it spread from the troubled companies to almost all those engaged in a nuclear building program, regardless of whether or not an underlying problem existed. Retirees, widows, and others, who for decades counted on the steady high payouts, discovered that utility common stocks were not immune to market fluctuations.

A prime example was LILCO (Long Island Lighting Company), which when faced with staggering costs, actually eliminated its dividend, which had been an income mainstay for many years.

As the trouble spread throughout the industry, investors were forced to examine utility companies in a new, more critical light. The tide began to shift back again two years ago as interest rates declined and many utilities hit new highs. Wall Street began to realize that not every company was endangered by the nuclear issue, but only those segments with troubled construction programs. This has led today to a "three-tiered market," offering a broad range of yields as well as risks.

THE THREE-TIERED MARKET

What has always been true in other industries is now true for the utilities. They, too, are subject to the basic premise that risks

UTILITIES WITH NUCLEAR PLANTS UNDER CONSTRUCTION

As these nuclear plants go on line, the company's need for capital will decline, internally generated cash will increase, and the need for external financing will be reduced. With these lowered expenses, the potential for improved earnings and increased dividends will be greatly improved. *Note:* Many of these are ranked low in safety and are not for conservative portfolios.

COMPANY	VALUE-LINE SAFETY RATING	YIELD
Central & Southwest Corp.	1	6.0%
Central Hudson	3	7.5
Illinois Power	3	8.8
Kansas City P&L	3	6.3
Kansas G&E	4	6.0
Ohio Edison	4	8.7
Southern Indiana G&E	2	5.0
Toledo Edison pfd	4	9.9

SOURCE: Shearman Ralston, Inc., 17 Battery Place, New York, NY 10004.

UTILITIES WITH NUCLEAR PLANTS IN OPERATION

Most electric utility companies are involved in either construction or generation of nuclear power. The 1979 accident at Three Mile Island resulted in major construction revisions to all nuclear projects, pushing up costs and magnifying financial as well as political problems. But once a nuclear plant is completed, its operation is far less expensive than that of a comparable oil, gas, or coal facility. Nuclear fuel sells for only about 10% of the cost of fossil fuel.

COMPANY	PERCENT NUCLEAR	VALUE-LINE SAFETY RATING	YIELD
Baltimore G&E	59%	1	5.3%
Iowa Ill. G&E	43	2	6.3
Iowa Resources	38	1	5.9
Northern States Power	41	1	5.1
FPL Group, Inc.	20	1	5.0
Wisconsin Electric	28	1	4.2
Wisconsin P&L	23	1	5.0
Wisconsin Public Ser	20	1	4.8
Southern Calif. Ed.	1	1	6.0

SOURCE: Shearman Ralston, Inc., 17 Battery Place, New York, NY 10004.

2 The utilities with nuclear plants in operation
3 The utilities with nuclear plants under construction

The emergence of these three groups has made selection of stocks more speculative than ever.

The key today to making intelligent choices lies in understanding the relative risks of individual utilities.

The accompanying three lists can be used as a starting point for stock selection. Those in the no-nuke and plant-in-operation categories obtain Value Line's highest ranking for safety. Those in the final list vary in safety, with none being ranked high. Before purchasing any utility, read Value Line or Standard & Poor's recent analysis of the company.

GUIDELINES FOR SELECTION

In the past, utility stocks moved pretty much as a group, but today the difference between the best and the poorest has

NO NUKES

COMPANY	VALUE-LINE SAFETY RATING	YIELD
Allegheny Power	1	5.4%
Central Illinois Public Service	1	5.6
Hawaiian Electric Company	1	5.0
Idaho Power Company	1	5.9
Ipalco Enterprises	1	5.2
Kansas Power & Light	1	5.0
Louisville G&E	1	5.7
Oklahoma G&E	1	5.4
Orange & Rockland	1	5.5
Potomac Electric Power	1	4.1
South West Public Service	1	5.4
Teco Energy	1	4.8

SOURCE: Shearman Ralston, Inc., 17 Battery Place, New York, NY 10004.

and rewards go hand in hand, which means that you will generally find the highest yields in what are regarded as the riskiest companies. The best yielding utilities are not appropriate for the conservative investor, since they tend to be heavily involved with large nuclear construction programs. This once homogeneous group now falls into three risk categories:

1 The no-nukes—the safest

widened and skepticism should be your guiding principle. When making a utility selection you should ask:

- How good is management?
- Is the dividend safe?
- What is the nuclear situation?
- What is the regulatory environment?
- What is the reserve margin? [The power capacity above peak-load usage; if especially high, the company may have unused plants and high costs. (The industry-wide average hovers around 25%.)]

Moreover,

- Don't select a utility stock based only on its yield. (A high return often reflects Wall Street uncertainty about the safety of the dividend.)
- Do select stocks that have expectations for higher earnings and growth rates.
- If all other things are equal, select a utility that has a dividend reinvestment plan. You will save on commissions.
- Diversify. Buy utilities from several states, to avoid any one state's unfavorable regulatory policies.

With stocks of quality utilities, the wise investor can look for total returns of about 14%: 8 to 9% from dividends and the balance from appreciation. At some point, most shares will become fully valued and should be sold, typically after 3 or 4 years.

To achieve such returns, you must be selective and be armed with plenty of information such as:

- **Bond rating,** as determined by Standard & Poor's or Moody's. This is a measure of the company's financial strength.
- **Regulatory climate.** The attitude of state authorities toward permitting the utility to earn an adequate rate of return is an important factor.
- **Return on equity.** This is that basic standard of quality—the ability of management to make money with your money. It is often a reflection of the state authorities, who may or may not permit an adequate rate of return.
- **AFDC (allowance for funds during construction).** Under this form of accounting, new construction and

---

THE BELL COMPANIES

Now that the great breakup is history, there are eight different Bell companies. Shares of all are traded on the NYSE. As in the past, their greatest attraction is relatively high yields: from 5.6% down to 4.6%. In most cases, the shareholders are the same people who were willing to plod along with safety.

There is growth potential: with Ma Bell, its superb research, ample finances, and willingness to invade foreign markets via joint ventures; with the regional companies, strong franchises and, in some cases, management that is eager to move into allied and more profitable areas.

COMPANY	RECENT PRICE	P/E RATIO	YIELD
AT&T	$ 23	16	5.1%
Ameritech	48	13	4.8
Bell Atlantic	74	13	4.8
Bell South	66	13	4.6
NYNEX	71	12	4.9
Pacific T	61	13	5.0
Southwest B	114	12	5.6
U.S. West	61	12	5.0

SOURCE: Barron's, August 22, 1986.

---

equipment expenses are shifted off the income statement (where they reduce earnings) onto the balance sheet (where they become part of the base used to ask for higher rates). This is legal, logical, and generally acceptable by regulatory authorities, but it's a yellow light for investors, because these are not *true* earnings.

AFDC is a noncash, bookkeeping transaction that lowers the quality of corporate profits. This data is available from Moody's Investor Services or your broker.

- **Main fuel.** This is a key criterion for

many analysts. Utilities that use water (hydroelectric) have no cost worries; those that use coal seldom have major problems with the supply or price of their fuel; those that rely on gas or oil are subject to conditions beyond their control; and those with nuclear plants are regarded as questionable to dangerous. This pessimism stems from the huge overrun costs and final abandonment of projects involving Public Service of New Hampshire and Long Island Lighting.

Note: With utilities, state laws often prescribe actions that in other industries would be management's prerogative.

MUTUAL FUNDS

If you're uncertain about which utility stocks to invest in, you might consider one of the mutual funds specializing in utilities. You will benefit from both diversity and professional management. Call each of the following for a copy of the prospectus and information on their returns for 1 and 5 years.

Fidelity Select Portfolios: Utilities
1-800-225-6190
1-617-523-1919 (in Massachusetts)

Energy & Utility Shares
1-215-542-8025

GOING GLOBAL:
Foreign Investments

Today, almost half the world's publicly traded stocks are registered *outside* the United States, which means that unless you take some of these issues under consideration, you are working with less than half your total investment opportunity. In fact, with the expansion of world trade, foreign business and investments are becoming increasingly important and will be more so in the years ahead. At various times and in certain economic cycles, astute investors are able to make substantial profits by "going global" because of the international ripple effect: each country's economic cycle is a separate one, so when one nation is in the midst of a poor stock market, others inevitably are thriving. Wise investors realize the advisability of not locking themselves into a narrow geographical investment situation.

The pull toward foreign investments is also being fueled by the growing number of international mergers and joint ventures, by the reduction in geographical distances, and by the closing in of what has come to be known as the *information gap.* This gap is the elapsed time between a political, financial, or business event and the public's recognition of the event.

An investment in a foreign stock offers at least two ways to make a profit or loss:

1   The price of the stock can go up (or down) in its local currency.
2   The value of the foreign country's currency may rise (or drop) relative to the U.S. dollar, thereby increasing or decreasing the value of your stock.

The best situation obviously exists when the price of the stock rises *and* the value of the country's currency likewise rises against the dollar. An important fact to keep in mind is that a rising currency can sometimes save you

from the pitfalls associated with a poor or only mediocre foreign stock.

Despite these compelling reasons for international investing, many otherwise clever investors still remain unschooled in the mechanics of successful investing in foreign stocks. The necessary guidelines, given below, can be mastered by those with the time and inclination to do so. But let's first examine the key pros and cons of international investing.

With all companies that have substantial foreign interests, there are extra risks resulting from gains or losses through foreign exchange. Since the company's earnings are in local currencies, they can lose a portion of their value when transferred back into dollars. The stronger the dollar, the lower the net earnings reported by the parent company. The impact can reduce profits by as much as 10%. Some international or foreign companies try to hedge against these currency swings by geographical and/or product diversification, but this can be expensive and not always effective. (See section on multinationals that follows.)

Currency fluctuations also affect the value of a company's nonmonetary assets (plant, equipment, inventories). When the dollar's value rises, that of the foreign currency declines. But the assets are shown at the exchange rates that were in effect when these items were purchased. That's why constant monitoring of the dollar's value is so important when going global. A good stockbroker or the international division of a large bank can keep you abreast of currency fluctuations and how they may impact on your investments. (See sources of information at the end of this chapter.)

Although there are several methods for investing in foreign stocks, the three most popular

FOREIGN INVESTMENTS

PROS

↑ Provides diversification

↑ Provides additional investment opportunities not available in U.S. markets

↑ Provides hedge against U.S. monetary or economic troubles such as inflation, dollar depreciation, slump in stock market

↑ As vitality shifts from one country to another, foreign firms may represent attractive alternatives

CONS

↓ Knowledge about currency fluctuations is required

↓ Foreign stocks are affected by local political situations

↓ There is less information available on foreign companies than there is on U.S. firms

↓ Foreign firms are not required to provide the same detailed type of information as are U.S. firms

↓ Accounting procedures are different from those of the United States, which can make accurate evaluation complex

↓ Foreign brokers and foreign exchanges are seldom bound by regulations as strict as those imposed by the SEC. Every country, in fact, has its own set of regulations

↓ Quotes are sometimes difficult to locate

↓ There is a risk of currency fluctuations

are: American Depository Receipts (ADRs), mutual funds, and multinational companies.

AMERICAN DEPOSITORY RECEIPTS (ADRs)

ADRs are negotiable receipts representing ownership of shares of a foreign corporation which is traded in an American securities market. They are issued by an American bank, but the actual shares are held by the American bank's foreign depository bank or agent. This custodian bank is usually but not always an office of the American bank (if there is one in the country involved). If not, the bank selected to be custodian is generally the foreign bank closest to the foreign company for whom the ADRs are being issued.

ADRs allow you to buy, sell, or hold the foreign stocks without actually, physically taking possession of them. They are registered by the SEC and are sold by stockbrokers. Each ADR is a contract between the holder and the bank, certifying that a stated number of shares of the overseas-based company has been deposited with the American bank's foreign office or custodian and will be kept there as long as the ADR remains outstanding. The U.S. purchaser pays for the stock in dollars and receives dividends in dollars.

When the foreign corporation has a large capitalization so that its shares sell for the equivalent of a few dollars, each ADR may represent more than 1 share: 10, 50, or even 100 shares in the case of some Japanese companies, where there are tens of millions of shares of common stock. Very often the most popular ADR group is the South African gold mining stocks, because that country is the major gold mining nation in the free world.

ADRs are generally initiated when an American bank learns that there is a great deal of interest in the shares of a foreign firm. Or a foreign corporation may occasionally initiate action if it wants to enter the American market. In either case, the bank then purchases a large

HOW ADRs ARE PURCHASED

1 Investors give a buy order to their broker.

2 Brokers place a buy order abroad.

3 Foreign brokers buy the stock.

4 The stock is deposited with the custodian banks in the foreign country.

5 Custodians instruct the American depository bank (Citicorp, Chemical, Irving Trust, Morgan Guaranty, for example) to issue an ADR.

6 The ADR is issued to the American investors.

block of shares and issues the ADRs, leaving the stock certificates overseas in its custodian bank.

Brokerage houses can also initiate ADRs through a foreign branch or a correspondent broker. The foreign liaison buys the shares and turns them over to the foreign branch of an American bank. That bank, in turn, has its American office (usually in New York) issue ADRs for the U.S. brokerage firm.

The most important test for whether or not a foreign company is selected for an ADR is whether a market exists in the United States for the shares. In other words, the ADR process is not designed to make a market for the shares of a foreign company so much as it is to follow the market.

$ IF YOU DARE: For risk-oriented investors, ADRs offer excellent opportunities for *arbitrage* (the simultaneous purchase and sale of identical or equivalent investments

SELECTED ADRs

COUNTRY	COMPANY	INDUSTRY	EXCHANGE AND SYMBOL
Australia	The Broken Hill Proprietary Co., Ltd.	Mining and oil	OTC:BRKNY
Denmark	Novo Industries A/S	Industrial enzymes; drugs	NYSE:NVO
Great Britain	Courtaulds plc	Rayon yarn	ASE:COU
	Glaxo Holdings plc	Drugs, foods	OTC:GLXOY
	Imperial Chemical Industries	Chemicals	NYSE:ICI
	Imperial Group plc	Tobacco	ASE:IMT
	The Plessey Company plc	Telecommunications	NYSE:PLY
	The Rank Organization plc	Electronic equipment	OTC:RANKY
Ireland	Elan Corp. plc	Drug research and technology	OTC:ELANY
Israel	Teva Pharmaceutical Industries, Ltd.	Veterinary products	OTC:TEVIY
Japan	Canon Inc.	Cameras	OTC:CANNY
	Fuji Photo Film Co., Ltd.	Photo products	OTC:FUJIY
	Hitachi, Ltd.	Electrical manufacturing	NYSE:HIT
	Honda Motor Co., Ltd.	Motorcycles and autos	NYSE:HMC
	Kubota, Ltd.	Agricultural machinery	NYSE:KUB
	Matsushita Electric Industrial Co.	Electronics equipment	NYSE:MC
	Pioneer Electronic Corp.	Audio equipment	NYSE:PIO
	Sony Corporation	Electronic products	NYSE:SNE
	TDK Corporation	Video and audio tapes	NYSE:TDK
	Tokio Marine-Fire	Insurance	OTC:TKIOY
Mexico	Tubos de Acero de Mexico, S.A.	Steel	ASE:TAM
Netherlands	N.V. Philips Gloeilampenfabrieke	Electronics	OTC:PGLOY
South Africa	Anglo-American	Gold, diamonds	OTC:ANGLY
	Blyvooruitzicht Gold Mining	Gold, uranium	OTC:BLYVY
	DeBeers Consolidated	Diamond mining	OTC:DBRSY
	Free State Geduld	Gold producer	OTC:FREEY
	President Steyn Gold	Gold mining	OTC:PSTYY
	President Brand Gold	Gold mining	OTC:PRESY
	St. Helena Gold Mines	Gold mining	OTC:SGOLY
	Western Deep Levels	Gold mining	OTC:WDEPY
Sweden	Gambro, Inc.	Medical devices and systems	OTC:GAMBY
	Ericsson (L.M.) Telephone Co.	Telecommunications	OTC:ERICY
	Pharmacia A.B.	Medical science products	OTC:PHABY

PROS AND CONS OF ADRs

PROS

↑ ADRs eliminate a lot of headaches that generally accompany direct investment in foreign stocks that are not sold as ADRs. An ADR enables you to make your purchase simply and quickly. If you do not buy an ADR, then you must place an order with your local broker, who then forwards it to a New York broker or correspondent, who sends it overseas for execution. You can have the certificate left in the country of issue or it can be sent to you, which may take 2 to 3 months. Since you generally cannot sell your stock until you have possession of the certificate, you could lose money should you wish to sell that particular stock before the certificate arrives. Even when the certificates are held abroad, transfers can take as long as 6 to 8 weeks. All this is eliminated when trading ADRs, because you are dealing with foreign companies in American markets.

↑ ADRs reduce language and accounting problems. Foreign companies registering with the SEC are required to publish their annual reports in English and also use standard accounting systems.

↑ ADRs are registered as regular stocks, with the owner's name printed on the ADR. Most foreign securities are issued in bearer form. If they are lost or stolen, they can be sold by anyone who presents them to a broker.

↑ ADRs are almost always more liquid than the underlying stock.

↑ Your dividends are paid in dollars. If you buy foreign shares directly, you will receive dividend payments in yen, francs, pounds, etc.; and if you are living outside a major metropolitan area, you may be forced to wait several weeks to receive your money.

↑ Immediate price quotes are available for ADRs.

↑ ADRs eliminate routine problems. In some countries there is a stamp tax, and when investors sell their securities abroad, they must send in the shares and wait for their money.

↑ The bank handles all the mechanical details of dividends, receiving and reporting stockholder voting, etc.

↑ Although foreign investments have additional political and economic risks not part of U.S. stocks, most of the corporations which have ADRs are large international organizations not likely to be severely affected by shifts in their own country. For the average investor who does not have access to extensive research facilities, ADRs are a handy way to buy a position in the expanding world economy.

CONS

↓ Quotations can be misleading. Sometimes if the price of the underlying foreign stock is particularly low, its ADR may be issued in equivalents. For example, a Fuji Photo ADR selling at $13 represents 2 Japanese shares. A Cannon ADR selling at $31 represents 5 shares. The underlying stock in both cases is selling at approximately $6 per share on the Tokyo Exchange.

↓ ADRs do not protect you against currency fluctuations. For example, if you buy an ADR worth 1,000 yen and a year later the yen has dropped against the dollar, even if your investment is still worth 1,000 yen, you will have a dollar loss if you sell.

↓ ADR owners may not exercise rights issued by foreign corporations unless the new stock is registered with the SEC (a rare situation). Such rights are automatically sold by the depository bank.

in order to profit from the price difference). You can take advantage of the price differences between the stocks traded locally and the ADRs selling in New York.

With gold shares, for example, there can be three different quotations: London, Johannesburg, and New York. A sharp trader, noting the wide spread, can buy shares in London and sell short ADRs in the United States. Generally, it's better to start with New York, because in London,

new shares are often sold at a discount through rights issued to old shareholders.

$ IF YOU DON'T: Stick with mutual funds

THE LEADING INTERNATIONAL MUTUAL FUNDS

Canadian Fund
1 Wall Street
New York, NY 10005
1-800-221-5757 (outside NY)
1-212-513-4200 (in NY)

Dean Witter World Wide Investment Trust
One World Trade Center
New York, NY 10048
1-212-938-4554

Fidelity Overseas Fund
82 Devonshire
Boston, MA 02109
1-800-544-6666

Financial Group Portfolios, Inc.
Pacific Basin Portfolio
P.O. Box 2040
Denver, CO 80201
1-800-525-9831

First Investors Corp.
120 Wall Street
New York, NY 10005
1-212-208-6000

G.T. Pacific Fund, Inc.
601 Montgomery Street
San Francisco, CA 94111
1-800-824-1580 (outside CA)
1-800-821-8361 (in CA)

Kemper International Fund, Inc.
120 South LaSalle Street
Chicago, IL 60603
1-800-621-1048

Keystone International Fund
99 High Street
Boston, MA 02104
1-800-225-1587

Merrill Lynch International Holdings, Inc.
633 Third Avenue
New York, NY 10017
1-212-692-2939

New Perspective Fund, Inc.
333 South Hope Street
Los Angeles, CA 90071
1-213-486-9200

Paine Webber ATLAS Fund, Inc.
140 Broadway
New York, NY 10005
1-800-544-9300

T. Rowe Price International Fund, Inc.
100 East Pratt Street
Baltimore, MD 21202
1-800-638-5660

Prudential Bache Global Fund, Inc.
2 Heritage Drive
North Quincy, MA 02171
1-800-225-1852

Putnam International Fund
265 Franklin Street
Boston, MA 02110
1-800-225-1581

Scudder International
175 Federal Street
Boston, MA 02110
1-800-225-2470

Shearson Global Mutual Fund
Shearson Lehman/American Express
14 Wall Street
New York, NY 10005
1-212-577-5822

Templeton Funds, Inc.
(Templeton World, Global I, & Global II Funds)
405 Central Avenue
St. Petersburg, FL 33731
1-800-237-0738

Transatlantic Fund, Inc.
100 Wall Street
New York, NY 10005
1-212-747-0440

specializing in foreign stocks and let someone else do the decision making and trading for you.

MUTUAL FUNDS

Perhaps the easiest way to go global, especially if you do not have the time or inclination to do your own research, is to purchase shares in one of the mutual funds specializing in foreign investments. In this way, you can participate in a diversified portfolio and, as with domestic mutual funds (see Chapter 14), you reap the advantages of professional management—in this case with foreign expertise. Although many of these funds are American owned and operated, they have foreign consultants providing up-to-date material on specific stocks as well as on the country's political situation and outlook.

Some funds consist entirely of foreign stocks; others mix foreign and American stocks. Most are members of a larger family of funds and thus offer the advantage of free switching from one fund to another.

$HINT: Before signing on with any of these mutual funds, write or call for a copy of the prospectus. Investment philosophies of the funds vary widely from conservative to very aggressive. Scudder International, for example, selects the country first, the industry second, and finally the individual stock. On the other hand, First Investors looks for undervalued stocks anywhere in the world, including politically troubled geographical areas.

FOREIGN MUTUAL FUNDS OR UNIT TRUSTS

A viable but less well-known way to invest globally is through foreign mutual funds, which are also known as "unit trusts." Outside the United States, unit trust refers to a mutual fund in which your American dollars buy shares of a large international portfolio of stocks.

Unit trusts range widely in their investment portfolios and objectives. Some invest only in given geographical regions, say, North America or the Far East, or in one particular country. Some funds, on the other hand, are devoted to specific industries in many different countries.

Few investors are aware of foreign unit trusts because they do not advertise or promote themselves in the United States. They are not allowed to ask you to become an investor *unless* they are registered with the SEC, and many elect not to become involved in that much red tape. Consequently, they do not seek out American investors. Keep in mind that unregistered foreign unit trusts do not have to abide by the SEC regulations, although they must, of course, follow the rules of their own country.

$IF YOU DARE: It is possible to set up a foreign bank account and use the banker broker as the middleperson. This enables a foreign fund to avoid selling directly to an American.

$IF YOU DON'T: Stick with American-based mutual funds.

SELECTED FOREIGN MUTUAL FUNDS OR UNIT TRUSTS

Great Britain	Barclays Unicorn Group Ltd.
	Unicorn House
	252 Romford Road
	London E7 9JB
	Britannia Group of Unit Trusts Ltd.
	Salisbury House
	29 Finsbury Circus
	London EC2M 5QL
	Lloyds Bank Unit Trust Managers, Ltd.
	71 Lombard Street
	London EC2 2XL
Canada	The Investors Group
	280 Broadway Avenue
	Winnipeg, Manitoba R3C 3B6
Netherlands	The Robeco Group
	Postbus 973
	3000AZ Rotterdam
	Holland

MULTINATIONAL CORPORATIONS

In 1980, the U.S. dollar started a climb that lifted it to historic highs against the pound, the lira, and the franc. Then, starting in late 1985, it began to slowly decline in value.

Multinational corporations, those companies with substantial portions of their earnings and profits derived from foreign business, stand to reap the greatest benefit from the decline and offer sound long-term investment choices. Multinationals also provide you with another way to diversify your investment portfolio and to invest globally at the same time.

The key factor to keep in mind when investing in multinationals is: when foreign currencies rise relative to the dollar, earnings from an American company's foreign subsidiary or division are instantly worth more.

WHO ARE THE MULTI-NATIONALS?

A number of companies depend heavily on international sales for at least one-third of their earnings. They tend to manufacture either popular products or necessities. These companies for the most part fall into five basic categories: cosmetics and household products, drugs, food, industrials, and chemicals.

$HINT: A strong dollar tends to hurt the multinational stocks: it makes U.S. products expensive for foreign buyers and foreign products cheap for American consumers. A strong dollar also creates an "exchange loss"; that is, if the money an American company earns abroad loses value against the dollar, the earnings for the company and its stockholders are reduced. The more a U.S. multinational depends on exports for sales, the more it will benefit from a weaker dollar. Thus, multinationals are a good hedge against a declining dollar.

INVESTING DIRECTLY

It is, of course, possible to trade directly by having your broker buy individual shares of foreign stocks listed on the major exchanges: in Britain, France, Germany, Italy, Japan, or Hong Kong (see table on page 249). This approach, however, makes sense only for those placing substantial dollar investments in well-known, widely traded stocks whose prices can be followed in the financial pages and is not suggested for the general investor.

MULTINATIONALS

INDUSTRY	PERCENT OF FOREIGN BUSINESS
Chemical	
Dow Chemical	54
Du Pont	32
Cosmetics or Household Products	
Colgate Palmolive	50
Gillette	50
International Flavors & Fragrances	62
Procter & Gamble	30
Revlon	30
Drugs	
Abbott Laboratories	23
American Home Products	28
Bristol-Myers	32
Johnson & Johnson	40
Merck	43
Pfizer	52
Foods	
Coca-Cola	40
CPC International	58
General Foods	25
H.J. Heinz	35
International Multifoods	33
McDonald's	22
Ralston-Purina	19
Industrials	
Caterpillar Tractor	46
Control Data	24
Hoover	59
IBM	42
Ingersoll-Rand	44
ITT Corp	47
Levi Strauss	24
MMM	35

U.S. BROKERAGE FIRMS WITH FOREIGN EXPERTISE

COMPANY	LOCATION
Bear Stearns & Co.	New York
Arnhold & S. Bleichroeder, Inc.	New York
Cazenove Inc.	New York; San Francisco
Drexel Burnham Lambert, Inc.	New York
A.C. Goode Co., Inc.	New York
Grieveson, Grant International, Ltd.	Boston
Merrill Lynch Pierce Fenner & Smith	New York
Nomura Securities International, Inc.	New York
Oppenheimer & Co., Inc.	New York
Prudential Bache Securities	New York
Rowe & Pitman, Inc.	Boston; San Francisco
Salomon Bros.	New York
Shearson Lehman, Inc.	New York
Smith Barney Harris Upham & Co.	New York
J.B. Were & Co.	New York
Wood Gundy & Co., Inc.	New York

SPECIAL FOREIGN SECURITIES

There are also foreign debt securities that provide high yields, short maturities, and generally low risk. They include:

➤ YANKEE BONDS These are debt issues of foreign governments and corporations funded in U.S. dollars and registered with the SEC. Their yields have been as much as 1% higher than equivalent domestic debt; their maturities are relatively short (6 to 15 years); and many have mandatory requirements for redeeming the whole issue in equal annual amounts, usually after a grace period of 5 years. Thus, a 15-year issue would be retired in 10 equal payments between the sixth and the fifteenth year.

➤ COMMON MARKET DEBT These are bonds of government or industry groups such as the European Investment Bank and the European Community. The combine borrows in dollars and then lends the proceeds to individual companies for expansion and modernization. They are safe and carry yields 1% more than those of comparable U.S. issues but have limited marketability. They are best for major investors.

➤ CONVERTIBLE DEBT To raise capital, some foreign companies offer special convertible bonds. Inco, Ltd., the huge nickel company, shares foreign exchange risks with investors by means of a 25-year bond with a $15\frac{3}{4}\%$ coupon. The plus is that the payment at maturity can be either in dollars or in sterling at the set rate of $1.98 per pound.

CANADIAN SECURITIES

Canadian securities are so similar to those of U.S. companies that the same criteria for buying and selling apply. The stocks of most major Canadian corporations are listed on American exchanges, but there are many other securities that can be considered for diversification. Most of these are of relatively small local companies that serve the limited north-of-the-border market. A few, primarily involved with natural resources, are large and active in international trade.

For Americans, Canadian securities are not overly attractive because: (1) in a push for greater control by domestic investors, the government has discouraged outside capital by restrictions and by withholding taxes on dividends and interest; (2) of the declining value of the Canadian dollar; (3) with few exceptions, publicly owned Canadian corporations do not meet quality standards: their capital is limited and their profits are erratic and relatively meager; and their managements are influenced by a small group of dominant financial institutions and individuals.

Most Canadian stocks are generally better speculations than they are investments, but if you do add these securities to your portfolio, heed these checkpoints:

DO invest and not gamble. Look for companies that will benefit from the long-term growth of the country. Forget about "penny" oil, gas, or mining stocks. There is almost no way that you can be sure of the integrity of the promoter or the authenticity of the seller's claims.

DO deal with a broker with good research facilities. Information on many Canadian issues is limited in the United States. Look for a major American brokerage firm with offices north of the border.

DO subscribe to a factual investment advisory service such as Canadian Business Service, 133 Richmond Street, West Toronto, M5H 3M8 Canada.

DON'T deal in shares of Canadian companies listed only on Canadian stock exchanges until you are familiar with the corporation. There are plenty of Canadian firms listed on American exchanges.

DON'T buy any security over the telephone. Despite attempts of authorities to control bucket shop operations, they still exist and continue to lure naïve speculators.

DO make all investments in U.S. currency (unless you own property or travel frequently in Canada). The Canadian dollar is often worth less than the U.S. dollar.

DON'T make any commitments on the basis of rumors or tips. By the time you get the word, every sharpie will be in the act and ready to sell out for a quick profit.

MORE ABOUT DIVERSIFICATION

As with any investment, diversification greatly reduces the level of risk involved. With foreign stocks, it is especially important to avoid reliance on the performance of any one stock, one industry, or even one country. Risk reduction is best achieved by spreading out your investment dollars in at least one of the following ways:

- *By country*. When certain foreign stock markets fall, it is inevitable that others will rise. Keep in mind that the U.S. market tends to be an anticipatory one, reflecting what the American investor thinks will happen in the forthcoming months. In addition, diversification by country offers a hedge against a poor economic climate in any one area.
- *By type of industry*. Buying shares in more than one industry, i.e., high tech, computers, oil, automobiles, etc., likewise provides protection.

- *By company within the industry*. For example, an energy portfolio could include stocks from a number of companies located in Great Britain's North Sea, Southeast Asia, Canada, the Middle East, and the United States.
- Buy stocks with P/E ratios which are lower than those of comparable U.S. companies. There should always be a compelling reason to purchase a foreign security, such as a low P/E or a unique industry position, as is the case currently with Sony and Honda Motors.
- Use a currency weighting system to balance your portfolio. The *U.S. dollar* block, which consists of U.S., Canadian, and occasionally Mexican stocks, should be about 45%. The *Pacific Rim* block, which includes Japanese stocks plus those of Hong Kong, Singapore, and Australia, should be 35%. The *European Common Market* (EEC) is made up of member countries such as West Germany, Switzerland, Sweden, etc. It should represent 20% of your portfolio. If the dollar declines, then reduce the U.S. bloc to 35% and increase all others.
- Diversify among the regions of the world. Never become too dependent on any one area.

FOR FURTHER INFORMATION

MULTI-NATIONAL COMPANIES & FOREIGN STOCKS

➤ BOOKS You can add to your list of multinationals by studying one of the standard reference books such as Moody's *Investor Handbook* and Standard & Poor's *Stock Market Guide* or *Value Line*. All three give the percentage of a company's earnings and sales derived from foreign operations. You should also read various company annual reports to learn what areas their sales come from. Earnings from Western Europe and Japan are currently more stable than those from Latin America.

FOREIGN STOCK EXCHANGES

Amsterdam Stock Exchange
Vereniging voor de Effechtenhandel
Postbus 19163
1000 GD Amsterdam
The Netherlands

Frankfurt Stock Exchange
Frankfurter Wertpapierbörse
6 Frankfurt a. M.
Postfach 2913
Germany

Johannesburg Stock Exchange
P.O. Box 1174
Johannesburg 2000
South Africa

London Stock Exchange
The Exchange
London EC2N 1HP
England

Bourse de Luxembourg
Boite postale 165
2011 Luxembourg

Milan Stock Exchange
Comitato Direttivo
degli Agenti di Cambio
Borsa Valori di Milano
Piazza degli Afferi, 6
20123 Milan
Italy

Paris Stock Exchange
Bourse de Paris
4, place de la Bourse
75080 Paris Cedex 02
France

Singapore Stock Exchange
16 Raffles Quay, #16-03
Hong Leong Building
Singapore 0104

Sydney Stock Exchange
20 Bond Street
Sydney
Australia

Tel Aviv Stock Exchange
54, Ahad Haam Street
Tel-Aviv 65543
Israel

Tokyo Stock Exchange
6, Nihombashi-Kabuto-cho
I-chome, Chuo-kes
Tokyo
Japan

Toronto Stock Exchange
2 First Canadian Place
Toronto, Ontario
Canada M5X 1J2

Vienna Stock Exchange
Wiener Börsekammer
Wipplingerstrasse 84
1011 Wien 1
Austria

Zurich Stock Exchange
Bleicherwege 5
CH-8021 Zurich
Switzerland

Moody's International Manual & News Reports
Moody's Investors Service
99 Church Street
New York, NY 10007
2 volumes annual; $1,095.00
Contains financial information on over 5,000 companies and institutions in 100 countries.

▶ PERIODICALS The following periodicals provide coverage of foreign markets as well as individual stocks:

The Wall Street Journal

Barron's National Business & Financial Weekly

The Economist

Investor's Chronicle (London)

Far East Economic Review

Japan Economic Journal

The Financial Times (London)
Bracken House
10 Cannon Street
London EC4P 4BY
$420 per year; daily Monday through Saturday

The Asian Wall Street Journal
Dow Jones & Company
22 Cortlandt Street
New York, NY 10007
$144 per year

Euromoney
Nester House, Playhouse Yard
London EC4V 5EX
U.S. Subscriptions: Business Press
                    International
                    205 East 42nd Street
                    New York, NY 10017
$108 per year; monthly

➤ NEWSLETTERS The following newsletters regularly cover foreign stocks. Also see Chapter 42 on evaluating newsletters.

Capital International Perspective
Capital International, S.A.
3, Place des Bergues
CH 1201 Geneva, Switzerland
SF 1,850; monthly and quarterly editions

Dessauer's Journal of Financial Markets
P.O. Box 718
Orleans, MA 02653
$150 per year; 24 issues

The International Advisor
The Global Investment Guide
P.O. Box 2289
Winter Park, FL 32790
$67.00 per year; monthly

The International Harry Schultz Letter
c/o FERC
P.O. Box 141
Clarens-Montreux
1815 Switzerland

Worldwide Investment Notes: The International Investment Advisory Letter
Worldwide Investment Research, Ltd.
7730 Carondelet Avenue
St. Louis, MO 63105
$195 per year; 24 issues

Tony Henrey's Gold Letter
P.O. Box 5577
Durban 4000
South Africa

International Bank Credit Analyst
BCA Publications Ltd.
3463 Peel Street
Montreal, Quebec, Canada H3A 1W7
$475.00 per year; monthly

The International Advisor
WMP Publishing Company
P.O. Box 2289
Winter Park, FL 32790
$125 per year; monthly

FOREIGN-BASED MUTUAL FUNDS OR UNIT TRUSTS

➤ BOOKS AND NEWSLETTERS

International Investment & Business
  Exchange
139A Sloane Street
London SW1, England

This service organization publishes a newsletter and *The World Wide Directory of Mutual Funds* ($39.95). Membership costs $99 a year plus a one-time entry fee, also $99. Their United States contact is:

INEX Educational Services
Crayton Cove
1185 Eighth Street South
P.O. Box 1427
Naples, FL 33940

Unit Trust Yearbook
Financial Times Business Publishing Ltd.
102 Clerkenwell Road
London EC1M 5SA
$35

➤ ANNUAL REPORTS For copies of annual reports of foreign companies, contact:

Worldwide Investment Research, Ltd.,
7730 Carondelet Avenue
St. Louis, MO 63105

For a fee, they will send you copies of the 15,000 annual reports on file.

30 BETTING ON A DECLINING DOLLAR

Over the past 4 years, and indeed until the early months of 1985, the value of the U.S. dollar in relation to the major foreign currencies rose approximately 50%, registering historic highs against the pound, lira, franc, and mark and prompting many to call it the "superdollar."

This strong dollar was sustained by several key factors, in particular a sharp decline in the rate of inflation, high interest rates (especially in relation to many other countries), and a continually improving American economy. The high interest rates in combination with the overall political stability of the United States were responsible for attracting a flood of overseas money into the United States as foreigners purchased dollar-denominated securities and U.S. property. Demand by foreigners for dollar-denominated assets remains strong. This influx of capital has helped finance the trade deficit as well as a major part of our federal deficit. It has been accelerated by the repeal of U.S. withholding tax on interest paid to foreigners.

Starting back in the spring of 1985, the dollar began to trend downward, albeit slowly and irregularly. And, of course, when that movement begins, speculative fever on Wall Street starts immediately to rise. The extent to which the dollar will decline is naturally difficult to predict. And although the dollar has fallen in value by 30%, many leading economists still regard it as overvalued—and feel it will drop an additional 6% to 10% over the next year. It seems inevitable that, as foreign portfolios are overweighted with dollar assets and as foreign economies grow at a faster pace than ours, the dollar will indeed continue to depreciate somewhat. Foreign demand for dollars could also beat a retreat if U.S. interest rates remain at their present levels and if the trade deficit continues to grow.

As the dollar declines, it is likely to have a positive effect on a number of investments, because:

- Domestic manufacturing companies that

LEADING UNITED STATES EXPORTERS

	EXPORT SALES (% OF TOTAL SALES)		FOREIGN OPERATING INCOME (% OF TOTAL)		5-YEAR GROWTH RATE
	1984	1985	1984	1985	
Boeing Co.	35%	43%	N.A.	N.A.	8%
Crown Cork & Seal	40	37	45%	39%	13
Exxon	72	71	57	59	5
Heinz (H.J.)	35	34	36	31	12
Polaroid Corp.	41	40	61	58	15
Squibb Corp.	40	41	46	44	26
Wrigley (Wm.)	32	31	35	30	13

SOURCE: Standard & Poor's *The Outlook*, June 4, 1986.

weathered stiff foreign competition will be able to boost their domestic sales

- Earnings of multinationals, when translated into dollars, will be enhanced
- Leading U.S. exporters will once again be competitive (see table on page 253)

A more stable dollar will not only help companies with substantial foreign business (see Multinational Corporations, pages 248ff.), but will also slow down the severe inroads foreign producers and manufacturers have made in this country. For example, computers and office equipment imports rose by 50% in 1984 over prior years.

However, investment decisions should not be made solely on the basis of the dollar's movement. Stock selection should always include the fundamentals emphasized throughout this book. In order to help you take advantage of the opportunities a lower dollar may provide, the top recommendations of several leading investment services are listed below.

Avery International	H. J. Heinz
Boeing	IBM
Burroughs	Kellogg Co.
Coca-Cola	MMM
Colgate Palmolive	Merck
Data General	Schlumberger Ltd.
Digital Equipment	Sealed Air
Gillette	Squibb

SOURCE: Shearman Ralston Inc., 17 Battery Place, New York, NY 10004

DOLLAR DROP SIDE EFFECTS

- Modest rise in inflation
- Healthier U.S. stock market
- Long-term rise in interest rates
- Possible rise in gold stocks
- Rise in prices of foreign stocks

PART SIX

TECHNIQUES FOR SMART INVESTING

Techniques, like research, are tools that are useful in making investments and essential when speculating. Concerned primarily with timing, techniques are most effective in enhancing gains and reducing losses. They are *never* substitutes for quality or value in the selection or sale of securities.

Some techniques rely on historical patterns of the stock market; i.e., what has happened before is likely to be repeated again under similar circumstances, and a trend in motion will continue until exhausted or reversed. Others require careful analysis, frequent monitoring, and more time and hard work than most people are willing to devote to the management of their money. And still others eliminate judgment and rely on programs based on rote.

Whether and how you use techniques depends on you. At best, the right techniques properly used can boost your profits; at worst, they can add to the excitement and fun of trying to make more money with your savings.

This section explains such techniques as:

- Forecasting
- Timing your trades
- Stop orders and selling short
- Formula plans
- Dividend reinvestment
- How to make money in takeovers

31 FORECASTING

J. P. Morgan said it, and it's 100% correct: "The only sure thing about the stock market is that it will fluctuate." Over the short term, the actions are almost unpredictable (if you guess right, it's usually due more to luck than to skill).

The daily, even weekly, swings in market prices are caused by transient, often meaningless, fears and, in special situations such as takeovers, greed. They reflect temporary developments or current events: international tensions, death of a prominent government leader, rise or fall of the values of major currencies, quarterly earnings of major corporations and, most important these days, the trend of interest rates. They are most significant to speculators but obviously have an impact on investors. As long as you are convinced of the long-term growth and profitability of the company, hold those stocks regardless of sudden down movements. Be patient, and try to take advantage of unwarranted pessimism to buy and of overoptimism to sell.

Long-term trends, however, usually follow established patterns. Some of these may not be clear until they are well under way, but there are areas where actions can be forecast with reasonable accuracy and utilized to add profits and reduce losses.

Patterns should never be taken as gospel. There have been major changes in the American economy, so that forces that were powerful in the past may not be so important today. Still, in the stock market, past is prologue—most of the time.

Traditionally, December has been an *up* month, but not in 1978 and 1981. Over the years, September has been a *down* month, but in 1982, the market was roaring up. You have to play the averages. Before you make any major commitment, check the seasonal pattern of the market, as shown by a major stock average, and of the industry group of the company whose shares you plan to buy or sell.

If there's no rush, wait for a month which has historically moved up if you plan to sell, down if you plan to buy. It is generally wise to unload before May or June, when prices are likely to fall.

The table shows that from 1897 through 1983 (with the exception of 1914 when the NYSE was closed), the DJIA rose in 581 months and fell in 447: 57% up, 43% down. But monthly figures can be deceptive, because one day can make a big difference in the month's performance.

The same forces obviously do not apply at all times, but the shifts appear to be the result

MONTHLY ADVANCES AND DECLINES IN THE DJIA SINCE 1897

	NUMBER OF TIMES	
MONTH	UP	DOWN
January	53	33
February	40	46
March	50	36
April	47	39
May	42	44
June	42	44
July	53	33
August*	58	27
September*	39	46
October*	45	40
November*	50	35
December	62	24

* Market closed in 1914.

of: (1) in January, a heavy flow of year-end dividends and bonuses into the market; (2) the drain of income tax payments reflected in the frequent lows in May; (3) summertime optimism often sparked by anticipation of a pickup of business in the fall; (4) frequent tax selling and switching in November and December; (5) relatively strong markets at the end of quarters (March, June, etc.), when institutional investors buy stocks that have had a big move in the last 2 months. Since they seldom report when these winners were acquired, they "paper" their performance.

➤ MONTHLY PATTERNS Based on advances, the best months to *buy* are February and September (if you can catch the low points); to *sell*, December, January, August, and July.

➤ SUMMER RALLY Since World War II, June opening prices have been lower than those at the close of August three times as often as they have been higher. Since 1960, declines have occurred in only 8 of the 24 summers. In most years, the gains have been modest but, thanks to a couple of big periods, have averaged almost +10%. The few losses have averaged −7.0%.

➤ YEAR-END SURGE December is almost always a good month for investors. Since 1897, the market has risen in 62 years and declined in 24. The high usually came around the middle of the month before year-end tax selling started to depress prices.

➤ JANUARY INDICATOR This is always a key month. Even fundamentalists place considerable faith in its forecasting ability: what happens in the first 5 days, or better in the full month, predicts the year's trend.

Some technicians focus on the action of the first trading day, but this indicator has limited value for most investors. When there has been a disparity between the first day's movement and the 5-day movement, the latter has been 50% more accurate. Anyway, after the first day, you can start to make decisions.

If you're an eager beaver, watch that 5-day figure. Its forecasting accuracy has been almost as good as that of the full month. It has correctly indicated the direction of the stock market 80% of the time since 1945 but has not done quite that well in the past decade.

Since 1900, there have been 32 years during which the DJIA declined in January. In 16 of

SUMMER RALLY

YEAR	PERCENT CHANGE: JUNE–AUGUST
1960	+0.3
1961	+4.9
1962	+8.0
1963	+4.6
1964	+1.3
1965	+3.7
1966	−9.1
1967	+3.5
1968	−0.6
1969	−2.4
1970	+11.3
1971	+3.5
1972	+2.6
1973	−4.7
1974	+0.1
1975	+0.1
1976	−17.4
1977	−6.4
1978	+5.9
1979	+5.4
1980	+9.5
1981	−10.0
1982	+14.9
1983	+0.6

those years, the market went on to record a loss over the next 11 months (average decline: −12%), but in the other 16 years, the market advanced (average: +19%).

But there have been years of failure: 1978, when January was down −6.2% but the full year ended up slightly +1.1%; and in 1982, when the first month was down −2.0% but the year was an ebullient +15%.

In January 1984, the market was off −3.0%, but technicians were not overly impressed, because this was a presidential election year when the market has historically risen twice as often as it has declined.

To put these percentages in perspective: a 3% gain for the DJIA at 1,000 means a rise of 30 points. Keep this in mind when you check the market action in January.

The January indicator is not always right,

but the odds are with you when you follow its signal.

SPECIAL INDICATORS

There are scores of other signals that are used by professionals. Most of them have been reliable over a limited period of time and involve calculations too complex for amateurs. But there is one indicator that has had a 60-year perfect predictive record: the "two tumbles and a jump" concept developed by Norman G. Fosback, editor of *Market Logic*. Whenever the Federal Reserve Board (Fed) lowers one of its three policy variables—discount rate, bank reserve requirement, brokerage house margin—over any time period, stock prices will jump the next year. Two cuts signify a decisive shift toward easier credit and a bull market. According to this theory, the market will be higher in 6, 9, and 12 months with an average gain of +17.8%, 23%, and +32%, respectively (with one exception in the Great Depression).

Fosback has recognized that the single most powerful force in the stock market is the interest rate as determined by the Fed. When the cost of money goes down, the price of securities— bonds and stocks—goes up. And vice versa when the interest rate rises. When you remember that the prime rate was $21\frac{1}{2}\%$ in early 1981 and was recently down to $10\frac{1}{2}\%$, it's logical to look for a stronger market in the future.

SPECIAL PRICE PATTERNS

Heavy institutional buying has confused the daily market pattern, but you may be able to pick up a few extra dollars by timing your purchases or sales with these not-so-well-documented market actions:

➤ WITHIN ANY MONTH Stock is often stronger around the end of the month: just before and after. It rises more often on the last day of the month and for the next 3 days, with the second trading day of the month the best: up 66.7% of the time.

Institutional money managers operate on a monthly fiscal basis. They place their orders in anticipation of an inflow of funds that takes place early each month.

➤ WITHIN ANY WEEK You will do better to buy on Monday morning and to sell on Friday afternoon. Over more than 40 years, the DJIA was down 54% of the Mondays, up on 63% of the Fridays (or last trading day of the week).

Specifically, one study showed that the average investment was 0.12% higher at the Friday close than on Thursday's close and about 0.22% lower at the close on Monday than on Friday's.

➤ WITHIN ANY DAY The first and last hours are likely to be the most active. The opening hour volume is boosted by overnight decisions, and it appears that many professionals review their holdings around 2 P.M and make their moves before closing.

On the other hand, there's little price movement between 11 A.M. and 2 P.M.—apparently because of time out for lunch.

But stock prices often decline in the last hour of trading because the professionals take their day's profits—or losses. And a strong close will usually be followed by higher opening prices.

➤ BEFORE HOLIDAYS The market tends to rise. The DJIA has risen two-thirds of the time before a 1-day holiday and about three-quarters of the time before a 3-day weekend.

➤ BLUE MONDAYS Historically, on the first trading day of the week, the market has gone down 61% of the time and up 39%.

If you are in doubt about carrying a long position over the weekend, don't. Sell on Friday and consider buying on Monday.

And here are some special forecasts, patterns, or techniques which show you how esoteric professionals can be:

➤ FULL MOON Over a 10-year period, the DJIA declined from one trading day before the full moon through the third day afterward. Five days after the celestial wonder, the Dow rose more often than it fell.

➤ SPREADS Buy when the spread between the high and low was greater than that of the previous day and if the market closed at or near the top of the day's trading range. The next opening will be strong.

Sell when the low-high spread is less than that of the previous day, especially when the market is topping. A reversal is coming.

When there's an extra-wide spread between the close and the low, look for a weak opening the next day.

STOCK-MARKET FORECASTING

According to John C. Touhey in his book *Stock Market Forecasting for Alert Investors,* the stock market can be forecast 80% of the time. His comments do not fully qualify as forecasts, but they are close enough to be summarized here. Here are some of the checkpoints he recommends:

- **Brokers' cash accounts.** When these increase for 2 consecutive months, *buy.* When they decline for the same period, *sell.*
- **Call loan interest rate.** When this declines by more than 3% in any one month, *buy.* When there are 3 consecutive monthly increases, *sell.*
- **Brokers' margin credit.** *Buy* when the monthly totals for the past 60 days are greater than those of the previous 2 months. *Sell* (or sell short) when they are less for 2 months.
- **Prime interest rate.** When this is lower than the yield of AAA corporate bonds, *buy.* When it is higher, be cautious and, generally, *sell* or do not buy.

William E. Donoghue, the editor and publisher of money market and mutual fund letters and books, recommends the *12% solution:* when the yield of money market funds falls below 12%, the outlook for stocks is favorable, and money should be shifted from fixed income securities or funds to equities. And when the money fund returns rise above 12%, it's time to ease savings back into money funds. Like most formulas, it works only when the investor exercises discipline.

BUYING AND SELLING:
Types of Orders

To ensure flexibility and protection, stock exchanges and brokers have developed trading techniques and regulations for buying and selling securities and contracts. All are governed by strict regulations. You don't have to know or understand them all, but here are some of the most widely used stock market orders:

➤ MARKET ORDER This specifies that brokers must buy or sell at the best price obtainable. If the order is to buy, they must keep bidding at advancing prices until they find a willing seller. Vice versa if the order is to sell. The customer can be certain the market order will be executed.

When you buy at market, you may make or lose a fraction of a point over a day's trading, but when you are shooting for 50% profit, that's not important. In selling at market, you may have to accept a lower than anticipated price.

As a general rule, when you are dealing with 100 shares, enter a market order. With larger lots, you will usually do better to set a specific price for the transaction.

➤ LIMIT OR LIMITED PRICE ORDER To buy or sell a stated amount of a security at a specific (or better) price.

➤ DAY ORDER To buy or sell during the day or expire at the end of that trading period.

➤ GOOD UNTIL CANCELED (GTC) ORDER Also known as open order. To buy or sell until the order is either executed or canceled. It is automatically canceled at the end of each month.

➤ SCALE ORDER To buy or sell a security with specified amounts and at specified price variations.

➤ STOP LIMIT ORDER To *buy*, placed above the current market price. It becomes a market limit order when the price of the stock trades at or above the stop limit price. To *sell*, it is placed below the current price and specifies a price below which the order must not be executed.

➤ STOP ORDER TO BUY Placed above the current market price. It becomes a market order when the stock trades at or above the stop buy price.

➤ STOP ORDER TO SELL The sell price is placed below the current price. It becomes a market order when the price of the stock is at or below the stop sell price.

HOW TO USE STOP ORDERS

Stop orders can be an important tool for traders and a useful aid for investors. They provide protection against the unexpected; they can force you to admit mistakes and thus cut your losses. Many veterans, both professional and amateur, rely on stop orders. They review them periodically, raise or lower them according to their view of the future, and, in many cases, *never* cancel them. They recognize a basic truth: like most investors, they will not close out a position that has gone against them unless it is done automatically by a stop order to sell and, occasionally, to buy.

Usually, the decline in the price of a stock will be the result of investor pessimism, but once in a while, snowballing can occur when there is a temporary imbalance between supply and demand. Here's what can happen:

GC trades at 50¼ after a sharp drop. Specialists have in their book orders to sell 1,000 shares at 50 stop, 300 shares at 49¾ stop, 1,000 shares at 49½ stop, and 1,200 shares at 49¼ stop.

The sale at 50 is made by the specialists (in their role of making an orderly market). The next sale, of 300 shares, is at 49¾. Now the snowballing starts and, if warranted, the floor governors of the NYSE will step in and suspend top orders. This cancels all orders already received and prohibits acceptance of additional stop orders until further notice. This ban goes into effect only after the close of the market.

Similarly, the AMEX outlaws the use of stop orders on round lots only (not odd lots). Stop limit orders are permitted on both types when the stop and limit prices are the same.

HOW TO SET STOP PRICES

Broadly speaking, there are two techniques to use:

➤ SET THE ORDER AT A PRICE THAT IS A FRACTION OF A POINT ABOVE THE ROUND FIGURE At 50⅛, for example. Your order will be executed before the stock drops to the round figure (50) which most investors will designate.

Remember: There is no guarantee that your stock will be sold at the exact stop price. In a fast-moving market, the stock may drop rapidly and skip the stop price, and thus the sale will be at a lower than anticipated figure. (See "snowballing" example above.)

➤ RELATE THE STOP PRICE TO THE VOLATILITY OF THE STOCK This is the *beta.* In making calculations, the trader uses a base of 1, indicating that the stock has historically moved with the market. A stock with a beta of 1.1 would be 10% more volatile than the overall market; one with a beta of 0.8 would be 20% less volatile than the market.

Andrew Kern of Avatar Associates uses these criteria for shares with a *beta:*

- Under 0.8, the sell price is 8% below the purchase price
- Between 0.8 and 1, the stop loss is set at 10% below the cost or recent high
- 1.1 to 1.3: 12% below
- 1.4 to 1.6: 14% below
- Over 1.6: 16% below

Example: XYZ stock is acquired at 50. Its beta is 1.2, so the stop loss is set at 44: 12% below 50. If the market goes up, the stop is raised for every 20% gain in the stock price. At 60, the sell order would be 53: 12% below 60.

Says Kern: "The lower the price of the stock, the greater the probable fluctuations; the higher the price of the stock, the smaller the swings are likely to be."

Thus Teledyne, at 150 with a 1.1 beta, would normally have a stop loss price of 132, but because of its high price, it would probably be about 139.

USES FOR STOP ORDERS

Stop orders are useful for the following purposes.

➤ TO LIMIT LOSSES ON STOCKS YOU OWN You buy 100 shares of Allied Wingding at 50 in hopes of a quick gain. You are a bit queasy about the market, so at the same time you enter an order to sell the stock at 47⅞ stop. If AW drops to 47²/₈, your stop order becomes a market order and you've limited your loss to 2⅝ points per share.

With investments, the problem is where to set the stop. Unless you plan to hold a quality stock for years—for your children or for your retirement-plan portfolio—always set stop prices that will keep your losses low. The trigger point depends on the type of stock, the market conditions, and the percentage of loss you are willing to accept. Always be ready to take quick, small losses if the stock or market does not do what you expected.

Traders generally set their loss target at 10% below cost or recent high. Investors who are concerned with long-term gains are more cautious and prefer a loss figure of about 15%: for a stock bought at 50, 42⅜. *For best results, set stop prices on the downside and have courage enough to back up your decisions.* Once any stock starts to fall, there's no telling how far down it will go. And if you are like most people, you will hang on in hope (and embarrassment). Only rarely will such a loser bounce back within the next 6 to 12 months. *Cut losses short and let your profits run.*

➤ TO LIMIT LOSSES WHEN YOU SELL SHORT In anticipation of a bear market, you sell short 100 shares of AW at 50. To reduce your risk if you are wrong and the market rises, you enter an order to buy 100 shares of AW at 52⅞ stop. If the stock price advances that high, you'll limit your loss to $287.50 (plus commissions).

With a stop limit price you specify a price below which the order must *not* be executed. This is useful with a volatile stock in an erratic market. If the price of the stock slips past the stop price, you won't be sold out.

You enter an order to sell 100 AW at 50

stop, 50 limit. The price declines from 50½ to 50. At that point, your order becomes a *limit* order at 50, *not a market order.* Your stock will *not* be sold at 49⅞, as can happen with a stop order at 50.

Traders also use a variation of this technique by specifying two different prices, one for the stop and one for the limit. You tell your broker to sell 100 shares of AW at 50 stop, limit 48. Thus, if AW falls to 50 or below, your order to sell at 48 takes over. The broker will sell, hopefully at a price above 48, but if the decline continues, the stock will not be sold.

➤ TO ENSURE A PROFIT A year ago you bought 100 shares of General Cocktail at 50 and it is now 55. You are planning a vacation trip and do not want to lose too much of your paper profit, so you give your broker an order to sell at 50 stop, good until canceled. If the market declines and the sale is made, you are sure of a 15-point per share gain.

Similarly, the stop order can protect a profit on a short sale. This time, you sell GC short at 55. The price falls to 40, so you have a $15 per share profit. You look for a further price decline but want protection while you're away. You enter a buy order at 45 stop. If the stock price does jump to 45, you will buy 100 shares, cover your short position, and have a $1,000 profit (assuming that the specialist is able to make the purchase on the nose).

You can apply the same technique in a series of steps, going up on purchases, down on short sales. This provides a continuous guarantee of sliding scale profits. But be cautious. These machinations can be very tricky.

➤ TO TOUCH OFF PREDETERMINED BUY, SELL, AND SELL-SHORT ORDERS If you rely on technical analysis and buy only when a stock breaks through a trendline on the upside and sell or sell short when it breaks out on the downside, you can place advance orders to "buy on stop," "sell on stop," or "sell short on stop." These become market orders when the price of the securities hits the designated figure.

Example: AW stock is at 48¾ and appears likely to shoot up. But you want to be sure that the rise is genuine, because over the years there's been resistance at just about 50. You set a *buy stop order* at 51⅜. This becomes a *market order* if the stock hits the peak.

BREAKING EVEN

Before you hang on to a stock in hopes that its price will rise so that you can break even, check this table. A stock must rise 100% to correct a 50% decline! If your stock declines from 100 to 50, it has dropped 50%. But it will take a doubling in price (a 100% move) to rise from 50 back to 100. *Moral:* take losses early; set stop orders to protect profits; stop dreaming.

IF A STOCK DROPS THE FOLLOWING PERCENTAGE	IT NEEDS TO RISE THIS PERCENTAGE FOR YOU TO BREAK EVEN
5% (100 to 95)	5% (95 to 100)
10% (100 to 90)	11% (90 to 100)
15% (100 to 85)	17% (85 to 100)
20% (100 to 80)	25% (80 to 100)
25% (100 to 75)	33% (75 to 100)
30% (100 to 70)	42% (70 to 100)
40% (100 to 60)	66% (60 to 100)
50% (100 to 50)	100% (50 to 100)
60% (100 to 40)	150% (40 to 100)
75% (100 to 25)	300% (25 to 100)

SPACE YOUR TRANSACTIONS

If you are making a large investment (500 shares or more) in any one stock, consider spacing out your purchases over a period of several days or even weeks. The commissions will be higher (roughly 15% more to buy five 100-share lots than one 500-share block), but in many cases you'll save money, because with modest fluctuations, your average cost will be lower. And if you decide that your choice was wrong, you can cancel the rest of the order.

EX-DIVIDEND DATE

Always check the ex-dates before you sell. This will ensure extra income benefits.

Ex-dividend means without dividend. On the stock tables, this is shown by the symbol "x" after the name of the company under the "sales" column.

The buyer of a stock selling ex-dividend does not receive the recently declared dividend. The payment goes to the shareholder whose name is recorded on corporate books on a date fixed by the company's directors. With Southwestern Public Service, here's how the date is shown in Standard & Poor's *Stock Guide:*

NAME OF ISSUE	DATE	EX-DIV.
Southwestern Public Service	9–1–86	8–11

But since 5 business days are allowed for delivery of the stock in "regular way" transactions, the NYSE would declare its stocks "ex-dividend" earlier—e.g., if the official date was Friday, the NYSE would list the stock with an "x" on Monday.

Once you have decided to sell a stable stock, delay the sale until a few days after the ex-dividend date, because on that day the price of the stock will usually dip to reflect the loss of income. Similarly, when you have decided to sell, check the ex-dividend date and delay the sale until after you are entitled to the payout.

(*Note:* With securities traded on Canadian exchanges, the time span is 3 business days.)

Ex-rights means without rights. As outlined earlier, rights offer stockholders the opportunity to buy new or additional stock at a discount. The buyer of a stock selling ex-rights is not entitled to this bargain after the announced date.

Ex-interest means without interest. It applies to the interest paid on certain types of income bonds. Here again, the payment is made only to bondholders of a set date.

To check the ex-dates, consult your broker.

ODD-LOT TRANSACTIONS

When you deal with odd lots of stocks—fewer than 100 shares—you may have to pay a premium, typically $1/8$ of a point. This goes to the specialist handling the transaction. There are exceptions where no charge is made:

- When the issue is handled directly by the broker, usually involving shares of a company for which the firm makes a market

- When the security is of a company listed on the NYSE when the order is placed 10 minutes before the 10 A.M. opening of the exchange
- With a short sale of a volatile stock in a volatile market. The prevailing round-lot price for a short sale is determined by odd-lot brokers every minute, but in a busy market, many round-lot sales can be made in those 60 seconds

Since round-lot sellers must wait their turn in the specialist's book, the price of their short sale may be lower than the "minute" price, especially when short sales can be made only on the "uptick." When prices are dropping fast, a short sale of up to 99 shares at a stated price can be executed by the odd-lot broker on the next registered uptick, which may occur before the specialist reaches the round-lot order.

BUYING AND SELLING FOR EXTRA PROFITS

Check the advice in the chapter on timing and keep these comments in mind. They are not always applicable but often can add a few dollars to your profits and save you from unnecessary losses.

➤ HOLD THE STOCK AS LONG AS YOUR ORIGINAL REASONS FOR BUYING STAND UP But not a minute longer. T. Rowe Price, one of the most successful professional money managers, puts it this way: "I learned that I did not have the ability to guess the ups and downs of the stock market averages. . . . I saw that most of the big fortunes were made by people retaining ownership of successful business enterprises which continued to grow and prosper over a long period of years."

➤ WATCH THE MARKET ACTION OF MAJOR STOCKS About 2 weeks before the end of a calendar quarter (March 31, June 30, etc.), buy high-grade stocks that have had a big move in the past 30 days. These are the stocks that will be bought by institutional investors to enhance their reports. (No one can be sure when, at what price, they bought, but the inference is that they were smart and bought early and low.)

This extra demand will boost the prices of these favorites; you can pick up a couple of

---

FOR EXTRA PROFITS

Watch the last hour of trading on the NYSE. With the net change in the DJIA between 3 and 4 P.M., construct a cumulative average, adding today's figure to yesterday's total.

If the market is +12 points at 3 P.M. and only +6 points at close, that's a disappointing day and not bullish for tomorrow. What happens is that, in that last hour, the specialists try to position themselves for the next day's business and the traders make their moves.

---

points quickly and, since the uptrend is likely to continue, should fare even better in the future.

Similarly, keep an eye on block transactions of institutionally favored blue chips. These used to be published weekly in *Barron's,* but so many transactions have recently been big ones, you'll have to get the information elsewhere: from statistical services or your broker.

When there are more sales in upticks (at prices higher than those of previous trades), it's a bullish signal—sometimes. Major investors follow their leaders . . . often blindly.

➤ DON'T GET OVERLY CONCERNED ABOUT TEMPORARY PRICE SWINGS Unless you are trading. Quality and value will always prove profitable when you are patient. But do relate the short-term fluctuations to the market's trend. With a strong upswing, almost all stocks will move up. Vice versa when the market is weak.

➤ IS THE STOCK OVERBOUGHT OR OVERSOLD? When an advancing stock rises far ahead of its rising trendline, it is temporarily overbought and some profit-taking is imminent. Avoid buying at this point. Conversely, a weak stock may be temporarily oversold and a technical rally is likely.

➤ CHECK THE LONG-TERM CHARTS TO SEE HOW THE STOCK HAS REACTED IN THE PAST If the rise has been rapid, be cautious. If the fall has been precipitous, don't buy or, if you are a trader, sell short.

➤ WATCH FOR EARLY WARNING SIGNALS Slackening volume with a strong upmoving stock means that buyers are becoming wary; heavier volume with a downtrender indicates that the big boys are unloading.

According to some analysts, a bull market generally lasts $2\frac{1}{2}$ years and is followed by $1\frac{1}{2}$ years of a bearish market.

➤ STUDY THE CHART PATTERNS As explained in the chapter on technical analysis, stocks develop patterns of their own. Utilities tend to move within a relatively narrow range; speculative stocks swing widely and rapidly; quality stocks fluctuate in a repetitive manner.

➤ SET SIGHTS ON WHOLE NUMBERS Traders are more likely to give their broker an order to buy at a whole number (40, 45, 50) than at a fraction ($40\frac{1}{2}$, $45\frac{1}{4}$, $50\frac{1}{8}$). When the price of a stock hits that round number, there will usually be a flood of orders that may create a support or resistance level.

➤ CONCENTRATE ON INDUSTRIES IN THE NEWS Not the stocks alone. Groups of stocks tend to move together. First action comes from the industry leaders (because of institutional interest), then the public moves in, generally preferring secondary companies in popular industries.

➤ WATCH THE EARNINGS ESTIMATES Of the corporate officers, not the analysts. Smart management never estimates earnings but will prefer to suggest a range. Aggressive stock-market-minded executives can seldom be trusted.

➤ TRADE WITH THE TREND In a rising market, take a position on the upside. Vice versa on the downside breakout.

When news is negative, specialists sell or sell short from the opening bell. They do not come back into the market and by day's end have made money. Too often, amateur investors start selling but during the day have second thoughts and start to buy again. They lose money.

➤ HAVE A SYSTEM AND STICK TO IT Presumably you selected the system after study and expert recommendations. Follow it closely until there are strong logical reasons to change. Jumping around is a matter of luck, not skill. Be patient. Even in trading, profits usually take time to develop.

➤ BUY ON WEAKNESS This is classic investment counsel but is easier said than done.

➤ DOUBLE UP ON LOW-PRICED STOCKS If the price of a stock selling under 10 rises quickly, double your commitment and watch its action twice as carefully. At the beginning, a trend is more likely to continue than to reverse itself, but *be sure that the direction of the stock's price is clearly established.*

➤ ACT PROMPTLY Successful trading can be a matter of hours or days. If you cannot keep close watch, don't trade.

Consider the tax consequences when selling. Short-term losses can be offset, dollar for dollar, with other income, to a maximum of $3,000. Long-term losses (when held over 6 months) generate only a $1 deduction for every $2 loss.

SPECIFIC GUIDELINES

Here are some excellent checkpoints as set by John Winthrop Wright, a leading fundamentalist:

- **Buy a stock** when it is selling well below the average price-earnings ratio of the past decade and there are good prospects for rising earnings and greater popularity.
- **Review a stock** when its P/E ratio goes to, or above, its average annual high for the last 5 years. For example, at a P/E of 14, it will probably be wise to sell unless there are strong reasons to anticipate a special situation such as a takeover. Very few stocks continue to trade far above the P/E ratios of their industry or their past averages.
- **Sell a stock** when it becomes fully priced in relation to past performance, future prospects, and again, its historical P/E ratio. When any stock that has sold at 8 to 12 times earnings gets to a multiple of 12, watch out.

Concludes Wright, "It is always better to make Baron Rothschild's famous mistake of making a little less by selling too soon than to take the greater risk of overstaying the market with an overpriced stock."

To these can be added two other checkpoints used by analysts for determining sell points:

- *When the price of the stock rises to more than double the shareholder's equity at corporate book value per common share.* When buyers are willing to pay much more than twice the tangible value of a company, they are adding a substantial premium for future growth. This caveat applies primarily to manufacturing firms with large investments in plants, equipment, etc. Drug/service/financial companies usually have small tangible assets in relation to their total revenues.
- *When the dividend yield falls below 3%.* If the company is utilizing its cash for R&D and expansion, that's good. But the growth must be sustained to justify such a low return for the use of your money.

SELLING SHORT

Selling short is a technique that seeks to sell high and buy low—the opposite of what most investors do. It's speculative but can be used as a protective device. You usually sell stock you do not own at the market price and hope to cover your position at a lower profit and thus rack up a pleasant profit.

Example: The stock of Nifty-Fifty, a high technology company, has soared from 20 to 48 in a few months. At this price, volume is declining and the chart shows that a resistance level is beginning to form. A report from your broker questions whether NF can continue its ever-higher earnings. From your own research—of the company and the industry—you agree and decide that after the next quarter's report the price of the stock will probably fall sharply. You arrange with your broker to borrow 500 shares from one of the firm's customers (as provided in the margin agreement which most customers sign) and sell these shares at 48.

Two months later, the company announces lower profits, and the stock falls to 40. Now, you buy 500 shares and pocket a $4,000 profit (less commissions). Or if you're persuaded that the price will continue to go down, you hold out for a lower purchase price.

This technique seems easy and logical, but short selling is one of the most misunderstood of all types of securities transactions and is often considered un-American and dangerous, as indicated by the Wall Street aphorism "He who sells what isn't his'n, buys it back or goes to pris'n." Yet when properly executed, selling short can preserve capital, turn losses into gains, defer or minimize taxes, and be profitable. *With few exceptions, the only people who make money with stocks in a bear market are those who sell short.*

Short selling is not for the faint of heart or for those who rely on tips instead of research. You may have some nervous moments if your timing is poor and the price of the stock jumps right after you sold short. But if your projections are correct, the price of that stock will fall—eventually. You must have the courage of your convictions and be willing to hang in there for months, even years.

The idea of profiting when a stock goes down may be hard to take, so when you decide to sell short, find a brokerage firm with an experienced trader.

Professionals who pay no commissions and can move in and out of positions quickly sell short in buoyant markets to take advantage of the almost inevitable temporary fluctuations. Amateurs will do well, and sleep easier, by selling short only in primary bear markets . . . *with the trend.*

RULES AND CONDITIONS FOR SELLING SHORT

Because it's a special technique, short selling of all securities is subject to strict operational rules:

➤ MARGIN All short sales must be made in a margin account, usually with stock borrowed from another customer of the brokerage firm under an agreement signed when the margin account was established. If you own stock, you can sell "against the box," as will be explained.

The minimum collateral must be the greater of $2,000 or 50% of the market value of the shorted stock but not less than $5 per share on issues selling at $5 or more nor less than either $2.50 per share or 100% of market for stocks trading under $5 per share. These provisions take care of any dividends or rights due the lender of the stock.

For amateurs who may have to wait out a temporary price rise, it's best to maintain a margin balance equal to 90% of the short sale commitment. This will eliminate the necessity for coming up with more collateral.

➤ COMMISSIONS You pay regular commissions, taxes, and fees on the initial short sale and subsequent purchase of the stock. If you deliver your own stock, you save the buying costs.

➤ INTEREST There are no interest charges on the margin account.

➤ PREMIUMS Once in a while, if the shorted stock is in great demand, your broker may have to pay a premium for borrowing, usually $1 per 100 shares per business day.

➤ DIVIDENDS All dividends on shorted stock must be paid to the owner. That's why it's best to concentrate on warrants and stocks that pay low or no dividends.

➤ RIGHTS AND STOCK DIVIDENDS Because you are borrowing the stock, you are not entitled to the use of rights or the receipt of stock dividends.

If you know or suspect that a company is going to pass or decrease its payout, you can get an extra bonus by selling short. The price of the stock is almost sure to drop. *But be careful.* The decline may be too small to offset the commissions.

➤ SALES PRICE Short sales must be made on the uptick or zero tick: that is, the last price of the stock must be higher than that of the previous sale. If the stock is at 70, you cannot sell short when it drops to $69^7/_8$ but must wait for a higher price: $70^1/_8$ or more. Or with a zero tick, the last two sales must have been at the same price.

Exception: the broker may sell at the same price, 70, provided that the last previous change in the price was upward. There might have been three or four transactions at 70. A short sale can be made when the last different price was $49^7/_8$ or lower. This is called selling on an even tick.

CANDIDATES FOR SHORT SALES

In choosing stocks for short sales, professionals use computers to analyze economic, industry, and corporate factors—plus guesswork based on experience. Amateurs must rely on simpler indicators such as:

■ *Insider transactions:* where officers and directors of the corporation have sold stock in the previous few months. The assumption is that when the number of insiders selling exceeds the number buying, the stock is at a high level and these knowledgeable people believe a decline is ahead.

- *Volatility:* as measured by the *beta* of the stock. This is the historical relation between the price movement of the stock and the overall market. A stock that moves with the market has a beta of 1.0; a more volatile issue (such as Holiday Corp.) is rated 1.5 because it swings 50% more than the market; a stable stock (General Foods) has a beta of 0.7 as it moves about 30% less than the overall averages.

   The more volatile the stock, the better it may be for short selling. You can hope to make your profit more quickly.

- *Relative strength:* how the stock stacks up with other companies in the same or similar industries. This calculation takes into account the consistency and growth of earnings and whether the last quarter profits were lower or higher than anticipated by Wall Street. These data are available from statistical services such as *Value Line* and *Standard & Poor's Earnings Forecast.*

   When corporate earnings are lower than the professional forecasts, the stock will almost always fall sharply. Helene Curtis Industries stock dropped over 11 points, even though its annual earnings rose to $1.96 from $1.40—all because this was below expectations. Catching such a situation so that you can sell short early will depend on your own projections, which can be based on news stories or information that you have gleaned from your personal contacts.

   As a rule of thumb, the best candidates for short selling are: (1) stocks that have zoomed up in a relatively short period; (2) one-time glamour stocks that are losing popularity; after reaching a peak, these stocks will be sold rapidly by the institutions, and since these "professionals" follow the leader, the prices can drop far and fast; (3) stocks that have already begun to decline more than the market averages, which occurs when an industry falters; they have started to show weakness and will soon have little or no sponsorship; (4) warrants of volatile stocks, which are low-priced, pay no dividends, and can swing sharply, so you can profit with declines of 2 or 3 points.

   The short seller should basically look for stocks that are beginning to be unpopular because of slower or lower earnings or institutional disfavor.

   The least attractive stocks for short selling are: (1) thin issues, where there are only a few hundred thousand outstanding shares; a little buying can boost their prices so that you can get caught in a squeeze and have to pay to borrow, or buy back, shares; (2) stocks with a large short interest: more than the volume of 3 days' normal trading; they have already been pressured downward and when the shorts are covered, this extra demand will force prices up; (3) shares of companies that are candidates for takeovers or buy-outs; to make a deal, the buyers will have to offer a premium price, but sharp traders sell short when they believe the proposal will be rejected, as the stock is almost sure to react unfavorably.

GUIDELINES FOR SUCCESSFUL SHORT SELLING

DON'T buck the trend. Do not sell short unless both the major and intermediate trends of the market—or, on occasion, those of an industry—are down. Make the market work for you. You may be convinced that an individual stock is overpriced, but do not take risks until there is clear, confirmed evidence of a fall in the market and in your target stock.

DON'T sell short at the market when the stock price is heading down. Place a limit order at the lowest price at which you are willing to sell short.

DO set protective prices. *On the upside,* 10 to 15% above the sale price depending on the volatility of the stock. In most cases, a quick small loss will be wise.

Be careful with stop orders. You may be picked off if the stock price rises to the precise point of the stop order and then declines. To maximize your profits, move that stop price with the decline: to $38\frac{1}{2}$ or $38\frac{1}{4}$ if the stock falls to 45 from 50.

DON'T short several stocks at once until you are experienced and have ample funds and time enough to check daily. Start with one failing stock, and if you make money, you will be ready for further speculations.

DO short when insiders, such as stock

exchange members and specialists, are active. They usually sell short before major declines and buy ahead of big rallies. Member short selling should exceed 85% of total round-lot short sales. Cover when that figure is below 60%.

Similarly, go short when short sales, by specialists, exceed 65% of total round-lot short sales; cover when this is below 40%.

You can get this information from your broker and many financial publications.

DO rely on the odd-lot selling indicator. This is available from several technical advisory services or can be set up on your own. It is calculated by dividing the total odd-lot sales into the odd-lot short sales and charting a 10-day moving average. When the indicator stays below 1.0 for several months, it's time to consider selling short. When it's down to 0.50, start selling.

Conversely, when the indicator rises above 1.0, do not sell short and cover your positions. And if you hesitate, cover all shorts when a 1-day reading bounces above 3.0.

DO set target prices but be ready to cover when there's a probability of an upswing. There will usually be a resistance level. If this is maintained with stronger volume, take your profit. You can't afford to try to outguess the professionals.

DO be patient for both the short sale and buy-back. Wait for the stock to top out and start to decline. Once you've taken your position, hang in there as long as you are convinced your original decision was right and the major trend—of the market and your stock—is down. For the

---

SELLING AGAINST THE BOX

This is a favorite year-end tactic that can freeze your paper profits or postpone taxes. You sell short against shares you own. The short sale brings in immediate cash and the profit (loss) is deferred until the short position is covered—next year or even 2 or 3 years hence. Here's how it works:

On March 1, Mary buys 100 shares of Geewhiz Electronics at 40. By July the stock is at 60, but the market is weakening and Mary gets nervous. She sells short 100 shares of GW with her own shares as collateral.

- If the price of GW stays around 60, she will lock in her gains minus commissions. She will sell the stock at 60 for a $20 per share profit: the 60 sale price minus the 40 cost.
- If the price of GW rises to 70, she'll still do OK. She delivers her own stock. She won't make that extra 10-point profit (from 60 to 70), but she will still have a $2,000 gain: the difference between her 40 cost and the 60 selling price.
- If the price of GW drops to 50, Mary has two choices:

1 To cover her short position by purchasing new shares. She will break even because her 10-point profit on the short sale will be offset by a 10-point loss on the value of the stock. Her net will be cut by the commissions.

2 To cover her short position with the shares she owns. She makes $1,000 profit on the short sale but has a smaller profit on the stocks she owns: $1,000 versus the $2,000 gain she had before.

This may sound like a get-rich-quick-with-little-risk scheme, but be cautious because:

- Commissions can eat up profits rapidly.
- Once the trend of the stock turns up, it is more likely to continue to rise than to fall. You may postpone some taxes, but you may also find that your year-end profit, from a lower than sold price, will be narrowed or eliminated.
- Under the wash sale rule (see Chapter 35), there will be no tax loss if the short sale is covered by buying the same or identical securities within 31 days after the date of the original short sale.

amateur, this can be rough, because there may be temporary last-gasp upmoves and the ultimate decline may be slower than you believe justified. If you cannot keep the faith, don't sell short.

Note: Most brokers encourage short sales because they get commissions for transactions on stocks that the seller does not own and, in effect, get two commissions on the same shares—already owned by a customer.

HEDGING FOR PROTECTION

To protect against wrong projections or unexpected rises in the price of the stock sold short, concentrate short selling on shares of companies where listed options are available. Immediately after you sell short, buy out-of-the-money calls on the same number of shares. Since the option permits you to cover your position by buying the stock at a not-much-higher price, your loss will be limited.

Example: Susan shorts 300 shares of HTH at 38 and buys 3 calls, exercisable at 40 in 7 months, for 3 ($900). If the stock drops to 30, Sue covers for a $2,400 profit (38 sale price minus 30 purchase price $\times$ 3). But she will lose $900 on the calls, because they will be worthless, so her net is $1,500.

If the stock rises to 45 before the option exercise date, she covers for a loss of $2,100 (38 at sale; 45 at purchase). But she can sell the calls for at least 5 ($1,500 for 3), so her loss is cut to $600. None of these examples counts commissions. This $600 compares with an uncovered loss of $2,100.

FORMULA PLANS

Formula plans are a convenient, better than "lock-'em-in-the-safe-deposit box" approach, usually superior to random, impulsive choices but seldom as effective as thoughtful well-planned selections and sales. They help you to average out, to miss maximum profits, and to skip big losses. If they are carried out consistently (which rarely happens), most formula plans buy relatively cheap and become profitable only when the prices of the securities rise over a period of time. They are handy for those who want to make regular small investments; they eliminate the decision about when stocks are cheap; and they are best for shares of mutual funds because their prices tend to reflect the long-term rise that has always characterized the stock market. Over the years, the average cost of all shares will be less than the average price at which you bought them. But you lose the fun and pride of judgment-based investing.

In volatile markets, buying by rote can be soothing, and profitable, for long-term investors. There's no system that can guarantee that a fool won't lose money, but when carried out properly, formula plans can avoid the two most common investment mistakes: buying too high and selling too low. Still, when stock prices are falling, consistent purchases are a form of averaging down—generally a poor policy unless you are convinced that there will be a turnaround soon.

Formula plans sound simple, but they can be difficult to maintain in practice. Most investors cannot convince themselves to sell when things are going well and to buy when the market action is unfavorable. These plans will seldom let you achieve a big killing, but they can stop you from being killed.

With investment by rote, there are two broad categories: (1) ratio plans, where action is taken on predetermined buy and sell signals, and (2) automatic plans, where commitments are based on a specific number of dollars or predetermined time period; that is, investing fixed dollars and/or in fixed time periods.

RATIO PLANS

Ratio plans compel caution in bull markets and bravery in bear markets. They force purchases as prices rise and switches or sales as prices decline. They are best for cyclical stocks in cyclical markets. The goal—to buy low and sell high—can usually be achieved over several years but is difficult over the short term. Here are the methods most widely acclaimed by professionals:

▶ PERCENTAGE OF STOCKS With this plan, you decide what percentage of your investment funds should be in stocks: 25%, 50%, 75%, etc., and how much in reserves. You then set intervals—months, quarters, years—at which you sell or buy to restore or maintain the set ratio. This must be done regardless of the level of security prices.

Example: You start with $25,000 and plan to have 75% in quality common stocks and the remaining 25% in a money market fund (or if you have large savings, in bonds or a bond fund). You buy $18,750 in stocks and put $6,250 in a money market fund.

After 6 months, the market goes up so that your stocks are now worth $22,000 and the money market fund shares are up to $6,700. The total portfolio is now $28,700. To keep the set ratio, $21,525 (75% of $28,700) must be in stocks, so you sell $475 worth of stocks and deposit the proceeds in the fund.

If the market goes down so that the stocks are worth only $15,000 (but the money market shares are still up to $6,700), you take $1,275 from the fund and buy stocks, so that the equity portion goes up to $16,275 (75% of $21,700). Now the reserve assets are down to $5,424.

You obey the formula no matter how scared you are that the market is going to drop more. With all formula plans, you must learn to regard falling prices as a chance to buy more stocks at lower prices to help make up for paper losses. That's not easy. Most investors cannot convince themselves to sell every time the portfolio is doing well and to buy each time the market is acting poorly.

An easy way to follow this system is to buy shares of a stock mutual fund. Because of its diversification, their value will bounce back faster than will a single stock (unless you pick a big winner). Conversely, the decline of the fund shares is likely to be slower than that of a single stock.

➤ PERCENTAGE CHANGES With this type of formula plan, actions are taken when the value of the portfolio increases or decreases by a set percentage. The change can be the same each way or varied—e.g., sell when the value of the portfolio goes up 25%; buy when it drops 20%. You start with $2,000, equally divided between stocks and bonds. When you have a 25% gain, sell some stocks and buy bonds. Or when the value dips 20%, sell some bonds and buy stocks to get back to the original balance.

Compared with a buy-and-hold strategy, this plan provides a 5% gain. With wider swings, the profits can be greater. For most people, this is more interesting than practical. Most of us are not willing to accept such strictures, because we believe that a rising stock (and market) will continue to go up and that a falling stock (or market) will somehow reverse its trend. But statistically, over several market cycles, this will work out well.

A variation is the 10% approach. There are no value judgments or complicated calculations. Each week, you add up the worth of your portfolio based on the closing prices. Then you set up a 30-day moving average (MA) (see Chapter 17). As long as the MA continues to rise or hold steady, you maintain a fully invested position. When there's a dip of 10% or more below the previous high, sell out, or if you're cautious, sell the losers. Do not start buying again until the MA rises 10% above the monthly low point. Then go back to a fully invested position.

This sounds better for trading than for investing, but surprisingly it doesn't work out that way. Most trends continue longer than anticipated, and with a diversified portfolio of quality stocks, that 10% decline will not come as quickly or as often as you may think. Vice versa for that 10% upswing. But not with volatile holdings, where you can be whipsawed and hurt by too many commissions.

➤ VARIABLE RATIOS These apply primarily to mixed portfolios. The key is the percentage of stocks held; up as stock prices decline, down as they rise. It's a defensive plan that works best when the market moves within a fairly limited range. In a bull market, the percentage of stocks might drop from 75 to 50% or less. Toward the end of a bear market, the buying starts again. In each case, the shift is from stocks to fixed income holdings.

The focal point is a central average that calls for investments half in stock, half in fixed income holdings: e.g., when the DJIA is at 1,000. You buy more stocks at low prices and sell more at high prices.

The problem, of course, is to determine that central price average. If stock prices roar up past your selected median, you'll soon be out of stocks and miss maximum appreciation. On the downside, however, you will always build protection, but you will not get back into stocks at the right time . . . at least not by formula.

HOW TO IMPROVE FORMULA PLAN RESULTS

The essence of all formula plans is to sell most stocks before bull market peaks and to buy most stocks before bear market bottoms. Since you are operating under a formula, you cannot use judgment in deciding whether a bull or bear market will continue. But there are some supplementary techniques which can help improve your profits.

- **Wait 30 to 60 days before buying or selling.** Once the formula has given a signal, wait for confirmation of this trend. You will have to develop your own timing schedule, but a month is minimal and 2 months may be too long.

- **Act only at the midpoint of the zone.** This is another delaying tactic. It shifts the action point up or down.

- **Use stop orders.** When your formula stock selling point is reached in the rising market, place stop orders to sell a few points below the current market level. If the uptrend continues, you will not sell your stocks too soon.

  In the opposite direction, when your formula buying point is reached in a declining market, put in an order to buy at a few points above the current market. If the downtrend continues, you will not buy too soon.

- **Change ratios or zone.** When you find that the formula plan is out of step with realities, you probably have been too conservative. Any change at or near the top of a bull market will not be effective. You will be almost out of stocks anyway. This is the wrong time to invest more heavily in stocks.

  It is probably more effective to make a zoning change at the time when the market drops into the middle or lower ranges. You will hold more stocks, so your profits should increase as the prices rise.

  But anytime you substitute judgment for the formula, you are risking errors that can prove costly.

DOLLAR COST AVERAGING (DCA)

This is the most widely used direct-investment formula plan. It eliminates the difficult problem of timing. You invest a fixed amount of dollars at specific time intervals: 1 month, 3 months, or whatever time span meets your savings schedule. Your average cost will always be lower than the average market price during the accumulation period.

For example, when you invest $600 regularly, regardless of the price of the shares, the lower the market value, the more shares you buy; thus, the average cost per share may be $5.73, while the average price is $6.20. Your profits come only when the value of the shares rises over a period of time.

With DCA, the type of stock acquired is more important than with strict formula plans. You want quality stocks that have these general characteristics:

- **Volatility** . . . but not too much. Preferably, the 10-year-high price should be $2\frac{1}{2}$ times the low. These swings are more common with cyclical stocks such as motors, machinery, and natural resources, but they can also be found with industries whose popularity shifts: drugs, electronics, and food processors.

  In bear markets, your dollars buy more shares, but your paper losses on already held stock will be high, so you will have to have a stout heart and confidence enough to maintain your commitment. That's where quality counts.

- **Long-term growth.** These are stocks of companies that can be expected to continue to boost revenues and earnings and outperform the overall stock market. If your stock fails to keep pace with the market comeback, you will lose the main advantage of DCA. Look for stocks that are more volatile on the upside than on the downside.

- **Steady ample dividends.** It is true that dividends, as such, have little to do with formula plans, but they can help to provide regular sums needed for periodic investments, especially when you find it difficult to scrape up spare cash.

  With the right stocks and modest commitments, you may find that in a few years, the dividends will be enough to meet those periodic payments. *Timing hint:* Start your program a week or two before the date you expect to receive a dividend check from the company whose stock you plan to buy.

  When you use margin, you can buy more shares with the same savings but you will have to pay interest which will be partially offset by the dividends you receive.

STOCKS FOR DOLLAR-COST AVERAGING

Archer-Daniels-Midland	Melville Corp.
Becton Dickinson	Merck & Co.
CBS, Inc.	Penney (J.C.)
Champion International	PepsiCo, Inc.
Chesebrough-Pond's	Pitney-Bowes
Coca-Cola	Quaker State Refining
Deere & Co.	Procter & Gamble
Eaton Corp.	RCA, Inc.
Emhart Corp.	Richardson-Vicks
General Foods	Rollins, Inc.
Goodyear Tire	Rubbermaid, Inc.
Holiday Inns	Scott Paper
Houston Natural Gas	Sonat, Inc.
Illinois Tool	Times Mirror
Kimberly-Clark	Upjohn Co.
Lilly (Eli)	Winn Dixie Stores
Long's Drug Stores	Xerox Corp.

- **Better-than-average profitability.** The average profit rate of the company over a decade should be at least 10%. It's fine to be able to buy more stock when the price is low, but there's little benefit if its value does not move up steadily over the years. Corporations able to show consistent profitable growth will always be worth more in the future. With DCA, you are striving to accumulate greater wealth. This can always be done best by buying stocks of companies that make better than average profits.
- **Good quality.** This means stocks of companies rated A− or higher by Standard & Poor's. With such criteria, you will avoid companies with high debt ratios and usually those whose prices swing sharply.

  Shares of mutual funds are excellent vehicles for DCA. They provide diversification, generally stay in step with the stock market as a whole, and usually continue to pay dividends.

Note: A study by *Forbes* magazine raised doubts about the true value of DCA. A survey of 12 NYSE stocks over a 5-year period found that: (1) the average cost under DCA exceeded the median for all purchase prices; (2) with eight of the stocks, the investor would have beaten DCA by buying a single block on any randomly chosen date; (3) the gains of the four "successes" averaged only 7.9% a year; (4) the commissions of DCA cut the gains in half.

➤ REVERSE DCA   This is a technique that is best after retirement when you begin to liquidate shares of a mutual fund. Instead of drawing a fixed dollar amount (as most retirees do), you sell a fixed number of shares. The average selling price will come out higher that way.

For illustration only, the table below shows the values of fund shares that fluctuate widely over a 6-month period. To get $100 income, you must sell 10 shares in the first month, 20 in the second, etc. Over the half year, you liquidate 75 shares at an average price of $8.

But if you sell a fixed number (10) of shares each month, your income will vary: $100 in month 1, $50 in month 2, $200 in month 4. Overall, you will cash in only 60 shares at an average redemption price of $10.

This can be dangerous because: (1) you won't get the same dollars every month, but over the same period of time, you will receive as much and have more shares still invested; but when the price of the shares drops, you have to unload more shares and will have fewer assets for future years; (2) you cannot know in advance the correct number of shares to sell; if you have to change the formula, you may be in trouble.

REVERSE DOLLAR-COST AVERAGING

SHARE PRICE	$100 PER MONTH NO. SHARES SOLD	10 SHARES PER MONTH $ INCOME
10	10	$100
5	20	50
10	10	100
20	5	200
10	10	100
5	20	50
	75	$600
Average redemption price per share	$8	$10

➤ DIVIDEND REINVESTMENT This is a variation of DCA that involves prompt reinvestment of dividends, often with a discount on new stock purchases. This service is offered by a number of corporations to strengthen stockholder relations and raise additional capital at low cost; for investors, it is a handy, inexpensive means for regular savings. It avoids the nuisance of small dividend checks and forces regular investments. It's good for growth but not for current income, because you never see the dividend check. Many companies offer these new shares at a discount, and some permit extra cash deposits, typically to a maximum of $3,000 each dividend time.

Under such a plan, all dividends are automatically reinvested in the company's stock. With the shareholder's OK, a bank or broker buys the required number of shares in the open market. The company then credits the full or fractional shares and pays dividends on the new total holdings. The commissions are prorated among participating shareholders and average about 1% of the value of the investment; there is also a service charge of about 5%, with a

SOME CORPORATIONS OFFERING 5% DISCOUNT WITH DIVIDEND REINVESTMENT PLANS

Ball Corp.	Hexcel Corp.
Bankers Trust	Mellon Bank
Bank of Boston	NICOR
Bank of Virginia	Norton Co.
Briggs & Stratton	Norwest Corp.
Carter Hawley Hale	Oneida Ltd.
Chase Manhattan	Safeway Stores
Chemical New York	Santa Anita Cos.
CP National	Southern Co.
Dravo Corp.	TECO Energy
Federal Realty	Tenneco
Investment Trust	Timken
First Virginia Banks	Travelers Corp.
Fleming Cos.	Universal Foods
Green Mountain	Universal Leaf Tobacco
Power	

SOURCE: Standard & Poor's *The Outlook.*

RULES FOR SUCCESSFUL TRADING (THANKS TO WILLIAM D. GANN)

- Never risk more than 10% of your capital on any one trade.
- Protect your position with a stop-loss order 3 to 5 points below cost or recent high.
- Never overtrade. This would violate the capital rule.
- Do not buck the trend. Never buy or sell if you are not *convinced* of the trend in motion.
- When in doubt, get out. And don't get in until you're sure.
- Trade only in active stocks.
- Diversify your risk with five stocks.
- Trade at the market, not with limit prices to buy or sell.
- Build a surplus with your winnings and use these reserves only in emergencies.
- Never buy solely to get a dividend: with stocks or funds.
- Never average down your losses.
- Be patient: never go into the market because you're simply tired of waiting or get out because your temper is thin.
- Look for big profits and small losses.
- Never cancel a stop-loss order when making a trade.
- Be ready to sell short when the market trend shifts.
- Never buy because a stock price is low or sell because it seems too high.
- Be careful about pyramiding until the uptrend is clear and confirmed.
- When you do pyramid, concentrate on stocks with small volume of shares outstanding on the buying side and those with larger volume of stock outstanding to sell short.
- Never hedge to protect a position. Do so only when you have carefully calculated the potential returns and protection.
- Never change your market position without a sound reason that meets your overall objectives.
- Don't go overboard with trades simply because you hit some big winners.

maximum of $2.50 per transaction. The savings are welcome: with $100 in dividends from a stock selling at $20 per share, the 5 new shares would carry a commission cost of $7.25 plus tax if they were bought directly. The bank charges only about $3.81. You get credit for fractional shares, and your dividend rate is adjusted accordingly. On closeouts, you receive the shares or cash. And under current IRS regulations, the service charge can be taken as a deduction in computing your federal income tax.

These dividend reinvestment plans were best with shares of qualified utilities, because through 1985, there were tax benefits: investors could exclude from taxable income dividends of $750 for a single return, $1,500 for a couple filing jointly.

33 | SPECIAL SITUATIONS

This is a catchall chapter for opportunities that at one time may be investments and at another may be speculations. The definition depends on the type of security, the quality of the corporation, and the trading techniques used.

- Companies that split their stocks or pay stock dividends can be excellent investments when these extras are justified by profitable growth. But the techniques used in buying and selling can be speculative: that is, when it appears that a company may split its stock, the price of its shares will usually rise rapidly and, after the split, fall sharply. The long-term investor who bought the shares when undervalued will probably retain his holdings and welcome such growth. A trader, however, would buy as the prospects of a split catch Wall Street's fancy and sell at a quick profit right after the announcement.
- With takeover situations, the investor might continue to hold shares of the acquiring company and look forward to enjoying the benefits of the purchase. But the speculator would try to pick up quick gains by buying the shares of the target firm.
- Companies with a small number of shares can be investments when you know, and have confidence in, the owners, but they can be speculations when there are problems because of limited capital, poor management, or threats of acquisition.

COMPANIES THAT SPLIT THEIR STOCKS FREQUENTLY

One of the most rewarding and exciting investments can be a corporation that increases the number of its shares of common stock: issuing one, two, three, or more shares for each outstanding share. Such splits usually occur when:

- The price of such a stock moves to a historic high so that individual investors are unwilling or unable to buy shares. Psychologically, a stock trading at 50 will attract far more than double the number of investors who are willing to pay 100.
- A small, growing company, whose shares are traded OTC, wants to list its stock on an exchange where the rules, for the NYSE, for example, require a minimum of 1 million common shares and at least 2,000 shareholders with 100 shares or more.

    Such a listing broadens investment acceptance as many institutions prefer the liquidity of an established market and more individuals can use the shares as collateral for margin loans.
- A corporation seeks to make an acquisition with minimal cash or debt.

Stock splits take place most often when:

- The price of the stock is about $75 per share. The most attractive range for most investors is $35 to $50 a share, so few splits are declared when the stock price is at a low level.
- There is a probability that more shareholders will benefit the business of the corporation by attracting more customers: retail stores or franchise operations moving into new markets; food and drug manufacturers adding new products; financial institutions making acquisitions in new areas.
- Management becomes fearful of an unfriendly takeover. When the top officials hold only a small percentage of the outstanding shares, a stock split will make more shares available at a lower price and

thus, hopefully, lessen the likelihood of a raid.

- Earnings are likely to continue to grow so that the price of the shares will keep rising. With more stock, the per share profits will appear smaller —for a while.
- The company has a record of stock splits. This indicates that the directors recognize, and are familiar with, the advantages of adding shares to keep old stockholders and attract new ones.

COMPANIES WITH A SMALL NUMBER OF SHARES

When corporations have a limited number of shares, their stock prices can move sharply: UP when there's heavy buying; DOWN when there's concerted selling. Theoretically, when a company has fewer than 500,000 shares, it should be an excellent speculation. Typically, the price-earnings ratios are low, the dividends relatively high, and, with concentrated ownership, these firms are targets for merger or acquisition and thus profitable speculations.

In practice, however, most small firms prefer to stay single and thus their stocks are seldom worthwhile. Usually, they are better for investment than trading. This is proven by the list of companies with small capitalization that has been a regular feature of *Your Investments* since 1974. About one-third of the firms have remained on the list; another one-third have issued more shares; and almost all the others have merged or gone out of business. Only a handful of these companies have grown sufficiently to be listed on a stock exchange.

That means that it pays to buy shares of small corporations only when you know, and are impressed by, the officers and directors and their ability to manage the business. The hopes of hefty profits are small, and the risks of losses, or, at best, small gains, is substantial.

COMPANIES WITH LOW PRICE-EARNINGS RATIOS

Buy a stock when nobody else wants it and wait for the "inevitable" turnaround or return to fashion. That's the stock selection strategy of many fundamental investors. The degree of speculation depends on the quality and prospects of the company.

STOCK DIVIDENDS

Stock dividends are extra shares issued to current shareholders, usually on a percentage basis: that is, a 5% stock dividend means that 5 new shares are issued for every 100 old shares. Such a policy can be habit forming, and most companies continue the extra distributions year after year because it conserves cash, keeps shareholders happy, and providers an easy, inexpensive way to expand the number of publicly owned shares and, usually, stockholders.

It's pleasant to receive such a bonus, but be sure that such a payout is justified. The actual dollar profits of the corporation should keep rising. If they stay about the same or decline, stock dividends may be better for show than growth. To evaluate a stock dividend in terms of a company's earning power and the stock's current price:

1 Find the future earnings yield on the current stock price. Use anticipated earnings per share for the current year. If the projected profits are $3 per share and the current price of the stock is 50, the earnings yield is 6%: $3 divided by 50 = .06.

2 Add the stock dividend percentage declared for the current year to the annual cash dividend yield. If the stock dividend is 5% and the cash dividend is 2%, the figure is 7%—the total dividend yield.

If the number 2 figure (7%) exceeds number 1 (6%), a shareholder faces earnings dilution and probable price weakness *unless* the corporate prospects are strong.

But if the profits are $5 per share, the earnings yield is 10%. Since this is more than the total dividend yield (7%), the stock dividend is not excessive.

With stocks selling at low multiples, it's important to do your research. That low price may be a sign of real trouble that can continue longer than anticipated. When you start with stocks at low price-earnings ratios, take the next step and check the estimates of future profits

COMPANIES WITH SMALL CAPITALIZATION
Less than 500,000 Shares of Common Stock

EXCHANGE	COMPANY	SHARES
OTC	AFA Protective System	282,000
OTC	American Underwriters	463,000
OTC	Bonray Drilling	433,000
AS	Clarostat Mfg.	476,000
OTC	Danners, Inc.	488,000
AS	Esquire Radio & Electric	483,000
AS	Frantz Mfg.	382,000
AS	Hastings Mfg.	420,000
OTC	Kahler Corp.	475,000
AS	Kenwin Shops	406,000
AS	Presidential Realty (A)	406,000
NY	Wheeling & Lake Erie	340,000

SOURCE: Standard & Poor's.

(available from your broker or Standard & Poor's). If there are not strong prospects of a corporate comeback, the stock price will probably continue to decline.

The table below shows typical speculations that could turn into investments. All the companies are well rated and have the potential of becoming quality corporations.

STOCKS SELLING BELOW BOOK VALUE

As noted earlier, book value is the net worth per share of common stock: all assets minus all liabilities. When the stock price is below book value, it is at a bargain level in that: (1) the corporation may be worth more dead than alive; if it were liquidated, shareholders would get more from the sale of assets than the current value of the stock; (2) the company may be a candidate for a takeover: when Gulf Oil was acquired by Socal, Gulf stock was selling at about 60% of its book value; (3) this may be a low base if corporate profits improve.

The usefulness of book value as a criterion depends on the type of corporation. Steel firms and manufacturers of heavy machinery have huge investments in plants and equipment so that they usually have a high book value. But they rarely make much money.

On the other hand, a drug manufacturer or retailer will have a low book value but will often turn in excellent earnings. The trick in using book value effectively is to find a company whose stock is trading below that figure and is making a comeback that has not yet been recognized in the marketplace.

In such a situation, you will get a double

BARGAINS?
Some Stocks Whose P/E Ratios Are Low and Whose Profits Are Expected To Rise

COMPANY	PRICE/EARNINGS ON LAST 12 MONTHS	EARNINGS LAST 12 MONTHS	1985	RECENT PRICE
Ahmanson (H. F.) & Co.	7.2	$3.00	$2.63	21
Ashland Oil	9.9	5.81	4.12	57
Bank of New York	9.7	6.69	6.39	65
Citicorp	8.8	6.97	7.12	61
Dayco Corp.	9.7	2.09	2.04	20
First Chicago	9.9	3.22	2.84	32
General Dynamics	9.0	8.50	9.05	77
General Public Util.	9.4	2.02	1.54	19
Great West'n Fin'l.	6.9	5.97	5.02	41
Irving Bank	8.6	6.32	6.14	54
Lockheed Corp.	8.6	6.15	6.10	53
Marine Midland Bks.	8.0	6.58	6.06	53
Mellon Bank Corp.	8.6	7.80	7.13	67

SOURCE: Standard & Poor's.

SELECTED STOCKS SELLING BELOW BOOK VALUE

COMPANY	PRICE	PERCENT BOOK VALUE
Apache Corp.	$9	81%
Armstrong Rubber	15	71
Berkey Inc.	6	79
Chase Manhattan	42	88
Control Data	24	83
Dresser Indus.	18	86
Firestone Tire & Rubber	24	83
First Mississippi	7	84
International Paper	56	84
Kaiser Alum. & Chem.	20	84
Kerr-McGee	30	86
Mesa Petroleum	3	82
Playboy Enterprises	7	82
Timken Co.	48	74
Zale Corp.	34	88

SOURCE: Standard & Poor's.

plus: buying assets at a discount and a higher stock price due to better profits. Just make sure that the assets are real and that the earnings are the result of management's skill, not accounting legerdemain.

OTHER OPPORTUNITIES

For those who can afford extra risks, there are special situations that can be very profitable if you guess right, have ample capital, buy at the right time and the right price, and watch developments closely.

➤ OUT OF BANKRUPTCY These are companies that have gone through the wringer and so start off on a solid base. If new management is competent, the value of the stock will rise, occasionally quickly but usually slowly. It takes time for the improved performance to be recognized.

Ten years ago, when Miller-Wohl, a retail chain, came out of bankruptcy, its shares were at 12½%. They rose to over 56, split 2 for 1, and then fell to about 14. Speculators did well if they bought low and sold near the peak.

In discovering such bargains:

■ *Look for corporations that have resources and a strong position in their field.* The broader the customer base, the greater the chance of success.

■ *Diversify with at least three holdings.* If you're lucky, one will prove to be a winner, the second will stay about even, and the loss on the third will be small. Hopefully, that right choice will pay off well enough to make all the risks worthwhile.

■ *Buy soon after emergence from chapter 11.* At that point, there's the greatest uncertainty and maximum risk but also a low base for future gains.

➤ RESTRICTED STOCKS These are closely held shares that cannot be sold publicly except under SEC rules to prevent potential abuses that involve speculation rather than legitimate investment capital-raising.

Rule 144 bars insiders from selling restricted stock in less than 2 years after issue and mandates that the sale must be made in 90 days and that the number of shares sold must not exceed: (1) 1% of the outstanding shares or (2) the average weekly trading volume for 4 weeks before the sale. The founder can sell at any time if there's need for cash.

Usually, these stocks are of small new companies and are originally sold at 40% or more below market value. If the company is successful, the profits can be high, but it's a tricky business unless you are privy to full information about the company and its plans and progress. When a large block comes to market, the price will usually decline.

➤ SPIN-OFFS These can be good deals when the parent firm is well managed and the new company proves profitable. The goal is generally to sell off shares to raise capital. The old company retains substantial ownership, so if all goes well, everyone wins. But there's no guarantee of success.

Example: National Steel, which over the years had diversified into financial services, sold 3 million shares of FN Financial S&L, to obtain money to modernize its steelmaking facilities. So far, neither the old nor the new shares have been overly profitable.

With spin-offs, the publicity is usually better than the profits.

34 | WINNING THE TAKEOVER GAME

Mergers and acquisitions appear to be here to stay. The tremendous surge of takeover activity on Wall Street has been prompted in part by the basic assumption that it's quicker, easier, and cheaper to buy assets than it is to build them. Every investor hopes to be part of this scene, and yet making money in takeover targets is not an automatic given for you or for anyone else.

The risks are greatest when it's an unfriendly takeover, because this is when the professionals move in and set up arbitrage situations: usually buying the stock of the acquiring company and selling short the stock of the other company. If the merger is completed, the speculator turns in the stock of the winner and receives shares of the surviving firm, which are sold to pay back the loan on the short sale. Once in a while, the positions are reversed. In both cases, there must be ample capital (at least $50,000) and recognition that a wrong guess, delay, or cancellation can cost a bundle: lost capital plus heavy interest charges. Amateurs can have more fun, and lose less, in Atlantic City or Las Vegas.

When you hold stock in the target company, your profits can be welcome, but it's wise to sell quickly and avoid the risks of waiting. *Example:* the stock of Crum & Forster, the big insurance company, sold between 21 and 36 in 1980. When Xerox announced a takeover, the price jumped to 55. This was the time to sell, because no matter how ideal the combination might appear, it would take years for management to settle down and boost total earnings.

On the other hand, takeover offers may fail, so you can lose money if you do not act quickly. On the day that Penn Central offered to buy GK Technologies, GK stock jumped 8¾ points. Because of opposition to the deal, nothing happened for 4 months. Then, PC called off the offer from

fear of lawsuits involving the tragic fire at MGM Grand Hotel, whose electrical system had been installed by GK many years before. At this news, GK stock fell 11 points and the professional arbitrageurs lost $30 million!

Arbitrage is relatively simple when only two firms are involved. The battle becomes a poker game. The professional has to decide only which stock to sell short. Even then, there can be extra risks: long delays (while the interest charges on loans mount) and the danger of a proration pool in the event that more shares are tendered than the buyer wants. Such a situation can play havoc with previous calculations.

When a third (or fourth) party joins the fray, arbitrage becomes more complex, and luck is often more important than skill. *Example:* Bendix went after Martin Marietta which, in turn, enlisted the aid of United Technologies to fight back by offering to take over Bendix.

Along came Allied Corp., which picked up Bendix, kept the Martin stock, and froze out United. The final offer had two tiers: (1) cash for 51% of Bendix shares; (2) an after-the-merger stock package. Some arbitrageurs made out well by buying Bendix at 55 and selling at 85. Others did nothing, so they acquired Allied stock that proved to be worth less than the cash received by the early actors. Now do you see why takeovers and arbitrage are not for amateurs?

If you own stock in a takeover target, you must be prepared to act quickly in order to get the best deal. Your broker will explain your options, and the management of the company will tell you if it approves or disapproves of the proposal—in other words, if it's a friendly or unfriendly takeover.

The acquirer, or firm trying to buy shares in another company, solicits the target company's shareholders through a tender offer. The information that must appear in this offer includes:

- The price to be paid
- The number of shares that will be accepted
- The method of payment—cash or securities or both
- The date when the offer opens
- The date when the offer expires
- Whether shareholders have a right to withdraw shares that have been tendered
- Who is making the tender offer
- Where one gets further information

A tender offer is not written in stone: it can be amended or even canceled if not enough shareholders offer their shares, or if another acquirer makes a better bid.

If you hold a stock that is the subject of a takeover, you'll find that it's not easy to sort out the value of the offer and decide what to do. Even the professional arbitrageurs have trouble in the most intricate deals; after all, the takeover game is rife with fast plays and unpredictable maneuvers. Its uncertainties and complications are so intricate that even the most skillful can lose. Clues are given along the way, but you must first understand the type of offer that you're dealing with.

FRIENDLY TAKEOVERS

A friendly tender offer, as opposed to the unfriendly version, is often unopposed. The terms are outlined in the initial announcement and are seldom changed, with management of the company about to be taken over generally agreeing to them.

LEVERAGED BUYOUTS

Over the past several years, this variation on the friendly takeover theme has become increasingly popular. A leveraged buyout is initiated by a company's management in order to:

- Avoid takeover by another corporation
- Keep control of the company
- Take the company private

In this type of deal, the company's assets and earnings capacity are used in order to secure loans to finance the purchase. Debt is used in a highly leveraged way to buy out almost all the common shareholder equity.

If you own stock in a company which is offered a leveraged buyout, you have no choice but to sell your stock. Frequently the announcement creates additional interest in the stock, which may drive up the price. You will obtain the best price by waiting until the offer is close to closing.

Of course, there is risk in holding the stock, too. If the deal becomes unglued because of government regulations, licensing problems in transferring assets, or any other complication, your shares could fall in price.

BUY-BACKS

This type of tender offer is almost always successful. In a buy-back the company offers to purchase some of its own stock back from its stockholders. In this way, a company can reduce its cash on hand—cash that might make it a likely candidate for a hostile bidder; and it also increases its earnings per share.

Frequently the price of a stock rises upon news of a buy-back. If you have faith in the company, you may not want to tender your shares. Your broker or a good financial service, such as Standard & Poor's or Value Line, can advise you further.

UNFRIENDLY TAKEOVERS

GREENMAIL

Pursuing and purchasing a stock based purely on takeover rumors can often mean you're skating on thin ice. Look at the bath you would have taken in Walt Disney stock after Reliance's attempted takeover. Here's what happened.

In 1984, financier Saul P. Steinberg and a small group of investors, over a period of 2½ months, bought about 11% of Disney shares. Then in the spring of that year, Steinberg bid $67.50 per share for an additional 37.7% of Disney. During the first 3 weeks of the offer, those who owned Disney stock saw their holdings soar some 25%. As it turned out, the wisest course of action was to sell, for those who hesitated lost. Why? Because Disney management, in a surprise move, bought back Steinberg's 11% holdings for $77.50 per share. Steinberg and his company, Reliance Group Holdings, Inc., had a nifty profit of $31.7 million, plus Disney

GREENMAILING: 1984

INVESTORS	COMPANY STAKE	BUY-BACK PRICE, MILLIONS OF DOLLARS	INVESTORS' PROFIT, MILLIONS OF DOLLARS
Saul Steinberg	Walt Disney (11%)	325.5	32
Charles Hurwitz	Castle & Cooke (12%)	70.6	14
Saul Steinberg	Quaker Oats (9%)	47.1	11
Bass Brothers	Texaco (10%)	1,280.0	400
Rupert Murdoch	Warner (9%)	180.6	50
Sir James Goldsmith	St. Regis (9%)	160.0	50

SOURCE: Reprinted from *U.S. News & World Report,* issue of June 25, 1984. Copyright, 1984, *U.S. News & World Report.*

agreed to pay Steinberg $28 million for legal and financing fees. The news for the shareholders was far less pleasant: within only 2 days, Disney stock temporarily fell from $60+ to a little above $45 per share.

The case just described is a classic example of greenmail. This term, a play on the word blackmail, refers to money paid by a corporation to make a potential acquirer go away. It buys the greenmailer's stock at a higher price than the going market price and leaves the rest of the shareholders with stock that usually drops in price.

The corporation, in order to save itself, buys back its stock and the only winner is the greenmailer. The stockholders in such a situation seldom make money, unless they move very quickly. The thousands of Disney shareholders, in fact, were furious not only because they were denied the greenmailer's premium price but also because their shares dropped in price. The incident forced changes in Disney management, which resulted in higher prices for the stock in the long run.

When an offer to buy is unwanted, the game obviously becomes intense, with the poten-

HOW TO EVALUATE A TENDER OFFER

- Read the offer-to-purchase statement sent by the bidder to all shareholders
- Is the offer friendly or hostile? Friendly deals are more likely to be accepted by management, but a hostile offer may attract other offers at higher prices. Consider tendering at any rate, but be alert to what professional arbitrageurs are doing. If they're not tendering, neither should you, and vice versa.
- Find out if you do tender your shares how long you have to take them back—should you have a change of heart.
- Note if the bid price applies to all shares tendered or if it's only a partial tender. Tenders for all stock are generally more profitable than partial tenders. You'll also be faced with the prospect that not all the shares that you tender will be accepted if the offer is oversubscribed.
- Is the takeover for cash, securities, or some of each? Cash is more certain in value than securities, which tend to fluctuate in price. Any newly issued securities may weaken the credit rating of the company.
- Are there possible antitrust problems? It's more likely if the company is part of a regulated industry such as banking, communications, insurance, utilities, etc.
- Does the acquirer have a successful or poor record for completing mergers? Or has he or she sold out for greenmail in the past?

tial risks and rewards much greater than those in a friendly situation. The price of the stock can go sky high. Then again, the whole deal can be shattered.

Because tender offers work quickly (1 month versus 3 to 6 months for a merger), they are popular with hostile bidders. Shareholders, however, must be told by the target company within a 10-day period whether the tender is hostile or friendly.

TO TENDER OR NOT TO TENDER?

After reading this voluminous material, you're still faced with the million dollar question: Should you tender or not?

You have three choices:

1 Tender to the bidder
2 Wait to see if a higher bid is made by a rival company
3 Sell in the market

You must decide between selling your shares upon announcement of the tender offer or waiting until the final settlement—often 3 to 6 months. As the deal comes closer to completion, the price spread tends to narrow. The chances of the deal's being successful are greater if the terms are presented in a formal contract. An agreement in principle is still not a signed deal.

Professional arbitrageurs engage in the business of buying stock after a deal is announced, gambling that a bidding war or a merger will push up the price. They have huge financial resources and exhaustive research facilities and calculate every aspect of a deal, including the cost of their money and the possibility of the deal's breaking up.

One way to handle the situation is to follow what the arbitrageurs are doing. Another is to sell up to half your stock once the takeover intention has been announced, thus protecting your gain against the deal's collapsing. Hang on to the rest of the shares until you're within 10 to 15% of the acquisition bid . . . then sell.

THE CASE FOR SELLING

Begin by noticing how the price of the stock is reacting to the offer and whether or not the deal is likely to go forward. If the price soars, give very serious consideration to selling in the market,

especially if the premium is 50% or better. Another occasion for selling: if you're nervous that the deal will collapse, then you're better off to take the money and run, putting aside any thoughts that you have about making a few extra points if the takeover is successful.

Sometimes, of course, holding on can involve risks. If the deal falls through, the stock may drop to the trading level it was at prior to the tender offer.

THE CASE FOR TENDERING

In many deals the initial offering is merely an open gambit in what becomes an intense, fierce battle for control of the company. How can you tell if there is likely to be a better offer? Value Line suggests these guidelines:

- If management does not endorse the offer, then a better deal or no deal at all is likely.
- If management has been holding discussions with the company making the initial offering, it's likely that the deal will be sweetened.
- If a major shareholder is dissatisfied with the initial terms of the offer, he or she will try to bring pressure to bear for better terms.
- If there are other overtures from serious contenders, a better deal is likely.

With the exception of 1978, about half the time an offer has been successful the deal was sweetened, points out Value Line.

With all takeovers, you must be ready to act quickly on the basis of answers to questions such as these:

- Is this a friendly or hostile takeover? If it's hostile, there's likely to be a battle and higher offers. This can be profitable but will be nervewracking, and there's always a chance that the deal will be called off and you'll be left with little or no gain. *Many takeovers fail: in 1982, of 52 tender offers, only 38 were completed.*
- Is the offer for cash, securities, or both? For most people, cash is best, because it's sure. But if you are in a high tax bracket (as you should be to be involved in such maneuvers), acceptance of cash for shares held for less than 1 year will result in a big tax bill.

- What is the *real* value of the offer—as calculated in the financial press or, better, by your broker's research department? If the stock price of the target company keeps moving up, insiders expect another bidder will move in.

- Who owns large blocks of stock? When the officers or directors of the acquiring company are major shareholders, they will probably stay the course. When a substantial portion of the shares of the target company is closely held, these insiders will call the shots.

- Does the tender offer apply to all or part of the shares? When Sunbeam was acquired by Allegheny International, the winning bid was $41 per share for 50% of the common stock. The rest was swapped for convertibles worth $29 each.

When you own shares of the acquiring company, it's usually wise to sell. Management is using your money for what it believes is a more profitable future, but let 'em prove it first! Du Pont spent billions to take over Conoco and 3 years later had yet to report a nickel profit.

When you own shares of the target company, the odds are in your favor but can be improved by watchful waiting. Once a tender offer has been announced:

- *Sit tight.* Wait until all offers are in before you make any decision. Most offers are originally viewed as unfavorable by management. There's an irate outcry that the price is too low and a scurry to find another potential partner (white knight) to boost the proposed purchase price. Usually these maneuvers will boost the bid.

- *If the deal involves exchanging securities,* consider whether you want to own shares of the acquiring company. Usually, as with Du Pont, the stock price will fall.

- *After the bidding has stopped and there's a firm offer,* sell on the open market rather than wait for full details. This eliminates risks that: (1) the tender will be withdrawn (which can be done without legal penalties); (2) only part of your shares will be acquired and you will end up with a mix of securities you don't want; (3) poor timing will cost you money. Further comments from Terence L. Dono-

ghue, arbitrage specialist with Wood Gundy brokerage firm:

"The risks in takeover stocks are enormous but the rewards can make the standard stock market returns look like pocket change. If you get a 4% spread on nine winning trades, you have a 36% return (less for amateurs who have to pay commissions). But one 20% loser can cut your profits, and if you're wrong twice, you're in trouble.

"If government is going to be involved, whether for antitrust or regulatory approval, skip the deal. This will slow the completion, and lost time can decimate profits.

"Be careful about following corporate raiders ... like T. Boone Pickens, chairman of Mesa Petroleum. He made a lot of money when he bought Superior Oil and sold his shares back to the company, but amateurs who bought because he was in the deal didn't do well."

FINDING TAKEOVER TARGETS

The current wave of corporate takeovers has certainly encouraged private investors as well as institutions to play the "guess who's coming to our company" game. Companies likely to become takeovers possess certain common characteristics (see box on page 284).

If you're looking for takeover candidates, try thinking as an acquirer does and gather as much data as possible: annual reports, 10-ks, proxy statements, research reports, etc. No one factor alone makes for a takeover, but in combination, you may find a winner. Yet never buy

---

TAKEOVERS

In 1985, there were 3,001 transactions, which includes all U.S. mergers, acquisitions, and takeovers. That's the highest number since 1974, when there were 4,040. The amount of money involved in 1985 was $179.8 billion, an all-time record.

SOURCE: W. T. Grimm & Co., Chicago (merger and acquisition consultants).

TAKEOVER INGREDIENTS

- A stock selling below book value per share. Purchase of this type of company provides the buyer with assets that can easily be sold, or it can result in the acquisition of assets far below the present cost of constructing them.
- Low debt when compared with equity. This gives a company untapped borrowing power for financing a leveraged buyout.
- Selling at less than 5 times cash flow.
- Selling below 10 times earnings. A low P/E enables the acquirer to more readily pay for the acquisition.
- Large cash holdings. Enable the purchaser to help pay for the acquisition.
- Hidden assets. (Assets carried on the balance sheet at less than their current value.)
- Business value. (Worth of the business to an acquirer, based on historical earning power, product line, market penetration.)
- Small number of shares outstanding.
- History of takeover interest and previous bids.
- Owners who may be willing to sell.

any company if it is not a good investment in and of itself. Select a stock with solid fundamentals—one that, should there never be a takeover, you'd be happy owning or one whose basic qualities fit your investment goals.

Start by looking at a company's balance sheet, which is a matter of public record. The ingredients for identifying a firm that is appealing to an acquirer are readily identifiable. One item alone, such as plenty of cash, is unlikely to capture a suitor's fancy, but in combination with other ingredients, it may tempt a knight or two.

OTHER SIGNS OF A TAKEOVER

➤ THE 5% SIGN Whenever a company buys 5% or more of another company's stock, that could be an indication of takeover interest.

The company must report its 5%+ purchase

to the SEC within 10 days in a 13D filing. You can read about it in the daily *SEC News Digest* and in the monthly *SEC Official Summary of Security Transactions and Holdings.* These can be purchased from the SEC or read in regional SEC offices.

Under SEC regulations, a company planning to seek control of another company must make its offer known within 5 days of filing the 13D. The company naturally does not want to tell the world of its intentions, so many times they will file the 13D but indicate that they're doing so for investment purposes only. Then later on they change direction and make the tender offer.

➤ INSIDER TRADING When corporate insiders trade in a stock, it must be reported to the SEC. Every week the commission compiles a list of stock purchases, sales, and exercises of options by corporate insiders. This is public information and also appears in the *SEC Official Summary of Security Transactions and Holdings.*

Insider movement may indicate that something is afoot, especially if the trading increases or decreases sharply. Insider buys are obviously a better indication of takeover possibilities than insider sales.

➤ OPTION TRADING If news of a takeover is floating around Wall Street and option trading in the stock has increased, it *may* mean the story has substance.

➤ TRADING An unusual amount of stock trading activity may signal takeover activity.

💲IF YOU DARE: Play the options as one way to guard against losing if a takeover deal falls apart.

💲IF YOU DON'T: Sell in the marketplace as soon as the stock hits your target goal.

FOR FURTHER INFORMATION

The 1986 Merger & Acquisition Sourcebook
Quality Services Company
5290 Overpass Road
Santa Barbara, CA 93111
$115

A 675-page looseleaf directory which lists financial data on the buyers and sellers involved in the year's mergers as well as facts on the deals that fell through.

MAJOR INSIDER TRANSACTIONS

TIMELINESS RANK	RECENT PRICE	COMPANY	INSIDER, TITLE	SHARES TRADED	DATE	PRICE RANGE	SHARES CURRENTLY HELD
PURCHASES							
2	19	Caesars World	M.T. Sosnoff*	198,600	7/8/86– 7/28/86	$18.00–$19.75	3,643,000
2	20	National Education	H.D. Bright, Pres.	1,500	7/11/86	$18.25	447,225
3	47	Olin Corp.	S.D. Medhus, V.P.	1,000	7/22/86	$42.63–$43.00	1,000
2	64	Pitney Bowes	D.T. Kimball, Dir.	500	7/7/86	$59.25	3,000
SALES							
2	28	Anheuser-Busch	J.H. Purnell, V.P.	16,540	7/31/86	$28.50–$28.56	22,710
3	42	Chrysler	E.T. Pappert, V.P.	17,750	7/15/86	$34.75	10,000
3	322	Teledyne, Inc.	G. Kozmetsky, Dir.	3,000	7/1/86– 7/2/86	$335.75–$336.00	602,902
–	83	Time Inc.	J.J. Collins, V.P.	3,744	7/9/86	$84.63	5,794

* Beneficial owner of more than 10% of common stock.

SOURCE: Value Line, August 29, 1986 (© 1986 Value Line, Inc.).

WHEN RAIDERS STRIKE—NOTABLE TAKEOVER ATTEMPTS

TARGET COMPANY	ORIGINAL SUITOR	ULTIMATE BUYER	PRICE PAID, (BILLION $)
Gulf Oil	T. Boone Pickens	Chevron	$13.2
Phillips Petroleum	T. Boone Pickens, Carl Icahn	remained independent	$ 4.5
Continental Group	James Goldsmith	Kiewit-Murdock Investment Group	$ 2.7
American Natural Resources	Coastal Corp.	Coastal Corp.	$ 2.5
St. Regis	James Goldsmith	Champion International	$ 1.8
Stauffer Chemical	Carl Icahn	Chesebrough-Pond's	$ 1.3
Avco	Irwin Jacobs	Textron	$ 1.2
Bergen Brunswig	Leucadia National	National Intergroup	$ 0.7
Scovill	Belzberg Brothers	Belzberg Brothers	$ 0.5

SOURCE: U.S. News & World Report, April 8, 1985.

ACQUISITION-SPEAK

A bewildering assortment of elaborate techniques and strategies has been developed by target companies to fend off corporate raiders. In the process, a brand new lexicon has blossomed full grown.

- **Bear hug.** An offer that's so good the directors of the takeover target company can't refuse.
- **Crown jewel.** A takeover target company often sells its most prized subsidiary in order to discourage the raider.
- **Front loading.** Quickly acquiring control of a company by making a high cash offer to insiders and then paying off other shareholders with securities or a combination of securities and cash that is worth less.
- **Gray knight.** A company that enters uninvited into the scene of a hostile merger and offers to buy the target company. It's regarded as gray until its terms are revealed.
- **Pac-man.** A maneuver in which the takeover target firm "bites" back at the raider by turning the tables and trying to take it over. A counterbid for control.
- **Poison pill.** A new issue of preferred stock that gives holders the right to redeem it at an enormous premium after a takeover. It boosts the cost to an acquiring company and is meant to discourage them.
- **Porcupine provisions.** Also known as shark repellent, these are corporate bylaws designed to put obstacles in the way of an acquiring company.
- **Risk arbitrage.** The purchase of shares of a takeover candidate at the market price in the hope that the merger or takeover will go through at a higher price.
- **Saturday night special.** A maneuver in which raiders elect their own candidates to a board of directors to help take control of the company.
- **Scorched-earth policy.** Means by which a company tries to turn itself into an ugly duckling and therefore appear unattractive to any buyer. *Example:* arranging for all debts to come due right after a merger.
- **Shark repellents.** Defensive methods used by companies to fend off takeovers; see also porcupine provisions.
- **Staggered boards.** A shark repellent in which companies adopt bylaws that permit only half the board of directors to come up for election each year. This prevents a *Saturday night special.*
- **Supermajority.** Requires a supermajority of stockholders' approval for a takeover. The corporation determines what constitutes a supermajority—it can be as much as 90 to 99%.
- **Two-tier bid.** A maneuver in which a combination of cash now and securities later is offered to pressure shareholders into surrendering their stock early on in the game and before another corporation makes a counter offer. The SEC ruling gives stockholders a minimum of 20 business days to respond to this type of offer.
- **White knight.** A company that will block an unfriendly merger, often at the suggestion of the target company, by taking it over on more favorable terms.

Babson's Investment & Barometer Letter
Babson's Reports
Wellesley Hills, MA 02181
$96

The section "Action Items—Our Advice" discusses tender offers now in progress and what to do about them. Newsletter is a weekly, but this column may or may not appear weekly.

Acquisition/Divestiture Weekly Report
Quality Services Company
5290 Overpass Road
Santa Barbara, CA 93111
$225

A weekly newsletter which provides data on companies involved in mergers plus a list of companies looking to buy and looking to sell.

Business & Acquisition Newsletter
2600 South Gessner Road
Houston, TX 77063
$100

A monthly newsletter reporting on companies up for sale.

Mergers & Acquisitions
229 South 19th Street
Philadelphia, PA 19103
$95

A quarterly magazine devoted to professional analysis of mergers.

The Value Line OTC Special Situations
    Service
711 Third Avenue
New York, NY 10017
$300

Bimonthly newsletter with facts on OTC mergers.

Consensus of Insiders
P.O. Box 10247
Fort Lauderdale, FL 33334
$247

Monthly newsletter which reports on insider trading in corporate stock options.

The Insiders
3471 North Federal Highway
Fort Lauderdale, FL 33306
$49

Semimonthly newsletter ranks companies and industries by insider trading activity.

Insider Indicator
2230 N.E. Brazee Street
Portland, OR 97212
$145

Semimonthly lists firms in which company officials are trading in the same way: buying or selling.

Street Smart Investing
P.O. Box 173
Katonah, NY 10536
$350

Newsletter tracks the 13D filings with the SEC made by any shareholder who acquires 5 percent or more of a company's stock.

PART SEVEN

TAXES AND EVERY INVESTOR

Last fall, the U.S. Congress passed the 1986 tax bill, the most massive tax overhaul seen in decades. And, unless you master the basic points of the new bill, you could unwittingly lose hundreds of dollars to the IRS. It is particularly crucial that every financial decision you make during 1987 be made only after reading the following four chapters.

These next sections not only explain the pertinent changes in the law but also show investors how to take advantage of these changes. Among the topics covered are:

- Social Security, IRAs, 401(K) plans, and pension benefits
- Home ownership and real estate opportunities
- Legitimate tax shelters
- Estate planning
- Life insurance and annuities

35 | THE NEW TAX BILL AND YOUR INVESTMENTS

The sweeping revisions of the 1986 Tax Reform Bill, achieved after months of congressional haggling and compromise, touch the lives of virtually every American. In broad terms, the bill shifts about $120 billion of tax burden from individuals to business over a period of 5 years. More specifically, it slashes personal tax rates. To pay for these rate reductions, the legislators either cut or eliminated a huge lineup of previously popular tax breaks, including a host of deductions, tax credits, and shelters.

The most radical change, of course, is the drop in the top tax rate for individuals from 50 to 28%, the lowest maximum rate the country has seen since 1931. In addition, cherished deductions, long used by middle and upper income taxpayers, have been wiped away, including deductions for interest on consumer loans (credit cards and auto loans) and state sales tax. IRA deductions have been reduced, home equity loans restricted, and the advantages of charitable giving diminished. Capital gains from the sale of stocks and other assets, whether long- or short-term, will be taxed at the same rate as dividends, wages, and interest income.

This chapter is designed to show you *as an investor* how to wade through the new regulations, find ways to save on taxes, and, at the same time, invest profitably. Tax considerations are clearly important when it comes to investing, but they should never be allowed to eclipse the basics. Further ramifications of the new bill are analyzed in Chapter 13 on tax-exempt bonds, Chapter 36 on tax shelters, and Chapter 38 on retirement.

INDIVIDUAL TAX RATES

The key change, and the one that appeals most to Americans, is the sharp drop in the top tax rate on individual income, from 50% down to 28%. In addition, the number of tax rates is reduced from 15 (ranging from 11 to 50%) to only 2: 28% and 15%. The lowest rate, 15%, applies to all taxable income for married couples up to $29,750. The top rate, 28%, applies to income above $29,750. For single taxpayers, the breaking point between 15% and 28% is $17,850. These cuts won't take full effect until 1988.

During 1987, a transition year, the rates blend old and new, with the top rate dropping from 50 to 38.5%.

► THE TRUE TOP RATE To some extent, the top 28% rate is misleading, because certain high-income families—those earning $71,900 (joint) or $43,150 (single)—pay a 5% surcharge, or 33% total rate. When income rises above $149,250, this 5% surcharge is replaced by the flat 28% rate from the first dollar. The surcharge serves to phase out the lower 15% rate for high-income people.

MARGIN LOANS

Under the new tax bill, if you borrow on margin from your broker, the interest you pay is deductible only to the extent that it is offset by investment income (from dividends, capital gains, and limited partnerships.) For example, if you want to deduct $1,500 worth of interest on your margin loan, you must report at least $1,500 of investment income to the IRS.

Another new ruling: you must use the money borrowed to make an investment. (Previously, you could borrow for any purpose.) Keep careful records to document the fact that you used the money for an investment.

$ HINT: Determine your monthly and year-to-date margin interest expense versus income from stocks and bonds. If your investment expense is larger than your

TAX RATES FOR 1987 ONLY

SINGLES	TAXED AT RATE OF:	MARRIED COUPLES FILING JOINT RETURN
$54,000 and above	38.5%	$90,000 and above
$27,000 to $54,000	35%	$45,000 to $90,000
$16,000 to $27,000	28%	$28,000 to $45,000
$ 1,800 to $16,800	15%	$ 3,000 to $28,000
Under $1,800	11%	Under $3,000

income, then talk to your broker about converting low-yielding stocks to convertible bonds or switching tax-free munis into taxable investments.

THE NEW LANDSCAPE AND YOUR INVESTMENTS

At first glance, the new tax laws seem merely to move the burden of $120 million from individuals onto corporate America. And indeed, the reform erases most of the special incentives and shelters cherished by industry for years, reversing a 35-year trend in which businesses have been paying less and less of the federal tax burden. In the early 1950s, for example, corporate America paid approximately 34% of total taxes; in 1985 its share had shrunk to just 13%! The lawmakers contend that, with the revisions, market efficiency will return to industries that have been propped up by tax shelters and other loopholes, which encouraged investors to finance money-losing operations in all kinds of deals, from energy to farming. With these loopholes closed, investment capital theoretically will flow into areas where profits are high, and economic growth will ensue.

In reviewing your investment portfolio, the impact of tax reform on individual industries is a key consideration. Most importantly, the bill has freed investment decision making from tax considerations in three distinct ways: (1) all capital gains will be taxed at the same rate as dividend and regular income; (2) there will be no tax advantage to holding a stock for 6 months or longer since the favorable long-term capital gains rate is being eliminated; and (3) most tax shelters have been given the kiss of

death. (Note that, under the transition rule, any long-term capital gains collected in 1987 will be taxed no higher than 28%, even though short-term gains from assets held 6 months or less will be taxed as high as 38.5%. Starting in 1988, long-term gains will receive no special treatment and will be taxed as high as 33%.)

Over the long run, therefore, financial assets

FIVE STEPS FOR EVERY INVESTOR

Based on the Tax Reform Bill of 1986, you should take the following five steps immediately in consultation with your broker or accountant.

1. Review your portfolio with an eye to increasing income-producing assets. Long-term capital gains have lost favorable tax treatment.
2. Consider more frequent trading, again because holding a stock 6 months or more no longer has any tax benefits.
3. Keep contributing to your IRA, but at the same time study the benefits of tax-deferred annuities as a viable alternative.
4. Review all tax shelters.
5. Review your retirement plans, keeping in mind that lump sum payments not rolled over into an IRA are subject to a 10% penalty and that 10-year forward averaging has been reduced to 5 years.

will gain in appeal, and tax considerations will be less important in buying and selling securities. High-yielding investments in particular make more sense than ever, since lower rates allow investors to keep more of this income and since the distinction between short- and long-term capital gains has been eliminated. (Of course, any stock that increases in value should not be overlooked. Appreciation remains as solid a way to make money as before reform.)

Lower tax rates are not the only reason to consider dividend-yielding stocks. Capital gains are now taxed like ordinary income. In the past, the top rate on capital gains was only 20%. Starting in 1987, 100% of capital gains will be taxed; the top rate will be 28%.

Under the new tax law, you will still be able to use capital losses to offset your regular income. For example, $1,500 worth of long-term losses can offset the same amount of wages. However, the amount of ordinary income that can be offset by capital losses each year is limited to $3,000.

So the marketplace, rather than our tax code, is now shaping investment decisions. As John H. Bryan, Jr., chairman of the Sara Lee Corp., said in response to the massive reform: "The way we conduct business will be vastly more along economic lines and less along tax-motivated lines." And so it should be for you as an investor. You must reexamine a whole parade of decisions—from selecting stocks and bonds to planning your retirement. The elimination of special capital gains treatment gives new glow to income-producing investments.

SELECTING STOCKS

The massive overhaul of the tax law created far-reaching changes in the attractiveness of a number of investments. The five key rulings to keep in mind as you plan your portfolio are:

1. The top corporate tax rate was reduced from 46 to 34% for taxable years beginning January 1, 1987. Companies with taxable income below $50,000 have a tax rate of only 15%; those between $50,000 and $75,000 are taxed at a rate of 25%. (For taxable years including July 1, 1987, blended rates apply.)
2. The investment tax credit (ITC) has been repealed.
3. Depreciation schedules are less generous.

4. Incentives for risk-oriented investors to finance start-up companies or venture capital deals or to partake in tax shelters have been virtually eliminated.
5. A 20% alternative minimum tax (AMT) now applies to all corporations.

The AMT is an important consideration for investors, because companies that for years have paid little or no tax, such as General Electric, W. R. Grace, and Boeing, will now have to pay up. The AMT requires each company to figure out its taxes twice, once using the standard formula and once using the AMT formula, and to pay the higher of the two amounts. An exemption of $40,000 is given to small businesses, but this is phased out for firms with more than $150,000 in income subject to the AMT.

The AMT actually reduces the value of some so-called "preference" items, such as accelerated depreciation of plant and equipment and tax-exempt bond interest. It also cuts in half the difference between book income (the profits of the company as reported to shareholders) and actual income. Industries that in the past paid low taxes and also benefited from accelerated depreciation include aerospace, forestry, mining, paper, railroads, and in some cases property-casualty insurers.

The AMT is not the only major change affecting stocks. Capital intensive industries have been hurt by loss of the investment tax credit (ITC), which ranged from 6 to 10% of the actual cost of equipment. Repeal of this tax break increases the effective cost of new plants and consequently reduces a company's cash flow.

Depreciation allowances were also reduced, since the new law lengthens write-off periods for many assets. The longer write-off periods mean, of course, smaller yearly tax deductions for companies.

As an investor, you should shift your emphasis away from heavy industry and those companies that spend massive amounts on facilities and equipment (see box) and into companies involved in consumer and/or nondurable goods: information, recreation, entertainment, advertising, and other services. Here's how some of the major industries are likely to react to the new tax law over the next year:

➤ ADVERTISING Big taxpayers under the old law, ad agencies should benefit from reform. Spending for advertising is likely to rise over

---

INDUSTRIES HURT BY ITC REPEAL

Aerospace/	Electronics	Rails
Defense	Leasing	Steel
Air Transport	Companies	Textile
Aluminum	Machinery	Mfgrs.
Autos & Parts	Metals	Tire &
Chemicals	Oil Service	Rubber
Coal	Paper	Trucks
Computers	Pollution	Utilities
Electrical	Control	
Equipment		

SOURCE: Standard & Poor's *The Outlook*, August 27, 1986.

---

the next two years as retailers and consumer goods manufacturers have more income to spend on promotion. One negative: loss of foreign tax credits will hurt those agencies doing a large percentage of business overseas.

➤ AIRLINES/RAILROADS Airlines will feel the loss of the ITC and tax-subsidized leasing arrangements for planes. However, increases in consumer spending due to the cut in individual tax rates could boost business. Railroads, a capital intensive industry, will be hard hit without exception.

➤ AUTOMOBILES Greater disposable income is expected to offset loss of the ITC and a less generous depreciation schedule. Lower financing deals offered by the Big Three should also increase sales.

➤ BANKS Although the key to this industry's prosperity has been and continues to be the overall economy, several new provisions are worrisome, in particular the elimination of the deductibility of reserves for loan losses. Previously banks could avoid paying taxes but under the revisions banks with assets of $500 million or more are allowed to deduct loan losses from income *only* when they are charged off as bad debts. In addition, banks can no longer deduct allocations to reserves for future bad loans.

Another key change eliminates the ability of banks to deduct the interest they pay on money used to finance holdings of tax-exempt securities. This affects regional banks in particular, which are large holders of municipals. These changes could be partially offset if the new tax bill stimulates a healthier economy.

➤ ELECTRONICS The cut in the research and development tax credit from 30 to 25% is likely to squeeze profit margins here. The credit permits companies to deduct from their tax payment a percentage of any increased amounts spent on research. (Note: the credit is based on *increases* in research spending, not on the overall amount.) Because it is a credit and therefore comes directly off the amount of tax owed, it is more valuable than a mere deduction.

Electronic companies will also suffer from the death of the ITC, which reduced the after-tax cost of capital spending. New rulings not only affect the companies themselves but are likely to discourage sales of computers to the public.

The computer software segment, a high-tax industry, is expected to fare better from the rate reduction in corporate taxes.

➤ FOOD/BEVERAGES/TOBACCO The corporate tax rate cut helps these industries as does increased consumer spending. Standard & Poor's analysts suggest looking at CPC International, Conagra, H. J. Heinz, Hershey Foods, Coca-Cola, PepsiCo, Anheuser-Busch, RJR Nabisco, and Philip Morris.

➤ HEAVY INDUSTRY On the whole, capital intensive industries are hurt by the bill, which discourages new investments and hinders plant and factory modernization and expansion. Repeal of the ITC for dollars spent on machinery and plants, plus reduction of depreciation levels, is having a negative impact on industries such as steel, appliances, farm equipment, and paper/forest products.

Efforts to upgrade plants are being sharply curtailed and as Burnell R. Roberts, chief executive of the Mead Corp., said, "Anything that discourages investment to maintain world competition is certainly ... a detriment." The changes affect leasing as well as purchasing of new equipment.

➤ INSURANCE Earnings from cash-value life insurance continue to receive tax-deferred treatment. Annuities, which are sold by insurance companies, guarantee future payments, and taxes on this annuity income continue to be deferred until you begin receiving payments. Property and casualty insurers now must pay taxes on 20% of unearned premiums and on 15% of tax-exempt income, most of which stems from their extensive municipal bond portfolios.

➤ MILITARY INDUSTRY Large defense contractors

could benefit because of the drop in the tax rate. In addition, a number of big contracts (C-5 cargo plane, F16 fighter, and B-1 bomber) come due in the next few years. Companies such as McDonnell Douglas and General Dynamics have set aside millions in anticipation of paying taxes at the old higher rate. Yet the law now allows them to pay taxes at the new lower rates. The long-term prospects are less positive, however, since these companies will no longer be able to defer most of their taxes until a project's completion.

➤ OIL INDUSTRY The new tax bill is still very much overshadowed by the 1985 plunge in the price of crude, which in turn caused sharp cutbacks in capital spending. Prior to tax reform, depressed oil prices had forced companies to trim spending.

A negative for independent producers: the restriction on tax shelters. Now, only owners of working interest in a well (as opposed to royalty owners) can deduct losses in excess of income. (See Chapter 36 on tax shelters.)

➤ PUBLISHING These companies could see a 10% or more earnings increase because of the reduction in the corporate tax rate. Capital spending here is minimal, so repeal of the ITC has little effect. Increased advertising by retailers should help the bottom line for newspapers and magazines. Companies to research: Dow Jones, Harcourt Brace Jovanovich, Houghton Mifflin, Knight Ridder, Lee Enterprises, Meredith Corp., and Tribune Co.

➤ REAL ESTATE Construction of office and apartment buildings, often financed through tax shelter programs, is hard hit by the new law. Write-offs for nonresidential property have been lengthened from 19 to 21½ years, which is bound to reduce the amount of investment dollars in development and new construction. Family home demand, however, is expected to remain healthy, since home ownership is one of the few remaining legitimate tax shelters. Mortgage interest deductions will increase in relative importance since there are so few other deductions available. The rise in disposable income will also benefit this sector. (See also Chapter 37 on real estate.)

➤ RETAILING This industry, which has historically paid among the highest taxes, is one of the biggest beneficiaries from the drop in corporate tax rates. The anticipated rise in disposable income should also widen profit margins.

Drug retailers, for whom the ITC was not a major feature, could post impressive earnings. Large retailers that do a great deal of business on credit could suffer somewhat, however, since consumers are no longer able to deduct interest on their credit card and/or installment debts. According to analysts at Standard & Poor's, Sears Roebuck and J.C. Penney could be hurt, whereas the outlook for Federated Department Stores, Ames, K Mart, The Limited, and Woolworth is positive.

➤ SECURITIES/FINANCIAL SERVICES Brokerage firms, which pay high taxes, should benefit from the reduction in rates. Most Wall Streeters expect a boost in the brokerage business, especially as investors shift out of tax shelters and over into equities. The ending of the 6-month holding period for long-term capital gains may also lead to greater trading and more commission revenues for this non-capital intensive industry.

➤ UTILITIES Public utility companies were primary beneficiaries of the investment tax credit. The full effect of this loss will probably not be felt until several years from now. In the meantime, investors seeking high-yielding stocks will do well with utilities, but monitor them carefully. (See Chapter 28.)

THE ALTERNATIVE MINIMUM TAX

This tax was designed to make certain that Americans with high incomes and high deductions would still have to pay at a rate of 20% on their adjusted gross income. The 1986 Tax Reform Bill increased the AMT to 21%. So, no matter how rich you are, no matter how many loopholes or tax shelters your accountant finds for you, if you have a high income, you may still have to pay some federal income tax.

You can easily determine if you are subject to the alternative minimum tax by following these steps:

1   Add all your preference items (see following list) to your adjusted gross income.

2   From this amount, subtract $40,000 if you are married and filing jointly, $30,000 if you are single, or $20,000 if you are married and filing separately.

3   Multiply this amount by a flat 21%. The result is your minimum tax.

If your standard tax is less than this figure, you

must pay the alternative minimum tax. The AMT is imposed only when it is greater than the regular tax, reduced by certain credits.

Certain preference items (line items that get favorable treatment on your regular income) increase your chances of being vulnerable to the AMT. These include:

1   Accelerated depreciation on property you own that is placed in service after 1986
2   Certain costs associated with tax shelters, such as research and development costs and intangible drilling costs
3   Local taxes and interest on investments that do not generate income
4   Tax-exempt interest on newly issued private activity bonds
5   Untaxed appreciation on charitable contributions of appreciated property

Deductions that reduce your AMT are:

1   Medical expenses at the point that they exceed 10% of your gross income
2   Charitable contributions, generally up to 50% of your gross income
3   Casualty losses in excess of 10% of gross income
4   Interest costs on your home
5   Certain estate taxes
6   Interest costs to the extent that they do not exceed your net investment income

With the new alternative minimum tax, there is a danger that certain tax shelters may reduce your regular taxable income to such an extent that you will wind up paying the larger alternative minimum tax. Monitor any sheltering you do with your accountant on a continual basis.

$ HINT: Since 1985, the IRS has required taxpayers to make estimated tax payments to cover taxes due under the AMT category. This affects investors with large portfolios. If you have substantial capital gains and/or tax shelter write-offs, figure your AMT liability using IRS Form 6251 and then make certain this amount is covered through withholding or quarterly estimated tax payments.

BORROWED MONEY & BONDS

In the past, the IRS allowed you to borrow money to buy bonds, and to the extent that the interest rate on your loan exceeded the interest income from the bond, you had a deduction. This deduction could then be used to offset other current income.

Beginning in 1984, write-off of interest for bonds purchased on margin was limited. Now interest cannot be deducted until the bonds are redeemed and the income to be offset is actually reported.

This ruling killed one of the most popular year-end tax saving strategies of all times. In the past, you could borrow money to buy a Treasury bond or note that matured after the end of the year. The interest on the borrowed money was deductible in the current year, yet you were not taxed on it until you sold the T-bill in the next year.

Now, however, to the extent that you have unrealized income on the T-bill, you are not allowed to deduct the interest expense. Your deduction is deferred until you sell the T-bill. This also applies to other debt instruments.

DIVIDEND INCOME

In the eyes of the IRS, not every bit of your dividend and interest income is the same, and the way in which you report it can make a big difference—with respect to not only how much income tax you must pay but also whether or not you will be audited.

If you received any dividend income during the year, then you must fill out Schedule B, Part II, in order to report it.

➤ CASH DIVIDENDS If you received dividends from IBM, Ford Motors, General Electric, or any other corporation, the amount is reported by the company directly to the IRS. You, in turn, receive Form 1099 information slips from each corporation telling precisely how much you received for the year. Report this same amount, exactly, on Schedule B.

➤ STOCK DIVIDENDS There are times, of course, when you receive a stock dividend rather than cash. Your original cost is now allocated over a greater number of shares.

➤ DIVIDEND REINVESTMENT PLANS As was described in Chapter 32, you may sign up for automatic reinvestment of your dividends if you own stock in certain companies. In such cases, the corporation pays your regular dividend with stock, *not* cash. The IRS maintains that since you could have had cash but elected not to, you will be taxed the same year you receive the dividend.

➤ RETURN OF CAPITAL Corporations sometimes give a return of capital distribution. If this is the case it will be so designated on your 1099 slip. Any return of capital is not taxed; however, your basis of stock must be reduced by whatever the amount is.

➤ INSURANCE DIVIDENDS Any dividends you may receive on veterans' insurance are *not* taxed, and dividends received from regular life insurance are generally not taxed. However, if you are in doubt, check with your accountant or insurance company.

➤ OTHER TYPES OF DIVIDENDS Money market mutual funds pay what is called a dividend, and you should list it as such on your tax return.

If you have an interest-bearing checking account with a savings and loan or a credit union, you may collect interest, although it is sometimes referred to as dividend income. Be

CORPORATIONS THAT PAY NO DIVIDENDS

COMPANY	STANDARD & POOR'S RATING
Anderson Clayton	B
Bally's Park Place	NR (no rating)
Blair (John)	B+
Burndy Corp.	B+
Circus Circus	NR
Clayton Homes	NR
Control Data	B
Crown Cork & Seal	B+
Data General	B
Federal Express	B
Golden Nugget	B
La Quinta Motor Inns	B+
Litton Industries	B+
National Semiconductor	B−
Paradyne Corp.	B−
Ramada Inns	B−
Rohr Industries	B
Teledyne Inc.	B+
Toys R Us	B+

SOURCE: Standard & Poor's.

DEDUCTIONS FOR THE INVESTOR

Section 212 of the Tax Reform Act of 1984 allowed you to deduct certain expenses incurred to produce and collect income and to manage or maintain property held to make income. Among the deductible items are:

- Subscriptions to investment publications
- Cost of books on investing and taxes
- Clerical expenses
- Insurance
- Safety deposit box rent
- Fees for accounting or investment advice and for legal advice if related to tax or investment matters
- Related taxes
- Expenses directly related to tax (but not investment) seminars, including transportation
- Travel expenses to visit your broker, your safe deposit box, and your tax accountant or lawyer
- Computers: the cost of a computer used in managing your investments is sometimes deductible. (If you use your computer for business over 50% of the time, you can depreciate it over 5 years and get a tax credit of up to 10% on the cost.) For more information, write for the pamphlet *The Personal Computer Tax Shelter,* Research Press, Inc., Box 8137-K, Prairie Valley, Kansas 66208.
- Losses: if you sell assets at a loss, you can deduct up to $3,000 of net losses annually.
- IRA or Keogh account custodian fees
- Securities that became worthless

INTEREST DEDUCTIONS
- Penalties paid on early savings withdrawals
- Mortgage prepayment penalties
- Points paid on loan financing for primary residences

aware: if this interest is reported on the 1099 slip as dividends, then you too should report it as dividend income.

TIMELY MOVES: WISE YEAR-END INVESTMENT STRATEGIES

TAX STRATEGIES

- If you have bond losses, you can consider swapping these bonds for other similar bonds. This gives you a deductible loss without changing your financial situation.
- If you have been buying or selling commodities, a different set of tax rules applies. Any gain or loss is treated as short term, no matter how long you held the commodity contract.
- If you own stock in a corporation whose long-term outlook is favorable but whose stock has dropped in price, you may want to take a loss for tax purposes but not give up your position entirely. You can buy more stock now at the lower price and sell your original holdings 31 days later. (You must wait the 31 days in order to avoid the "wash sale rule," which prevents loss deductions on sale or repurchase transactions made within 31 days.) The risk involved is of course that the stock could continue to fall in price.
- If you own stock that has gone way up in price since you purchased it and you feel it is near its peak and you want to lock in your profit but not pay taxes this year, you can "sell short against the box." In other words, you can keep your stock until the covering date next year when you then will be taxed.

BOND SWAPS

Another year-end strategy that can help save on taxes is a bond swap. You'll find that under certain circumstances it pays to sell bonds worth less than their initial cost in order to set up a tax loss and then reinvest that same money in a similar bond. By converting a paper loss to an actual loss, you can offset any taxable gains earned in more profitable investments. In the process of swapping, you may also be able to increase your yield.

If you're thinking of doing a bond swap, don't wait until the last days of the year. It may take your broker several weeks to locate an appropriate bond.

Bond swaps involve two steps:
- Selling assets that are worth less now than their original purchase price
- Replacing these assets with similar (but not the same) assets

Although you can use any asset, municipal bonds are the favorite, primarily because there are so many available. It's relatively easy to find a bond of a different issuer with the same interest rate, maturity date, and degree of safety as your original bond. By immediately purchasing similar bonds for approximately the same price as the ones you sold, you restore your market position and your income.

Even if you didn't make a killing in the market this year but you took some investment profits, a bond swap can help reduce your tax bite. Here's how it works.

If you own bonds purchased when interest rates were lower, they are probably worth less in the secondary market today. If you sell them, you can take a long-term capital loss which can be used dollar for dollar to offset any gains (first against any long-term gains and if there are none, against short-term gains). If you have no long- or short-term capital gains, the loss can be used to offset up to $3,000 of taxable income, on a $1-to-$1 basis. If your loss is greater than that, it can be carried over into the next year.

Any of these steps involves taking a loss to reduce your taxes, but at the same time you've lost your position in the bond market along with any income that you were receiving from the bonds. A bond swap enables you to keep your position by buying comparable bonds selling for approximately the same price.

➤ STATE INCOME TAX A bond swap is also useful if you move from a state with no income tax to one that has an income tax. Buy municipal bonds issued by the new state that are not subject to state taxes.

➤ DEALING WITH THE IRS The Internal Revenue Service does not recognize a loss for tax purposes if you have swapped for a new bond that is identical to the one that you've been holding.

In order for the IRS to recognize a loss for tax purposes, you must buy bonds of a different issuer or with a different maturity date or coupon.

➤ SWAPPING COSTS Unlike stocks and most

other securities, where commissions are noted quite separately from the purchase or sale price, municipal bonds have their commission included in the price of the bond. Commissions range from 1 to 3%, i.e., $10 to $30 per $1,000 face value bond, which means that a swap involving $50,000 worth of bonds could entail a commission somewhere between $50 and $150.

SHIFTING INCOME TO CHILDREN

According to the new law, unearned income of a child aged 14 or less that is derived from assets, including stocks and bonds, transferred from parent to child is taxed at the parent's rate when this income exceeds $1,000 per year. If, on the other hand, the child is over 14, the income is taxed at the child's rate, presumably lower than the parent's.

The new bill in effect has put an end to the Clifford trust, which was one of the most popular ways to reduce taxes by transferring assets to children.

If you wish to give money to your children but you don't want it to be taxed at your rate, then you are limited to a handful of choices. One, of course, is tax-free municipal bonds. Another is U.S. EE savings bonds. In the latter case, interest is not taxed until the bonds are cashed in. Then, when your child turns 14, you can change the portfolio mix and periodically cash in the bonds, since the income will then be taxed at the child's rate.

$ IF YOU DARE: To avoid being taxed at your rate, have a grandparent or someone else give money to your child for investment. Caution: you could be in trouble with the IRS if the money is a disguised gift from you via grandparents. The amount that taxpayers can bequeath directly to grandchildren without paying the generation-skipping tax has been limited to $2 million. This limit ends in 1990.

$ TAX HINT: Earnings in Clifford trusts set up after March 1, 1986, will be taxed to the donor regardless of the beneficiary's age.

If you have already transferred investments to a child under age 14, you may want to put these investments into municipals or zero coupon bonds.

$ TAX HINT: You can still make a tax-free loan up to $10,000 ($20,000 for a couple) to each member of your family per year. It is also possible to loan up to $100,000 if tax avoidance is not one of the principal purposes. Imputed interest is then equal to the borrower's investment income. This is a popular way for parents to help children buy property.

If you are involved in income shifting, keep careful records indicating that you have separate accounts for your children. Segregate gifts from you, grandparents, and others. Income from gifts from relatives other than parents is taxed at the child's rate, regardless of age.

OTHER NEW RULINGS TO KEEP IN MIND

➤ THE TWO-EARNER OR MARITAL DEDUCTION In the past, a married couple was able to exclude from taxation 10% of the earned income of the lesser earning spouse. This benefit has been eliminated.

➤ DIVIDEND EXCLUSION The old exclusion from taxation of $200 ($100 for singles) of dividend income has been repealed. All dividend income is taxed.

➤ INCOME AVERAGING This technique, which allowed you to reduce taxes by averaging income over a 3-year period, thus smoothing out the differences between high- and low-income years, has been eliminated.

➤ STATE AND LOCAL TAXES Except for sales tax, these taxes continue to be fully deductible.

➤ INVESTMENT EXPENSES These, including tax planning, the cost of this book, tax-return preparation, investment publications, and other miscellaneous items are deductible only for amounts in excess of 2% of your adjusted gross income.

➤ PENSION PLANS Employees must now be vested (or guaranteed participation) in pension plans after 5 years of employment, not 10 as was the case.

➤ CHARITABLE DEDUCTIONS Unless you itemize, you cannot deduct your charitable contributions.

➤ MEDICAL EXPENSES You can deduct medical expenses only to the extent that they exceed 7½% of your adjusted gross income.

36 TAX SHELTERS

The simplest and usually the best tax shelter for most people is tax-exempt bonds, as explained earlier. These are *investments* whose interest is free of federal and often state taxes. But most other tax shelters are complex. They rely on tax laws to provide deductions or deferrals of income and realized appreciation. *Before you make any investment in a tax shelter, do your homework and consult your tax adviser.*

Tax shelters initially were approved by Congress to encourage investments in areas that otherwise might not attract sufficient capital. With real estate, the deductions for interest, taxes, and depreciation made it possible to encourage building and owning apartment houses, office buildings, and other structures. These benefits proved to be so attractive that Congress has sharply slimmed down the tax advantages. Due to tax reform, the emphasis has shifted now to shelters that generate income and defer payment of taxes.

LIMITED PARTNERSHIPS

The most common tax shelter is built around a limited partnership. This involves a *general partner* who has expertise in the operations of the business and *limited partners* who are the investors seeking specific profit opportunities and tax benefits.

The general partner assumes management responsibilities and makes all decisions. Generally, the general partner is a knowledgeable individual who puts up some money, receives a sizable share of the profits, is assured of income while the project operates, and accepts liability for losses in excess of partnership capital.

Private offerings, involving about 35 partners, start with an investment of $25,000 or often much more. Public offerings, with a larger number of participants, must file a prospectus with the SEC and meet certain financial standards established to protect the public. Many states set minimum requirements for investors in public offerings in order to prevent those who are unable to sustain the risk/loss factor involved from participating. In California, for example, you must have $200,000 in assets. Increasingly, investors are getting greater protection. Members of the National Association of Security Dealers (NASD) must exercise "due diligence": discovering whether the general partner is competent and honest, comparing the proposal with similar deals, evaluating the likelihood of the proposed tax benefits, and determining the fairness of the proposed method of sharing profits and expenses.

In all tax shelters, be wary and use common sense.

THE 1986 TAX REFORM BILL

Just about the toughest provision in the tax reform package centers around a great favorite, tax shelters. Although shelters are not totally extinct, the deals that were set up primarily to generate large paper losses are a thing of the past. The new rulings put a crimp in using paper losses generated by shelters to reduce tax liability. Losses from most so-called "passive" investments—ones in which the taxpayer does not "materially" participate—can no longer be used to offset income from salary, dividends, capital gains, royalties, or interest. In other words, passive losses can be used only to offset income from other passive investments—most often, limited partnerships. Unusable passive losses, however, are not totally without merit: they can be carried forward to offset passive income in the future or be deducted when the investment is finally sold.

Tax-sheltered investments and limited part-

299

nerships you already own get a break, since the new rulings are being phased in over 5 years. In 1987, 35% of losses not offsetting passive income are allowed; in 1988, it will be 60%; in 1989, 90%; and in 1991, 100%.

The following shelters escaped reform.

OIL AND GAS PROGRAMS

Senators and various interested groups from the big oil states lobbied hard in 1986 and were able to get a special exemption for those with "working interest" investments in oil and gas drilling. Investors here are still able to use their losses to shelter ordinary income, *even* if they are not active participants in these oil and gas operations.

➤ OIL AND GAS DRILLING Investors can probably write off 80% of their total investment on personal tax returns in the first year. Income in later years from successful wells may be partially offset by depletion and depreciation. Stay away from programs that spin off no income until the wells come in. If the well turns out to be dry, you'll never see a dollar.

➤ OIL AND GAS INCOME PROGRAMS Although taxes must be paid when the program ends, investors can possibly earn income annually equal to 8 to 10% of their investment. Most specialists regard income programs as safer than oil and gas drilling, where one merely hopes to see oil.

MASTER LIMITED PARTNER- SHIPS (MLPs)

An MLP, which is set up instead of a corporation to run a business, enables investors to sidestep the high corporate tax rate. Investors can also write off start-up costs plus losses (if any) on their personal returns.

MLPs trade on the major stock exchanges and therefore offer greater liquidity than a straight tax shelter. Among those in the oil industry are: Mesa Limited Partnership (NYSE), Samson Energy Limited Partnership (ASE), and Transco Exploration Partners (NYSE).

GOLD MINES

Several gold mining companies that trade OTC offer investors direct interest in the gold produced. Earnings can be paid in bullion, coins, or gold certificates, all of which the IRS deems a "return of capital assets" and

---

HOW TO READ A PROSPECTUS FAST

By law, every major tax shelter or limited partnership must submit a prospectus to shareholders. The prospectus may appear to be formidable and dull, but it will pay you to spend a few minutes reviewing the facts, figures, and statements. For those who are in a hurry:

- Read the opening summary word for word.
- Check the accounting projections and footnotes.
- Check the use of proceeds: how much will go for fees; how much will go to work for your interests?
- Check the compensation to the general partner.
- Review line by line the track record of the sponsors, participants, and employees.
- Read with help from your tax adviser the discussion of tax consequences. This can be tough going, but never invest in anything that you do not fully understand.
- *Do business only with reputable, established firms* that exercise "due diligence" when reviewing the general partner's financial statement, track record, experience, and technical expertise as well as the fairness of the deal itself. To double-check, get information from special services such as:

Limited Partners Letter, P.O. Box 1146, Menlo Park, CA 94025

The Stanger Report, 623 River Road, Fair Haven, NJ 07701

Brennan Reports, P.O. Box 882, Valley Forge, PA 19482

---

thus not taxable. However, when you convert them into cash you must pay taxes.

CATTLE

At the present time, you can buy cattle on a December 31 and at the same time prepay the cost of keeping the animals for their lifetime. You can then deduct half of these prepaid costs in the first year. (Check with your accountant first regarding the status of this shelter.)

EQUIPMENT LEASING

In these partnerships you buy equipment, lease it to a user, and then shelter some of the income through depreciation. The new rules allow you to write off some assets even faster than before. Keep in mind, however, that the tax reform stretches out depreciation in most cases.

REAL ESTATE

All rental income is now subject to the loss limitation rules, whether or not the taxpayer participates in managing the property.

There is one small break, however: under a special exemption, as much as $25,000 of losses from rental real estate can be used annually by those who actively participate in the rental activity *and* whose adjusted gross income is less than $100,000. For every dollar that your adjusted gross income is over $100,000, this $25,000 loss allowance is reduced by 50¢. So if you have $150,000 of income, you cannot claim a rental loss against your other income unless it's against passive income. For example, if your income is $125,000, you can take up to $12,500 in losses on rental real estate.

➤ LOW-INCOME HOUSING Under the new law, tax credits are available to those who buy, build, or rehabilitate low-income housing. The credits could work out to be equal to 90% of your investment over 10 years. The credits can offset regular income but are phased out if your adjusted gross income is over $200,000. If your income exceeds $250,000, there are no credits.

➤ REHABILITATION The tax credit for rehabilitating older buildings has been reduced. In the past, three credits (15%, 20%, and 25%) were allowed, depending on the type and age of the buildings. Now there are only two credits: 10% for nonresidential buildings put into service prior to 1936 and 20% for all historic structures.

$HINT: Low-income and rehab participation also entitle you to the $25,000 exemption. This benefit is phased out for those with adjusted gross incomes between $200,000 and $250,000. It's available whether or not you actively participate.

These new rules have hurt the real estate industry, which traditionally financed development via limited partnerships that provided tax losses to those who invested during the first years of a project. But the new rules affect others as well—no one who invests in a business without participating in its operations "on a regular, continuous, and substantial basis" can take losses to offset other income. (See also Chapter 37 on real estate.)

37 REAL ESTATE

For generations, owning a piece of the American dream has meant buying a home: steady appreciation, tax benefits, shelter—all rolled into one. But the new tax bill and a changing economy make it necessary to think twice about real estate as a surefire investment. Lower individual tax rates have reduced the value of mortgage interest deductions, and elimination of the capital gains preference results in higher taxes when real estate is sold at a profit. So before you leap, read this chapter and discuss the implications with your accountant.

A key to success in this area is choosing the right type of real estate. Your first choice is whether to invest directly or indirectly. If, for example, you don't want the bother and hassle of owning and caring for property, then a real estate investment trust (REIT) or limited partnership (RELP) might be the answer. In any case, you should understand the new tax rulings before making a move.

In 1981, Congress voted exceptionally lucrative tax breaks for real estate developers, builders, and those seeking tax-sheltered investments. That same year, Congress also enacted accelerated depreciation allowances, giving birth to a great flurry of building activity that resulted in hundreds of office buildings, shopping centers, and nursing homes. Building rehabilitation also grew in popularity under the special rules for certified historic structures.

The 1986 Tax Reform Bill essentially curbs these tax benefits, especially in the area of commercial real estate. It also touches upon one of America's most sacred cows, the home mortgage, by limiting its use for personal loans. Yet if you make the right decisions, you can still benefit handsomely from real estate investments.

YOUR HOME AS A TAX SHELTER

Unlike interest on consumer loans, your mortgage interest and property taxes are still fully tax-deductible. And you can continue to *postpone gains made on the sale of your principal residence,* as long as you buy another that costs at least as much as the one you sold *and* you do so within 2 years of sale date. If your new home costs less, then you must pay taxes on the lesser of either the house sale profits or the difference between the price of the old and the new home. Deferring these profits is particularly important, since any profit from a home sale is now taxed at your regular income tax rate and no longer at a favorable long-term capital gains rate. It is possible to keep deferring taxes by moving, and if you do so until you are age 55 you can then take advantage of the following special break: a one time $125,000 capital gains exemption from taxes on home sale profits for those age 55 and over.

One point to keep in mind, however, is that the cut in the top individual tax rates from a high of 50% to a high of 28% actually reduces the value of mortgage deductions, in particular for those who formerly were in the 50% bracket. That means you will now be paying more after-tax dollars to buy the same house.

YOUR HOME AS A FINANCING TOOL

Under the new rules, you can deduct interest on first and second mortgages, including loans for capital improvements and home equity lines of credit. There are no restrictions on the use of the money borrowed *if* the total does not exceed the purchase price plus the cost of improvements. But interest on loans above that amount is not deductible *unless* the money is used for medical or educational expenses. *This is an important restriction.* To state it another way, the new regulation permits deduction of interest on home loans only up to the price the owner paid for the house plus the value of any improvements made. The sole exceptions are loans made for medical and educational purposes. For example, if you paid $100,000 for your home and you added $15,000 worth of improvements, you can now deduct interest expense on a loan up to $115,000. Of course, the actual cash you can raise is reduced by the amount of any outstanding mortgage. The new law basically sanctions tax-deductible borrowing using your home as collateral. Be sure to keep careful records of your expenditures as well as detailed invoices from contractors and repair men to document the cost of home improvements for the IRS.

Under the old rules, home loans were most often written against the appraised *value* of the house, not the purchase price. Therefore, in geographical areas where there's been a rapid increase in real estate values, the new ruling is restrictive.

$HINT: If you have already borrowed against your house and have exceeded the limit under the new law, a grandfather clause permits interest deduction on loans outstanding *before* August 17, 1986, for "up to the fair market value" of the house, no matter what the money is used for.

RENTAL INCOME

Rental property, whether it's a condo in Florida, a ski house in Montana, or a center hall colonial in the suburbs, if purchased after January 1, 1987, does not fare as well as before. It must be depreciated over a much longer period of time. The write-off period, formerly 19 years on residential property, has been stretched out to 27½ years (to 31½ years for commercial property). In the past, as a landlord, you could deduct the total value of your investment over 19 years, writing off greater amounts in the

first years, but now you must take deductions in equal amounts each year over 27½ years.

If property produces rent, then the income or losses generated are considered "passive," which means you cannot offset salary or investment income with these rental losses, with one exception: if your adjusted gross income is under $100,000, the new tax law allows you to write off up to $25,000 a year in rental property tax losses against other income, including your salary—*provided you actively manage the property.* This special $25,000 allowance is phased out as you become wealthier, i.e., if your adjusted gross income exceeds $150,000 ($75,000 for marrieds filing separately), there is no such break.

$HINT: Recalculate the return you receive on any property, keeping in mind that the new lower tax brackets reduce the value of deductions. If your property generates a loss *and* your income is less than $150,000, make certain you satisfy the IRS requirement of being an "active" participant in order to get the loss allowance.

To be considered an active manager, you must own 10% of the property involved as well as make decisions on repairs, rents, and tenants. If you hire a manager but guide him or her, you will still be considered active provided you can document your involvement to the IRS.

In considering rental property, keep in mind that the new restrictions for deducting losses mean you must invest in property that produces a positive cash flow, i.e., rents must be greater than costs.

If you make more than $150,000 annually, you can still reap some benefits, because the new changes pertain to tax reporting, not to

---

DEDUCTIONS YOU MAY TAKE ON RENTAL PROPERTY

- maintenance
- depreciation
- repairs
- utility bills
- insurance

your cash flow. This means that if your rental income covers mortgage payments, the only plus you've lost is the tax shelter aspect. In the meantime, keep a running account of your losses and apply them when you eventually sell the property.

PROPERTY AS A TAX SHELTER

Hardest hit by the new regulations are real estate limited partnerships (RELPs), which make up about 70% of all limited partnerships. These shelters traditionally generated large amounts of passive or phantom losses. Now these losses can be used *only* to offset other passive income and not your salary or portfolio income. But you do have several years before passive losses are completely phased out. For example, this year (1987), up to 65% of losses in a real estate partnership can be taken against other income. In 1988, it drops to 40%; to 20% in 1989; and finally to only 10% in 1990.

This grace period allows you (and your accountant) to devise ways to use these losses productively, perhaps by tying them in with another passive partnership, one that generates income, such as a RELP in mortgages. This requires an expert in the field—don't undertake it on your own. But in the future you can expect to see more syndications that generate cash returns rather than tax benefits. Public limited partnerships, registered with the SEC, are usually sold in $5,000 denominations ($2,000 for IRAs), and liability is limited to the amount invested.

Private programs, not SEC registered, have larger minimum investments ($10,000 to $100,000). Many of these will no longer be viable investments, since you cannot deduct losses over and above the amount of your passive income. If you bought a program prior to the new law, you can deduct a percentage of the losses that exceed passive income: 65% in 1987, declining to 0% in 1991 as described on pages 299–300.

What to look for: partnerships purchasing real estate for cash (since borrowing now generates unusable write-offs) and generating rental income which is now sheltered by depreciation. Example: miniwarehouses.

REAL ESTATE INVESTMENT TRUSTS (REITs)

REITs are corporations that operate basically like mutual funds but invest in managed, diversified portfolios of real estate properties and mortgages. These properties or mortgages generate cash flows, 95% of which (in terms of earnings) must be passed on to shareholders.

REITs were little affected by the tax overhaul, because they never really did center around tax benefits. Now they are as competitive as those real estate shelters that lost their tax benefits and sometimes more so. The new bill also gives REITs a boost: they now can have a role in managing their own property and have greater flexibility in setting rental fees.

Although REITs shares can and do appreciate in price, they are primarily suggested for their high yields and as a way to participate in real estate. With lower individual tax rates, REIT investors can now keep more of these dividends.

There are three types of REITs: *Equity REITs*, which build and develop properties, are less speculative than *mortgage REITs*, which lend money to developers and involve greater risk. *Hybrid REITs* combine both properties and mortgages. REITs trade on the major exchanges. Further information is available in *Value Line Investment Survey* or from *Realty Stock Review*, a twice-monthly newsletter which tracks the performance of 100 REITs ($264/year; Audit Investments, 136 Summit Avenue, Montvale, NJ 07645).

GUIDELINES FOR SELECTING REITs

Read the annual report and talk to your broker about:
- How long the REIT has been in business
- What the dividend payout record has been
- Whether dividends are covered by cash flow (they should be) rather than one-time sale of property
- Location of properties: avoid depressed and overbuilt areas
- Type of property: look for an adequate mix; office buildings now overbuilt
- Experienced management

The time to start planning for a financially secure retirement is the day you receive your first paycheck, something few of us ever do. But don't agonize over the fact, just avoid further delays and start now. This chapter is not intended to be a complete retirement guide, but the information here will help you lay the financial groundwork that makes the difference between merely getting along and continuing life at full tilt.

SOCIAL SECURITY

In order to plan your retirement investments intelligently, start by taking a close look at your Social Security situation. Then build around this basic data. It may seem like a nuisance, but ignoring Social Security records could lead to lower benefits than you're legitimately entitled to, since benefits are based on the Social Security Administration's records of what you have earned. It's up to you, and not the Social Security Administration, to find out if your records are accurate. Serious errors could cost you thousands of dollars in benefits.

➤ STEP 1. REQUEST A WRITTEN STATEMENT OF EARNINGS   Call, visit, or write your local Social Security office to get a copy of form SSA 7004, "Request for Social Security Statement of Earnings." Send it in and at the same time request an estimate of the monthly payment you will be entitled to at age 65. Do this every 3 years. You'll receive a computerized statement in 4 to 6 weeks showing all earnings credited to your account.

If you suspect errors on your statement, contact your Social Security office. Provide as much data as possible, including dates of employment, wages received, employer's name and address, copies of W-2 forms, and check stubs.

➤ STEP 2. CALCULATE YOUR BENEFITS   If you're near retirement, the Social Security estimate of your monthly benefits will be fairly accurate. If you're younger, make your own rough estimate.

➤ STEP 3. DETERMINE WHAT PERCENTAGE OF YOUR FINAL SALARY YOU'LL NEED TO LIVE ON   Financial advisors suggest between 50 and 80%; obviously Social Security alone will not be adequate. Gerald Richmond, associate pension actuary at New England Mutual Life Insurance Co., says that for the average wage earner, the 41% of earnings replaced by Social Security benefits should be supplemented by 20 to 25% from a pension plan and at least 10% from personal savings.

➤ POINTS TO REMEMBER ABOUT SOCIAL SECURITY

- Working spouses who pay Social Security taxes earn their own benefits.
- Nonworking spouses qualify for a retirement benefit that is equal to half what their retired spouses receive.
- You can supplement your retirement income by working, but any amount earned over $7,320 will reduce benefits for

---

FOR ADDITIONAL HELP

Several hundred lawyers specialize in resolving Social Security problems, such as denial of disability benefits and errors in retirement benefits. They are members of the National Organization of Social Security Claimants' Representatives, which operates a nationwide referral service. Call 1-800-431-2804 to get names of members in your area. In New York State, call collect: 1-914-735-8812.

retirees aged 65 to 70; earnings above $5,400 reduce benefits for those under age 65. The limits rise each year.

■ Benefits may be taxed. A married couple filing a joint federal return with a gross adjusted income (including tax-exempt bond interest and half their Social Security benefits) that totals more than $32,000, will have half of the excess taxed. However, the tax cannot be more than half the Social Security benefit. For singles, the benchmark is $25,000.

Now that you know what you're likely to receive from Social Security, you're undoubtedly impressed with the fact that you will need a great deal more to continue a comfortable lifestyle after age 65!

THE 1986 TAX REFORM BILL

Congress did not have a very soft spot for employees when it came to reform. Business expenses are now harder to deduct, stock incentive plans are less appealing and IRAs took it on the shoulder.

As you read through this chapter, keep in mind the following alterations made by Congress.

■ The new law changes the income tax treatment of withdrawals from tax-deferred savings plans. Now, each withdrawal must consist of (1) contributions made by you; (2) contributions made by your employer; (3) some of the account's earnings. In addition, a 10% penalty applies to all early withdrawals.

■ It appears that the best way to get money out of a company-sponsored tax plan is by borrowing, since there is no 10% penalty involved. Check with your accountant about the maximum you may borrow as well as repayment schedules.

■ The new bill requires corporate pension plans to fully vest employees after five years.

■ The maximum amount of annual compensation your company can use in determining your pension is only $200,000. Previously there was no limit. This does not affect benefits that have been building up before 1987.

■ The amount you can collect if you retire early has been cut:

1 If you retire before age 62, the maximum you can receive a year is $90,000.

2 If you retire between 61 and 55, the maximum is gradually reduced to $75,000 per year.

3 If you retire before 55, the maximum is $40,000 per year.

4 If you retire at 65, the maximum is $90,000 per year

■ There is a new 15% penalty on taxable distributions in excess of $112,000 per year from your pension, company-sponsored plan, tax-sheltered annuities, and even your IRA.

$ HINT: To avoid the 15% penalty, roll over the lump sum into an IRA and then make certain your withdrawals are less than $112,000 per year.

■ Ten-year forward averaging, which saved dollars for taxpayers receiving lump-sum distributions when they retired or quit a job, has been cut to five.

INDIVIDUAL RETIREMENT ACCOUNTS (IRAs)

When the Tax Act of 1981 made IRAs available to all workers, it seemed like a pleasant but insignificant tax break. But if you've been stashing away $2,000 a year since then, you have a sizeable amount of money on hand. Your philosophy should be shifting too—away from thinking of your IRA as a savings account to be ignored or placed in a CD, toward realizing that it's an investment requiring diversification and thoughtful management.

Where you should invest it depends on several factors: the current economic environment, your age, other sources of income, and your appetite for risk. The closer you are to retirement, of course, the less risk you should take. You must also decide if you are temperamentally suited to manage your account or if you need a professional. In general, high-yield conservative investments should form the basic core of most IRAs, but there are exceptions and variations. At a certain point, part of your IRA should go into other vehicles such as growth

---

HOW AN IRA CAN PAY OFF

The second column shows the results achieved by Investor A, who invests his $2,000 on January 1 every year. The third column shows the results realized by Investor B, who waits until the last minute, April 15, to make his contribution. The last column shows Investor C's position. He invests at the beginning of the year, but outside an IRA. He invests only $1,000. There's no question about the winner—Investor A, who proves that the early bird gets the worm.

VALUE OF $2,000 ANNUAL INVESTMENT ASSUMING 10% ANNUAL YIELD

INVESTMENT PERIOD	IRA INVESTOR A MAKES ANNUAL INVESTMENT ON JAN. 1	IRA INVESTOR B MAKES ANNUAL INVESTMENT ON APRIL 15 OF FOLLOWING YEAR	NON-IRA INVESTOR C IN 50% TAX BRACKET MAKES ANNUAL $1,000 INVESTMENT ON JAN. 1
10 years	$ 35,062	$ 29,195	$13,207
20 years	$126,005	$109,989	$34,719
30 years	$361,886	$319,548	$69,761

SOURCE: Merrill Lynch.

---

stocks, which protect your nest egg from reduced returns when interest rates are low and yet take advantage of a rising stock market.

Only a few investments are excluded by law from IRAs: collectibles, commodities (such as gems, stamps, art, antiques, and oriental rugs), and leveraged investments (those made with borrowed cash). The 1986 law permits inclusion of U.S. American Eagle gold bullion coins but they must be held by a custodian, not the IRA owner. You may borrow money to put in your IRA, but margined stocks, commodity futures, and mortgaged real estate are out. Among the tax advantaged investments that make no sense in an IRA are municipal bonds, tax shelters, and deferred annuities. (See Investment Choices for Pension Plans, pages 313–314.)

One of the most disappointing changes in the new tax bill is the cutback in deductions for individual retirement accounts. In the past the $2,000 annual deduction was available to all who earned at least that much in salary form. For an estimated 25% of taxpayers that deduction no longer exists.

- If your gross adjusted income (before IRA contribution) is over $50,000 ($35,000 for singles) *and* you are covered by an employer's pension plan, you are no longer entitled to the IRA tax deduction.

- If your gross adjusted income (before IRA contribution) is between $40,000 and $50,000 ($25,000 to $30,000 for singles) *and* you are covered by an employer's pension plan, your IRA deduction is reduced.

- If you have no pension plan coverage you can still deduct the full $2,000 IRA contribution.

- Full deduction available now to workers covered by a pension plan only if their income is below $25,000 for singles and $40,000 for those filing jointly.

$ HINT: Even if you are not allowed to make a tax-deductible contribution, you can still contribute up to $2,000 (nondeductible) to your IRA. Taxes on interest or other earnings are still deferred. Deposits for which you do not receive a tax deduction must be paid into a separate IRA to avoid confusion.

The following retirement programs disqual-

IRA BASICS

- Annual contribution: $2,000 of earned income if under age 70½.
- You can wait until April 15 to make your contribution for the previous year.
- If you and your spouse both work, you may each have an IRA.
- You can contribute a total of $2,250 to a spousal account; this amount can be split between accounts as long as neither gets over $2,000.
- IRA money must be invested with an IRS-approved custodian, such as a bank, savings and loan, stockbroker, mutual fund, or insurance company.
- You can open as many IRA accounts as you like using a different custodian or investment each year and thus spreading out your risk.
- There is a 10% penalty for withdrawing money before you are 59½.
- Money withdrawn is taxed as ordinary income. If you withdraw before age 59½, you pay both the tax *and* the 10% penalty.
- You must withdraw money starting at age 70½ or be penalized.

ify you from making a fully deductible IRA contribution: Keogh, SEP, money purchase pension plan, profit sharing plan, defined benefit plan, 401(K), employee stock option plan, government employee retirement plan, 403(b) (teachers' annuity), 457s (municipal employee retirement plan), and Taft-Hartley plan (union employee retirement plan).

HINT: If you can only make nondeductible IRA contributions, you may want to consider a deferred annuity contract. These, too, allow you to accumulate interest and dividend earnings tax free. Two added pluses: there is no limitation on the amount you can invest, and the early withdrawal penalty is only 5% versus 10% for an IRA.

Lump-sum payouts from company pension or profit-sharing plans in the past qualified for ten-year forward averaging. This has been elim-

inated for most people. Therefore, rolling over these monies into an IRA is a strategic tax-free transaction that should not be overlooked.

SELF-DIRECTED IRAs

When your IRA contains $5,000 to $10,000 you're ready to benefit from diversification. Consider doing so through a self-directed account, which can be set up at a brokerage firm for $25 to $30 plus a yearly fee. Designed for those who want to guide their own account, it allows you to invest in stocks, bonds, limited partnerships, options, Treasuries, zeros, or mortgage-backed securities. If you want advice on managing the

A SELF-DIRECTED IRA

PROS
- ↑ Allows for diversification
- ↑ Offers greatest variety of investments
- ↑ Has appreciation potential
- ↑ Enables you to adjust portfolio to take advantage of changes in economic environment
- ↑ All income and capital gains accumulate free of taxes during lifetime of the IRA
- ↑ Custodian fee is tax-deductible

CONS
- ↓ Takes time, knowledge, and continual supervision to avoid losses
- ↓ Must pay commissions on every transaction
- ↓ Risk level high
- ↓ Withdrawals prior to age 59½ subject to 10% penalty plus ordinary federal income tax
- ↓ Long-term profits made on stock held outside an IRA taxed at more favorable capital gains rate; capital losses outside an IRA can be used to offset capital gains, but inside an IRA, such a loss has no tax benefits
- ↓ Shelters short-term gains from taxation

FAVORITE CHOICES
Zero coupon bonds, Ginnie Maes, convertible bonds, and high-yielding common stocks, particularly utilities.

WHEN IT PAYS TO PAY A PENALTY

Cashing in an IRA before age 59½ entails a 10% tax penalty. The figures below show how many years you must hold an IRA to cover both the penalty and federal income taxes and still get back more than you would have made on a taxable investment.

TAX BRACKET	YIELD ON INVESTMENT			
	8%	10%	12%	14%
25%	8 years	7 years	6 years	5 years
38%	7	6	5	4
45%	6	5	5	4
50%	6	5	5	4

SOURCE: US News & World Report.

COMPOUNDING OF IRA BENEFITS

AFTER:	CONTRIBUTIONS DEPOSITED ON:		
	JAN. 2	DEC. 31	APRIL 15*
5 years	$12,963	$12,003	$11,033
10 years	32,010	29,639	27,974
15 years	59,997	55,553	50,793
20 years	101,119	93,629	87,303

* Of the following year
SOURCE: United Retirement Bulletin, March 1986.

portfolio, use a full service broker; otherwise save on commissions with a discount broker. A self-directed account takes time and vigilance on your part, yet it offers the greatest degree of flexibility along with the greatest potential for appreciation. It also involves the most risk.

$ WARNING: Avoid investments that are attractive largely for tax advantages, such as tax-exempt municipal bonds. Since IRAs are already sheltered from taxes, the exemption is wasted. In addition, all income, including tax-free yields, will be taxed when withdrawn.

$ HINT: The Cleveland Electric Illuminating Co. was the first company to establish an IRA for those who buy the stock through its dividend reinvestment plan. There are no brokerage commissions, and dividends can be automatically reinvested. Check with the electric utility company in your area.

The following table illustrates the difference in results when contributions are made on the first or the last of the year or 3½ months into the next year (the last date legally possible), assuming $2,000 is deposited annually at 10%. At the end of 20 years the IRA owner is 16% better off if contributions are made at the earliest possible date each year.

YOUR IRA AND YOUR HEIRS

If you're blessed with sufficient income from other sources, you may want to leave IRA funds to your heirs. The revised rules passed as part of the 1984 tax act will help. Although the IRS views IRAs primarily as a retirement benefit, not a death benefit, the new mortality tables help those who want to leave money behind by making it possible for them to withdraw less money from their IRA. You must start withdrawing money by April 1 of the year after you turn 70½; otherwise you face a stiff 50% excise tax on excess accumulations. Study the table below and check with your accountant or financial planner to determine your withdrawals.

CALCULATING MINIMUM IRA WITHDRAWALS

AT AGE:		DIVIDE ACCOUNT
MEN	WOMEN	BALANCE BY:
65	70	15.0
70	75	12.1
75	80	9.6
80	85	7.5
85	90	5.7
90	95	4.2
95	100	3.1

Note: other figures are used for joint life expectancy.

SOURCE: IRS.

§HINT: If you contribute $2,000 annually to an IRA, assuming a 25-year growth period, accumulations at 10%, and that you are in the 28% tax bracket, your IRA will be worth $113,253 more than a similar taxable investment.

IRA ROLLOVER

This is a special form of withdrawal of pension assets that can be used to shelter money withdrawn early from a Keogh or corporate plan. The original payment must be in a lump sum and can be part or all of the individual's vested assets. Once in the IRA Rollover, the savings continue to accumulate tax-free until payouts start—permissible after age 59½, mandatory at 70½. The IRA Rollover must be established and maintained by the owner of the IRA (except in the case of a divorced spouse); there can be no additional contributions; the assets cannot be invested in a life insurance policy; and the transfers must be made within 60 days after the distribution and must go directly into the new IRA. *If any of the money is deposited in your personal account, the entire withdrawal will be taxable.*

Note: If the distribution from a pension plan includes life insurance, you will probably owe a tax on the cash value. To avoid this, borrow against the cash value, roll that money over into an IRA, and keep the policy for protection. Check with your accountant first.

AVOID PENALTIES

If for any reason you have inadvertently put too much money into your IRA, take it out immediately. For each year the excess remains in the account, a 6% excise tax is levied on both it and earnings. Earnings on the excess must be reported as income in the year earned. The excess and earnings on the excess may also be subject to a 10% penalty when withdrawn.

§HINT: There's a new type of insurance on the market: IRAsure insures against long-term unemployment or disability that could prevent you from funding your IRA. Not available in all states. Call: Signature Group 1-800-621-0393; in IL 1-800-572-2416.

KEOGH PLANS

Designed for the self-employed and proprietors of small companies, Keoghs work much like IRAs but have several added advantages. You can put away as much as $30,000 a year and, as with an IRA, your Keogh contribution is deductible from income when calculating your taxes. Earnings are not taxed until withdrawn. If you have a Keogh you may also have an IRA.

To get your annual deduction, however, you must have a Keogh in place by the end of that year, although contributions don't have to be completed until you file your tax return.

If you, as a self-employed person, establish a Keogh for yourself, you must extend its benefits to your employees. Employees must get comparable benefits on a percentage basis; e.g., if you put in 15% of earned income for yourself, you must match that 15% for each employee.

There are two basic types of Keoghs: (1) defined-contribution plans and (2) defined-benefit plans.

MOVING YOUR IRA

As your IRA account grows or as market conditions change you may want to invest your dollars elsewhere. The IRS has strict rules to follow.

IRA TRANSFER

- If you arrange for a direct transfer of funds from one IRA custodian to another, there is no limit on the number of switches you can make.

- Plan on transfers taking at least a month. Banks, brokerage firms, and even some mutual funds are often backlogged with paperwork.

- Get instructions early on, ideally in writing, from both the resigning and accepting IRA sponsor. Pay fees and notarize necessary papers immediately. Keep track of details as well as deadlines; don't depend on the institution to do this for you.

IRA ROLLOVER

- You may take personal possession of your IRA money once a year for 60 days.

- If you hold the money longer than 60 days you'll be subject to the 10% penalty.

> DEFINED-CONTRIBUTION PLAN The more common and the simpler of the two is one in which you decide how much to put in. In other words, the annual contribution is predetermined and what you receive upon retirement is variable, depending upon how well you've invested your deposits. Contributions are set forth in the plan's document by formula—usually it's a percentage of earned income up to a maximum of 25% of compensation, not to exceed $30,000 a year. Sometimes this figure is given as 20%, which is also accurate: it's 25% of compensation minus your Keogh contribution, which works out to be 20% of net earnings. For example, if you make $100,000, you can contribute $20,000 ($100,000 − $20,000 contribution = $80,000 compensation; 25% of $80,000 = $20,000). This is known as a "money purchase" plan, and the percentage contribution initially established continues in the future. In a "profit-sharing" plan, you can set aside up to 13% of your income, up to $30,000 a year. Under this plan the percentage contribution can vary. It may make sense to combine these two plans in order to avoid being locked into paying the same percentage each year. This is called a "paired plan."

> DEFINED-BENEFIT PLAN This is almost the equivalent of a corporate pension plan. Designed to pay a predetermined benefit each year after you retire, it allows you to put aside up to 100% of your self-employment income annually. A pension actuary determines how much you need to deposit each year to provide for your benefits, which can be up to $90,000 a year under current law. This type of Keogh makes particularly good sense for the investor who is over fifty since there are fewer years left in which to put aside retirement funds.

SIMPLIFIED EMPLOYEE PENSION PLANS (SEPs)

There is another type of tax-saving retirement plan that has received far less publicity than either the IRA or Keogh. Yet it permits contributions greater than $2,000 a year. Called a *Simplified Employee Pension Plan* (SEP), it is suitable for small businesses and sole proprietors. Designed to cut red tape, it's considerably easier to set up and administer than a Keogh. Although its initial purpose was to encourage small and new firms to establish reitrement programs, self-employeds without Keoghs can use them too. The deadline for setting up a SEP is April 15, just as it is with a regular IRA. (With a Keogh, the date is December 31.)

When an employer—which can be you as a sole proprietor—establishes a SEP, the employee then opens an IRA at a bank, mutual fund, or other approved institution. The employer can put up to 15% of an employee's annual earnings in the SEP.

401(K) PLAN

This plan, also called a "salary-reduction" plan, was authorized by Congress in 1980, but due to an IRS delay in issuing rules for it, it got off to a slow start. By now, however, nearly three out of four major firms offer it as a fringe benefit. Employers like it because it reduces the firm's pension costs by encouraging employees to save more themselves. Some companies set it up in addition to an already existing pension plan. The main attraction is the plan's tax break along with the fact that employers often add dollars to it for their employees. Here's how it works:

1 Your employer sets up the plan with a regulated investment company, a bank trust department, or an insurance company.
2 You set aside part of your salary into a special savings/investment account. You

---

KEOGH PAPERWORK

Form 5500: Starting in 1985, one-person Keogh owners were required to file an annual report with the IRS. It's called Form 5500.

Form 5500-C: This lengthy document must be filed when the Keogh plan is established and every third year thereafter.

Form 5500-R: Must be filed in the years the 5500-C is not filed.

KEOGHS AND SEPs COMPARED

	KEOGH	SEP
Eligible individuals	Sole proprietor, partnership, incorporated business, self-employed, freelancers subchapter S	Sole proprietor, partnership, incorporated business
Contributions	Up to 25% of earned income with maximum of $30,000	Up to 15% of earned income with maximum of $30,000; if self-employed, up to 13.04% with maximum of $30,000; 20% money purchase Keogh
Deadlines	December 31 to establish filing date for funding	April 15 of following year
Distribution	May begin at 59½ or regular retirement age, whichever is later. Must begin April 1 following year you turn 70½. May also begin at disability or death.	May begin at age 59½ or earlier due to disability or death. Must begin April 1 following year you turn 70½.
Taxes	Contributions are tax-deductible. Earnings tax-deferred. Lump sum distributions eligible for 5-year forward averaging.	Contributions are tax-deductible. Earnings tax-deferred. All distributions treated as ordinary income.
Reports	Annually must file 5500 forms and summary reports. Initially must file a summary plan and notice to interested parties.	Employees should be notified of amount contributed for them each year.
Loans	May be available	Not available
Penalties:		
Overcontribution	Excess may be carried over to subsequent years	6%
Early withdrawal	10% for 5% owners of business	10%
Late distribution	50%	50%

have several options, usually a guaranteed fixed rate income fund, a portfolio of stocks or bonds, or short-term money market securities. The amount set aside is *not* counted as income when figuring your federal income tax. For example, if you earn $50,000 and put $5,000 into a 401(K), you report only $45,000 compensation. In addition, earnings that

accumulate in the 401(K) plan do so free of tax—until withdrawn.

3 Many companies match employee savings, up to 5 or 6%. Most often a firm chips in 50¢ for each $1 the employee saves.

4 The maximum you can contribute is $7,000 a year and there is a 10% penalty for withdrawing funds before age 59½.

5 If you change jobs or take out the balance

in a lump sum after age 59½, you can take advantage of 5-year averaging, another tax break. (You treat the total payout as though you received it in 5 annual installments.)

INVESTMENT CHOICES FOR PENSION PLANS: A SHOPPER'S BAZAAR

There are many places to invest your IRA, Keogh, or 401(K) dollars. This section explains the most popular choices.

➤ CERTIFICATES OF DEPOSIT (CDs) If low risk is your goal, then bank or savings and loan certificates of deposit offer that plus convenience, safety (they are insured up to $100,000), and low cost. CD rates are locked in, and recent low rates have made them less attractive. While interest rates are down, buy short-term CDs with 6-month to 1-year maturities.

$ HINT: Most banks allow IRA customers over age 59½ to cash in their CDs early without incurring a penalty. Check with your bank about its policy.

➤ ZERO COUPON BONDS Ideal for pension plans because there is no need to report the annual appreciation. When held in personal portfolios, the individual investor must pay taxes on the assumed interest.

The yields (currently from about 9 to 13%) are locked in but there are risks that: (1) interest rates will soar and thus denigrate the value of the bonds; (2) the company may not be able to pay off at maturity; (3) the true value of the paid-up loan will be reduced by inflation.

One alternative: buy stripped U.S. government bonds. Their prices are a bit higher so their yields will be lower, but you're sure of getting your money at maturity (see page 104).

➤ U.S. GOVERNMENT RETIREMENT BONDS These are sold by Federal Reserve Banks and the U.S. Treasury in denominations of $50, $100, and $500. They are eligible only for retirement plans. They yield 9% compounded annually. If they are redeemed prior to age 59½ (except for disability), the proceeds are taxed as income in the year they are cashed plus there is a penalty of 10% of the proceeds. After age 59½, they can be redeemed with taxation of the proceeds as income in the year of redemption.

These are poor investments but may have some use as a continuing tax shelter after retirement. They are safe—but little more.

➤ COMMON STOCKS Select only quality corporations that have made lots of money and have logical prospects of continuing to do so in the near future. You can choose income-oriented stocks (primarily utilities and banks) or stocks for total returns (modest dividends and substantial appreciation). It's best to look for some income because it's not taxed. You'll find lists of both types of stocks throughout this guide. As explained elsewhere, convertibles qualify as common stocks and can be excellent long-term holdings.

➤ MUTUAL FUNDS Here your savings are pooled for investment according to your goal. Funds offer a wide range of choices, from high-risk stock funds to conservative money market funds. Mutual funds that contain government agency issues, such as Ginnie Maes, Freddie Macs, and Fannie Maes, are particularly popular because of their high yields and comparative safety. Ginnie Maes, but not Freddie and Fanny, are backed by the full faith and credit of the U.S. Treasury. There are also stock funds for appreciation, bond funds for income, and much in between. In most cases you can switch funds under the same management for little or no fee. A full explanation of mutual funds is found in Chapter 14.

➤ DEBT ISSUES Government bills, notes, and bonds; corporate notes and bonds. Be sure that their interest is taxable, because your pension plan is a tax shelter. If you go this route, select a debt issue that will mature when cash will be needed for retirement.

For total returns, buy discount bonds that will ensure good income and steady appreciation. Ask your broker for bonds from his inventory, because this will save commissions; insist on A-rated issues; select your maturity date and work backward: e.g., if you plan to retire in 1999, have your broker find a 15-year maturity. Remember, bonds preserve capital and lock in yields.

➤ REAL ESTATE *Only* for the more aggressive investor! One of the better ways to make such investments with pension fund assets is to buy the land and let the promoter or builder own the building and take any applicable tax deductions. Then lease the land on a percentage of rent basis with an escalator clause so that your investment will benefit from higher rentals and, on sale, from a share of the capital gains. Builders always need cash so you can make a profitable deal. Be sure that this is an arm's length transaction: that you do not have any personal money in the deal.

If you prefer to invest in pooled projects, Real Estate Investment Trusts (REITs) and limited partnerships are available, but these are generally more suitable for personal holdings which can benefit from tax deductions.

Be cautious with all real estate. It is always easier to get in than to get out. A well-structured pension plan should be flexible and liquid enough to provide money quickly to pay for benefits due participants at severance, death, or retirement. Do not invest fiduciary money in real estate until total assets are $100,000, and then keep the percentage below 20%.

ANNUITIES

Annuities are often a part of retirement planning, either directly or indirectly, and although this book does not evaluate insurance per se, it is important to be aware of what annuities can and cannot do. The top annuities are monitored annually by A. M. Best Company. (Check for a copy of *Best Insurance Reports* at your library or from your insurance agent.)

ANNUITIES AND THE NEW TAX BILL

Annuities have increased investment appeal since the tax reform of 1986, because the new bill eliminates most tax shelters and reduces the benefits of IRAs for many. Deferred annuities offer a viable alternative to IRAs. Although contributions are not tax-deductible, the earnings accumulate tax-deferred, and, unlike an IRA, there is no dollar limit on the amount you can invest each year. In addition, without preferential treatment of capital gains, it makes more sense than before to buy securities through a tax-sheltered program.

An annuity is basically a tax-deferred retirement savings plan, purchased from an insurance company, with no cap on the annual contribution. If the annuity holder dies during the so-called "accumulation period," the designated beneficiary is guaranteed the amount invested. You make one (single premium) or a series of contributions to the annuity and in return the insurance company guarantees that your money will grow at a certain rate. Then, on a specified date, you begin receiving regular payments, or you may elect to take the money out in a lump sum. This money is then subject to ordinary income tax, although it has accumulated on a tax-deferred basis. Payments vary in size depending on how much you put in, how long your money was invested, and the rate of return. Options vary greatly from company to company and from plan to plan.

There are two general types of deferred annuities: variable and fixed.

▶ FIXED ANNUITY Here the insurance company guarantees that your money will grow at a specific rate for a specific period of time—often for one year. After that, the interest rate generally fluctuates annually, although it cannot drop below a set minimum. The company also guarantees to pay back your principal.

▶ VARIABLE ANNUITY Here the rate of return varies based upon the performance of the mutual funds you choose from a selection offered by the insurance company. In fact, investing in a variable annuity is similar to investing in a family of mutual funds: you can switch among funds and/or divide your money over several of them. Your return fluctuates daily. This is a riskier investment than a fixed annuity in that your principal is NOT guaranteed.

$ HINT: If your money is in a taxable CD and you do not need the income, a fixed

---

VARIABLE ANNUITIES

PRO
↑ You can conceivably earn more money in a variable annuity.

CON
↓ If the mutual funds perform poorly, your original principal could diminish.
↓ Most variable annuities offer a limited number of mutual funds, and switching may be restricted to several times per year.

annuity could be a better investment. Example: Metropolitan Life 5-year annuity with a current rate of 7.85% or 3-year with a rate of 7.40%. Upon maturity there are no surrender penalties and you can roll it over.

➤ SINGLE PREMIUM WHOLE LIFE INSURANCE This relatively new vehicle combines insurance with four basic tax benefits: tax-deferred accumulation of cash values, tax-free withdrawals of principal, tax-free loans or withdrawals of interest, and tax-free death benefits.

You pay the entire premium up front in a lump sum with this type of plan. Your money is invested at a guaranteed rate of interest—usually guaranteed for one year with a minimum floor. This cash value compounds on a tax-deferred basis. You can borrow the interest, starting in the second year, and these loans are exempt from income tax. (Nor does the loan ever have to be repaid.) It is also possible to borrow up to 90% of the principal at low rates (2 to 3%). The death benefit increases at a slow rate, depending upon how much you have borrowed.

When the contract matures, which is generally when the holder dies, the proceeds are passed on to the beneficiary *outside of probate* and therefore with no income tax due. If, however, the contract is "cashed out," you pay ordinary income tax on the gain from day one. This is to be avoided at all costs.

Points to keep in mind:

- Interest rate is usually guaranteed only for one year.
- Principal is guaranteed at all times.
- Life insurance coverage is a secondary consideration.
- The older one is, the less insurance is provided.
- Taxes are hefty if you surrender the policy.
- Through policy loans, you can essentially get tax-free income on a regular basis.

Single premium whole life should be regarded only as a lifetime investment, one which will also help your beneficiaries. When selecting a policy, look for one that has been consistently rated A+ by A.M. Best. Choose a company with at least $1 billion in assets that has been in business for a number of years.

$ HINT: If you borrow from your variable life insurance policy and if at the same time the underlying investments are doing poorly, you may be required to pay additional premiums in order to keep your policy going.

➤ EXPENSES The minimum investment amount for a variable annuity is generally $5,000 to $10,000, although many single premium annuities require a one-time lump sum of $25,000. Most companies have annual management fees of .5 to 3% of total assets. Some have high sales charges as well as an additional charge to pay for the management of the mutual funds. Policies vary with regard to surrender fees.

$ HINT: Because of the early withdrawal penalty and the capture of taxes, annuities are long-term investments and best for those aged 50 or older. Remember, too, that most variable annuities offer a limited number of mutual funds and switching is often restricted to several times per year.

➤ DEFERRED COMPENSATION Under the previous tax law, highly paid executives benefited by deferring part of their income into the future, generally until after retirement when they would be in a lower tax bracket. Of course, the new tax rates change this, since for most the maximum rate is now 28% (or 33% in some cases). This narrows or even eliminates the gap between taxes paid now and in the future. For some executives who fear taxes will rise in future administrations, this may be the lowest rate they'll see for some time.

PENSION PLANS

Under the previous tax laws, companies could pay out up to $75,000 a year from a funded plan to those who retired at age 55. For those who waited until 65 to retire, the maximum payout rose to $90,000 a year.

Under the new law, the maximum payouts are $72,000 for 62-year-old retirees; $60,000 for those 60 years old; $40,000 for 55-year-olds. The cap of $90,000 remains in effect for 65-year-olds.

Some companies may try to make up the difference through payments from unfunded pension plans that do not have to abide by the new regulations. (These plans are less secure and not guaranteed.) Consequently, look for cash or bonuses in lieu of unfunded pension payouts.

STOCK OPTIONS

Tax overhaul has reduced but not eliminated the appeal of stock options. They remain a key way to motivate top executives and at the same time tie in their professional performance with the performance of the company. In fact, executive compensation plans that include stock options tie management directly to the return offered to stockholders. By offering stock options, the company can also offer executives the possibility for impressive gains—gains that probably no company would consider giving in cash. (Stock options are essentially the right to buy a company's stock at some point in the future at a fixed price. For example, if an executive is given an option in 1987 to buy stock at $15/share by 1990 and the stock rises to $20/share by then, if he exercises the option he will have a $5 gain.)

In the past, there were tax advantages to options because the gains were taxed at the maximum capital gains rate of 20% versus the top tax rate then of 50%. The 1986 Tax Reform Bill makes stock options less attractive in two ways: it eliminates the favorable capital gains rate and reduces the top rate from 50% to 28%.

$ IF YOU DARE: Negotiate for actual stock in your company instead of cash payments and bonuses. Use stock options when the market is healthy or if you work for a growing company.

TAKING YOUR PENSION IN A LUMP SUM

The new legislation makes taking lump sum pension dollars all at once upon retirement less appealing than in the past, especially for those covered by "defined-benefit" plans.

The lump sum choice causes cash flow problems for some companies. When an employee opts to take his/her pension in a lump sum, the employer considers the estimated life span of the retiree, using standard mortality tables. Then the employer estimates the interest rate the retiree could earn. The higher the rate, the less money the company has to turn over to the retiree up front.

The Retirement Equity Act of 1984 requires companies to use the rate stated monthly by the Pension Benefit Guarantee Corp., a federal agency. But some companies say this is not binding and use a much higher rate.

The new tax law okays using the higher rate, retroactive to the end of 1984, for calculating sums above $25,000.

ANNUITIES AND YOUR PENSION

If you're close to retirement or changing jobs, you're faced with the issue of how to handle the balance in your pension account. There are three basic choices: (1) cashing it in for a lump sum distribution, (2) taking it in monthly payments, and (3) rolling it over into an IRA. Your accountant should be consulted prior to making a final decision.

- With a *lump sum payment* you will have control over your investment choices and you will also be able to take advantage of the 5-year averaging tax formula.
- If you decide on *monthly payments,* then your employer uses your pension dollars to buy an annuity. As mentioned above, annuity returns vary widely. Find out. Of course you can also buy your own individual annuity—see sources at the end of this chapter.
- With an *IRA rollover* your money will grow tax-free until withdrawn, starting no later than age 70½.

If you elect an annuity, you can specify how your pension savings will be invested: for *fixed income,* where the holdings will be bonds and mortgages to provide a set sum each month, or *variable income,* where the investments are split between bonds and stocks and the returns will fluctuate but will never be below a guaranteed minimum.

GUARANTEED INVESTMENT CONTRACTS (GICs)

Few people realize that the most popular investment in most defined benefit plans and company pension funds is a *guaranteed investment contract* or GIC. GICs are fixed rate, fixed term debt instruments sold by insurance companies to corporate pension plans. They offer a stated, fixed rate of return for a specific period.

GICs run as long as the retirement manager likes, generally 1 to 10 years. The insurance company invests the cash it raises in a number of conservative investments, such as long-term bonds, public utility bonds, real estate and mortgages, and, to some extent, stocks. GICs are guaranteed by the issuer, so any default of an underyling issue or drop in interest rates would be absorbed by the insurance company.

Most employees who select where to invest their retirement funds select GICs but know little about them since the contracts are sold to institutions, not individuals. Make sure you do. (They also may go by other names such as "guaranteed income" or "fixed income.")

Three-year GICs currently pay about 8%, about 2 points above money market funds. If rates rise, as with any fixed income vehicle, you are locked into a lower yield. If rates fall, you benefit.

CHECK THE QUALITY

A. M. Best Co. publishes ratings of insurance companies, including those that sell GICs. In addition, both Capitoline Investment Services, Inc. of Richmond, VA, and Standard & Poor's monitor them. Check at your library and with your broker, accountant, or pension officer at work. Now that interest rates are low, insurance companies that guaranteed double-digit rates are vulnerable to having bonds in their GIC portfolios called. In some cases, the insurance company will be forced to use its capital to pay the guaranteed rate. Those with a large portion in Ginnie Maes are also in possible trouble: as homeowners pay off high-rate mortgages, yields are dropping. Says Kenneth L. Walker, president of Capitoline Investment Services: "This will be the year that separates the weak [insurance companies] from the strong." Make certain your pension portfolio is with the strong.

Capitoline advises individuals to distribute their retirement funds among several well-rated GIC issuers. If you're a younger employee it makes greater sense to distribute your funds into equities or other investments, heeding the age-old wisdom of never putting all your eggs in one basket.

NURSING HOME INSURANCE

As you (or members of your family) approach your late 60s or 70s, part of retirement planning should deal with long-term care. Depending upon your financial situation, you may want to consider this new type of insurance. Nursing homes are expensive—average cost of care $65 a day or nearly $24,000 a year. Many senior citizens incorrectly believe Medicare will pick up the total bill. It does not. At present Medicare

---

KINDS OF POLICIES

INSURER	LENGTH OF COVERAGE	DAYS OF PRIOR HOSPITALIZATION REQUIRED
Aetna Life & Annuity 203-273-4475	4 consecutive years skilled and custodial; 2 years at home	zero, or 3 within 30 days of nursing home admittance
AIG Life 800-424-4582	5 years skilled and custodial; 2 years at home	3 within 30 days of nursing home admittance
CNA 312-822-5944	1,000 consecutive days of skilled; 60 days custodial	3 within 30 days of nursing home admittance
Fireman's Fund American Life 800-321-9352	4 consecutive years skilled and custodial; 180 days at home	3 within 90 days of nursing home admittance
Prudential 800-245-1212	3 years skilled or custodial; 365 home visits	3 within 30 days of nursing home admittance
United Equitable 800-323-7645	4 years skilled; 2 years custodial	zero

pays only for the first 20 days and a varying amount for the following 80 days. After 100 days, you must pick up the tab. Most so-called Medigap policies (private supplementary insurance) only pay for a limited service.

A number of the major insurance companies have nursing home policies, which help cushion the costs. Premiums are lowest when you're least likely to need such care. According to a recent insurance company study, the odds are 1 in 100 that you'll need a nursing home between ages 65 and 74; that jumps to 7 in 100 for ages 74 to 84, and 23 in 100 after age 85.

Although a number of insurance companies offer some type of nursing home coverage, they vary greatly in their cost and coverage. The data in the accompanying chart is intended to be informative rather than analytical. Prior to taking out a policy, discuss the matter with your insurance agent or financial planner and study at least two different plans before making a final decision.

FOR FURTHER INFORMATION

Retirement Income Guide
A.M. Best Company
Oldwick, NJ 08858
Twice a year; $42.00 per year

United Retirement Bulletin
Business Service Co.
210 Newbury Street
Boston, MA 02116
Monthly; $21 per year

IRA Owner's Guide
Fidelity Investments
82 Devonshire Street
Boston, MA 02109
Free

Marketing Single Premium Whole Life (booklet). Written and published by Frank H. Miller, 1985 ($11.95; P.O. Box 542, Cherry Hill, NJ 08003).

PART EIGHT

INVESTING LIKE A PRO: INFORMATION AND ADVICE

Information is the solid base for all successful money management. Advice is an extension of that information framed by the experience and knowledge of someone else.

As you have probably learned by experience, most losses are the result of the failure to check all pertinent data before you make a decision. What appeared to be bullish in January may be neutral in May.

Most information relevant to the stock market is readily available and understandable. Do not be intimidated by self-styled "experts" who will guide you up the "road to riches." If you have been successful in business, government, or a profession, you are better informed and more sophisticated about *your* world than anyone else.

You may not speak the jargon of Wall Street, but you understand that to preserve and enhance your capital you must get the facts and use common sense. To meet your present needs and future wants, you must plan ahead, which, in turn, requires information. You cannot achieve a goal until you prepare some sort of road map. Says Venita Van Caspel, a successful money manager and author, "*In all my years of financial planning, I have never met a person who planned to fail. But I have met many who failed to plan.*"

That plan should be yours, not a prepackaged deal served off the assembly line. You are different from any other person. You have different assets and different objectives, pay different taxes, and have a different temperament than anyone else. *Make your own investments.*

Perhaps the best way to emphasize the value of financial information and advice is to ask you to assume that two people in your family each have inherited $100,000 and have asked you to select and manage their portfolios. One is a lively 62-year-old widow and the other is a 19-year-old nephew who will be working in the Peace Corps in Nepal for the next 3 years.

For both, you will need the same basic information, but each portfolio will require a different emphasis, and your method of management will benefit from advice from different counselors.

In order to make the best decisions: (1) start with general summaries available from news stories and statistical services; (2) select 20 corporations whose securities appear attractive; (3) get detailed data from annual reports, research analyses, and advisory letters; (4) make comparisons to narrow your choices; (5) seek outside counsel if you need extra explanation or clarification; (6) with the final list, check criteria against specific goals of income and growth, time frame, risk-reward ratios, etc.; (7) use a computer to make the final review before acting. *If you're not confident, don't proceed any further.* That's what information is for.

In this section you will find material on:

- Sample portfolios for different times in your life
- Reading annual reports
- Finding the best professional help
- Selecting an investment newsletter
- Investing by computer
- Using market indicators

39

A LIFETIME PORTFOLIO

The following sample portfolios contain securities that are suitable for pension plans—holdings chosen for two or more years on the basis of fundamental quality and current undervalue; or flexible holdings that are generally suitable for all age groups. The choices depend on your personal resources, goals, and style. If you're 32 and conservative, take a look at the stocks in the portfolio for the 50s or 60s. If you're 67 and have extra savings, buy some of the growth stocks listed in the portfolio for the 30s. All the suggestions are quality corporations, but conditions can shift rapidly, so stay alert and actively manage your money.

It's exciting and sometimes profitable to speculate with securities: to buy new or high-tech issues and watch the values of the shares double or triple in a few months (usually in a strong market). But such success is more luck than skill. And the long-term odds are *always* against you: only a handful of fledging firms ever grow into quality corporations.

Investments can be almost sure winners over the years when you stick to quality. Buy when the securities are undervalued and have bright prospects and sell them when you can get full price or, if you make a mistake, suffer only a small quick loss. Be aware of quality, value, and, nowadays especially, timing.

This chapter furnishes a list of the kinds of securities that should be the core of every pension and most personal portfolios. The target goal should be a 20% total return with the realization that in flat or down markets the returns will be less, so that your average annual yield will be about 16% or, after commissions, about 15%. *At that rate, you'll double your money every 5 years.*

In the portfolios that follow, few debt securities or speculations are included: debt securities because they should be selected for income

and modest growth; speculations because, by definition, they are not investments. Few provide adequate income and even fewer have records that can justify realistic projections (no matter what your broker's research department may guesstimate). What that means is DON'T be foolish and listen to siren calls of hope; DO be wise and make your decisions on facts and logical anticipations.

HIGHLY PROFITABLE COMPANIES

The table on the next page shows some companies that have had unusually high records over the past years in growth of earnings and dividends. They should continue to be profitable investments. Some are major corporations with worldwide interests but most are smaller companies with greater potential because it's a lot easier to double $250 million sales than it is to double $1 billion.

These firms are managed by tough-minded professionals who must produce or be replaced. At times, their executives may be slow to move, but all have ample resources in personnel, money, facilities, products, distribution, or service. They know how to make money with your money so that shareholders should benefit: from appreciation and ever-higher dividends. These are the types of stocks that are in the portfolios of major institutional investors and that should be part of the holdings of every individual who wants to hold assets. But they are slightly more risky than the big blue chips.

This doesn't mean that you should buy these stocks and lock them in a safe deposit box. Review them frequently, compare their returns with your investment goals, and do not hesitate to sell when the company appears to be living on its reputation rather than on profits or when

HIGHLY PROFITABLE COMPANIES

COMPANY	EARNINGS PER SHARE GROWTH	DIVIDEND GROWTH	RETURN ON EQUITY
Barnett Banks of Florida	16%	15%	22%
ChemLawn	9	22	27
Clorox Co.	17	10	30
Dow Jones & Co.	11	14	39
Dun & Bradstreet	14	16	47
Dunkin' Donuts	14	20	19
Gannett Co.	9	11	54
GEICO	7	18	27
Hathaway Corp	27	40	36
Heinz (H.J.)	12	17	25
McGraw-Hill	8	13	35
Meredith Corp.	13	17	27
Nat'l Convenience Stores	−7	16	25
Pioneer Group	20	31	55
Republic Gypsum	64	55	42
Rubbermaid, Inc.	16	13	20
Sara Lee Corp.	10	10	25
ServiceMaster Ind.	14	22	45
Subaru of America	25	63	53
Wal-Mart Stores	33	45	35
Waste Management	12	27	26

Figures represent 5-year averages.

SOURCE: Standard & Poor's.

major investors start selling. In a broad sense, follow the leaders: buy when they buy; sell when they sell. Your broker can keep you up to date on such activities, or watch the most active list. With wise timing of both buying and selling, you will be able to outscore the market and retire with financial security—or travel more after you retire.

STOCKS FOR HIGH INCOME

This has been an ever-changing mix over the years: first REITs, then bank stocks and convertibles, and now primarily utilities. Here the investor can look for income that is about 25 to 30% below that available from debt securities plus potential appreciation that over the years should average from 5 to 10%. Thus, total returns can be satisfactory. In a few cases, there may be greater and more rapid appreciation, but that's the exception and will probably be the result of a takeover offer rather than corporate progress.

Historically, most of these companies have paid above-average dividends, but *do not take this for granted.* Check the quarterly reports to see if profits are rising enough to warrant higher payouts. Make a note when there's one poor or flat quarter; double-check when there are two in succession; and unless there are good reasons to anticipate that this downtrend has ended, consider selling.

With income stocks, hold as long as the yield is as good or better than at the outset; but when there's a dip or lack of progress, remember that stop-loss rule: get ready to sell with a 10 to 15% drop. Unless you plan to hold the stocks

SMALLER COMPANIES: PROJECTED RISING PROFITS

COMPANY	STANDARD & POOR'S RATING	COMPOUND ANNUAL GROWTH RATE: 1984–89	RECENT PRICE
Angelica Corp.	A–	18	19
Comm. Psychiatric	A–	23	32
Cullinet Software	B+	35	30
Electronic Data	A–	25	28
HBO & Company	NR	40	20
Luby's Cafeterias	A–	20	32
National Data	B+	20	18
Pic'n Save Corp.	B+	25	17
Safeguard Business Sys.	NR	25	16
Safety-Kleen	A–	20	31
Shared Medical	A–	25	30

SOURCE: Dean Witter Reynolds; Standard & Poor's.

a long time, don't argue with Wall Street. And when this decline comes with heavier volume, it means that the professionals are unhappy and that price can continue to plummet.

SAMPLE PORTFOLIOS

This has been one of the most popular features of *Your Investments.* The results over the 13 years that they have been included have been excellent: average annual rates of return of over +20%. They illustrate the wisdom of hewing to the basic principles of quality and value and timing purchases according to clearly defined criteria. The choices are made in July, read by investors after January the next year, and revised the following spring. There have been mistakes, but overall the results have been substantially better than those of stock market averages. The important point to remember is that these are the *types* of securities to look for, but decisions should be made only after you have done a careful review and have made projections based on past performance and long-term market trends.

These sample portfolios are for illustration only: to explain the standards or data used in the selection of profitable securities, to spotlight the importance of proven performance, and to emphasize that successful investment is a long-term process.

QUALITY STOCKS WITH HIGH DIVIDENDS*

COMPANY	RECENT YIELD
Apache Petroleum	9.8%
Bunker Hill Inc. Sec.	10.1
Calif. REIT SBI	11.1
Centerior Energy	11.1
Cenvill Investors	10.6
CNA Income Shares	10.4
Commonwealth Edison	9.8
ENSERCH Corp.	10.6
Exxon Corp.	6.1
General Motors	6.5
Hatteras Income Sec.	9.2
Illinois Power	10.8
John Hancock Inv. Trust	9.2
Mesa Limited Partnership	13.2
Ohio Edison	10.1
Philadelphia Electric	12.4
Sabine Royalty Trust UBI	14.7
Tenneco, Inc.	8.0
Texaco Inc.	9.1
USLIFE Income Fund	10.2
Wells Fargo Mtg./Eqty.	11.0

* All companies are A or A+ ranked.

SOURCE: Standard & Poor's.

CANDIDATES FOR DIVIDEND INCREASES

	CURRENT ANNUAL DIVIDEND RATE	PROBABLE NEW ANNUAL RATE	APPROX- IMATE PRICE	YIELD (%) ON CURRENT RATE	YIELD (%) ON PROBABLE NEW RATE	PAYOUT RATIO†
American Brands	$3.90	$4.00	64	6.1	6.3	47%
American Home Prod.	2.90	3.00	63	4.6	4.8	55
American Medical Int'l	0.72	0.80	20	3.6	4.0	39
★Ameritech	6.60	7.00	100	6.6	7.0	56
Assoc. Dry Goods	1.40	1.48	36	3.9	4.1	39
AZP Group	2.72	2.80	27	10.1	10.4	[1]68
Baltimore Gas & Elec.	1.70	1.80	24	7.1	7.5	[1]63
Bell Atlantic	6.80	7.20	101	6.7	7.1	60
BellSouth	2.80	3.00	46	6.1	6.5	55
Carlisle Corp.	1.08	1.16	33	3.3	3.5	32
Central & South West	2.02	2.14	27	7.5	7.9	54
Chesebrough Pond's	2.00	2.12	39	5.1	5.4	67
Chemical New York	2.48	2.65	45	5.5	5.9	33
Citicorp	2.26	2.40	50	4.5	4.8	28
Clorox	1.36	1.44	45	3.0	3.2	38
Coca-Cola	2.96	3.16	79	3.7	4.0	49
Connecticut Nat. Gas	2.60	2.70	34	7.6	7.9	72
★Consolidated Edison	2.40	2.64	38	6.3	6.9	57
Continental Telecom	1.80	1.86	26	6.9	7.2	[1]57
CSX Corp.	1.16	1.20	32	3.6	3.8	34
Dana Corp.	1.28	1.36	27	4.7	5.0	39
Dart & Kraft	1.56	1.72	40	3.9	4.3	43
Diversified Energy	1.40	1.50	21	6.7	7.1	52
Duke Power	2.60	2.70	36	7.2	7.5	65
Echlin Inc.	0.44	0.50	15	2.9	3.3	34
Federal Co.	1.84	2.00	54	3.4	3.7	37
★Federated Dept. Strs.	2.54	2.64	65	3.9	4.1	37
First Bank System	1.60	1.80	41	3.9	4.4	28
First Interstate Bancorp	2.50	2.60	54	4.6	4.8	34
FPL Group	1.96	2.08	27	7.3	7.7	[1]61
Gillette	2.60	2.70	71	3.7	3.8	46
Houston Industries	2.64	2.80	28	9.4	10.0	[1]62
IC Industries	1.44	1.60	37	3.9	4.3	42
IPALCO	3.04	3.20	37	8.2	8.6	[1]78
Irving Bank	1.96	2.05	44	4.5	4.7	[1]33
Kimberly-Clark	2.32	2.40	63	3.7	3.8	37
Lear Siegler	2.00	2.12	51	3.9	4.2	38
May Dept. Stores	1.88	2.04	61	3.1	3.3	32

	CURRENT ANNUAL DIVIDEND RATE	PROBABLE NEW ANNUAL RATE	APPROX-IMATE PRICE	YIELD (%) ON CURRENT RATE	ON PROBABLE NEW RATE	PAYOUT RATIO†
★Mellon Bank	2.68	2.78	55	4.9	5.1	37
Minnesota Min. & Mfg.	3.50	3.60	88	4.0	4.1	51
Monsanto	2.48	2.56	47	5.3	5.4	50
National Fuel Gas	2.08	2.20	30	6.9	7.3	50
Niagara Mohawk Power	2.08	2.18	20	10.4	10.9	[1]74
★Norfolk Southern	3.40	3.60	78	4.4	4.6	40
★Northeast Utilities	1.58	1.70	18	8.8	9.4	60
Northern States Power	3.52	3.80	51	6.9	7.5	[1]61
NYNEX	6.40	6.80	94	6.8	7.2	54
Pacific Gas & Elec.	1.84	1.96	20	9.2	9.8	[1]69
★Pacific Telesis	5.72	6.00	79	7.2	7.6	58
★Parker Hannifin	1.12	1.16	37	3.0	3.1	33
Peoples Energy	1.20	1.30	19	6.3	6.8	53
Philip Morris	4.00	4.50	92	4.3	4.9	33
§PNC Financial	1.32	1.40	35	3.8	4.0	30
Potomac Electric	2.16	2.30	34	6.4	6.8	55
Procter & Gamble	2.60	2.80	66	3.9	4.2	57
Public Svc. Elec. & Gas	2.84	2.92	31	9.2	9.4	71
Republic N.Y.	1.64	1.80	53	3.1	3.4	27
Rohm & Haas	2.20	2.32	73	3.0	3.2	33
San Diego Gas & El.	2.24	2.40	28	8.0	8.6	[1]69
★Security Pacific	1.34	1.44	32	4.2	4.5	29
South Jersey Indus.	2.48	2.56	30	8.3	8.5	86
So. Calif. Edison	2.16	2.34	25	8.6	9.4	64
★Southwestern Bell	6.00	6.20	80	7.5	7.8	57
Sterling Drug	1.20	1.28	37	3.2	3.5	47
TECO Energy	2.36	2.54	34	6.9	7.5	[1]66
Texas Utilities	2.52	2.70	30	8.4	9.0	56
★Thomas & Betts	1.36	1.40	39	3.5	3.6	51
Tucson Electric	3.00	3.35	41	7.3	8.2	[1]69
Union Pacific	1.80	1.90	51	3.5	3.7	39
USG Corp.	1.68	1.80	47	3.6	3.9	24
§U.S.Bancorp	1.00	1.04	32	3.1	3.3	29
US West	5.72	6.00	85	6.7	7.1	54
§Washington Energy	1.76	1.84	23	7.7	8.0	63
★Wisconsin Elec. Power	2.48	2.66	39	6.4	6.8	22

★Master List issue. § Over the counter. †Current indicated dividend as a percentage of estimated 1986 earnings. [1]Based on 1985 earnings.

SOURCE: Standard & Poor's *The Outlook.*

We are assuming that:

- There are no deductions for the costs of commissions and fees.
- Sales are almost always made when the price of the stock falls 15% below cost or recent high (or when the chart shows a distinct reversal of its uptrend).
- The investor keeps abreast of financial news and takes appropriate action: selling utilities with heavy commitments to nuclear plants when such fears hit the headlines.
- Income taxes are not an important consideration, so that there's no need to take short-term rather than long-term losses—or profits.
- The total lists include more issues than an individual can follow. Generally, 20 stocks should be the maximum; 10 to hold, 10 for the future.

A PORTFOLIO FOR YOUR 30s: ORIENTED TOWARD GROWTH

Because this portfolio is for young investors who have 30 or more years to build assets, these securities are selected primarily for growth rather than income. The fact, however, that they are all quality issues makes them suitable at any stage of your life when appreciation is called for. Regard these stocks as long-term holdings, yet monitor their earnings trends continually and be prepared to sell if earnings deteriorate or if there is a negative change in industry fundamentals. As long as earnings advance and their overall financial picture remains strong, these stocks should be held.

SELL

➤ BARRY WRIGHT (BRA) This company is a supplier of products for computers and other information media, which has been in a slump. It is not expected to see wider profit margins until the end of the 1980s.

➤ BURNDY CORP (BDC) This manufacturer of electrical and electronic connectors has been hurt by the slowdown in domestic business. Its tubing operation has been hit especially hard.

➤ HUMANA INC. (HUM) The nation's third largest hospital management company posted poor results for the year, primarily in its HMO division called Care Plus. In general HMOs are expected to have continuing problems.

HOLD

➤ JOSTEN'S, INC. (JOS) This manufacturer of school jewelry and printer of school books has increased its sales and earnings for 29 consecu-

A PORTFOLIO FOR YOUR 30s

SHARES PER COMPANY	ORIGINAL COST	PRICE AUGUST 1986	DIVIDEND	YIELD	P/E
Buy					
100 Comm. Psychiatric	$ 34	$ 34	$0.32	1.0%	21
100 IBM	138	138	4.40	3.2	13
Sell					
200 Barry Wright	25	19	0.60	3.2	17
200 Burndy Corp.	17	14	—	—	—
100 Humana Inc.	33	23	0.76	3.3	11
Hold					
150 Josten's Inc.	25	35	0.88	2.5	18
100 Mead Corp.	42	57	1.20	2.1	20
100 Montgomery St. Inc.	19	23	1.80	7.8	—
100 Travelers	46	46	2.16	4.7	12

tive years. Management has wisely decided to move into foreign markets: Japan, UK, France. Earnings per share were $1.76 in 1985 and are estimated to reach $1.90 in 1986 and $2.10 by 1987. JOS may not be a buy at this time, but it is worth holding.

➤ MEAD CORP (MEA) A diversified paper and forest products company, Mead has several areas of strength: catalog paper, school supplies, and orders from businesses. It has been hurt recently by the strong dollar, but a decline in the strength of the dollar plus anticipated healthier paper markets by the late 1980s make the shares of this well-run company an attractive buy.

➤ MONTGOMERY STREET INCOME SECURITIES, INC. (MTS) A closed-end diversified investment company, 70% of its assets are in high-quality debt instruments. These shares are a solid 2- to 4-year holding for even the most conservative investors.

➤ TRAVELERS CORP (TIC) Based in Hartford, CT, Travelers offers a full line of life, accident, health, fire insurance, annuities, and mutual funds. Travelers was selling in the high 50s until its recent registration of 6 million additional shares. Despite this potential dilution, the fundamentals remain strong.

BUY

➤ COMMUNITY PSYCHIATRIC (CMY) This company owns and manages 25 psychiatric hospitals and 54 artificial-kidney centers and also operates a home health care business. Management has proposed conversion into a limited partnership. The initial annual dividend rate would be $2.40 per share or a yield of 7%.

➤ IBM (IBM) Investors should buy and hold this premier blue chip stock. Although earnings per share tends to fall during periods of slow economic growth, it should improve during the latter half of 1987. In the meantime, the dividend is secure and likely to rise.

A PORTFOLIO FOR YOUR 40s: INCOME PLUS GROWTH

This sample portfolio is designed for individuals who are beginning to have it made, can afford steady savings, and, because of family responsibilities, are becoming somewhat more conservative than they were in their 30s. They look, therefore, for income plus growth, not the other way around. Total performance of the portfolio is up significantly from last year, so we're

A PORTFOLIO FOR YOUR 40s

SHARES PER COMPANY	ORIGINAL COST	PRICE AUGUST 1986	DIVIDEND	YIELD	P/E
Buy					
100 Dun & Bradstreet	$112	$112	$2.56	2.3%	26
100 Oklahoma Gas & Electric	38	38	2.08	5.4	16
Sell					
100 Archer-Daniels-Midland	18	21	0.10	0.5	13
100 AZP Group	28	32	2.72	8.6	9
Hold					
100 Amer. Capital Bond Fund	20	25	2.20	8.8	—
100 CPC International	38	70	2.20	3.1	22
150 EG&G Corp.	20	30	0.52	1.7	15
100 Emhart Corp.	18	34	1.40	4.1	13
100 Exxon Corp.	34	65	3.60	5.5	9
150 Mutual of Omaha	14	16	1.44	8.9	—
100 Stanley Works	22	40	1.04	2.6	14
100 United Telecommun.	19	30	1.92	6.4	13

staying fully vested, with the exception of AZP and Archer-Daniels.

SELL

➤ ARCHER-DANIELS-MIDLAND (ADM) A processor and marketer of agricultural commodities, this company has *not* turned in expected earnings increases. Poor agribusiness not likely to improve radically during next 12 months.

➤ AZP CORP. (AZP) Formerly Arizona Public Service Company, this electric utility also owns 29.1% of the Palo Verde #1 nuclear power plant. This element of risk, especially in light of the Russian nuclear accident, makes these shares unnecessarily risky to hold.

HOLD

➤ CPC INTERNATIONAL (CPC) The stock of this worldwide food products and corn refining company has moved from $38 per share when we first placed it in the 40s portfolio to its July 1986 price of $67. Its well-known brand names include Knorr soups, Hellmann's, Skippy peanut butter, Mazola corn oil, Karo syrup, and Thomas' baked goods. Several new plants coming on stream are expected to reduce costs and improve profit margins. The company offers respectable growth prospects over the next 3 to 5 years.

➤ EG&G CORP (EGG) This company, which manufactures electronic components and scientific instruments, has benefited from the growing defense program, chalking up a 15-year record of double-digit earnings. Its future appears equally bright with numerous government contracts and a recent $5-million contract with Xerox. The price of this stock moves relatively slowly albeit steadily upward, so it should be regarded as a long-term holding.

➤ EMHART CORP. (EMH) This well-run manufacturer of hardware, do-it-yourself items, shoe machinery and tools, as well as chemical products reports that international sales account for 41% of business, and will benefit from the declining dollar. These shares have a 3- to 5-year appreciation potential.

➤ EXXON CORP. (XON) The world's largest integrated oil company, Exxon continues to reach new highs largely because of its stock buy-back program. Management is wisely concentrating on cost controls. The stock offers a respectable

dividend return approaching 7%. Given the major risk inherent in all the oils, Exxon is probably the best of the group at this time.

➤ STANLEY WORKS (SWK) A well-established manufacturer of consumer tools and hardware, and a leading supplier of the fast-growing do-it-yourself market. With more housing starts and better control of production and distribution, SWK is projected to have earnings per share in 1986 of $3.50, up from $2.60 in 1984. Mac Tools, the company's professional auto mechanics division, is growing at a double-digit rate. Future prospects appear secure.

➤ UNITED TELECOMMUNICATIONS (UT) This is the second largest non-Bell telephone company and is aggressively expanding in the communications field by buying 9.8% of Southern New England Telephone Co. and undertaking joint ventures with AT&T and Control Data. Despite the conservative nature of this investment, UT has moved from $19 when we first recomended it to $51, while its yield of 8.1% is very respectable at this time.

➤ AMERICAN CAPITAL BOND FUND (ACB) This diversified, closed-end management fund states as its investment objective: income and conservation of capital. It invests solely in nonconvertible debt securities. Approximately 80% of its assets are in high-quality instruments. These shares, with their 11% yield, should be held as an income investment only.

➤ MUTUAL OF OMAHA INTEREST SHARES (MUO) This closed-end fund invests over 50% of its assets in conservative U.S. government debt issues and the rest in aggressive corporates. This balanced approach has been successful: note the 10.4% yield. These shares bear watching for any significant drop in the return.

BUY

➤ OKLAHOMA GAS & ELECTRIC (OGE) This utility offers both security and a good current dividend. It has an exceptionally strong balance sheet and no nuclear plants.

➤ DUN & BRADSTREET (DNB) This leader in the information business is expanding its international operations. D&B owns Reuben H. Donnelley, Moody's, and A. C. Nielson. Earnings could increase as much as 15 to 18% this year.

A PORTFOLIO FOR YOUR 50s: LOOKING TOWARD RETIREMENT

Here the thrust becomes more conservative because most people are still paying college bills and beginning to think seriously now about the capital needed for their retirement. The portfolio selections reflect this growing conservativism and desire for safe, steady income.

HOLD

➤ BRIGGS & STRATTON CORP. (BGG) The world's largest manufacturer of air-cooled gasoline engines keeps its inventories low. Although the company was hard hit by the recession, it seems to be turning around slowly yet steadily. Management is making impressive investments in new plant and equipment, keeping it one step ahead of the competition. Shares of this well-run, solid company have a 3- to 5-year capital gains potential.

➤ FLORIDA POWER & LIGHT 8s, '99 These income-producing bonds have appreciated from last year's price of $62½ to $77 and as the bond approaches its maturity date (1999) the price will move closer to its par value of $1,000. Hold these bonds for even further appreciation. The current yield at today's price is 10.37%, an above average return in view of declining interest rates.

➤ K-MART 6s, '99 Recommended last year at a price of $90, these CVs are now selling at $114. They are convertible into 28.17 shares of common at a conversion price of $35.50. These bonds have appreciated along with the price of the common and now yield 5.3%. We recommend that they be held for further appreciation as this leading retailer continues its exemplary record.

➤ DELUXE CHECK PRINTERS, INC. (DLX) The country's largest check printer appears headed for another record-breaking year. Demand is high and a 7 to 10% increase is expected to push sales up and earnings per share to $2.85 from $2.43 in 1985. Diversification is an added plus: the company has a 43% holding in Data Card Corp., a leading plastic card manufacturer. A solid near- and long-term holding.

➤ JOHN HANCOCK INVESTORS TRUST (JHI) A closed-end diversified trust whose primary goal is income. The portfolio consists of corporate fixed income securities and some convertibles. Preferred and common stocks cannot exceed 20% of the fund's total assets. John Hancock has a substantial commitment to long-term debt issues, which look increasingly attractive as interest rates decline.

A PORTFOLIO FOR YOUR 50s

SHARES PER COMPANY	ORIGINAL COST	PRICE AUGUST 1986	DIVIDEND	YIELD	P/E
Buy					
300 Pioneer Corp.*	$20½	$23	$2.76	12%	—
Sell					
200 Sonat, Inc.	27	26	2.00	7.7	—
Hold					
200 Briggs & Stratton Corp.	27	34	1.60	4.7	15
200 Deluxe Check Printers	39	69	1.28	1.9	26
10 Florida P&L 8s, '99	62½	92	—	9.0†	—
300 John Hancock Inv. Trust	15	24	2.14	9.0	—
10 K-Mart 6s, '99 (CVs)	90½	147	—	4.1	—
200 Ohio Edison	15	22	1.92	8.9	9

* Mesa Ltd. Partners pref A (see text)
† Yield to maturity

A PORTFOLIO FOR YOUR 60s

SHARES PER COMPANY	ORIGINAL COST	PRICE AUGUST 1986	DIVIDEND	YIELD	P/E
Buy					
10 Commonwealth Ed. 9½s, 2016	$100	$100	—	9.5%	—
Hold					
10 AT&T 8¾s, '00	67	99½	—	8¾	—
200 Amer. Electric Power	24	31	2.26	7.3	13
200 Drexel Bond-Deb. Fund	21	23	2.00	8.8	—
300 Southern Company	22	27	2.04	7.6	9
100 J.P. Morgan	63	93	2.45	2.6	10
Sell					
300 Texas Utilities	20	37	2.68	7.2	9
200 Rochester Telephone	18½	49	2.56	5.2	13

➤ OHIO EDISON CO. (OEC) The risk factor associated with this electric utility is reflected in its high yield of 12.1%. Monitor carefully and sell if there is negative news or evidence that the dividend is in trouble. In the meanwhile, hold for the excellent yield.

SELL

➤ SONAT, INC. (SNT) The stock of this aggressive gas and drilling company has been hurt by the drop in the price of crude. Sell and take the modest profit.

BUY

➤ PIONEER CORP (PNA) These 300 shares were exchanged for 552 Mesa Ltd. Partnership preference A units when Mesa acquired Pioneer Corp. in the summer of 1986. The new units receive first rights to cash distributions as MLP units. (The MLP was a spinoff of Mesa Petroleum Co. into a limited partnership.) Each unit will have an annual distribution of $1.50 and yield over 12%.

A PORTFOLIO FOR YOUR 60s: EMPHASIS ON SAFETY

In this age bracket, the emphasis should be on income plus some growth. Safety should be paramount unless you have money to spare from an inheritance or sale of your home. This is the best place for debt issues, preferably with intermediate to not-too-long maturities that take into account the actuarial life expectancies of both husband and wife: at age 65, 14.4 years for men and 18.8 for women.

- *Treasury bonds.* As we go to press, U.S. Treasury bonds with the longer maturities (i.e., those due in 2010 to 2015) are yielding 7.4% and those with 10-year maturities, 7.5%. We suggest, therefore, that those investors seeking the highest level of safety turn to Treasury notes and bonds. For those seeking higher yields *and* willing to assume the risk of owning Baa bonds, buy Marathon Oil 12½s, '94 at $102, yielding 12%.

- *Zero coupon bonds* to mature at or soon after retirement date. These are only for pension plans and trusts where there are no taxes to be paid. In personal portfolios, there are no interest checks, but you must pay annual taxes on the imputed income—a complex calculation that will not be welcomed by your accountant.

- *Pass-throughs* such as Ginnie Maes or Fannie Maes that pay a high yield via monthly checks (frequently enhanced by mortgage repayments). Be wary of relying on those until you are over age 70 with a life expectancy of 11.5 years for men and 15.2 for women. Most pass-throughs are paid out in less than 15 years.

40

BEHIND THE SCENES:
Reading Annual Reports

Some are flashy, some are plain; some are fat and some are thin; but all annual reports are the single most important tool in analyzing corporations to decide whether to buy, hold, sell, or pass by their securities. In a few minutes, you can check the corporation's quality and profitability and, with closer study, can learn a great deal about the character and ability of management, its methods of operation, its products and services, and, most important, its future prospects. If you own securities of the corporation, you will receive a copy of the annual report about 4 months after the close of its operating year. If you are considering becoming a shareholder, get a copy from your local library or your broker or by writing the company (get the address from reference books at your library).

First, skim the text, check the statement of income and earnings to see how much money was made and whether this was more than that of previous years, and review the list of officers and directors for familiar names. Later, if you're still interested, you can follow up the points of interest.

The amount of information is amazing; scores of figures show the source of: revenues and earnings of major divisions; foreign and domestic activities; off-balance sheet financing such as store, plant, and equipment leases; depreciation, tax credits (gained or sold), effects of inflation, allocations of expenses for interest, research, and so on and on. Almost all the data needed to make wise judgments are available in these annual summaries and in capsulated form for updates in quarterly reports.

The statements will always be factually correct, but the interpretations, especially those in the president's message, will naturally attempt to present the most favorable view within legal and accounting limits.

Here's what to look for.

➤ TRENDS In sales, earnings, dividends, accounts receivable. If they continue to rise, chances are that you've found a winner. It's like a chart where the timing is indicated by the trend: to *buy* when it's moving up; to *review* when it plateaus; to consider *selling* when it's down.

As you review the trends, keep in mind the external forces that can have an impact on the future: with financial institutions, interest rates; with hospital firms, the impact of mandated cost ceilings; with oil and gas companies, new federal legislation affecting tax benefits, etc.

➤ INFORMATION *From the tables:* corporate financial strength and operating success or failure; *from the text:* explanations of what happened during the year and what management projects for the future. If you don't believe management, do not hold the stock.

➤ POSITIVES New plants, products, personnel, and programs. Are the total assets greater and liabilities lower than in previous years? If so, why? Through tighter controls or decreases in allocations for R&D, marketing, etc.?

If the profits were up, was the gain due to fewer outstanding shares (because of repurchase of stock), to nonrecurring income from the sale of property, or to higher sales and lower costs?

➤ NEGATIVES Plant closings, sales of subsidiaries, discontinuance of products, and future needs for financing. Not all these will always be adverse, but they can make a significant difference with respect to what happens in the next few years.

If the profits were down, was this due to the elimination of some products or services? of price wars? of poor managerial decisions?

➤ FOOTNOTES Read these carefully because this is where you can spot problems. Be cautious if there were heavy markdowns of inventory, adverse governmental regulations, rollovers of debt, and other unusual events.

➤ BALANCE SHEET To see whether cash or liquid assets are diminishing and whether accounts receivables, inventories, or total debt are rising. This will usually be a yellow rather than a red flag.

➤ FINANCIAL SUMMARY Not only for the past year but for the previous 5 years. This will provide an overall view of corporate performance and set the stage for an analysis of the most recent data.

In the stock market, past is prologue. Few companies achieve dramatic progress or fall on hard times suddenly. In most cases, the changes have been forecast. The corporation with a long, fairly consistent record of profitable growth can be expected to do as well, or better, in the years ahead and thus prove to be a worthwhile holding. The erratic performer is likely to move from high to low profits (or losses). And the faltering company will have signs of deterioration over 2 or 3 years.

READING THE REPORT

When you review the text, you can get an idea of the kind of people who are managing your money, learn what they did, or did not, do and why, and get some idea of future prospects.

➤ READ THE REPORT CHINESE STYLE From back to front. Start with the auditor's report. If there are hedging phrases such as "except for" or "subject to," be wary. These phrases can signal the inability to get accurate information and may forecast future write-offs.

➤ READ THE PRESIDENT'S MESSAGE If there were failures, there should be logical explanations. Management is not always right in its decisions, but in financial matters, frankness is the base for confidence. If previous promises were unfulfilled (and that's why you should keep your annual reports), find out why. If the tone is overly optimistic, be wary. Modern business is too competitive, and too subject to external pressures, to ensure swift progress. If you are skeptical, do not hold the stock.

➤ CHECK SIGNIFICANT COMMENTS AGAINST THE FINANCIAL FACTS In its 1981 annual report, Baldwin-United boasted of a 36% growth in earnings per share and a 91% gain in assets. But the back of the report revealed that in the past 2 years, the cash drains were $87 million and $105 million, respectively. *No wonder the company went belly-up!*

➤ WATCH FOR DOUBLE-TALK Clichés are an integral part of business writing, but they should not be substitutes for proper explanations. If you find such meaningless phrases as "a year of transition" or some of the deathless prose listed in the box, start getting ready to unload. There are better opportunities elsewhere.

HOW TO TRANSLATE THE PRESIDENT'S MESSAGE

Here are some of the techniques used in writing annual reports to phrase comments in terms that tend to divert the reader's attention away from problems.

WHAT THEY SAY	WHAT THEY MEAN
"The year was difficult and challenging."	"Sales and profits were off, but expenses (including executive salaries) were up."
"Management has taken steps to strengthen market share."	"We're underselling our competitors to drive them out of the market."
"Integrating the year's highs and lows proved challenging."	"Sales were up; profits went nowhere."
"Management worked diligently to preserve a strong financial position."	"We barely broke even but were able to avoid new debts."
"Your company is indebted to the dedicated service of its employees."	"We don't pay 'em much, but there's not much else to cheer about."

➤ STUDY THE QUALITY AND SOURCE OF EARNINGS When profits are entirely from operations, they indicate management's skill; when they are partially from bookkeeping, look again. But do not be hasty in drawing conclusions. Even the best of corporations may utilize "special" accounting.

Examples: In valuing inventories, LIFO (last in, first out), current sales are matched against the latest costs so that earnings can rise sharply when inventories are reduced and those latest costs get older and thus lower. When oil prices were at a peak, Texaco cut inventories by 16%. The LIFO cushion, built up over several years, was a whopping $454 million and transformed what would have been a drop in net income into a modest gain.

Such "tricks" are one reason why stocks fall or stay flat after annual profits are reported. Analysts are smart enough to discover that earnings are more paper than real.

➤ TAKE A GOOD LOOK AT FOREIGN CURRENCY TRANSACTIONS These can be tricky and often difficult to understand. Under recent revisions

INFLATION-ADJUSTED ACCOUNTING: MERCK & CO., INC.

	($ IN MILLIONS EXCEPT PER SHARE AMOUNTS)				
	1983	1982	1981	1980	1979
Sales					
As reported	$3,246	$3,063	$2,929	$2,734	$2,385
1983 constant dollars	3,246	3,161	3,207	3,305	3,275
Net Income					
As reported	$ 451	$ 415	$ 398	$ 415	$ 382
1983 constant dollars	381	347	340	411	414
Current costs	420	400	423	457	466
Earnings per Share					
As reported	$ 6.10	$ 5.61	$ 5.36	$ 5.54	$ 5.06
1983 constant dollars	5.15	4.69	4.56	5.48	5.49
Current costs	5.68	5.41	5.69	6.11	6.18
Common Stock Dividends Paid per Share					
As reported	$ 2.80	$ 2.80	$ 2.60	$ 2.30	$ 1.90
1983 constant dollars	2.80	2.89	2.85	2.78	2.61
Net Assets at Year-End					
As reported	$2,435	$2,204	$2,001	$1,863	$1,665
1983 constant dollars	3,080	2,933	2,797	2,779	2,674
Current costs	3,041	2,931	2,800	2,826	2,780
Purchasing Power Gain on Net Monetary Liabilities	$ 11	$ 6	$ 6	$ 2	$ 2
Market Price per Common Share at Year-end					
Actual	$90.38	$84.63	$84.75	$84.75	$72.25
1983 constant dollars	88.85	86.35	89.85	97.90	94.00
Average Consumer Price Index	298.4	289.1	272.4	246.8	217.4

Note: With inflation down to below 5%, these figures are no longer overly significant. Some companies are skipping such comparisons, but these summaries give you a good idea of the impact of inflation when it was at a high level.

of accounting rules, it's possible to recast them retroactively when, of course, they can be favorable. One major firm whose domestic profits had been lagging went back 4 years with its overseas reports and boosted its per share profits to $7.08 from the previously reported $6.67 per share.

Most international corporations have elaborate systems for hedging against fluctuations in foreign currencies. These are relatively expensive, but they tend to even out sharp swings in the value of the dollar. Wall Street hates uncertainty and tends to prefer stocks of corporations that try to protect their monetary positions. That's a good example to follow.

You may have to burrow in the footnotes, but with major companies, find out about the pension obligations: the money which the firm must pay to its retirees. One way to boost profits (because this means lower annual contributions) is to raise the assumed rate of return on pension fund investments. When General Motors increased its projected rate of return to 7% from 6% a year, it added 69¢ per share to its reported earnings. This is OK as long as the higher yield is justified by investment performance.

➤ CALCULATE THE CASH FLOW The after-tax earnings plus annual depreciation on fixed assets minus preferred dividends, if any. Then compare with previous years. Cash flow is indicative of corporate earning power because it shows the dollars available for profits, new investments, etc.

➤ KEEP AN EYE ON DEBT If the total loans drop sharply, find out if this was due to a redemption of the securities with extra cash or from the proceeds of the sale of assets or from assets-shifting such as defeasance. With this technique, the debt is retired via an irrevocable trust of risk-free investments such as T-bills or U.S. bonds. The trust pays the interest on the old debt and eventually retires the principal. But since the old bonds were swapped at a discount, the spread between that cost and par is shown as "earnings": e.g., Company E owes $10,000 in bonds to be repaid in 5 years; it uses defeasance to shift the debt for $50,000 and so reports $50,000 in extra profits. Nice deal for the company but not too good for the investor.

➤ BEWARE OF OVERENTHUSIASM ABOUT NEW PRODUCTS, PROCESSES OR SERVICES Usually, it takes 3 years to translate new operations into sizable sales and profits. And the majority of new projects are losers.

➤ PAY SPECIAL ATTENTION TO THE RETURN ON EQUITY (PROFIT RATE) This is the best measurement of management's ability to make money with your money. Any ROE above 15% is good; when below, compare the figure with that of previous years and other firms in the same industry. Some industries seldom show a high rate of return: heavy machinery because of the huge investment in plants and equipment; utilities because of the ceiling set by public commissions.

➤ WATCH OUT FOR EQUITY ACCOUNTING Where earnings from other companies, which are more than 20% owned, are included in total profits. There are no cash dividends, so the money cannot be used for expansion or payouts to shareholders. This maneuver can massage the reported earnings, but that's about all. Teledyne, a major conglomerate, reported $19.96 per share profits, but a close examination revealed that $3.49 of this was from equity accounting—phantom, not real, earnings.

To get the most from ownership of securities in a company, take advantage of special offers: booklets, explanatory folders, products sold at discounts, dividend reinvestment plans, etc. *Remember:* as a stockholder, you are part owner of the business.

41 FINDING THE BEST PROFESSIONAL HELP

Many people who are willing to spend some time in research and analysis, to adhere to principles such as are outlined in this guide, and to use common sense can be successful investors. But there are times when advisers can be useful: for *direction* when you are starting out; for *confirmation* when you become more experienced; and for *management* when you have substantial assets.

Be slow to let anyone else manage your money without your approval or at least knowledge. It's your savings. You worked hard to earn these dollars, and in most cases, you know your goals and needs better than anyone else does.

There are four general categories of people to help you with your investments, as well as various institutional planning departments.

➤ STOCKBROKERS These are representatives or agents of a buyer or seller of stocks or bonds. Brokers, who receive commissions for their services, are sometimes partners in a brokerage firm, but if not, they are called registered representatives (reps) and are regular employees. Brokers and registered reps must first be employed by a member firm of the National Association of Security Dealers (NASD) and then pass a comprehensive exam. Only upon successful completion of the exam is the broker allowed to buy and sell securities for customers.

➤ INVESTMENT ADVISERS An all-inclusive term covering pension fund managers, publishers of investment newsletters, and personal money advisers. The SEC requires all investment advisers to register, although it does not impose any special requirements or qualifications in order to register. Professional money managers fall within this category.

These are individuals or groups; some operate independently, but most are associated with other financially oriented organizations. Roughly, their fees are 1% of portfolio value with a minimum of $500 a year. Above $1 million, the fees are scaled down. Small savings, under $250,000, are usually handled through standard portfolios designed for various investment objectives. Larger holdings receive personal attention.

Their biggest plus: You have someone to talk to, someone who can keep you up to date on economic and financial developments, back up recommendations with research reports, and explain the pros and cons of various opportunities or options.

Investment advisers are worthwhile when: (1) they provide factual, intelligible, useful information; (2) you have substantial assets that require more attention than you are willing, or able, to give; (3) you can afford the luxury of someone to hold your hand with respect to investment. In most cases, for most sophisticated people, the benefits of investment advice are more psychological than real.

It is essential to *use advisers in related areas:* a competent lawyer to set up a retirement plan or trust; a tax expert to make certain that you are taking advantage of legitimate ways to reduce taxes; and an experienced accountant to prepare complicated tax returns. A professional money manager can be valuable when you are involved with large sums in a fiduciary capacity, but for personal and pension savings, the primary role of the investment adviser should be to establish a system that will enable you to make your own decisions. Once you have a sound base, you can decide whether you want to handle your savings directly or with help, or to turn management over to someone else—for a fee.

With small sums, such as $10,000 in an IRA, any intelligent individual can make his or her own decisions. When assets grow larger, information—from broker's research reports, financial publications, and advisory letters—can be helpful. And when your savings total over $100,000, it may be wise to seek professional assistance. At this point, the right kind of investment advice can help you to increase your wealth and teach you how to be your own money manager. The fees paid will be returned many times over, in dollars and in peace of mind.

➤ FINANCIAL PLANNERS These generalists, who theoretically help you develop an overall financial plan and then implement it with you, are not licensed, registered, or regulated. Planners receive a fee for their services, which can range from $150 to several thousand dollars, depending on the size of your portfolio. Almost anyone can be a financial planner, although planners tend to be insurance salespeople, brokers, bankers, and/or lawyers. They may or may not have taken special courses.

➤ CERTIFIED FINANCIAL PLANNER (CFP) This designation is awarded individuals who pass a series of long, detailed examinations on various aspects of investing and financial planning at the College for Financial Planning in Denver. Typically, the CFP reviews the portfolio and prepares specific recommendations for present and future action . . . at a cost of from $60 to $150 an hour. This service can be valuable when you have ample assets and expect more in the future, but unbiased CFPs are hard to find. To make a living, most have to rely on income from the sale of insurance, tax shelters, or limited partnerships. At worst, you'll get a better idea of how to plan your investments and financing; at best, you will learn how to handle your wealth more profitably.

FINDING THE BEST

When you feel the need of an adviser, choose carefully, and if your selection is not satisfactory, make a change. Avoid counsel from those with selfish interests: *any stockbroker* who relies excessively on commissions from buying and selling securities; *the insurance agent* whose livelihood depends on the ability to sell only certain policies and packages; *the banker* whose institution provides savings and trust services.

The number one consideration in choosing any type of investment adviser is comfort: to select someone whom you respect, whose advice you are willing to follow, who operates in a professional manner (with integrity, intelligence, and information), and who eases your doubts and fears.

These criteria eliminate brokers hustling for commissions; salespeople who make quick recommendations without considering your assets, income obligations, and goals; and everyone who promises large, fast returns.

Look for the following:

➤ PERFORMANCE OVER THE LONG TERM Select someone with at least 10 years' experience in order to cover both bull and bear markets. Anyone can be lucky with a few stocks for a few years, but concentrate on an individual or firm whose recommendations have outpaced market averages by at least 2 percentage points: higher in *up* markets; lower in *down* periods. This applies to total returns—income plus appreciation or minus depreciation—and refers primarily to stocks but is a sound guideline for debt securities. A minimum expectation from an investment adviser should range between 15% and 20% including income and appreciation. The cost of this advice, including commissions and fees, will be at least 2%, according to veteran money manager Harold C. (Bill) Mayer.

Superior performance should be a continuing criterion. Every 6 months, compare the returns of your investments with those of a standard indicator: with *bonds,* the Dow Jones bond average or, for tax-frees, the Dow municipal bond average; with *stocks,* the Standard & Poor's 500 (which is broader and more representative than the Dow Jones industrial average). Then, subtract the commissions you paid to see whether you're getting your money's worth.

➤ REPUTATION As indicated by the longevity of the organization and the judgments of non-competing professionals. Comments from old customers are most valuable for helping you learn how you are likely to be treated and about the promptness and efficiency of service and reports. Is extra cash moved quickly into a money market fund? Are orders executed promptly and correctly? Are dividends posted immediately? Are monthly reports issued on time?

➤ COMPATIBILITY An overall investment philosophy to match your objectives of income or growth. If you're conservative, stay away from a swinger who constantly comes up with new issues, wants you to trade frequently, suggests speculative situations, and scoffs at interest and dividends.

If you're aggressive, look for someone who keeps up on growth opportunities and is smart enough to recognize that no one should always be fully invested in equities and not to recommend bonds or liquid assets under unfavorable stock market conditions.

➤ STRATEGY/TECHNIQUES Find out by asking questions such as:

- **Where do you get investment ideas?** From in-house research or from brokerage firms?

- **What are your favorite stock-picking strategies?** Out-of-favor stocks with low price-earnings ratios? Small company growth stocks? Larger corporations whose shares are now undervalued based on predictable earnings expectations?

- **How diversified are the portfolios?** Do you shoot for big gains from a few stocks or seek modest profits from a broader list?

➤ WILLINGNESS TO SELL Successful investing relies on two factors: how much you make and how little you lose. Check the composition of all portfolios for the past 10 years. If they are still holding glamor stocks bought at peaks and now near lows, move on! Don't stick with professionals who ignore their losses.

Finally—and this applies to your attitude after you've made a choice—**DON'T be afraid to say no** if you neither understand nor have confidence in the recommendations. Nothing is more important than trust when you are dealing with money. You can forgive a few mistakes, but when they mount up, cancel the agreement.

INTERVIEWING POTENTIAL ADVISERS AND BROKERS

Whatever you do, don't select someone to help you with your investments by walking into a firm cold, off the street. And never sign on with the first person you talk with. Set up interviews with several candidates. Go to the interview prepared with a series of questions and compare how each of your potential advisers answers them.

Jay J. Pack, a broker and author of *How to Talk to a Broker*, suggests the following six basic questions:

- What do you suggest that I do with my $25,000 (or whatever amount you have)?

Beware of the person who suggests you put it all in one product.

- How long have you been in business? With this firm?
- Will you give me several references so I may check on your record?
- What will it cost me to use your help? Get specifics about fees and commissions, in writing.
- What sort of return can I expect from my investment?
- What research materials do you rely upon?

Any good planner, adviser, or broker should:

- Be willing to meet with you in person for a free consultation
- Provide you with references or sample portfolios
- Ask you about your net worth, financial goals, and tolerance for risk
- Offer you several alternatives, and say why
- Be able to refer you to other professionals for specific help
- Set up a schedule for reviewing your securities, assets, and overall financial picture
- Answer your phone calls

WHERE TO GO

➤ INVESTMENT COMPANIES OR MUTUAL FUNDS As explained earlier, these are professionally managed pools of funds that invest in a diversified group of securities for specific goals: growth, income, balance, or a combination. In most cases, the initial investment is small and you can make additional purchases easily and can buy and sell shares quickly.

Realistically, of course, you seldom get advice, because the fund managers do what they think best. But you can call the 800 number for information on the various types of funds and their performance.

➤ BROKERS Despite the advertisements and fancy titles that are being bestowed on registered representatives, brokers are still commission men and women. They earn their living by persuading customers to buy and sell. Directly or indirectly through their firm's research department, they can provide statistical information and will make recommendations. An honest broker can make your portfolio grow.

Some brokerage firms promote discretionary accounts, where all decisions are made by "professionals." These are designed primarily for aggressive portfolios seeking to profit from special situations, trading, and other forms of speculation. In bull markets, these fare well, but in see-saws, profits can disappear. Use only if you have ample funds, because the minimum portfolio is typically $200,000.

➤ INSURANCE COMPANIES Here again, there's a strong push for agents to become "financial advisers." What this really means is that investments are handled by the home office according to specific preset goals. Your funds are commingled with those of others, so what you're buying is a special type of mutual fund. Your savings are allocated to meet your investment goals: for *fixed income,* holdings in a mix of debt and dividend paying stocks; for *variable income,* debt and equity securities, real estate, oil and gas deals, etc.; for *tax shelters,* real estate and oil and gas deals.

Only a handful of these types of insurance packages have been around long enough to build a performance record, and most offers include life insurance. Furthermore, the costs are high: commissions of 5 to 20% plus management fees; and, in some cases, there are penalties for early withdrawals.

➤ BANKS, TRUST COMPANIES, AND THRIFT INSTI-TUTIONS Their "advice" departments are organized to *manage* large savings such as pension funds or estates. With few exceptions, their performance records have been excessively conservative.

Fortunately, with competition, there are beginning to be major changes: bank holding companies are setting up special departments to sponsor public-invited investment seminars, provide free "personal" financial counsel to high-balance depositors, and offer more-or-less standard counseling by a bank executive who reviews your portfolio and makes recommendations with the hope that you will turn management over to the bank's "experienced" staff. Typical charges at Chase Manhattan Bank: $100 an hour with a $250 minimum.

➤ FUND ADVISORY SERVICES These are a new development, where publishers of specialized newsletters track the performance of mutual funds and recommend those that they think will perform best in the near future. Their comments are more interesting than profitable. It's a new version of racing forms.

➤ MODEL PORTFOLIOS These are available from investment advisory services that publish weekly reports and letters. You don't have to follow their recommendations, but when you do, you are, in effect, turning over control of the management of your money.

SETTLING DISPUTES

ARBITRATION
As with all businesses, there are individuals who either deliberately or carelessly give poor advice. In the brokerage business, integrity is paramount, so that all American exchanges have strict rules, and most firms have

---

BEFORE YOU UNDERTAKE ARBITRATION YOU SHOULD KNOW THAT:

- The odds for an arbitration settlement in your favor are typically about 50:50. (In 1983, for example, the NYSE's arbitration group decided 137 cases in the client's favor and 139 for the broker.)
- Arbitration is not the only way to settle an unresolved broker dispute, regardless of what your contract with the brokerage house states. The SEC has ruled that clients can, if they prefer, address violations of federal securities law in a court.
- If you decide to go to arbitration and the case is not decided in your favor, you cannot turn around and sue the broker. You can sue only if you do not choose arbitration first.
- One advantage of suing is that you are permitted to use discovery procedures to find other clients who may support your case.
- Act immediately if you are planning to sue or go to arbitration. Arbitrators and judges won't look favorably upon your complaint if you wait to see if the investment in question goes up in price.

SOURCE: Jay J. Pack, *How to Talk to a Broker,* New York: Harper & Row, 1985.

compliance officers whose responsibility is to monitor trading, make sure that full information is provided to all clients, and act promptly when there are deviations.

The trouble comes when the customer does not understand an investment or when the broker is not clear about all the facts. When the price of the securities goes down, recriminations start. If you take a flier, you can't blame the brokers for your mistake. But they may be at fault if they cross the line between optimism and misrepresentation.

If you have had a misunderstanding with your broker that cannot be resolved, you may wish to go to arbitration, which is a "uniform binding arbitration procedure." Your case will be reviewed by an impartial board for a nominal fee. Fees range from $15 (if resolved by mail) to $550 for cases involving $100,000, or more.

DISCOUNT STOCKBROKERS

If you like to make your own buy-and-sell decisions, do your own research, and can operate independently of a full service brokerage firm, then it is possible to save between 30 and 80% on your commissions by using a discount broker.

These no-frills operations are able to offer lower rates because they do not provide research, they hire salaried order clerks and not commissioned brokers, and they maintain low overheads. Yet many have a surprisingly complete line of investment choices available: in addition to stocks and bonds, many handle Treasury issues, municipals, options, and mortgage-backed securities and will set up self-directed IRAs or Keoghs. The country's largest discounter, Charles Schwab & Co., also offers to trade mutual fund shares. Shearman Ralston and Securities Research have distinguished themselves in the field by publishing a monthly market report newsletter and offering modest amounts of research free to customers.

Several discounters have also moved into the computer field: Max Ule and Fidelity Brokerage Services market software programs enabling customers to place trades from their home computers, to receive stock quotes, and even to evaluate their portfolios.

As a general rule, you will be able to save $25 to $75 when doing a 300-share trade. But

---

SHOULD YOU USE A DISCOUNT BROKER?

YES, IF:
- You have investment savvy
- You enjoy following the stock market and have time to do so
- You have clear ideas about what to buy and sell, and when
- You subscribe to an investment service or serious professional periodicals
- You follow technical indicators
- You read market news on a regular basis
- You trade often
- You are not afraid to make mistakes

NO, IF:
- You cannot decide what to buy and sell
- You require investment advice
- You are too busy to follow the market
- You are nervous about things financial
- You are inexperienced

SOURCE: Jay J. Pack, *How to Talk to a Broker*, New York: Harper & Row, 1985.

---

discounters set up varying schedules, so it definitely pays to shop around when selecting a firm. With some—called value brokers—the rates escalate with both the number of shares and their price. With others—called share brokers—rates are tied solely to the number of shares traded. You will save more with lower priced shares if you use a value broker and with share brokers for higher priced stocks.

As guidelines, use a discount broker if you:
- Have a portfolio of $100,000
- Trade at least twice a month in units of 300 shares or more
- Feel so confident of your stock market skill that you do not want someone else to monitor or question your decisions
- Are sure that the savings in commissions are worthwhile: at least 20% below rates negotiated with regular stock brokerage firms
- Are not involved with special securities such as convertibles, options, or warrants, where accurate information is difficult to obtain

COMMISSIONS: FULL-RATE FIRMS VS. DISCOUNT BROKERS

	100 SHARES @ 51	200 SHARES @ 28	300 SHARES @ 38	500 SHARES @ 60
Merrill Lynch	$92	$122	$204	$435
E.F. Hutton	90	120	201	430
Shearson-Amex	97	124	206	440
Paine Webber	90	121	205	435
Chas. Schwab	45	70	91	156
Fidelity Source	40	62	93	150
Quick & Reilly	48	63	89	189
Pace Securities	35	35	45	60

If you are a heavy trader, play it both ways: get information from your regular broker and handle large deals through the discount house.

THE BIG THREE

If you decide to do your own research or you want to supplement that offered by your stock-broker or financial adviser, you will find that three publication services will be enormously helpful. They are expensive, so you may want to use them at your library or broker's office before buying your own copies.

MOODY'S

Moody's Investor Service
99 Church Street
New York, NY 10007
1-212-553-0300

A leading research and information service aimed primarily at the business community, Moody's (a Dun & Bradstreet Corporation company) is known throughout the world for its bond ratings and factual publications. It is not an investment advisory service.

➤ MOODY'S MANUALS The company publishes seven manuals on an annual basis. Each is continually updated, some as often as twice a week. The manuals cover 20,000 U.S. and foreign corporations and 14,000 municipal and

DISCOUNTERS

J. Alexander
Securities
Los Angeles, CA
1-213-687-8400
$30 minimum

Baker & Co.
Cleveland, OH
1-800-321-1640
1-800-362-2008
(OH)
$35 minimum

Fidelity
Boston, MA
1-800-225-2097
1-800-882-1269
(MA)
$30 minimum

Haas Securities
Corp.
Chicago, IL
1-800-621-1410
1-800-572-1139
(IL)
$25 minimum

Pacific Brokerage
Services
Beverly Hills, CA
1-800-421-8395
1-800-421-3214
(CA)
$25 minimum

Quick & Reilly
New York, NY
1-800-221-5220
1-800-522-8712
(NY)
$35 minimum

Rose & Company
Chicago, IL
1-800-621-3700
$25 minimum

Charles Schwab & Co.
San Francisco, CA
1-800-648-5300
1-800-792-0988 (CA)
$34 minimum

Shearman Ralston,
Inc.
New York, NY
1-800-221-4242
1-212-248-1160 (NY)
$30 minimum

Securities Research,
Inc.
Vero Beach, FL
1-800-327-3156
$30 minimum

Muriel Siebert & Co.
New York, NY
1-212-248-0600
$30 minimum

StockCross, Inc.
Boston, MA
1-800-225-6196
1-800-392-6104
(MA)
$25 plus 8½% per
share minimum

Max Ule
New York, NY
1-800-223-6642
1-212-687-0705 (NY)
$39 minimum

Wilmington Brokerage
Services
Wilmington, DE
1-800-345-7550
1-302-651-1011 (DE)
$39 minimum

government entities. Each one gives financial and operating data, company histories, product descriptions, plant and property locations, and lists of officers. The seven are:

- *Banks and finance.* Covers 11,000 financial institutions, including insurance companies, mutual funds, banks, and real estate trusts.
- *Industrial.* Covers every industrial corporation on the NYSE and AMEX plus 500+ on regional exchanges.
- *OTC industrial.* Covers 3,200 industrial companies traded on NASDQ or OTC.
- *Public utility.* Covers every publicly held U.S. gas and electric utility, gas transmission, telephone, and water company.
- *Transportation.* Covers airlines, railroads, oil pipelines, bridge and tunnel operators, bus and truck lines, and auto and truck rental and leasing firms.
- *International.* Covers 5,000+ international corporations in 100 countries.
- *Municipal and government.* Covers 14,000 bond-issuing municipalities and government agencies; includes bond ratings.

➤ MOODY'S HANDBOOKS Soft-cover books are published quarterly that give concise overviews of 2,000 corporations. Useful to retrieve instant facts and financial summaries. They are called *Handbook of Common Stocks* and *Handbook of OTC Stocks.*

➤ OTHER PUBLICATIONS *Moody's Dividend Record.* Detailed reports on current dividend data of 14,700 stocks; updated twice weekly.

Moody's Industry Review. Ranks 4,000 leading companies in 145 industry groups.

Moody's Bond Record. Monthly guide to 40,700 fixed income issues including ratings, yield to maturity, and prices.

Moody's Bond Survey. Weekly publication on new issues.

➤ A WORD ABOUT MOODY'S BOND RATINGS Their purpose is to grade the relative quality of investments by using nine symbols ranging from Aaa (the highest) to C (the lowest). In addition, each classification from Aa to B (for corporate bonds) sometimes has a numerical modifier: the number 1 indicates that the security ranks at the highest end of the category; the number 2,

in the middle; and the number 3, at the lower end. (See Chapter 11.)

STANDARD & POOR'S

Standard & Poor's Corp.
25 Broadway
New York, NY 10004
1-212-208-8000

For over 120 years Standard & Poor's has been providing financial information, stock and bond analysis, and bond rating and investment guidance. Its materials are used by investors as well as the professional and business community.

➤ MAJOR PUBLICATIONS

- *Corporation Records.* Seven volumes covering financial details, history, and products of 1,000 corporations. One volume, *Daily News,* provides continually updated information 5 days a week on 10,000 publicly held corporations.
- *Stock Reports.* Analytical data on 4,000 corporations. Includes every company traded on the NYSE and AMEX plus 2,000 over-the-counters. There are two-page reports on each company.
- *Industry Surveys.* This two-volume looseleaf is continually updated and covers 65 leading U.S. industries. Surveys cover all aspects of an industry including tax rulings.
- *Stock Guide.* A small paperback containing 44 columns of statistical material on 5,000 stocks. A broker's Bible.
- *The Outlook.* A weekly advisory newsletter covering the economic climate, stock forecasts, industry predictions, buy-and-sell recommendations, etc. Presents a "master list of recommended stocks" with four separate portfolios: one, long-term growth; two, promising growth; three, cyclical and speculative stocks; four, income stocks.
- *Trend-line Publications.* Publishes marketing behavior charts providing investors with a visual look at a company's performance. Includes charts of indexes and indicators.

➤ OTHER PUBLICATIONS *Credit Week, Bond Guide, Commercial Paper Ratings Guide, Poor's Register of Corporations, Directors and Execu-*

tives, Security Dealers Handbook and Statistical Service.

➤ A WORD ABOUT STANDARD & POOR'S FIXED INCOME RATINGS   Standard & Poor's rates bonds from AAA (the highest) to D (bonds in default). Those with ratings between AAA to BBB are considered of investment quality. Those below BBB fall into the speculative category. Ratings between AA and B often have a + or − to indicate relative strength within the larger categories (see Chapter 11).

VALUE LINE

Value Line, Inc.
711 Third Avenue
New York, NY 10017
1-212-687-3965

An independent investment advisory, Value Line, Inc., publishes one of the country's leading investment advisory services, *The Value Line Investment Survey,* as well as several other publications and the Value Line index.

➤ MAJOR PUBLICATION   *The Value Line Investment Survey,* begun in 1935, is a weekly advisory service published in a two-volume looseleaf binder. It covers reports on each of 1,700 common stocks divided into 92 industry groups.

➤ OTHER PUBLICATIONS   *The Value Line OTC Special Situations Service.* Covers fast-growing smaller companies. Published 24 times a year.

Value Line Options. Evaluates and ranks nearly all options listed on the U.S. exchanges.

Value Line Convertibles. Evaluates and ranks for future market performance 580 companies. and 75 warrants.

FOR FURTHER INFORMATION

ARBITRATION

Director of Arbitration
New York Stock Exchange
11 Wall Street
New York, NY 10006

Director of Arbitration
National Association of Security Dealers
2 World Trade Center
New York, NY 10048

Office of Consumer Affairs
Securities & Exchange Commission
450 Fifth Street, N.W.
Washington, D.C. 20549

BROKERS

Jay J. Pack. *How to Talk to a Broker.* New York: Harper & Row, 1985

70% Off! The Investor's Guide to Discount Brokerage. New York: Facts on File, 1984

EVALUATING INVESTMENT NEWSLETTERS

Promises of 100% annual returns on your investments; guarantees of market success; predictions of great riches—these and other flamboyant bits of advertising have tempted more than a million people to subscribe to one of the 500 investment newsletters on the market. Are they worth the price of subscription? Some are, but many have not done better than the averages. Yet, a well-written carefully selected newsletter along with other sources of information can boost your investment awareness and consequently your performance.

Today, when the need for sound financial advice is so crucial, you're apt to be bombarded by a barrage of newsletters, each one claiming to be the answer to making a killing on Wall Street. Here are guidelines to help avoid the charlatans and opportunists and cash in on the wiser, more seasoned advisers.

A key factor to keep in mind is that, from year to year, the performance success of all newsletters changes. And the selection of one or two issues that either take off or bomb has enormous impact on the performance of a letter.

Before plunking down the full price of admission, take out a trial subscription to several (see suggested lists below), which will run from $10 to $55. Compare them and see if any suit your investment philosophy *and* income level. Ask your stockbroker, banker, accountant, or reliable friend for recommendations. During the trial period, keep a record of the recommendations made.

Newsletters that do not represent a brokerage firm are no longer required to register as investment advisers with the SEC, so you can expect to see newsletter editors claiming more than they can deliver. This is especially true in

a bull market, when the number of publications increases dramatically.

Often newsletters will twist their material in order to make it appear as though they've made a winning prediction. If the editor claims he or she called a market change or picked an outstanding stock, go back to the issue and make certain it really was the case.

Although last year's success does not automatically guarantee the same for the next 12 months, it's one of the few benchmarks available. Try to determine the newsletter's overall track record.

The top five newsletters in 1985–86, based on a hypothetical $10,000 portfolio invested by

---

CHECKLIST OF POINTS TO CONSIDER

DOES THE NEWSLETTER:
- Contradict itself from one issue to the next
- Explain changes in recommendations
- Evaluate its mistakes
- Update its mistakes
- Take credit for predictions it did not make
- Present stale news, dated prices and statistics
- Offer a hotline service
- Include commissions/fees in its performance results
- Leave you feeling confused—or is the advice clear, especially sell decisions
- Provide sample portfolios with instructions, rather than just lists of equities with no advice

Mark Hulbert, who tracks the performance of 95 newsletters were:

BI Research   +79%
P.O. Box 30
South Salem, NY 10590
1-914-763-5816

McKeever Strategy Letter   +69%
P.O. Box 4130
Medford, OR 97501
1-503-773-5123

Personal Finance   +63%
1300 North 17th Street
Arlington, VA 22209
1-703-276-7100

OTC Insight   +54%
P.O. Box 1329
El Cerrito, CA 94530
1-415-276-7100

Medical Technology Stock Letter   +43%
155 Montgomery Street
San Francisco, CA 94104
1-415-781-4595

Another way to study the newletter industry is to read the reports of those who rank the publications or provide summaries of their contents. These include:

> *Hulbert Financial Digest*
> 409 First Steet, S.E.
> Washington, D.C. 20003
> 1-202-546-2164

Tracks 95 newsletters based on their stock recommendations

> *Dick Davis Digest*
> P.O. Box 2828
> Ocean View Street
> Miami, FL 33140
> 1-305-531-7777

Summarizes tips given by other investment services

> *Focus on Wall Street*
> Select Information Exchange
> 2095 Broadway
> New York, NY 10023
> 1-212-874-6408

Ranks stock selections of 400 newsletters and financial magazines and publishes top 50

> *Timer Digest*
> P.O. Box 030247
> Ft. Lauderdale, FL 33308
> 1-305-764-8499

Follows 40 market timers

Among those newsletters that have had solid long-term records are:

> *Prudent Speculator* (Al Frank, ed.)
> P.O. Box 1767
> Santa Monica, CA 90406
> 1-213-395-5275

> *Growth Stock Outlook* (Charles Allmon, ed.)
> 4405 East West Highway
> Bethesda, MD 20814
> 1-301-654-5205

> *Cabot Market Letter* (Carlton Lutts, ed.)
> P.O. Box 1013
> Salem, MA 01970
> 1-617-745-5532

> *Zweig Forecast* (Marty Zweig, ed.)
> 747 Third Avenue
> New York, NY 10017
> 1-212-644-0040

> *Professional Tape Reader*
> (Stan Weinstein, ed.)
> P.O. Box 2407
> Hollywood, FL 33022
> 1-305-923-3733

> *Dow Theory Letters* (Richard Russell, ed.)
> P.O. Box 1759
> La Jolla, CA 92037
> 1-619-454-0481

TRACKING INSIDER TRADING

The sales and purchases of any company's stock by the firm's officials can be an indication of stock price trends. It's not foolproof, but if you have time to do the research, you may unearth some interesting situations. A handful of newsletters chart this so-called insider trading.

> *Consensus of Insiders* (Perry Wysong, ed.)
> P.O. Box 10247
> Fort Lauderdale, FL 33334
> 1-305-563-6827

The Insider (Norman Fosback, ed.)
3471 North Federal Highway
Fort Lauderdale, FL 33306
1-305-563-9000

The Insider's Edge Highlights Report
(Richard A. Horowitz, ed.)
122 Spanish Village
Dallas, TX 75248
1-214-380-1334

Insider Indicator (J. Michael Reed, ed.)
2230 N.E. Brazee Street
Portland, OR 97212
1-503-281-8626

Value Line
711 Third Avenue
New York, NY 10017
1-212-687-3217

Street Smart Investing (Kiril Sokoloff, ed.)
P.O. Box 173
Katonah, NY 10536
1-914-962-4646

Emerging & Special Situations
(Robert Natale, ed.)
Standard & Poor's Corp.
25 Broadway
New York, NY 10005
1-212-208-8000

FOR FURTHER INFORMATION

The best way to check out any newsletter is to ask for a sample issue or a trial subscription. Or take advantage of one of the two special sample offer deals:

Select Information Exchange
2095 Broadway
New York, NY 10023
20 services for $11.95

The Hirsch Organization
6 Deer Trail
Old Tappan, NJ 07675
25 services for $25

43 BITS AND BYTES: Investing by Computer

Although most investors still turn to their brokers for help in picking stocks and to newspapers for quotations, much important information previously available only to Wall Street professionals is now at the fingertips of Every Investor, if he or she has a computer, modem, and cash to spend. Today, with most personal computers (IBM, Apple, Commodore, etc.) you can tap into thousands of bits of relevant investment data, turning your home almost into a full service brokerage firm. Among the applications of a computer with proper software are:

- Access to huge electronic libraries, called data bases
- Current stock prices, bond yields, and portfolio updates
- News on companies, the economy, and industry developments
- Personalized spreadsheets to track investments
- Recall of company stock histories

Programs and equipment are expensive, however, and you must plan to spend time putting the information you gather to work. The primary benefit of the computer is its ability to access news and facts instantly. It's then up to you to interpret the data. The various services are not cheap, and not worth the expenditure for the small, average investor. If you fall under that rubric, you should stick with spending a few cents for the daily paper and $100 or $200 a year on financial publications.

If you're running a sizable portfolio, however, or if you're truly interested in the market, then go on line, but only *after* reading the following suggestions. Start out by learning about the various data bases.

FOUR DATA BASES

There are three major data bases that store information of use to investors. In most cases you can access this material with the proper software and a modem (a small electronic device that enables computers to communicate via telephone lines). The three major data bases have various packages and fees. They bill you for the amount of time you spend using the system. In most areas of the country, a local phone call connects you with the data base, but check it out first. The material below is general and should be confirmed by a call to the company. All three data bases work much the same way: you locate the information you want by selecting various menus or topics and typing numbers in. Shortcuts that bypass menus exist, and the right software can reduce accessing almost to one step.

CompuServe (available at most computer stores)
500 Arlington Centre Boulevard
P.O. Box 20212
Columbus, OH 43220
1-800-848-8199

Hourly rate: $12.50 prime time
$6.00 off hour
(extra charges for financial news)

Offers: S&P, Value Line data, 20-minute-delayed quotes on 9,000 stocks, earnings forecasts on 2,400 companies, historical data on 50,000 securities

Dow Jones News/Retrieval (choice of most investors)
P.O. Box 300
Princeton, NJ 08540
1-800-257-5144

Hourly rate: $1 to $2.30 per minute
$60 to $138 per hour

Offers: 39 different services: news from *Wall Street Journal, Barron's,* Dow Jones ticker; news as it breaks; S&P's data base; brokerage firm research reports; SEC filings; Wall Street Week's TV show transcripts

The Source
1616 Anderson Road
McLean, VA 22102
1-800-336-3366

Hourly rates: $7.75 to $25.80

Offers: prices on 10,000 securities, AP & UPI financial news, abstracts from *Fortune, Harvard Business Review, Institutional Investor.* In addition to financial news, includes weather, sports, movie reviews, airline schedules. "Bizdate" taps into 9 categories of financial news updated 80 times a day. Weekly mutual fund data provided by the Donoghue Organization.

One smaller, less detailed, but also less expensive data base you should know about is:

Warner Computer Systems
Hackensack, NJ
1-212-986-1919 (NY)
1-201-489-1580 (NJ)
1-800-626-4635

Hourly rate: $1.70 per minute to 6 PM
M–F
$0.60 per minute off peak and weekends

Offers: less extensive than Dow Jones News/Retrieval, Warner focuses on securities prices. Information is updated weekly and covers Dow Jones averages, all S&P indexes, AMEX and NASDAQ, interest rates, gold and silver prices, options, and mutual funds.

SOFTWARE PACKAGES

There are over 250 types of software programs, covering every area of investing and speculating.

To update the basic material, you buy services that will provide additional information such as the latest quotes, volume, price changes, earnings, etc. The following is a representative sampling of the types of software available. Inclusion on this list is not a product endorsement. Study the list and then talk to colleagues and computer pros for additional ideas.

➤ PORTFOLIO MANAGEMENT SOFTWARE

The Personal Investor
PBL Corporation
P.O. Box 559
Wayzata, MN 55391
1-612-473-8998

Designed for individual investors, updates portfolios containing stocks, bonds, options, mutual funds, Treasuries. Can transfer data onto spreadsheets. Not overwhelming to noncomputer users. Has built-in capacity to link up with Dow Jones News/Retrieval.

PEAR Portfolio Management System
Hale Systems; Remote Computing Division
1044 Northern Boulevard
Roslyn, NY 11576
1-800-645-3120
1-718-895-3810

Designed initially for brokers, handles up to 200 portfolios on a disc. Summarizes realized and unrealized capital gains and losses and appraises portfolios.

➤ STOCKS

Option X
Crawford Data Systems
P.O. Box 705
Soomis, CA 93066
1-805-484-4159

Option X unearths overpriced and underpriced stock options. Compares, analyzes options to give investor best opportunity.

➤ BONDS

Bond Yielder
C.E. Software
801 73rd Street
Des Moines, IA 50312
1-515-224-1995

Evaluates and compares fixed income securities, including yield to maturity, yield after capital gains, taxable returns, etc.

➤ REAL ESTATE

>   Investor III
>   Good Software Corp.
>   12900 Preston Road
>   Dallas, TX 75230
>   1-214-239-6085

Evaluates real estate as an investment, giving figures for depreciation, mortgages, recapture, taxes, etc.

➤ RETIREMENT/EDUCATION

>   IFDS, Inc.
>   P.O. Box 88870
>   Atlanta, GA 30356
>   1-404-256-6447

Covers retirement, education, income taxes, and risk management.

➤ TAXES

>   Tax Mini-Miser
>   Sunrise Software
>   36 Palm Court
>   Menlo Park, CA 94025
>   1-415-441-2351

Computes various tax strategies.

>   Aardvark Software, Inc.
>   783 North Water Street
>   Milwaukee, WI 53202
>   1-414-289-9988

"Estate Tax Plan" calculates tax liabilities, reviews alternatives, and computes complex figures. "Professional Tax Planner" is a problem solving program that answers the "what if" questions surrounding tax issues.

➤ TECHNICAL ANALYSIS

>   Market Analyst
>   Anidata, Inc.
>   7200 Westfield Avenue
>   Pennsauken, NJ 08110
>   1-609-663-8123

Can chart your own indicators; also calculates and charts volume, moving averages, etc. Can download data from CompuServe or Warner.

>   TechniFilter
>   RTR Software Systems
>   444 Executive Systems
>   El Paso, TX 79902
>   1-915-544-4397

Works with Dow Jones Market Analyzer. Can construct your own formulas if you like. Covers trendlines, volume charts, moving averages.

➤ FUNDAMENTAL ANALYSIS

>   Stockpak II
>   Standard & Poor's Corp.
>   25 Broadway
>   New York, NY 10004
>   1-800-852-5200
>   1-212-208-8000 (NY)

Screens stocks on fundamentals, covering more than 4,500.

>   The Evaluation Form
>   Investor's Software
>   Box N
>   Bradenton Beach, FL 33510
>   1-813-778-5515

Uses approach developed by National Association of Investment Clubs. Contracts on selection of undervalued stocks for long term.

➤ GETTING ON-LINE BROKERAGE FIRM REPORTS

>   Business Research Corp.
>   12 Farnsworth Street
>   Boston, MA 02210
>   1-800-662-7878
>   1-617-787-2205

"Investext" of Boston includes research from 36 leading brokerage firms and the work of 300+ analysts. Adds 2,000 pages of research per week. Can tap in directly, through Dailog Information Services (1-800-227-1927), or The Source (one of the four data bases listed above).

$ HINT: When you buy a modem or other equipment, try to get free trial time. All three major data bases will consider making such arrangements with serious prospective customers.

Before you buy, figure out what you need or what you will actually use. Do you tend to invest long term? Short term? Are you interested in options? Do you need to keep track of 250 portfolios? More? Less? Do you use graphs?

In addition to talking to colleagues and friends who already use computers for investing, join one of the computer user groups that exist in most major cities. For additional sources of information about these groups, contact:

The New York PC User Group
80 Wall Street (Suite 614)
New York, NY 10005

The Big Apple User Group
P.O. Box 490
Bowling Green Station
New York, NY 10274

American Association of Microcomputer Investors
P.O. Box 1384
Princeton, NJ 08542

American Association of Individual Investors
612 North Michigan Avenue
Chicago, IL 60611

(The latter two associations publish directories and other helpful material about various programs.)

WHERE, WHAT, WHEN:
Exchanges, Indexes, and Indicators

In keeping with Wall Street jargon and financial reporting, initials are used frequently. Here are some of the most widely used:

EXCHANGES

➤ NYSE: NEW YORK STOCK EXCHANGE This is the major auction market for common stocks and corporate bonds. To be listed, a corporation must:

- Demonstrate earning power of $2.5 million before federal income taxes for the most recent year and $2 million pretax for each of the preceding two years
- Have net tangible assets of $16 million
- Have market value of publicly held shares of $16 million.
- Report a total of one million common shares publicly held
- Have 2,000 holders of 100 shares or more. OR, under new provisions:
- For firms with 2,200 owners, the shareholders need no longer be round-lot owners. In addition: (1) the company's stock must have had an average monthly volume of 100,000 shares for the 6 months prior to application; (2) the company must have a 3-year cumulative pretax income of $6.5 million with $4.5 million in the most recent year.

➤ AMEX: AMERICAN STOCK EXCHANGE These corporations are generally smaller and less financially strong than those on the NYSE. The firm must have:

- Earnings of $400,000 after all charges and taxes and not including nonrecurring items
- Corporate net worth of $4 million
- 500,000 shares of common, exclusive of holdings of officers or directors, including 150,000 shares held in lots of 100 or more
- 1,000 public stockholders with 500 owning 100 or more shares
- Market price of $5 minimum with $3 million market value

➤ BOS: BOSTON STOCK EXCHANGE
➤ MID: MIDWEST STOCK EXCHANGE
➤ MSE: MONTREAL STOCK EXCHANGE
➤ PE: PHILADELPHIA STOCK EXCHANGE This lists both stocks and options.
➤ TSE: TORONTO STOCK EXCHANGE
➤ PSE: PACIFIC STOCK EXCHANGE
➤ OTC: OVER THE COUNTER This is the market for securities that are not listed on major exchanges. The trading is conducted by dealers who are members of NASD (National Association of Securities Dealers) and who may or may not be members of other exchanges. Trading is by bid and asked prices. The primary market is NASDAQ (National Association of Securities Dealers Automated Quotations) which consists of about 200 of the most actively traded issues. Some 2,500 other stocks are quoted in daily financial summaries.
➤ CBOE: CHICAGO BOARD OF OPTIONS EXCHANGE The major auction market for calls and puts, primarily on NYSE stocks, and recently for special types of options such as those on Treasury bonds.
➤ AMEX OPTIONS EXCHANGE The division of AMEX that trades puts and calls, almost entirely on NYSE listed stocks.
➤ CBT: CHICAGO BOARD OF TRADE A major market for futures contracts: commodities, interest rate securities, commercial paper, and so forth.
➤ CME: CHICAGO MERCANTILE EXCHANGE Futures contracts for commodities, T-bills, etc., and the Standard & Poor's 500 Index.

➤ COMEX (FORMERLY NEW YORK COMMODITY EXCHANGE) Futures and options of a limited number of commodities and metals (gold, silver, and copper).

➤ CTN: NEW YORK COTTON EXCHANGE Trading in futures in cotton and orange juice.

➤ IMM: INTERNATIONAL MONETARY MARKET This is located at the Chicago Mercantile Exchange and trades in futures of foreign currency and U.S. Treasury bills.

➤ KC: KANSAS CITY BOARD OF TRADE Trades in futures of commodities and Value Line futures index.

➤ NYFE: NEW YORK FUTURES EXCHANGE A unit of the NYSE that trades in the NYSE composite futures index.

➤ NYM: NEW YORK MERCANTILE EXCHANGE Trading in futures of petroleum and metals.

FEDERAL AGENCIES

➤ SEC: SECURITIES AND EXCHANGE COMMISSION A federal agency established to help protect investors. It is responsible for administering congressional acts regarding securities, stock exchanges, corporate reporting, investment companies, investment advisers, and public utility holding companies.

➤ FRB: FEDERAL RESERVE BOARD The federal agency responsible for control of such important investment items as the discount rate, money supply, and margin requirements.

➤ FDIC: FEDERAL DEPOSIT INSURANCE CORPORATION An agency which provides insurance of bank deposits.

➤ FSLIC: FEDERAL SAVINGS AND LOAN INSURANCE CORPORATION A similar insurance-of-deposits agency for savings and loan associations.

➤ CFTC: COMMODITY FUTURES TRADING COMMISSION This is a watchdog for the commodities futures trading industry.

STOCK MARKET AVERAGES

➤ DOW JONES INDUSTRIAL AVERAGE (DJIA) The oldest and most widely used stock market average. It shows the action of the stocks of 30 major corporations, representing about 15% of NYSE values, on a weighted basis: e.g., IBM at 110 carries more than three times the weight of Woolworth at 35.

Furthermore, cash dividends tend to reduce the average as each stock passes its ex-dividend date, and, percentagewise, a stock that falls from 100 to 50 loses 50% of its value; but when it moves back, the gain is 100%.

STOCKS IN DOW JONES AVERAGES

Industrials (DJIA)

Allied Corp.	International Harvester
Aluminum Co.	International Paper
American Brands	Merck & Co.
American Can	Minnesota Mining &
American Express	Mfg.
American Tel. & Tel.	Owens-Illinois
Bethlehem Steel	Procter & Gamble
Du Pont, E.I.	Sears, Roebuck
Eastman Kodak	Standard Oil (Calif.)
Exxon Corporation	Texaco, Inc.
General Electric	Union Carbide
General Foods	U.S. Steel
General Motors	United Technologies
Goodyear Tire	Westinghouse Electric
Inco, Ltd.	Woolworth (F.W.)
International Business Machines	

Transportation (DJTA)

AMR Corp.	Pan American World
Burlington Northern	Airways
Canadian Pacific	Rio Grande Industries
Carolina Freight	Santa Fe Southern
CSX Corp.	Pacific
Delta Airlines	Transway International
Eastern Airlines	Trans World
Federal Express	UAL, Inc.
Norfolk & Southern	Union Pacific Corp.
Northwest Airlines	U.S. Air Group
Overnite Transportation	

Utilities (DJUA)

American Electric Power	Niagara Mohawk Power
Cleveland Electric	Pacific Gas & Electric
Columbia Gas System	Panhandle Eastern Corp.
Commonwealth Edison	Peoples Energy
Consolidated Edison	Philadelphia Electric
Consolidated Natural Gas	Public Service E & G
Detroit Edison	So. California Edison
Houston Industries	

MARKET INDICATORS, INDEXES, AND AVERAGES

Whether you're bullish, bearish, or uncertain, you can get a reading on the direction of the market, interest rates, and the overall economy by following some of the key statistics (or indicators) regularly churned out by Wall Street and Washington. These should be regarded not as gospel but rather as tools to help you make informed and intelligent decisions about your investments and for timing moves between stocks, bonds, and cash equivalents. Make a point of jotting down these numbers on your own chart and track the trends. You will see definite patterns between the market, interest rates, and the money supply. (The indicators are presented in alphabetical order.)

ECONOMIC INDICATOR	COMPOSITION	WHAT IT PREDICTS
Consumer price index (CPI)	Measures changes in the average price of consumer goods and services	The direction of inflation and changes in the purchasing power of money
Dollar index	Consists of value of the dollar as measured against major foreign currencies	Domestic corporate profits and multinational earning power
Dow Jones industrial average (DJIA)	30 major companies whose stock is held by many institutions and individuals; index is price-weighted so that moves in high-priced stocks exercise more influence than those of lower priced stock on the average	Action of the stock market, which in turn anticipates future business activity
Employment figures and payroll employment	Number of people working or on company payrolls	Foretells consumer spending, which in turn affects corporate profits
Gross national product (GNP)	Total goods and services produced in United States on an annual basis; inflation can distort the accuracy of this figure, so subtract inflation from GNP to get "real" rate of GNP	General business trends and economic activity are forecast by changes in real GNP
Index of industrial production (IIP)	Shown as a percentage of the average, which has been tracked since 1967; base is 100	Amount of business volume
Money supply:		
M1	Currency held by public plus balances in checking accounts, NOW accounts, travelers checks, money market funds	Extent of consumer purchasing power and liquidity of public's assets
M2	M1 plus time deposits over $100,000 and repurchase agreements	Used by Federal Reserve as a gauge for predicting as well as
M3	M2 plus T-bills, U.S. savings bonds, bankers' acceptances, term Eurodollars, commercial paper	controlling pace of economy; when M1 shows a big increase, Fed usually reduces the money supply, which sends interest rates up; Fed reduces M1 by selling Treasuries; tightening of M1 serves to curb inflation; an increase in M1 fuels inflation
Standard & Poor's 500 stock index	Indexed value of 500 stocks from NYSE, AMEX, and OTC; more useful than the	Direction of the economy and the market; because the market tends

ECONOMIC INDICATOR	COMPOSITION	WHAT IT PREDICTS
	Dow Jones industrial average because it's broader; includes 400 industrials, 40 public utilities, 20 transportations, and 40 financials; stocks are market-value-weighted, i.e., price of each stock is multiplied by the number of shares outstanding	to anticipate future economic conditions, this is a good leading indicator
Three-month Treasury bill rate	Interest rate paid to purchasers of T-bills	General direction of interest rates; gives indication of the Federal Reserve system's fiscal policy; for example, during a recession, Fed increases the amount of currency in circulation, which serves to lower the T-bill rate; during inflation, currency is reduced and T-bill rate rises; rising interest rates tend to reduce corporate profits because of the increased costs of borrowing; therefore, a continual rise in T-bill rates presages a decline in the stock market; falling rates help stock and bond prices
Wage settlements	Percentage changes in wages that come about because of new labor contracts	Predicts price changes for goods and services; sharply higher wage settlements result in higher inflation rates

According to Lou Stone, senior analyst with Shearson-American Express, "Most of the big gains are simply recoveries in value, not actual profits realized. Out of 313 million shares of GM outstanding, only 62 million shares traded in 1982 . . . more than half were duplications so that less than 10% of the shares changed hands during the year."

In recent years, the composition of the average has been changed to reflect the growing scientific, consumer, and international roles of American business: IBM replaced Chrysler and Merck was substituted for Esmark, Inc.

The DJIA is determined by dividing the closing prices by a divisor that compensates for past stock splits and stock dividends. In mid-1983, this was 1.292. This meant that a 10-point change in the average represented an actual price shift of $12.92.

➤ DOW JONES TRANSPORTATION AVERAGE (DJTA) This is made up of the stocks of 20 major transportation companies. Recent changes have substituted a trucking firm (Carolina Freight) and an airline (U.S. Air, Inc.), for merged railroads. The recent divisor was 1.574.

➤ DOW JONES UTILITIES AVERAGE (DJUA) This consists of 15 major utilities to provide geographic representation. With more firms forming holding companies to engage in oil and gas exploration and distribution, its value is greater as a point of reference than as a guide to the market's evaluation of producers of electricity and distributors of gas. The recent divisor was 2.709.

➤ STANDARD & POOR'S PRICE INDEX Of 500 leading NYSE-listed corporations: 425 industrials, 20 railroads, and 55 utilities. It is weighted in that it is based on the market value of all outstanding shares of these companies, so that it reflects the action of a comparatively few large firms. For example: IBM accounts for 3.9% of the index; Foster Wheeler for only .06%. The recent value was 152.85.

➤ WILSHIRE EQUITY INDEX This is a value-weighted index derived from the dollar value of 5,000 common stocks including all those listed on the NYSE and AMEX and the most active OTC issues. It is the broadest index and thus is more representative of the overall market.

➤ NYSE COMMON STOCK INDEX A composite index covering price movements of all common stocks listed on the big board. It is based on the close of the market December 31, 1965, and is weighted according to the number of shares listed for each issue. Point changes are converted to dollars and cents to provide a meaningful measure of price action.

➤ DOW JONES BOND AVERAGE This consists of bonds of 10 public utilities and 10 industrial corporations.

➤ DOW JONES MUNICIPAL BOND YIELD AVERAGE This is a changing average but it basically shows the yields of low-coupon bonds in 5 states and 15 major cities.

INDEX